D1451788

CREDIT RISK

Models and Management

CREDIT RISK

Models and Management

Published by Risk Books, a specialist division of Risk Publications.

Haymarket House
28-29 Haymarket
London SW1Y 4RX
Tel: +44 (0)171 484 9700
Fax: +44 (0)171 484 9758

Every effort has been made to secure the permission of individual copyright holders for inclusion.

Introductory overviews © Financial Engineering Ltd 1999
This compilation © Financial Engineering Ltd 1999

ISBN 1 899332 32 4

British Library Cataloguing in Publication Data
A catalogue record for this book is available from the British Library

Risk Books Commissioning Editor: Conrad Gardner
Project Editor: Lisa Carroll

Desk editing and typesetting by Special Edition, London.

Printed and bound in Great Britain by Bookcraft (Bath) Ltd, Somerset.

CONTENTS

AUTHORS

Edward I. Altman is the Max L. Heine Professor of Finance at the Stern School of Business, New York University. Since 1990, he has directed the research effort in Fixed Income and Credit Markets at the NYU Salomon Center and is currently the Vice-Director of the Center. Prior to this he chaired the Stern School's MBA program for 12 years. He has been a visiting Professor at the Hautes Etudes Commerciales and Université de Paris-Dauphine in France, at the Pontificia Catolica Universidade in Rio de Janeiro, at the Australian Graduate School of Management in Sydney and at the Luigi Bocconi University in Milan. He has an international reputation as an expert on corporate bankruptcy and credit risk analysis and has published over a dozen books and more than 100 articles in scholarly finance, accounting and economic journals. Edward is one of the founders and an Executive Editor of the *Journal of Banking and Finance* and Advisory Editor of the John Wiley *Frontiers in Finance Series*. He received his MBA and PhD in finance from the University of California, Los Angeles.

Angelo Arvanitis heads the Quantitative Credit, Insurance & Risk Research team at Paribas. His responsi-

bilities include the development of pricing and hedging models for Credit Derivatives, Convertible Bonds, Insurance Derivatives and credit risk management tools for managing the bank's overall credit exposure. Prior to joining Paribas he worked at Lehman Brothers in New York and BZW in London. Angelo received a BSc in physics from the University of Athens in Greece. He continued his studies at the University of California, the London School of Economics and the PhD program in finance at the University of Chicago.

Tanya Styblo Beder is a Managing Director at Caxton Corporation. Previously she was a principal of Capital Market Risk Advisors, Inc. Tanya has also been a vice-president of the First Boston Corporation and was a consultant in the financial institutions practice at McKinsey and Company. She holds an MBA in finance from Harvard University and a BA in mathematics from Yale University. Her academic work focuses on global capital markets, off-balance sheet instruments and the future of the financial system. Tanya has written several articles in the financial area, which have been published in *The Financial Analysts Journal*, *Harvard Business Review* and *The Journal of Financial Engineering*.

Fischer Black was Professor of Finance at the University of Chicago's Graduate School of Business from 1971 and, in 1975, joined the MIT's Sloan School of Management. In 1984 he joined Goldman Sachs, where he later became a partner. He will be best remembered for developing the Black–Scholes option pricing formula with Myron Scholes. He died in August 1995, at the age of 57.

Marshall E. Blume is Howard Butcher III Professor of Finance, Director of the Rodney L. White Center for Financial Research and Past Chairman of the Finance Department at the Wharton School of the University of Pennsylvania. He has been a visiting Professor of Finance at the New University of Lisbon, the Stockholm School of Economics and the European Institute for Advanced Studies in Management in Brussels. He received his MBA and PhD from the University of Chicago. He is a member of the Board of Managers of the Measey Foundation and a past chairman of the NASD Economic Advisory Board. He served on the US Government Accounting Office advisory committee that investigated the October 1987 stock market crash. He is a past managing editor of the *Journal of Finance* and is currently an editor of the

Journal of Fixed Income and the *Journal of Pension Fund Management & Investment*.

Lea V. Carty is a Managing Director in Moody's Investor Services' Risk Management Services Group. He has published research articles concerning various aspects of corporate credit risk as well as trends in corporate credit quality in academic journals, professional journals and books. Prior to joining Moody's in 1992, Lea worked at Bear, Stearns, and Company, Inc., New York, and Thomson-CGR, Paris. He holds a BA in mathematics and French from Washington University in St. Louis, an MA in mathematics from the University of Colorado and a PhD in economics from Columbia University. His thesis, written in the academic disciplines of corporate finance and economic history, was awarded distinction.

Diane Cooke is a research associate at the Salomon Center of the Stern School of Business at New York University.

John C. Cox is the Nomura Professor of Finance in the Sloan School of Management at MIT. He received his PhD from the Wharton School at the University of Pennsylvania. He has published a number of articles in finance and economics journals and is co-author of the book *Options Markets*. His research interests include derivatives markets, the term structure of interest rates, dynamic investment strategies and optimal security design.

Michel Crouhy is Senior Vice President in the Global Analytics, Market Risk

Management Division, at CIBC. Prior to his current position at CIBC, Michel was a Professor of Finance at the HEC School of Management in Paris, where he was also Director of the MS HEC in International Finance. He has been a visiting professor at the Wharton School and at UCLA. Michel holds a PhD from the Wharton School and is a graduate of the Ecole Nationale des Ponts et Chaussées, France. He has published extensively in academic journals in the areas of banking, options and financial markets, and is editor of the collection *Banque & Bourse* at Presses Universitaires de France. He is also associate editor of the *Journal of Derivatives*, the *Journal of Banking and Finance*, the *Journal of Risk* and *Financial Engineering and the Japanese Markets*.

Darrell Duffie is a Professor of Finance in the Graduate School of Business at Stanford University and has written articles on economics, finance and applied mathematics for various journals, as well as several books, including *Dynamic Asset Pricing Theory*. He received his PhD in 1984 and has remained on the faculty at Stanford University. His current research interests are in the design and valuation of financial securities, the modelling of credit risk and interest rates, and risk management.

Christopher C. Finger is a partner in the RiskMetrics Group LLC. He is primarily responsible for research on the CreditMetrics methodology and also contributes to research into market risk, simulation methods and the application of risk models in emerging markets. Before

joining the RiskMetrics Group he worked in Risk Management Services at JP Morgan, where he co-authored the CreditMetrics Technical Document, contributed to the RiskMetrics Technical Document and wrote various articles pertaining to the two methodologies. In addition, he worked on advisory assignments, implementing risk management methodologies for JP Morgan clients. Christopher holds a PhD in applied mathematics from Princeton University and a BS in mathematics and physics from Duke University.

Lawrence Fisher is the First Fidelity Bank Research Professor of Finance in the Graduate School of Business at Rutgers University.

Jerome S. Fons is a Managing Director in the Banking and Sovereign Group at Moody's Investor Services in New York. He is currently responsible for Moody's ratings for East Asian banks, including Japanese banks. From 1990 through 1994 he was the principal author of Moody's corporate bond and commercial paper default studies and has published widely in the field of credit risk. In 1994 Jerome became chief mortgage economist at Moody's, where he provided analytic support to the mortgage pass-through team. Prior to joining Moody's he was an Economic Advisor at Chemical Bank, New York, and an Economist with the Federal Reserve Banks of New York and Cleveland. He holds a PhD in economics from the University of California at San Diego.

Dan Galai is the Abe Gray Professor of Finance and

Business Administration at the Hebrew University, School of Business Administration, in Jerusalem. He was a Visiting Professor of Finance at INSEAD and has also taught at the University of California, Los Angeles, and the University of Chicago. He holds a PhD from the University of Chicago and undergraduate and graduate degrees from the Hebrew University. He has served as a consultant for the Chicago Board of Options Exchange and the American Stock Exchange as well as for major banks. He has published numerous articles in leading business and finance journals on options, financial assets and corporate finance and was a winner of the first Annual Pomeranze Prize for excellence in options research presented by the CBOE. Dan is a Principal in SIMGA P.C.M., which is engaged in portfolio management and corporate finance.

Jon Gregory is a quantitative analyst in the Credit, Insurance and Risk research team at Paribas, based in London. He is experienced in designing and building credit risk models. His current responsibilities include developing models for pricing, hedging and actively trading credit risk at a portfolio level. Prior to joining Paribas, Jon worked for Salomon Brothers. He has a BSc from the University of Bristol and received his PhD from the University of Cambridge in 1996.

Andrew Hickman is an Assistant Vice President in the Risk Measurement and Management Department at Credit Suisse First Boston, with responsibility for counterparty exposure analysis in

the Americas. Andrew is involved in the ongoing development of the CreditRisk+ model. He received a BS in finance from the Wharton School of Business. Prior to joining CSFB he specialised in risk management with Oliver, Wyman & Company, a management consultancy to the financial services industry.

Frank Iacono is a Vice President of Chase Securities, Inc., in the Credit Derivatives Group in New York. His responsibilities include the structuring and marketing of synthetic asset-backed securities and other credit derivative products. Prior to joining Chase in June 1998, he was a Vice President at Capital Market Risk Advisors, Inc. At CMRA Frank specialised in quantitative issues in derivatives and financial risk management including value-at-risk, stochastic processes and contingent claim analysis. He has published articles on credit derivatives, value-at-risk and corporate finance and has spoken at numerous conferences on cutting-edge issues in pricing and risk management. Frank earned a Juris Doctor degree, Cum Laude, from Harvard Law School, and a Bachelor of Science degree, Summa Cum Laude, from Yale College in applied mathematics. He is a member of the New York State bar.

Robert Jarrow is the Ronald P. and Susan E. Lynch Professor of Investment Management at the Johnson Graduate School of Management, Cornell University. He is also Managing Director and Director of Research at the Kamakura Corporation. He was the 1997 IAFE/SunGard Financial Engineer of the

year. He is a graduate of Duke University, Dartmouth College and MIT. Robert is known for his pioneering work on the Heath–Jarrow–Morton model for pricing interest rate derivatives. His current research includes the pricing of exotic options and other derivative securities as well as investment management theory. He is currently a co-editor of *Mathematical Finance* and the *Journal of Derivatives* and an associate editor of the *Review of Financial Studies,* the *Journal of Financial and Quantitative Analysis,* the *Review of Derivatives Research, Journal of Fixed Income,* the *Financial Review* and *The Review of Futures Markets*. He is an advisory editor for *Asia-Pacific Financial Markets.*

Vellore Kishore is a research associate at the Salomon Center of the Stern School of Business at New York University.

H. Ugur Koyluoglu is a consultant at Oliver, Wyman & Company, where his responsibilities include developing and implementing quantitative tools for better risk and capital management at banks and re/insurance companies. Ugur received his BS in civil engineering from Bogazici University, Istanbul, and his MA and PhD in civil engineering and operations research from Princeton University. Previously, he taught applied mathematics and engineering at Princeton, Koc and Aalborg Universities and conducted research on the random vibration of structures due to earthquakes and on risk measurement and management. He is author of more than 40 publications in journals and conference proceedings.

David X. Li is a partner in the RiskMetrics Group, where he concentrates on credit modelling. He worked for CIBC/Oppenheimer for two and half years – first as a Senior Manager in Global Analytics, where he validated trading models, then as an Executive Director in the Financial Products group, where he was responsible for credit derivative trading models. Prior to that he was a Senior Analyst, Manager, with risk management of the Royal Bank of Canada. He was an assistant professor in actuarial science and finance before he left academia. David has a PhD in statistics from the University of Waterloo and master's degrees in economics, finance and actuarial science. He is an Associate of the Society of Actuaries (SOA) and an elected Council Member of the Investment Section of the SOA.

Felix Lim is currently a Senior Fixed Income Analyst with the Vanguard Group, with responsibilities in foreign corporate and government bond investments. Prior to joining Vanguard he was a Senior Associate with Morgan Stanley Institutional Investment Management. He received his undergraduate and graduate degrees from the Wharton School of the University of Pennsylvania. His contribution to this volume was written while he was a doctoral candidate in finance at Wharton.

Francis Longstaff is Professor of Finance at the Anderson School at UCLA. He received his PhD in finance from the University of Chicago. He is a Certified Public Accountant (CPA) and a Chartered Financial Analyst (CFA). From 1995 to 1998,

Francis was Head of Fixed Income Derivative Research at Salomon Brothers Inc. in New York. His research includes term structure theory, fixed-income derivative valuation and risk management. Other interests include the effect of liquidity on the valuation of securities. He has published more than 30 articles in academic journals. He serves on the Board of Directors of Simplex Capital Ltd, an Asian-based hedge fund.

A. Craig MacKinlay is the Joseph P. Wargrove Professor of Finance at the Wharton School of the University of Pennsylvania, where he has been a faculty member since 1984. He also is on the Board of Directors of the American Finance Association, a Research Associate of the National Bureau of Economic Research, a member of the ITG Scientific Advisory Board, a member of the Journal Investment Consulting Advisory Board and a former member of the NASD Economic Advisory Board. His research interests include empirical implementation and validation of asset pricing models, measuring investment performance, pricing of futures contracts, microstructure of financial markets, assessment of credit risk, and statistical methods in finance. He has served as an Associate Editor of the *Review of Financial Studies* and the *Journal of Business and Economic Statistics* and is currently an editorial board member of the *Pacific Basin Finance Journal* and an associate editor of *Review of Quantitative Finance and Accounting*.

Robert M. Mark is an Executive Vice President at

the Canadian Imperial Bank of Commerce (CIBC). His responsibilities at CIBC encompass Corporate Treasury and Risk Management functions. Prior to this, he was the partner in charge of the Financial Risk Management Consulting practice at Coopers & Lybrand (C&L). He has also worked as a managing director in the Asia, Europe, and Capital Markets Group (AECM) at Chemical Bank and as a senior officer at Marine Midland Bank/Hong Kong Shanghai Bank Group (HKSB), where he headed the technical analysis trading group within the Capital Markets Sector. He earned his PhD, with a dissertation in options pricing, from New York University's Graduate School of Engineering and Science, graduating first in his class. He subsequently received an Advanced Professional Certificate (APC) in accounting from NYU's Stern Graduate School of Business. He was also appointed chairperson of the National Asset/Liability Management Association (NALMA) and an Adjunct Professor at NYU's Stern Graduate School of Business.

Aidan McNulty is a partner in the RiskMetrics Group LLC. He is primarily responsible for marketing to the corporate market and the investment banking community. Before joining the RiskMetrics Group, Aidan worked in Risk Management Services at JP Morgan, specialising in credit risk management. Prior to his five years in JP Morgan he was a principal and co-founder of a financial services software company specialising in FX margin trading. Aidan was educated at Trinity College

Dublin, where he obtained a BBS and MA.

Robert C. Merton is currently the John and Natty McArthur University Professor at the Harvard Business School. After receiving a PhD in economics from MIT in 1970, he served on the finance faculty of MIT's Sloan School of Management until 1988, when he moved to Harvard. Robert is the author of numerous scholarly articles, the book *Continuous-Time Finance* and co-author *of Casebook in Financial Engineering: Applied Studies of Financial Innovation, The Global Financial System: A Functional Perspective* and *Finance*. He is past President of the American Finance Association and a member of the National Academy of Sciences. He received the Alfred Nobel Memorial Prize in the Economic Sciences in 1997.

Ross Miller is president of Miller Risk Advisors, a credit and portfolio risk management consultancy. Previously he was Senior Vice President and Director of Research at NatWest Markets, where he managed the development of new quantitative investment products. He founded General Electric's quantitative finance group and led the quantitative risk management task force at GE Capital. He taught finance and economics at the California Institute of Technology and Boston University, where he performed seminal research in the application of experimental economics to financial markets. He has written one book, *Computer-Aided Financial Analysis*, and 20 journal articles. He received a BS from the California Institute of Technology and a PhD from Harvard University.

Paul Narayanan is a credit and financial risk consultant based in Bryn Mawr, Pennsylvania. He currently advises banks and insurance companies in the US and abroad on risk models. He has developed and implemented risk systems for commercial lending, residential mortgages and consumer loans. He worked for many years in credit risk and interest rate risk management as Vice President in Chase Manhattan Bank, Bank of Boston and Meritor PSFS. More recently, he managed an asset disposition unit in the Resolution Trust Corporation (RTC) and supervised the servicing of RTC's very substantial assets. The Commonwealth of Pennsylvania uses his bank model in the supervisory process of the department of banking. He has co-authored articles in the *Journal of Banking and Finance, Financial Analysts Journal* and *Financial Markets, Institutions and Instruments*. He has been a speaker in various forums, including NYU Stern School's Executive Development program and Fundação Getulio Vargas, São Paulo, Brazil. He is also a co-builder of the Zeta credit risk model and is the author, with John A. Caouette and Edward I. Altman, of the book *Managing Credit Risk: The Next Great Financial Challenge*.

Krishna Ramaswamy is Professor of Finance at the Wharton School of the University of Pennsylvania. He received degrees of PhD from Stanford University, MBA from Duke University and BTech from the Indian Institute of Technology, Kharagpur, India.

Eduardo S. Schwartz is the California Professor of Real Estate and Professor of Finance, Anderson Graduate School of Management at the University of California, Los Angeles. He has an engineering degree from the University of Chile and a Masters and PhD in finance from the University of British Columbia. He has been on the faculty at the University of British Columbia and visiting at the London Business School and the University of California at Berkeley. He has published more than 80 articles in finance and economic journals, as well as monographs, chapters, conference proceedings and special reports. He is an associate editor for many journals, including the *Journal of Finance* and the *Journal of Financial and Quantitative Analysis*. He is past president of the Western Finance Association and the American Finance Association. He has also been a consultant to governmental agencies, banks, investment banks and industrial corporations.

David C. Shimko joined Bankers Trust in 1997 and is now a Principal and Head of the Risk Management Advisory Group. Currently, David is focused on developing CoVar, an initiative of Bankers Trust designed to provide credit risk management services to the energy industry. Prior to joining Bankers Trust, he was Vice President and Head of Risk Management Research at JP Morgan Securities, responsible for ongoing research into strategic and analytical risk management questions for JP Morgan and its clients. Previously he was responsible for Commodity Derivatives Research on Morgan's trading desk. He has worked extensively with clients around the world in evaluating, designing and implementing risk management strategies and programmes and putting in place strategic frameworks for the evaluation of business risks and capital deployment. Before joining Morgan David was Assistant Professor of Finance at the University of Southern California and a private consultant to financial institutions. He has published over 60 academic and trade articles on strategic issues and the practice of risk management, produced financial software packages and written a technical textbook at the PhD level entitled *Finance in Continuous Time: A Primer*. He writes a monthly end-user column in *Risk* magazine. David holds a PhD in managerial economics/finance and a BA in economics from Northwestern University.

Suresh Sundaresan is the Chase Manhattan Bank Foundation Professor of Financial Institutions in the department of Finance & Economics, Graduate School of Business, at Columbia University. He holds a PhD and an MS from Carnegie Mellon and joined Columbia Business School in 1980.

Naohiko Tejima is a PhD candidate in German literature at the University of Tokyo, where he has also studied towards a PhD in mathematics. His undergraduate major was also in mathematics at the University of Tokyo. He has worked part time in the Tokyo office of Kamakura for the past eight years.

Stuart M. Turnbull is Vice President of Global Analytics, at CIBC, where he is in charge of developing the next generation of credit and market risk management models. Previously he was the Bank of Montreal Professor of Banking and Finance, Queen's University (Canada), and a Research Fellow, Institute for Policy Analysis (Toronto). He is a graduate of the Imperial College of Science and Technology (London) and the University of British Columbia. He is the author of *Option Valuation*, and (with Robert A. Jarrow) *Derivative Securities*. He has published over 30 articles in major finance and economics journals and in law journals, as well as many articles in practitioner journals. He is an associate editor of *Mathematical Finance*, the *Journal of Financial Engineering* and the *International Journal of Theoretical and Applied Finance*, and has served as an associate editor for the *Journal of Finance*.

Donald R. van Deventer founded the Kamakura Corporation in April 1990 and is currently President. His emphasis is on the expansion of the company's software product lines and its international risk management and financial advisory businesses. He is the co-author of two books and his professional and research papers have been widely published. Prior to this he was senior vice president in the investment banking department of Lehman Brothers (then Shearson Lehman Hutton), and previously treasurer for First Interstate Bancorp in Los Angeles, where he also served as senior planning officer for acquisitions, new ventures and corporate strategy. Prior to this, Donald was a vice president in the risk management department of Security Pacific National Bank. He holds a PhD in business economics from the Harvard University Department of Economics and the Harvard Graduate School of Business Administration and a degree in mathematics and economics from Occidental College.

Thomas C. Wilson is a Principal with Swiss Re New Markets, where he is responsible for Risk Management and Risk Controlling globally, covering both financial and insurance risks. Prior to joining Swiss Re New Markets, Tom was a partner in the consulting firm of McKinsey & Company, where he focused primarily on serving financial institutions in the areas of risk and performance measurement and management. He was also responsible for McKinsey's Global Risk Management Practice. He previously worked with the Union Bank of Switzerland in Zurich as a swap-option trader and risk manager. Tom has a doctorate in economics from Stanford University and a bachelor's degree in business administration from the University of California at Berkeley.

Introduction

David Shimko

Bankers Trust

In the field of financial economics, credit risk management has traditionally fallen squarely between two camps. Traditionalists argued that credit risk assessment was more art than science. *Nouveau* financial engineers claimed that contingent claims (read "options") pricing could explain all that was interesting about bond pricing. Until recently it appeared that the traditionalists were right. The analytic models for credit risk assessment were hopelessly inadequate to deal with the complexities of bond pricing in the real world. After all, how do you determine the fair value of a risky bond? The answer was: determine the default probability and the recovery in default! Imagine – determining the value of one unknown quantity, the price of a bond, by substituting two unknown quantities in its place . . . . Clearly, although tremendous strides had been made in the determination of default probabilities and recoveries, the resulting analytic was less than satisfactory.

The perseverance of academics and analysts has paid off in spades in the last few years. Models used to be either too simplistic or too complex, with a surfeit of unobservable parameters. Real progress has been made in credit analytics, both at the individual loan or bond level and at the portfolio level. Part of this progress can be attributed to the published work on contingent claims, but the integration of this literature into the financial mainstream has yielded even better results.

While financial economics basked in its progress over the last two decades, the financial markets followed a parallel path. Suddenly, traditional credit departments at major banks, who used to rely on internal credit scoring systems and processes that were fundamentally qualitative in nature, found their analytic foundations being shaken. New technologies in credit risk evaluation, some borrowed from academics, challenged the traditional wisdom. Some were less successful than others. But although the analytic services (BARRA, KMV) had varying levels of success, nothing changed the traditional credit departments more than the advent of credit derivatives. After all, theoretical models go only so far. It is when you have a chance to transact on differences in opinion about different credit events that you seriously examine the analytics on which you base your opinion.

Once you have good analytics, of course, you are wasting your time unless you plan to use them. Some managers manage risk while keeping an eye on return, while others do the opposite. Still others prefer to arbitrage small credit differentials or trade risky bonds against equity. Some do this without preparation, and may even be successful. For the rest of us, this volume aims to provide not only the complete analytic background to the measurement of credit risk but guidance on how to manage it, whether you are a bond portfolio manager, a trader on a credit derivatives desk or a hedge fund manager.

What questions does the modern credit risk professional need to have answers to? They are as follows:

❏ What is the state of the credit market – now and from the perspective of the last 20 years?

❑ What do default rates and recoveries look like in general?

❑ What systematic tendencies can one see in those default rates and recoveries?

❑ What can basic contingent claims models offer in the way of understanding bond prices?

❑ Where are these models deficient?

❑ Can corrections be made to the basic models to make them more realistic?

❑ How do the advanced models perform?

❑ Can contingent claims models be integrated with term structure models?

❑ How can term structure models be adapted to model the risk structure of interest rates?

❑ How can one use all the best available models to price credit-sensitive instruments?

❑ Assuming we have a good model for pricing and risk assessment, how should we manage credit risks?

❑ How should our management of credit risk incorporate model information?

❑ What part of credit risk management rightfully belongs to "managerial judgement"?

Like you, I hate lists of questions without answers. Continue reading this book to gain much insight and some answers on these topics. I urge you, when you have finished, to revisit these questions and ask how your intuition and judgement have improved as a direct result of working through the many contributions therein.

The book is organised into five sections. The first, *Risky bonds in the portfolio and market context*, serves as a general introduction to the credit markets. Beginners and advanced practitioners alike will benefit from this introduction – beginners for the exposure to market statistics, and advanced practitioners for an introduction to credit based on macroeconomic analysis.

The second section, *Valuation of risky debt*, contains the classical sequence of papers in the style of Merton's oft-cited work. From the initial observation (Merton's) that shareholders have the right to "put" the firm to the debtholders to satisfy debt obligations, we see that debt has option-like characteristics. Putting that simple observation into practice requires that all the restrictive assumptions Merton makes generally need to be removed, from considering different kinds of debt, or the effect of coupons or stochastic (changing) interest rates. The other papers in the section all follow in Merton's tradition, while generalising the work to be of more practical importance to us today.

The third section, *Credit ratings*, explores and develops the traditional approach to credit risk management, highlighting both its strengths and its weaknesses. No credit professional should be without a complete understanding of these strengths and weaknesses. Even the theoretical "quant" who wants to model credit using the most sophisticated contingent claims pricing techniques needs to be aware of the impact that credit ratings analysis has had on the credit profession.

The fourth section, *Credit risk mitigation alternatives*, applies the analytic methods developed in the preceding sections to the pricing of credit risk mitigation alternatives, with an emphasis on credit derivatives. This section brings theoretical calculations into practical reality. For example, when we price a bond we need not worry too much about separating the probability of default from the recovery on default. But when we write a credit derivative that pays off only in the event of default we need to know precisely what probability of default to use and how to hedge our bets. No doubt, credit derivatives have changed both the marketplace and credit analytics, and, as noted in one contribution, some of these changes may be very subtle indeed.

The fifth section, *Practitioner's guide to managing credit risk*, is a collection of articles directed at credit risk managers. It is the least analytically complex of the last four sections. To reach the broadest possible audience – the manager seeking guidance, and the analyst wondering where the analytics lead and how his or her analysis will be used – the section contains two papers from the literature and two that were specially commissioned. In the spirit of this book, one should not have credit risk measurement without credit risk management. It is ironic that many banks today have strong credit departments and equally strong but separate credit analytics groups. Hopefully, this text and others like it will contribute to the ultimate convergence of these efforts.

The introductions to each section provide more detail on the papers they contain, highlighting important points and showing how they contribute to the section's overall theme. The introductions are "easy reads" and non-quantitative in nature to ensure that the non-technical professional gets the key points of each paper and understands why they are important. In many cases they also suggest further reading options for those who want to enrich their study further.

Some more sophisticated readers will no doubt come to the conclusion that we have missed an important paper or one that summarised the issues well. I concede in advance that this is likely to be true. Some papers we failed to consider in the proper context or light or simply missed. Others we thought were brilliant but had not yet stood the test of time, or had perhaps appeared only in working paper form without the benefit of the peer review and editorial processes that tend to sharpen (and shorten) our efforts. Throughout the section introductions, and in the bibliographies of each chapter, you will find many more papers and references that will help you to expand your credit risk management knowledge beyond the confines of this text.

In our defence, however, you will find a complete treatment of credit risk assessment and management in this volume. We have drawn from both academics and practitioners to produce a state-of-the-art reference work and educational guide for the modern credit risk practitioner. The book addresses both theoretical models and their practical application in day-to-day credit risk management. We have avoided pure interest rate risk – obviously a key component of any bond pricing model – as this topic has been dealt with comprehensively in the Risk Publications volume *Vasicek and Beyond: Approaches to Building and Applying Interest Rate Models*, edited by Lane Hughston (1996).

RISKY BONDS IN THE PORTFOLIO AND MARKET CONTEXT

Introduction

Risky Bonds in the Portfolio and Market Context

David Shimko

You will find option pricing theorists who can price any kind of option you name but cannot quote the market price of a single option! So that you do not become one of these theorist-asters in credit risk management we have included a comprehensive and timely survey of the bond markets. Edward Altman, with Diane Cooke and Vellore Kishore, agreed to a reprint of their latest "Report on Defaults and Returns on High-Yield Bonds" in this volume. The report is updated annually by the Salomon Center at the Leonard N. Stern School of Business, New York University. The annual subscription fee is well worth the price.

The study, which opens this section, contains all the anecdotal information you will need to describe credit risk to the non-specialist. For example, the 1998 default rate for all US issues was 1.10% in 1998, compared to 0.65% in 1997. Defaults are on the rise, you might say, particularly in the wake of the Asian meltdown in late summer of that year. In the 20-year perspective, however, that rate was pretty low. From 1978 to 1998 the average default rate was 1.82% per year, a large part of which came from 1986–92. Recovery rates showed an interesting twist in 1998 (35.9%), falling below both the 1997 levels (54.2%) and the 20-year average (40–42%).

Altman and his colleagues show yet again that credit ratings may have some predictive power just prior to default but that as one increases the time prior to default that predictive power wanes substantially. For example, 8.2% of defaulted issues in 1998 were considered investment grade one year before default! Furthermore, 7% of issues rated AAA by Standard & Poor's have defaulted since 1971, and the number will grow with time. This suggests that the relationship between credit rating and credit quality is at best complex – ratings alone are not sufficient to gauge default probabilities.

The authors also report yield spread results – ie, "How much are you earning net of default risk by investing in high-yield bonds?" The results for 1998 are not terrific given the results for late summer, but the longer-term results are informative (see their Table 13 and Figure 2). For example, $1 in 1977 would have grown to $11 in 1998 had you invested in high-yield bonds as against $7 if you had invested in high-quality bonds.

Finally, the study shows how default rates and recoveries differ by industry. Leading defaulters in 1998 were financial services, leisure and manufacturing. The lowest recoveries were seen in miscellaneous and diversified manufacturing, and the highest were from chemicals, petroleum companies and utilities.

The report is fascinating, but it raises more questions than it answers. For example, some of the highest default rates occurred in years when the stock market crashed and during the Gulf War. The Altman analyses have found their niche, and I wouldn't change a word now or in future updates. But the present report recognises its limitations – that there are significant systematic effects present in default rates and recoveries for which the authors have not accounted.

A macro-view of credit

Altman, Cooke and Vellore's study could be criticised on the grounds that it provides data for only the most elementary bond pricing models – historical default frequencies and recoveries. Thomas Wilson explains, in his two-part thesis first published in 1997, why this approach fails to perform well in the aggregate. For example, if an analyst estimated default probabilities, recoveries and correlations among bonds, would not his model be sufficient to price bond portfolios and assess their risks? Wilson shows us why this is not enough. Even though macroeconomic effects may have a small influence on whether an individual bond issue defaults, the importance in the aggregate is staggering. We cannot evaluate bond prices and risks without a sense of how aggregate economic performance affects the assumptions that underlie risky bond pricing.

Wilson also demonstrates that analysts should not be happy approximating credit loss distributions with bell-shaped curves. Credit losses are fundamentally asymmetric because one can experience windfall losses but not windfall gains. Wilson shows how to build up a discrete distribution of outcomes from a model where the incidence and severity of default are conditional on the state of the macroeconomy. The result is a multifactor systematic risk model that induces default correlations between individual loans and bonds and which determines default likelihoods and recoveries according to market risk factors rather than requiring the analyst to assume default correlations exogenously.

The systematic default factor, it turns out, is responsible for 77.5% of the variation in average default rates and induces a large part of the correlation between those defaults. Other factors are also important. Simulating these factors, one can construct a distribution of future default probabilities for any state of the market today.

In part two of his exposition Wilson explains how to derive these distributions and expands the analytic technique to cover illiquidity, variable recovery rates and country defaults. The author twice expresses skepticism about "all-singing, all-dancing" models, yet it is not beyond the realm of imagination that his framework could serve as the basis for such a model.

Wilson's paper does not give us all the answers, but it provides a useful framework on to which we can overlay debt pricing models that recognise the option-like features of debt. The next section, *Valuation of risky debt*, reviews the history and current practice of a contingent claims approach to the pricing of risky bonds.

Report on Defaults and Returns on High-Yield Bonds: Analysis through 1998 and Default Outlook for 1999–2001

Edward I. Altman with Diane Cooke and Vellore Kishore

Leonard N. Stern School of Business, New York University

Nineteen-ninety-eight was a year of mixed performance for the high-yield bond market in the United States, with much below average returns and spreads over default-risk-free Treasury bonds but continued relatively low default rates and losses and another record year of new issuance. Returns and new issuance were excellent through the first seven months of the year, but returns reversed and new issues dried up, temporarily, in the wake of the Russian default in August and the turmoil in emerging markets, causing another short-term flight to quality. Returns in 1998 on high-yield bonds in the US were slightly above 4.0% for the entire year, about 8.5% lower than historical averages. Return spreads also were much below average (–8.7%).

The default rate was again relatively low – 1.60% – and losses from default 1.1%. Despite 1998's low relative return, net returns (after deducting losses from defaults) over the last two decades continue to show a compounded result of more than 12% per year and spreads over US Treasuries of more than 2.5% per year. New issuance of high-yield debt in 1998 totalled a record $140 billion, with $115 billion of the total in the first seven and a half months.

This report documents the high-yield debt market's risk and return performance by presenting default and mortality statistics and providing a matrix of average returns and other performance statistics over the relevant periods of the market's evolution. Our analysis covers the period 1971–98 for defaults and 1978–98 for returns. In addition, we present our annual forecast of expected defaults for the next three years (1999–2001). Two other reports, published by the NYU Salomon Center,[1] comprehensively document the performance of defaulted public bonds and bank loans and the default rate experience on syndicated bank loans.

Default rates

During 1998, $7.464 billion of domestic US high-yield straight bonds defaulted or were exchanged under distressed conditions. This amount comprised 53 issues from 37 defaulting companies and resulted in a default rate of 1.60%. This compares to 29 issues

This paper was first published as New York University Salomon Center Working Paper S/99/10, 1999. The authors wish to thank Chris McHugh of New Generation Research, Wilson Miranda and Elizabeth Tompkins of Salomon Smith Barney Inc. for their assistance with data and also the many securities dealers for their price quotations. Finally, this report benefits from the assistance of Luis Beltran and Lourdes Tanglao of the NYU Salomon Center.

Table 1. Historical default rates – straight bonds only excluding defaulted issues from par value outstanding, 1971–98

Year	Par value outstanding ($ million) (a)	Par value defaults ($ million)	Default rates (%)
1998	465,500	7,464	1.603
1997	335,400	4,200	1.252
1996	271,000	3,336	1.231
1995	240,000	4,551	1.896
1994	235,000	3,418	1.454
1993	206,907	2,287	1.105
1992	163,000	5,545	3.402
1991	183,600	18,862	10.273
1990	181,000	18,354	10.140
1989	189,258	8,110	4.285
1988	148,187	3,944	2.662
1987	129,557	7,486	5.778
1986	90,243	3,156	3.497
1985	58,088	992	1.708
1984	40,939	344	0.840
1983	27,492	301	1.095
1982	18,109	577	3.186
1981	17,115	27	0.158
1980	14,935	224	1.500
1979	10,356	20	0.193
1978	8,946	119	1.330
1977	8,157	381	4.671
1976	7,735	30	0.388
1975	7,471	204	2.731
1974	10,894	123	1.129
1973	7,824	49	0.626
1972	6,928	193	2.786
1971	6,602	82	1.242

			Standard deviation (%)
Arithmetic average default rate			
1971–98		2.577	2.515
1978–98		2.790	2.753
1985–98		3.592	2.999
Weighted average default rate (b)			
1971–98		3.054	3.308
1978–98		3.075	2.890
1985–98		3.166	2.921
Median annual default rate, 1971–98		1.552	

(a) As of mid-year.
(b) Weighted by par value of amount outstanding for each year.
Source: Authors' compilation and various dealer estimates.

from 21 companies in 1997. A list of 1998 defaults appears in Appendix A.[2] The 1998 default rate is somewhat higher than last year's rate (1.25%), but it remains considerably below the historic weighted average annual rate from 1971–98 of 3.1% per year (2.6% arithmetic average rate) and is slightly above the median annual rate (1.55%) over the same 28-year period (Table 1 and Figure 1). The face value of defaults was about $3.3 billion higher in 1998 than one year earlier (an increase of 78%, but the mid-year base population of high-yield bonds also increased from $335 to $466 billion (39%); hence, the modest increase in the rate of default). The default rate in 1998 continued a six-year string of rates below 2.0%, and in four of the six years the rate was below 1.5%. Over the period 1992–98 the long-term annual weighted-average default rate has declined from 4.2% to 3.1% per year.

Default rates and ageing bias

The 1998 default rate of 1.60% is based on a mid-year population estimate of $465.5 billion – an amount that does not include issues that defaulted prior to 1998 but were still outstanding. This population total was swelled by a tremendous surge in new issuance in the second half of 1997 and the first half of 1998 (public and 144a issues), further adjusted for upgrades from high-yield to investment grade and downgrades to high-yield

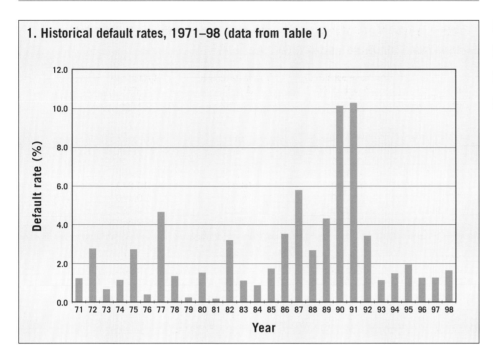

1. Historical default rates, 1971–98 (data from Table 1)

status and, finally, by calls and other redemptions. Therefore, despite considerably higher default amounts in 1998, the default rate increased only modestly from the 1997 level.

Whenever there is a relatively large increase in new issuance in the high-yield market, you will observe a downward bias in the default rate due to the "ageing effect" of defaults. This will be clearly seen, at a later point, when we present our mortality statistics and observe that the marginal default/mortality rates in the first three years after issuance start out quite low, increase considerably until the third year and then, for the most part, level off. This new issuance ageing effect is not possible to observe in the Moody's (dynamic cohort) or Standard & Poor's (static-pool) approaches.[3]

Our mortality calculations take into account the ageing bias that can manifest during abnormally high new issuance periods. Despite all this we observe that the bias, though observable, was not very substantial in 1998 now that the high-yield market is as large as it is. For example, if the population base had not grown at all from the mid-year 1997 figure, the 1998 default rate would have been 2.23%.

Quarterly and industry defaults
Appendix B calculates default rates on a quarterly basis (since 1990). It can be observed that the quarterly rates in 1998 fluctuated considerably, with the fourth quarter's rate (0.47%) the second highest. As noted in our earlier reports, quarterly rates are almost never indicative of trends except possibly back in the period 1990–91, when default rates skyrocketed to record levels over several consecutive quarters. For example, the fourth quarter's rate would have been considerably higher had we included all issues which missed interest payments in December but still had some grace period time remaining at year end.

Appendix C lists the defaults since 1970 by industry affiliation. The "leading" sectors in 1998 include general manufacturing (6), financial services (6), communications (6), retailing (6) and leisure/entertainment (5). We do not calculate default rates by industrial sector although we have analysed industrial sector recoveries (see Altman and Kishore, 1996; updated data from that study are given in Appendix D).

Default losses and recovery at default
Default losses did rise substantially in 1998 compared to 1997 (1.10% versus 0.65%) but were still far below the average from 1978–98 of 1.82% per year (2.05% weighted average annual rate). Table 2 shows the 1998 loss rate, which includes the loss of one-half of the average annual coupon. Default losses for the last 21 years are shown in Table 3.

Table 2. Default loss rate, 1998 (%)

Background data

Average default rate 1998	1.603
Average price at default (a)	35.863
Average loss of principal	64.137
Average coupon payment	9.460

Default loss computation

Default rate	1.603
× loss of principal	64.137
Default loss of principal	1.028
Default rate	1.603
× loss of half of coupon	4.730
Default loss of coupon	0.076
Default loss of principal and coupon	1.104

(a) If default date price is not available, end-of-month price is used.
Source: Authors' compilations and various dealer quotes.

Table 3. Default rates and losses, 1978–98 (a)

Year	Par value outstanding (a) ($ million)	Par value of default ($ million)	Default rate (%)	Weighted price after default ($)	Weighted coupon (%)	Default loss (%)
1998	465,500	7,464	1.60	35.9	9.46	1.10
1997	335,400	4,200	1.25	54.2	11.87	0.65
1996	271,000	3,336	1.23	51.9	8.92	1.10
1995	240,000	4,551	1.90	40.6	11.83	1.24
1994	235,000	3,418	1.45	39.4	10.25	0.96
1993	206,907	2,287	1.11	56.6	12.98	0.56
1992	163,000	5,545	3.40	50.1	12.32	1.91
1991	183,600	18,862	10.27	36.0	11.59	7.16
1990	181,000	18,354	10.14	23.4	12.94	8.42
1989	189,258	8,110	4.29	38.3	13.40	2.93
1988	148,187	3,944	2.66	43.6	11.91	1.66
1987	129,557	7,486	5.78	75.9	12.07	1.74
1986	90,243	3,156	3.50	34.5	10.61	2.48
1985	58,088	992	1.71	45.9	13.69	1.04
1984	40,939	341	0.84	48.6	12.23	0.48
1983	27,492	301	1.09	55.7	10.11	0.54
1982	18,109	577	3.19	38.6	9.61	2.11
1981	17,115	27	0.16	12	15.75	0.15
1980	14,935	224	1.50	21.1	8.43	1.25
1979	10,356	20	0.19	31	10.63	0.14
1978	8,946	119	1.33	60	8.38	0.59
Arithmetic average 1978–98			2.79	42.5	11.38	1.82
Weighted average 1978–98			3.07			2.05

(a) Excludes defaulted issues.
Source: Tables 1 and 2.

The average recovery rate on the issues for which we had end-of-default month prices was 35.9% – somewhat below the venerable 40-42% historical average recovery rate (Tables 3 and 4) and considerably lower than last year's figure (54.2%). This was surprising since 44 of the 53 defaulting issues were senior secured or senior unsecured and less than 10 were subordinated; seven were discounted bonds, where we use accreted values as the base. About 70% of all new issuance in the high-yield market since 1991 has been senior in priority. This lower than average 1998 recovery rate is a caution to investors, who cannot assume that senior bonds will always result in above-average recovery rates. For example, the senior unsecured recovery rate in 1998 was 39.57%, as against an historical average of over 48%. Table 4 lists the recovery rates (prices just after default) by seniority for 1998 and for the past 21 years. Most of the seniority levels recovered lower amounts in 1998 than the historical 21 year average, with the exception of the senior secured group. The overall arithmetic average 21-year recovery rate of $40.41 is based on more than 800 issues (42.5% average, weighted by the amount outstanding in each year – see Table 3).

In Table 5 we list the average recovery at default stratified by original bond rating for the period 1971–98. The weighted recoveries for investment-grade bonds definitely show higher rates than for non-investment grade debt, but the three "junk" bond classes continue to show very little difference. This is also true after adjusting for seniority bias.

Table 6 lists the original Standard & Poor's ratings of defaulting issues, as well as the one year and six months prior to default ratings. Of the 756 issues tabulated, 77.1% were original issue high-yield bonds and 22.9% were originally rated as investment grade but eventually defaulted; 8.2% of the defaulted issues were still rated investment grade one year prior to default and 6.9% six months prior (multiple issues from a few, large, high-grade issuers, eg, Columbia Gas System, however, accounted for a large proportion of the 12- and six-month-prior investment grade defaults), and most of these were BBB.

Table 7 shows that the time it takes for an issue to default compared to its issuance date makes virtually no difference in the recovery rate. The possible exception is the $47.63 weighted recovery in the first year, which is almost matched by the figure of just over $50 in the ninth year. Most other weighted recoveries by year are in the high $30s to low $40s range.

Table 4. Weighted average recovery rates on defaulted debt by seniority per $100 face amount, 1978–98

Default year	Senior secured No.	$	Senior unsecured No.	$	Senior subordinated No.	$	Subordinated No.	$	Discount and zero coupon No.	$	All seniorities No.	$
1998	6	70.38	21	39.57	6	17.54	0	0	7	21.03	40	35.89
1997	4	74.90	12	70.94	6	31.89	1	60.00	2	19.00	25	53.89
1996	4	59.08	4	50.11	9	48.99	4	44.23	3	11.99	24	51.91
1995	5	44.64	9	50.50	17	39.01	1	20.00	1	17.50	33	41.77
1994	5	48.66	8	51.14	5	19.81	3	37.04	1	5.00	22	39.44
1993	2	55.75	7	33.38	10	51.50	9	28.38	4	31.75	32	38.83
1992	15	59.85	8	35.61	17	58.20	22	49.13	5	19.82	67	50.03
1991	4	44.12	69	55.84	37	31.91	38	24.30	9	27.89	157	40.67
1990	12	32.18	31	29.02	38	25.01	24	18.83	11	15.63	116	24.66
1989	9	82.69	16	53.70	21	19.60	30	23.95	–	–	76	35.97
1988	13	67.96	19	41.99	10	30.70	20	35.27	–	–	62	43.45
1987	4	90.68	17	72.02	6	56.24	4	35.25	–	–	31	66.63
1986	8	48.32	11	37.72	7	35.20	30	33.39	–	–	56	36.60
1985	2	74.25	3	34.81	7	36.18	15	41.45	–	–	27	41.78
1984	4	53.42	1	50.50	2	65.88	7	44.68	–	–	14	50.62
1983	1	71.00	3	67.72	–	–	4	41.79	–	–	8	55.17
1982	–	–	16	39.31	–	–	4	32.91	–	–	20	38.03
1981	1	72.00	–	–	–	–	–	–	–	–	1	72.00
1980	–	–	2	26.71	–	–	2	16.63	–	–	4	21.67
1979	–	–	–	–	–	–	1	31.00	–	–	1	31.00
1978	–	–	1	60.00	–	–	–	–	–	–	1	60.00
Total/Average	99	59.38	258	48.12	198	34.46	219	31.71	43	20.76	817	40.32
Median		59.85		50.11		35.2U		33.39		19.00	–	41.77
Std dev.		23.18		26.16		24.75		22.53		6.34	–	25.77

Source: Authors' compilation from various dealer quotes.

Table 5. Average price after default by original bond rating, 1971–98

Rating	Number of observations	Average price ($)	Weighted average price ($)	Median price ($)	Standard deviation ($)	Minimum price ($)	Maximum price ($)
AAA	7	68.34	76.99	71.88	20.82	32.00	97.00
AA	20	59.59	76.52	54.25	24.59	17.80	99.88
A	56	60.63	47.59	61.32	25.53	10.50	100.00
BBB	84	49.05	49.59	50.00	23.40	2.00	103.00
BB	79	39.25	39.20	34.50	22.08	1.00	98.75
B	416	37.84	36.72	34.38	24.46	0.50	112.00
CCC	121	38.23	35.22	30.00	27.67	1.00	103.25
Total	783	41.70	40.16	37.00	25.73	0.50	112.00

Source: Authors' compilation.

Table 6. Rating distribution of defaulted issues at various points prior to default, 1971–98 (a)

	Original rating Number	%	Rating one year prior to default Number	%	Rating six months prior to default Number	%
AAA	5	0.7	0	0.0	0	0.0
AA	25	3.3	0	0.0	0	0.0
A	66	8.7	5	0.8	2	0.3
BBB	77	10.2	48	7.4	45	6.6
Total investment grade	173	22.9	53	8.2	47	6.9
BB	90	11.9	80	12.3	62	9.1
B	385	50.9	325	50.1	287	42.0
CCC	104	13.8	174	26.8	240	35.1
CC	4	0.5	12	1.8	41	6.0
C	0	0.0	5	0.8	6	0.9
Total non-investment grade	583	77.1	596	91.8	636	93.1
Total	756	100	649	100	683	100

(a) Based on Standard & Poor's bond ratings.
Source: Authors' compilation.

Table 7. Weighted average price at default by numbered years after issuance, 1971–98

Years to default	Number of observations	Average price ($)	Weighted avg. price ($)	Median price ($)	Standard deviation ($)
1	34	44.53	47.63	34.50	26.26
2	105	38.90	36.75	36.50	22.58
3	130	39.41	36.62	35.00	25.83
4	121	42.52	42.27	39.00	25.00
5	103	42.03	41.03	37.00	26.78
6	82	39.25	39.25	35.00	25.71
7	41	37.60	44.71	35.75	25.87
8	33	36.75	34.51	27.00	27.35
9	19	41.99	50.22	33.00	27.34
10	25	38.52	42.69	32.00	23.47
All	693	40.18	39.76	36.00	25.31

Source: Authors' compilation.

We also observe (not illustrated here) that the number of years remaining in the maturity of a bond issue is not at all related to its likelihood of defaulting. In other words, companies usually default because of their inability to meet interest payments and not the repayment of principal at maturity. A related key factor to observe is the date when non-cash pay deferred-interest bonds do become cash pay – for example, after three years from issuance. Many new recent issues in certain industries (eg, telecommunications) have this feature.

Interest payment grace periods and accreted values: effect on default rates and losses

It is well known that the calculation of meaningful default rates and losses is more of an art than a science and that the number of possible alternative methods is staggering when you consider all of the subtleties. Two factors that we have consistently considered over the years in the calculation of default rates are the treatment of interest payment grace periods and accreted values on discounted bond defaults. A "legal" default in public bond markets involves the missing of an interest payment when it comes due and the failure to "cure" that missed payment within a specified grace period (usually 30 days). We have always applied this rule, and in 1998 there were two bond issuers (with a face

Table 8. Mortality rates by original rating – all rated corporate bonds,* 1971–98 (%)

		\multicolumn{10}{c}{Years after issuance}

		1	2	3	4	5	6	7	8	9	10
AAA	Yearly	0.00	0.00	0.00	0.00	0.05	0.00	0.00	0.00	0.00	0.00
	Cumulative	0.00	0.00	0.00	0.00	0.05	0.05	0.05	0.05	0.05	0.05
AA	Yearly	0.00	0.00	0.36	0.22	0.00	0.00	0.00	0.00	0.03	0.03
	Cumulative	0.00	0.00	0.36	0.58	0.58	0.58	0.58	0.58	0.62	0.65
A	Yearly	0.00	0.00	0.03	0.10	0.05	0.10	0.04	0.12	0.08	0.00
	Cumulative	0.00	0.00	0.03	0.13	0.18	0.28	0.32	0.44	0.53	0.53
BBB	Yearly	0.02	0.29	0.27	0.61	0.28	0.42	0.16	0.07	0.07	0.29
	Cumulative	0.02	0.31	0.58	1.19	1.46	1.88	2.03	2.10	2.17	2.45
BB	Yearly	0.36	0.73	2.65	1.65	2.29	1.14	2.11	0.25	1.52	3.38
	Cumulative	0.36	1.09	3.71	5.30	7.47	8.52	10.46	10.68	12.04	15.02
B	Yearly	1.14	3.00	5.71	6.24	4.59	3.36	2.93	1.88	1.54	1.04
	Cumulative	1.14	4.10	9.57	15.22	19.11	21.83	24.12	25.55	26.70	27.45
CCC	Yearly	2.03	13.60	15.16	8.27	2.96	9.59	4.02	3.36	0.00	3.71
	Cumulative	2.03	15.36	28.19	34.13	36.07	42.21	44.53	46.39	46.39	48.38

*Rated by Standard & Poor's at issuance.
Based on 681 issues.

value of $461 million) that did indeed miss an interest payment but managed to cure that miss within the grace period (All Star Gas Corp. and Service Merchandise Company). In addition, during December 1998 there were interest payment misses amounting to $836 million in face value that had a grace period extending into 1999. Since the grace period did not expire by year end, in most cases, we will only include these bonds as defaults in January 1999, assuming the payments are not cured.[4] If we had included both the cured interest payment misses and December's "misses," the default rate in 1998 would have been 1.88%.

With respect to accreted values of discounted bonds, we feel that it is not appropriate to use the full face value of the issue in our default rate and default loss calculations. Only the accreted value – ie, the value that investors could theoretically have sold their bonds for at the time of default (if there were no credit problems) – is appropriate. In 1998 seven discounted bonds defaulted (see Appendix A), an unusually large number. The difference between the face and accreted values of these issues was $600 million. In addition, our calculation of the recovery rate (Tables 2, 3 and 4) is based on the price that the bonds traded at just after default as a percentage of the accreted value, not the face value. This procedure results in a higher recovery rate and a lower loss rate than would be the case if face values were used.

Mortality rates, losses and simulated return spreads

Updated mortality rates and losses for the period 1971–98 are reported in Tables 8 and 9. Our total defaulted issue population that had a rating upon issuance and a price at default now numbers 682 issues. The methodology for these calculations comes from Altman (1989) and adjusts for calls, sinking funds and other redemptions. Similar to actuarial insurance calculations, our mortality method measures default experience for major rating categories from the "birth" of the issue and is market- (not issuer-) weighted. It clearly adjusts for the ageing bias (discussed below).

The relatively low 1998, and last six-year, default rates have reduced cumulative mortality rates slightly and losses throughout the entire spectrum of ratings and horizons. For example, the five-year cumulative rates through 1998 versus 1994 were for BBB (1.46% versus 2.39%), for BB (7.47% versus 10.79%), for B (19.11% versus 23.71%), and for CCC (36.07% versus 45.63%). Also, all of the five- and ten-year cumulative rates were lower through 1998 versus 1997, reflecting the continued drop in default rates in recent years. For example, the five-year single-B rate dropped to 19.11% from 21.95%.

Table 9. Mortality losses by original rating – all rated corporate bonds,* 1971–98 (%)

		Years after issuance									
		1	2	3	4	5	6	7	8	9	10
AAA	Yearly	0.00	0.00	0.00	0.00	0.01	0.00	0.00	0.00	0.00	0.00
	Cumulative	0.00	0.00	0.00	0.00	0.01	0.01	0.01	0.01	0.01	0.01
AA	Yearly	0.00	0.00	0.07	0.08	0.00	0.00	0.00	0.00	0.02	0.02
	Cumulative	0.00	0.00	0.07	0.15	0.15	0.15	0.15	0.15	0.17	0.19
A	Yearly	0.00	0.00	0.02	0.06	0.04	0.07	0.02	0.07	0.05	0.00
	Cumulative	0.00	0.00	0.02	0.08	0.12	0.19	0.21	0.28	0.32	0.32
BBB	Yearly	0.02	0.17	0.15	0.32	0.10	0.26	0.14	0.05	0.04	0.20
	Cumulative	0.02	0.19	0.33	0.66	0.76	1.01	1.15	1.19	1.24	1.44
BB	Yearly	0.25	0.46	1.99	1.26	1.19	0.92	1.12	0.15	0.85	1.75
	Cumulative	0.25	0.70	2.68	3.91	5.05	5.92	6.98	7.12	7.90	9.52
B	Yearly	0.67	1.99	4.45	4.23	3.36	2.12	1.80	1.39	0.82	0.67
	Cumulative	0.67	2.65	6.97	10.91	13.90	15.72	17.24	18.39	19.05	19.60
CCC	Yearly	1.02	11.09	10.66	4.98	1.85	6.60	3.60	2.67	0.00	3.09
	Cumulative	1.02	12.00	21.39	25.30	26.68	31.52	33.98	35.75	35.75	37.73

*Rated by Standard & Poor's at issuance.
Based on 681 issues.

Table 10. Mortality rates by original rating – all rated corporate bonds,* 1983–98 (%)

		Years after issuance									
		1	2	3	4	5	6	7	8	9	10
AAA	Yearly	0.00	0.00	0.00	0.00	0.00	0.00	0.00	0.00	0.00	0.00
	Cumulative	0.00	0.00	0.00	0.00	0.00	0.00	0.00	0.00	0.00	0.00
AA	Yearly	0.00	0.00	0.44	0.25	0.00	0.00	0.01	0.00	0.00	0.00
	Cumulative	0.00	0.00	0.44	0.69	0.69	0.69	0.70	0.70	0.70	0.70
A	Yearly	0.00	0.00	0.03	0.11	0.06	0.02	0.02	0.05	0.05	0.00
	Cumulative	0.00	0.00	0.03	0.15	0.21	0.23	0.25	0.30	0.36	0.36
BBB	Yearly	0.02	0.29	0.26	0.68	0.24	0.41	0.09	0.05	0.00	0.00
	Cumulative	0.02	0.31	0.58	1.25	1.49	1.89	1.99	2.04	2.04	2.04
BB	Yearly	0.38	0.75	2.69	1.54	2.42	1.01	2.19	0.30	1.83	0.96
	Cumulative	0.38	1.13	3.78	5.26	7.56	8.49	10.50	10.77	12.40	13.24
B	Yearly	1.16	3.03	5.85	6.14	4.62	2.99	2.80	1.18	0.72	0.59
	Cumulative	1.16	4.15	9.75	15.30	19.21	21.62	23.82	24.72	25.26	25.70
CCC	Yearly	2.06	13.82	15.30	8.42	3.04	9.75	3.84	2.86	0.00	0.00
	Cumulative	2.06	15.60	28.51	34.53	36.52	42.71	44.91	46.48	46.48	46.48

*Rated by Standard & Poor's at issuance.
Based on 573 issues.

As for the ageing effect of bond defaults (mentioned earlier), we do find evidence of this for BBB- and B-rated bonds during the first four years after issuance and for BB- and CCC-rated bonds for three years, but no relationship thereafter. This can be observed in the yearly (marginal) mortality rates in Table 8. The BB marginal rates are somewhat erratic, rising for the first three years and fluctuating thereafter. Single-B marginal rates rise for the first four years, reach a steady state of about 4–6% per year for years three through seven, and fall off subsequently.

Similar results can be found for the mortality losses given in Table 9. These are actual losses adjusted for recoveries at default and the loss of one semi-annual interest payment. Recall that these marginal and cumulative mortality rates and losses reflect underlying cohort populations that are adjusted each year for defaults, distressed restructurings and redemptions (calls).

In addition to the mortality rates and losses for the period 1971–98, we have also calculated those statistics for the period when the high-yield bond market began its significant new issuance trend (1983). Tables 10 and 11 present the mortality statistics for the 1983–98 timespan. Note from Table 1 that in 1983 the amount outstanding increased by about 50% when new issuance that year was about $15 billion.

Comparing mortality statistics from our traditional starting point (1971) to the later starting date (1983), we can observe that, in general, cumulative mortality rates are essentially the same for the non-investment grade ratings in the shorter, more recent, sample period (ie, the 1983–98 period).

Table 12 lists a type of "simulated actual" return spread of corporate bonds (per $100 of investment) over long-term US Treasuries for up to 10 years after issuance, covering the period 1971–98. This analysis assumes that the investor bought the indicated rating category and held for 10 years (semi-annual holding periods). The return spread changes over time as interest rates change and returns are adjusted for reinvested cashflows, at the then prevailing rate, from coupon payments and recoveries on defaults. Prices of individual issues, however, do not change unless a default occurs. Data on defaults and losses are derived from the authors' database, which is the same source as that used in Tables 8–11.

Results through 1998 for 10-year-horizons continue to indicate that the double-B class performs best, followed closely by triple-B bonds. This is confirmation of the now more commonly found "cross-over" investment strategy, which involves purchasing split BBB/Ba or Baa/BB bonds as well as double Bs. Single-B return spreads are lower than the

Table 11. Mortality losses by original rating – all rated corporate bonds,* 1983–98 (%)

		Years after issuance									
		1	2	3	4	5	6	7	8	9	10
AAA	Yearly	0.00	0.00	0.00	0.00	0.00	0.00	0.00	0.00	0.00	0.00
	Cumulative	0.00	0.00	0.00	0.00	0.00	0.00	0.00	0.00	0.00	0.00
AA	Yearly	0.00	0.00	0.09	0.09	0.00	0.00	0.00	0.00	0.00	0.00
	Cumulative	0.00	0.00	0.09	0.17	0.17	0.17	0.18	0.18	0.18	0.18
A	Yearly	0.00	0.00	0.02	0.07	0.04	0.01	0.00	0.02	0.04	0.00
	Cumulative	0.00	0.00	0.02	0.09	0.14	0.15	0.15	0.17	0.21	0.21
BBB	Yearly	0.02	0.17	0.14	0.36	0.07	0.24	0.09	0.04	0.00	0.00
	Cumulative	0.02	0.19	0.33	0.68	0.76	0.99	1.09	1.13	1.13	1.13
BB	Yearly	0.25	0.48	2.01	1.23	1.26	0.84	1.09	0.18	1.02	0.79
	Cumulative	0.25	0.73	2.72	3.92	5.13	5.93	6.95	7.12	8.07	8.79
B	Yearly	0.67	2.02	4.56	4.14	3.39	1.91	1.69	0.96	0.28	0.34
	Cumulative	0.67	2.68	7.11	10.96	13.98	15.62	17.05	17.85	18.07	18.36
CCC	Yearly	1.04	11.27	10.76	5.07	1.88	6.70	3.44	2.72	0.00	0.00
	Cumulative	1.04	12.19	21.64	25.61	27.01	31.90	34.24	36.03	36.03	36.03

*Rated by Standard & Poor's at issuance.
Based on 573 issues.

Table 12. Return spread of corporate bonds over risk-free governments for the period 1971–98 ($)

Years after issuance	Bond rating at issuance						
	AAA	AA	A	BBB	BB	B	CCC
0.5	0.22	0.36	0.51	0.12	0.13	1.45	(3.19)
1.0	0.46	0.05	0.02	0.03	1.61	4.12	(6.52)
1.5	0.71	1.05	1.66	2.13	1.86	5.00	(10.01)
2.0	0.99	1.45	2.25	2.87	1.14	5.73	(10.20)
2.5	1.30	1.87	2.94	3.69	0.35	6.51	(10.40)
3.0	1.62	2.41	3.68	4.76	3.56	7.62	(7.80)
3.5	1.98	2.99	4.57	5.93	4.36	8.80	(4.81)
4.0	2.36	3.62	5.39	7.07	5.67	9.19	(4.39)
4.5	2.78	4.31	6.29	8.30	7.15	(4.69)	(3.78)
5.0	3.24	5.05	7.33	9.75	8.34	(3.79)	0.70
5.5	3.73	5.86	8.53	11.32	9.62	(2.83)	5.64
6.0	4.27	6.74	9.71	13.14	12.23	(1.14)	8.64
6.5	4.84	7.69	11.07	15.11	15.07	0.68	
7.0	5.46	8.70	12.47	17.26	17.21	3.51	
7.5	6.13	9.79	14.09	19.60	19.53	6.61	
8.0	6.86	10.96	15.80	21.72	21.00	9.44	
8.5	7.64	12.23	17.72	24.01	22.56	12.53	
9.0	8.48	13.63	19.72	27.04	26.78	17.54	
9 5	9.41	15.19	22.19	30.40	31.50	23.15	
10.0	10.40	16.87	24.59	34.03	36.66	29.35	

*Net Investment each period adjusted for cumulative mortality rates, calls and sinking fund redemptions. Assume sale of defaulted debt at the average price at the end of the month after default, minus loss of one semi-annual coupon payment. Assume reinvestment of all cashflows at the actual average annual YTM for the appropriate bond-rating class; long-term average annual YTM used for government bonds. Returns are expressed in dollars per $100 of investment.
Source: authors' compilations, Standard & Poor's and Tables 7 and 8.

BB and BBB classes, but they improved from earlier results. Although BB bonds continue to perform better than B-rated issues, the differential narrowed in 1998 relative to the 1994–97 results. Note that Table 12 does not include the effect of price changes caused by interest rate fluctuations or those caused by overall market perceptions. Hence, the results are "simulated" in that market risk is not factored in.

Total returns

Tables 13–15 and Figure 2 document the actual total returns and spreads on high-yield bonds compared to 10-year US Treasuries for the period 1978–98 inclusive.[5] Table 13 shows each year's return and return spread as well as the promised yield to maturity and yield spread at year end. The high-yield bond return spread over US Treasuries was

−8.73% in 1998, considerably below the 1978–98 arithmetic annual average of 2.53% (2.57% compound annual average). The returns are net of defaults. Returns and spreads in 1998 were much below average, primarily due to the precipitous drop and only modest recovery from the flight to quality effects of August and September.

The compound average annual return spread decreased to 2.57% in 1998. The 2.57% return spread can be compared to the average annual yield spread of 4.53%. The difference (just under 200 bp per year) is very close to our average annual default loss (2.05% per year) found in Table 3.

Table 13. Annual returns, yields and spreads on 10-year treasury and high-yield bonds,* 1978–98

Year	Return (%) High-yield	Treasury	Spread	Promised yield (%) High-yield	Treasury	Spread
1998	4.04	12.77	(8.73)	10.04	4.65	5.39
1997	14.27	11.16	3.11	9.20	5.75	3.45
1996	11.24	0.04	11.20	9.58	6.42	3.16
1995	22.40	23.58	(1.18)	9.76	5.58	4.18
1994	(2.55)	(8.29)	5.74	11.50	7.83	3.67
1993	18.33	12.08	6.25	9.08	5.80	3.28
1992	18.29	6.50	11.79	10.44	6.69	3.75
1991	43.23	17.18	26.05	12.56	6.70	5.86
1990	(8.46)	6.88	(15.34)	18.57	8.07	10.50
1989	1.98	16.72	(14.74)	15.17	7.93	7.24
1988	15.25	6.34	8.91	13.70	9.15	4.55
1987	4.57	(2.67)	7.24	13.89	8.83	5.06
1986	16.50	24.08	(7.58)	12.67	7.21	5.46
1985	26.08	31.54	(5.46)	13.50	8.99	4.51
1984	8.50	14.82	(6.32)	14.97	11.87	3.10
1983	21.80	2.23	19.57	15.74	10.70	5.04
1982	32.45	42.08	(9.63)	17.84	13.86	3.98
1981	7.56	0.48	7.08	15.97	12.08	3.89
1980	(1.00)	(2.96)	1.96	13.46	10.23	3.23
1979	3.69	(0.86)	4.55	12.07	9.13	2.94
1978	7.57	(1.11)	8.68	10.92	8.11	2.81
Arithmetic annual average						
1978–98	12.65	10.12	2.53	12.89	8.36	4.53
Compound annual average						
1978–98	12.03	9.46	2.57			

*End of year yields.
Source: Salomon Smith Barney Inc.'s High-Yield Composite Index.

Table 14. Compound average annual returns on high-yield bonds, 1978–98 (%)

Base period (Jan 1)	1978	1979	1980	1981	1982	1983	1984	1985	1986	1987	1988	1989	1990	1991	1992	1993	1994	1995	1996	1997	1998
1978	7.57	5.61	3.36	4.39	9.48	11.45	11.02	12.80	13.21	12.31	12.58	11.65	9.96	12.05	12.46	12.82	11.85	12.41	12.35	12.45	12.03
1979		3.69	1.32	3.36	9.97	12.14	11.61	13.57	13.93	12.85	13.09	12.03	10.16	12.41	12.82	13.18	12.12	12.70	12.62	12.71	12.26
1980			(1.00)	3.19	12.14	14.48	13.26	15.30	15.47	14.05	14.18	12.90	10.77	13.17	13.55	13.89	12.71	13.29	13.17	13.23	12.73
1981				7.56	19.36	20.17	17.11	18.87	18.47	16.38	16.24	14.56	12.02	14.55	14.86	15.12	13.76	14.32	14.12	14.13	13.54
1982					32.45	27.01	20.52	21.88	20.79	17.92	17.53	15.47	12.53	15.27	15.54	15.77	14.25	14.81	14.57	14.55	13.91
1983						21.80	14.96	18.55	18.04	15.21	15.22	13.23	10.26	13.51	13.98	14.37	12.85	13.56	13.39	13.45	12.84
1984							8.50	16.96	16.81	13.62	13.94	11.86	8.70	12.51	13.14	13.65	12.07	12.90	12.77	12.88	12.26
1985								26.08	21.20	15.38	15.35	12.54	8.73	13.10	13.73	14.24	12.43	13.31	13.13	13.22	12.54
1986									16.50	10.37	11.98	9.39	5.56	11.07	12.07	12.84	11.01	12.02	12.01	12.21	11.56
1987										4.57	9.78	7.12	2.99	10.01	11.35	12.32	10.35	11.62	11.59	11.83	11.16
1988											15.25	8.41	2.47	11.42	12.76	13.67	11.20	12.54	12.39	12.58	11.78
1989												1.98	(3.38)	10.17	12.14	13.35	10.53	12.16	12.04	12.29	11.43
1990													(8.46)	14.50	15.75	16.39	12.33	13.95	13.56	13.65	12.54
1991														43.23	30.16	26.09	18.23	19.05	17.71	17.21	15.48
1992															18.29	18.31	10.90	13.67	13.18	13.36	11.98
1993																18.33	7.38	12.17	11.94	12.40	10.96
1994																	(2.55)	9.21	9.89	10.97	9.54
1995																		22.40	16.69	15.88	12.80
1996																			11.24	12.74	9.77
1997																				14.27	9.04
1998																					4.04

Source: Salomon Smith Barney Composite Index; Edward I. Altman, New York University Salomon Center.

2. Cumulative value of $1,000 investment, 1978–98: high-yield bonds versus 10–year US Treasury bonds

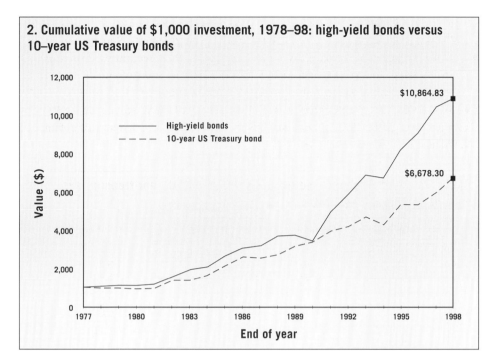

Table 13 also shows promised yields and spreads. At the end of 1998 the yield spread was 5.39%, up considerably from 1997's 3.45% and also above the historic average of 4.53%. During 1998 the yield spread increased by almost 200 basis points as yields on Treasuries dropped and high-yield bond yields increased from 9.20% to 10.04%. Again, the flight to quality was the primary cause. We note that the above-average 1998 12.77% return on 10-year US Treasuries was due to the fairly sharp decrease in interest rates.

Tables 14 and 15 are matrices of high-yield compound returns and spreads over 10-year US Treasuries for all possible beginning-of-year and end-of-year points. Note the relatively high absolute compound returns for most investment horizons, translating to double-digit absolute returns. Return spreads are mostly positive, although not for all horizons.

Figure 2 shows that $1,000 invested in high-yield bonds at the end of 1977 and compounded over the 21-year period January 1978 to December 1998 would be worth $10,865 – considerably more than the $6,678 the same amount would have been worth if invested in 10-year US Treasuries.

Table 15. Compound annual return spreads between high-yield and LT government bonds, 1978–98 (%)

Base period (Jan 1)	1978	1979	1980	1981	1982	1983	1984	1985	1986	1987	1988	1989	1990	1991	1992	1993	1994	1995	1996	1997	1998
1978	8.68	6.60	5.01	5.51	3.17	5.82	4.13	3.10	1.99	2.57	3.15	1.64	0.19	1.77	2.43	2.66	2.88	2.68	3.15	3.14	2.57
1979		4.55	3.23	4.48	1.71	5.22	3.32	2.23	1.08	1.84	2.55	0.94	(0.57)	1.20	1.95	2.23	2.49	2.29	2.81	2.83	2.24
1980			1.96	4.45	0.67	5.39	3.05	1.79	0.51	1.46	2.30	0.54	(1.08)	0.88	1.73	2.04	2.34	2.14	2.70	2.72	2.10
1981				7.08	(0.13)	6.74	3.36	1.75	0.22	1.37	2.35	0.36	(1.43)	0.77	1.70	2.05	2.37	2.15	2.75	2.77	2.42
1982					(9.63)	6.49	1.93	0.18	(1.39)	0.29	1.59	(0.58)	(2.46)	0.07	1.16	1.58	1.97	1.76	2.44	2.48	1.79
1983						19.57	6.62	2.97	0.39	1.94	3.13	0.49	(1.73)	0.96	2.05	2.42	2.75	2.48	3.14	3.13	2.37
1984							(6.32)	(5.94)	(6.48)	(2.59)	(0.22)	(2.73)	(4.75)	(1.40)	0.08	0.68	1.23	1.04	1.87	1.96	1.23
1985								(5.46)	(6.56)	(1.30)	1.34	(2.00)	(4.50)	(0.69)	0.89	1.47	1.98	1.72	2.56	2.60	1.76
1986									(7.58)	0.48	3.28	(1.26)	(4.32)	0.00	1.67	2.23	2.68	2.33	3.18	3.17	2.24
1987										7.24	8.05	0.61	(3.61)	1.38	3.08	3.51	3.84	3.34	4.16	4.06	2.98
1988											8.91	(2.99)	(7.41)	(0.24)	2.15	2.82	3.31	2.80	3.78	3.71	2.56
1989												(14.74)	(15.07)	(3.32)	0.44	1.58	2.38	1.93	3.14	3.14	1.93
1990													(15.34)	2.59	5.68	5.82	5.82	4.76	5.73	5.41	3.80
1991														26.05	18.45	14.26	11.80	9.40	9.72	8.78	6.51
1992															11.79	9.06	7.84	5.83	6.94	6.32	4.14
1993																6.25	6.00	3.87	5.76	5.25	2.89
1994																	5.74	2.76	5.61	5.01	2.26
1995																		(1.18)	5.50	4.69	1.22
1996																			11.20	7.29	1.93
1997																				3.11	(2.93)
1998																					(8.73)

Source: Salomon Smith Barney Composite Index; Edward I. Altman, New York University Salomon Center.

Outlook for the supply and demand of distressed securities

We have observed that there has been a considerable reduction in the size of the public and private distressed debt market in the past few years, which is certainly clear in the diminished size of our defaulted debt indexes.[6] The supply of new defaults clearly did not keep pace with those firms that emerged in one form or another from distressed restructuring. Also, the relatively low default rate in recent years (Table 1) did not add sizeable amounts to our indexes and to the population of defaulted securities.

As for the future, we expect the market for distressed and defaulted securities to increase considerably. The huge new-issue supply of non-investment grade debt in the last seven years of over $460 billion should result in an increase of default amounts in the coming years. While we do not expect the near-term default rates and numbers to approach the record years of 1990 and 1991, or perhaps even to reach the weighted average levels of 1971–98 (3.1% per year), the net supply of distressed and defaulted issues will almost certainly increase. This is partially a function of the considerable number of defaults that have already emerged, leaving a relatively small number of existing issues, compared to our expected larger number of new defaults.

A critical question for high-yield bond and distressed security investors is the likely supply of new defaulted and distressed paper. We do not use a formal econometric model for predicting near-term default rates. We feel, however, that a reasonable method would be to extrapolate default totals on the basis of the amount of new issuance in the recent past and the relationship between new issuance, segregated by original bond credit ratings, and expected defaults of these new issues. A method for doing just this is the mortality rate approach, first developed in the late 1980s (Altman, 1989) and updated each year. As discussed earlier, mortality rates – based on new issuance from 1971–97 and defaults through 1998 – are given in Table 8. Based on this method, we estimated $9.7 billion of defaults in 1998 – about $2 billion higher than actual defaults.

On the basis of actual new issuance by bond rating from 1989 to 1998 and expected new issuance in 1999 and 2000,[7] as well as the *marginal* mortality rate results in Table 8, we estimate that the new *publicly traded* bond default totals will increase substantially and have a face value of approximately $46 billion over the next three years (Table 16).

Table 16. Expected supply of new defaulted debt: US only, public and private markets, 1999–2001,[1] face value ($ billion)

	1999	2000	2001	Total
Public defaulted debt	11.30	16.76	18.15	46.21
Private defaulted debt[2]	27.12	40.22	43.56	110.90
Total defaulted debt	38.42	56.98	61.71	157.11

1. Estimates are based on marginal mortality rates (Table 8), actual and expected new corporate bond issues by bond rating.
2. Assumes private/public ratio of 2.4.
Source: New issues by bond rating compilation from Salomon Smith Barney Inc. and SDC Group.

Due to the high proportion of senior bonds issued in the high-yield debt market since 1992 – about 70% of the total new issuance – the expected average price at default is expected to be close to 50% of par value (compared to the venerable 40% for all defaults). This implied a market value estimate of about $23 billion of new public defaults over the period 1999–2001 (Table 17).

From Table 16, we observe that expected defaults for 1999 are $11.3 billion, about 50% above the amount from 1998. Assuming a modest increase in the population of high-yield bonds to $500 billion by mid-1999, the resulting default rate is 2.26% – still below historic averages.

According to our methodology, these public defaults will be accompanied by a new *private* defaulted debt face value total of about $111 billion. This is based on a 2.4 to 1.0 ratio of private to public debt of defaulting companies (Altman with Beltran, 1999). The resulting expected total of public and private defaulted debt at face value for the

Table 17. Expected supply of new defaulted debt: US only, 1999–2001 ($ billion)

	Defaulted debt	
Debt type	Face value	Market value[1]
Public straight debt	46.21	23.11
Private senior debt[2]	110.90	77.63
Total defaulted debt	157.11	100.74

1. Assumes market value at default at 50% of face value for public debt and at 70% of face value for private debt.
2. Assumes a ratio of 2.4:1 of private to public debt.
Source: New issues by bond rating compilation from Salomon Smith Barney Inc. and SDC Group.

next three years is therefore approximately $157 billion ($101 billion market value). Incidentally, although these numbers look quite large, the implied default rate in these estimates for the US high-yield debt market is in the range 2.3% (1999) to 3.0% by the year 2001. These rates are below or equal to the historical annual weighted average and assume that the population of high-yield bonds rises to $600 billion by the year 2001.

Summary and outlook

In conclusion, 1998 was a below-average year for high-yield debt in terms of absolute and relative returns. On the positive side, default rates were again below 2.0% and new issues again set a record. Investor concern with high-yield bonds was reflected in a relatively high promised yield spread at the end of 1998, but this spread was considerably lower than it was a few months earlier.

As noted above, our forecasts are based on extrapolation of historical default rates by bond rating and the past 10 years and expected next two years of new issuance. The forecast defaults are demonstrably greater than recent experience and may be viewed as unnecessarily pessimistic given these recent low defaults. On the other hand, recent new issuance data cast a very different light on the forecast. Low-grade new issuance (eg, rated B or below) swelled in 1998 to the highest proportion of total high-yield new issuance since the late 1980s, and the CCC-rated category alone contributed almost $10 billion of new issues in 1998 (not to mention significant net downgrades to CCC in recent years). Combined with the non-rated, new-issue segment of about $15 billion in 1998, these two categories are likely to contribute large numbers of defaults, especially if the economy and the stock market sag.

We have been estimating higher default rates for the last two years, but our estimates have been below actual results. We again expect higher default amounts in 1999–2001, and probably higher default rates as well. These rates will, however, more than likely remain below or eventually rise to the historic average of 3.0% per year.

Dr Altman is the Max L. Heine Professor of Finance and Vice Director of the New York University Salomon Center, Leonard N. Stern School of Business. Diane Cooke and Vellore Kishore are research associates at the NYU Salomon Center.

Appendix A

Defaulted corporate straight debt, 1998 (a)

Company	Bond issue	Coupon (%)	Maturity date	Outstanding amount ($ million)	Default date
Greate Bay Hotel and Casino	First mortgage notes	10.875	1/15/04	182.5	1/5/98
PRT Funding Corp. (Pratt)	Senior notes	11.625	4/15/04	85.0	1/5/98
Home Holdings, Inc.	Senior notes	7.750	12/15/98	100.0	1/15/98
Home Holdings, Inc.	Senior notes	8.625	12/15/03	178.8	1/15/98
Westbridge Capital Corp.	Senior subordinated notes	11.000	3/1/02	20.0	1/15/98
Venture Stores, Inc.	Medium-term notes	Various	Various	60.9	1/20/98
APS Holding Corporation	Senior subordinated notes	11.875	1/15/06	100.0	2/2/98
Brunos Inc.	Senior subordinated notes	10.500	8/1/05	400.0	2/2/98
United States Leather Inc.	Senior notes	10.250	7/31/03	135.0	2/2/98
American Rice Inc.	Mortgage notes	13.000	7/31/02	100.0	2/28/98
Salant Corporation	Senior secured notes	10.500	12/31/98	111.9	2/28/98
Grand Union Co.	Junior subordinated notes	0.000	3/2/99	7.2	3/1/98
Grand Union Co.	Senior notes	12.000	9/1/04	595.5	3/1/98
Unison Healthcare Corp.	Senior notes	12.250	11/1/06	100.0	3/2/98
Unison Healthcare Corp.	Senior notes	13.000	12/1/99	20.0	3/2/98
Royal Oak Mines, Inc.	Senior subordinated Yankee note	11.000	8/15/06	175.0	3/23/98
Australis Holdings (b)	Senior discount notes	0.000	11/1/02	80.2	4/8/98
Australis Holdings (c)	Senior secured guaranteed PIK	15.750	5/15/03	193.1	4/8/98
Heartland Wireless Communications, Inc.	Senior notes	13.000	4/15/03	100.0	4/15/98
Heartland Wireless Communications, Inc.	Senior notes	14.000	10/15/04	125.0	4/15/98
American Telecasting (d)	Senior discount notes	0.000	6/15/04	141.0	5/13/98
American Telecasting (e)	Senior discount notes	0.000	8/15/05	135.9	5/13/98
Cityscape Financial	Senior notes	12.750	6/1/04	300.0	6/1/98
Geotek Communications (f)	Senior secured discount notes	0.000	7/15/05	143.6	6/30/98
CAI Wireless Systems, Inc.	Senior notes	12.250	9/15/02	275.0	7/30/98
CAI Wireless Systems, Inc.	Senior notes	12.000	10/1/05	30.0	7/30/98
Renaissance Cosmetics, Inc.	Senior notes	11.750	2/15/04	200.0	8/19/98
Olympia & York Maiden Lane	Secured notes	10.375	12/31/95	200.0	8/31/98
International Wireless Communications Holdings (g)	Senior secured discount notes	0 000	8/15/01	139.0	9/3/98
Golden Books Family Entertainment	Senior notes	7.650	9/15/02	150.0	9/15/98
Acme Metals, Inc. (h)	Senior discount notes	13.500	8/1/04	0.7	9/28/98
Acme Metals, Inc.	Senior secured notes	12.500	8/1/02	17.5	9/28/98
Acme Metals, Inc.	Senior notes	10.875	12/15/07	200.0	9/28/98
Ionica Group PLC	Senior notes	13.500	8/15/06	150.0	9/28/98
Ionica Group PLC (i)	Senior discount notes	0.000	5/1/07	250.0	9/28/98
ERLY Enterprises, Inc.	Subordinated debentures	12.500	12/1/02	4.9	9/29/98
Southern Pacific Funding Corp.	Senior notes	11.500	11/1/04	100.0	10/1/98
Criimie Mae, Inc.	Senior notes	9.125	12/1/02	100.0	10/3/98
National Energy Group	Senior unsecured notes	10.750	11/1/06	164.7	11/2/98
AmeriTruck Distribution Corp.	Senior subordinated notes	12.250	11/15/05	100.0	11/9/98
Wilshire Financial Services Group Inc.	Senior notes	13.000	1/1/04	84.2	11/13/98
Wilshire Financial Services Group Inc.	Senior notes	13.000	8/15/04	100.0	11/13/98
Livent, Inc.	Senior notes	9.375	10/15/04	125.0	11/18/98
Pioneer Finance Corp. (Santa Fe Gaming)	Guaranteed first mortgage	13.500	12/1/98	60.0	11/18/98
HealthCor Holdings	Senior notes	9.375	10/15/04	125.0	11/30/98
Florida Coast Paper Co. LLC	First mortgage notes	12.750	6/1/03	165.0	12/7/98
Penn Traffic Company	Senior notes	8.625	12/15/03	200.0	12/15/98
Penn Traffic Company	Senior subordinated notes	9.625	4/15/05	400.0	12/15/98
Penn Traffic Company	Senior notes	10.250	2/15/02	125.0	12/15/98
Penn Traffic Company	Senior notes	10.375	10/1/04	100.0	12/15/98
Penn Traffic Company	Senior notes	10.650	11/1/04	100.0	12/15/98
Penn Traffic Company	Senior notes	11.500	4/15/06	100.0	12/15/98
P & C Food Markets	Senior notes	11.500	10/15/01	107.2	12/15/98

Total 7,463.7

(a) 63 international issues with an aggregate amount of $9,781.3 million and 14 convertible bond defaults with an aggregate amount of $1,377.5 million are not included. *Source:* Moody's Investor Services, Inc.
(b) Zero coupon until 11/01/00, 15.00% thereafter. Face value $131.2 million. Accreted value at default, $80.2 million.
(c) Secured guaranteed PIK at 1.75% per month of accreted value to 5/15/00. 15.75% cash coupon thereafter. Face value $343.2 million. Accreted value at default, $193.1 million.
(d) Zero coupon until 12/15/99, 14.50% thereafter. Face value $183.0 million. Accreted value at default, $141.0 million.
(e) Zero coupon until 8/15/00, 14.50% thereafter. Face value $201.7 million. Accreted value at default, $135.9 million.
(f) Zero coupon until 7/15/00, 15.00% thereafter. Face value $207 million. Accreted value at default, $143.6 million.
(g) Zero coupon. Face value $196.7 million. Accreted value at default, $139.0 million.
(h) Zero coupon until 8/97, 13.50% thereafter. Face value $0.7 million. Accreted value at default, $0 7 million.
(i) Zero coupon until 2002, 15.00% thereafter. Face value $420.0 million. Accreted value at default, $250.0 million.

Appendix B

Quarterly default rates: high-yield debt market, 1989–98

Year/quarter		Par value debt outstanding (a) ($ billion)	Debt defaulted by quarter ($ billion)	Quarterly default rates (%)
1989	1Q	n.a.	1.03	n.a.
	2Q	n.a.	1.13	n.a.
	3Q	n.a.	3.54	n.a.
	4Q	n.a.	2.41	n.a.
			8.11	
1990	1Q	185.00	4.16	2.25
	2Q	185.00	2.51	1.36
	3Q	181.00	6.01	3.32
	4Q	181.00	5.67	3.13
			18.35	
1991	1Q	182.00	8.74	4.80
	2Q	182.00	2.75	1.51
	3Q	183.00	5.01	2.74
	4Q	183.00	2.36	1.29
			18.86	
1992	1Q	183.20	3.33	1.82
	2Q	151.10	1.26	0.83
	3Q	163.00	0.37	0.23
	4Q	151.89	0.59	0.39
			5.55	
1993	1Q	193.23	0.38	0.20
	2Q	193.23	1.33	0.69
	3Q	206.91	0.05	0.03
	4Q	190.42	0.52	0.27
			2.29	
1994	1Q	232.60	0.67	0.29
	2Q	230.00	0.16	0.07
	3Q	235.00	0.41	0.17
	4Q	235.00	2.18	0.93
			3.42	
1995	1Q	240.00	0.17	0.07
	2Q	240.00	1.68	0.70
	3Q	240.00	0.98	0.41
	4Q	240.00	1.72	0.72
			4.55	
1996	1Q	255.00	0.44	0.17
	2Q	255.00	0.89	0.35
	3Q	271.00	0.41	0.15
	4Q	271.00	1.59	0.59
			3.34	
1997	1Q	296.00	1.85	0.63
	2Q	318.40	0.60	0.19
	3Q	335.40	1.48	0.44
	4Q	335.40	0.27	0.08
			4.20	
1998	1Q	379.00	2.37	0.63
	2Q	425.70	1.22	0.29
	3Q	465.50	1.62	0.35
	4Q	481.60	2.26	0.47
			7.46	

(a) Par value at beginning of quarter; n.a. = not available.
Source: Appendix A.

Appendix C

Corporate bond defaults by industry (number of companies)

Industry	1970–80	1981	1982	1983	1984	1985	1986	1987	1988	1989	1990	1991	1992	1993	1994	1995	1996	1997	1998	Total
Auto/Motor carrier	1								3	3	3									10
Conglomerates	0		2							1	1		3	3		1			1	12
Energy	1		2	3	5	7	12	2	4		7	4								47
Financial services	2	1	1	1	1	1			4	11	8	8	3	3	4	3	1	2	6	60
Leisure/Entertainment	0			1	1	2	6	2	4	4	8	2	4	3		8				45
General manufacturing	2		7					3	3	1	5	8	8	7	3	8	6	7	6	84
Health care	0							1	2					1	1	1	1	3	2	12
Miscellaneous industries	2	1		1	2	6	3	1		1	4	4	3	1	1	1	1		3	36
Real estate/Construction	5		2		1	1		1	1	3	7	5	1	1	1	2	1		1	33
REIT	10		1	1								1								13
Retailing	5		1	1		1	1		1	2	6	6	6	4	5	6	3	6	6	67
Communications	6	1		2	2	1	1	3	1	4	3	4	1	1	3	2	2	1	6	40
Transportation (non-auto)	2	1	1	2		1	1	1			1	2			2	1	1	2	1	17
Utilities								1	1				1				1	1		5
Total	36	4	17	12	19	23		15	24	26	47	62	34	22	19	28	15	29	37	444

Appendix D

Weighted average recovery rates by industry, 1971–98

Industry	Sample	Weighted average price ($)	Average price ($)	Price range ($) Low	High	Standard deviation ($)	Median ($)
Mining	47	31.78	32.93	9.50	99.00	17.85	32.00
Food and kindred products, tobacco	22	38.81	44.83	14.50	88.50	20.16	43.75
Textile mill, apparel and related products	37	39.20	35.62	5.00	89.30	18.69	32.88
Lumber, wood products, furniture and fixtures, paper and allied products	11	27.96	32.95	2.00	75.00	25.45	43.50
Chemical, petroleum and energy, rubber, plastic and leather products	41	73.74	59.67	12.00	98.75	28.03	67.50
Stone, clay, glass, concrete, metals and fabricated products	74	29.45	38.16	2.00	101.50	22.84	35.75
Machinery, electrical, electronic and transportation equipment, instruments and related products	47	43.38	45.48	4.40	86.00	21.83	44.50
Miscellaneous and diversified manufacturing	23	25.35	38.32	1.00	94.13	26.63	31.50
Transportation (rail road, bus, air, water, freight), pipeline and transportation services	49	40.42	40.37	5.00	103.25	29.23	38.00
Printing and publishing, communication and movie production	64	34.45	36.17	3.75	97.00	21.79	33.00
Utilities	57	61.56	70.01	17.75	99.88	19.78	79.00
Wholesale and retail trade	123	35.33	37.24	0.50	98.50	23.01	36.00
Finance, insurance and real estate	114	36.57	36.31	1.00	103.00	26.23	31.59
Services	68	43.25	41.80	2.00	112.00	28.40	34.25
Total	777	40.32	41.66	0.50	112.00	25.89	37.00

Source: Appendices A and C and Table 4.

1 *These reports are available to Associates of the Salomon Center and to subscribers to the monthly defaulted debt indexes; specifically, Altman and Suggitt (1997) and Altman with Beltran (1999).*

2 *We have not included Eurobonds and other international defaults in these calculations since the international high-yield market is not large or, indeed, clear in terms of size and coverage. We do list the aggregate amount of international issue defaults in Appendix A, which was considerable (over $9 billion) in 1998. In addition, consistent with our past approach, we do not include those issues that missed interest payments in 1998 but cured their delinquencies within the typical 30-day grace period or that missed an interest payment in December and still had a grace period remaining into 1999 (see discussion at a later point).*

3 *For an in-depth discussion of the various default rate methodologies and results, see Caouette, Altman and Narayanan (1998).*

4 *Penn Traffic Company missed an interest payment on $200 million of bonds on December 15, triggering cross-default clauses on an additional $932 million. Since the grace period was only 15 days, we include it in the 1998 results.*

5 *Note that these statistics are somewhat different than those found in the comparable exhibits (tables and figures) in previous years' reports. We are now using the returns, yields and spreads from Salomon Smith Barney Inc.'s high-yield Composite Index comprising about 1400 bonds (December 1998).*

6 *See the NYU Salomon Center Annual Report "The Investment Performance of Defaulted Bonds and Bank Loans: 1987-1998" by Altman with Beltran (1999).*

7 *We have projected new issuance by bond rating for 1999 and 2000 by using arithmetic averages for the previous five-year period. 1994-98.*

BIBLIOGRAPHY

Altman, E. I., 1989, "Measuring Corporate Bond Mortality and Performance", *Journal of Finance* XLIV(4), September.

Altman, E. I., and V. Kishore, 1996, "Almost Everything You Wanted to Know About Recoveries on Defaulted Bonds", *Financial Analysts Journal* November/December.

Altman, E. I., and H. Suggitt, 1997, "Default Rates in the Syndicated Bank Loan Market: A Mortality Analysis", Working paper series S-97-39, NYU Salomon Center; forthcoming in the *Journal of Banking and Finance* (1999).

Altman, E. I., with L. Beltran, 1999, "The Performance of Defaulted Bonds and Bank Loans: 1987-1998", NYU Salomon Center Special report, January.

Caouette, J., E. I. Altman and P. Narayanan, 1998, *Managing Credit Risk: The Next Great Financial Challenge* (New York: John Wiley & Sons).

2

Portfolio Credit Risk (I)

Thomas C. Wilson
Swiss Re New Markets

Financial institutions are increasingly measuring and managing the risk from credit exposures at a portfolio level, as well as the usual transaction level. This is happening for various reasons: the rise of portfolio credit risk management; the fall in profitability of traditional credit products; and increased opportunities (through credit derivatives) to manage the institution's exposure after it has been originated.

However, to exploit these opportunities, management must answer several questions. What is the risk of a given portfolio? How do different macroeconomic scenarios – at both regional and industry sector level – affect the portfolio's risk profile? What is the effect of changing the portfolio mix? How could risk-based pricing at the individual contract and portfolio levels be influenced by the level of expected losses and credit risk capital?

In this chapter and in chapter 3 we describe a new, intuitive and practical method that can provide answers to these questions by tabulating the exact loss distribution from correlated credit events. The importance of tabulating the exact loss distribution is highlighted by the fact that counterparty defaults and rating migrations (upgrades and downgrades) cannot be predicted and are not perfectly correlated, implying that management faces a distribution of potential losses rather than a single potential loss (see Figure 1). To make the definition of credit risk more precise in the context of loss distributions, the financial industry is converging on risk measures that summarise relevant aspects of the entire loss distribution. Two distributional statistics have become increasingly relevant for measuring credit risk: expected loss and some critical value of the loss distribution, often defined as the portfolio's credit risk capital. Each measure serves a distinct and useful role in supporting management decision-making and control.

Expected losses, illustrated as the mean of the distribution in Figure 1, are often the basis for management's reserve policies: the higher the expected losses, the higher the reserves that must be set aside. As such, expected losses are also an important component for determining whether the pricing of the credit risk position is adequate. Usually, each transaction or netted credit portfolio should be priced with enough margin to cover its contribution to the portfolio's expected credit losses, as well as to other operating expenses.

Credit risk capital, defined as the maximum loss within a known confidence interval (eg, 99%) over an orderly liquidation period, is often interpreted as the additional economic capital that must be held against a given portfolio, above and beyond the level of credit reserves, to cover its unexpected credit losses. As it would be uneconomic to hold capital against *all* potential losses (this would imply that equity is held against 100% of all credit exposures), some level of capital must be chosen to support the portfolio of transactions in most, but not all, cases. Just as with expected losses, credit risk capital is also important for determining if the credit risk of a particular transaction is appropriately priced: typically, each transaction must be priced with enough margin to

This article was originally published in Risk *magazine, September 1997.*

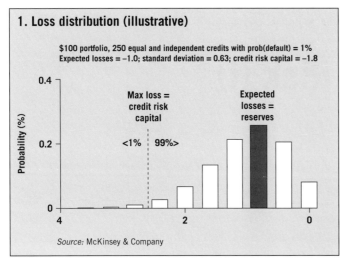

1. Loss distribution (illustrative)

$100 portfolio, 250 equal and independent credits with prob(default) = 1%
Expected losses = –1.0; standard deviation = 0.63; credit risk capital = –1.8

Max loss =
credit risk
capital

Expected
losses =
reserves

<1% 99%>

Probability (%)

0.4

0.2

0

4   2   0

Source: McKinsey & Company

cover not only its expected losses but also the cost of its marginal risk capital contribution.

Most industry professionals split the challenge of credit risk measurement into two questions: what is the (joint) probability of a credit event occurring and what is the loss should it occur?

Measuring potential losses, given a credit event, is simple for many standard commercial banking products. For example, the exposure of a $100 million unsecured loan is roughly equal to $100 million, subject to any recoveries and discounting effects. For derivatives portfolios, committed but unutilised lines, collateralised transactions etc, it is more difficult. In this article, we focus on tabulating these loss distributions for an arbitrary portfolio, *given* the level of exposure. Readers interested in the complexities of exposure measurement for derivatives should consult JP Morgan (1997), Lawrence (1995) and Rowe (1995).

We will develop an approach here for measuring expected and unexpected losses that differs from other approaches in several important ways. First, it models the actual discrete loss distribution, and therefore the amount of risk capital required to support the portfolio, according to the number and size of credits, rather than using a normal distribution or mean-variance approximation. This is important because, in the case of an unbalanced, concentrated portfolio, the loss distribution is discrete and multinomial, rather than continuous and unimodal, and it is highly skewed rather than symmetric. In addition, its shape changes dramatically as other positions are added.

Because of this, the usual measure of unexpected losses, standard deviations, is like a rubber ruler: it can be used to give a sense of the uncertainty of loss, but its actual interpretation in terms of dollars-at-risk depends on the degree to which the ruler has been "stretched" by diversification or large exposure effects. In contrast, the model developed here tabulates the actual, discrete loss distribution for any given portfolio, thus also allowing explicit and accurate tabulation of a "large exposure premium" in terms of risk-adjusted capital for less diversified portfolios.

Second, the losses (or gains) are measured on a *discounted default basis* for credit exposures that *cannot* be liquidated (eg, most mid-market or retail loans and some corporate over-the-counter trading lines), as well as on a marked-to-market basis (recognising the economic impact of both credit migrations and defaults) for those that can be liquidated before the maximum maturity of the exposure (eg, traded corporate loans or debt securities). This implies that the model can be used to cover the credit exposures from liquid secondary market positions, as well as from illiquid commercial positions. Also, because we model both the average default and migration rates and correlations for single, rated counterparty names, as well as average loss rates on portfolios of non-rated retail counterparties, we can integrate retail exposures such as mortgage or credit card pools, which often make up the lion's share of a commercial bank's risk profile, into the same risk measurement framework.

The third difference is that the tabulated loss distributions are conditional on the current state of the economy, rather than being based on unconditional or 20-year averages that do not reflect the portfolio's true current risk. This allows us to capture the cyclical default effects that constitute the largest source of risk for diversified portfolios. Specific country and industry influences are recognised on the basis of empirical relationships, rather than assuming a constant correlation between counterparty segments or correlations determined by equity price movements, thereby allowing the model to mimic the actual, historical default correlations between corporates in different industries and regions as well as retail portfolios.

Some models, including many developed in-house, rely on one systematic risk factor to capture default correlations or, equivalently, on a constant correlation between all counterparties. Our approach is based on a true multifactor systematic risk model, which better captures reality. Finally, the loss distributions can be tabulated to incorporate not only random recovery rates, but also country events that can trigger technical default on an obligation, regardless of the counterparty's credit quality.

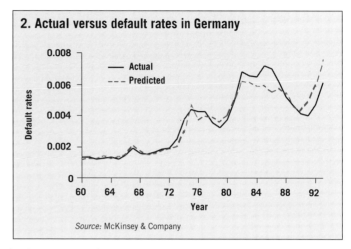

2. Actual versus default rates in Germany

Source: McKinsey & Company

Intuition behind the model

In terms of modelling the joint default behaviour or systematic risk of a portfolio of counterparties over time, the model developed here leverages several intuitive observations on the behaviour and impact of individual, as well as aggregate, credit events. These observations are more complex than they might first appear; for a more complete justification and analysis, see Wilson (1997). In chapter 3, we will show how to tabulate losses for an arbitrary portfolio of exposures based on these systematic risk indexes.

The first observation is that diversification helps to reduce loss uncertainty, all else being equal. Second, there is still substantial loss uncertainty – the systematic risk – for even the most diversified portfolios. Third, a portfolio's systematic risk is mostly driven by the "health" of the macroeconomy – in recessions, one expects defaults (and downgrades) to increase.

This relationship between average default rates and the state of the macroeconomy is shown in Figure 2, which plots the actual default rate versus one predicted using only macroeconomic aggregates such as GDP growth and unemployment rates. The macroeconomic factors explain much of the overall variation in the average default rate series, as reflected by Logit regression equation R^2 (see equation (1)) of more than 90% for most of the countries investigated in Wilson (1997), including the US, Germany, Japan and France as well as domestic retail mortgage portfolios in many of the same countries. Similar analysis also shows that different sectors of the economy react differently to macroeconomic shocks and cycles. For example, the intuitive expectation that the construction sector would be more adversely affected during a recession than other sectors is supported by data for a wide variety of different countries analysed in Wilson (1997).

More specifically, we model speculative default rates by estimating the parameters of a Logit function where the dependent variable is the probability of default for speculative grade counterparties and the independent variable is a segment-specific index depending on current macroeconomic variables, such as:

$$p_{j,t} = \frac{1}{1 + \exp(y_{j,t})} \tag{1}$$

where $p_{j,t}$ is the probability of default for a speculative grade counterparty in segment j at time t, and $y_{j,t}$ is the segment-specific macroeconomic index, whose parameters must be estimated. This functional form was chosen over linear and exponential representations for two reasons: first, because it offered, on average, a better fit (as measured by R^2) and second, because, for any value of the index y, it yields a probability within the interval [0, 1]. The latter is important not only because it is a desirable property for a probability, but also because we will be simulating these index values over a multi-year horizon and extreme economic cycles using Monte Carlo methods: without this, we cannot guarantee the resulting probability of default will be between [0, 1].

The macroeconomic index, which measures the health of the country's macroeconomy, is determined by such variables as overall unemployment, GDP growth rate, the rate of government spending, regional housing price indexes and unemployment rates

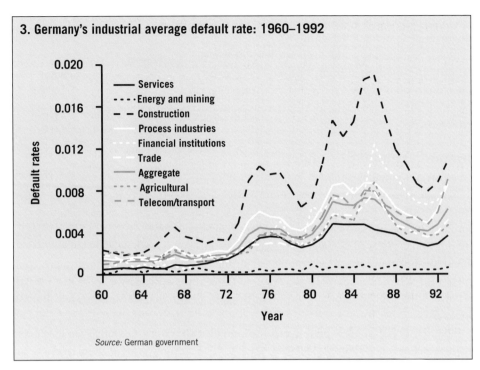

3. Germany's industrial average default rate: 1960–1992

Source: German government

for mortgage portfolios and so on. More specifically, the index takes the following form:

$$y_{j,t} = \beta_{j,0} + \beta_{j,1} X_{j,1,t} + \beta_{j,2} X_{j,2,t} + \beta_{j,3} X_{j,3,t} + \upsilon_{j,t} \tag{2}$$

where $y_{j,t}$ is the index value specific for the jth segment at time t,
$\beta_j = (\beta_{j,0}, \beta_{j,1}, \beta_{j,2}, \beta_{j,3})$ is a set of regression coefficients to be estimated for the jth segment, $X_{j,t} = (X_{j,1,t}, X_{j,2,t}, X_{j,3,t})$ is the set of explanatory variables at time t for the jth segment (eg, GDP growth rates and unemployment) and $\upsilon_{j,t}$ is a random variable assumed to be independent and identically normally distributed, for example:

$$\upsilon_{j,t} \sim N\left(0, \sigma_j\right) \quad \text{or} \quad \upsilon_t \sim N\left(0, \Sigma_\upsilon\right) \tag{3}$$

where υ is the vector of stacked index innovations and Σ_υ is the $j \times j$ covariance matrix of the index innovations. This formulation can be viewed as a multifactor model for determining segment-specific average speculative default rates: the systematic risk component is captured by the (weighted) influence of the macroeconomic variables with a segment-specific "surprise" captured by the error term υ. To make the model segment-specific, we estimate individual functions for each country/industry/retail pool segment whenever data is available,[1] allowing the explanatory variables to differ between segments.

The fourth observation is that these relationships hold not only for each country but also for different segments within each country. Figure 3 plots the average default rates by segment for Germany, all of which move very strongly with the overall German credit cycle but with different amplitudes, construction being the most volatile (or highest "beta") industry and energy and mining being the least volatile (or lowest "beta") industry. Similar, strong regression results also hold for these industries.

The final observation is also both intuitive and empirically verifiable: rating migrations are linked to the macroeconomy – both default and credit downgrades are more likely in a recession. Our starting point is an unconditional Markov transition matrix (which we denote (ϕM)), calculated using rating agency data, own experiences or JP Morgan's estimated transition matrix (JP Morgan, 1997). This matrix gives the average probability of migrating from one credit class to another within a year and is estimated using several years' data across many countries and industries (see Table 1). The matrix is therefore unconditional, representing the long-run average probability of migrating

Table 1. Unconditional credit migration probabilities

Initial rating				Final rating				
	AAA	AA	A	BBB	BB	B	CCC	Default
AAA	0.894	0.098	0.006	0.002	0.001	0.000	0.000	0.000
AA	0.009	0.909	0.071	0.008	0.001	0.002	0.000	0.000
A	0.001	0.026	0.901	0.060	0.008	0.004	0.000	0.001
BBB	0.001	0.003	0.063	0.851	0.063	0.015	0.002	0.003
BB	0.000	0.002	0.006	0.074	0.789	0.102	0.012	0.015
B	0.000	0.001	0.004	0.006	0.061	0.830	0.038	0.061
CCC	0.002	0.000	0.002	0.010	0.015	0.120	0.660	0.191
Default	0.000	0.000	0.000	0.000	0.000	0.000	0.000	1.000

Source: Moody's Investors Service

and ignoring the current state of the economic cycle. In reality, however, the probabilities, like the ratings, will vary with the economic cycle in a predictable manner and can therefore be made conditional.

Figure 4 plots rating migrations against average speculative default rates – a good proxy for the economy's health. One important observation from this figure is that rating migrations are not only volatile, but are also correlated with changes in the average speculative default rate: if the speculative default rate is higher than average, then downward migrations increase and upward migrations decrease, and vice versa; these observations are confirmed by the correlations between the two.

These empirical relationships between the speculative default rates and the credit migration, as well as default rates for other rating classes discussed earlier, can be used to make the *un*conditional Markov rating transition matrix *conditional* on the current speculative default rate (see Wilson (1997) for more details).

Intuitively, we model the relationship in the following manner: if the ratio of the actual speculative default rate to its unconditional mean ($SDP_t / \phi SDP$) equals one, then the conditional transition matrix is equal to the unconditional matrix. If this ratio is greater than one (ie, more defaults than average), then more of the probability mass is shifted into downgraded and default states; and vice versa if the ratio is less than one.[2]

Based on these conditional one-year Markov transition matrices, we can calculate the cumulative conditional probabilities of migrating from one rating class to another over any (yearly) time frame using the following formula:

$$M_t = \Pi_{i=1,\dots,t} M \left(SDP_t / \phi SDP \right) \qquad (4)$$

where M_t represents the t-year conditional cumulative rating distribution for a given future path of the speculative default rates, $M(SDP_t / \phi SDP)$ is the conditional one-year rating transition matrix dependent upon the speculative default rate, SDP_t is the realised speculative default rate at time t, ϕSDP is the average speculative default rate and $\Pi_{i=1,\dots,t}$ is the multiplication operator.

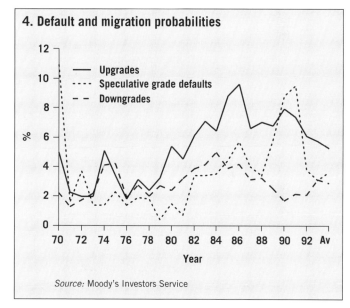

4. Default and migration probabilities

Source: Moody's Investors Service

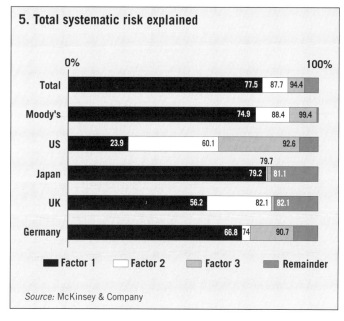

5. Total systematic risk explained

Source: McKinsey & Company

In terms of our modelling strategy, the multiple factors driving our multifactor model of systematic credit risk are the correlated macroeconomic variables (eg, GDP growth, unemployment rates) for the various countries in our sample, as well as industry-specific "shocks". Figure 5 shows the need for a multifactor, rather than a single-factor model, for systematic risk. A factor analysis of country-average default rates – a good surrogate for systematic risk by country – shows that the first "factor" captures only 77.5% of the total variation in systematic default rates for Moody's, the US, UK, Japanese and German markets.

This corresponds to the amount of systematic risk "captured" by most single-factor models; the rest of the variation is implicitly assumed to be independent and uncorrelated. Unfortunately, the first factor only explains 23.9% of the US systematic risk index, 56.2% of the UK's and 66.8% of Germany's. The substantial correlation remaining is explained by the second and third factors, covering an extra 10.2% and 6.8% respectively of the total variation and the bulk of the risk for the US, the UK and Germany. This shows that a single-factor systematic risk model, eg, one based on asset betas or agency data alone, is not enough to capture all correlations.

The multiple factors driving our multifactor model of systematic credit risk are, in fact, the correlated macroeconomic variables for the various countries in our sample, as well as industry-specific "shocks".

Multifactor systemic risk model

Using these, as well as other historical relationships, we can construct a multifactor model for the evolution of default and credit migration probabilities. We do this in three steps: first, describing the evolution of the global macroeconomy; second, mapping this into country/industry-specific one-year speculative default rates or default indexes; finally, mapping these into country and industry-specific cumulative rating migration probabilities.

Defining the state of the economy

At the beginning of any period t, the economy's health is drawn from a (conditional) distribution. Using our Logit models for determining the country/industry-specific speculative default rates, the economy's condition is defined by the various macroeconomic explanatory variables discussed earlier (eg, GDP innovations, changes in housing price indexes, etc). For illustrative purposes, we use a set of univariate, autoregressive equations of order 2 (AR(2)) to model the development of the individual macroeconomic time series describing the economy's health.[3] More precisely, we assume that the evolution of each of the macroeconomic series is governed by

$$X_{j,i,t} = k_{i,0} + k_{i,1} X_{j,i,t-1} + k_{i,2} X_{j,i,t-2} + \varepsilon_{j,i,t} \qquad (5)$$

where $X_{j,i,t}$ is the value of the ith macroeconomic variable in the jth segment at time t, $k_{i,j}$ (where $j = 1, \ldots, 3$) are the three constants to be estimated for each of the i macroeconomic variables and $\varepsilon_{j,i,t}$ is the error term, assumed to be distributed $N(0, \sigma_i)$.

The constant parameters (k) are estimated using historical data, ie, data for which $t < 0$. Once the constant parameters have been estimated, the $\varepsilon_{j,i,t}$ terms for $t \geq 0$ can be considered as the forecast errors or "surprises" for the t-step ahead forecast and are the variables which need to be simulated. As the forecast "surprises" are correlated (eg, a surprisingly poor showing for GDP growth will most likely be associated with an unpleasant surprise in terms of unemployment rates), we also need to estimate the joint covariance matrix for the forecast error terms to simulate the joint development of the different macroeconomic variables. More specifically, based on the assumptions made earlier, it follows that

$$\varepsilon \sim N\left(0, \Sigma_\varepsilon\right) \qquad (6)$$

where ε is the stacked vector of errors from each of the i AR(2) equations and Σ_ε is the covariance matrix of ε.

Defining segment default indexes

Based on this state of the economy, we determine the average speculative default rate for each country/industry segment. The macroeconomic forecast and simulated forecast error terms are used to drive the Logit functions described in equations (1) and (2); these, in turn, are used to construct the t-step ahead cumulative rating distributions using the empirical regularities specified in equation (4).

Combining the earlier equations, we derive the speculative default rates for all of the j country/industry segments, given a particular realisation of the various macroeconomic innovations and innovations to the Logit functions. More specifically, we define a system of equations governing the joint evolution of the country/industry-specific speculative default rates and associated macroeconomic variables:

$$p_j\left(y_{j,t}\right) = \frac{1}{1 + \exp\left(y_{j,t}\right)}$$

$$y_{j,t} = \beta_{j,0} + \beta_{j,1}X_{j,1,t} + \beta_{j,2}X_{j,2,t} + \beta_{j,3}X_{j,3,t} + \upsilon_{j,t}$$

$$X_{j,i,t} = k_{i,0} + k_{i,1}X_{j,i,t-1} + k_{i,2}X_{j,i,t-2} + \varepsilon_{j,i,t}$$

$$E = \begin{pmatrix} \upsilon \\ \varepsilon \end{pmatrix} \sim N\left(0, \Sigma\right) \qquad \Sigma \equiv \begin{bmatrix} \Sigma_\upsilon & \Sigma_{\upsilon,\varepsilon} \\ \Sigma_{\varepsilon,\upsilon} & \Sigma_\varepsilon \end{bmatrix}$$

where E is the $(j+i) \times 1$ vector of innovations affecting the system of equations given above and Σ is the $(j+i) \times (j+i)$ covariance matrix of macroeconomic variable forecast errors (υ), and segment-specific speculative default rate "shocks" (ε).

Defining A as the $n \times n$ Cholesky decomposition of Σ so that $\Sigma = AA'$, we can now simulate the joint speculative default rates across all segments over some time horizon, T. This is done by:

❏ drawing a sequence of realisations for z_t, $t = 1$ to T, of $(j+i)$ $N(0, I)$ random variables, where I is the $(j+i) \times (j+i)$ identity matrix;

❏ calculating the realisations E_t, incorporating the correlations between the various macroeconomic and segment-specific default innovations, using the relationship $E_t = A^*z_t$; and

❏ calculating $P(t)$ using the above system of equations.

Figure 6 gives an example of five simulations of the speculative default rates for Germany over a 10-year horizon. For example, we can interpret the uppermost simulation as representing an immediate recession followed by a gradual recovery and the lowermost simulation run as being an immediate and sustained improvement in the German economy.

Tabulating the cumulative migration distributions

Once the speculative default rates for each country/industry segment have been simulated, we then calculate the unique Markov transition matrix for each segment for any time horizon by using equation (4). Using the relationships outlined in equation (4) and the simulated speculative default rates, we can calculate the rating distribution for any initial rating at different points in time in the future, conditional on the simulated macroeconomic cycle over that time horizon. Figure 7 shows the histogram of simulated cumulative default probabilities for a five-year, single-A counterparty in Germany, based on 500 simulations.

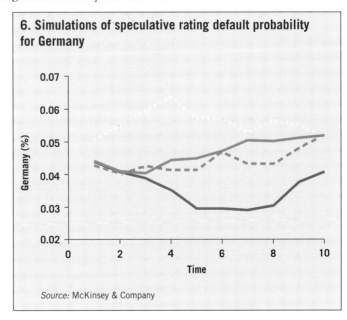

6. Simulations of speculative rating default probability for Germany

Germany (%)

Time

Source: McKinsey & Company

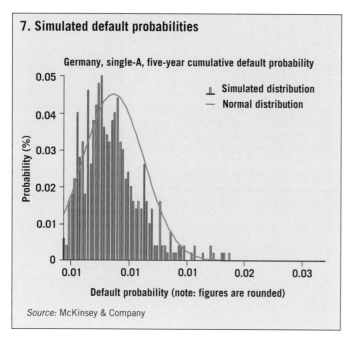

7. Simulated default probabilities

Germany, single-A, five-year cumulative default probability

Probability (%)

- Simulated distribution
- Normal distribution

Default probability (note: figures are rounded)

Source: McKinsey & Company

Similar histograms can be tabulated for both cumulative default probabilities and cumulative credit rating migration probabilities for any maturity, rating class, country and industry combination. Interestingly, the histogram in Figure 7 does not look "normal": it is truncated at zero (a natural phenomenon, as probabilities should not in general be negative) and, because of this, it is skewed. In general, this phenomenon occurs most with higher rated, shorter maturity exposures, which tend on average to have lower cumulative default probabilities. The distributions for lower rated, longer maturity portfolios tend to be more symmetric in shape (since the mean is quite a bit higher).

Systematic risks

Given the simulated default probability distribution for each of the segments, by rating, we can tabulate several interesting distribution parameters such as the expected conditional default probability and maximum possible default probability for each segment, by rating. Table 2 shows the conditional expected cumulative default rates for the German index portfolio for exposures of any maturity up to 10 years and any initial rating from triple-A to default, conditional on the macroeconomic environment in Germany in 1995. It is interesting to note that if the *long run average* levels of the macroeconomic explanatory variables are used for the initial conditions for simulating the AR(2) processes given in equation (5), then the cumulative default probabilities given in Table 2 would be *equal* to the unconditional cumulative default probabilities implied by the migration matrix given in table A. Thus, our approach explicitly allows one the choice of whether or not to recognise where we are currently in the credit cycle explicitly when tabulating the portfolio's loss distribution.

Table 2 *could* represent the conditional expected portfolio loss rates if, and only if, four conditions are met: the portfolio is diversified to the extent that it mimics the German index portfolio (eg, a large number of small German exposures in all industries); recovery rates are zero; the exposure for each individual counterparty is constant over its entire life; and the losses are treated on a non-discounted basis. As these assumptions are restrictive in practice for an arbitrary portfolio of credit exposures, we present the cumulative expected default probabilities here only to illustrate the properties of the systematic risk model; we will relax each of these restrictive assumptions in chapter 3, demonstrating then how to tabulate the actual loss distributions for any arbitrary portfolio.

According to this table, the average conditional cumulative default rates for a three-year, single-A diversified German index position is 0.780, conditional on the current macroeconomic environment. The last row of this table is equal to 100 because it represents counterparties that are currently in default and the model assumes that default

Table 2. Cumulative conditional average default probability

					Maturity					
1	2	3	4	5	6	7	8	9	10	Rating
0.000	0.008	0.035	0.093	0.193	0.345	0.562	0.863	1.252	1.741	AAA
0.000	0.055	0.178	0.382	0.684	1.094	1.628	2.315	3.143	4.122	AA
0.121	0.364	0.780	1.385	2.206	3.241	4.493	5.999	7.697	9.579	A
0.575	1.610	3.153	5.121	7.483	10.135	13.013	16.148	19.367	22.633	BBB
2.872	7.087	12.160	17.510	22.941	28.209	33.227	38.094	42.599	46.750	BB
11.798	22.170	31.473	39.438	46.340	52.253	57.333	61.858	65.755	69.120	B
26.999	44.020	55.545	63.445	69.169	73.446	76.760	79.494	81.726	83.582	CCC
100	100	100	100	100	100	100	100	100	100	D

Source: McKinsey & Company

Table 3. Cumulative excess loss probability

					Maturity					
1	2	3	4	5	6	7	8	9	10	Rating
0.00	0.01	0.02	0.06	0.12	0.24	0.41	0.63	0.83	1.08	AAA
0.00	0.04	0.10	0.22	0.36	0.64	1.00	1.43	1.77	2.17	AA
0.05	0.17	0.36	0.68	1.03	1.67	2.40	3.19	3.72	4.30	A
0.25	0.74	1.35	2.24	3.05	4.39	5.68	6.85	7.38	7.91	BBB
1.26	3.06	4.57	6.29	7.35	9.05	10.27	11.05	10.92	10.79	BB
5.16	7.79	8.84	9.87	9.97	10.67	10.88	10.72	9.96	9.31	B
7.07	8.37	7.94	7.75	7.11	7.03	6.78	6.42	5.83	5.36	CCC
0	0	0	0	0	0	0	0	0	0	D

Source: McKinsey & Company

Table 4. Total risk

					Maturity					
1	2	3	4	5	6	7	8	9	10	Rating
0.00	0.01	0.06	0.15	0.31	0.58	0.97	1.49	2.08	2.82	AAA
0.00	0.09	0.28	0.60	1.05	1.74	2.63	3.75	4.91	6.29	AA
0.17	0.54	1.14	2.06	3.23	4.91	6.89	9.19	11.41	13.87	A
0.83	2.35	4.50	7.37	10.54	14.53	18.69	23.00	26.75	30.54	BBB
4.13	10.15	16.73	23.80	30.29	37.25	43.50	49.14	53.52	57.54	BB
16.96	29.96	40.31	49.31	56.31	62.92	68.21	72.58	75.71	78.43	B
34.07	52.39	63.49	71.19	76.28	80.48	83.54	85.91	87.55	88.94	CCC
100	100	100	100	100	100	100	100	100	100	D

Source: McKinsey & Company

is an absorbing state. In a similar manner, we can also tabulate other critical values of the index loss distribution.

In Table 3, we have tabulated the additional probability of default within a 99% confidence interval, above and beyond the expected default probability, for the German index portfolio conditional on the current macroeconomic environment. As with the previous exhibit, this table could be interpreted as the credit risk capital for a portfolio of German exposures if and only if the portfolio mimicked the German index, had no recovery potential in the case of default, had constant exposures over the life of the commitments and if the losses were to be treated on a non-discounted basis. Again, we will demonstrate how to calculate the credit risk capital from an arbitrary portfolio of exposures in part two of this article.

Tables 2 and 3 show two interesting and connected phenomena: the excess maximum default probability above the expected probability of default does not increase monotonically by rating category or by maturity as one might expect given the close relationship between maximum possible default rates and credit risk capital. These observations are reflected most clearly in the declining cumulative excess loss probabilities for the triple-C rating category for maturities longer than two years and for the profile by rating for eight-year exposures, which peaks at the double-B class and declines thereafter.

The explanation for this phenomenon is straightforward: for lower rated exposures, the uncertainty of loss relative to the expected loss actually decreases with maturity after some point, reflecting the fact that more of the exposure will be lost with increasing certainty as the maturity is extended. This interesting effect disappears, however, if one focuses on the total maximum risk, defined as the total maximum default probability within a 99% confidence interval, which, like expected losses, increases monotonically in maturity for all rating classes (see Table 4).

1 *Typically, data can come from own portfolio experiences, public rating agencies or publicly available average default rate statistics. If not available, equity price data can be used as a surrogate in order to generate sector correlations, in the same way as they are used in CreditMetrics (JP Morgan, 1997).*

2 *An alternative starting point may have been to model the one-year probability of default for each rating class rather than the one-year Markov rating transition matrix. But we chose the latter approach because*

we are interested in measuring the credit risk of multi-year engagements and positions that are managed on a mark-to-market basis; for multi-year engagements, credit migrations leading to later defaults can be just as important as immediate defaults, implying that modelling one-year default rates would have been inappropriate; the same situation holds true for mark-to-market positions, where credit migrations as well as default events cause losses (or gains) which need to be recognised.

3 *In practice, we actually use univariate ARIMA*(p,d,q) *processes. While it is clear that a better modelling strategy might have been to estimate a vector autoregressive moving average (VARMA*(p,q)*) model or even a multi-country structural equation model, we chose the independently estimated ARIMA representation because of its simplicity. Further work on improving the macroeconomic models should be undertaken.*

BIBLIOGRAPHY

JP Morgan, 1997, CreditMetrics technical documentation.

Lawrence, D., 1995, "Aggregating Credit Exposures: The Simulation Approach", *Derivative Credit Risk: Advances in Measurement and Management,* Risk Publications, London.

Rowe, D., 1995, "Aggregating Credit Exposures: The Primary Risk Source Approach", *Derivative Credit Risk: Advances in Measurement and Management,* Risk Publications, London.

Wilson, T., 1997, "Measuring and Managing Credit Portfolio Risk", Unpublished paper.

3

Portfolio Credit Risk (II)

Thomas C. Wilson
Swiss Re New Markets

In the previous chapter we developed a multifactor model for systemic default and
credit migration risk based on historical macroeconomic and average default rate
time series for different country/industry segments. In developing this model for
systematic or non-diversifiable credit risk, we made use of several intuitive observations
that credit managers very often take for granted.

We formulated each of these intuitive observations into a rigorous statistical model,
which we then estimated. While the resulting distributions of correlated average
default probabilities are interesting, we still need a way to tabulate explicitly the loss
distribution for any arbitrary portfolio of credit risk exposures. To this end, we will
now turn our attention to developing an efficient method of doing this, which is
capable of handling:

❑ portfolios with large, undiversified positions and/or diversified positions;

❑ portfolios with non-constant exposures (such as those found in derivatives trading
books) and/or constant exposures (such as those found in commercial lending
books); and

❑ portfolios comprising liquid credit-risky positions (such as secondary market debt or
loans) and/or illiquid exposures that must be held to maturity (such as some commercial loans or trading lines) and/or retail portfolios such as mortgages, overdrafts
and credit cards.

Table 1. A numerical example

1. Determine state	State	GDP	Prob
	Expansion	+1	33.33%
	Average	0	33.33%
	Recession	−1	33.33%

2. Determine segment probability default	State	"Low-beta" Prob A	"High-beta" Prob B
	Expansion	2.50%	0.75%
	Average	2.97%	3.45%
	Recession	4.71%	5.25%

3. Determine loss distributions

In our model,[1] time is divided into discrete periods, indexed by t, and there are three
steps in each period. To make these more tangible, we will consider a single-period,
three-state, two-segment numerical example (see Table 1). In practice, we simulate a
10–20-year horizon, 10,000–100,000 states and up to 300 customer segments in order
to capture the true risk characteristics of a typical portfolio. The steps are:

Determine the state
The first step during any given period is to determine the state of the world, ie, the
macroeconomic health of the economy. In our simple example, there are three possible states of the economy that can occur: an economic "expansion" (with GDP

This article was originally published in Risk *magazine, October 1997.*

Table 2. Numerical example: two counterparty exposures

	Expansion				Average				Recession			
Loss distribution	A	B	A + B	Prob	A	B	A + B	Prob	A	B	A + B	Prob
	−100	−100	−200	0.01%	−100	−100	−200	0.03%	−100	−100	−200	0.08%
	−100	0	−100	0.83%	−100	0	−100	0.96%	−100	0	−100	1.49%
	0	−100	−100	0.24%	0	−100	−100	1.12%	0	−100	−100	1.67%
	0	0	0	32.26%	0	0	0	31.23%	0	0	0	30.10%
	Corr(A, B) = 0%				Corr(A, B) = 0%				Corr(A, B) = 0%			
					Conditional corr(A, B) = 1%							

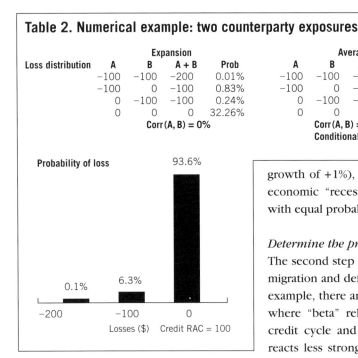

Probability of loss

93.6%

6.3%

0.1%

−200   −100   0

Losses ($)   Credit RAC = 100

growth of +1%), an "average" year (with GDP growth of 0%) and an economic "recession" (with GDP growth of -1%). Each can occur with equal probability (33.33%).

Determine the probability of default for each segment
The second step is to translate the state of the world into conditional migration and default probabilities for each customer segment. In this example, there are two counterparty segments: a "low-beta" segment, where "beta" relates to the segment's default rates relative to the credit cycle and not to an equity cycle, whose default probability reacts less strongly to macroeconomic fluctuations than a high-beta segment. These default probabilities would be driven by the statistical systematic risk models described in chapter 2.

Determine loss distributions
The third step is to determine the actual loss distribution for the portfolio. We will demonstrate this by tabulating the (non-discounted) loss distribution for portfolios that are constant over their life, cannot be liquidated and have known recovery rates; later, we will show how to incorporate liquid traded assets, retail portfolios, random recovery rates and country defaults into the analysis.

Undiversified portfolios

The conditional loss distribution in the simple two-counterparty, three-state numerical example is tabulated by recognising that there are three independent "draws" (or states) of the economy and that, conditional on each of these states, there are only four possible default scenarios (ie, A defaults, B defaults, both A and B default or neither defaults), as shown in Table 2.

The conditional probability of each of these loss events for each state of the economy is calculated by convoluting or aggregating each position's marginal loss distribution under the assumption of independence for each state. Thus, the conditional probability of a $200 loss in the expansion state is 0.01%, whereas the unconditional probability of achieving the same loss, given the entire distribution of future economic states (ie, expansion, average, recession) is 0.1%. For the example shown in Table 2, the expected portfolio loss is $6.50 and the credit risk capital is $100 (since this is the maximum potential loss within a 99% confidence interval across all possible future states of the economy).

Our approach for tabulating loss distributions is, therefore, first to tabulate the conditional portfolio loss distribution for each state of the world, given that counterparty defaults and credit migrations are independent, conditional on that state of the world; then, we aggregate these conditional loss distributions to an unconditional loss distribution by recognising that each was generated by an independent, random draw from the possible states of the world. The implicit assumption underlying our calculation of the conditional loss distributions is that all default and migration correlations are fully determined by the systematic risk model. That is, no further information beyond country, industry, rating and the state of the economy is useful in terms of predicting the default correlation between any two counterparties.

Table 3. Numerical example: diversified counterparty exposures

	NA = 1 and NB = infinity			
	Loss			
	A	B	A + B	Prob
Expansion	−2.50	−0.75	−3.25	33.33%
Average	−2.97	−3.45	−6.42	33.33%
Recession	−4.71	−5.25	−9.96	33.33%
	Unconditional Corr(A,B)			91%
	Credit RAC = 9.96			

	NA = 1 and NB = infinity			
	Loss			
	A	B	A + B	Prob
Expansion	−100	−0.75	−100.75	0.83%
	0	−0.75	−0.75	32.50%
Average	−100	−3.45	−103.45	0.99%
	0	−3.45	−3.45	32.30%
Recession	−100	−5.25	−105.25	1.57%
	0	−5.25	−5.25	31.80%
	Credit RAC = 105.25			

To underscore this point, suppose that management were confronted with two single-A counterparties in the German construction industry with the prospect of either a recession or an economic expansion in the near future. Using the traditional approach, which ignores the impact of the economy in determining the default probabilities for this and other segments, we would conclude that the counterparty default rates were correlated. Using our approach, we observe that the probability of default for both counterparties is significantly higher in a recession than in an expansion since credit cycles are "caused" by macroeconomic cycles, leading to correlated defaults. However, because we assume that default and migration correlations are fully determined by the segment's systematic risk, no other information beyond the counterparties' country, industry and rating (the counterparties' segmentation criteria, say) are useful in determining their joint default correlation once the state of the economy is determined. Using our approach, we know that the two German, single-A construction companies both have a higher probability of default during a recession but, given that we are in a recession, actual defaults for the two are independent. This is the identical assumption implicitly made by other multifactor models such as CreditMetrics (JP Morgan, 1997) and KMV's portfolio model (Kealhofer, 1995a and 1995b), but ours extends the framework by allowing the systematic risk profile of different corporate and retail segments to be estimated using actual loss histories as well as information from equity markets, allowing the institution to capture better the correlations and momentum found in actual default data.

As an aside, if the recovery rate were known with certainty, we could adjust the conditional loss distributions appropriately, to reflect the fact that a default event did not imply that the full exposure was lost. For example, if the recovery rate was 71.57% (Standard & Poor's average recovery rate for triple-B senior secured debt), then the expected losses would be $1.85 and the credit risk capital would be $28.43. Note that the assumption of a constant recovery rate will be relaxed later.

Portfolio diversification

Intuitively, we should be able to diversify away all idiosyncratic risk as we increase the number of counterparties in each segment, leaving only systematic (non-diversifiable) risk. Put more succinctly, as we diversify our holdings within a particular segment, that segment's loss distribution will converge to the loss distribution implied by the segment index. This logic is consistent with other single-factor or multifactor models in finance, eg, the behaviour of an equity portfolio under the capital asset pricing model.

Our multifactor model for systemic default risks is qualitatively similar, except that there is no single risk factor. Rather, there are multiple factors that fully describe the complex correlation structure between countries, industries and ratings. In our simple numerical example in Table 3, for a well-diversified portfolio consisting of many counterparties in each segment (NA + NB = infinity), all idiosyncratic risk in each segment is diversified away, leaving only the systematic risk in each segment.

In other words, because of the law of large numbers, the actual loss distribution for the portfolio will converge to the expected loss for each state of the world, implying that the unconditional loss distribution has only three possible outcomes, representing each of the three states of the world. Each occurs with equal probability and with a loss per segment consistent with the conditional probability of loss for that segment, given that state of the economy. While the expected losses from the portfolio would remain constant, this remaining systematic risk would generate a credit risk capital value of only $9.96 for the $200 million exposure in this simple example, demonstrating not only the benefit to be derived from portfolio diversification but also the fact that not all systematic risk can be diversified away.

In the second case in Table 3 (NA = 1 and NB = infinity), all of the idiosyncratic risk is diversified away within segment B, leaving only the systematic risk component. The segment A position, on the other hand, still contains idiosyncratic risk, since it comprises only a single risk position. Thus, for each state of the economy, two possible outcomes are possible: either the counterparty in segment A goes bankrupt or it does not. The unconditional probability that counterparty A will default in the economic expansion state is 0.83% (a 33.33% probability that the expansion state occurs, multiplied by a 2.5% probability of default for a segment A counterparty, given that state). Regardless of whether counterparty A goes into default or not, the segment B position losses will be known with certainty (given the state of the economy), since all idiosyncratic risk within that segment has been diversified away.

To illustrate the results using our simulation model, suppose we had equal $100, 10-year exposures to single-A counterparties in each of five country segments – Germany, France, Spain, the US and the UK – at the beginning of 1996. The aggregate simulated loss distribution for this portfolio of diversified country positions, conditional on the then-current macroeconomic states for the different countries at the end of 1995, is given in Figure 1. This portfolio has an expected loss of $37.5 million and would require an additional $24 million in risk capital to support it over the life of the commitments.

We now introduce a single large, undiversified exposure into the same portfolio. The impact is clearly visible in Figure 2. The return distribution has become bimodal, reflecting the fact that, for each state of the world, two events might occur. Either the large counterparty will go bankrupt, generating a "cloud" of portfolio loss events centred around –140, or it will not, generating a similar, but higher probability, "cloud" centred around –40. This calculation therefore demonstrates the risk capital premium needed to support the addition of a large, undiversified exposure.

Variable exposures and discounted losses

The calculations above illustrate how to tabulate the (non-discounted) loss distributions for non-liquid portfolios with constant exposures. While useful in many instances, these portfolio characteristics differ from reality in two important ways. First, the potential

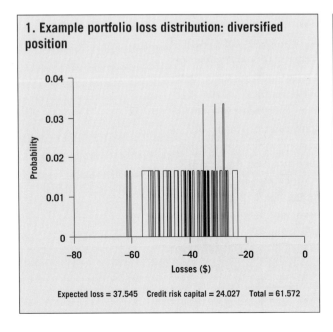

1. Example portfolio loss distribution: diversified position

Expected loss = 37.545   Credit risk capital = 24.027   Total = 61.572

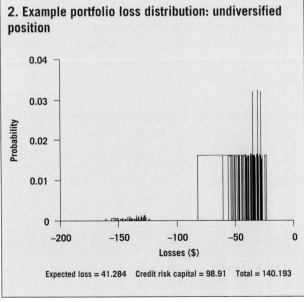

2. Example portfolio loss distribution: undiversified position

Expected loss = 41.284   Credit risk capital = 98.91   Total = 140.193

exposure profiles generated by trading products are not typically constant (as pointed out in Wilson, 1997, Lawrence, 1995, and Rowe, 1995). Second, the calculations ignore the time value of money, so a potential loss in the future is deemed as "painful", in terms of today's value, as a loss today.

In reality, the value of potential economic loss in the event of default varies over time. This poses a further challenge for our model, even supposing that the potential exposure envelope has been calculated for all counterparties and their netting/collateral sets – a difficult enough task in its own right.

This can be seen in Figure 3. If the counterparty had gone into default some time during the first year, the present value (PV) of the portfolio's loss would be $100 in the case of non-constant exposures and $100 e$(-r_1 \times 1)$ in the case of discounted exposures, where r_1 is the continuously compounded, one-year, zero-coupon rate. If one counterparty were to default in year two, however, the PV of the portfolio's loss would be $50 in the case of non-constant exposures and $100 e$(-r_2 \times 2)$ in the case of discounted exposures. Unlike the case of constant, non-discounted exposures, where the timing of the default is inconsequential, non-constant exposures or discounting of the losses imply that the timing of the default is critical in terms of tabulating the potential economic loss.

Addressing both of these issues requires us to work with marginal, rather than cumulative, default probabilities. Whereas the cumulative default probability is the probability of observing a default in any of the prior years, the marginal default probability is the probability of observing a loss in each specific year (assuming that the loss has not already occurred in a previous period).

Figure 4 illustrates the impact of non-constant loss exposures in terms of tabulating loss distributions. With constant exposures, the loss distribution for a single exposure is bimodal. Either it goes into default at some time during its maturity – with a cumulative default probability covering the entire three-year period equal to $p_1 + p_2 + p_3$ in the figure, implying a loss of 100 – or it does not. If the exposure varies, however, you stand to lose a different amount depending upon the exact timing of the default event. In the above example, you would stand to lose 100 with probability p_1, the marginal probability that the counterparty goes into default during the first year, 50 with probability p_2, the marginal probability that the counterparty goes into default during the second year, and so on.

Until now, we have simulated only the cumulative default probabilities; the tabulation of the marginal default probabilities from the cumulative is a straightforward exercise. Once done, the portfolio loss distribution can be tabulated by convoluting the individual loss distributions, in the same manner as described earlier. The primary difference between our model and other models is that we explicitly recognise that loss distributions for non-constant exposure profiles are not binomial but multinomial, due to the fact that the timing of default is just as important in terms of tabulating the position's loss distribution.

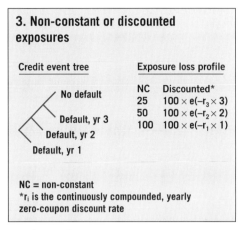

3. Non-constant or discounted exposures

Credit event tree		Exposure loss profile	
No default		NC	Discounted*
		25	$100 \times e(-r_3 \times 3)$
Default, yr 3		50	$100 \times e(-r_2 \times 2)$
Default, yr 2		100	$100 \times e(-r_1 \times 1)$
Default, yr 1			

NC = non-constant
*r_i is the continuously compounded, yearly zero-coupon discount rate

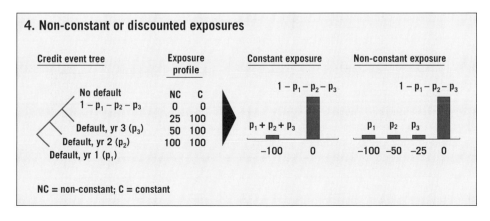

4. Non-constant or discounted exposures

Credit event tree — Exposure profile — Constant exposure — Non-constant exposure

		NC	C		
No default		0	0		
$1 - p_1 - p_2 - p_3$		25	100		
Default, yr 3 (p_3)		50	100		
Default, yr 2 (p_2)		100	100		
Default, yr 1 (p_1)					

Constant exposure: $1 - p_1 - p_2 - p_3$; $p_1 + p_2 + p_3$ at -100, 0

Non-constant exposure: $1 - p_1 - p_2 - p_3$; p_1 p_2 p_3 at -100 -50 -25 0

NC = non-constant; C = constant

Liquid assets

Until now, we have also assumed that the counterparty exposure must be held until maturity and that it cannot be liquidated at some market price before its maturity or expiry. This assumption is inadequate for three reasons:

❑ Many financial institutions are faced with the increasing probability that a bond name will also show up in their loan portfolio. As such, they want to measure the credit risk contribution arising from their secondary bond trading operations and integrate it into an overall credit portfolio perspective.

❑ While this assumption has been appropriate historically for many traditional asset classes (especially corporate loans and credit lines to support off-balance-sheet products), there has been a sharp increase in tools that allow credit exposures to be managed after their origination. Examples of such emerging tools include secondary and securitised loan trading; credit portfolio exchanges or "swaps"; credit derivatives; third party guarantees or insurance, etc. Having said this, it is nonetheless the case that most of the credit risk held by many retail and commercial banks – in the relatively opaque retail and mid-market segments – remains illiquid, especially in Europe and Asia.

❑ Finally, many financial institutions choose to tabulate the actual loss distribution for holding period horizons that might differ from the "liquidation" period of the commitment, reflecting, say, the periodicity of their capital allocation planning and budgeting process.

In all three cases, management is presented with two specific measurement challenges. First, as with market risk capital or value-at-risk, management must decide on the appropriate time horizon over which to measure the potential loss distribution. In the previous examples, the relevant time horizon coincided with the maximum maturity of the exposure, based on the assumption that management could not liquidate the position prior to its expiry. This assumption is commonly relaxed either by specifying a common holding period consistent with the institution's planning and budgeting process, thereby ignoring the risk capital needed to support the positions beyond the first year, or by specifying a position-specific holding period horizon, coinciding with the time it would take management to recognise a problem and liquidate the position in an orderly manner. This latter approach requires that management has a clear perspective regarding the market liquidity for each individual position.[2]

The second challenge arises in regard to tabulating the marked-to-market value losses should a credit event occur. Until now we have defined the loss distribution only in terms of default events (although default probabilities have been tabulated using rating migrations as well). It is clear, however, that if the position can be liquidated prior to its maturity, then other credit events (eg, credit downgrades and upgrades) may affect its marked-to-market value at any time before its expiry. For example, if you lock in a single-A spread and the credit rating of the counterparty decreases to triple-B, you suffer an economic loss.

To calculate the marked-to-market distribution for positions that can be liquidated prior to maturity, we need to modify our approach in two important ways. First, we must simulate not only the cumulative default probabilities for each rating class but also store in memory the probabilities of counterparty rating migrations. This is straightforward, although it is memory-intensive. Complicating this calculation, however, is the fact that, if the time horizons are different for different asset classes, a continuum of rating migration probabilities might need to be stored – one for each possible maturity or liquidation period. To reduce the complexity of the task, we tabulate migration probabilities for yearly intervals only and make the assumption that the rating migration probabilities for any liquidation horizon that falls between years can be approximated by some interpolation method.[3]

Second, and more challenging, we need to be able to tabulate the change in marked-to-market value of the exposure for each possible change in credit rating. In the case of

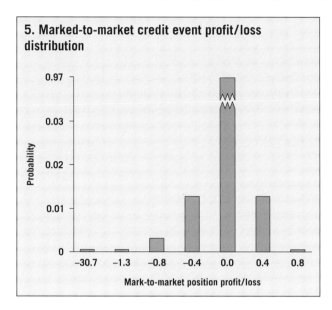

5. Marked-to-market credit event profit/loss distribution

Mark-to-market position profit/loss

6. Distribution of defaulted bond prices

Prices

Source: Moody's Investors Service

traded loans or debt, a pragmatic approach is simply to define a table of average credit spreads, in basis points per year, as a function of rating and the maturity of the underlying exposure. The potential loss (or gain) from a credit migration can then be tabulated by calculating the change in marked-to-market value of the exposure due to the changing of the discount rate implied by the credit migration.[4]

The results of applying this approach are shown in Figure 5, where we have tabulated the potential profit and loss profile from a single traded credit exposure, originally rated triple-B, which can be liquidated prior to one year. For this example, we have used a recovery rate of 71.57%, the average recovery rate for senior secured credits rated triple-B. As is clear from Figure 5, it is inappropriate to talk about "loss" distributions in the context of marked-to-market loan or debt securities, since it is also possible to *profit* from an improvement in the counterparty's credit standing.

Although this approach allows one to capture the impact of credit migrations while holding the level of interest rates and spreads constant, it must be seen as a complement to a market risk measurement system that accurately captures the potential profit or loss impact of changing interest rate levels and average credit spread levels. If your market risk measurement system does not capture these risks, a more complicated approach could be used, eg, simulating jointly interest rate levels, average credit spread levels and credit rating migrations. While potentially desirable, such an approach may come close to the fabled "all singing, all dancing" models that our grandmothers warned us about.

Variable recovery rates and country defaults

Throughout our discussions so far, we have also assumed that the amount that could be recovered in the event of default was a known constant, dependent only upon the rating of the counterparty. In reality, however, the actual amount that one can recover is neither constant nor is it dependent solely on the rating of the counterparty, as demonstrated by the Moody's Investors Service (1994) data plotted in Figure 6. Clearly, the market's expectation of potential recovery from defaulted securities depends upon the individual security.

One way to model the impact of random recovery rates is to simulate jointly defaults and recovery rates. As is apparent from Figure 6, however, we must first specify a recovery distribution for each of the relevant recovery classes. We do this for various classes (senior secured, subordinated, unsecured, etc), by using Moody's, Standard & Poor's or your own portfolio's historical experiences. For every simulation of the systematic risk factors, we then take a random draw on this recovery distribution to tabulate the exposure's loss in the event of default. This technique implicitly assumes that the random recovery rates can be drawn independently from one another across different macroeconomic scenarios and counterparties. This assumption clearly breaks down, however, in two cases of interest:

❏ The first is when we are tabulating potential losses in the event of default arising from trading exposures. It is quite probable that the recovery rates for two client exposures are highly correlated, depending upon the compositions of their portfolios. For example, both might be corporate counterparties hedging liabilities with long-dated dollar interest rate swaps. The solution would again be to develop a model that jointly simulates the portfolio's potential exposure (driven by market rates) and credit events – ie, another "all singing, all dancing" model.

In addition to its inherent modelling complexity, however, this approach might also suffer from some concrete system constraints. To implement such an approach, all the counterparty's transactions, including netting and collateral information and valuation methods, would have to reside in a common system. While for many institutions this may be the ultimate objective, very few could currently implement such a system. More importantly, given the current state of financial disclosure, which provides little transparency regarding the hedge transactions concluded by a corporation, we may not know whether defaults and market rates are positively or negatively correlated for a particular counterparty.

❏ The second case is for certain asset classes, most notably mortgages and some collateralised loans, where the recovery rate is highly negatively correlated with the probability of default. Residential homeowners rarely default on their property when there is still much positive equity in the home. In these cases, it is sometimes useful to either add regional property price indexes to the set of explanatory variables used in the Logit modelling of our systematic risk indexes or to make the recovery distributions dependent upon the state of the economy.

In addition, our loss tabulation framework allows an institution easily to incorporate country or political risk. This is accomplished by associating each asset with a specific risk country and then simulating (correlated) country events. If a country event occurs, then all assets that bear that country's risk revert to their recovery distributions.

1 *McKinsey & Company has implemented this model within an application which will be made available free of charge. Contact McKinsey & Company for details.*

2 *Complicating this process is the fact that, while any credit exposure can be liquidated for a price, its actual liquidation depends on the price offered. Very often, management is far more willing to acknowledge the possibility of liquidating a credit risky position than to actually do it.*

3 *Clearly, this assumption can be relaxed if the Markov migration probability matrix can be calculated for time horizons of higher frequency; the problem one might face is that this calculation may introduce more noise than explanatory power, due to the higher frequency of the data.*

4 *For credit-risky exposures, such as the potential exposure from trading lines that can only be liquidated via other methods (such as credit guarantees or credit derivatives), one would have to provide a "cost of credit insurance" table or liquidation, again as a function of the exposure's maturity and credit rating.*

BIBLIOGRAPHY

JP Morgan, 1997, CreditMetrics technical documentation.

Kealhofer, S., 1995a, "Managing Default Risk in Portfolios of Derivatives", *Derivative Credit Risk: Advances in Measurement and Management,* Risk Publications, London.

Kealhofer, S., 1995b, "Portfolio Management of Default Risk", proprietary documentation, KMV Corporation, San Francisco.

Lawrence, D., 1995, "Aggregating Credit Exposures: The Simulation Approach", *Derivative Credit Risk: Advances in Measurement and Management,* Risk Publications, London.

Moody's Investors Service, 1994, *Corporate Bond Defaults and Default Rates 1970-1993,* Moody's Investors Service.

Rowe, D., 1995, "Aggregating Credit Exposures: The Primary Risk Source Approach", *Derivative Credit Risk: Advances in Measurement and Management,* Risk Publications, London.

Wilson, T., 1997, "Measuring and Managing Credit Portfolio Risk", Unpublished paper.

VALUATION OF RISKY DEBT

Introduction

Valuation of Risky Debt

David Shimko

In the celebration of Fischer Black and Myron Scholes' seminal paper "The Pricing of Options and Corporate Liabilities" (1973) and Robert Merton's "A Rational Theory of Option Pricing" (1973), it seems that the world concentrated on the high value of a pricing model that was useful to both academics and practitioners. For the academics, the option pricing model was rigorous and consistent with general equilibrium theory, while for the practitioner this model approximated reality and used variables that were mostly observable. The contemporaneous emergence of option markets in Chicago benefited from, and contributed to, new research in the option pricing literature.

A re-reading of the original Black and Scholes paper, however, will convince you that the authors' main goal was not necessarily to value options, which were in their view a relatively small part of the marketplace. Rather, their main goal was to value corporate liabilities - options on a grander scale. In this vein Merton's 1974 paper, which opens this section, restates and expands the original Black–Scholes–Merton framework papers, focusing specifically on the application of the option pricing model to a simple corporate liability.

Today the analogy seems quite simple to us, a testament to how we now take these things for granted. Suppose that a firm has a single issue of discount debt (no coupons) in its capital structure. In this case, when the debt matures the equity holders will pay off the debt if there is any residual value; otherwise they will default. Put another way, the equity holders have a call option on the assets of the firm, which they can buy back from the lenders by paying the face value of the debt at maturity. If they choose not to exercise their call option they default, and the bondholders receive the liquidation value of the firm.

In simple equations, one could say

$$\text{Value of firm} = \text{Equity value} + \text{Debt value} \qquad \text{(1A)}$$

$$\text{Value of firm} = \text{Call option on the firm's assets} + \text{Debt value} \qquad \text{(1B)}$$

In Merton's model, the value of the firm is given exogenously (outside the model). The call option is valued using the Black–Scholes–Merton formula, and the debt is simply the residual value. Alternatively and equivalently, using put–call parity, debt can be seen as the value of default-free debt minus the value of the shareholder's right to "put" the assets to the debtors to satisfy their nominal obligations:

$$\text{Value of risky debt (Debt value)} = \text{Value of risk-free debt} - \text{Value of put option} \qquad \text{(2)}$$

Both equations (1B) and (2) are useful in making statements about the value of risky debt. For example, Merton shows by analogy to options that an increase in the riskiness of assets always hurts debt value. Equation (2) is also useful when one is trying to determine the impact of a firm's characteristics on the credit spread, which is defined as the yield on the risky debt under the assumption that it is paid in full.

Discussions of the "credit spread" as a function of term to maturity normally use the phrase "risk structure of interest rates", which was first coined in Merton's article and is now a standard part of our vocabulary. To keep the analysis simple, Merton assumed perfect markets and a flat term structure. Perfect markets allow continuous, costless trading and seamless arbitrage; and a flat term structure provides that the risk-free rate of interest is constant regardless of maturity. There are no coupon payments in Merton's model, nor does he discuss the effect of bond indenture provisions (although he does evaluate one case in which coupons are paid continuously and perpetually).

Despite the theoretical limitations of the assumptions of Merton's model, the paper has stood the test of time. Indeed, several academics have committed a significant amount of their research to extricating certain assumptions from Merton's models or submitting them to rigorous testing. Some of the products of these efforts have been reprinted in this volume.

One logical extension of the Merton characterisation is supplied by Fischer Black and John Cox in their 1976 paper "Valuing Corporate Securities: Some Effects of Bond Indenture Provisions". In that study, which follows Merton's here, Black and Cox examine the impact on risky bond value of safety covenants, subordination agreements and restrictions on the financing of payments to stakeholders. By "safety covenants" the authors mean the early liquidation rights of bondholders in the event of perceived mismanagement by equity holders. "Subordination" refers to the rights of equity holders to issue debt that is junior to existing debt. Finally, restrictions on payment financing prohibit firms from increasing their leverage to make payments and require that they meet any additional requirements with equity prior to the retirement of debt.

The valuation approach, in spite of the apparent complexity, is completed in the style of Merton's paper – perfect markets and closed-form solutions. The value of bonds with these provisions follows the blueprint of Cox, Ingersoll and Ross (1985a), which separates the value of an asset into three parts: payment when bad events occur (safety provisions); payments when good events occur (reorganisation); and, absent these events, payments in the ordinary course of time.

The conclusions are not simple or trivial. Safety covenants are great for bondholders, not surprisingly. It turns out that the valuation of subordinated debt is quite difficult. For example, one would be tempted to assume that increasing asset volatility is bad for all debtholders, yet Black and Cox show that this may not be true: increasing volatility may be a good thing for subordinated debtholders if it increases their likelihood of getting paid after the senior debtholders. That is, subordinated debt may look like equity or it may look like debt.

There are several other immediate extensions of Merton's analysis along these lines. Brennan and Schwartz's "Analyzing Convertible Bonds" (1980) and Ingersoll's "A Contingent Claims Valuation of Convertible Securities" (1977) are highly recommended to the interested reader but are not included in this volume because they concentrate on the option aspects of corporate debt more so than the credit characteristics.

Another logical extension to the Merton paper that is not reprinted here is Geske's "The Valuation of Corporate Liabilities as Compound Options" (1977). The main point made by Geske was that a coupon bond subject to default cannot be valued as if it were a sequence of zero-coupon bonds. That is, the payment of a coupon could be thought of as giving up the value of the option to default until the next coupon date. The valuation of compound options, of course, becomes analytically complex.

But the issue of the importance of coupon payments as an empirical matter is explored in the paper by Joon Kim, Krishna Ramaswamy and Suresh Sundaresan (1993), "Does Default Risk in Coupons Affect the Valuation of Corporate Bonds: A Contingent Claims Approach Model", which appears here as chapter 6. Their general observation is that models of the Merton variety cannot generate the yield spreads observed in bond markets. For example, using Merton's model one could generate a spread of up to 120 basis points (bp) by torturing the parameter ranges. Yet, AAA bond credit spreads in their sample reached 215 bp with an average of 77 bp, and BAA spreads reached 787 bp with an average of 198 bp!

The authors deduced that either default risk in coupons or stochastic interest rates could be an explanatory factor – allowing Merton's results to be consistent with real-market observations after making a few small theoretical changes. They assumed perfect markets (as Merton did), and furthermore applied Cox, Ingersoll and Ross's (1985b) model for short-term interest rates to characterise the movements in the term structure. (This model assumes that the short rate follows a mean-reverting process, with volatility proportional to the square root of the interest rate.)

Because of the coupons and stochastic interest rates, Kim and his co-authors were not able to find a closed-form solution for the bond pricing problem but used numerical techniques to establish their results. In broad terms, they found that the inclusion of coupon payments, stochastic (variable) interest rates and call provisions common in most corporate bonds were able to make Merton's basic results fit the more broadly observed credit spreads.

Although Kim, Ramaswamy and Sundaresan were able to demonstrate the effect of stochastic risk-free interest rates on risky debt valuation, some have criticised the Cox–Ingersoll–Ross (CIR) model as one that is not able to fit observed term structures. One such criticism was made by Hull and White (1993) in "Single Factor Interest Rate Models and the Valuation of Interest Rate Derivative Securities". Hull and White recommended that for valuation purposes researchers use the Vasicek (1977) model instead of the CIR model. The Vasicek model has the unfortunate theoretical (and small) possibility of negative short-term interest rates, but it also has the fortunate practical feature that it can be parameterised to fit almost any observed term structure.

Taking this advice to heart, David Shimko, Naohiko Tejima and Donald van Deventer (1993) showed that the replacement of the CIR model with Vasicek's not only has the desirable practical properties mentioned by Hull and White but it also allowed the computation of a closed-form solution for zero-coupon bond prices. Using their model, it is easy to show how the credit spread responds to different assumptions about asset volatility and interest rate volatility, or the correlation between the two. For reasonable parameter values, it is easy to exceed the 120 bp maximum credit spread under the Merton model. In other words, even without the coupon payments and call provisions of Kim, Ramaswamy and Sundaresan, it is possible to explain market credit spreads by modelling asset prices and interest rate changes more robustly. Shimko, Tejima and van Deventer's paper is reprinted here as chapter 7.

In the next chapter Philip Jones, Scott Mason and Eric Rosenfeld perform an empirical analysis, originally published in 1994, in line with that of Kim and co-workers, and conclude that models based on contingent claims analysis (CCA) do not add much value when valuing investment-grade debt but add some value when dealing with sub-investment-grade debt. For example, in a price level regression of market prices on model prices (CCA versus a "naïve" model), they found that the following regression fits:

$$\text{Actual price} = 0.0117 + 0.6911 \times \text{Naïve model price} \quad (R^2 = 95\%)$$

or

$$\text{Actual price} = 0.0029 + 0.8627 \times \text{CCA Model price} \quad (R^2 = 98\%)$$

Of course, the R^2 measures are misleading when dealing with price levels, but considering the standard error of the slope estimates (~ 0.01 in each case), the CCA model performed much better in replicating the actual bond prices.

Although there is some supporting evidence favouring the CCA model, Jones and his colleagues also point to misspecification problems by regressing the model pricing errors on the bond parameters. Some of these problems could be alleviated by considering tax aspects and stochastic interest rates. All in all, this study adds value as an update of the authors' previous work and provides a blueprint for further work.

In Lawrence Fisher's discussion of the paper, he states that Jones, Mason and Rosenfeld cannot be considered a test of the CCA approach because of its inherent inability to consider the effect of three of Merton's most important assumptions: perfect liquidity, the irrelevance of taxes and stochastic interest rates. His other objections and suggestions make for good reading, especially for researchers looking for a new angle on the valuation of risky bonds.

In chapter 9 Francis Longstaff and Eduardo Schwartz (1995) make good on their claim to provide "A Simple Approach to Valuing Risky Fixed and Floating Rate Debt". Combining valuation features from Shimko, Tejima and van Deventer (1993) – ie, using the Vasicek interest rate model – and bond characteristics from Kim, Ramaswamy and Sundaresan (1993) and Jones, Mason and Rosenfeld (1994), they are able to derive a closed-form solution for risky debt, with or without coupons, and with fixed or floating rate provisions.

They also explain why the correlation between asset value and interest rates is so important. Normally, practitioners think of credit ratings as indicators of the likelihood of default and attribute different credit spreads by industry to different expected recovery rates. The authors expand this observation further, suggesting that when asset values are correlated with interest rates, higher rates may precipitate a firm's default because of increased cashflow obligations but, at the same time, increase its recovery value.

Finally, they provide a simple empirical model with observed credit spreads to demonstrate the overall consistency of their model with the data observed in practice. The empirical portion should not be seen as a test of the model *per se* but rather as an empirical exploration of the consistency of model predictions with market experience.

The final chapter, "Credit Risk Revisited", by Michel Crouhy, Dan Galai and Robert Mark (1998), is a reminder that, complex as the bond pricing analytics become, we can still learn much from the original Merton model. For example, recent work by Jarrow and Turnbull (1995; chapter 16 of this volume) and Duffie and Singleton (1994) used the observation that credit spreads are the product of default rates and recovery rates to broaden the study of corporate bond valuation. This subtle observation can be recreated in the Merton framework – as can the traditional analytics: hedge ratios and market betas, for instance.

Overall, this section cannot be considered a complete survey of the literature on corporate bond pricing derived from the option pricing framework. Nevertheless, the body of work presented here will give the reader an understanding and appreciation of the major issues – both theoretical and practical – in developing bond pricing formulas from options theory.

BIBLIOGRAPHY

Black, F., and M. Scholes, 1973, "The Pricing of Options and Corporate Liabilities", *Journal of Political Economy* 81, pp. 637-59.

Brennan, M. J., and E. S. Schwartz, 1980, "Analyzing Convertible Bonds" *Journal of Financial and Quantitative Analysis* November, pp. 907-29.

Cox, J. C., J. E. Ingersoll and S. A. Ross, 1985a, "An Intertemporal General Equilibrium Model of Asset Prices", *Econometrica* 53, pp. 363-84.

Cox, J. C., J. E. Ingersoll and S. A. Ross, 1985b, "A Theory of the Term Structure of Interest Rates", *Econometrica* 53, pp. 385-407.

Duffie, D., and K. Singleton, 1997, "Modeling Term Structures of Defaultable Bonds", Graduate School of Business, Stanford University, Stanford, California.

Geske, R., 1977, "The Valuation of Corporate Liabilities as Compound Options", *Journal of Financial and Quantitative Analysis*.

Hull, J., and A. White, 1993, "Single Factor Interest Rate Models and the Valuation of Interest Rate Derivative Securities", *Journal of Financial and Quantitative Analysis* 28, pp. 235-54.

Ingersoll, J. E., 1977, "A Contingent Claims Valuation of Convertible Securities", *Journal of Financial Economics* 4, pp. 289-322.

Merton, R. C., 1973, "A Rational Theory of Option Pricing", *Bell Journal of Economics and Management Science* 4, pp. 141-83.

Vasicek, O. A., 1977, "An Equilibrium Characterization of the Term Structure", *Journal of Financial Economics* 5, pp. 177-88.

4

On the Pricing of Corporate Debt: The Risk Structure of Interest Rates

Robert C. Merton

Harvard Business School

The value of a particular issue of corporate debt depends essentially on three items: (1) the required rate of return on riskless (in terms of default) debt (eg, government bonds or very high grade corporate bonds); (2) the various provisions and restrictions contained in the indenture (eg, maturity date, coupon rate, call terms, seniority in the event of default, sinking fund, etc.); (3) the probability that the firm will be unable to satisfy some or all of the indenture requirements (ie, the probability of default).

While a number of theories and empirical studies have been published on the term structure of interest rates (item 1), there has been no systematic development of a theory for pricing bonds when there is a significant probability of default. The purpose of this paper is to present such a theory, which might be called a theory of the risk structure of interest rates. The use of the term "risk" is restricted to the possible gains or losses to bondholders as a result of (unanticipated) changes in the probability of default and does not include the gains or losses inherent to all bonds caused by (unanticipated) changes in interest rates in general. Throughout most of the analysis, a given term structure is assumed and, hence, the price differentials among bonds will be caused solely by differences in the probability of default.

In a seminal paper, Black and Scholes (1973) present a complete general equilibrium theory of option pricing which is particularly attractive because the final formula is a function of "observable" variables. Therefore, the model is subject to direct empirical tests, which they (Black and Scholes, 1972) performed with some success. Merton (1973) clarified and extended the Black–Scholes model. While options are highly specialised and relatively unimportant financial instruments, both Black and Scholes (1973) and Merton (1970, 1973) recognised that the same basic approach could be applied in developing a pricing theory for corporate liabilities in general.

In the second section of the paper, the basic equation for the pricing of financial instruments is developed along Black–Scholes lines. In the third section, the model is applied to the simplest form of corporate debt, the discount bond where no coupon payments are made, and a formula for computing the risk structure of interest rates is presented. In the fourth section, comparative statics are used to develop graphs of the risk structure, and the question of whether the term premium is an adequate measure of the risk of a bond is answered. In the fifth section, the validity in the presence of bank-

This paper was first published in the Journal of Finance *29, pp. 449–70 (1974) and is reprinted with the kind permission of Blackwell Publishers. The author thanks J. Ingersoll for doing the computer simulations and for general scientific assistance. Aid from the National Science Foundation is gratefully acknowledged.*

ruptcy of the famous Modigliani–Miller (Modigliani and Miller, 1958) theorem is proven, and the required return on debt as a function of the debt-to-equity ratio is deduced. In the sixth section, the analysis is extended to include coupon and callable bonds.

On the pricing of corporate liabilities

To develop the Black–Scholes-type pricing model, we make the following assumptions:

A.1 There are no transactions costs, taxes, or problems with indivisibilities of assets.

A.2 There are a sufficient number of investors with comparable wealth levels so that each investor believes that he can buy and sell as much of an asset as he wants at the market price.

A.3 There exists an exchange market for borrowing and lending at the same rate of interest.

A.4 Short sales of all assets, with full use of the proceeds, is allowed.

A.5 Trading in assets takes place continuously in time.

A.6 The Modigliani–Miller theorem that the value of the firm is invariant to its capital structure obtains.

A.7 The term structure is "flat" and known with certainty. In other words, the price of a riskless discount bond which promises a payment of one dollar at time τ in the future is $P(\tau) = \exp[-r\tau]$, where r is the (instantaneous) riskless rate of interest, the same for all time.

A.8 The dynamics for the value of the firm, V, through time can be described by a diffusion-type stochastic process with stochastic differential equation

$$dV = (\alpha V - C)dt + \sigma V dz$$

where α is the instantaneous expected rate of return on the firm per unit time; C is the total dollar payouts by the firm per unit time to either its shareholders or liabilities-holders (eg, dividends or interest payments) if positive, and it is the net dollars received by the firm from new financing if negative; σ^2 is the instantaneous variance of the return on the firm per unit time; and dz is a standard Gauss–Wiener process.

Many of these assumptions are not necessary for the model to obtain but are chosen for expositional convenience. In particular, the "perfect market" assumptions (A.1–A.4) can be substantially weakened. A.6 is actually proved as part of the analysis and A.7 is chosen so as to clearly distinguish risk structure from term structure effects on pricing. A.5 and A.8 are the critical assumptions. Basically, A.5 requires that the market for these securities is open for trading most of time. A.8 requires that price movements are continuous and that the (unanticipated) returns on the securities be serially independent, which is consistent with the "efficient markets hypothesis" of Fama (1970) and Samuelson (1965).[1]

Suppose there exists a security whose market value, Y, at any point in time can be written as a function of the value of the firm and time, ie, $Y = F(V, t)$. We can formally write the dynamics of this security's value in stochastic differential equation form as

$$dY = \left[\alpha_y Y - C_y \right] dt + \sigma_y Y dz_y \tag{1}$$

where α_y is the instantaneous expected rate of return per unit time on this security; C_y is the dollar payout per unit time to this security; σ_y^2 is the instantaneous variance of the return per unit time; and dz_y is a standard Gauss–Wiener process. However, given that $Y = F(V, t)$, there is an explicit functional relationship between the α_y, σ_y, and dz_y in (1) and the corresponding variables α, σ and dz defined in A.8. In particular, by Itô's lemma,[2] we can write the dynamics for Y as

$$dY = F_V dV + \tfrac{1}{2} F_{VV} (dV)^2 + F_t dt$$

$$= \left[\tfrac{1}{2} \sigma^2 V^2 F_{VV} + (\alpha V - C) F_V + F_t \right] dt + \sigma V F_V dz \quad \text{from A.8} \tag{2}$$

where subscripts on F denote partial derivatives. Comparing terms in (2) and (1), we have that

$$\alpha_y Y = \alpha_y F \equiv \tfrac{1}{2}\sigma^2 V^2 F_{vv} + (\alpha V - C)F_v + F_t + C_y \tag{3a}$$

$$\sigma_y Y = \sigma_y F \equiv \sigma V F_v \tag{3b}$$

$$dz_y \equiv dz \tag{3c}$$

Note: from (3c) the instantaneous returns on Y and V are perfectly correlated.

Following the Merton derivation of the Black–Scholes model presented in (1973, p. 164), consider forming a three-security "portfolio" containing the firm, the particular security, and riskless debt such that the aggregate investment in the portfolio is zero. This is achieved by using the proceeds of short sales and borrowings to finance the long positions. Let W_1 be the (instantaneous) number of dollars of the portfolio invested in the firm, W_2 the number of dollars invested in the security, and W_3 ($\equiv -[W_1 + W_2]$) the number of dollars invested in riskless debt. If dx is the instantaneous dollar return to the portfolio, then

$$dx = W_1 \frac{(dV + Cdt)}{V} + W_2 \frac{\left(dY + C_y dt\right)}{Y} + W_3 r dt$$

$$= \left[W_1(\alpha - r) + W_2 \left(\alpha_y - r\right) \right] dt + W_1 \sigma dz + W_2 \sigma_y dz_y$$

$$= \left[W_1(\alpha - r) + W_2 \left(\alpha_y - r\right) \right] dt + \left[W_1 \sigma + W_2 \sigma_y \right] dz \quad \text{from (3c)} \tag{4}$$

Suppose the portfolio strategy, $W_j = W_j^*$, is chosen such that the coefficient of dz is always zero. Then, the dollar return on the portfolio, dx*, would be non-stochastic. Since the portfolio requires zero net investment, it must be that to avoid arbitrage profits the expected (and realised) return on the portfolio with this strategy is zero. In other words:

$$W_1^* \sigma + W_2^* \sigma_y = 0 \qquad \text{(No risk)} \tag{5a}$$

$$W_1^*(\alpha - r) + W_2^*(\alpha_y - r) = 0 \qquad \text{(No arbitrage)} \tag{5b}$$

A non-trivial solution ($W_j^* \neq 0$) to (5) exists if and only if

$$\left(\frac{\alpha - r}{\sigma} \right) = \left(\frac{\alpha_y - r}{\sigma_y} \right) \tag{6}$$

But, from (3a) and (3b), we substitute for α_y and σ_y and rewrite (6) as

$$\frac{\alpha - r}{\sigma} = \frac{\left(\tfrac{1}{2}\sigma^2 V^2 F_{vv} + (\alpha V - C)F_v + F_t + C_y - rF \right)}{\sigma V F_v} \tag{6'}$$

and, by rearranging terms and simplifying, we can rewrite (6') as

$$0 = \tfrac{1}{2}\sigma^2 V^2 F_{vv} + (rV - C)F_v - rF + F_t + C_y \tag{7}$$

Equation (7) is a parabolic partial differential equation for F which must be satisfied by *any* security whose value can be written as a function of the value of the firm and time. Of course, a complete description of the partial differential equation requires, in addition to (7), a specification of two boundary conditions and an initial condition. It is precisely these boundary condition specifications which distinguish one security from another (eg, the debt of a firm from its equity).

In closing this section, it is important to note which variables and parameters appear in (7) (and, hence, affect the value of the security) and which do not. In addition to the value of the firm and time, F depends on the interest rate, the volatility of the firm's value (or its business risk) as measured by the variance, the payout policy of the firm, and the promised payout policy to the holders of the security. However, F does *not* depend on the expected rate of return on the firm nor on the risk preferences of investors nor on the characteristics of other assets available to investors beyond the three mentioned. Thus, two investors with quite different utility functions and different expectations for the company's future but who agree on the volatility of the firm's value will, for a given interest rate and current firm value, agree on the value of the particular security, F. Also all the parameters and variables except the variance are directly observable and the variance can be reasonably estimated from time-series data.

On pricing "risky" discount bonds

As a specific application of the formulation of the previous section, we examine the simplest case of corporate debt pricing. Suppose the corporation has two classes of claims: (1) a single, homogeneous class of debt; and (2) the residual claim, equity. Suppose further that the indenture of the bond issue contains the following provisions and restrictions: (1) the firm promises to pay a total of B dollars to the bondholders on the specified calendar date T; (2) in the event this payment is not met, the bondholders immediately take over the company (and the shareholders receive nothing); (3) the firm cannot issue any new senior (or of equivalent rank) claims on the firm nor can it pay cash dividends or do share repurchase prior to the maturity of the debt.

If F is the value of the debt issue, we can write (7) as

$$\tfrac{1}{2}\sigma^2 V^2 F_{vv} + rVF_v - rF - F_\tau = 0 \qquad (8)$$

where $C_y = 0$ because there are no coupon payments; $C = 0$ from restriction (3); $\tau \equiv T - t$ is length of time until maturity so that $F_t = -F_\tau$. To solve (8) for the value of the debt, two boundary conditions and an initial condition must be specified. These boundary conditions are derived from the provisions of the indenture and the limited liability of claims. By definition, $V \equiv F(V, \tau) + f(V, \tau)$, where f is the value of the equity. Because both F and f can only take on non-negative values, we have that

$$F(0, \tau) = f(0, \tau) = 0 \qquad (9a)$$

Further, $F(V, \tau) \le V$, which implies the regularity condition

$$\frac{F(V, \tau)}{V} \le 1 \qquad (9b)$$

which substitutes for the other boundary condition in a semi-infinite boundary problem where $0 \le V \le \infty$. The initial condition follows from indenture conditions (1) and (2) and the fact that management is elected by the equity owners and, hence, must act in their best interests. On the maturity date T (ie, $\tau = 0$) the firm must either pay the promised payment of B to the debtholders or else the current equity will be valueless. Clearly, if at time T, $V(T) > B$, the firm should pay the bondholders because the value of equity will be $V(T) - B > 0$, whereas if they do not the value of equity would be zero. If $V(T) \le B$, then the firm will not make the payment and default the firm to the bondholders because otherwise the equity holders would have to pay in additional money and the (formal) value of equity prior to such payments would be $(V(T) - B) < 0$. Thus, the initial condition for the debt at $\tau = 0$ is

$$F(V, 0) = \min[V, B] \qquad (9c)$$

Armed with boundary conditions (9), one could solve (8) directly for the value of the debt by the standard methods of Fourier transforms or separation of variables. However, we avoid these calculations by looking at a related problem and showing its correspondence to a problem already solved in the literature.

To determine the value of equity, $f(V, \tau)$, we note that $f(V, \tau) = V - F(V, \tau)$ and substitute for F in (8) and (9) to deduce the partial differential equation for f. Namely:

$$\tfrac{1}{2}\sigma^2 V^2 f_{vv} + rVf_v - rf - f_\tau = 0 \qquad (10)$$

subject to

$$f(V, 0) = Max[0, V - B] \qquad (11)$$

and boundary conditions (9a) and (9b). Inspection of the Black–Scholes equation (1973, p. 643, (7)) or Merton (1973, p. 65) equation (34) shows that (10) and (11) are identical to the equations for a European call option on a non-dividend-paying common stock where firm value in (10)-(11) corresponds to stock price and B corresponds to the exercise price. This isomorphic price relationship between levered equity of the firm and a call option not only allows us to write down the solution to (10)-(11) directly but, in addition, allows us to immediately apply the comparative statics results in these papers to the equity case and, hence, to the debt. From Black–Scholes equation (13) when σ^2 is a constant, we have that

$$f(V, \tau) = V\Phi(x_1) - Be^{-r\tau}\Phi(x_2) \qquad (12)$$

where

$$\Phi(x) \equiv \frac{1}{\sqrt{2\pi}} \int_{-\infty}^{x} \exp\left[-\tfrac{1}{2}z^2\right] dz$$

and

$$x_1 \equiv \frac{\log[V/B] + \left(r + \tfrac{1}{2}\sigma^2\right)\tau}{\sigma\sqrt{\tau}}$$

and

$$x_2 \equiv x_1 - \sigma\sqrt{\tau}$$

From (12) and F = V - f, we can write the value of the debt issue as

$$F[V, \tau] = Be^{-r\tau}\left\{ \Phi\left[h_2\left(d, \sigma^2\tau\right)\right] + \frac{1}{d}\Phi\left[h_1\left(d, \sigma^2\tau\right)\right] \right\} \qquad (13)$$

where

$$d \equiv \frac{Be^{-r\tau}}{V}$$

$$h_1(d, \sigma^2\tau) \equiv -\frac{\left[\tfrac{1}{2}\sigma^2\tau - \log(d)\right]}{\sigma\sqrt{\tau}}$$

$$h_2(d, \sigma^2\tau) \equiv -\frac{\left[\tfrac{1}{2}\sigma^2\tau + \log(d)\right]}{\sigma\sqrt{\tau}}$$

Because it is common in discussions of bond pricing to talk in terms of yields rather than prices, we can rewrite (13) as

$$R(\tau) - r = \frac{-1}{\tau} \log \left(\Phi\left[h_2(d, \sigma^2 \tau)\right] + \frac{1}{d} \Phi\left[h_1(d, \sigma^2 \tau)\right] \right) \qquad (14)$$

where

$$\exp[-R(\tau)\tau] \equiv \frac{F(V, \tau)}{B}$$

and $R(\tau)$ is the yield-to-maturity on the risky debt provided that the firm does not default. It seems reasonable to call $R(\tau) - r$ a *risk premium*, in which case equation (14) defines a risk structure of interest rates.

For a given maturity, the risk premium is a function of only two variables: (1) the variance (or volatility) of the firm's operations, σ^2; and (2) the ratio of the present value (at the riskless rate) of the promised payment to the current value of the firm, d. Because d is the debt-to-firm value ratio where debt is valued at the riskless rate, it is a biased-upward estimate of the actual (market-value) debt-to-firm value ratio.

Since Merton (1973) has solved the option pricing problem when the term structure is not "flat" and is stochastic (by, again, using the isomorphic correspondence between options and levered equity), we could deduce the risk structure with a stochastic term structure. The formulae (13) and (14) would be the same in this case except that we would replace "$\exp[-r\tau]$" by the price of a riskless discount bond which pays one dollar at time τ in the future and "$\sigma^2\tau$" by a generalised variance term defined in (1973, p. 166).

A comparative statics analysis of the risk structure

Examination of equation (13) shows that the value of the debt can be written, showing its full functional dependence, as $F[V, \tau, B, \sigma^2, r]$. Because of the isomorphic relationship between levered equity and a European call option, we can use analytical results presented in Merton (1973) to show that F is a first-degree homogeneous, concave function of V and B.[3] Further, we have that[4]

$$F_v = 1 - f_v \geq 0; \qquad F_B = -f_B > 0$$

$$F_\tau = -f_\tau < 0; \qquad F_{\sigma^2} = -f_{\sigma^2} < 0$$

$$F_r = -f_r < 0 \qquad (15)$$

where again subscripts denote partial derivatives. The results presented in (15) are as one would have expected for a discount bond: namely, the value of debt is an increasing function of the current market value of the firm and the promised payment at maturity, and a decreasing function of the time to maturity, the business risk of the firm, and the riskless rate of interest.

Since we are interested in the risk structure of interest rates, which is a cross-section of bond prices at a point in time, it will shed more light on the characteristics of this structure to work with the price ratio $P \equiv F[V, \tau]/B \cdot \exp[-r\tau]$ rather than the absolute price level, F. P is the price today of a risky dollar promised at time τ in the future in terms of a dollar delivered at that date with certainty, and it is always less than or equal to one. From equation (13), we have that

$$P[d, T] = \Phi\left[h_2(d, T)\right] + \frac{1}{d} \Phi\left[h_1(d, T)\right] \qquad (16)$$

where $T \equiv \sigma^2 \tau$. Note that, unlike F, P is completely determined by d, the "quasi" debt-to-firm value ratio, and T, which is a measure of the volatility of the firm's value over the life of the bond, and it is a decreasing function of both. In other words:

$$P_d = -\frac{\Phi(h_1)}{d^2} < 0 \tag{17}$$

and

$$P_T = -\frac{\Phi'(h_1)}{2d\sqrt{T}} < 0 \tag{18}$$

where $\Phi'(x) \equiv \exp[-x^2/2]/\sqrt{2\pi}$ is the standard normal density function.

We now define another ratio which is of critical importance in analysing the risk structure: namely, $g \equiv \sigma_y/\sigma$, where σ_y is the instantaneous standard deviation of the return on the bond and σ is the instantaneous standard deviation of the return on the firm. Because these two returns are instantaneously perfectly correlated, g is a measure of the relative riskiness of the bond in terms of the riskiness of the firm at a given point in time.[5] From (3b) and (13), we can deduce the formula for g to be

$$\frac{\sigma_y}{\sigma} = \frac{VF_v}{F}$$

$$= \frac{\Phi[h_1(d,T)]}{P[d,T]d}$$

$$\equiv g[d,T] \tag{19}$$

In the fifth section, the characteristics of g are examined in detail. For the purposes of this section, we simply note that g is a function of d and T only, and that from the "no-arbitrage" condition, (6), we have that

$$\frac{\alpha_y - r}{\alpha - r} = g[d,T] \tag{20}$$

where $(\alpha_y - r)$ is the expected excess return on the debt and $(\alpha - r)$ is the expected excess return on the firm as a whole. We can rewrite (17) and (18) in elasticity form in terms of g to be

$$dP_d/P = -g[d,T] \tag{21}$$

and

$$TP_T/P = \frac{-g[d,T]\Phi'(h_1)\sqrt{T}}{2\Phi(h_1)} \tag{22}$$

As mentioned in the third section, it is common to use yield to maturity in excess of the riskless rate as a measure of the risk premium on debt. If we define $[R(\tau) - r] \equiv H(d, \tau, \sigma^2)$, then, from (14), we have that

$$H_d = \frac{1}{\tau d} g[d,T] > 0 \tag{23}$$

$$H_{\sigma^2} = \frac{1}{2\sqrt{T}} g[d,T] \frac{\Phi'(h_1)}{\Phi(h_1)} > 0 \tag{24}$$

$$H_\tau = \left(\log[P] + \frac{\sqrt{T}}{2} g[d,T] \frac{\Phi'(h_1)}{\Phi(h_1)} \right) \Big/ \tau^2 \gtrless 0 \tag{25}$$

Table 1. Representative values of the term premium, R – r

σ²	Time until maturity = 2 d	R – r (%)	σ²	Time until maturity = 5 d	R – r (%)
0.03	0.2	0.00	0.03	0.2	0.01
0.03	0.5	0.02	0.03	0.5	0.16
0.03	1.0	5.13	0.03	1.0	3.34
0.03	1.5	20.58	0.03	1.5	8.84
0.03	3.0	54.94	0.03	3.0	21.99
0.10	0.2	0.01	0.10	0.2	0.12
0.10	0.5	0.82	0.10	0.5	1.74
0.10	1.0	9.74	0.10	1.0	6.47
0.10	1.5	23.03	0.10	1.5	11.31
0.10	3.0	55.02	0.10	3.0	22.59
0.20	0.2	0.12	0.20	0.2	0.95
0.20	0.5	3.09	0.20	0.5	4.23
0.20	1.0	14.27	0.20	1.0	9.66
0.20	1.5	26.60	0.20	1.5	14.24
0.20	3.0	55.82	0.20	3.0	24.30

σ²	Time until maturity = 10 d	R – r (%)	σ²	Time until maturity = 25 d	R – r (%)
0.03	0.2	0.01	0.03	0.2	0.09
0.03	0.5	0.38	0.03	0.5	0.60
0.03	1.0	2.44	0.03	1.0	1.64
0.03	1.5	4.98	0.03	1.5	2.57
0.03	3.0	11.07	0.03	3.0	4.68
0.10	0.2	0.48	0.10	0.2	1.07
0.10	0.5	2.12	0.10	0.5	2.17
0.10	1.0	4.83	0.10	1.0	3.39
0.10	1.5	7.12	0.10	1.5	4.26
0.10	3.0	12.15	0.10	3.0	6.01
0.20	0.2	1.88	0.20	0.2	2.69
0.20	0.5	4.38	0.20	0.5	4.06
0.20	1.0	7.36	0.20	1.0	5.34
0.20	1.5	9.55	0.20	1.5	6.19
0.20	3.0	14.08	0.20	3.0	7.81

As can be seen in Table 1 and Figures 1 and 2, the term premium is an increasing function of both d and σ^2. While, from (25), the change in the premium with respect to a change in maturity can be either sign, Figure 3 shows that for $d \geq 1$ it will be negative. To complete the analysis of the risk structure as measured by the term premium, we show that the premium is a decreasing function of the riskless rate of interest. In other words:

$$dH/dr = H_d \, \partial d/\partial r = -g[d, T] < 0 \qquad (26)$$

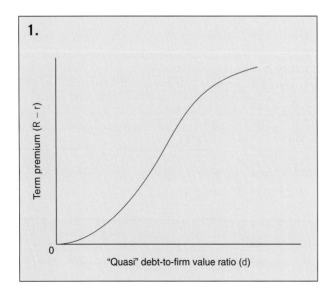

1.

Term premium (R – r)

0

"Quasi" debt-to-firm value ratio (d)

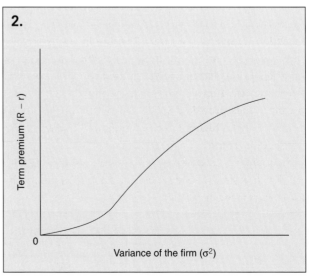

2.

Term premium (R – r)

0

Variance of the firm (σ^2)

It still remains to be determined whether R – r is a valid measure of the riskiness of the bond. In other words, can one assert that if R – r is larger for one bond than for another, then the former is riskier than the latter? To answer this question, one must first establish an appropriate definition of "riskier." Since the risk structure, like the corresponding term structure, is a "snapshot" at one point in time, it seems natural to define the riskiness in terms of the uncertainty of the rate of return over the next trading interval. In this sense of riskier, the natural choice as a measure of risk is the (instantaneous) standard deviation of the return on the bond, $\sigma_y = \sigma g[d, T] \equiv G(d, \sigma, \tau)$. In addition, for the type of dynamics postulated, I have shown elsewhere[6] that the standard deviation is a sufficient statistic for comparing the relative riskiness of securities in the Rothschild–

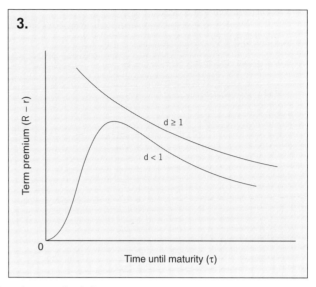

3.

Stiglitz (1970) sense. However, it should be pointed out that the standard deviation is not sufficient for comparing the riskiness of the debt of different companies in a portfolio sense[7] because the correlations of the returns of the two firms with other assets in the economy may be different. However, since R – r can be computed for each bond without the knowledge of such correlations, it cannot reflect such differences except indirectly through the market value of the firm. Thus, as at least a necessary condition for R – r to be a valid measure of risk, it should move in the same direction as G does in response to changes in the underlying variables. From the definition of G and (19), we have that

$$G_d = \frac{\sigma g^2}{\sqrt{T}} \frac{\Phi(h_2)}{\Phi(h_1)} \left[\frac{\Phi'(h_2)}{\Phi(h_2)} + \frac{\Phi'(h_1)}{\Phi(h_1)} + h_1 + h_2 \right] > 0^8 \qquad (27)$$

$$G_\sigma = \frac{g \left(\Phi(h_1) - \Phi'(h_1) \left[\frac{\sqrt{T}}{2}(1-2g) + \frac{\log d}{\sqrt{T}} \right] \right)}{\Phi(h_1)} > 0 \qquad (28)$$

$$G_\tau = \frac{-\sigma^2 G}{2\sqrt{T}} \frac{\Phi'(h_1)}{\Phi(h_1)} \left[\frac{1}{2}(1-2g) + \frac{\log d}{T} \right] \gtreqless 0 \text{ as } d \lesseqgtr 1 \qquad (29)$$

Table 2 and Figures 4–6 plot the standard deviation for typical values of d, σ, and τ. Comparing (27)–(29) with (23)–(25), we see that the term premium and the standard deviation change in the same direction in response to a change in the "quasi" debt-to-firm value ratio or the business risk of the firm. However, they need not change in the same direction with a change in maturity, as a comparison of Figures 3 and 6 readily demonstrates. Hence, while comparing the term premiums on bonds of the same maturity does provide a valid comparison of the riskiness of such bonds, one cannot conclude that a higher term premium on bonds of different maturities implies a higher standard deviation.[9]

To complete the comparison between R – r and G, the standard deviation is a decreasing function of the riskless rate of interest, as was the case for the term premium in (26). Namely, we have that

$$dG/dr = G_d \, \partial d/\partial r$$

$$= -\tau d \, G_d < 0 \qquad (30)$$

Table 2. Representative values of the standard deviation of the debt, G, and the ratio of the standard deviation of the debt to the firm, g

	Time until maturity = 2				Time until maturity = 5		
σ^2	d	g	G	σ^2	d	g	G
0.03	0.2	0.000	0.000	0.03	0.2	0.000	0.000
0.03	0.5	0.003	0.001	0.03	0.5	0.048	0.008
0.03	1.0	0.500	0.087	0.03	1.0	0.500	0.087
0.03	1.5	0.943	0.163	0.03	1.5	0.833	0.144
0.03	3.0	1.000	0.173	0.03	3.0	0.996	0.173
0.10	0.2	0.000	0.000	0.10	0.2	0.021	0.007
0.10	0.5	0.077	0.024	0.10	0.5	0.199	0.063
0.10	1.0	0.500	0.158	0.10	1.0	0.500	0.158
0.10	1.5	0.795	0.251	0.10	1.5	0.689	0.218
0.10	3.0	0.989	0.313	0.10	3.0	0.913	0.289
0.20	0.2	0.011	0.005	0.20	0.2	0.092	0.041
0.20	0.5	0.168	0.075	0.20	0.5	0.288	0.129
0.20	1.0	0.500	0.224	0.20	1.0	0.500	0.224
0.20	1.5	0.712	0.318	0.20	1.5	0.628	0.281
0.20	3.0	0.939	0.420	0.20	3.0	0.815	0.364

	Time until maturity = 10				Time until maturity = 25		
σ^2	d	g	G	σ^2	d	g	G
0.03	0.2	0.003	0.001	0.03	0.2	0.056	0.010
0.03	0.5	0.128	0.022	0.03	0.5	0.253	0.044
0.03	1.0	0.500	0.087	0.03	1.0	0.500	0.087
0.03	1.5	0.745	0.129	0.03	1.5	0.651	0.113
0.03	3.0	0.966	0.167	0.03	3.0	0.857	0.148
0.10	0.2	0.092	0.029	0.10	0.2	0.230	0.073
0.10	0.5	0.288	0.091	0.10	0.5	0.377	0.119
0.10	1.0	0.500	0.158	0.10	1.0	0.500	0.158
0.10	1.5	0.628	0.199	0.10	1.5	0.573	0.181
0.10	3.0	0.815	0.258	0.10	3.0	0.691	0.219
0.20	0.2	0.196	0.088	0.20	0.2	0.324	0.145
0.20	0.5	0.358	0.160	0.20	0.5	0.422	0.189
0.20	1.0	0.500	0.224	0.20	1.0	0.500	0.224
0.20	1.5	0.584	0.261	0.20	1.5	0.545	0.244
0.20	3.0	0.719	0.321	0.20	3.0	0.622	0.278

On the Modigliani–Miller theorem with bankruptcy

In the derivation of the fundamental equation for pricing of corporate liabilities, (7), it was assumed that the Modigliani-Miller theorem held so that the value of the firm could be treated as exogenous to the analysis. If, for example, due to bankruptcy costs or corporate taxes, the M-M theorem does not obtain and the value of the firm does depend on the debt-equity ratio, then the formal analysis of the paper is still valid. However, the linear property of (7) would be lost and, instead, a non-linear, simultaneous solution, $F = F[V(F), \tau]$, would be required.

Fortunately, in the absence of these imperfections, the formal hedging analysis used in the second section to deduce (7), simultaneously, stands as a proof of the M-M theorem even in the presence of bankruptcy. To see this, imagine that there are two firms which are identical with respect to their investment decisions, but one firm issues debt and the other does not. The investor can "create" a security with a payoff structure identical to the risky bond by following a portfolio strategy of mixing the equity of the unlevered firm with holdings of riskless debt. The correct portfolio strategy is to hold $(F_V V)$ dollars of the equity and $(F - F_V V)$ dollars of riskless bonds, where V is the value of the unlevered firm, and F and F_V are determined by the solution of (7). Since the value of the "manufactured" risky debt is always F, the debt issued by the other firm can never sell for more than F. In a similar fashion, one could create levered equity by a portfolio strategy of holding $(f_V V)$ dollars of the unlevered equity and $(f - f_V V)$ dollars of borrowing on margin, which would have a payoff structure identical to the equity issued by the levering firm. Hence, the value of the levered firm's equity can never sell for more than f. But, by construction, $f + F = V$, the value of the unlevered firm. Therefore, the value of the levered firm can be no larger than the unlevered firm, and it cannot be less.

Note, unlike in the analysis by Stiglitz (1969), we did not require a specialised theory of capital market equilibrium (eg, the Arrow–Debreu model or the capital asset pricing model) to prove the theorem when bankruptcy is possible.

In the previous section, a cross-section of bonds across firms at a point in time was analysed to describe a risk structure of interest rates. We now examine a debt issue for a single firm. In this context, we are interested in measuring the risk of the debt relative to the risk of the firm. As discussed in the fourth section, the correct measure of this relative riskiness is $\sigma_y/\sigma = g[d, T]$ defined in (19). From (16) and (19), we have that

$$\frac{1}{g} = 1 + \frac{d\Phi(h_2)}{\Phi(h_1)} \qquad (31)$$

From (31), we have $0 \leq g \leq 1$. In other words, the debt of the firm can never be more risky than the firm as a whole, and, as a corollary, the equity of a levered firm must always be at least as risky as the firm. In particular, from (13) and (31), the limit as $d \rightarrow \infty$ of $F[V, \tau] = V$ and of $g[d, T] = 1$. Thus, as the ratio of the present value of the promised payment to the current value of the firm becomes large and, therefore, the probability of eventual default becomes large, the market value of the debt approaches that of the firm and the risk characteristics of the debt approach that of (unlevered) equity. As $d \rightarrow 0$ the probability of default approaches zero, and $F[V, \tau] \rightarrow B\exp[-r\tau]$, the value of a riskless bond, and $g \rightarrow 0$. So, in this case, the risk characteristics of the debt become the same as riskless debt. Between these two extremes the debt will behave like a combination of riskless debt and equity, and will change in a continuous fashion. To see this, note that in the portfolio used to replicate the risky debt by combining the equity of an unlevered firm with riskless bonds, g is the fraction of that portfolio invested in the equity and $(1 - g)$ is the fraction invested in riskless bonds. Thus, as g increases the portfolio will contain a larger fraction of equity until, in the limit as $g \rightarrow 1$, it is all equity.

From (19) and (31), we have that

$$g_d = \frac{g}{d}\left[-(1-g) + \frac{1}{\sqrt{T}}\frac{\Phi'(h_1)}{\Phi(h_1)}\right] > 0 \qquad (32)$$

that is, the relative riskiness of the debt is an increasing function of d, and

$$g_T = \frac{-g\Phi'(h_1)}{2\sqrt{T}\Phi(h_1)}\left[\tfrac{1}{2}(1-2g) + \frac{\log d}{T}\right] \gtreqless 0 \quad \text{as } d \lesseqgtr 1 \qquad (33)$$

4.

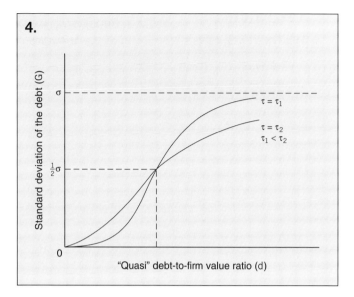

"Quasi" debt-to-firm value ratio (d)

5.

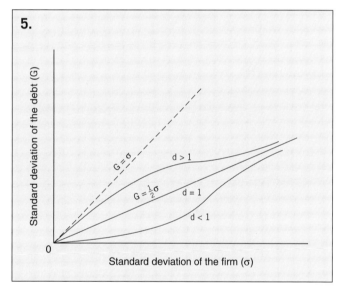

Standard deviation of the firm (σ)

6.

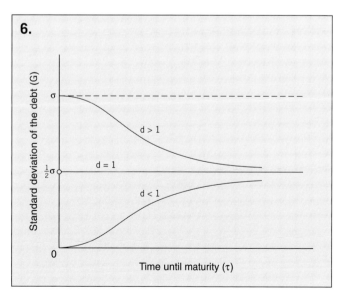

Time until maturity (τ)

Further, we have that

$$g[1, T] = \tfrac{1}{2}, \quad T > 0 \tag{34}$$

and

$$\lim_{T \to \infty} g[d, T] = \tfrac{1}{2}, \quad 0 < d < \infty \tag{35}$$

Thus, for d = 1, independent of the business risk of the firm or the length of time until maturity, the standard deviation of the return on the debt equals half the standard deviation of the return on the whole firm. From (35), as the business risk of the firm or the time to maturity gets large, $\sigma_y \to \sigma/2$ for all d. Figures 7 and 8 plot g as a function of d and T.

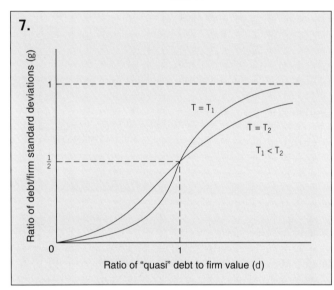

7.

Ratio of debt/firm standard deviations (g)

$T = T_1$

$T = T_2$

$T_1 < T_2$

Ratio of "quasi" debt to firm value (d)

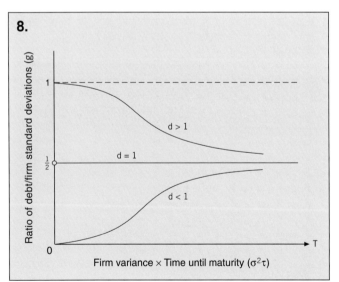

8.

Ratio of debt/firm standard deviations (g)

$d > 1$

$d = 1$

$d < 1$

Firm variance × Time until maturity ($\sigma^2 \tau$)

Contrary to what many might believe, the relative riskiness of the debt can decline as either the business risk of the firm or the time until maturity increases. Inspection of (33) shows that this is the case if d > 1 (ie, the present value of the promised payment is less than the current value of the firm). To see why this result is not unreasonable, consider the following: for small T (ie, σ^2 or τ small), the chances that the debt will become equity through default are large, and this will be reflected in the risk characteristics of the debt through a large g. By increasing T (through an increase in σ^2 or τ), the chances are better that the firm value will increase enough to meet the promised payment. It is also true that the chances that the firm value will be lower are increased. However, remember that g is a measure of how much the risky debt behaves like equity versus debt. Since for g large the debt is already more aptly described by equity than riskless debt (eg, for d > 1, g > ½ and the "replicating" portfolio will contain more than half equity). Thus, the increased probability of meeting the promised payment dominates, and g declines. For d > 1, g will be less than a half, and the argument goes just the opposite way. In the "watershed" case when d = 1, g equals a half, the "replicating" portfolio is exactly half equity and half riskless debt, and the two effects cancel, leaving g unchanged.

In closing this section, we examine a classical problem in corporate finance: given a fixed investment decision, how does the required return on debt and equity change as alternative debt–equity mixes are chosen? Because the investment decision is assumed fixed, and the Modigliani–Miller theorem obtains, V, σ^2, and α (the required expected return on the firm) are fixed. For simplicity, suppose that the maturity of the debt, τ, is fixed, and the promised payment at maturity per bond is $1. Then, the debt–equity mix is determined by choosing the number of bonds to be issued. Since in our previous analysis F is the value of the whole debt issue and B is the total promised payment for the whole issue, B will be the number of bonds (promising $1 at maturity) in the current analysis, and F/B will be the price of one bond.

Define the market debt-to-equity ratio to be X, which is equal to (F/f) = F/(V − F). From (20), the required expected rate of return on the debt, α_y, will equal r + (α − r)g.

Thus, for a fixed investment policy

$$d\alpha_y / dX = (\alpha - r)\frac{dg}{dB} \bigg/ \frac{dX}{dB} \tag{36}$$

provided that $dX/dB \neq 0$. From the definition of X and (13), we have that

$$dX/dB = \frac{X(1+X)(1-g)}{B} > 0 \tag{37}$$

Since $dg/dB = g_d d/B$, we have from (32), (36), and (37) that

$$d\alpha_y / dX = \frac{d(\alpha-r)g_d}{X(1+X)(1-g)} > 0$$

$$= \frac{(\alpha-r)}{X(1+X)}\left[-g + \frac{1}{\sqrt{T}}\frac{\Phi'(h_2)}{\Phi(h_2)}\right] \tag{38}$$

Further analysis of (38) shows that σ_y starts out as a convex function of X, passes through an inflection point where it becomes concave, and approaches α asymptotically as X tends to infinity.

To determine the path of the required return on equity, α_e, as X moves between zero and infinity, we use the well-known identity that the equity return is a weighted average of the return on debt and the return on the firm. In other words:

$$\alpha_e = \alpha + X(\alpha - \alpha_y)$$

$$= \alpha + (1-g)X(\alpha - r) \tag{39}$$

α_e has a slope of $(\alpha - r)$ at $X = 0$ and is a concave function bounded from above by the line $\alpha + (\alpha - r)X$. Figure 9 displays both α_y and α_e. While Figure 9 was not produced from computer simulation, it should be emphasised that because both $(\alpha_y - r)/(\alpha - r)$ and $(\alpha_e - r)/(\alpha - r)$ do not depend on α, such curves can be computed up to the scale factor $(\alpha - r)$ without knowledge of α.

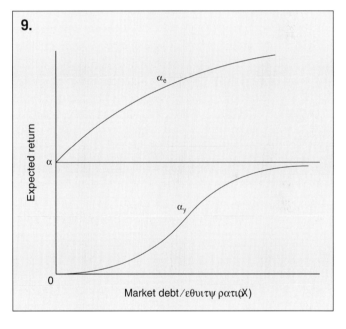

9.

On the pricing of risky coupon bonds

In the usual analysis of (default-free) bonds in term structure studies, the derivation of a pricing relationship for pure discount bonds for every maturity would be sufficient because the value of a default-free coupon bond can be written as the sum of discount bonds' values weighted by the size of the coupon payment at each maturity. Unfortunately, no such simple formula exists for risky coupon bonds. The reason for this is that if the firm defaults on a coupon payment, then all subsequent coupon payments (and payments of principal) are also defaulted on. Thus, the default on one of the "mini" bonds associated with a given maturity is not independent of the event of default on the "mini" bond associated with a later maturity. However, the apparatus developed in the previous sections is sufficient to solve the coupon problem.

Assume the same simple capital structure and indenture conditions as in the third section except modify the indenture condition to require (continuous) payments at a coupon rate per unit time, $\bar{C}$. From indenture restriction (3), we have that in equation (7) $C = C_y = \bar{C}$ and, hence, the coupon bond value will satisfy the partial differential equation

$$0 = \tfrac{1}{2}\sigma^2 V^2 F_{VV} + \left(rV - \bar{C}\right)F_V - rF - F_\tau + \bar{C} = 0 \tag{40}$$

subject to the same boundary conditions (9). The corresponding equation for equity, f, will be

$$0 = \tfrac{1}{2}\sigma^2 V^2 f_{vv} + \left(rV - \overline{C}\right) f_v - rf - f_\tau \tag{41}$$

subject to boundary conditions (9a), (9b), and (11). Again, equation (41) has an isomorphic correspondence with an option pricing problem previously studied. Equation (41) is identical to equation (44) in Merton (1973, p. 170), which is the equation for the European option value on a stock which pays dividends at a constant rate per unit time of $\overline{C}$. While a closed-form solution to (41) for finite τ has not yet been found, one has been found for the limiting case of a perpetuity ($\tau = \infty$), and is presented in Merton (1973, p. 172, equation (46)). Using the identity $F = V - f$, we can write the solution for the perpetual risky coupon bond as

$$F(V, \infty) = \frac{\overline{C}}{r} \left\{ 1 - \frac{\left(\dfrac{2\overline{C}}{\sigma^2 V}\right)^{2r/\sigma^2}}{\Gamma\left(2 + \dfrac{2r}{\sigma^2}\right)} M\left(\frac{2r}{\sigma^2},\ 2 + \frac{2r}{\sigma^2},\ \frac{-2\overline{C}}{\sigma^2 V}\right) \right\} \tag{42}$$

where $\Gamma(\ )$ is the gamma function and $M(\ )$ is the confluent hypergeometric function. While perpetual, non-callable bonds are non-existent in the US, there are preferred stocks with no maturity date and (42) would be the correct pricing function for them.

Moreover, even for those cases where closed-form solutions cannot be found, powerful numerical integration techniques have been developed for solving equations like (7) or (41). Hence, computation and empirical testing of these pricing theories is entirely feasible.

Note that, in deducing (40), it was assumed that coupon payments were made uniformly and continuously. In fact, coupon payments are usually only made semi-annually or annually in discrete lumps. However, it is a simple matter to take this into account by replacing "$\overline{C}$" in (40) by "$\Sigma_i \overline{C}_i \delta(\tau - \tau_i)$", where $\delta(\ )$ is the Dirac delta function and τ_i is the length of time until maturity when the ith coupon payment of $\overline{C}_i$ dollars is made.

As a final illustration, we consider the case of callable bonds. Again, assume the same capital structure but modify the indenture to state that "the firm can redeem the bonds at its option for a stated price of $K(\tau)$ dollars", where K may depend on the length of time until maturity. Formally, equation (40) and boundary conditions (9a) and (9c) are still valid. However, instead of the boundary condition (9b) we have that for each τ there will be some value for the firm, call it $\overline{V}(\tau)$, such that for all $V(\tau) \geq \overline{V}(\tau)$ it would be advantageous for the firm to redeem the bonds. Hence, the new boundary condition will be

$$F\left[\overline{V}(\tau), \tau\right] = K(\tau) \tag{43}$$

Equation (40), (9a), (9c), and (43) provide a well-posed problem to solve for F provided that the $\overline{V}(\tau)$ function were known. But, of course, it is not. Fortunately, economic theory is rich enough to provide us with an answer. First, imagine that we solved the problem as if we knew $\overline{V}(\tau)$ to get $F[V, \tau; \overline{V}(\tau)]$ as a function of $\overline{V}(\tau)$. Second, recognise that it is at management's option to redeem the bonds and that management operates in the best interests of the equity holders. Hence, as a bondholder, one must presume that management will select the $\overline{V}(\tau)$ function so as to maximise the value of equity, f. But, from the identity $F = V - f$, this implies that the $\overline{V}(\tau)$ function chosen will be the one which minimises $F[V, \tau; \overline{V}(\tau)]$. Therefore, the additional condition is that

$$F[V, \tau] = \min_{\{V(\tau)\}} F[V, \tau; V(\tau)] \tag{44}$$

To put this in appropriate boundary condition form for solution, we again rely on the isomorphic correspondence with options and refer the reader to the discussion in Merton (1973), where it is shown that condition (44) is equivalent to the condition

$$F_v\left[\overline{V}(\tau), \tau\right] = 0 \qquad (45)$$

Hence, appending (45) to (40), (9a), (9c) and (43), we solve the problem for the $F[V, \tau]$ and $\overline{V}(\tau)$ functions simultaneously.

Conclusion

We have developed a method for pricing corporate liabilities which is grounded in solid economic analysis, requires inputs which are on the whole observable, and can be used to price almost any type of financial instrument. The method was applied to risky discount bonds to deduce a risk structure of interest rates. The Modigliani–Miller theorem was shown to obtain in the presence of bankruptcy provided that there are no differential tax benefits to corporations or transactions costs. The analysis was extended to include callable, coupon bonds.

1 *Of course, this assumption does not rule out serial dependence in the earnings of the firm. See Samuelson (1973) for a discussion.*

2 *For a rigorous discussion of Itô's lemma, see McKean (1969). For references to its application in portfolio theory, see Merton (1973).*

3 *See Merton (1973, Theorems 4, 9, 10), where it is shown that* f *is a first-degree homogeneous, convex function of* V *and* B.

4 *See Merton (1973, Theorems 5, 14, 15).*

5 *Note, for example, that in the context of the Sharpe–Lintner–Mossin capital asset pricing model,* g *is equal to the ratio of the "beta" of the bond to the "beta" of the firm.*

6 *See Merton (1973, Appendix 2).*

7 *For example, in the context of the capital asset pricing model, the correlations of the two firms with the market portfolio could be sufficiently different so as to make the beta of the bond with the larger standard deviation smaller than the beta of the bond with the smaller standard deviation.*

8 *It is well known that* $\Phi'(x) + x\Phi(x) > 0$ *for* $-\infty < x \leq \infty$.

9 *While inspection of (25) shows that* $H_\tau < 0$ *for* $d \geq 1$, *which agrees with the sign of* G_τ *for* $d > 1$, H_τ *can be either signed for* $d < 1$, *which does not agree with the positive sign on* G_τ.

BIBLIOGRAPHY

Black, F., and M. Scholes, 1972, "The Valuation of Option Contracts and a Test of Market Efficiency", *Journal of Finance* 27, pp. 399–417.

Black, F., and M. Scholes, 1973, "The Pricing of Options and Corporate Liabilities", *Journal of Political Economy* 81, pp. 637–59.

Fama, E. F., 1970, "Efficient Capital Markets: A Review of Theory and Empirical Work", *Journal of Finance* 25, pp. 383–417.

McKean, H. P., 1969, *Stochastic Integrals*, New York, Academic Press.

Merton, R. C., 1970, "Dynamic General Equilibrium Model of the Asset Market and Its Application to the Pricing of the Capital Structure of the Firm", Sloan School of Management working paper no. 497-70, MIT.

Merton, R. C., 1973, "A Rational Theory of Option Pricing", *Bell Journal of Economics and Management Science* 4, pp. 141-83.

Modigliani, F, and M. Miller, 1958, "The Cost of Capital, Corporation Finance, and the Theory of Investment", *American Economic Review* 48, pp. 261-97.

Rothschild, M., and J. E. Stiglitz, 1970, "Increasing Risk: I. A Definition", *Journal of Economic Theory* 2 (3), pp. 225-43.

Samuelson, P. A., 1965, "Proof that Properly Anticipated Prices Fluctuate Randomly", *Industrial Management Review* 6, pp. 41-49.

Samuelson, P. A., 1973, "Proof that Properly Discounted Present Values of Assets Vibrate Randomly", *Bell Journal of Economics and Management Science* 4, pp. 369-74.

Stiglitz, J. E., 1969, "A Re-Examination of the Modigliani-Miller Theorem", *American Economic Review* 59, pp. 78-93.

5

Valuing Corporate Securities: Some Effects of Bond Indenture Provisions

Fischer Black[†] and John C. Cox

Sloan School of Management, Massachusetts Institute of Technology

I n one of their papers, Black and Scholes (1973) presented an explicit equilibrium model for valuing options. In this paper they indicated that a similar analysis could potentially be applied to all corporate securities. In other papers, both Merton (1973) and Ross (1976) noted the broad applicability of option pricing arguments. At the same time Black and Scholes also pointed out that actual security indentures have a variety of conditions that would bring new features and complications into the valuation process.

Our objective in this paper is to make some general statements on this valuation process and then turn to an analysis of certain types of bond indenture provisions that are often found in practice. Specifically, we will look at the effects of safety covenants, subordination arrangements and restrictions on the financing of interest and dividend payments.

Throughout the paper we will make the following assumptions:

❑ Every individual acts as if he can buy or sell as much of any security as he wishes without affecting the market price.
❑ There exists a riskless asset paying a known constant interest rate r.
❑ Individuals may take short positions in any security, including the riskless asset, and receive the proceeds of the sale. Restitution is required for payouts made to securities held short.
❑ Trading takes place continuously.
❑ There are no taxes, indivisibilities, bankruptcy costs, transaction costs or agency costs.
❑ The value of the firm follows a diffusion process with instantaneous variance proportional to the square of the value.

This last assumption is quite important and needs some amplification. Until very recently this was the standard framework for discussions of contingent claim pricing. Increasing evidence, however, indicates that it may not be completely appropriate.[1] The instantaneous variance may be some other function of the firm value and possibly dependent on time as well.[2] It may also depend on other random variables. Furthermore,

This paper was originally published in the Journal of Finance, *vol. 31, 1976, and is reprinted here with the kind permission of Blackwell Publishers. The authors would like to thank Robert Merton, Stephen Ross, and Mark Rubinstein for many helpful discussions. They are also grateful to Andrew Christie and Johannes Mouritsen for technical assistance. This research was partially supported by a grant from the Dean Witter Foundation to Stanford University, and by the Center for Research in Security Prices, sponsored by Merrill Lynch, Pierce, Fenner and Smith, Inc., at the University of Chicago.*
[†]*Fischer Black died in August 1995. Fischer Black, January 11, 1938–August 30, 1995.*

discontinuities associated with jump processes may be important.[3] Nevertheless, this assumption provides a useful setting for the points we want to make and facilitates comparison with earlier results.

With these assumptions, the standard hedging or capital asset pricing arguments lead to a valuation equation. For the process we are considering here, it is derived in its most general form in Merton (1974) as

$$\frac{1}{2}\sigma^2 V^2 f_{vv} + \left(rV - p(V,t)\right)f_v - rf + f_t + p'(V,t) = 0 \tag{1}$$

where f is a generic label for any of the firm's securities, V is the value of the firm, t denotes time, σ^2 is the instantaneous variance of the return on the firm, $p(V, t)$ is the net total payout made, or inflow received, by the firm, and $p'(V, t)$ is the payout received or payment made by security f.

Suppose the firm has outstanding only equity and a single bond issue with a promised final payment of P. At the maturity date of the bonds, T, the stockholders will pay off the bondholders if they can. If they cannot, the ownership of the firm passes to the bondholders. So at time T, the bonds will have the value $\min(V, P)$ and the stock will have the value $\max(V - P, 0)$.

Now this formulation already implicitly contains several assumptions about the bond indenture. The fact that σ^2, $p(V, t)$ and $p'(V, t)$, and P were assumed known (and finite) implies that the bond contract renders them determinate by placing limiting restrictions on, respectively, the firm's investment, payout and further financing policies.

Furthermore, it assumes that the fortunes of the firm may cause its value to rise to an arbitrarily high level or dwindle to nearly nothing without any sort of reorganisation occurring in the firm's financial arrangements. More generally, there may be both lower and upper boundaries at which the firm's securities must take on specific values. The boundaries may be given exogenously by the contract specifications or determined endogenously as part of an optimal decision problem.

The indenture agreements that we will consider serve as examples of a specified or induced lower boundary at which the firm will be reorganised. An example of an upper boundary is a call provision on a bond.[4] Also, the final payment at the maturity date may be a quite arbitrary function of the value of the firm at that time, $\xi(V(T))$.

It will be helpful to look at this problem in a way discussed in Cox and Ross (1975, 1976).[5] The valuation equation (1) does not involve preferences, so a solution derived for any specific set of preferences must hold in general. In particular, the relative value of contingent claims in terms of the value of underlying assets must be consistent with risk neutrality.[6]

If we know the distribution of the underlying assets in a risk-neutral world, then we can readily solve a number of valuation problems.[7] We can in our problem think of each security as having four sources of value: its value at the maturity date if the firm is not reorganised before then, its value if the firm is reorganised at the lower boundary, its value if the firm is reorganised at the upper boundary, and the value of the payouts it will potentially receive. Although the first three sources are mutually exclusive, they are all possible outcomes given our current position, so they each contribute to current value. The contribution to the total value of a claim of any of its component sources will in a risk-neutral world simply be the discounted expected value of that component.

For any claim f, let $h_i(V(t), t)$, $i = 1, \ldots, 4$, denote, respectively, the four components referred to above, so $f(V(t), t) = \Sigma_{i=1}^4 h_i(V(t), t)$. Let $g_1(\tau)(g_2(\tau))$ be the value of f, as given by the contract, if the firm is reorganised at the lower (upper) boundary $C_1(\tau)(C_2(\tau))$ at time τ. Denote the distribution in a risk-neutral world of the value of the firm at time τ, $V(\tau)$, conditional on its value at the current time t, $V(t)$, $C_1(t) < V(t) < C_2(t)$, as $\Phi(V(\tau), \tau \mid V(t), t)$. Then taking the indicated expectations we can write

$$h_1\left(V(t), t\right) = e^{-r(T-t)} \int_{\kappa(T)} \xi(V(T)) d\Phi\left(V(T), T \mid V(t), t\right) \tag{2}$$

and

$$h_4\big(V(t),t\big) = \int_t^T e^{-r(s-t)}\left[\int_{\kappa(s)} p'\big(V(s),s\big)d\Phi\big(V(s),s\,|\,V(t),t\big)\right]ds \qquad (3)$$

where $\kappa(\cdot)$ denotes the interval $(C_1(\cdot), C_2(\cdot))$.

The contribution of the potential value at the reorganisation boundaries is somewhat different. Formerly we knew the time of receipt of each potential payment but not the amount that would actually be received. Here the amount to be received at each boundary is a known function specified by the contract, but the time of receipt is a random variable. However, its distribution is just that of the first passage time to the boundary, and the approach taken by Cox and Ross can still be applied.

Let $\Psi_1(t^*\,|\,V(t),t)$ be the distribution of the first passage time t^* to the lower boundary and $\Psi_2(t^*\,|\,V(t),t)$ denote the corresponding distribution for the upper boundary. Then

$$h_{i+1}\big(V(t),t\big) = \int_t^T e^{-r(t^*-t)}g_i(t^*)d\Psi_i\big(t^*\,|\,V(t),t\big) \qquad i=1,2 \qquad (4)$$

This development also disposes of uniqueness problems, since economically inadmissible solutions to the valuation equation are automatically avoided by the probabilistic approach. However, it cannot be applied directly to situations where the boundaries must be determined endogenously as part of an optimal stopping problem.

Actual payouts by firms, of course, occur in lumps at discrete intervals. In many situations it is more convenient and perfectly acceptable to represent these payouts as a continual flow. Many other times, however, it is preferable to explicitly recognise the discrete nature of things. This is particularly true in optimal stopping problems when the structure of the problem dictates that decisions will be made only at these discrete points. An example in terms of options would be an American call on a stock paying discrete dividends. Restrictions on the financing of coupon payments to debt, which we will discuss later, provides an example in terms of corporate liabilities.

To solve these problems we could work recursively, with the terminal condition at each stage determined by the solution to the previous stage. Start at the last payment date. If a decision is made to stop at this point, the claim holder receives a payoff given by the terms of the contract. If he does not stop, his payoff is the value of a claim with one more period to go, given that the value of the firm is its current value minus the payment. This value is determined by the payment to be received at the maturity date. The claim holder can then determine his optimal decision rule. With the optimal decision rule specified, we can find the value of the claim as a function of firm value at the last decision point. At the next-to-last decision point we would face an identical problem except that the value function we just found would take the place of the function giving the payment to be received at the maturity date. By working backwards we can find the value of the claim at any time. Note that this gives only an approximate solution when the optimal decision points are actually continuous in time. However, we could always get a better approximation by adding more discrete decision points, even though no payouts are being made at these additional points.

Throughout the paper we will make use of the relationship between the equilibrium expected return on any of the individual securities of the firm, ν, and the (exogenously determined) equilibrium expected return on the total firm, μ. As given in Black and Scholes (1973) and Merton (1974), this is $\nu - r = (Vf_v/f)(\mu - r)$. Furthermore, since the process followed by any individual security is a transformation of that governing the total value of the firm, its instantaneous variance will be $\sigma^2 V^2[f_v]^2$. Thus we can write the ratio of the instantaneous standard deviation of the rate of return on any individual security to that of the firm as Vf_v/f. Another way to say this is that in equilibrium the excess expected return per unit of risk must be the same for all of the firm's securities. The elasticity Vf_v/f thus conveys the essential information about relative risk and expected return. In subsequent use of the term elasticity, we will always be referring to this function.

Bonds with safety covenants

In this section we will consider the effects of safety covenants on the value and behaviour of the firm's securities. Safety covenants are contractual provisions that give the bondholders the right to bankrupt or force a reorganisation of the firm if it is doing poorly according to some standard. One standard for this may be the omission of interest payments on the debt. However, if the stockholders are allowed to sell the assets of the firm to meet the interest payments, then this restriction is not very effective. In this situation a natural form for a safety covenant is the following: if the value of the firm falls to a specified level, which may change over time, then the bondholders are entitled to force the firm into bankruptcy and obtain the ownership of the assets. In this form of agreement, interest payments to the debt do not play a critical role, so we will assume that the firm has outstanding only a single issue of discount bonds. We will, however, assume that the contractual provisions allow the stockholders to receive a continuous dividend payment, aV, proportional to the value of the firm. With a continuous time analysis, it is quite reasonable for the time dependence of the safety covenant to take an exponential form, so we will let the specified bankruptcy level, $C_1(t)$, be $Ce^{-\gamma(T-t)}$.

The relevant form of the valuation equation (1) for the bonds, B, will be

$$\tfrac{1}{2}\sigma^2 V^2 B_{vv} + (r-a)VB_v - rB + B_t = 0 \tag{5}$$

with boundary conditions
$$B(V, T) = \min(V, P)$$

$$B(Ce^{-\gamma(T-t)}, t) = Ce^{-\gamma(T-t)}$$

Similarly, the value of the stock, S, must satisfy

$$\tfrac{1}{2}\sigma^2 V^2 S_{vv} + (r-a)VS_v - rS + S_t + aV = 0 \tag{6}$$

with boundary conditions
$$S(V, T) = \max(V - P, 0)$$

$$S(Ce^{-\gamma(T-t)}, t) = 0$$

To apply the probabilistic approach to valuation we need $\Phi(V(\tau), \tau \mid V(t), t)$, the distribution in a risk-neutral world of the value of the firm at time τ, $V(\tau)$, conditional on its value at the current time t, $V(t) = V$. Under our assumptions, this will be the distribution of a lognormal process with an (artificial) absorbing barrier at the reorganisation boundary $C_1(\tau) = Ce^{-\gamma(T-\tau)}$. The probability that $V(\tau) \geq K$ and has not reached the reorganisation boundary in the meantime is given by

$$N\left(\frac{\ln V - \ln K + \left(r - a - \tfrac{1}{2}\sigma^2\right)(\tau - t)}{\sqrt{\sigma^2(\tau - t)}}\right)$$

$$- \left(\frac{V}{Ce^{-\gamma(T-t)}}\right)^{1 - \left(\frac{2(r-a-\gamma)}{\sigma^2}\right)} N\left(\frac{2\ln Ce^{-\gamma(T-t)} - \ln V - \ln K + \left(r - a - \tfrac{1}{2}\sigma^2\right)(\tau - t)}{\sqrt{\sigma^2(\tau - t)}}\right) \tag{7}$$

where $N(\cdot)$ is the unit normal distribution function. Setting $K = Ce^{-\gamma(T-\tau)}$ gives the probability in a risk-neutral world that the firm has not been reorganised before time τ. This is the complementary first passage time distribution. That is, if t^* is the first passage time to the boundary, the probability that $t^* \geq \tau$ is obtained from (7) by letting $K = Ce^{-\gamma(T-\tau)}$.

By using these distributions to find the expected discounted value of the payments, we can obtain the valuation formula for B as

$$B(V,t) = Pe^{-r(T-t)}\left[N(z_1) - y^{2\theta-2}N(z_2)\right] +$$

$$Ve^{-a(T-t)}\left[N(z_3) + y^{2\theta}N(z_4) + y^{\theta+\zeta}e^{a(T-t)}N(z_5) +\right.$$

$$\left. y^{\theta-\zeta}e^{a(T-t)}N(z_6) - y^{\theta+\eta}N(z_7) - y^{\theta-\eta}N(z_8)\right] \quad (8)$$

where

$$y = \frac{Ce^{-\gamma(T-t)}}{V}$$

$$\theta = \frac{r - a - \gamma + \frac{1}{2}\sigma^2}{\sigma^2}$$

$$\delta = \left(r - a - \gamma - \frac{1}{2}\sigma^2\right)^2 + 2\sigma^2(r-\gamma)$$

$$\zeta = \frac{\sqrt{\delta}}{\sigma^2}$$

$$\eta = \frac{\sqrt{\delta - 2\sigma^2 a}}{\sigma^2}$$

$$z_1 = \frac{\ln V - \ln P + \left(r - a - \frac{1}{2}\sigma^2\right)(T-t)}{\sqrt{\sigma^2(T-t)}}$$

$$z_2 = \frac{\ln V - \ln P + 2\ln y + \left(r - a - \frac{1}{2}\sigma^2\right)(T-t)}{\sqrt{\sigma^2(T-t)}}$$

$$z_3 = \frac{\ln P - \ln V - \left(r - a + \frac{1}{2}\sigma^2\right)(T-t)}{\sqrt{\sigma^2(T-t)}}$$

$$z_4 = \frac{\ln V - \ln P + 2\ln y + \left(r - a + \frac{1}{2}\sigma^2\right)(T-t)}{\sqrt{\sigma^2(T-t)}}$$

$$z_5 = \frac{\ln y + \zeta\sigma^2(T-t)}{\sqrt{\sigma^2(T-t)}}$$

$$z_6 = \frac{\ln y - \zeta\sigma^2(T-t)}{\sqrt{\sigma^2(T-t)}}$$

$$z_7 = \frac{\ln y + \eta\sigma^2(T-t)}{\sqrt{\sigma^2(T-t)}}$$

$$z_8 = \frac{\ln y - \eta\sigma^2(T-t)}{\sqrt{\sigma^2(T-t)}}$$

This formula holds for all $Ce^{-\gamma(T-t)} \le Pe^{r(T-t)}$. An interesting choice is $Ce^{-\gamma(T-t)} = \rho Pe^{-r(T-t)}$, with $0 \le \rho \le 1$, so that the reorganisation value specified in the safety covenant is a constant fraction of the present value of the promised final payment. For clarity in making comparisons, we will use only this form below.

Merton (1974) has extensively studied in this setting the properties of discount bonds when there are no safety covenants and no dividends. Rather than repeat parts of his analysis, we will focus on properties that are particular to the existence of safety covenants. The most basic properties, such as the fact that B is an increasing function of V and t and a decreasing function of σ^2, r and a, remain the same.

It is easy to verify that B is an increasing function of ρ. Contrary to what is sometimes claimed, premature bankruptcy is not in itself detrimental for the bondholders. It is in their interests to have a contract that will force bankruptcy as quickly as possible. If bankruptcy occurs, the total ownership of the firm will pass to the bondholders, and this is the best they can achieve in any circumstances. A second look shows that B is a convex function of ρ, going to $Pe^{-r(T-t)}$, the riskless value, as ρ goes to one. The elasticity of B is a decreasing concave function of ρ, going to zero as ρ goes to one, so a high bankruptcy level always makes the debt safer. The elasticity of the stock is an increasing convex function of ρ.

Safety covenants provide a floor value for the bond which limits the gains to stockholders from somehow circumventing the other indenture restrictions. For example, as either σ^2 or a goes to infinity, the value of the bonds goes to $\rho Pe^{-r(T-t)}$ rather than zero. Similarly, if we compare the riskiness of bonds of firms differing only in investment policy or dividend policy, we find important differences for large values of a and σ^2. If $\rho = 0$, the elasticity is an increasing concave function of a, going to one as a goes to infinity. If $\rho > 0$, the elasticity has an initial increasing concave segment, but then reaches a maximum, followed successively by decreasing concave and convex segments going to zero as a goes to infinity. The behaviour of the elasticity with respect to the variance is for small values of σ^2 qualitatively the same as the case with no safety covenant, but as σ^2 becomes large, it approaches zero rather than one-half.

The behaviour of the elasticities with respect to the value of the firm is also interesting and is shown in Figure 1. When the stock is entitled to receive dividends, as the value of the firm declines, we find that the riskiness and expected return of the stock first increases, then decreases, and finally increases again as the value approaches the bankruptcy boundary. Intuitively we could think of this in the following way. For values of V near the boundary it is quite likely that the stockholders will lose everything and their claim is accordingly quite risky. As V increases, we reach a stage where bankruptcy is no longer imminent, but it is most unlikely that anything will be left for the stockholders at the maturity date. The value of the stock derives almost solely from the value of the dividends it is entitled to receive, and these are proportional to the value of the firm and hence have unitary elasticity. As V increases further, the major part of the stock's value becomes due to the uncertain amount it may receive at the maturity date, and hence the riskiness increases. Finally, as V reaches a very high level, it becomes virtually certain that the bonds will be redeemed in full and the stock becomes equivalent to a levered position in the firm as a whole, with degree of leverage $V/(V - Pe^{-r(T-t)})$.

Subordinated bonds

Another common form of indenture agreement involves the subordination of the claims of one class of debt holders, the junior bonds, to those of a second class, the senior bonds. At the maturity date of the bonds, payments can be made to the junior debt holders only if the full promised payment to the senior debt holders has been made. Suppose that both classes of bonds are discount bonds, and

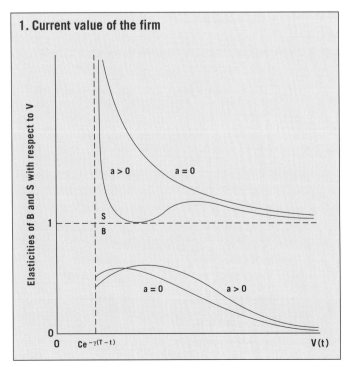

1. Current value of the firm

Elasticities of B and S with respect to V

a > 0   a = 0

S
1
B

a = 0   a > 0

0
0    $Ce^{-\gamma(T-t)}$ V(t)

Table 1. Values of claims at maturity

Claim	$V < P$	$P \leq V \leq P+Q$	$V > P+Q$
Senior bonds	V	P	P
Junior bonds	0	V – P	Q
Stock	0	0	V – P – Q

let the promised payments to senior and junior debt be, respectively, P and Q. Then at the maturity date the value of each of the firm's securities will be as shown in Table 1.

This problem could be solved separately by the methods used earlier, but this is unnecessary since we can write the solution in terms of (8). To see this, note that the value of the senior bond (or stock) is the same as the corresponding security of an identical firm with a single bond issue having a promised payment of P (or (P + Q)). Let $B(V, t; P, \rho Pe^{-r(T-t)})$ denote the formula given in (8) for a single bond issue with promised payment P and a safety covenant boundary given by $\rho Pe^{-r(T-t)}$. Then the value of the junior debt, J, can be written as

$$J(V, t) = B(V, t; P+Q, \rho Pe^{-r(T-t)}) - B(V, t; P, \rho Pe^{-r(T-t)}) \quad \rho < 1$$

$$= B(V, t; P+Q, \rho Pe^{-r(T-t)}) - Pe^{-r(T-t)} \quad 1 \leq \rho \leq \frac{P+Q}{P}$$

$$= Qe^{-r(T-t)} \quad \rho > \frac{P+Q}{P} \tag{9}$$

The discussion in the first section suggested that the values of junior and senior discount bonds, and correspondingly of options with different exercise prices, could be given a geometric interpretation. Consider the case with no payouts and no safety covenants. Depict graphically the distribution function $\Phi(V(T), T|V(t), t)$. Then, as shown in Figure 2, the values of the firm's securities can be interpreted as areas above the distribution function, when these areas are multiplied by the discount factor $e^{-r(T-t)}$.

To see this, consider, for example, the senior bonds. Since

$$\int_0^P V(T)d\Phi = \int_0^P \left[1 - \Phi(V(T))\right]dV(T) - P\left[1 - \Phi(P)\right]$$

then

$$\int_0^\infty \min(V(T), P)d\Phi = \int_0^P \left[1 - \Phi(V(T))\right]dV(T)$$

which is represented by the indicated area.

Subordination does indeed achieve its anticipated effect of giving the senior bonds a larger value than they would have if they were the corresponding fraction of an undifferentiated bond issue. That is, the value of the senior bonds will be greater than P/(P + Q) times the value of a single issue with promised payment P + Q. This follows directly from the concavity of discount bonds in the final payment.

The effects of a safety covenant on the subordinated debt are just as we would expect. J is initially a decreasing convex function of ρ, reaching a minimum when $\rho = 1$. For $\rho > 1$, it is an increasing convex function, reaching a maximum when $\rho = P + Q$. For values of $\rho < 1$, the benefits of the safety covenant accrue entirely to the senior bondholders and are partly at the expense of the junior bondholders as well as the stockholders. As ρ increases, the junior

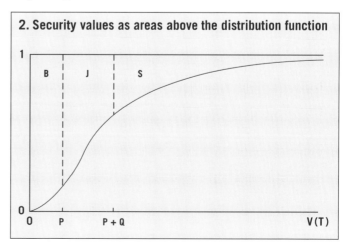

2. Security values as areas above the distribution function

bondholders begin to receive benefits as well, and finally the entire expense falls upon the stockholders. In the remainder of this section we will let $\rho = 0$.

Further analysis shows that the subordinated debt has many characteristics that are quite different from those normally associated with bonds. While senior bonds are always a concave function of V, the junior bonds are initially a convex function of V, becoming a concave function for larger values of V. The inflection point, V^*, occurs at

$$V = \left[P(P+Q) \right]^{\frac{1}{2}} \exp \left[-(r - a - \tfrac{1}{2}\sigma^2)(T - t) \right] \qquad (10)$$

Again unlike the senior debt, the value of the junior debt can be an increasing function of σ^2. Analysis of the function shows J as an increasing (decreasing) function of σ^2 for V less than (greater than) V^*. This means that the bondholders as a group may under some circumstances have conflicting interests with respect to changes in the total riskiness of the firm's investment policy. To fully protect the value of their claims, the senior bondholders must insist on the sole right to approve investment policy changes that will increase the business risk of the firm.

As we might now expect, J can be an increasing function of time to maturity. Unlike the senior debt, it is possible for the junior debt to be worthless at maturity, and if such a development is imminent, the junior bondholders would find it in their interests to try to extend the maturity date of the entire bond issue. Although it is possible for the value of the junior bonds to be either a decreasing or an increasing function of the interest rate, it is always a decreasing function of the dividend rate.

Turning now to the characteristics of risk and expected return, we find that the junior bonds behave partly like a senior bond and partly like a stock. We normally think of a bond as being less risky than the assets of the firm, that is, having an elasticity of less than one, and of the stock as being more risky than the assets. However, we find that the elasticity, ε, of J is a decreasing convex function of V which goes to zero as V goes to infinity and to infinity as V goes to zero. Further inspection shows that

$$\varepsilon \gtrless 1 \quad \text{as} \quad PN(z_1; P) \gtrless (P+Q)N(z_1; P+Q) \qquad (11)$$

The behaviour of the elasticity with respect to time until maturity for the relevant firm and parameter values is shown in Figure 3.

Restrictions on the financing of interest and dividend payments

Suppose now that the firm has interest-paying bonds outstanding. In this section we will see that it is quite important how the stockholders are allowed to raise the money to make the payments to the bondholders. Previous studies of interest-paying bonds have assumed that the stockholders are allowed to sell the assets of the firm to make these payments. Many bonds have contractual provisions that limit the extent to which this can be done. To focus on the effects of these restrictions, suppose that the sale of assets for this purpose is in fact completely forbidden. Interest payments, and any dividend payments, must be financed by issuing new securities. To protect the value of their claim the bondholders must also require that the new securities be equity or subordinated bonds.

To clarify further, suppose the bonds have a promised final payment of P and make periodic interest payments of $c = Pe^{rt'}$, where t' is the interval between payments. If an interest payment is not made, the firm is in default and the promised payment P becomes due immediately. The bonds would

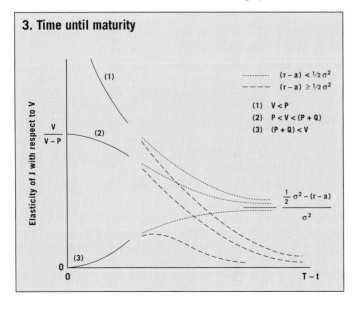

3. Time until maturity

(1)

$\dfrac{V}{V-P}$ (2)

.... $(r-a) < \tfrac{1}{2}\sigma^2$
- - - - $(r-a) \geq \tfrac{1}{2}\sigma^2$

(1) $V < P$
(2) $P < V < (P+Q)$
(3) $(P+Q) < V$

$\dfrac{1}{2}\sigma^2 - (r-a)$

σ^2

Elasticity of J with respect to V

(3)

0

0 $\qquad\qquad$ T – t

then be worth $\min(V, P + c)$. Since this is the maximum value the bonds can possibly have, the bondholders would always be glad to see a payment missed, and correspondingly the stockholders would always want to make the payment if there were any way they possibly could. However, they may not be able to. This would happen whenever the value of the equity after the payment is made, if it is made, was less than the value of the payment. Even if the present stockholders offered an equity issue that would dilute their own interest to virtually nothing, they would still find no takers for it. All of this can occur when the assets of the firm still have substantial value. It provides one explanation, along with the safety covenants discussed earlier, of the observed fact that many firms end up in bankruptcy and reorganisation even though their total value may be quite significant.

Under these circumstances the use of junior debt, and the exact terms of the junior debt, have important implications. Suppose that because of legal restrictions or diffusion of ownership the junior bondholders are forced to play a purely passive role. They cannot at some late later date agree to a change in their contract or take an active part in the firm. To protect themselves in these circumstances, the junior bondholders must require that any subsequent debt issues be subordinated to their own.

However, issuing any junior debt at all in this situation would actually help the senior bondholders and hurt the stockholders. This is because it would then be more likely that a payment will be missed and the bondholders will take over the firm. To see this, consider the value of the claims after a payment has been made. In an attempt to raise the money to in fact make that payment the stockholders were formerly able to offer up for sale the total value of the firm less the value of the senior bonds, while now they can offer only the total value less the value of both the senior and junior bonds. The senior bondholders would be better off, and assuming that the junior debt was sold at a fair price, the difference would have to come out of the pockets of the stockholders.

If it is possible for the junior debt holders to subsequently voluntarily change their status, things will be different. They may find it in their interests to permit the issue of additional unsubordinated debt rather than allow a payment to be missed. In fact, the disadvantages of junior debt could be completely circumvented by a contract of the following kind. Suppose that in the junior debt indenture it is specified that if the stockholders find that they cannot make a payment by issuing new equity, they will sign their entire interest over to the junior bondholders. The junior bondholders could then immediately reorganise the firm as one having only equity and senior bonds. If such an arrangement is possible, there would then be no disadvantage to issuing junior debt, since the firm would in effect switch back to equity at exactly the moment when the debt would have been a disadvantage.

We have stated the discussion in terms of extreme cases in order to highlight the issues. Often there may be only partial restrictions on the sale of assets, such as those allowing the sale of assets added by current earnings, or the junior bondholders may be able to partly change their status. While these considerations would have a quantitative impact, the qualitative results would not be affected.

The relevant form of equation (1) for our problem is

$$\tfrac{1}{2}\sigma^2 V^2 F_{vv} + rVF_v - rF + F_t + \sum_{j=1}^{n} c_j \delta(t - t_j) = 0 \qquad (12)$$

where c_j is the jth interest payment, t_j is the time at which the jth interest payment is made, n is the total number of interest payments, and $\delta(\cdot)$ is the Dirac delta function. The first derivative term does not involve the outflow of interest or dividend payments because they are exactly offset by the inflow of new financing. The standard terminal condition and the stopping condition described above complete the specification of the problem.

The solution can be obtained by the recursive technique discussed in the first section. For example, consider the situation immediately before the last payment is due. Let $s(V, t_n)$ be the value of the firm's stock if the payment is made. This is the solution to the standard problem with terminal condition $\max(V - P, 0)$. Then the minimum value of the firm at which the payment can be made, $\overline{V}$, is the root of $s(V, t_n) = c$. The value of the stock just before the payment is made, $\overline{s}(V, t_n)$, will be $s(V, t_n) - c$ if $V \geq \overline{V}$ and zero if $V < \overline{V}$. The value of the bonds will be $V - \overline{s}(V, t_n)$. For the situation just before the next-to-last payment is due, we apply the same analysis with $\overline{s}(V, t_n)$ replacing $\max(V - P, 0)$. By working recursively in this way, we can obtain a complete solution to the problem, but in general no closed form expression will be available.

To obtain a better perspective on the behaviour of F, consider the case of a perpetual bond with continual interest payments of c per unit time. Equation (1) now has the form

$$\tfrac{1}{2}\sigma^2 V^2 F_{VV} + rVF_V - rF + c = 0 \qquad (13)$$

From our earlier discussion we know that there will be some point at which no more equity can be sold and the bondholders will take over the firm. To find this point, think of things in the following way. In equilibrium new equity financing must sell at a fair price, so it makes no difference whether we think of it as being purchased by new investors or by the original stockholders. So we can think of this as a situation where the stockholders will make payments into the firm to cover the interest payments to the bondholders, but at any time they have the right to stop making payments and either turn the firm over to the bondholders or pay them c/r. It is clear that the critical value of the firm at which they will do this, $\overline{V}$, is independent of the current value of the firm and will be chosen by the stockholders to minimise the value of the bonds and hence maximise the value of their own claim.

While a solution could be obtained and interpreted by the probabilistic approach discussed earlier, in the perpetual case it may be clearer to proceed formally with the ordinary differential equation (13). The solution to (13) can be written as the sum of a particular solution to the full inhomogeneous equation and the general solution to the corresponding homogeneous equation. A particular solution is c/r. Combining this with the corresponding general solution gives

$$F(V) = \frac{c}{r} + K_1 V + K_2 V^{-\alpha} \qquad (14)$$

where $\alpha = 2r/\sigma^2$ and K_1 and K_2 are arbitrary constants to be determined by the boundary conditions. As the value of the firm goes to infinity, the bonds must approach their riskless value and further increases in value must accrue solely to the stockholders, so $F_V(\infty) = 0$ and hence $K_1 = 0$.

The lower boundary condition then gives

$$K_2 \overline{V}^{-\alpha} + \frac{c}{r} = \min\left(\overline{V}, \frac{c}{r}\right) \qquad (15)$$

so $K_1 = \overline{V}^{\alpha+1} - (c/r)\overline{V}^\alpha$ if $\overline{V} < (c/r)$ and $K_2 = 0$ if $\overline{V} \geq (c/r)$. Choosing $\overline{V} \geq (c/r)$ gives the bonds their maximum possible value, so the optimal $\overline{V}$ must be an interior point and the value of the bonds will be

$$F(V) = \frac{c}{r} + \left(\overline{V}^{\alpha+1} - \frac{c}{r}\overline{V}^\alpha\right)V^{-\alpha} \qquad (16)$$

Solving the first-order condition for minimising F(V) gives $\overline{V} = (\alpha/\alpha + 1)c/r$. Substitution and rearranging then gives

$$F(V) = \frac{c}{r} - \left[\left(\frac{\alpha}{\alpha+1}\right)^\alpha - \left(\frac{\alpha}{\alpha+1}\right)^{\alpha+1}\right]\left(\frac{c}{r}\right)^{\alpha+1} V^{-\alpha} \qquad (17)$$

For comparison consider now the corresponding case where the assets of the firm can be sold to make interest and dividend payments. The valuation equation for the bonds, G, will take the form

$$\tfrac{1}{2}\sigma^2 V^2 G_{vv} + \left[(r-a)V - (c+d)\right]G_v - rG + c = 0 \tag{18}$$

where c again represents the continuous interest payments to the bonds and the stock is entitled to receive dividend payments of $aV + d$. The upper boundary condition will again be $F_v(\infty) = 0$ and the lower boundary condition is now $G(0) = 0$. The solution is

$$G(V) = \frac{c}{r}\left[1 - \frac{\Gamma\!\left(k - \frac{2(r-a)}{\sigma^2} + 2\right)\left(\frac{2(c+d)}{\sigma^2 V}\right)^k}{\Gamma\!\left(2k - \frac{2(r-a)}{\sigma^2} + 2\right)} M\!\left(k, 2k - \frac{2(r-a)}{\sigma^2} + 2, -\frac{2(c+d)}{\sigma^2 V}\right)\right] \tag{19}$$

where $M(\cdot,\cdot,\cdot)$ is the confluent hypergeometric function. $\Gamma(\cdot)$ is the gamma function, and k is the positive root of

$$\sigma^2 k^2 + [\sigma^2 - 2(r-a)]k - 2r = 0 \tag{20}^8$$

When $a = 0$, $k = (2r/\sigma^2) = \alpha$, so with $d = 0$ this reduces to formula (42) in Merton (1974). In this case (19) can be written in the more convenient form

$$G(V) = \frac{c}{r}[1 - \Gamma(\alpha, Z)] + \left(\frac{cV}{c+d}\right)\Gamma(\alpha+1, Z) \tag{21}$$

where $Z = (2(c+d)/\sigma^2 V)$ and $\Gamma(n, x)$ is the gamma distribution function with parameter n, $\Gamma(n, x) = \int_0^x e^{-s}s^{n-1}ds/\Gamma(n)$.[9]

Analysis of the solutions show that F is always greater than G, so the financing restrictions do increase the value of the bonds. When V is large, F is less sensitive to changes in V than is G, and it is less risky in the sense of having a lower elasticity, but when V is small the relationships are reversed. The premium due to the restrictions achieves its maximum at $\bar{V}$ and is a decreasing convex function of V. For the case with financing restrictions, we find that the value at which the stockholders would abandon the firm is a linear increasing function of c and a decreasing convex function of σ^2 and r.

We would suspect that the premium of F over G is due partly to the increase in asset value from the inflow of new financing and partly to the implicit safety covenant which places the firm in the hands of the bondholders at some positive value. To get some idea of the different effects, consider a bond, H, which allows the sale of assets but which has a safety covenant giving the bondholders control of the firm at $\bar{V}$. It is easy to verify that

$$H(V) = \frac{c}{r} + \lambda\left[G(V) - \frac{c}{r}\right] \tag{22}$$

where

$$\lambda = \left[\frac{\bar{V} - \frac{c}{r}}{G(\bar{V}) - \frac{c}{r}}\right]$$

Inspection shows that $F \geq H > G$. At $\bar{V}$, F and H have the same value by construction. As V increases, the spread between them at first widens and then narrows to zero as the value of each claim approaches that of riskless debt, c/r. The sensitivity and riskiness of F compared to H is qualitatively the same as its comparison to G.

Further examination of the functions shows that both F and G are increasing concave functions of V and c. They are both decreasing functions of σ^2, having an initial concave segment followed by a convex segment. Similarly, both elasticities are increasing functions of V, c and σ^2.

Conclusion

In this chapter we first discussed some general issues in the valuation of contingent claims. We outlined some solution methods that could be applied even when the problem possesses inherent discreteness and discussed an intuitive way of interpreting the solutions. We then investigated the effects of three specific provisions often found in bond indentures. These were safety covenants, subordination arrangements, and restrictions on the financing of interest and dividend payments. We found that these provisions do indeed increase the value of bonds and that they may have a quite significant effect on the behaviour of the firm's securities.

The most important qualifications to our results involve the assumptions about the absence of bankruptcy costs and about the probabilistic process governing the value of the firm. Most of our general results should hold for other stochastic processes, but of course the specific formulas and quantitative impact would be different. It should be noted that if the value of the firm follows a jump process, the value of a safety covenant may be drastically altered since the value of the firm could then reach points below the bankruptcy level without first passing through it.

The introduction of bankruptcy costs might have a more important effect. This would depend on the specific form of the bankruptcy costs and also on the influence of other factors, such as taxes, which would have to be introduced into the analysis to justify the existence of debt in a world with positive bankruptcy costs. However, their impact on our analysis should not be exaggerated. We are considering bankruptcy as simply the transfer of the entire ownership of the firm to the bondholders. The physical activities of the firm need not be affected. The bondholders may not want to actively run the company, but probably the stockholders did not either. The bondholders could retain the old managers or hire new ones, or they could refinance the firm and sell all or part of their holdings. Certain legal costs may be involved in the act of bankruptcy, but if contracts are carefully specified in the first place with an eye towards minimising these costs, then their importance may be significantly reduced.

1 *See Black (1975).*

2 *See Cox and Ross (1976) for a discussion of some models of this type.*

3 *Processes with discontinuous sample paths are examined in Cox and Ross (1975, 1976) and Merton (1976).*

4 *Call provisions on bonds have recently been examined by Brennan and Schwartz (1975) and Ingersoll (1976). All of our results could be extended to include such upper boundaries as well.*

5 *For a related discussion, see Black and Scholes (1970).*

6 *The ability to form a perfectly hedged portfolio is a sufficient condition for the derivation of a valuation equation free of preferences. Note that this does not say that the value of the underlying assets in terms of the values of other assets is independent of preferences.*

7 *In a risk-neutral world the instantaneous mean total return must be* rV, *so the instantaneous mean of the price component must be* $rV - p(V, t)$. *For a diffusion process, this, together with the instantaneous variance and behaviour at accessible boundaries, completely specifies the processes. The value of the assets of the firm would in general have only a lower barrier, an absorbing one at the origin. However, our interest is in probabilities for paths of firm value that have not previously reached one of the reorganisation boundaries. A convenient way to introduce this is by considering the distribution with the boundaries taken as artificial absorbing barriers, and we will adopt this convention.*

8 *Let* $Z = (2(c + d)/\sigma^2 V)$ *and* $G(V) = Z^k e^{-Z} h(Z)$. *This reduces the homogeneous part of the equation to*

$$Z h_{zz} + [(\beta + k) - Z] h_z - \beta h = 0$$

where $\beta = k - (2(r - a)/\sigma^2) + 2$. *This is Kummer's equation, with general solution*

$$K_1 M(\beta, \beta + k, Z) + K_2 Z^{1-\beta-k} M(1 - k, 2 - \beta - k, Z)$$

Using the boundary conditions and well-known properties of the confluent hypergeometric function gives (19).

9 *The solution in this form was shown to us by John Barry. It has also been independently derived by Jonathan Ingersoll. That it is equivalent to the solution given by Merton can be seen by noting that*

$$M(A, A + 1, -Z) = AZ^{-A}\Gamma(A)\Gamma(A, Z)$$

and

$$M(A, A + 2, -Z) = (A + 1)M(A, A + 1, -Z) - AM(A + 1, A + 2, -Z)$$

$$= \Gamma(A + 2)Z^{-A}\Gamma(A, Z) - A\Gamma(A + 2)Z^{-(A+1)}\Gamma(A + 1, Z)$$

BIBLIOGRAPHY

Black, F., 1975, "Forecasting Variance of Stock Prices for Options Trading and Other Purposes", Seminar on the Analysis of Security Prices, University of Chicago, November.

Black, F., and M. Scholes, 1970, "A Theoretical Valuation Formula for Options, Warrants, and Other Securities", Financial Note No. 16B, Associates in Finance, October.

Black, F., and M. Scholes, 1973, "The Pricing of Options and Corporate Liabilities", *Journal of Political Economy* 81, No. 3, May–June.

Brennan, M. J., and E. S. Schwartz, 1975, "Convertible Bonds: Valuation and Optimal Strategies for Call and Conversion", Working paper 336, University of British Columbia, October.

Cox, J. C., and S. A. Ross, 1975, "The Pricing of Options for Jump Processes", Rodney L. White Center Working paper 2-75, University of Pennsylvania, April.

Cox, J. C., and S. A. Ross, 1976, "The Valuation of Options for Alternative Stochastic Processes", *Journal of Financial Economics* 3, Nos 1-2, January–March.

Ingersoll, J. E., Jr, 1976, "A Contingent Claims Evaluation of Convertible Bonds and the Optimal Policies for Call and Conversion", PhD dissertation, Massachusetts Institute of Technology, February.

Merton, R. C., 1973, "The Theory of Rational Options Pricing", *Bell Journal of Economics and Management Science* 4, No. 1, Spring.

Merton, R. C., 1974, "On the Pricing of Corporate Debt: The Risk Structure of Interest Rates", *Journal of Finance* 29, No. 2, May.

Merton, R. C., 1976, "Option Pricing When Underlying Stock Returns are Discontinuous", *Journal of Financial Economics* 3, Nos 1-2, January–March.

Ross, S. A., 1976, "Options and Efficiency", *Quarterly Journal of Economics* 90, No. 1, February.

6

Does Default Risk in Coupons Affect the Valuation of Corporate Bonds? – A Contingent Claims Model

In Joon Kim, Krishna Ramaswamy and Suresh Sundaresan

Korea Advanced Institute of Science and Technology, Seoul;
The Wharton School of the University of Pennsylvania, Philadelphia;
Graduate School of Business, Columbia University, New York

In their pioneering papers, Black and Scholes (1973) and Merton (1973) emphasised the correspondence between corporate liabilities and options and indicated how the theory of option pricing might be used to value corporate liabilities. This correspondence has been the cornerstone of a number of studies: Merton (1974) examined the risk structure of interest rates; Black and Cox (1976) provided significant extensions by explicitly modelling some indenture provisions; and Brennan and Schwartz (1980) and Ingersoll (1977) used this correspondence to value convertible and callable corporate liabilities. This list is only partial, but it illustrates the range of issues which may be addressed using option pricing theory.

While the insights offered by this research are beyond questioning, the ability of this approach to explain the yield spreads between corporate bonds and comparable default-free Treasury bonds has been questioned in recent papers. In a paper which is closely related to our work, Jones, Mason and Rosenfeld (1984) sought to test the predictive power of a contingent claims pricing model based on some simplifying assumptions which included non-stochastic interest rates, strict "me-first" rules and the sale of assets to fund bond-related payments; they also permitted interaction of multiple call and sinking fund provisions. The empirical findings of Jones, Mason and Rosenfeld (1984) indicate that such versions of contingent claims pricing models do not generate the levels of yield spreads that one observes in practice.[1] Over the 1926–86 period, the yield spreads on high-grade corporates (triple-A rated) ranged from 15 to 215 basis points and averaged 77 bp; and the yield spreads on BAAs (also investment-grade) ranged from 51 to 787 bp and averaged 198 bp. We show later in this paper that the conventional contingent claims model due to Merton (1974) is unable to generate default premiums in excess of 120 bp, *even* when excessive debt ratios and volatility parameters are used in the numerical simulation.

This paper was originally published in Financial Management, *Vol. 22 (3), Autumn 1993, published by Financial Management Association International, College of Business Admin, University of South Florida, Tampa, FL 33620-5500, telephone (813) 974 2084. The authors are grateful to Stephen Buser, Bruce Grundy, Kose John, Eduardo Schwartz, Walter Torous and an anonymous referee for their comments and suggestions. Research support for Krishna Ramaswamy from the Geewax-Terker Program in Investments, for In Joon Kim from the Leonard N. Stern School of Business, and for Suresh Sundaresan from the Graduate School of Business is gratefully acknowledged. We are responsible for any errors.*

DOES DEFAULT RISK
IN COUPONS AFFECT
THE VALUATION OF
CORPORATE BONDS?
– A CONTINGENT
CLAIMS MODEL

The inability (at plausible parameter values) of contingent claims pricing models to account for the magnitude of the yield spreads between corporate and Treasury bonds provides the motivation for this paper. The focus is on two issues central to the valuation of corporate claims.

First, we make explicit assumptions about how and when bankruptcy occurs and we discuss the nature of the payoffs with regard to indenture provisions. Previous studies have generally placed the burden of bankruptcy on the principal payment at maturity and not on the coupon obligations along the way. Our focus, in contrast, is on: (i) the possibility of the firm defaulting on its coupon obligations; and (ii) the interaction between dividends and default risk.

Second, the values of Treasury and corporate bonds are influenced significantly by interest rate risk: Jones, Mason and Rosenfeld (1984) concluded that the introduction of stochastic interest rates might improve the performance of contingent claims pricing models. We model this source of uncertainty by specifying a stochastic process for the evolution of the short rate. We find that although the yields on both Treasury and corporate issues are significantly influenced by the uncertainty in interest rates, the yield spreads are quite insensitive to interest rate uncertainty. The role of call features in corporate and Treasury bonds is also studied. The call feature has a differential effect on Treasury issues relative to corporate issues: we find that the call feature is relatively more valuable in Treasury issues than it is in corporate issues. The differential effect of call provisions is a significant factor in explaining the observed yield spreads between non-callable ("straight") corporates and straight Treasuries on the one hand and callable corporates and callable Treasuries on the other.

Our study, by incorporating these features in a simple partial equilibrium setting, makes two contributions. First, it builds a contingent claims model with stochastic interest rates to accommodate the risk of default in the coupons in the presence of dividends and examines the effect of the call provision in this more realistic setting. Second, it provides evidence that these models are capable of generating yield spreads that are consistent with the levels observed in practice. To be sure, all the models presented here describe firms with extremely simple capital structures – firms with a single issue of debt outstanding. Given the results, however, we are hopeful that contingent claims models will be useful to studying the more complex liabilities of firms with complicated capital structures.[2]

This chapter is organised as follows. We begin by building the contingent claims valuation framework for pricing corporate and Treasury bonds and then discuss the differences between the models we study and the model in Merton (1974). In the next section we provide a numerical analysis of straight non-callable corporate and Treasury bonds. We characterise the behaviour of yield spreads with respect to changes in maturity, with respect to shifts in the debt ratios of the firm and with respect to the parameters that govern the stochastic process that drives interest rates. In the third section, we extend the model to callable bonds and examine optimal call policies in a stochastic term structure environment.

The valuation of non-callable corporate bonds

Corporate bonds are priced to yield a higher promised return than comparable Treasury issues due to the possibility of default. The credit quality of the issuing corporation, the nature of the issue (senior or subordinated, secured or unsecured, callable or non-callable, with or without sinking fund provisions, etc) and the contractual provisions specifying the payoffs in the event of a default all serve to determine the market value, and hence the promised yields on corporate bonds. We take up these issues now in the context of a contingent claims valuation model.

The model constructed here differs from the standard contingent claims model in the way in which we specify the occurrence and implications of bankruptcy. In other respects, however, it is similar to the models in Brennan and Schwartz (1980) and Jones, Mason and Rosenfeld (1985). We study the valuation of the single debt issue of a firm

79

DOES DEFAULT RISK

IN COUPONS AFFECT

THE VALUATION OF

CORPORATE BONDS?

– A CONTINGENT

CLAIMS MODEL

whose total market value follows a diffusion process, in a world in which the Miller-Modigliani (1958) theorems are understood to apply.[3]

The following assumptions are employed:

(A0) Trading occurs continuously in perfect and frictionless financial markets with no taxes, transaction costs or informational asymmetries. Investors act as price-takers.

(A1) The value of the firm, denoted V, follows the lognormal diffusion process

$$dV = (\alpha - \gamma)Vdt + \sigma_1 VdZ_1 \qquad (1)$$

where α is the instantaneous expected rate of return on the firm gross of all payouts, σ_1^2 is the instantaneous variance of the return on the firm, and Z_1 is a standard Wiener process. The dynamics of the value of the firm are such that γV has a natural interpretation: it is the *net cash outflow* from the firm resulting from optimal investment decisions. An important implication of this interpretation of γV is that it is independent of the capital structure of the firm. The firm's capital structure consists of equity and a single, coupon-bearing bond with principal P. This bond may be either callable or non-callable; in this section we assume it is non-callable.

(A2) The uncertainty in the term structure of interest rates is captured by the process on the nominal short rate r, given by

$$dr = \kappa(\mu - r)dt + \sigma_2 \sqrt{r}dZ_2 \qquad (2)$$

The scalar μ is the long-run mean rate of interest, κ is the speed with which the interest rate r approaches the long-run mean rate and the instantaneous variance of change in r is proportional to its level. Z_2 is a standard Wiener process. The instantaneous correlation between dZ_1 and dZ_2 is given by ρ. Default-free bonds are priced according to the local expectations hypothesis, ie, each bond's expected rate of return over the next instantaneous holding period is equal to r.

(A3) The bond's indenture provisions prohibit the stockholders from selling the assets of the firm to pay dividends. The bondholders have priority and must be paid their coupon continuously at the rate of $c. Otherwise, the firm is forced into bankruptcy, which is assumed to be costlessly enforced. Thus, the lower reorganisation boundary for the firm's value, denoted by V*, is given by c/γ. At this level, the total net cashflow per unit time will be just sufficient to pay the contractual coupon.

(A4) The payoffs to bondholders upon bankruptcy are defined as follows: when V = V*, the payoff is

$$\min\left[\delta(\tau)B(r, \tau; c), V^*\right] \qquad (3)$$

where $B(r, \tau; c)$ is the value of a comparable Treasury bond with a time-to-maturity given by τ, and $\delta(\tau)$ is a positive fraction. Relation (3) says that bondholders will recover upon bankruptcy either the total value of the firm or $\delta(\tau)$ fraction of the value of a comparable Treasury obligation (which is free of default risk), whichever is less. By assuming that $\delta(0) = 1$, we ensure that bondholders are promised P or V, whichever is less, at maturity.

Assumption (A0) is standard. Our goal is to demonstrate that the observed yield spreads between corporates and Treasuries can be generated in the context of models where market imperfections play no part. Assumption (A1) is a convenient way to represent the random evolution of the firm's value. In a more general setting, perhaps with stochastic investment opportunities, the dynamics of the firm's value will depend on the optimal investment decisions made by the managers. We have abstracted from those issues for simplicity: the *net cashflow* is understood to be the operating cashflow (cash revenues minus expenses in this no-tax world) less a predetermined investment outlay. The economic content of Assumption (A2) is that the uncertainty in the term structure can be

DOES DEFAULT RISK
IN COUPONS AFFECT
THE VALUATION OF
CORPORATE BONDS?
– A CONTINGENT
CLAIMS MODEL

modelled using a single state variable. The stochastic process defined in relation (2) has been used by Cox, Ingersoll and Ross (1985) and Richard (1978) and these papers provide the properties of the conditional moments of the process as well as the stationary distribution implied by relation (2).[4] This approach differs from that in Brennan and Schwartz (1980), who employ two state variables (the short rate and the long rate) to capture the uncertainty in interest rates. Since we are attempting to simultaneously model the stochastic evolution of the value of the firm and the evolution of interest rates, the problem already has two state variables. The introduction of an extra state variable, such as the long rate, would render the valuation problem virtually intractable. The assumption on the local expectations hypothesis enables us to avoid specifying investors' preferences and the nature of risk premiums; a complete discussion of this issue is in Cox, Ingersoll and Ross (1981).

The assumptions embodied in Assumption (A3) distinguish our study from the earlier contributions in the literature: we have modelled the fact that if and when the firm's cashflows are unable to cover its interest obligations, bankruptcy is precipitated. An essential feature of corporate bonds is that omission of a coupon payment precipitates bankruptcy – for a detailed treatment of the standard bond indenture provisions, see Smith and Warner (1979). To incorporate default risk of coupons and payment of common dividends, we recognise the firm's *net cashflow* as a fundamental variable in the analysis.[5] We have implicitly assumed that the process for the net cashflow of the firm and the preferences of investors are such that the value of the firm follows a lognormal diffusion process.

We offer a rather simple but internally consistent account of how bankruptcy occurs and how it is settled between bondholders and shareholders. The firm, by Assumption (A1), has equity and a single bond issue with bondholders receiving a coupon rate of $c and a promised final payment of $P. The bond indentures prohibit the firm from selling assets. Otherwise, it may be optimal for shareholders to sell the assets and pay themselves a liquidating dividend. We assume that the net cashflow is continuously distributed to both shareholders and bondholders. The bondholders are entitled to the contractual coupon and shareholders receive any residual cashflow if the net cashflow is large enough. Otherwise, the firm is forced into bankruptcy. The key to our approach, then, is the recognition that the cashflow problem is the source that precipitates bankruptcy. This approach is broadly consistent with the fact that many bond indenture provisions related to the incidence of bankruptcy are specified in terms of cashflows.[6] Since bankruptcy is defined in terms of cashflow alone, we do not rule out the possibility that at the time of bankruptcy, the value of the firm can be *higher* than the value of the remaining debt obligations evaluated as if they were default-free. It is sometimes argued that these models should permit the sale of assets in order to make coupon payments. This clearly alters the firm's investment policy and hence its future net cashflows. As a practical matter, the sale of assets is restricted with some exclusions (see Smith and Warner, 1979, p. 126).

In practice, due to the difficulty of objectively defining the optimal investment policy, managers acting on behalf of shareholders have an incentive to reduce the amount of planned investment and pay the coupon in order to avoid bankruptcy – or at least postpone it – and this may not be observable to bondholders. The deviation from the optimal investment policy will reduce the value of the firm and in turn the value of the corporate bond, and the conditions for the Miller–Modigliani theorem would no longer apply. In this model, however, there are no informational asymmetries, and both shareholders and bondholders agree to the optimal investment policy and hence agree as to the net cashflows of the firm.

A complete description of bankruptcy requires a description of rules on how the assets of the firm will be divided between bondholders and shareholders. The lower reorganisation boundary in relation (3) is very stylised, and it keeps the bondholders from reaping benefits from bankruptcy: they receive only a fraction of the value of a comparable default-free bond. One can justify this by appealing to the illiquidity of the market for real assets. The available evidence indicates (see Altman and Nammacher, 1985) that, on average, the market values of low-grade corporate bonds ("junk" bonds) are approximately 40% of their par values immediately after filing for bankruptcy. To be consistent with these observations, we have chosen the lower reorganisation boundary presented in equation (3). Brennan and Schwartz (1980) employ a similar distribution rule: they assume bondholders will take over the firm when the firm's value falls below a fraction of the par value of the bond. Under their rule, however, bankruptcy is not cash-flow driven, and it may work in favour of the bondholders because the fraction of par value can be larger than the value of an equivalent default-free bond when interest rates are high.

Assumption (A3) and relation (3) play an important role in our contingent claims pricing model, and therefore merit further discussion. The contingent claims pricing model presented here requires an *ex ante* specification of the occurrence of and payoffs from bankruptcy; it specifies the fraction $\delta(\tau)$ exogenously; and it does not allow for either new equity issues or side-payments (for example, in a mutually agreeable reorganisation, perhaps with changes in future investment policy) from stockholders to bondholders to alter this specification along the way. This rules out strategic decisions leading to agreements on the part of both bondholders and stockholders. Such a situation might arise, for example, if the payoff received by bondholders in relation (3), $\delta(\tau)B(\tau;c)$, was less than they would receive if they agreed to forgo coupons for the next n months and receive a higher level of coupons thereafter. For a description of US firms in reorganisation, and the difficulty in writing down a suitable payoff in bankruptcy, see Franks and Torous (1989). This is a limitation of the model presented here. Our concern, however, was to see how well the model might perform in the absence of strategic considerations during reorganisation.[7]

THE VALUATION EQUATION

The underlying state variables in this model are the value of the firm V and the interest rate r, so we represent the total value of the corporate bond as $W(V, r, \tau; c)$, where τ is the time to maturity of the bond. Given Assumptions (A1) and (A2), Brennan and Schwartz (1980) show that the value of the corporate bond must satisfy the following partial differential equation:[8]

$$\tfrac{1}{2}\sigma_1^2 V^2 W_{VV} + \rho\sigma_1\sigma_2\sqrt{r}VW_{rV} + \tfrac{1}{2}\sigma_2^2 rW_{rr} + \kappa(\mu - r)W_r + (r - \gamma)VW_V - rW + c = W_\tau \quad (4)$$

We need to append boundary conditions, in addition to the bankruptcy-relation condition (3), in order to complete the description of the bond's value. As V approaches infinity, the payoff function approaches the value of a comparable default-free bond. Thus,

$$\lim_{V \to \infty} W(V, r, \tau; c) = B(r, \tau; c) \quad (5)$$

Because we are considering a single (hence, seniormost) non-callable corporate bond, the bondholders will get the lower of the face value (P) or the market value of the firm at maturity. This leads to the following terminal condition:

$$W(V, r, \tau = 0; c) = \min[V, P] \quad (6)$$

In order to solve the valuation equation (4) subject to the boundary conditions (3), (5) and (6), one must first compute the prices of the default-free coupon bonds $B(r, \tau; c)$ since these appear as boundary values in equations (3) and (5). We can compute these prices by using the formula for default-free, zero-coupon bonds provided in Cox, Ingersoll and Ross (1985) and computing the value of a coupon-bearing, default-free bond as the sum of the values of the coupons and principal.

The valuation equation described here differs from Merton's equation for a firm with a single debt issue (see Merton, 1974), and extensions in Black and Cox, 1976) by:

DOES DEFAULT RISK
IN COUPONS AFFECT
THE VALUATION OF
CORPORATE BONDS?
– A CONTINGENT
CLAIMS MODEL

DOES DEFAULT RISK
IN COUPONS AFFECT
THE VALUATION OF
CORPORATE BONDS?
– A CONTINGENT
CLAIMS MODEL

(i) incorporating interest rate risk, and (ii) accounting for coupons and the attendant risk of default prior to maturity. It differs from the valuation equation in Brennan and Schwartz (1980) in the way in which default arises and the specification of the payoffs upon default, as discussed earlier.

SUBORDINATED BONDS AND LBOs

The framework developed in this study may be used to examine another topical issue in the market for corporate bonds: deeply subordinated bonds and their use in the funding of management buyouts. Although only a single debt security was considered in the model presented, we can value subordinated debt in the same model by using the ideas in Black and Cox (1976). In this paper, Black and Cox showed that junior (subordinated) debt may be represented as a portfolio of suitably specified senior debt (or equivalently, as a vertical spread[9]). The same logic extends to our setting with two important modifications:

❑ The senior and junior bonds in our model pay coupons and the portfolio arguments of Black and Cox will have to be modified to account for that feature.
❑ The lower reorganisation boundary will depend on the sum of the coupon cashflows of the two outstanding layers of debt. The lower reorganisation boundary may be specified so that it depends on the promised cashflows of either the senior bondholders alone or both bondholders – and the way in which one specifies the boundary will affect the qualitative results.

With these modifications, we can proceed with the pricing of junior or junk debt in the same way as Black and Cox (1976) have done in their paper.

This treatment of the valuation of junior debt leads to an implication that differs from that which Black and Cox (1976) found in their setting: the issuance of junior debt actually benefited the senior debt holders. In that model, Black and Cox considered only zero-coupon debt issues. As a result, the existence of a junior debt issue involved no additional cashflows from the firm.

In the setting suggested in our model, the junior debt is coupon-bearing and interest rates are stochastic. The firm pays periodic coupons to the junior as well as senior bondholders and this may leave the senior bondholders with a smaller value if and when bankruptcy occurs – for example, there may be sufficient cashflow to service the senior but not the junior bonds when interest rates are low. Thus, in our model there will be scenarios in which senior bondholders will be worse off with the presence of junior debt. This is broadly consistent with what one observes in practice: the issuance of junk bonds typically leads to the downgrading of existing senior debt issues.[10] We hope in future work to pursue the valuation of junior debt with these features.

Numerical solutions to the valuation equation for non-callable bonds

There is no known closed-form solution to the valuation equation (4), so we will display numerical solutions in this section. Before we do so, it will be useful to review the evidence on yield spreads for corporate bonds – these are the numbers which our numerical solutions should match.

Figure 1 displays the yields on AAA- and BAA-rated debt over long-term Treasury yields. The monthly data series are taken from the *Federal Reserve Bulletin*. The yield spreads on high-grade corporates ranged from 15 to 215 bp and averaged 77 bp, and the yield spreads on BAAs (also investment-grade) ranged from 51 to 787 bp and averaged 198 bp, over

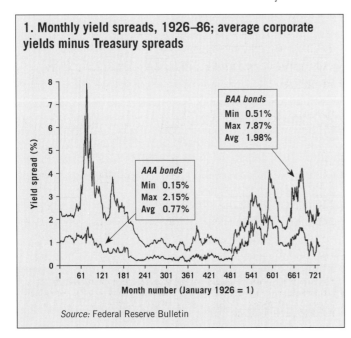

1. Monthly yield spreads, 1926–86; average corporate yields minus Treasury spreads

BAA bonds
Min 0.51%
Max 7.87%
Avg 1.98%

AAA bonds
Min 0.15%
Max 2.15%
Avg 0.77%

Month number (January 1926 = 1)

Source: Federal Reserve Bulletin

DOES DEFAULT RISK

IN COUPONS AFFECT

THE VALUATION OF

CORPORATE BONDS?:

A CONTINGENT

CLAIMS MODEL

the 1926-86 period. These yields are not separately available for non-callable and callable bonds – in fact, the majority of the existing corporate issues of long-term bonds are callable. For this reason, we are unable to construct a series of non-callable coupon-bearing bonds' yield spreads and hence to provide evidence on the relation between these yield spreads and the maturities of the bonds. However, Fama (1986) reports a negative relationship between average default premiums and maturities for short-term money market securities.

The numerical solutions to the valuation equation presented here are obtained from the alternating directions implicit method. The following parameter values are chosen for the stochastic process (in relation (2)) for the interest rate: $\kappa = 0.5$, $\mu = 9\%$, $\sigma_2 = 0.078$. At these parameter values, the yield to maturity of long-term, pure discount bonds approaches 8.89% as maturity increases; the steady state density of r has a mean of $\mu = 9\%$ and a standard deviation of 2.34%.[11] The speed of mean reversion in r is captured by the value of κ, and it indicates that if we start at a current value of r at 6%, then the conditional mean and conditional standard deviation of r in one year's time is 7.18% and 4.27%, respectively. The values of κ, μ, and σ, were chosen so that by varying the current value of r (as we do below, from 7% to 11%), we obtain rising, relatively flat, and declining term structure scenarios for default-free bonds. The parameter σ_1 for the standard deviation of the process on the firm's total value was varied around 0.15, the net cash-flow rate γ was fixed[12] at 0.05, and we used values of ρ of –0.2, 0, and 0.2. We report results with ρ of –0.2, consistent with the slight negative relationship between the returns of common stock indices and nominal Treasury bill returns; the results for ρ of 0 and 0.2 are virtually the same. The value of the "fraction to recover," $\delta(\tau)$, was kept constant (ie, time-invariant) at 0.8;[13] this is a relatively conservative number, given that Altman and Nammacher (1985) report a figure close to 0.4. We vary the capital structures by varying the ratio (P/V) between 0.5 and 0.25, which straddles observed debt ratios of 30 to 35%.[14] These are the central parameter values employed. We also examined the effects due to variation in these parameters, and we report on the relevant results below.

To fix matters, Table 1 shows the default premiums on a 9%, non-callable 10-year corporate bond with a face value P = $100 for: (i) Merton's valuation equation (with no interest rate uncertainty);[15] and (ii) for our model (also with no interest rate uncertainty, fixing $\sigma_2 = 0.0$, $r = \mu = 9\%$, and hence imposing a flat term structure). Thus, Table 1 serves as a useful point of departure for the subsequent results on stochastic term structure settings; and it *isolates* the influence of the assumption on premature default and the lower boundary condition in relation (3). As the table shows, Merton's model with a standard deviation σ_1 of 0.15 displays a default premium ranging from 7 bp (at V = 200, or a debt ratio of 50%) to one basis point (at V = 400).

By contrast, the numerical solutions to the valuation equation (4), assuming $\sigma_2 = 0$ and $r = \mu = 9\%$ (a flat term structure) display default premiums ranging from 205 bp to 5 bp, with a 26-bp "spread" at a debt ratio of 33%. In order to increase the spread to reasonable levels in Merton's model (48 bp at a debt ratio of 33%), we had to *double* the riskiness of the firm's assets. In order to get spreads closer to market spreads at conventional debt levels, it seems preferable to us to move the contingent claims modelling effort in the direction of valuing coupon-bearing bonds with the possibility of premature default, rather than increase the asset volatility.

We now turn to the results for the case with stochastic term structures. We show these results for three initial values for r, of 7, 9 and 11%. Figures 2, 3 and 4 plot the term structure of yield spreads[16] for

Table 1. Default premiums (bp) on 9%, 10-year corporate bonds under a flat, non-stochastic term structure

Firm value (V)	Merton's model		Our model*	
	$\sigma_1 = 0.15$	$\sigma_1 = 0.30$	$\sigma_1 = 0.15$	$\sigma_1 = 0.30$
200	7	120	205	294
220	4	98	127	251
240	2	80	82	217
260	1	67	55	189
280	1	56	37	167
300	1	48	26	148
320	1	41	18	132
340	1	35	13	119
360	1	31	10	108
380	1	28	7	98
400	1	25	5	89

*Solution to the valuation equation (4) subject to equations (3), (5) and (6) with σ_2 = 0 (non-stochastic interest rate case), net cashflow ratio (γ) = 0.05, and recovery factor (δ) = 0.8. Merton's model has non-stochastic interest rates. The yield curve is flat, at 9%, for both models.

2. Yield spread versus maturity for a non-callable 9% coupon bond

The debt ratio is fixed at 0.42; r is the current interest rate

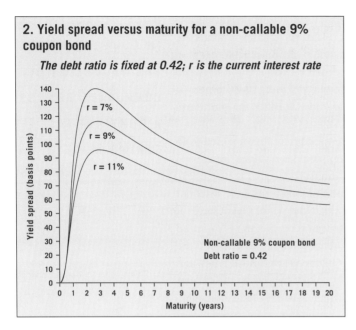

3. Yield spread versus maturity for a non-callable 9% coupon bond

The debt ratio is fixed at 0.33; r is the current interest rate

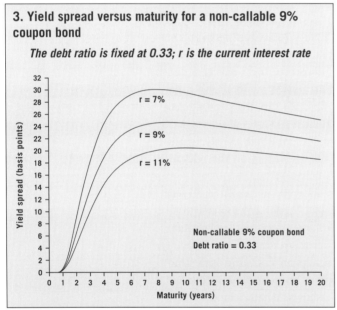

4. Yield spread versus maturity for a non-callable 9% coupon bond

The debt ratio is fixed at 028; r is the current interest rate

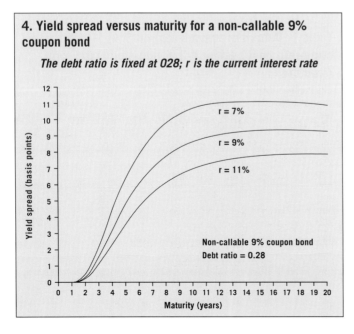

debt ratios corresponding to P/V = 0.42, 0.33 and 0.28. As expected, the capital structure of the firm has a significant effect on the shape of the term structure of yield spreads. For firms with a low debt ratio, the spreads on corporate bonds increase as time to maturity increases. In this case, long-term bonds are riskier than short-term bonds because more coupons are subject to default risk. With a high debt ratio, the spreads increase in the first place and then decrease as time to maturity increases. In this case, investors holding short-term bonds are exposed to the more significant possibility of default on the balloon payment.[17] As a consequence, short-term corporate bonds are priced to provide a higher yield than long-term corporate bonds. This results in a humped risk structure of interest rates. The levels of the yield spreads, however, decline significantly with reduced debt ratios across all maturities. For instance, with P/V = 0.42, a 10-year corporate bond may command a yield spread of 70 to 92 bp, depending on the level of interest rates. However, at a P/V ratio of 0.28, the range becomes 7 to 10 bp.

These results are fairly insensitive to variations in the values selected for the correlation coefficient (ρ) between the changes in the value of the firm and the interest rate.[18] The uncertainty in the interest rates (σ_2) significantly influenced the yields on *both* Treasury and corporate issues. Interest rate risk, however, is relatively independent of default risk so that the *spreads* remain unaffected. This can be seen by comparing Table 2 (which incorporates stochastic rates) with Table 1: as the value for σ_2 is *doubled* to 0.156, the yield spread for a 10-year, 9% corporate bond increases by only four basis points to 86 bp when the P/V = 0.42 and r = 9%. However, the location of the interest rate r relative to its long-run mean rate μ makes a significant difference, as can be seen in Figure 2. Comparing Figure 2 with Figures 3 and 4 suggests that interest rate expectations play an important role in the determining yield spreads when default risk is relatively high (a high P/V ratio).[19] Irrespective of the debt ratio, the spreads decrease with the level of the interest rates. Intuitively, when the rates tend to infinity, both the riskless and the risky bond are worthless and the spread should tend to zero. Similarly, when the rates tend to zero, the present value of default risk is maximised, *ceteris paribus*. This should cause the spread to widen significantly. Our results confirm this intuition. The yield spread is sensitive to changes in the recovery factor (δ) and the net cashflow ratio (γ). For a firm with $\gamma = 0.06$ and P/V = 0.42, the yield spread would be 37 bp for a 10-year, 9% bond when the short rate is 9%. This is 44 bp lower than the yield spread for a firm with $\gamma = 0.05$. That is, the higher is the net cashflow ratio, the lower is the yield spread. This makes sense, because given a firm's value, a higher net cashflow means the firm is more likely to meet coupon obligations. For Figures 2–4 and Tables 1 and 2, we maintained δ, the recovery factor, at 0.8. We show the yields to maturity of a 9%, 10-year, non-callable bond when δ = 0.4 in Table 3. In this case, the yield spread is as large as 823 bp given P/V = 0.5 and r = 7%. This suggests that the yield spread can be very large for low-grade bonds with a small recovery factor. Given the work of Altman and Nammacher (1985), these estimates of spreads are consistent with the evidence on the spreads of junk bonds.

These results are encouraging: they indicate that our model is capable of generating yield spreads that are empirically observed. We now study yield spreads for callable bonds. This is an important task – the majority of corporate debt is callable. The force of the call feature will be to raise the yields, *ceteris paribus*, so that the comparisons to real world bonds will actually come closer.

The numerical solutions for callable corporate bonds

Corporations typically issue debt with call features. One motivation is, of course, to have the necessary flexibility to refinance the debt should rates go down. Rational investors will naturally recognise this and anticipate the issuing firms to refinance in periods of low interest rates. They will pay a lower price for a corporate bond with a call feature than for an otherwise identical corporate issue without the call feature. In examining callable corporate bonds, we define the *total spread* as the yield differential between a callable corporate bond and an otherwise similar but non-callable Treasury bond; this is in contrast to the *call premium*, which is the difference in the yields of callable and non-callable, but similar (either corporate or Treasury) bonds. In the following analysis, interactions between default risk and the call provision play an important role in determining the total spread defined in this way.

We might expect the issuing firm to act rationally and call the debt issue when the rates reach a critical value.[20] It is beneficial for the issuing firm to retire the bond when the interest rate is low and the value of the firm is high. But if during periods of low interest rates, the value of the firm is also lower, then the firm may not be able to call the bonds. The foregoing arguments should also make it clear that the optimal call policy will depend on both the state variables V and r, and will represent a critical *surface* of firm values and interest rates for each maturity $\{C(\tau), R(\tau)\}$, which must be found endogenously.

Suppose that a bond (with remaining time τ) is called by the firm when the value of the firm is $C(\tau)$ and the interest rate is $R(\tau)$. The value of a callable corporate bond, denoted $G(V, r, \tau; c)$, corresponding to a call policy, $\{C(\tau), R(\tau)\}$, also satisfies the valuation equation (4). The conditions specified in equations (3) and (6) also apply to the callable corporate bond. However, the upper boundary condition will change to

$$G(C(\tau), R(\tau), \tau; c) = K \qquad (7)$$

Table 2. Yield spreads (bp) on 9%, 10-year non-callable corporate bonds* under a stochastic term structure

Firm value (V)	Interest rate (r)		
	7%	9%	11%
200	217	204	191
220	139	126	112
240	92	81	70
260	62	53	45
280	42	36	26
300	29	25	21
320	20	17	14
340	14	12	10
360	10	9	7
380	8	7	5
400	5	5	4

*Solution to the valuation equation (4) subject to equations (3), (5) and (6) with the following parameter values: Face value (P): 100; recovery factor (δ) = 0.8; volatility parameter for the firm value (σ_1): 0.15; net cashflow ratio (γ): 0.05; long-run mean rate of interest (μ): 9%; speed of adjustment parameter (κ): 0.5; volatility parameter for the interest rate (σ_2): 0.078; and correlation coefficient (ρ): −0.2.

Table 3. Yield spreads (bp) on 9%, 10-year non-callable corporate bonds* under a stochastic term structure (recovery factor (δ) = 0.4)

Firm value (V)	Interest rate (r)		
	7%	9%	11%
200	823	760	696
220	480	426	375
240	301	262	224
260	196	164	141
280	132	111	93
300	91	76	63
320	63	53	43
340	45	37	30
360	32	27	21
380	23	19	15
400	17	14	11

*Solution to the valuation equation (4) subject to equations (3), (5) and (6) with the following parameter values: Face value (P): 100; recovery factor (δ) = 0.4; volatility parameter for the firm value (σ_1): 0.15; net cashflow ratio (γ): 0.05; long-run mean rate of interest (μ): 9%; speed of adjustment parameter (κ): 0.5; volatility parameter for the interest rate (σ_2): 0.078; and correlation coefficient (ρ): −0.2.

Table 4. Values* and yield spreads† (bp) on 9%, 10-year callable corporate bonds (callable at par)

Firm value (V)	Interest rate (r)		
	7%	9%	11%
200	89.60	87.46	85.40
	226	214	201
220	93.71	91.55	89.39
	156	143	129
240	96.24	93.94	91.58
	115	103	91
260	97.75	95.35	92.84
	92	80	70
280	98.62	96.19	93.58
	78	66	58
300	99.12	96.70	94.03
	70	58	50
320	99.40	97.01	94.30
	66	53	46
340	99.55	97.20	94.47
	64	50	43
360	99.64	97.32	94.58
	63	48	41
380	99.69	97.39	94.65
	62	47	40
400	99.71	97.44	94.70
	61	47	39
Callable treasury bond	99.78	97.56	94.81
	60	44	37

For firm value, the first row gives the bond's value and the second its spread.
* Solution to the valuation equation (4) subject to equations (3), (5), (6) and (7) with the following parameter values: Face value (P): 100; recovery factor (δ) = 0.8; volatility parameter for the firm value (σ_1): 0.15; net cashflow ratio (γ): 0.05; long-run mean rate of interest (μ): 9%; speed of adjustment parameter (κ): 0.5; volatility parameter for the interest rate (σ_2): 0.078; and correlation coefficient (ρ): −0.2.
† Yield spreads between 9%, 10-year callable corporate bonds and comparable non-callable Treasury bonds.

5. Critical boundary for the optimal call policy for a 9% coupon bond

The bond will be called if the current interest rate falls to the boundary at the appropriate debt ratio (P/V) for the corporate bond

In equation (7), we have assumed for simplicity that K is the fixed call price at which the firm has the right to call the bond.[21] Typically, the call price declines to the par value over time.

The valuation equation (4), subject to equations (3), (5), (6) and (7), is solved numerically by the alternating direction implicit method, and the values of callable corporate bonds are presented in Table 4. The parameter values chosen are the same as those for non-callable bonds. The call price K was assumed to be equal to the par value of the bond. From Table 4, one can see that the total yield spread between a 10-year, 9% corporate bond and a comparable non-callable Treasury bond is 103 bp when the debt ratio is 42% and the interest rate is 9%. For the same parameter configuration, as Table 2 shows, the yield spread between a non-callable corporate bond and a non-callable Treasury bond is 81 bp. Therefore, we may conclude that out of 103 bp, only 22 bp can be attributable to the call provision of the bond. A significant part of the yield spread on callable corporate bonds, therefore, appears to be determined by default risk.

For debt ratios of 42 to 28%, the critical interest rate below which the corporate bond is optimally called is plotted in Figure 5. These are cross-sectional views of the critical surface for each debt ratio (this is made necessary because as the firm's value V changes, the debt ratio changes). The optimal call policy of the firm appears to be more sensitive to the interest rate than to the value of the issuing firm.[22] As the value of the firm falls, the critical interest rate also declines. This is consistent with one's intuition: at low firm values, the issuing firm waits much longer before calling the bonds. The trade-off here is that a decision to call forces an immediate cash outflow but relieves the firm of its (now) high coupon obligations.

The term structure of total yield spreads on a callable corporate bond (defined as the difference between the yield on the callable corporate bond and that on the straight default-free bond) is plotted in Figures 6, 7 and 8 for different debt ratios. The shape of the curves is the same regardless of the debt ratios, although the level of yield spreads is high when the debt ratio is high. This is in contrast to the results for non-callable bonds (see, for example, Figure 4) where the yield spread increases with maturity over a wider range. In Figures 6, 7 and 8, the yield spreads go through a maximum, hinting at a stronger interaction between call provisions and default risk at longer maturities. As the interest rates tend to very high values, the spreads decrease – but as the rates tend to go down, the incentive to call increases *and* the present value of default risk tends to increase. If the firm is solvent, the former effect dominates the latter. Otherwise, the firm defaults and loses the option to call. Note that both effects serve to increase the spread over non-callable Treasury bonds. This is exactly what we observe in Figures 6, 7 and 8.

We can compare this total spread with the yield spread on the non-callable corporate bonds that were analysed numerically in section two, and hence study the effect of the call provision. In order to isolate the effect of the call provision, however, it is necessary to estimate the impact of call provisions on default-free Treasury bonds. Given Assumptions (A0) and (A2) in first section, the value of a callable Treasury bond will depend on the single state variable r, and also the call policy employed by the Treasury. Just as in the case of the callable corporate bond, the value of the callable, coupon-bearing Treasury bond, denoted $H(r, \tau; c)$, will satisfy a valuation equation and reflect an optimal call policy $R^*(\tau)$. This valuation equation (which is equivalent to setting H_v to zero in relation (4)) and the associated boundary conditions are:[23]

$$\frac{1}{2}\sigma_2^2 r H_{rr} + \kappa(\mu - r)H_r - rH + c = H_\tau \qquad (8)$$

$$H(r, \tau = 0; c) = P \qquad (9)$$

$$\lim_{r \to \infty} H(r, \tau; c) = 0 \qquad (10)$$

$$H(R^*(\tau), \tau; c) = K \qquad (11)$$

The market value of the callable government bond is obtained by choosing $R^*(\tau)$ that minimises $H(r, \tau; c)$. The optimal call policy is, obviously, endogenous to the valuation problem.[24]

The valuation equation (8), subject to the boundary conditions (9) through (11), is solved by the finite difference implicit method to obtain the value of the callable government bond. The parameter values chosen are the same as those for the non-callable government bond. The contribution of the Treasury's call provision to the promised yield to maturity is measured by the difference in the yield to maturity between the callable government bond and the straight government bond. This turned out to be equal to about 45 bp for a 10-year, 9% coupon bond. This is *larger* than the yield differential between the callable corporate bond and the non-callable corporate bond which is 22 bp for comparable coupon and maturity. Thus, the call feature interacts with the risk of default in determining the total yield spread on a callable corporate bond. Our analysis suggests that the call feature reduces the value of government bonds by more than it reduces that of corporate bond, *ceteris paribus*.[25]

Figure 5 plots the critical level of interest rates below which the government bond is called optimally, and shows this to be a monotone decreasing function of time to maturity. With longer time to maturity, default-free bonds are called at lower interest rates. Comparing it with the critical interest

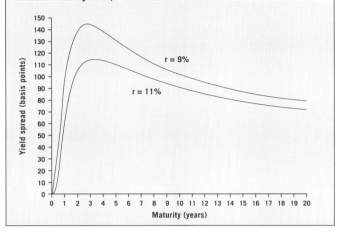

6. Total yield spreads versus maturity for a callable 9% coupon bond

The debt ratio is fixed at 0.42; the total yield spread is the difference between the yields of a callable corporate bond and a comparable non-callable Treasury bond; r is the current interest rate

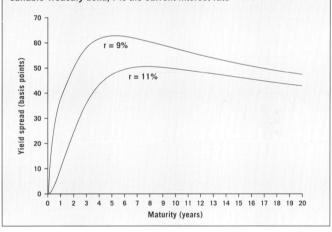

7. Total yield spreads versus maturity for a callable 9% coupon bond

The debt ratio is fixed at 0.33; the total yield spread is the difference between the yields of a callable corporate bond and a comparable non-callable Treasury bond; r is the current interest rate

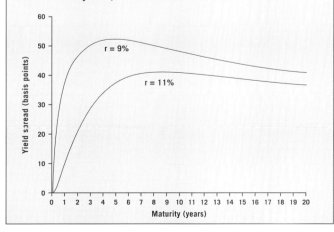

8. Total yield spreads versus maturity for a callable 9% coupon bond

The debt ratio is fixed at 0.28; the total yield spread is the difference between the yields of a callable corporate bond and a comparable non-callable Treasury bond; r is the current interest rate

DOES DEFAULT RISK
IN COUPONS AFFECT
THE VALUATION OF
CORPORATE BONDS?
– A CONTINGENT
CLAIMS MODEL

Table 5. The value* and yield spreads† (bp) on 9% callable Treasury bonds with call protection

Interest rate (r) (%)	Time to maturity (years)			
	5	10	15	20
5	NA‡	105.50	106.48	107.02
	NA	49	13	7
6	NA	103.77	104.70	105.23
	NA	26	13	7
7	NA	102.08	102.95	103.48
	NA	26	13	7
8	99.26	100.42	101.24	101.75
	62	26	13	7
9	98.20	98.79	99.56	100.06
	50	26	13	7
10	96.98	97.18	97.90	98.39
	41	25	13	8
11	95.69	95.60	96.28	96.76
	35	25	13	7
12	94.37	94.05	94.69	95.15
	31	24	13	7
13	93.03	92.52	93.12	93.57
	21	23	13	7
14	91.68	91.02	91.58	92.03
	23	24	13	8
15	90.33	89.55	90.07	90.51
	22	23	13	7

*Solution to the valuation equations (8), (9), (10) and (11) with the following parameter values: Face value (P): $100; call price (K): $100; long-run mean rate of interest (μ): 9%; speed of adjustment parameter (κ): 0.5; volatility parameter for the interest rate (σ_2): 0.078.
†Yield spreads between 9%, 10-year callable Treasury bonds which are callable during the last five years, and comparable non-callable Treasury bonds.
‡It is optimal to call the bonds.

rates for a callable corporate bond, we find that the critical level of interest rates is lower for the corporate bond. As default risk serves to *reduce* the value of the corporate bond, it takes lower interest rates to raise the value of the corporate bond to the call price.

All callable Treasury bonds have a call protection period which is in effect until the bonds have five years or less to maturity. To study its impact, we solved the valuation equation for Treasury bonds with and without the call protection period. Table 5 summarises the results when the bonds have a call protection feature. Corresponding to interest rates of 7%, 9% and 11%, these results for a 10-year Treasury bond may be contrasted with the yield to maturity of Treasury bonds without the protection feature in Table 4. With the call protection, yields are lower, *ceteris paribus*, since the protection feature works to the advantage of the buyers. The bond may sell *above* par (which is the call price) at sufficiently low interest rates: at r = 7%, the bond sells at 102.08, whereas the bond without call protection sells at 99.78. The yield spreads widen as the interest rates drop. Again, this is intuitive: the protection feature is most valuable under such circumstances.

We are now in a position to isolate the interaction between the call provision and default risk. It is instructive to do this by example. We consider a Treasury bond and a corporate bond, both with ten years to maturity when the current short rate is 9%. For the corporate bond, the debt ratio is 42%. Here is a summary of the yields to maturity for callable and non-callable bonds:

Security	Yield to maturity (%)
Straight government bond	8.93
Callable government bond	9.38
Straight corporate bond	9.74
Callable corporate bond	9.96

The total spread defined as the yield differential between the callable corporate bond and the straight government bond is 103 bp. The difference in the yield to maturity

DOES DEFAULT RISK
IN COUPONS AFFECT
THE VALUATION OF
CORPORATE BONDS?
– A CONTINGENT
CLAIMS MODEL

between the straight corporate bond and the straight government bond measures the portion of total spread that can be attributable to default risk: it is 81 bp. The contribution of the call provision to the total premiums is 45 bp and is the yield differential between the callable government bond and the straight government bond. Therefore, 81 + 45 – 103 = 23 bp is attributable to interaction between the call provision and default risk. These reductions in yield differentials due to interaction between the call provision and default risk are summarised in Table 6. Larger reductions are associated with higher debt ratios and lower interest rates.

Table 6. The effect of interaction* (bp) between default risk and call provision on the yield spread of 9%, 10-year callable corporate bonds[†]

Firm value	Interest rate (r)		
(V)	7%	9%	11%
200	51	34	27
220	43	28	20
240	37	23	16
260	30	18	12
280	24	15	9
300	19	12	8
320	14	9	5
340	10	7	4
360	7	6	3
380	6	5	2
400	4	3	2

*The interaction is the reduction in the total yield spread of a callable corporate bond due to the presence of the call provision. It is computed by subtracting the corporate bond's call premium from the Treasury bond's call premium.

[†] The following parameter values are used to compute the yields to maturity: Face value (P): 100; recovery factor (δ) = 0.8; call price (K): 100; volatility parameter for the firm value (σ_1): 0.15; net cashflow ratio (γ): 0.05; long-run mean rate of interest (μ): 9%; speed of adjustment parameter (κ): 0.5; volatility parameter for the interest rate (σ_2): 0.078; and correlation coefficient (ρ): –0.2.

Summary

We have developed a corporate bond valuation model which incorporates some important real world features. We have modelled stochastic interest rates and the importance of cashflow shortages in precipitating bankruptcy. The payoffs in bankruptcy in the real world are very complex. We have chosen a simple specification in order to demonstrate the viability of the contingent claims approach. The approach presented here is internally consistent and plausible in terms of generating the empirically observable magnitude of yield spreads on corporate bonds. The results also imply some testable implications for the shape of the term structure of yield spreads.

Stochastic interest rates seem to play an important role in determining the yield differentials between a callable corporate bond and an equivalent government bond due to the interactions between call provisions and default risk. This suggests that care should be taken in interpreting empirical results regarding the effect of default risk on the values of callable corporate bonds.

1 *Similar conclusions have been reported by Ramaswamy and Sundaresan for corporate floating rate instruments.*

2 *See Jones, Mason and Rosenfeld [1983], (1984) for a discussion of complicated capital structures. A useful discussion of this technique is in Cox and Rubinstein (1985, Ch. 7); see also Fisher (1984).*

3 *Black and Cox (1976) and Jones, Mason and Rosenfeld (1984) have discussed the implications of multiple issues of debt and "me-first" rules in this context.*

4 *An added advantage of this choice is that it permits the use of known solutions for the price of default-free, pure discount bonds to arrive at the value of coupon-bearing Treasuries, which are needed in defining the boundary conditions to our valuation problem. The parameters for this process have been estimated by Cox, Ingersoll and Ross (1979) and by Brown and Dybvig (1986).*

5 *Recall that net cashflow should be interpreted as the total cashflow less the optimal investment outlay, and is exogenous. This rules out the possibility that it might be in the interest of stockholders to deviate from optimal investment policy in order to avoid bankruptcy. With perfect information, if bondholders and shareholders agree on what cashflow is, it is not possible for shareholders to avoid bankruptcy by deviating from optimal investment policy.*

6 *In practice, bond covenants are also stated in terms of stock (as opposed to flow) variables, such as accounting net worth. In the contingent claims setting used here, it is difficult to impose these conditions.*

7 *Cox and Rubinstein (1985, pp. 402, 403) discuss the use of call provisions to circumvent some indenture provisions that might be restrictive on shareholders.*

8 *In the development of equation (4), we can admit a proportional factor risk premium for interest rate*

DOES DEFAULT RISK
IN COUPONS AFFECT
THE VALUATION OF
CORPORATE BONDS?
– A CONTINGENT
CLAIMS MODEL

risk. We have set the factor risk premium to zero, although our simulations indicate that our results are not sensitive to this specification.

9 *The face amount of the senior debt in the portfolio must be specified carefully. See, for example, Cox and Rubinstein (1985).*

10 *In the valuation of LBOs, our model may be used in the following way. As junior debt is issued to repurchase equity, wealth transfer begins to take effect across different security holders. By the Modigliani-Miller theorem, the total value of the issuing firm must remain the same. Therefore, the amount of junior debt that must be issued to effect an LBO is the outcome of an iterative process. Computationally, we must iterate with varying levels of junior debt issues and look for the fixed point where the value of junior debt issued just equals the value of equity that is outstanding.*

11 *The steady state density of* r *is a gamma; and the conditional distribution of* r(s) *given* r(t), s > t, *is a non-central Chi-square.*

12 *This value of* γ *is appropriate for a firm with a 30% debt ratio, a coupon rate of 9%, and a dividend yield of 3.5%. That is,* $\gamma = (0.3)(0.09) + (0.7)(0.035) = 0.0515$. *We report below the effect of varying* γ *around 0.05.*

13 *Keeping* $\delta(\tau) = 0.8$ *and retaining Assumption (A4) and equation (6), which relate to the boundary conditions at bankruptcy and expiration, will give rise to a discontinuity at expiration. We have found, however, that shapes and levels of yield curves are relatively unaffected by this specification, especially at longer maturities.*

14 *The ratio* B/V *might be an economically more meaningful measure of capital structure. We choose the ratio* P/V *as a measure of capital structure in order to examine the term structure of yield spreads for a given capital structure because the ratio* B/V *is dependent on* r *and* τ, *and will not be constant as these variables change.*

15 *Note that this model will permit the sale of assets to meet coupon payments in order to remain feasible.*

16 *It might be more useful to construct the term structure of yield spreads using Treasury and corporate bonds of various maturities, all selling at par. For this purpose, it is necessary to find coupon rates that give rise to par value for bonds. In the context of our model, this is not feasible because the value of corporate bonds for a given short-term interest rate and a given capital structure is not a monotonic function of coupon rates. We have varied the coupon levels, and we find that the resulting shapes of the term structure spreads are not sensitive to coupon rates around the coupon rate of 9%.*

17 *This phenomenon is sometimes called the "crisis at maturity".*

18 *In order to save space, we do not report the results from changing various parameter values. These results are available from the authors.*

19 *We have also computed yield spreads on non-callable (and callable) bonds generated from Merton's model with stochastic interest rates but with standard asset sales and bankruptcy rules. A comparison of these results with those reported in Table 1 shows that stochastic interest rates serve to increase the yields-to-maturity of both corporate and Treasury bonds but leave the yield spread relatively unchanged. This conclusion is also warranted if the bonds are callable.*

20 *Vu (1986) has studied call behaviour using a sample of non-convertible called bonds. He reports among other things that bond prices are, on average, slightly below the call price at the time of the call announcement. Ingersoll (1977) pointed out that, in practice, firms do not seem to follow the theoretically optimal policy in calling convertible bonds. This issue has been re-examined in recent years.*

21 *The optimality of the call policy* {C(τ), R(τ)} *is ensured by the smooth-pasting condition*

$$\lim_{\{V, r\} \to \{C(\tau), R(\tau)\}} G_v = \lim_{\{V, r\} \to \{C(\tau), R(\tau)\}} G_r = 0$$

22 *The optimal call policy is more sensitive to interest rates than to firm value in the sense that if the interest rate is fixed, it takes extremely high firm value to make the call worthwhile. In some cases, no matter how high firm value is, it will not be optimal to call the bond. When the interest rate is higher than seven per cent, it is suboptimal to call 10-year or longer maturity bonds regardless of the value of the firm.*

23 *Equation (9) says that, at maturity, the bond must sell at par. As* r $\to \infty$, *the bond becomes worthless, which is reflected in equation (10). Finally, at the critical interest rate, the bond must sell for the call price as shown in equation (11).*

24 *The smooth-pasting condition which guarantees the optimality of the call policy is*

$$\lim_{r \to R^*(\tau)} H_r = 0$$

DOES DEFAULT RISK
IN COUPONS AFFECT
THE VALUATION OF
CORPORATE BONDS?
– A CONTINGENT
CLAIMS MODEL

25 We should be careful to point out that the comparison with an "otherwise similar" government has been made using equal coupon and maturity. Because bankruptcy would effectively shorten the term of a bond, even if the corporate bond were default-free, the corporate bond in our formulation may be repaid prematurely – so the corporate bond's duration would not be equal to that of a "comparable" Treasury bond.

BIBLIOGRAPHY

Altman, E. I., and S. A. Nammacher, 1985, *The Default Rate Experience on High Yield Corporate Debt,* Morgan Stanley monograph, March.

Black, F., and J. C. Cox, 1976, "Valuing Corporate Securities: Some Effects of Bond Indenture Provisions", *Journal of Finance* May, pp. 351-67.

Black, F., and M. Scholes, 1973, "The Pricing of Options and Corporate Liabilities", *Journal of Political Economy* January/March, pp. 637-59.

Brennan, M. J., and E. S. Schwartz, 1978, "Finite Difference Methods and Jump Processes Arising in the Pricing of Contingent Claims: A Synthesis", *Journal of Financial and Quantitative Analysis* September, pp. 461-74.

Brennan, M. J., and E. S. Schwartz, 1980, "Analyzing Convertible Bonds", *Journal of Financial and Quantitative Analysis* November, pp. 907-29.

Brown, S., and P. Dybvig, 1986, "The Empirical Implications of the Cox, Ingersoll, Ross Theory of the Term Structure of Interest", *Journal of Finance* July, pp. 617-32.

Cox, J. C., J. E. Ingersoll, Jr., and S. A. Ross, 1979, "Duration and the Measurement of Basis Risk," *Journal of Business* January, pp. 51-61.

Cox, J. C., J. E. Ingersoll, Jr., and S. A. Ross, 1985, "A Theory of the Term Structure of Interest Rates," *Econometrica* March, pp. 385-407.

Cox, J. C., J. E. Ingersoll, Jr., and S. A. Ross, 1981, "A Reexamination of the Traditional Hypotheses of the Term Structure of Interest Rates", *Journal of Finance* September, pp. 769-99.

Cox, J. C., and M. Rubinstein, 1985, *Option Markets* (Englewood Cliffs, NJ: Prentice-Hall).

Fama, E. F., 1986, "Term Premiums and Default Premiums in Money Markets", *Journal of Financial Economics* September, pp. 175-96.

Fisher, L., 1984, "Discussion", *Journal of Finance* July, pp. 625-7.

Franks, J. R., and W. N. Torous, 1989, "An Empirical Investigation of U.S. Firms in Reorganization", *Journal of Finance* July, pp. 747-69.

Ingersoll, J. E., 1977, "A Contingent-Claims Valuation of Convertible Securities", *Journal of Financial Economics* May, pp. 289-322.

Jones, E. P., S. P. Mason, and E. Rosenfeld, 1983, "Contingent Claims Valuation of Corporate Liabilities: Theory and Empirical Tests", National Bureau of Economic Research, Working paper, 1143.

Jones, E. P., S. P. Mason, and E. Rosenfeld, 1984, "Contingent Claims Analysis of Corporate Capital Structures: An Empirical Investigation", *Journal of Finance* July, pp. 611-25.

Merton, R. C., 1973, "Theory of Rational Option Pricing", *Bell Journal of Economics and Management Science* Spring, pp. 141-83.

Merton, R. C., 1974, "On the Pricing of Corporate Debt: The Risk Structure of Interest Rates", *Journal of Finance* May, pp. 449-69.

Miller, M., and F. Modigliani, 1958, "The Cost of Capital, Corporation Finance and the Theory of Finance", *American Economic Review* June, pp. 261-97.

Ramaswamy, K., and S. Sundaresan, 1986, "The Valuation of Floating Rate Instruments: Theory and Evidence", *Journal of Financial Economics* December, pp. 251-72.

Richard, S. F., 1978, "An Arbitrage Model of the Term Structure of Interest Rates", *Journal of Financial Economics* March, pp. 33-57.

Smith, C. W., and J. Warner, 1979, "On Financial Contracting: An Analysis of Bond Indenture Provisions", *Journal of Financial Economics* June, pp. 175-219.

Vu, J. D., 1986, "An Empirical Investigation of Calls of Non-Convertible Bonds", *Journal of Financial Economics* June, pp. 235-66.

The Pricing of Risky Debt When Interest Rates Are Stochastic

David C. Shimko, Naohiko Tejima and Donald R. van Deventer

Bankers Trust; Kamakura Corporation; Kamakura Corporation

Determination of a corporation's cost of debt capital is an important exercise for both corporate treasurers and bankers. Term structure models have been widely applied to determine the term premium component in bond prices – Vasicek (1977), Cox, Ingersoll and Ross (1985), and Longstaff and Schwartz (1992) represent a short list.

Relatively less academic attention has been paid to the credit component of the cost of capital, however. Option-based models have been applied to corporate debt in order to understand the effects of credit variables on the spread. For example, a pioneering study by Merton (1974) adapts the Black–Scholes option pricing model to the pricing of risky discount debt. In spite of the assumption of a constant interest rate, Merton's model yields important insights into the determinants of the credit spread.

This chapter generalises Merton's risky debt pricing model to allow for stochastic interest rates. In this model, we examine the combined effect of term structure variables and credit variables on debt pricing.

To emphasise the marginal impact of the term structure volatility and correlation effects, we retain the structure of Merton's model, but generalise it to allow for stochastic interest rates as in Vasicek (1977). In Merton's model, the value of corporate assets follows a stationary lognormal process, and interest rates are assumed constant. In the Vasicek model, interest rates follow a mean-reverting process with constant volatility. Surprisingly, Merton's (1973) earlier valuation of options with stochastic interest rates and time-varying volatility can then be applied to find a closed-form expression for the value of risky debt.

Our bond pricing equation yields comparative static results that are consistent with Merton's: the credit premium increases with the face value of the debt and the volatility of the assets, and decreases with the value of corporate assets. Supplementing Merton's observations, we find that the credit spread is an increasing function of the (risk-free) term structure volatility for reasonable parameter values. Term structure effects, however, can cause the sign of the derivative to change.

We also find that changes in the correlation between interest rates and asset value may have a positive or negative impact on the credit spread; the comparative statics are parameter-sensitive. For reasonable parameter values, as the correlation increases, the credit spread increases.

Our analysis allows us to explore a series of critical issues that managers of financial institutions and financial managers of corporations face. These questions are fundamental to their task.

This paper was originally published by Institutional Investor in The Journal of Fixed Income, *September, 1993. The authors appreciate the helpful comments of Kamakura Corporation colleagues Ken Adams, Noriko Honda, Yuichiro Inagaki and Tony Kobauyashi.*

For example, how does the correlation between a bank's credit risk and interest rate movements affect its borrowing cost? What maturity debt (or face value) should a corporate treasurer issue to minimise fluctuations in the value of the corporation's stock price? How much capital should be allocated to activities within a bank that vary both in absolute degree of credit risk and in the correlation of that risk with movements in interest rate risks?

Options theory and the valuation of risky debt: Merton's model

We start by looking at a simplified case of a bank (or a corporation) whose assets have a market value V. The value of assets V is assumed to be uncertain because of factors such as basic business risk, credit risk, foreign exchange risk or the price risk of marketable securities held by the organisation. We ignore the existence of deposit insurance in some banking markets, such as the United States. We assume that the returns on the bank's assets are instantaneously normal, ie, that returns on the bank's assets follow the stochastic process:

$$\frac{dV}{V} = \alpha\, dt + \sigma_v\, dz_1$$

where α and σ are the constant drift and volatility of asset values.

This assumption, while commonly applied to corporate assets, is at best an approximation for the stochastic process followed by bank assets. For example, banks own fixed-income assets that by construction will not follow geometric Brownian motion processes.

For purposes of exposition, we initially assume that the risk-free interest rate is constant; this replicates Merton's results so that they may be compared to our results. (In the next section, we extend this approach to the case of stochastic risk-free interest rates.) We assume that the bank's assets are financed at time t by the issuance of zero-coupon bonds with principal B that is due to mature at time T. We also assume there are no cash distributions to equity until time T.

Given the risk inherent in the bank's balance sheet, what should be the pricing on this risky debt? In the words of a bank treasurer, what should be the spread to Treasuries (the risk-free rate) on the bank's debt?

We begin by assuming perfect markets, free of transaction costs, taxes and information differences among participants. In this Modigliani–Miller (1958) environment, the market value of the firm is the sum of debt and equity values; the value of the firm is independent of capital structure. We assume that all of the firm's assets can be or will be converted costlessly to cash at time T. If the value of the firm's assets at time T is greater than the principal value of the zero-coupon debt B, then the bonds will be paid off in full; otherwise, debtors receive the firm's assets.

The value of equity at time T is therefore

$$E = \max[V_T - B, 0]$$

The equity of the firm is equivalent to a call option on the assets of the firm.

Assuming that V can be traded or perfectly replicated, the well-known Black–Scholes call option pricing formula on an asset with value V, volatility σ, time to maturity τ, strike price B and riskless rate of interest r is

$$\text{Equity value} = VN(d_1) - Be^{-r\tau}N(d_2)$$

where

$$d_1 = \frac{\ln\left(\dfrac{V}{B}\right) + \left(r + \tfrac{1}{2}\sigma^2\right)\tau}{\sigma\sqrt{\tau}}$$

$$d_2 = d_1 - \sigma\sqrt{\tau}$$

where $N(z)$ is the cumulative normal density evaluated at z. Since the value of the firm consists only of debt and equity, the value of the risky debt is

$$D = VN(h_1) + Be^{-r\tau}N(h_2)$$

where

$$h_1 = \frac{\ln\left(\dfrac{Be^{-r\tau}}{V}\right) - \frac{1}{2}\sigma^2\tau}{\sigma\sqrt{\tau}}$$

$$h_2 = -h_1 - \sigma\sqrt{\tau}$$

The required rate of return on debt is given by

$$r_D = -\frac{1}{\tau}\ln\left(\frac{D}{B}\right)$$

It is well known that the credit spread, $r_D - r$, increases with the face value of the debt and the volatility of the assets and decreases with the value of the assets. For a more detailed derivation and discussion of this issue, see Ingersoll (1987) or Uyemura and van Deventer (1992).

The pricing of risky debt with stochastic interest rates

By making use of Merton's (1973) model for the pricing of options with stochastic interest rates, the pricing of risky debt can be extended to the case of stochastic risk-free interest rates. Merton's valuation formula for options when interest rates are stochastic is predicated on the assumption that the instantaneous variance of the return on a risk-free zero-coupon bond depends only on time to maturity, and "is otherwise assumed to be nonstochastic and independent of the level of P", the price of a risk-free bond. This requirement is consistent with the term structure model of Vasicek (1977), but not the models of Cox, Ingersoll and Ross (1985) or Longstaff and Schwartz (1992).

In order to take advantage of Merton's work, we assume that the risk-free term structure is consistent with the Vasicek model. The Vasicek model assumes that the short-term riskless interest rate is mean-reverting to long-run mean γ at speed k, and that its instantaneous volatility (σ_r) is constant:

$$dr = k(\gamma - r)dt + \sigma_r dz_2$$

The Vasicek model suffers from the implicit assumption that, at any given time, the future instantaneous interest rates are normally distributed. While this implies the possibility of negative interest rates in future time periods, this liability is offset by the Hull and White (1992) observation that the modified Vasicek model can be used to fit any observable term structure. They note that the Cox, Ingersoll and Ross model (1985), which avoids the possibility of negative interest rates, is unfortunately not sufficiently general to fit all possible term structures.

When movements in the short-term interest rate take the Vasicek form, the price of a zero-coupon bond is priced according to the Vasicek formula:

$$P(\tau) = \exp\left[\frac{1-e^{-k\tau}}{k}\left(R(\infty)-r\right) - \tau R(\infty) - \frac{\sigma_r^2}{4k^3}\left(1-e^{-k\tau}\right)^2\right]$$

where

$$R(\infty) = \gamma + \frac{\sigma_r}{k}\lambda - \frac{1}{2}\frac{\sigma_r^2}{k^2}$$

Note that lambda is the market price of risk for such risk-free bonds and must be independent of the bond maturity for no-arbitrage assumptions to prevail. We also assume that the stochastic factors driving the instantaneous returns on bank assets and movements in the instantaneous risk-free interest rates are correlated:

$$dz_1 dz_2 = \rho dt$$

The value of risky debt when interest rates are stochastic can be written:

$$F = V - VN(h_1) + BP(\tau)N(h_2)$$

where

$$\delta(s) = -\frac{1 - e^{-ks}}{k} \sigma_r$$

$$v^2(s) = \sigma_v^2 + \delta(s)^2 - 2\rho\sigma_v \delta(s)$$

$$T = \int_0^\tau v(s)^2 ds$$

$$= \tau\left(\sigma_v^2 + \frac{\sigma_r^2}{k^2} + \frac{2\rho\sigma_v\sigma_r}{k}\right) + \left(e^{-k\tau} - 1\right)\left(\frac{2\sigma_r^2}{k^3} + \frac{2\rho\sigma_r\sigma_v}{k^2}\right) - \frac{\sigma_r^2}{2k^3}\left(e^{-2k\tau} - 1\right)$$

and

$$h_1 = \frac{\ln\left(\dfrac{V}{P(\tau)B}\right) + \frac{1}{2}T}{\sqrt{T}}$$

$$h_2 = h_1 - \sqrt{T}$$

$N(z)$ is the cumulative normal distribution function; $\delta(s)^2$ is the instantaneous variance of the Vasicek model risk-free zero-coupon bond with maturity s; $v(s)^2$ is the instantaneous variance of the risky debt function F; and T is the integrated instantaneous variance of the risky debt function F over the life of the risky bond.

This intuitive derivation of the value of risky debt when rates are stochastic can be evaluated more formally by deriving the appropriate partial differential equation for risky debt pricing. The value of risky debt is a function of two stochastic factors V and r. One can use Itô's lemma and the standard no-arbitrage arguments to show that F must satisfy the partial differential equation

$$F_t + \frac{1}{2}F_{vv}V^2\sigma_v^2 + \frac{1}{2}F_{rr}\sigma_r^2 + F_{rv}\rho\sigma_r\sigma_v V + F_{r[k(\gamma-r)-\lambda]} - rF + rF_v V = 0$$

At maturity, the value of risky debt F must equal the smaller of the face value of the debt or the value of bank assets:

$$F(\tau = 0) = \min(B, V)$$

One can show that this solution satisfies the standard partial differential equation and the associated boundary condition.

Implications of the risky debt formula

A corporate treasurer or senior manager at a commercial bank is likely to ask some corporate finance strategy questions. How does leverage impact the "spread", the difference between the yield on the firm's risky debt and the corresponding maturity risk-free bond? How does the volatility of interest rates impact this credit spread? How does the riskiness of the underlying assets impact credit spread? How does the correlation of credit risk with interest rate risk impact financing costs? What maturity debt

...

should be selected to minimise the volatility of the firm's equity? How much capital should be allocated to finance assets of different riskiness so that the cost of debt financing for each asset class will be equal?

We address each of these issues in turn. We note that the debt issued by this hypothetical bank or corporation is zero-coupon debt with no covenants that would allow the debt holder to trigger bankruptcy, no matter what value assets may have prior to the maturity of the debt. We assume that the value of assets V is initially 100, and that debt policy is set by analysing a debt financing amount F at different maturities, which means that the principal amount B (which effectively includes the future value of interest as well as the up-front amount of "principal" F) will be different for each maturity.

The yield on risky debt and the yield on risk-free debt are calculated on a continuous basis, as is the "credit spread", which is equal to the difference between the two rates. The credit spread is algebraically defined as the difference between the continuously compounded (promised) debt yield and the comparable yield on a zero-coupon bond of the same maturity:

$$\text{Credit spread} = r_D - r_p$$
$$= -\ln(D/B)/\tau + \ln(P)/\tau$$
$$= \ln(PB/D)/\tau$$

THE IMPACT OF LEVERAGE

Figure 1 shows the increase in credit spread that results when leverage (the borrowing amount F) is increased from 50% of assets to 95% of assets assuming σ_r is 0.06, σ_v is 0.11, and the correlation between interest rate movements and the asset returns is 0.3. Given these assumptions, the credit spread is monotonically upward-sloping with maturity and with the amount of leverage.

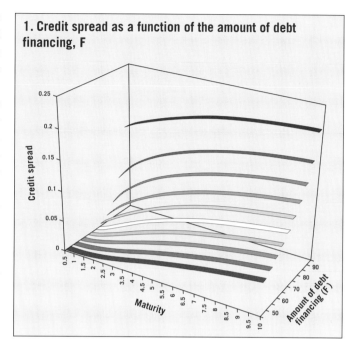

1. Credit spread as a function of the amount of debt financing, F

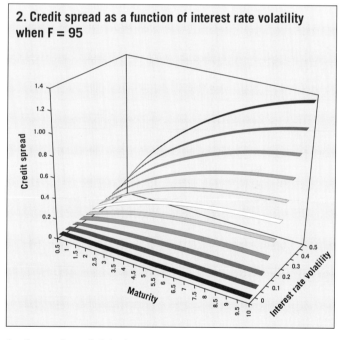

2. Credit spread as a function of interest rate volatility when F = 95

The property that the credit spread increases with the face value of debt is correct regardless of parameter choice. For some parameter choices, however, credit spread declines with debt maturity.

THE IMPACT OF INTEREST RATE VOLATILITY

Given the same base case assumptions and a financing amount F equal to 95%, increases in the volatility of the instantaneous risk-free interest rate dramatically increases the credit spread shown in Figure 2. This directional result is not universally correct. Changes in interest rate volatility affect the volatility of bond returns through changes in the slope of the term structure and through the correlation of interest rate changes with asset value changes. Of course, for prespecified parameter values, the partial derivative can be signed.

THE IMPACT OF ASSET VOLATILITY

Figures 3 and 4 show the impact of increasing asset volatility on the credit spread. Figure 3 shows the kind of monotonic increase in credit spread one might expect, both with

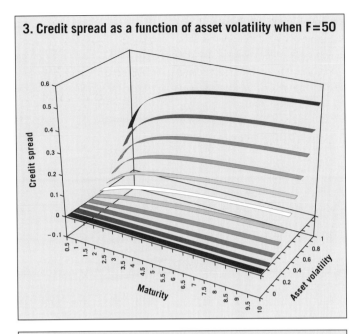

3. Credit spread as a function of asset volatility when F=50

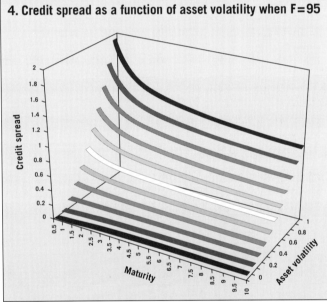

4. Credit spread as a function of asset volatility when F=95

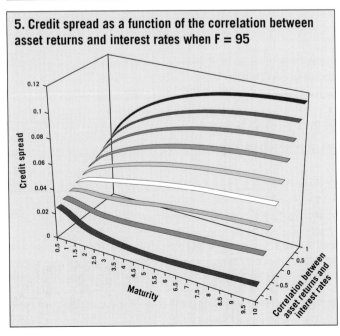

5. Credit spread as a function of the correlation between asset returns and interest rates when F = 95

respect to maturity and the amount of asset volatility. Figure 4 shows clearly, however, that the credit spread may well decrease with maturity if asset volatility is high enough and leverage (represented by F) is also high.

CORRELATION BETWEEN ASSET RETURNS AND INTEREST RATES

Figure 5 confirms that the impact of correlation between asset returns and the instantaneous interest rate increases credit spread for the base case assumptions as correlation increases, but it also demonstrates that credit spread need not increase with maturity if the correlation is strongly negative.

IMPLICATIONS FOR THE MINIMUM-RISK FUNDING STRATEGY

A commonly held assumption among corporate treasurers and bank management is that the "zero risk" funding strategy is for the maturity of the liability issued to be matched to the maturity of the asset being financed. In the context of our model, what does "zero risk" mean?

We take the zero-risk funding strategy to be the funding strategy that eliminates short-term interest rate volatility from the equity return. This leaves the part of asset volatility that is uncorrelated with interest rates unhedged.

Using Itô's lemma, and forcing the asset and debt sensitivities to interest rate changes to be identical in dollar terms, we find this implicit relation is satisfied at the minimum-risk point:

$$B = \frac{\left[1 - N(h_1)\right]\sigma_v \, \rho k V}{P\sigma_r N(h_2)\left(1 - e^{-k\tau}\right)}$$

That is to say, there exist combinations of face value and maturity for debt that eliminate interest rate risk for equity holders.

This formula shows that the minimum-risk funding strategy depends on the correlation between "credit risk" and the risk-free interest rate, as well as other parameters of the model. In general, that means that a strategy of matching maturities will *not* produce the minimum-risk funding strategy.

Using the risky debt formula for capital allocation and capital adequacy

The Bankers Trust Company has long used a formula labelled "risk-adjusted return on capital" to judge the internal profitability of diverse banking activities on a risk-equalised basis. This concept is explained at length in Uyemura and van Deventer (1992).

Briefly, each unit i within the organisation conducts business that results in cashflows with a standard deviation of S_i dollars per year. "Capital adequacy" is measured by determining the amount of capital necessary to assure that the unit on a standalone basis has a 99% probability of remaining solvent. Returns on the business activity are measured by calculating returns related to this risk-adjusted capital figure. The Bank for International Settlements capital adequacy regulations, as implemented by the Federal Reserve Board, are intended to achieve the same objective, although the regulations are set at arbitrary risk-weight levels.

How can the risky debt formula above be used for capital allocation? There are three steps in the process:

❑ Select the time frame for the analysis (say, one year).
❑ Choose B, the face amount of zero-coupon debt in the model, and F so that the continuous yield on cash proceeds of F to earn B in one year is the same as the bank's marginal cost of funds for a one-year horizon.
❑ Select the volatility of interest rates.
❑ Determine the underlying volatility of the asset class and its correlation with movements in the risk-free interest rate.
❑ Solve for V, the value of assets.

The amount of capital that would be allocated to this asset class would be $(V - F)/V$ as a ratio to the value of assets. All asset classes would have the same marginal cost of debt with a one-year maturity. In this sense, the capital ratios are risk-adjusted and properly consider credit risk, interest rate risk and the correlation between them.

Summary and suggestions for future research

We have shown the impact of interest rate movements and credit risk, broadly defined, on the pricing of risky debt. The correlation between interest rate movements and the returns on the underlying asset is clearly an important variable in determining the credit spread on risky debt. The formula has broad implications for financial strategy, optimal maturities in debt financing, and capital adequacy analysis and capital allocation.

This analysis can be extended in various ways. First of all, the analysis of a banking firm's risky debt valuation should not assume lognormality. The value of F given above is not lognormally distributed; a complete analysis of risky debt for banks would assume lognormality of asset returns at the borrower level and use the formula for F as the value of assets V to derive bank debt pricing.

Second, as pointed out by Ingersoll, one cannot conclude that the value of coupon-bearing debt is simply the sum of risky zero-coupon bonds, because each maturity of a zero-coupon bond changes the value of assets V. Nonetheless, the valuation formula for risky debt when rates are stochastic represents an important step forward in understanding the full complexity of credit analysis.

Appendix

DERIVATION OF THE PARTIAL DIFFERENTIAL EQUATION FOR THE PRICING
OF RISKY DEBT FORMULA IN THE VASICEK BOND PRICING MODEL

Let F be the value of the risky bond with maturity τ so $F = F(V, r, B, \tau)$. V is the value of underlying firm assets and r is the instantaneous risk-free interest rate. Using the stochastic processes for r and V and applying Itô's lemma gives this expression for the change in the value of risky debt:

$$dF = F_V\,dV + F_r\,dr + F_t\,dt + \tfrac{1}{2}F_{VV}(dV)^2 + \tfrac{1}{2}F_{rr}(dr)^2 + F_{rV}(dr\,dV)$$

$$= \left[\alpha V F_V + k(\gamma - r)F_r + F_t + \tfrac{1}{2}F_{VV}V^2\sigma_V^2 + \tfrac{1}{2}F_{rr}\sigma_r^2 + F_{rV}\rho\sigma_r\sigma_V V\right]dt$$

$$\quad + \left[F_V\sigma_V V\right]dz_1 + \left[F_r\sigma_r\right]dz_2$$

We then impose no-arbitrage conditions by selecting a portfolio such that interest rate risk and asset risk (credit risk in the case of a bank) are eliminated by taking positions in the underlying asset and the risk-free (except for interest rate risk) bond.

Assume the portfolio includes one unit of the risky bond and w_1 and w_2 units of the asset and riskless bond, respectively.

The value of the portfolio is $Q = F + w_1 V + w_2 P(\tau)$, where the riskless bond has the same maturity as the risky debt. We choose $w_1 = -F_V$. Now $dQ = dF + w_1 dV + w_2 dP$. To eliminate interest rate risk, choose $w_2 = -F_r/P_r$.

Once the portfolio has been made riskless, the instantaneous return on the portfolio must equal the risk-free instantaneous interest rate; dQ must equal $rQdt = r[F - F_V V - F_r/P_r P(\tau)]$, which means that

$$dQ = F_t \, dt + \tfrac{1}{2} F_{VV} V^2 \sigma_V^2 + \tfrac{1}{2} F_{rr} \sigma_r^2 + F_{rV} \rho \sigma_r \sigma_V V - \frac{F_r}{P_r}\left[-P_\tau + \tfrac{1}{2} P_{rr}(dr)^2\right]$$

$$= r\left[F - F_V V - \frac{F_r}{P_r} P(\tau)\right]$$

$$dQ = F_t + \tfrac{1}{2} F_{VV} V^2 \sigma_V^2 + \tfrac{1}{2} F_{rr}\left(\sigma_r\right)^2 + F_{rV} \rho \sigma_r \sigma_V V + \frac{F_r}{P_r} P_\tau - \frac{F_r}{P_r}\left[\tfrac{1}{2} P_{rr} \sigma_r^2\right]$$

$$= r\left[F - F_V V - \frac{F_r}{P_r} P\right]$$

So the fundamental pricing equation is

$$F_t + \tfrac{1}{2} F_{VV} V^2 \sigma_V^2 + \tfrac{1}{2} F_{Vr} \sigma_V^2 + F_{rV} \rho \sigma_r \sigma_V V + \frac{F_r}{P_r} P_\tau - \frac{F_r}{P_r} \tfrac{1}{2} P_{rr} \sigma_r^2 - rF + rF_V V + r\frac{F_r}{P_r} P = 0$$

To avoid riskless arbitrage in the riskless bond market, the expected return less the risk-free rate divided by the bond's volatility has to equal a constant risk aversion parameter lambda. From the partial differential equation for no-arbitrage equilibrium in the riskless bond market, we know

$$\frac{P_r(T)k(\gamma - r) + \tfrac{1}{2} P_{rr}(T) \sigma_r^2 - P_\tau(T) - rP(T)}{P_r(T)} = \lambda$$

We substitute this expression into the equation above to obtain the fundamental partial differential equation for the pricing of risky debt:

$$F_t + \tfrac{1}{2} F_{VV} V^2 \sigma_V^2 + \tfrac{1}{2} F_{rr} \sigma_r^2 + F_{rV} \rho \sigma_r \sigma_V V + F_r\left[k(\gamma - r) - \lambda\right] - rF + rF_V V = 0$$

BIBLIOGRAPHY

Cox, J. C., J. E. Ingersoll, Jr, and S. A. Ross, 1985, "A Theory of the Term Structure of Interest Rates", *Econometrica* 53, pp. 385–407.

Hull, J., and A. White, 1992, "One-Factor Interest Rate Models and the Valuation of Interest Rate Derivative Securities", University of Toronto.

Ingersoll, J., 1987, *Theory of Modern Financial Decision Making* (New York: Rowman & Littlefield Publishers, Inc).

Longstaff, F. A., and E. S. Schwartz, 1992, "Interest Rate Volatility and the Term Structure: A Two-Factor General Equilibrium Model", *Journal of Finance* 47, pp. 1259–82.

Merton, R. C., 1973, "Theory of Rational Option Pricing", *Bell Journal of Economics and Management Science* 4, pp. 141–83.

Merton, R. C., 1974, "On the Pricing of Corporate Debt: The Risk Structure of Interest Rates", *Journal of Finance* 29, pp. 449–70.

Modigliani, F., and M. H. Miller, 1958, "The Cost of Capital, Corporation Finance, and the Theory of Investment", *American Economic Review* 48, pp. 261–97.

Uyemura, D. G., and D. R. van Deventer, 1992, *Financial Risk Management in Banking* (Chicago: Probus Publishing).

Vasicek, O. A., 1977, "An Equilibrium Characterization of the Term Structure", *Journal of Financial Economics* 5, pp. 177–88.

8

Contingent Claims Analysis of Corporate Capital Structures: An Empirical Investigation

E. Philip Jones, Scott P. Mason and Eric Rosenfeld

Graduate School of Management, Rutgers University and Harvard University

In their seminal work Black and Scholes (1973) provide a significant insight which arguably is of more academic and practical value than their famous option pricing model. They demonstrate that corporate liabilities can be viewed as combinations of simple option contracts. This generalisation of option pricing, as refined by Merton (1974, 1977), has become known as Contingent Claims Analysis (CCA). While CCA has subsequently been used by many researchers as a theoretical framework in which to view the pricing of corporate liabilities, its empirical validity remains an open question. Ingersoll (1976, 1977b) has tested the model's ability to predict prices for dual-purpose funds and call policies for convertible bonds respectively. In a recent paper, Jones, Mason and Rosenfeld (1983), we tested CCA in one of its potentially most important applications, namely the valuation of debt in typical corporate capital structures. The objective of Jones, Mason and Rosenfeld (1983) was to test the predictive power of a prototypical model based on the usual set of assumptions in the CCA literature. The database used in Jones, Mason and Rosenfeld (1983) was made up primarily of investment-grade bonds, ie, bond rating of BBB or higher. This chapter extends that test of the prototypical model to a larger database which includes a number of non-investment-grade, or "junk", bonds. In addition, this chapter demonstrates that in the multiple bond problem the value of callable debt need not be a monotonic function of firm value.

Research attempting to explain corporate bond prices has had a long and varied history. One line of research (eg, Sloan (1963) and Jaffee (1975)) can be described as "macro" in that relative bond prices, or yield spreads, are posited to be functions of the supply and demand of various assets, and/or the position of the economy in the business cycle. Another line of research pioneered by Fisher (1959) views relative bond prices, or yield spreads, as functions of firm-specific, or "micro", characteristics such as financial or business risk. Contingent Claims Analysis is consistent with the approach of Fisher (1959) in that the model's inputs can be viewed as measures of financial and business risk. The advantage of CCA over the regression-based analysis of Fisher (1959) is that CCA provides a specific functional relationship to be tested. In addition, given the structure of the CCA model, it is straightforward to infer firm values or other security values from the values of traded claims, and to price different covenant structures separately.

In the second section of this chapter, a brief discussion of the CCA valuation problem for a firm with equity and multiple issues of callable non-convertible sinking fund coupon debt is presented. For such capital structures it is demonstrated that the value

This paper first appeared in The Journal of Finance, *Vol. 39 (3), July 1984, and is reprinted here with the kind permission of Blackwell Publishers.*

CONTINGENT
CLAIMS ANALYSIS
OF CORPORATE
CAPITAL
STRUCTURES:
AN EMPIRICAL
INVESTIGATION

of callable debt need not be a monotonic function of firm value. The data and estimation procedures are discussed in the following section and the fourth section is an analysis of the results.

Theory

The theoretical basis of CCA is developed in Black and Scholes (1973) and Merton (1974, 1977). The usual assumptions made in the CCA literature, eg, Ingersoll (1976, 1977) are:

❑ Perfect markets: The capital markets are perfect with no transaction costs, no taxes and equal access to information for all investors.

❑ Continuous trading

❑ Itô dynamics: The value of the firm, V, satisfies the stochastic differential equation

$$dV = (\alpha V - C)dt + \sigma V dz$$

where total cash outflow per unit time C is locally certain, α and σ^2 are the instantaneous expected rate of return and variance of return on the underlying assets.

❑ Constant σ^2.

❑ Non-stochastic term structure: The instantaneous interest rate $r(t)$ is a known function of time.

❑ Shareholder wealth maximisation: Management acts to maximise shareholder wealth.

❑ Perfect bankruptcy protection: Firms cannot file for protection from creditors except when they are unable to make required cash payments. In this case perfect priority rules govern the distribution of assets to claimants.

❑ Perfect anti-dilution protection: No new securities (other than additional common equity shares) can be issued until all existing non-equity claims are extinguished. Deals between equity and subsets of other claimants are prohibited.

❑ Perfect liquidity: Firms can sell assets as necessary to make cash payouts, with no loss in total value.

Under these assumptions it can be shown that corporate liabilities which are functions of the value of the firm and time obey a partial differential equation which depends on the known schedule of interest rates, $r(t)$, the variance, σ^2, of firm value and indenture provisions, eg, payouts and covenants. More importantly, the CCA pricing of corporate liabilities is not dependent on the equilibrium structure of risk and return, ie, α. Readers are referred to Black and Scholes (1973) and Merton (1974, 1977) for a derivation of the basic partial differential equation.

A starting point for the analysis of typical capital structures is the example of CCA applied to non-convertible corporate bonds, namely the formulation in Merton (1974) of a callable coupon bond with no sinking fund. Merton shows that the debt $D(V, t)$ in a firm with one issue of such debt obeys the following partial differential equation and boundary conditions

$$0 = \tfrac{1}{2}\sigma^2 V^2 D_{vv} + (rV - cP - d)D_v + D_t - rD + cP$$
$$D(0, t) = 0$$
$$D(V, t^*) = \min(V, P)$$
$$D(\bar{V}, t) = k(t)P$$
$$D_v(\bar{V}, t) = 0 \tag{1}$$

where $P = P(t)$ is the outstanding bond principal at time t, c is the coupon rate per unit principal, $k(t)$ is the call price schedule per unit principal, $d = d(V, t)$ is the known dividend policy and t^* is the maturity date of the bond. The upper free boundary, $\bar{V}(t)$, corresponds to the optimal call barrier at or above which the firm will call the bonds. Translating the standard set of assumptions listed above into an explicit model for valuing claims in a typical capital structure is considerably more difficult than suggested by

CONTINGENT

CLAIMS ANALYSIS

OF CORPORATE

CAPITAL

STRUCTURES:

AN EMPIRICAL

INVESTIGATION

equation (1). A typical capital structure consists of equity and multiple issues of callable non-convertible sinking fund coupon debt. This differs from the standard example of a single issue of non-convertible debt because of both the sinking fund and multiple issue features.

Most issues of corporate debt specify the mandatory retirement of bonds via periodic sinking fund payments. Typically the firm is required to required to retire a specified fraction of the initial bonds each period. Generally the firm has the option to redeem these bonds through either of two mechanisms: it can purchase the necessary bonds in the market and deliver them to the trustee, or it can choose the necessary bonds by lot and retire them by paying the standard principal amount to their owners. Often the firm also has the option to double the number of bonds retired each period if it wishes. Hence the firm faces the following choices each period:

❑ Should the bonds be called?

❑ Assuming the bonds are not called, should the mandatory number of bonds be sunk at market or par? (If this option exists.)

❑ Assuming the bonds are not called, should the sinking fund payment be doubled? (If this option exists.)

Unfortunately, incorporating the option to double the sinking fund payment in a capital structure with numerous debt issues dramatically increases the dimensionality of the valuation problem. Therefore, the option to double is ignored in the numerical approximations. This will lead to the underpricing of equity and the overpricing of debt. The reader is referred to Jones, Mason and Rosenfeld (1983) for a full analytic treatment of how the formulation of the debt valuation problem is affected by the presence of sinking funds.

Another major problem in the Contingent Claims Analysis of typical capital structures is the presence of multiple debt issues. This characteristic of typical capital structures introduces interactions among bonds that are not present in the standard example of one debt issue. Of particular importance is the interaction among the optimal call policies of the different bonds. The major complexity is the fact that minimising the market value of a particular bond via a call is not necessarily equivalent to maximising the value of the equity. To see this, consider a firm with two discount bonds of the same maturity and seniority. Let the first bond, D', be non-callable and have a promised principal of B'. Let the second bond, D, be callable at K for just the current point in time (then non-callable) and have a promised principal of B where $K < Be^{-r\tau}$, is the maturity of the bond, and r is the risk-free rate of interest. Given the current firm value, V, and the decision *not* to call D, then the value of the two bonds would be

$$D = \frac{Bg(V, \tau, B + B')}{(B + B')}$$

$$D' = \frac{B'g(V, \tau, B + B')}{(B + B')}$$

(2)

where $g(\cdot)$ is the risky discount bond function of Merton (1974).

Now consider that specific firm value, V^*, where the holder of the callable bond is indifferent to being called, ie,

$$D(V^*, \tau) = \frac{Bg(V^*, \tau, B + B')}{(B + B')} = K$$

$$D'(V^*, \tau) = \frac{B'g(V^*, \tau, B + B')}{(B + B')}$$

(3)

Should the callable bond be called when the firm value is V^*, then the value of the non-

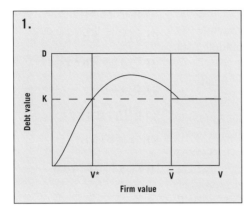

1.

Debt value / D / K

V* / V̄ / V

Firm value

callable bond would be $D'(V^*, \tau) = g(V^* - K, \tau, B')$. The holder of the non-callable bond would strictly prefer the decision to call if $g(V^* - K, \tau, B') > B'g(V^*, \tau, B + B')/(B + B')$, which by the homogeneity of $g(\cdot)$ and the fact that $g_V > 0$ is equivalent to $V^* - K > V^*B'/(B + B')$. But, given (3), this is equivalent to $V^* > g(V^*, \tau, B + B')$, which is always true.

Since the holder of the non-callable bond would strictly prefer a call and, by construction, the holder of the callable bond is indifferent, then the equity would be strictly worse off by calling. Therefore, by continuity, the firm value, V, at which equity would call is greater than V^* and the value of the callable bond, $D(V, \tau)$, can exceed K for $V > V^*$. But this implies that $D(V, \tau)$ will not be monotonic in firm value. To see this consider a $V \gg V^*$. While it is true that the holder of the non-callable bond will always prefer a call for $V > V^*$, as V becomes large the value of the non-callable bond approaches $B'e^{-r\tau}$, the value of a risk-free bond. This restricts the extent to which the non-callable bond can benefit from a call of D and will, for a sufficiently large V, result in the equity capturing some of the benefit. Therefore, as depicted in Figure 1, the value of the callable bond will not be monotonic in firm value.

Thus, in order to identify the optimal call policies, it is necessary to systematically consider all possible capital structure states and to choose that state which will result in the value of equity being maximised. The reader is referred to Jones, Mason and Rosenfeld (1983) for a complete and detailed discussion of this issue. It is important to understand the dimensionality of the n callable bond case. First note that there are 2^n possible capital structure states, including the trivial state of an all-equity firm. Furthermore, there are a number of securities to be valued in each state. Given n callable bonds, there are $\binom{n}{n} = 1$ capital structure states corresponding to no bonds having been called. In this one state there are $n + 1$ securities to be valued. There are $\binom{n}{n-1} = n$ capital structure states corresponding to one bond having been called. In each of these n states there are n securities to be valued. Continuing in this way, we find that there are

$$\sum_{j=0}^{n-1} \binom{n}{n-j} (n + 1 - j)$$

solutions in all. Hence one high priority line of research in terms of applying Contingent Claims Analysis to typical capital structures is the derivation of rational theorems which rule out various capital structure states – eg, which show that certain kinds of bonds are always called first.

Data and methodology

Data were collected for a total of 27 firms on a monthly basis from January 1975 through January 1981 when possible. The firms were selected according to a number of criteria at the beginning of 1975:

❏ Simple Capital Structures (ie, one class of stock, no convertible bonds, small number of debt issues, no preferred stock).

❏ Small proportion of private debt to total capital.

❏ Small proportion of short term notes payable or capitalised leases to total capital.

❏ All publicly traded debt is rated.

Based on these criteria the following firms were selected:

Firm name	Bond rating range
Allied Chemical	Double-A/A
Anheuser Busch	A
Braniff	Triple-B/double-C
Brown Group	A
Bucyrus Erie	A
Champion Spark Plug	Double-B
Cities Service	A
CPC	Double-A/A
Crane	Triple-B
Food Fair	Triple-B/B

CONTINGENT

CLAIMS ANALYSIS

OF CORPORATE

CAPITAL

STRUCTURES:

AN EMPIRICAL

INVESTIGATION

Fuqua	B
General Cigar	Double-B/B
Kane Miller	B
MGM	Triple-B/B
National Tea	B
NVF	B
Procter and Gamble	Triple-A
Pullman	Triple-B
Rapid American	B/double-C
Raytheon	Double-A/A
Republic Steel	A
Seagram	A
Tandy	Triple-B/B
United Brands	B
Upjohn	Triple-A
Whittaker	Double-B/B

CCA requires three kinds of data in order to solve for prices of individual claims as functions of total firm value: indenture data, standard deviation data and interest rate data. The bond indentures define the boundary conditions and payout terms which constitute the economic description of various claims. For example, the following data were collected for each bond for each firm: principal, coupon rate, call price schedule, call protection period, sinking fund payments, seniority and options to sink at market or par. The bond covenant data were collected from Moody's Bond Guide, except that sinking fund payments were collected from the monthly S&P Bond Guide. For purposes of testing the model, actual bond prices were also collected from the latter source.

Two procedures were used to estimate the standard deviation for each firm in the sample, as of each January from 1977 through to 1981. The first procedure (hereafter referred to as Method I) was based on forming a monthly time series for the value of the firm using 24 trailing months of data. The value of the firm was estimated as the sum of the market value of equity, the market value of traded debt and the estimated market value of non-traded debt. The market value of the non-traded debt was estimated by assuming that the ratio of book to market was the same for traded and non-traded debt. The logarithmic total return on the value of the firm, including any cash credits/debits, was calculated and the standard deviation of these returns determined.

The second procedure (hereafter referred to as Method II) is a maximum likelihood procedure based on the relationship between the standard deviations of the return to the firm and the equity. Given the assumptions of CCA, it follows from Itô's Lemma that the instantaneous standard deviation of equity, σ_E, is given by

$$\sigma_E = \sigma_V E_V V / E \qquad (4)$$

where V is the standard deviation of the return to the firm and E_V is the partial derivative of the value of equity with respect to the value of the firm. The Method II procedure was to run the model using the Method I estimate of standard deviation as a seed. The value of the firm, V, the value of equity, E, and the partial derivative of equity, E_V, with respect to the value of the firm which are implied by the observed total value of marketable claims are read from this pass of the model. Then the standard deviation of return to the equity is calculated, using the CRSP daily returns data, for the three month period, October–December, immediately preceding the January rest date. Given (4), a new estimate of σ_V is formed using E, E, V, and E_V. The model is then rerun using this new estimate of V. Table 1 summarises the Method II estimates of the standard deviation of returns to the firm.

The standard assumption in CCA is that the future course of interest rates, r(t), is known. Specifically, it is often assumed that the instantaneous rate of interest is constant through time, ie, a flat term structure. The assumption of a flat term structure results in a fundamental problem for the empirical test of the contingent claims model in that the model will misprice riskless bonds. Therefore, the test of whether CCA can price risky bonds is systematically flawed. This problem is handled by the assumption that the future course of the one-year rate of interest will be consistent with the one-

CONTINGENT

CLAIMS ANALYSIS

OF CORPORATE

CAPITAL

STRUCTURES:

AN EMPIRICAL

INVESTIGATION

Table 1. Estimates of annualised standard deviations of returns to firm: Method II

Name	1977	1978	1979	1980	1981
Allied Chemical	0.191	0.149	0.167	0.229	0.314
Anheuser Busch	0.343	0.276	0.219	0.184	0.221
Braniff	0.198	0.199	0.293	0.270	0.173
Brown Group	0.164	0.165	0.214	0.186	0.253
Bucyrus Erie	0.313	0.304	0.404	0.267	0.319
Champion Spark Plug	0.267	0.246	0.356	0.427	0.307
Cities Service	0.176	0.133	0.140	0.250	0.450
Crane	0.254	0.214	0.334	0.254	0.255
CTC	0.233	0.215	0.187	0.228	0.307
Food Fair	0.157	0.139	N/A	N/A	N/A
Fuqua	0.509	0.211	0.340	0.437	0.318
General Cigar	0.090	0.103	0.143	0.154	0.297
Kane Miller	0.136	0.121	0.146	0.169	0.167
MGM	0.176	0.240	0.535	0.464	0.610
National Tea	0.628	0.486	0.493	N/A	N/A
NVF	N/A	0.264	0.421	0.663	0.474
Procter & Gamble	0.171	0.142	0.191	0.168	0.235
Pullman	0.349	0.231	0.450	0.362	N/A
Rapid American	0.224	0.117	0.133	0.124	0.052
Raytheon	0.253	0.270	0.369	0.222	0.369
Republic Steel	0.120	0.116	0.170	0.178	0.125
Seagram	0.233	0.169	0.292	0.384	N/A
Sunbeam	0.372	0.240	0.351	0.365	0.324
Tandy	0.271	0.285	0.587	0.309	0.510
United Brands	0.177	0.176	0.276	0.170	0.215
Upjohn	0.247	N/A	N/A	N/A	0.241
Whittaker	0.161	0.171	0.436	0.400	0.318

year forward interest rates implied by the current term structure. The following procedure was used to estimate implied one-year forward interest rates as of each January from 1977 through to 1981. First, all par government bonds, adjusted for accrued interest, were identified as of that date. These data were gathered from the *Wall Street Journal*. If necessary, linear interpolation was used to complete the yield curve. Then this yield curve was solved for implied one-year forward rates. Hence the implied forward rates pertain to a par term structure, and this procedure will result in the model correctly pricing par government bonds.

The method of Markov chains is used to approximate solutions to the partial differential equations. Parkinson (1977), Mason (1979) and Cox, Ross and Rubinstein (1979) use Markov chains to approximate solutions to valuation problems similar to those considered in this chapter. The method of finite differences has been used by Brennan and Schwartz (1977a, 1977b) to treat similar contingent claims equations. The methods of Markov chains and finite differences are very similar, and in some cases identical, as demonstrated by Brennan and Schwartz (1978) and Mason (1978). Readers are referred to these papers for background on numerical analysis techniques.

If all claims are publicly traded, then the value of the firm can be observed and prices for all claims, relative to the observed firm value, can be predicted. However, since all claims on the test firms are not publicly traded, an alternative approach had to be taken. Namely, the total value of all traded claims is used to infer the firm value. In other words, what firm value is consistent with the observed value of all traded claims? This implied firm value is then used to predict bond prices. Counting each year from 1977 through to 1981, and counting each bond existing in each year for each of the 27 firms, we solved numerically for prices of 305 bonds.

Results

Tables 2–5 summarise the results. Percentage error is defined as the predicted price minus the actual

Table 2. Sign test of CCA model versus naïve (riskless) model

	Number of bonds	Number of times that $S_{CCA} < S_{naïve}$
Entire sample	305	256*
Investment grade	176	139*
Non-investment grade	129	117*

$S_{CCA} = |$ actual price – CCA model price $|$
$S_{naïve} = |$ actual price – naïve model price $|$
*Significant at the 99% level or greater

Table 3. Pricing results and comparisons: CCA model and naïve (riskless) model

	Number of bonds	Percentage error mean (standard deviation)		Absolute percentage error mean (standard deviation)	
		CCA model	Naïve model	CCA model	Naïve model
Overall results					
Entire sample	305	0.0452	0.0876	0.0845	0.1143
		(0.1003)	(0.1441)	(0.0705)	(0.1240)
Investment grade	176	0.0047	0.0149	0.0587	0.0574
		(0.0727)	(0.0703)	(0.0432)	(0.0432)
Non-investment grade	129	0.1005	0.1867	0.1197	0.1919
		(0.1063)	(0.1590)	(0.0840)	(0.1528)
High variance					
Entire sample	149	0.0214	0.0644	0.0763	0.0942
(>0.055)		(0.0918)	(0.1055)	(0.0554)	(0.0800)
Investment grade	85	−0.0101	0.0094	0.0603	0.0566
(>0.055)		(0.0738)	(0.0706)	(0.0438)	(0.0433)
Non-investment grade	64	0.0633	0.1375	0.0975	0.1443
(>0.055)		(0.0965)	(0.0996)	(0.0618)	(0.0896)
Low variance					
Entire sample	156	0.0679	0.1097	0.0923	0.1334
(0.055)		(0.1028)	(0.1701)	(0.0816)	(0.1522)
Investment grade	91	0.0185	0.0200	0.0571	0.0581
(0.055)		(0.0688)	(0.0696)	(0.0425)	(0.0431)
Non-investment grade	65	0.1371	0.2352	0.1416	0.2388
(0.055)		(0.1027)	(0.1889)	(0.0963)	(0.1843)
High financial leverage					
Entire sample	148	0.0857	0.1499	0.1061	0.1589
(>0.31)		(0.1049)	(0.1634)	(0.0843)	(0.1546)
Investment grade	90	0.0072	0.0207	0.0656	0.0625
(>0.24)		(0.0806)	(0.0760)	(0.0475)	(0.0480)
Non-investment grade	63	0.1173	0.2375	0.1332	0.2427
(>0.55)		(0.1182)	(0.1951)	(0.1001)	(0.1886)
Low financial leverage					
Entire sample	157	0.0070	0.0288	0.0641	0.0722
(0.31)		(0.0785)	(0.0897)	(0.0459)	(0.0606)
Investment grade	86	0.0020	0.0088	0.0515	0.0521
(0.24)		(0.0632)	(0.0631)	(0.0367)	(0.0368)
Non-investment grade	66	0.0843	0.1382	0.1069	0.1434
(0.55)		(0.0906)	(0.0909)	(0.0624)	(0.0826)
Long term					
Entire sample	153	0.0479	0.0949	0.0821	0.1190
(>14 years)		(0.0911)	(0.1417)	(0.0621)	(0.1222)
Investment grade	88	0.0157	0.0265	0.0590	0.0599
(>15 years)		(0.0716)	(0.0692)	(0.0434)	(0.0436)
Non-investment grade	66	0.1025	0.2066	0.1189	0.2070
(>12 years)		(0.0962)	(0.1442)	(0.0750)	(0.1438)
Short term					
Entire sample	152	0.0424	0.0802	0.0869	0.1095
(14 years)		(0.1087)	(0.1460)	(0.0779)	(0.1255)
Investment grade	88	−0.0063	0.0032	0.0583	0.0548
(15 years)		(0.0721)	(0.0694)	(0.0429)	(0.0427)
Non-investment grade	63	0.0983	0.1659	0.1206	0.1761
(12 years)		(0.1159)	(0.1707)	(0.0924)	(0.1601)
Senior bonds					
Entire sample	231	0.0327	0.0625	0.0780	0.0963
		(0.0949)	(0.1272)	(0.0633)	(0.1039)
Investment grade	158	0.0004	0.0105	0.0573	0.0562
		(0.0707)	(0.0689)	(0.0414)	(0.0412)
Non-investment grade	73	0.1027	0.1752	0.1227	0.1831
		(0.1027)	(0.1494)	(0.0776)	(0.1396)
Junior bonds					
Entire sample	74	0.0841	0.1657	0.1048	0.1703
		(0.1066)	(0.1644)	(0.0862)	(0.1596)
Investment grade	18	0.0422	0.0534	0.0708	0.0673
		(0.0790)	(0.0703)	(0.0549)	(0.0572)
Non-investment grade	56	0.0976	0.2017	0.1158	0.2033
		(0.1107)	(0.1696)	(0.0915)	(0.1677)
High coupon					
Entire sample	150	0.0600	0.1046	0.0886	0.1142
(>8.00%)		(0.0900)	(0.1015)	(0.0620)	(0.0906)
Investment grade	87	0.0189	0.0351	0.0586	0.0575
(>7.75%)		(0.0702)	(0.0621)	(0.0430)	(0.0423)
Non-investment grade	68	0.0911	0.1581	0.1099	0.1584
(>9.25%)		(0.0885)	(0.0957)	(0.0636)	(0.0952)

(Continued overleaf)

CONTINGENT

CLAIMS ANALYSIS

OF CORPORATE

CAPITAL

STRUCTURES:

AN EMPIRICAL

INVESTIGATION

Table 3 (continued). Pricing results and comparisons: CCA model and naïve (riskless) model

	Number of bonds	Percentage error mean (standard deviation)		Absolute percentage error mean (standard deviation)	
		CCA model	Naïve model	CCA model	Naïve model
Low coupon					
Entire sample	155	0.0309	0.0711	0.0805	0.1144
(8%)		(0.1074)	(0.1741)	(0.0776)	(0.1493)
Investment grade	89	–0.0092	–0.0049	0.0587	0.0573
(7.75%)		(0.0724)	(0.0721)	(0.0433)	(0.0441)
Non-investment grade	61	0.1109	0.2186	0.1307	0.2292
(9.25%)		(0.1223)	(0.2033)	(0.1009)	(0.1913)
High price					
Entire sample	150	0.0273	0.0494	0.0672	0.0772
(<82.5)		(0.0811)	(0.0892)	(0.0530)	(0.0667)
Investment grade	87	0.0186	0.0254	0.0535	0.0537
(>84.0)		(0.0650)	(0.0637)	(0.0413)	(0.0426)
Non-investment grade	64	0.0604	0.1206	0.0933	0.1310
(>78.5)		(0.939)	(0.1081)	(0.0612)	(0.0952)
Low price					
Entire sample	155	0.0626	0.1245	0.1012	0.1502
(82.5)		(0.1132)	(0.1743)	(0.0805)	(0.1527)
Investment grade	89	–0.0089	0.0046	0.0637	0.0609
(84.0)		(0.0771)	(0.0747)	(0.0443)	(0.0436)
Non-investment grade	65	0.1399	0.2519	0.1457	0.2519
(78.5)		(0.1029)	(0.1736)	(0.0946)	(0.1736)
High current yield					
Entire sample	155	0.0752	0.1448	0.1025	0.1561
(>9.75%)		(0.1076)	(0.1620)	(0.0821)	(0.1511)
Investment grade	102	0.0125	0.0270	0.0616	0.0598
(>8.50%)		(0.0753)	(0.0703)	(0.0451)	(0.0457)
Non-investment grade	69	0.1074	0.2255	0.1207	0.2255
(>10.50%)		(0.0997)	(0.1690)	(0.0831)	(0.1690)
Low Current Yield					
Entire sample	150	0.0142	0.0284	0.0659	0.0710
(9.75%)		(0.0813)	(0.0906)	(0.0496)	(0.0631)
Investment grade	74	–0.0061	–0.0018	0.0546	0.0540
(8.50%)		(0.0674)	(0.0668)	(0.0400)	(0.0394)
Non-investment grade	60	0.0924	0.1421	0.1186	0.1532
(10.50%)		(0.1129)	(0.1335)	(0.0850)	(0.1206)

price divided by the actual price. Absolute percentage errors and results from a naïve model are also reported. The naïve model essentially assumes that the value of the firm is sufficiently large to make all debt riskless. These results were obtained from the same runs of the model that produced the CCA estimates. Thus the naïve model prices simply reflect the magnitude and timing of promised payments discounted back by the risk-free interest rates, $r(t)$, plus the effects of the call provision and the sinking fund option to sink at the minimum of par or market. Incrementally, the CCA model prices attempt to capture the risk of default through the consideration of business risk, σ^2 and financial risk, ie, finite firm value relative to promised payouts. In addition, the CCA model introduces the distinction between senior and junior debt as well as the presence of equity which complicates (relative to the naïve model) the optimal call policy.

Table 2 presents a simple sign test of the CCA model versus the naïve model. The absolute pricing errors for the two models are compared and the number of times that the CCA model's error is less than the naïve model's error are counted. As is evident from Table 2, the CCA model's error significantly outperforms the naïve model. This is not a surprising result since the naïve model is perfectly nested within the CCA model and will (almost) always generate a higher predicted price (the exceptions having to do with the "cresting" of bond prices induced by the optimal call policy as depicted in Figure 1). Since the interest rates, $r(t)$, have been calibrated to replicate risk-free bond prices and since most of the actual bond prices reflect some risk premium, then the CCA model should significantly outperform the naïve model on a sign test.

Table 3 presents the pricing errors for the CCA and naïve models for various subsamples. Results are reported for investment-grade (bond rating of BBB or higher) and non-investment-grade subsamples as well as the entire sample. All splits are at the 50th percentile for each sample. As is evident from inspection, the CCA and naïve models are virtually indistinguishable for investment-grade bonds. This can be interpreted as evidence that firm value risk is not playing a significant role in explaining investment-grade bond prices. This also suggests that a stochastic interest rate model could be a better predictor of investment-grade bond prices. There do appear to be significant differences between the CCA and naïve models for non-investment-grade bonds. However, there is little evidence in Table 3 that the CCA model performs significantly better (in an absolute sense) for any particular subsample of non-investment-grade bonds.

Tables 4–5 present regression-based results which are consistent with earlier tables. Specifically, Table 4 demonstrates that the CCA model is virtually indistinguishable from the naïve model for investment-grade bonds. However, the CCA model does appear

Table 4. Regression results of actual prices versus CCA model and na ve model

Dependent variable = Actual price

	Constant	Na ve model price	CCA model price	R²
Entire sample	0.0056 (0.0008)	0.0832 (0.0301)	0.7781 (0.0355)	0.977
	0.0131 (0.0012)	0.7243 (0.0103)		0.942
	0.0050 (0.0008)		0.8746 (0.0077)	0.977
Investment grade	0.0025 (0.0007)	1.0022 (0.1780)	−0.0637 (0.1798)	0.985
	0.0025 (0.0007)	0.9392 (0.0087)		0.985
	0.0027 (0.0007)		0.9473 (0.0095)	0.983
Non-investment grade	0.0043 (0.0013)	0.1740 (0.0359)	0.6541 (0.0442)	0.983
	0.0117 (0.0020)	0.6911 (0.0136)		0.953
	0.0029 (0.0014)		0.8627 (0.0110)	0.981

Standard errors are in parentheses below coefficient estimates.

to have incremental explanatory power for non-investment-grade bonds. Table 5 presents the results of a multivariate regression of the percentage pricing error for the CCA model against the characteristics identified in Table 3 plus a year dummy variable. The presence of a year effect is indicated, with the effect being stronger for investment-grade bonds. This could be related to an intertemporal bias in variance estimation or interest rate uncertainty. Variance, or business risk, is significant for the entire sample,

Table 5. Regression of CCA model errors

Dependent variable = CCA model price − Actual price

Independent variables	Entire sample Coefficient	Mean	Investment grade Coefficient	Mean	Non-investment grade Coefficient	Mean
Constant	0.0234 (0.1351)		−0.0875 (0.2176)		0.5397 (0.2281)	
Variance	−0.4599 (0.0653)	0.084	−0.3465 (0.0797)	0.078	−0.5987 (0.1214)	0.092
Maturity	−0.0028 (0.0008)	14.260	−0.0021 (0.0009)	15.120	−0.0041 (0.0019)	13.100
Coupon	−0.0102 (0.0151)	7.880	−0.0071 (0.0256)	7.520	0.0314 (0.0233)	8.370
Price	−0.0008 (0.0016)	81.680	0.0006 (0.0026)	84.510	−0.0069 (0.0026)	77.810
Senior/junior (dummy) (junior = 1, senior = 0)	−0.0032 (0.0103)	0.240	0.0305 (0.0157)	0.102	−0.0084 (0.0143)	0.434
Bond rating (1–9 1 = triple-A, 9 = C)	0.0235 (0.0045)	4.101	0.0075 (0.0079)	2.830	0.0271 (0.0172)	5.830
Current yield	2.8015 (1.1678)	0.098	2.4934 (1.9982)	0.090	−0.2471 (1.7832)	0.109
Financial leverage	−0.0901 (0.0286)	0.372	−0.0621 (0.0363)	0.244	−0.1747 (0.0521)	0.547
1978 (dummy)	−0.0541 (0.0129)	0.193	−0.0654 (0.0134)	0.198	−0.0363 (0.0232)	0.186
1979 (dummy)	−0.1053 (0.0134)	0.203	−0.1012 (0.0149)	0.187	0.1075 (0.0234)	0.224
1980 (dummy)	−0.1001 (0.0166)	0.206	−0.0973 (0.0198)	0.198	−0.0965 (0.0287)	0.217
1981 (dummy)	−0.1664 (0.0197)	0.200	−0.1471 (0.0244)	0.210	−0.1763 (0.0372)	0.186
R²	0.539		0.453		0.502	

Standard errors are in parentheses below coefficient estimates.

CONTINGENT
CLAIMS ANALYSIS
OF CORPORATE
CAPITAL
STRUCTURES:
AN EMPIRICAL
INVESTIGATION

as well as for the investment and non-investment-grade bond subsamples. In all cases variance enters with a negative coefficient which suggests that a high estimated variance could be associated with an overestimate of the variance and therefore an underestimate of the bond price. Maturity is also significant and enters with a negative coefficient. This is undoubtedly related to the variance effect being amplified for long-term bonds.

Current yield is significant for the entire sample. This could be due to the fact that the IRS allows investors to amortise a secondary market premium against interest income while allowing realised gains due to secondary market discounts to be taxed at capital gains rates. However, current yield is not significant in the non-investment-grade subsample. This could be due to another dimension of the tax effect which has to do with risk.

Consider low-quality par bonds versus high-quality par bonds. The expected capital loss on the low-quality bonds is larger in absolute terms than the expected capital loss on the high-quality bonds. Hence the low-quality bonds will have a higher coupon rate than the high-quality bonds. Since the higher taxes on the low-quality bond are ignored, any tax effect will cause low-quality bonds to be overpriced relative to high-quality bonds. In particular, since government par bonds are perfectly safe, any tax effect will cause corporate par bonds to be overpriced in general. Similar considerations say that any tax effect will cause junior par bonds and long-maturity par bonds to be overpriced relative to senior par bonds and short-maturity pay bonds respectively.

Conclusions

The objective of this chapter is to test the predictive power of a CCA model of typical capital structures. A distinction is made between the model's performance *vis-à-vis* investment-grade and non-investment-grade bonds. The CCA model is not an improvement over a naïve (riskless) model for investment-grade bonds. However, the CCA model does appear to have incremental explanatory power over the naïve model for non-investment-grade bonds. These is evidence that introducing stochastic interest rates, as well as taxes, would improve the model's performance. Variance estimation errors, as with all option-based models, appear to be important.

Establishing the empirical validity of the CCA model is an important goal. Numerous problems remain, including better bond prices, more efficient numerical techniques and adjustments to the standard set of assumptions. We view the contributions of Jones, Mason and Rosenfeld (1983) and this study as: identifying and resolving a number of analytical issues in the formulation of the CCA valuation problem for typical capital structures, and demonstrating empirical results which are crucial in establishing research priorities in what will be a large and complex task.

BIBLIOGRAPHY

Black, F., and M. Scholes, 1973, "The Pricing of Options and Corporate Liabilities", *Journal of Political Economy* 81, pp. 637–59.

Brennan, M., and E. Schwartz, 1977a, "Convertible Bonds: Valuation and Optimal Strategies for Call and Conversion", *Journal of Finance* 32, pp. 1699–715.

Brennan, M., and E. Schwartz, 1977b, "The Valuation of American Put Options", *Journal of Finance* 32, pp. 449–62.

Brennan, M., and E. Schwartz, 1978, "Finite Difference Methods and Jump Processes Arising in the Pricing of Contingent Claims: A Synthesis", *Journal of Financial and Quantitative Analysis,* September, pp. 461–74.

Cox, J., S. Ross and M. Rubinstein, 1979, "Option Pricing: A Simplified Approach", *Journal of Financial Economics* 7, pp. 229–63.

Fisher, L., 1959, "Determinants of Risk Premium on Corporate Bonds", *Journal of Political Economy* 4, pp. 269–322.

111

CONTINGENT
CLAIMS ANALYSIS
OF CORPORATE
CAPITAL
STRUCTURES:
AN EMPIRICAL
INVESTIGATION

Ingersoll, J., 1976, "A Theoretical and Empirical Investigation of the Dual-purpose Funds", *Journal of Financial Economics* 3, pp. 83–123.

Ingersoll, J., 1977a, "A Contingent Claims Valuation of Convertible Securities", *Journal of Financial Economics* 4, pp. 269–322.

Ingersoll, J., 1977b, "An Examination of Corporate Call Policies on Convertible Securities", *Journal of Finance* 32, pp. 463–78.

Jaffee, D. M., 1975, "Cyclical Variations in the Risk Structure of Interest Rates", *Journal of Monetary Economics* 1, pp. 309–25.

Jones, E. P., S. P. Mason and E. Rosenfeld, 1983, "Contingent Claims Valuation of Corporate Liabilities: Theory and Empirical Tests", National Bureau of Economic Research Working Paper no. 1143.

Mason, S. P., 1978, "The Numerical Analysis of Certain Free Boundary Problems Arising in Financial Economics", Harvard Business School, Boston, MA.

Mason, S. P., 1979, "The Numerical Analysis of Risky Coupon Bond Contracts", Working Paper no. 79-35., Harvard Business School, Boston, MA.

Merton, R. C., 1974, "On the Pricing of Corporate Debt: The Risk Structure of Interest Rates", *Journal of Finance* 29, pp. 449–70; reprinted as Chapter 4 of the present volume.

Merton, R. C., 1977, "On the Pricing of Contingent Claims and the Modigliani–Miller Theorem", *Journal of Financial Economics* 5, pp. 147–75.

Parkinson, M., 1977, "Option Pricing: The American Put", *Journal of Business* 50, pp. 21–36.

Sloan, P. E., 1963, "Determinants of Bond Yield Differentials: 1954 to 1959", *Yale Economic Essays,* Spring.

Appendix

Discussion
Lawrence Fisher, Graduate School of Management, Rutgers University

"Contingent Claims Analysis of Corporate Capital Structures: An Empirical Investigation" by E. Philip Jones, Scott P. Mason, and Eric Rosenfeld ("JMR") is an ambitious project that shows substantial use of formal analytical skills. First, JMR extend Merton's (1974) contingent claims analysis (CCA) of a firm that has a single, callable debt issue to the case where the firm may have many such issues and where each issue may have sinking-fund requirements and be callable for redemption as a whole or for the sinking fund. Then they attempt to test the implications of their model for the prices of publicly traded debt securities against an alternative "naïve" model that assumes there is no risk of default.

It seems to me that there are three crucial assumptions at the heart of Merton's CCA – three assumptions that may be required to make the model tractable but which may not be sufficiently true for the model to provide useful estimates of security prices. These are:

❏ perfect liquidity (and irrelevance of firm size – cf. Fisher (1959, 1974);
❏ irrelevance of taxes;
❏ non-stochastic interest rates.

I had hoped that JMR would test one or more of these assumptions. If taken at face value, their empirical results would suggest that CCA takes account of risk in only a very rough and unsatisfactory manner. However, both the particular form of CCA model that JMR have used and their empirical methods are ill-suited for testing the three crucial assumptions. Hence, the applicability of Merton's CCA to corporate bond markets remains untested.

CONTINGENT

CLAIMS ANALYSIS

OF CORPORATE

CAPITAL

STRUCTURES:

AN EMPIRICAL

INVESTIGATION

FORMAL MODEL

One of the so-called "standard" assumptions that the authors use – indeed, they show that it implies strange behaviour by the firm because the value of a bond does not increase monotonically with the value of the firm – is needlessly unrealistic.[1] That is the assumption "Perfect [*sic*] anti-dilution protection," which requires that no new debt securities be issued until all existing non-equity claims have been extinguished. Another implication, which JMR do not notice, is that under that assumption, capital structures with multiple bond issues and a realistic variety of coupon rates – the topic under consideration – cannot come into existence. Moreover, actual indentures seldom contain such provisions. Instead, they are likely to impose an upper limit on the ratio of debt to equity, a lower limit on the ratio of operating income to fixed charges, or restrictions on dividend payments and the sale of assets. Before proceeding further, JMR should replace that assumption by another provision that would prevent dilution, allow reasonable behaviour by the firm and still let the model be tractable. Perhaps allowing refunding subject to a limitation on the debt/equity ratio (in market-value terms) and a requirement that the new issue not reduce the duration of liabilities would be a suitably realistic and tractable alternative.

Taking full account of the tax structure would be very complicated. For example, Brick and Fisher (1982, 1983) have analysed effects of asymmetries in personal income taxes similar to those noted by JMR with and without corporate income taxes and have derived a number of theoretical propositions. One proposition is that issuing risky debt and valuable equity is not value-maximising behaviour *unless* there is a corporate income tax. However, our formal analysis, which some readers find very difficult and complex, used a single, discrete time period and does not (and cannot) look at callability.

Either of the following approximate methods might be a feasible way to test the effects of personal taxes on bond prices in the context of CCA. Method one would take cash flows and the riskless rate of interest on alternative before-tax and after-tax bases. Method two would use only before-tax cash flows but would take the yield on a government with the same price or coupon and maturity or duration as the alternative riskless rate. Then the test of the relevance of personal income taxes would be to see which set of interest rates provided the better set of estimated bond valuations.

Moreover, JMR's "naïve" model ignores the literature of the last few decades. For example, the CCA model may be tested in the context of Fisher (1959), as modified by Tambini (1969, p. 221), by seeing whether the yield spreads implied by the CCA valuations replace my instrumental estimators or risk of default and whether the CCA's assumption that liquidity is irrelevant is correct.

EMPIRICAL METHODS

I have misgivings about most aspects of JMR's empirical analysis. Space permits little more than listing the topics.

❏ Sampling procedures: Selection of firms (random samples?) and time periods (why only the most recent five years?).
❏ Methods of measurement: Imputation of the value of non-marketable liabilities (errors in this variable affect the estimated risk of default); confounding of stock-price fluctuations that might indicate risk of default with direct effects of interest-rate fluctuations (to a first-order approximation, the latter do not affect risk of default if the duration of the firm is equal to the duration of the liabilities).
❏ Data sources for Corporate and Government bond prices and yields: Some of the S&P Bond Guide's "prices" are Standard & Poor's own valuations rather than actual quotations; the *Wall Street Journal*'s quotations have been received by telephone and contain frequent errors – machine-readable sources of government bond data are available.
❏ Analysis of errors: There are at most 135 independent observations available (27

CONTINGENT
CLAIMS ANALYSIS
OF CORPORATE
CAPITAL
STRUCTURES:
AN EMPIRICAL
INVESTIGATION

firms times five years), not 305; relative price errors tend to be heteroscedastic with respect to duration; the multiple regression contains two sets of mutually determined "independent" variables.

The problems with the empirical analysis further reinforce my conclusion that Merton's contingent claims analysis of risky bonds remains to be tested.

1 *The assumption may have been entirely satisfactory in the study from which HMR took it.*

BIBLIOGRAPHY

Brick, I., and L. Fisher, 1982, "Effects of Capital Structure on the Value of the Firm under Tax Asymmetry", Working paper, Rutgers University, April.

Brick, I., and L. Fisher, 1983, "Effects of Classifying Equity or Debt on the Value of the Firm under Tax Asymmetry", Working paper, Rutgers University, November.

Fisher, L., 1959, "Determinants of Risk Premiums on Corporate Bonds", *Journal of Political Economy* 67(3), June, pp. 217-37.

Fisher, L., 1974, "Discussion", *Journal of Finance* 29(3), May, pp. 488-92.

Merton, R. C., 1974, "On the Pricing of Corporate Debt: The Risk Structure of Interest Rates", *Journal of Finance* 29(2), May, pp. 449-70; reprinted as Chapter 4 of the present volume.

Tambini, L., 1969, "Financial Policy and the Corporation Income Tax", in *The Taxation of Income from Capital*, A. C. Harberger and M. J. Bailey, eds (Washington: The Brooking Institutions), p. 221.

9

A Simple Approach to Valuing Risky Fixed and Floating Rate Debt

Francis A. Longstaff and Eduardo S. Schwartz

Anderson Graduate School of Management, University of California at Los Angeles

The traditional Black–Scholes (1973) and Merton (1974) contingent claims-based approach to the valuation of corporate debt has become an integral part of the theory of corporate finance. In this approach, interest rates are assumed to be constant, and the default risk of a bond is modelled using option pricing theory. This framework for valuing risky debt has been applied in a number of articles, including Geske (1977), Ingersoll (1977a, 1977b), Merton (1977), Smith and Warner (1979) and many others.

One of the drawbacks of this approach is that default is assumed to occur only when the firm exhausts its assets. This is clearly unrealistic, since firms usually default long before their assets are exhausted. In addition, Jones, Mason and Rosenfeld (1984) and Franks and Torous (1989) show that this aspect of the model implies credit spreads that are much smaller than actual credit spreads. In an important article, Black and Cox (1976) relax this assumption and allow default to occur when the value of the firm's assets reaches a lower threshold. This feature makes the model consistent with either net worth- or cashflow-based insolvency. By incorporating this more realistic default condition, the Black and Cox model is able to generate credit spreads that are more consistent with those observed in corporate debt markets.

Despite this advantage, the Black and Cox model shares some of the other limitations of the traditional Black–Scholes–Merton framework for valuing risky debt. Specifically, this framework assumes that interest rates are constant. This assumption is difficult to justify in a valuation model for risky fixed-income securities. In addition, this framework assumes that assets are allocated among corporate claimants according to strict absolute priority rules if the firm defaults. However, recent evidence advanced by Franks and Torous (1989, 1994) Eberhart, Moore and Roenfeldt (1990), LoPucki and Whitford (1990), Weiss (1990), Betker (1991, 1992) and others shows that strict absolute priority is rarely upheld in distressed reorganisations.

This chapter develops a simple new approach to valuing risky debt by extending the Black and Cox (1976) model in two ways. First, this model incorporates both default risk and interest rate risk. Second, this approach explicitly allows for deviations from strict absolute priority. In developing the model architecture, our objective is to be able to provide tractable valuation models for risky debt securities. Accordingly, we present the simplest possible specification for the model rather than the most general. This has the important advantage of allowing us to derive simple closed-form expressions for both risky fixed-rate and floating-rate debt. These closed-form expressions provide a number of new insights into the properties of corporate debt prices.

We first apply our framework to value risky discount and coupon bonds. We show that

This paper was first published in The Journal of Finance *50(3), pp. 789–819 (1995), and is reprinted with the kind permission of Blackwell Publishers.*

the credit spreads implied by the model are consistent with many of the properties of actual credit spreads. For example, the model implies credit spreads that are comparable in magnitude to actual spreads and allows the term structure of credit spreads to be either monotonic increasing or hump-shaped. An important implication of our results is that credit spreads for firms with similar default risk can vary significantly if the assets of the firms have different correlations with changes in interest rates. This property of the model has the potential to explain why bonds with similar credit ratings but in different industries or sectors have widely differing credit spreads. Finally, we show that the properties of high-yield bonds can be very different from those of less risky debt. For example, the duration or interest rate sensitivity of a high-yield bond may actually increase as it gets closer to its maturity date.

We then derive closed-form expressions for the value of risky floating-rate debt. We find that the price of a floating-rate bond can be an increasing function of the maturity of the bond in some situations. Similarly, the value of floating-rate debt can be an increasing function of the level of interest rates. These results illustrate that the properties of floating-rate debt are fundamentally different from those of fixed-rate debt. In general, the price of a floating-rate bond need not equal its par value even on coupon payment dates because of the risk of default.

Using Moody's corporate bond yield averages, we examine whether the implications of our model are consistent with the actual properties of credit spreads. As implied by the model, we find that credit spreads are strongly negatively related to the level of interest rates. Furthermore, changes in interest rates account for the majority of the variation in credit spreads for most of the bonds in the sample. This drives home the importance of allowing for interest rate risk in addition to default risk in valuing risky debt securities. We also find that the differences in the duration of bonds across industries and sectors are consistent with the differences in correlations with changes in the interest rate. These results provide supporting evidence for the empirical implications of our valuation model.

There are a number of other articles focusing on the valuation of corporate securities that allow for both default risk and interest rate risk. These include Ramaswamy and Sundaresan (1986), Hull and White (1992), Maloney (1992), Jarrow and Turnbull (1992a, 1992b, 1992c, 1992d), Kim, Ramaswamy and Sundaresan (1992), Ginzburg, Maloney and Willner (1993), Shimko, Tejima and van Deventer (1993), Gennotte and Marsh (1993), and Nielsen, Saa-Requejo and Santa-Clara (1993). The present work distinguishes itself from each of these other contributions in that it is the only one that provides closed-form valuation expressions for risky coupon bonds as well as risky floating-rate debt. In addition, it is the only one that jointly allows for: default before the firm exhausts all its assets; complex capital structures, including multiple issues of debt; deviations from strict absolute priority; and empirical evidence supporting the implications of the model.

The valuation framework

In this section we extend the Black and Cox (1976) model to develop a simple continuous-time valuation framework for risky debt that allows for both default risk and interest rate risk. This framework is then used in later sections to derive closed-form valuation expressions for a variety of risky corporate debt securities. The basic assumptions of this framework, which are discussed individually below, parallel those of Black and Scholes (1973), Merton (1974) and Black and Cox (1976).

ASSUMPTION 1 *Let* V *designate the total value of the assets of the firm. The dynamics of* V *are given by*

$$dV = \mu V dt + \sigma V dZ_1 \qquad (1)$$

where σ *is a constant and* Z_1 *is a standard Wiener process.*

ASSUMPTION 2 *Let* r *denote the short-term riskless interest rate. The dynamics of* r *are given by*

$$dr = (\zeta - \beta r)dt + \eta dZ_2 \qquad (2)$$

where ζ, β *and* η *are constants and* Z_2 *is also a standard Wiener process. The instantaneous correlation between* dZ_1 *and* dZ_2 *is* ρdt.

This assumption about the dynamics of r is drawn from the term structure model of Vasicek (1977). Although consistent with many of the observed properties of interest rates, these dynamics can allow negative interest rates. There are several reasons, however, why this assumption may be justifiable in the context of this model. First, the probability of negative interest rates occurring is small for realistic parameter values. Second, given that the current value of r is positive, these dynamics always imply positive expected future values of r. This is important since the primary effect of r on credit spreads is through its expected future values. Note that our approach could be extended to allow for more general interest rate processes, although risky debt prices would then need to be solved for numerically.

ASSUMPTION 3 *The value of the firm is independent of the firm's capital structure.*

This is the standard assumption that the Modigliani–Miller theorem holds. This assumption also implies that changes in capital structure, such as payments of coupons and principal, have no effect on V. This is easily satisfied, for example, if coupons and principal payments are financed by issuing new debt. Implicit in this assumption is the notion that the capital structure of the firm is held constant over time or that the status quo is maintained.[1] This is reasonable in light of the fact that, in this frictionless continuous-time framework, the firm has no incentive to alter its capital structure.[2] We allow the capital structure of the firm to consist of a variety of contingent claims, including debt with different coupon rates, priorities and maturity dates.

ASSUMPTION 4 *Following Black and Cox (1976), we assume that there is a threshold value,* K, *for the firm at which financial distress occurs. As long as* V *is greater than* K, *the firm continues to be able to meet its contractual obligations. If* V *reaches* K, *however, the firm immediately encounters financial distress, defaults on all of its obligations, and some form of corporate restructuring takes place.*

An important implication of this assumption is that default occurs for all debt contracts simultaneously. This is realistic because, when a firm defaults on a debt issue, it typically defaults on other issues owing to cross-default provisions, acceleration of principal provisions or injunctions against making coupon payments on other debt issues. Although we assume that K is a constant, which is consistent with the assumption of a stationary capital structure, we could extend the analysis to allow K to depend on time and the riskless interest rate or to follow a separate stochastic process. However, since it is the ratio of V to K, rather than the actual value of K, that plays the major role in our analysis, allowing a more general specification for K simply makes the model more complex without providing additional insight into the valuation of risky debt.[3]

This definition of financial distress is consistent with both the case where the firm is insolvent because assets of V = K do not generate sufficient cashflow to meet current obligations, and that where assets of V = K imply a violation of minimum net worth or working-capital requirements. The distinction between flow-based and stock-based insolvency is discussed by Wruck (1990) and Kim, Ramaswamy and Sundaresan (1992).

Since financial distress is triggered when V = K, a reorganisation or bankruptcy is simply a mechanism whereby total assets of K are allocated to the various classes of corporate claimants. A corporate restructuring can occur in a variety of ways, including a Chapter 7 liquidation, a Chapter 11 reorganisation, a Chapter 11 liquidation or a private debt restructuring.[4]

The traditional approach to valuing corporate securities assumes that strict absolute priority holds. However, a growing amount of evidence shows that absolute priority rules are frequently violated in corporate restructurings. For example, Franks and Torous (1989) find that absolute priority is violated in 78% of the bankruptcies in their sample. Similar percentages are found by Eberhart, Moore and Roenfeldt (1990) and Weiss (1990). In addition, recent research suggests that the actual payoff to a bondholder in a reorganisation depends on a host of exogenous variables, such as firm size, the bargaining power of the bondholders, the existence of an equity committee and the strength of the ties between managers and shareholders.[5] Several recent authors have attempted to model some of the elements of the bargaining game among corporate claimants during financial distress and to incorporate them into a model for risky debt prices. These include Anderson and Sundaresan (1992), Mella and Perraudin (1993) and Leland (1994). Although insightful, these models are limited to their ability to capture the actual properties of corporate debt since they do not allow interest rates to be stochastic.

Rather than trying to model the complex bargaining process among corporate claimants during a restructuring or bankruptcy, we take the allocation of the firm's assets as exogenously given.

ASSUMPTION 5 *If a reorganisation occurs during the life of a security, the security holder receives* $1 - w$ *times the face value of the security at maturity.*

An equivalent way of specifying the payoffs in the event of a default would be to assume that the security holder receives N riskless zero-coupon bonds at the time of the default, where N equals $1 - w$ times the face amount of the debt and where the maturity date of the riskless bonds is the same as for the original debt. This equivalent specification is consistent with typical reorganisations in which security holders receive new securities rather than cash in exchange for their original claims. We note that there are other possible specifications for the payoff in reorganisation. For example, w could be allowed to depend on the remaining maturity of the bond or even on the level of interest rates at the time the firm defaults.

The factor w represents the percentage writedown on a security if there is a reorganisation of the firm during the life of the security. For limited liability securities, $w \le 1$. In general, w will differ across the various bond issues and classes of securities in the firm's capital structure. When $w = 0$, there is no writedown and the security holder is unimpaired. When $w = 1$, the security holder receives nothing in a restructuring. If $w < 0$, a security holder actually benefits from a restructuring.[6] Note that nothing in this assumption precludes w from being viewed as the expected outcome from a game theoretic model of the bargaining process.

In practice, the value of w for a particular class of securities could be estimated from actuarial information. For example, Altman (1992) finds that the average writedown, w, for secured, senior, senior subordinated, cash-pay subordinated and non cash-pay subordinated debt for a sample of defaulted bond issues during the period 1985 to 1991 is 0.395, 0.477, 0.693, 0.720 and 0.805, respectively. Franks and Torous (1994) find that the average writedown, w, for secured debt, bank debt, senior debt and junior debt for a sample of firms that reorganised under Chapter 11 during the period 1983 to 1990 is 0.199, 0.136, 0.530 and 0.711, respectively. Similar results are obtained by Betker (1992). The only constraint on the value of w is the adding-up constraint that the total settlement on all classes of claims cannot exceed K.[7]

Note that even when firms have many issues of debt outstanding, the bonds are usually grouped into a small handful of categories for the purposes of reorganisation. Thus, only two or three different values of w are usually necessary in valuing a firm's debt. For example, in December 1992 General Motors Acceptance Corp. had 53 out-

119

A SIMPLE

APPROACH TO

VALUING RISKY

FIXED AND FLOATING

RATE DEBT

standing long-term debt issues listed in *Moody's Bank and Finance Manual*. Of these, 42 issues were described as either not secured, or not secured and ranking *pari passu* with all other unsecured obligations of the company. The priority of the remaining 11 issues was not described but was probably the same as that of the other 42 issues since they were listed simply as notes or debentures.

Although we assume that w is a constant, this framework could easily be extended to allow for stochastic values of w provided that the risk of w is unsystematic. Since w represents the outcome of the bargaining process, the assumption that w is unsystematic may not be unreasonable. Because w affects payoffs linearly, allowing w to be random simply requires that we replace w with its expected value in the valuation expressions.

ASSUMPTION 6 *We assume perfect, frictionless markets in which securities trade in continuous time.*

This assumption allows us to invoke standard results to derive the fundamental partial differential equation defining the price, $H(V, r, T)$, of any derivative security with payoff at time T contingent on the values of V and r. This partial differential equation is

$$\frac{\sigma^2}{2}V^2 H_{VV} + \rho\sigma\eta V H_{Vr} + \frac{\eta^2}{2}H_{rr} + rVH_V + (\alpha - \beta r)H_r - rH = H_T \qquad (3)$$

where α represents the sum of the parameter ζ and a constant representing the market price of interest rate risk. As shown by Campbell (1986), this market price of interest rate risk can be derived within a simple general equilibrium framework in which the representative investor has logarithmic preferences. The value of the derivative security is obtained by solving equation (3) subject to the appropriate maturity condition.

The value of a riskless discount bond plays an important role in the derivation of valuation expressions for corporate securities. In this framework, the value of a riskless discount bond $D(r, T)$ is given by the Vasicek (1977) model

$$D(r, T) = \exp(A(T) - B(T)r) \qquad (4)$$

where

$$A(T) = \left(\frac{\eta^2}{2\beta^2} - \frac{\alpha}{\beta}\right)T + \left(\frac{\eta^2}{\beta^3} - \frac{\alpha}{\beta^2}\right)(\exp(-\beta T) - 1) - \left(\frac{\eta^2}{4\beta^3}\right)(\exp(-2\beta T) - 1)$$

$$B(T) = \frac{1 - \exp(-\beta T)}{\beta}$$

Valuing fixed-rate debt

In this section we derive valuation expressions for risky discount and coupon bonds and examine their implications for the term structure of credit spreads. Let $P(V, r, T)$ denote the price of a risky discount bond with maturity date T. The payoff on this contingent claim is 1 if default does not occur during the life of the bonds, and $1 - w$ if it does. This payoff function can be expressed as

$$1 - wI_{\gamma \leq T} \qquad (5)$$

where I is an indicator function that takes value one if V reaches K during the life of the bond, and zero otherwise. More formally, I takes value one if the first-passage time, γ, of V to K is less than or equal to T. In addition, let X denote the ratio V/K.

PROPOSITION 1 *The value of a risky discount bond is*

$$P(X, r, T) = D(r, T) - wD(r, T)Q(X, r, T) \qquad (6)$$

where

$$Q(X, r, T, n) = \sum_{i=1}^{n} q_i$$

$$q_1 = N(a_1)$$

$$q_i = N(a_i) - \sum_{j=1}^{i-1} q_j N(b_{ij}), \quad i = 2, 3, \ldots, n$$

$$a_i = \frac{-\ln X - M(iT/n, T)}{\sqrt{S(iT/n)}}$$

$$b_{ij} = \frac{M(jT/n, T) - M(iT/n, T)}{\sqrt{S(iT/n) - S(jT/n)}}$$

and where

$$M(t, T) = \left(\frac{\alpha - \rho\sigma\eta}{\beta} - \frac{\eta^2}{\beta^2} - \frac{\sigma^2}{2} \right) t + \left(\frac{\rho\sigma\eta}{\beta^2} + \frac{\eta^2}{2\beta^3} \right) \exp(-\beta T) \left[\exp(\beta t) - 1 \right]$$

$$+ \left(\frac{r}{\beta} - \frac{\alpha}{\beta^2} + \frac{\eta^2}{\beta^3} \right) \left[1 - \exp(-\beta t) \right] - \left(\frac{\eta^2}{2\beta^3} \right) \exp(-\beta T) \left[1 - \exp(-\beta t) \right]$$

$$S(t) = \left(\frac{\rho\sigma\eta}{\beta} + \frac{\eta^2}{\beta^2} + \sigma^2 \right) t - \left(\frac{\rho\sigma\eta}{\beta^2} + \frac{2\eta^2}{\beta^3} \right) \left[1 - \exp(-\beta t) \right]$$

$$+ \left(\frac{\eta^2}{2\beta^3} \right) \left[1 - \exp(-2\beta t) \right]$$

The term $Q(X, r, T)$ *is the limit of* $Q(X, r, T, n)$ *as* $n \to \infty$. $N(\cdot)$ *denotes the cumulative standard normal distribution function.*

A proof of Proposition 1 is given in the appendix.

This closed-form expression involves nothing more complex than the standard normal distribution function. Note that the q_i terms in equation (6) are defined recursively, which makes it straightforward to program this valuation expression and to calculate risky discount bond prices. Although $Q(X, r, T)$ is defined as the limit of $Q(X, r, T, n)$, the convergence is rapid; numerical simulations show that setting $n = 200$ results in values of $Q(X, r, T)$ and $Q(X, r, T, n)$ that are virtually indistinguishable.

Proposition 1 shows that the value of a risky discount bond depends on V and K only through their ratio, X. Thus, X provides a summary measure of default risk of the firm and can be viewed as a proxy variable for the credit rating of the firm. An important implication of this is that risky debt can be valued without having to specify separately the values of V and K. This feature dramatically simplifies the practical implementation of the model. From equation (6), the price of the risky discount bond is an explicit function of X, r and T and depends on the parameters w, α, β, η^2, σ^2 and ρ.

This closed-form expression has an intuitive structure. The first term in equation (6) represents the value the bond would have if it were riskless. The second term represents a discount for the default risk of the bond. The discount for default risk consists of two components. The first component, $wD(r, T)$, is the present value of the writedown on the bond in the event of a default. The second component, $Q(X, r, T)$, is the probability – under the risk-neutral measure – that a default occurs. It is important to recognise that the probability of a default, $Q(X, r, T)$, under the risk-neutral measure may differ from the actual probability of a default. This is because the upward drift of the actual process for

V in equation (1) is μV, while the upward drift of the risk-neutral process depends on the value of r and is independent of μ.

Since X is a sufficient statistic for default risk in this model, we do not need to condition on the pattern of cash payments to be made prior to the maturity date of a bond in order to value the bond. Intuitively, this is because we assume that financial distress triggers the default of all of the firm's debt. In contrast, the traditional approach implicitly assumes that a discount bond can only default at its maturity date. Because default risk is captured by a common state variable, X, in this model, bonds can be valued by conditioning on X directly rather than on the default status of other bonds. An important implication of this is that coupon bonds can be valued as simple portfolios of discount bonds.[8] This value-additivity feature is a major reason why this approach is significantly more tractable than the traditional approach to valuing risky fixed-rate debt securities.

The price of a risky bond is an increasing function of the default-risk variable X. This is intuitive since the higher the value of X, the further the firm is from the default threshold and the smaller the discount for default risk. Differentiation shows that bond values are decreasing functions of w. This is because an increase in w implies that the writedown on a bond in the event of financial distress is larger. Similarly, as T increases, the value of D(r, T) decreases and the risk-neutral probability of a default, Q(X, r, T), increases. Both of these effects tend to reduce the value of the risky bond. Hence, risky bonds are decreasing functions of T.

In general, the price of a risky bond is a decreasing function of r. Furthermore, the sensitivity of the price to changes in r provides a measure of the duration of the bond. As shown by Chance (1990) and others, the duration of a risky fixed-rate bond is shorter than that of an otherwise riskless bond. This property also holds for the fixed-rate bond prices implied by this model. The reason for this is that the riskless interest rate, r, plays two roles in the valuation of risky debt. In particular, an increase in r results in a lower value for D(r, T). However, an increase in r implies that the upward drift of the risk-neutral process for V is higher. This means that as r increases, V is expected to drift away from K at a faster rate, which reduces the risk-neutral probability of a default.

Another interesting implication of this model is that the duration of a risky discount bond need not be a monotonically increasing function of its maturity. For example, for a moderate level of default risk, the duration of a zero-coupon bond can first increase with T, level out, and then decrease with T. This also serves to illustrate how different the properties of risky bonds are from those of riskless bonds. In fact, for values of X and w very close to one, the effect of r on the drift can offset the effect of bond price, and a risky bond can be an increasing function of r. Thus, the duration of very risky fixed-rate debt can actually become negative, although it should be noted that this occurs only for extremely risky debt. This is shown in Figure 1, which plots the price of a zero-coupon bond when the value of X is very close to the default threshold. The value of the zero-coupon bond is an increasing function of r for maturities less than three years. In addition, the correlation between the assets of the firm and changes in the interest rate can be shown to have a major effect on the duration of risky fixed-rate debt.

Given the explicit solution for risky fixed-rate debt, we can solve for the credit spread. This is defined as the difference between the yields of a risky and a riskless bond with identical maturity dates and coupon rates. Figure 2 graphs the term

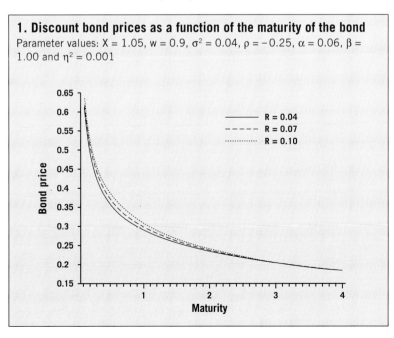

1. Discount bond prices as a function of the maturity of the bond

Parameter values: X = 1.05, w = 0.9, $\sigma^2 = 0.04$, $\rho = -0.25$, $\alpha = 0.06$, $\beta = 1.00$ and $\eta^2 = 0.001$

R = 0.04
R = 0.07
R = 0.10

Bond price

Maturity

2. Credit spreads for an 8% bond for different values of X

Parameter values: r = 0.04, w = 0.5, σ² = 0.04, ρ = −0.25, α = 0.06, β = 1.00 and η² = 0.001

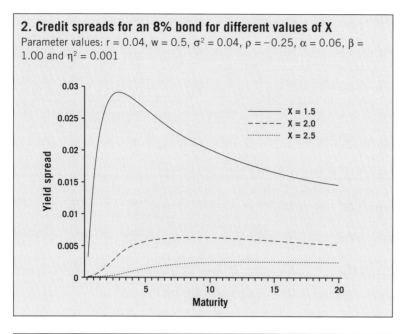

3. Credit spreads for an 8% bond for different values of w

Parameter values: X = 2.0, r = 0.04, σ² = 0.04, = ρ −0.25, α = 0.06, β = 1.00 and η² = 0.001

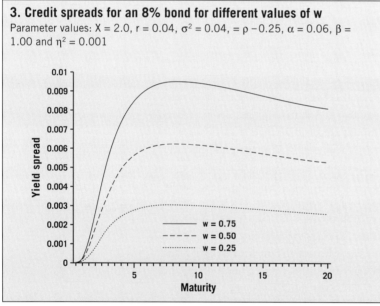

4. Credit spreads for an 8% bond for different values of r

Parameter values: X = 2.0, w = 0.50, σ² = 0.04, ρ = −0.25, α = 0.06, β = 1.00 and η² = 0.001

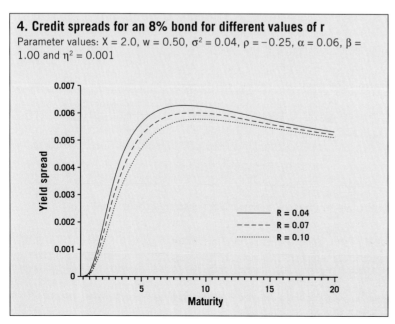

structure of credit spreads for an 8% coupon bond for various values of X. The values of the interest rate parameters used in these examples are chosen to match closely the observed moments of the short-term interest rate during the past 30 years. As shown, the term structure of credit spreads can be monotonic increasing as well as hump-shaped. This corresponds well with recent empirical evidence given by Sarig and Warga (1989), which suggests that the term structure of credit spreads is monotonic increasing for bonds with high ratings and humped-shaped for bonds with low ratings. In addition, the magnitudes of the credit spreads implied by this model are consistent with the average levels observed in debt markets. For example, Figure 2 shows that the average credit spread for a 10-year 8% coupon bond with X = 2.0 is about 60 basis points. This is close to the average spread of 48 basis points for Moody's AAA-rated industrial bond yield average during the period 1977–92.

Figure 3 shows the term structure of credit spreads for varying values of the writedown, w. As expected, the credit spread is an increasing function of w. However, as w increases the term structure of credit spreads can take on different shapes. For example, when w = 0.25, the maximum credit spread occurs for a bond with a maturity of about eight years. When w = 0.75, however, the maximum credit spread occurs for a bond with a maturity of nearly 10 years. Since w is related to priority, differences in the credit spreads shown in Figure 3 can be viewed as the term structure of priority. Note that priority matters for medium-term bonds.

The relation between credit spreads and the level of the short-term interest rate is shown in Figure 4. As discussed earlier, an increase in r tends to reduce the probability of a default because of the effect on the drift of the risk-neutral process for V. Thus, an increase in r results in a decrease in the credit spread. The magnitude of the decrease in the credit spread, however, depends on the value of ρ. This empirical implication of the model will be examined in the concluding section of this chapter.

Figure 5 graphs the credit spread for different values of the variance, σ², of the firm's assets. As σ^2 increases from 0.04 to 0.09 the maximum credit spread increases from approximately 60 basis points to approximately 300 basis points. Note that the maximum credit spreads occur at different maturities as σ^2 increases.

Figure 6 plots the relation between the term structure of credit spreads and the correlation coefficient between asset returns and changes in the interest rate. As shown, the effect of correlation can be very significant. For example, the credit spread for an 8% bond with a maturity of eight years widens by 27 basis points as the correlation increases from -0.50 to $+0.50$. The intuitive explanation for the increase in the credit spread with ρ is that the risk-neutral distribution of future values of V depends on r. Thus, the variance of changes in the value of the firm during the life of the bond depends on the correlation between asset returns and changes in the interest rate. When ρ is positive, the covariance term adds to the total variance and, therefore, increases the probability that the critical default threshold will be reached during the life of the bond. These results are consistent with empirical evidence that credit spreads for AAA-rated bonds vary across sectors. For example, the average yield for Moody's triple A-rated industrial bond index during 1977 to 1992 is 45 basis points less than the same measure for triple A-rated public utility bonds. The relation between credit spreads and correlations will also be examined in the concluding section.

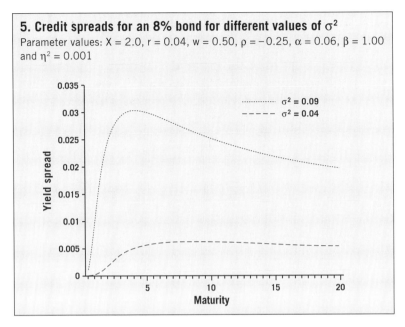

5. Credit spreads for an 8% bond for different values of σ^2
Parameter values: X = 2.0, r = 0.04, w = 0.50, ρ = -0.25, α = 0.06, β = 1.00 and η^2 = 0.001

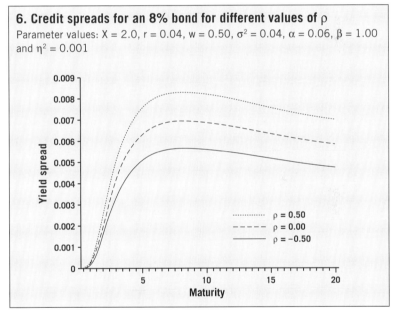

6. Credit spreads for an 8% bond for different values of ρ
Parameter values: X = 2.0, r = 0.04, w = 0.50, σ^2 = 0.04, α = 0.06, β = 1.00 and η^2 = 0.001

An important advantage of this model is that it is easy to implement in practice. For example, when firms have multiple issues of debt outstanding, the value of X can be implied from the market price of the most liquid bond and then used to value the other bonds. This is similar to the familiar technique of solving for the implied variance of an at-the-money option and using it to price the remaining options. The values of σ^2 and ρ, since they are determined by the nature of the firm's assets, can be determined on the basis of historical firm or industry data, or could even be implied along with the value of X from market data. The value of r and the three term structure parameters α, β and η^2 are easily obtained from term structure data.[9]

Valuing floating-rate debt

In this section we derive valuation expressions for floating-rate coupon payments. The value of a floating-rate note or bond can then be obtained by summing the values of the floating-rate coupons and the value of the terminal principal payment as given in the previous section. Let F(X, r, τ, T) represent the value of one floating-rate coupon payment to be made at time T, where the floating rate is determined at time τ, $\tau \leq$ T. The payoff on this claim at time T is the value of r at time τ if default does not occur prior to T, and $(1 - w)r$ if it does. This payoff function can be expressed as

124

A SIMPLE
APPROACH TO
VALUING RISKY
FIXED AND FLOATING
RATE DEBT

$$r(1 - w I_{\gamma \leq T})\qquad(7)$$

where I is again the indicator function. Note that the payoff received at time T is simply the value of r at time τ multiplied by the payoff function for a risky discount bond. This similarity will allow us to make direct comparisons between fixed- and floating-rate payments.

PROPOSITION 2 *The value of a risky floating-rate payment is*

$$F(X, r, \tau, T) = P(X, r, T) R(r, \tau, T) + w D(r, T) G(X, r, \tau, T)\qquad(8)$$

where

$$R(r, \tau, T) = r \exp(-\beta \tau) + \left(\frac{\alpha}{\beta} - \frac{\eta^2}{\beta^2}\right)\left[1 - \exp(-\beta \tau)\right]$$

$$+ \left(\frac{\eta^2}{2\beta^2}\right)\exp(-\beta T)\left[\exp(\beta \tau) - \exp(-\beta \tau)\right]$$

$$G(X, r, \tau, T, n) = \sum_{i=1}^{n} q_i \frac{C(\tau, iT/n)}{S(iT/n)} M(iT/n, T)$$

and where

$$C(\tau, t) = \left(\frac{\rho \sigma \eta}{\beta} + \frac{\eta^2}{\beta^2}\right)\exp(-\beta \tau)\left[\exp(\beta \min(\tau, t)) - 1\right]$$

$$- \frac{\eta^2}{2\beta^2}\exp(-\beta \tau)\exp(-\beta t)\left[\exp(2\beta \min(\tau, t)) - 1\right]$$

The term $G(X, r, \tau, T)$ *is the limit of* $G(X, r, \tau, T, n)$ *as* $n \to \infty$. *The remaining terms are as defined in Proposition 1.*

A proof of Proposition 2 is given in the appendix.

The value of a floating-rate coupon payment is an explicit function of X, r, τ and T. The ratio X is, again, a sufficient statistic for the riskiness of the firm. Numerical simulations show that $G(X, r, \tau, T, n)$ converges rapidly to $G(X, r, \tau, T)$.

This closed-form expression for $F(X, r, \tau, T)$ parallels that for $P(X, r, T)$. From equation (7), the floating-rate coupon payoff at time T is the value of r at time τ multiplied by the payoff function for a risky discount bond. Consistent with this, the first term in equation (8) is simply the price of a risky discount bond times the expected value of the value of r at time τ under the risk-neutral process. However, since r is correlated with X under the valuation measure, the price of a risky floating-rate payment must reflect this correlation. The second term in equation (8) adjusts for this correlation through the term $C(\tau, t)$, which is the covariance of the value of r at time τ with the value of ln X at the time, t, of its first passage to zero. Note that the correlation between r and X will generally not equal zero even if the instantaneous correlation coefficient, ρ, is zero. This is because the drift term for the risk-neutral process for X depends on r, which induces correlation between r and X when measured over discrete intervals of time.[10]

This valuation expression has many important implications for the values of floating-rate securities. To illustrate, recall that the price of a fixed-rate coupon payment is a decreasing function of T. In contrast, the value of a floating-rate coupon payment can be an increasing function of T. This is shown in Figure 7, where the price of the floating-rate coupon payment is plotted as a function of T. The intuition for this property is that when r is below its long-run average value, the expected value of the payoff equation (7) is an increasing function of T since r is mean-reverting. As T increases, however, the discount factor applied to the payoff tends to reduce the value of the floating-rate payment. For small values of T, the first effect can offset the second, resulting in a positive relation between the value of the floating-rate payment and T. As T → ∞, however, the value of the floating-rate payment approaches zero.

Another surprising implication of this model is that the value of the floating-rate coupon payment can be an increasing function of r. This is also shown in Figure 7. One reason for this is that an increase in r again has the effect of increasing the expected payment while reducing the discount factor applied to the payoff. For small values of T, the first effect can dominate the discount factor effect. A second reason for this property is related to the correlation between changes in interest rates and the returns of the firm. When the correlation is positive, an increase in r implies that larger values of X are more likely, which reduces the default risk of the firm and leads to an increase in the value of the floating-rate coupon payment. This feature illustrates that the correlation between interest rates and the returns of the firm can play a significant role in determining the values of risky corporate debt.

To provide some additional insights into the pricing of risky floating-rate debt, we compute the ratio of the price of a risky floating-rate coupon payment to that of a riskless floating-rate coupon payment. The ratio provides a measure of the percentage size of the discount for risk. The ratio of

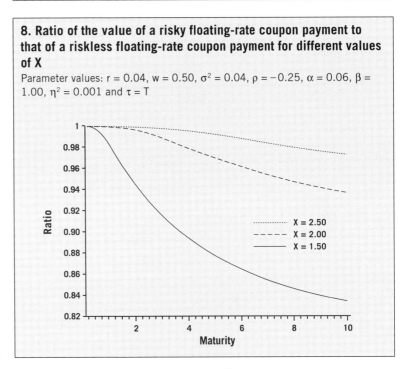

7. Values of floating-rate coupon payments for different values of r

Parameter values: X = 2.0, w = 0.50, σ^2 = 0.04, ρ = −0.25, α = 0.06, β = 1.00, η^2 = 0.001 and τ = T

8. Ratio of the value of a risky floating-rate coupon payment to that of a riskless floating-rate coupon payment for different values of X

Parameter values: r = 0.04, w = 0.50, σ^2 = 0.04, ρ = −0.25, α = 0.06, β = 1.00, η^2 = 0.001 and τ = T

the risky to riskless prices is shown in Figure 8 for different horizons and values of X. As illustrated, the shape of the relation between risky and riskless floating-rate payments depends critically on the value of X. The value of the ratio is also affected by the correlation coefficient ρ.

This expression for valuing floating-rate coupon payments can easily be extended to value coupon payments that are tied to a specific yield rather than to r, or to a specific yield plus a spread. For example, from equation (4), the yield on a t-maturity riskless bond is given by B(t)r/t − A(t)/t, which is a linear function of r. Thus, the value of a claim that pays the t-maturity yield determined at time τ as a floating-rate coupon at time T is simply B(t)F(X, r, τ, T)/t − A(t)P(X, r, T)/t. Again, the value of a stream of floating-rate payments equals the sum of the values of the individual payments.

Empirical analysis

The valuation framework for risky debt presented in this chapter has many empirical implications for fixed-income markets. One of the most important of these is that credit spreads for corporate bonds are driven by two factors: an asset value factor and an interest rate factor. Furthermore, the correlation between the two factors plays a critical role in determining the properties of credit spreads. In contrast, the traditional approach implies that credit spreads depend only on an asset value factor.

To provide some evidence on the properties of actual credit spreads for corporate bonds, we collected monthly data for Moody's industrial, utility and railroad corporate bond yield averages for the period 1977 to 1992 along with the corresponding yields for 10-year and 30-year Treasury bonds. Since the bonds used in the Moody's yield averages have varying maturities, we compute the average maturity of the bonds in the sample using the average maturity data reported in *Moody's Bond Record*. We then compute credit spreads by taking the average of the 10-year and 30-year Treasury yields that matches the maturity of the corporate yield average for that month and then subtracting the Treasury average from the corporate yield.[11] For most bonds, 190 months of data are available. For the AAA-rated utility yields, data for 10 months are missing. In addition, the railroad yield average was discontinued in 1989, resulting in a time series of 149 monthly observations for these bonds. In addition to computing credit spreads, we also calculate relative credit spreads by dividing the corporate yield by that for the Treasury bond with corresponding maturity.

Table 1 presents summary statistics for the credit spreads and relative credit spreads stratified by industry and credit rating. As expected, credit spreads increase in both absolute and relative terms as the credit rating of the bond decreases. In general, the same is true for the standard deviation of the credit spread. It is important to observe that bonds with the same credit rating but from different industries or sectors need not have similar credit spreads. This demonstrates that credit rating is not a sufficient statistic for the risk of a corporate bond.

To examine whether the properties of credit spreads are consistent with the implications of our two-factor framework, we regress changes in credit spreads on proxies for the two factors. As a proxy for the changes in the interest rate we use changes in the 30-year Treasury yield, and as a proxy for the return on the underlying assets we use the returns computed from Standard & Poor's industrial, utility and railroad stock indexes. Let ΔS denote the change in the credit spread. Similarly, let ΔY denote the change in the 30-year Treasury yield and let I denote the return on the appropriate equity index. The regression equation is

$$\Delta S = a + b\Delta Y + cI + \varepsilon \qquad (9)$$

where a, b and c are regression coefficients.

Table 1. Summary statistics for the credit spreads in Moody's utility, industrial and railroad bond yield averages

| | Credit spread | | Relative spread | | Number of |
	Mean	Std deviation	Mean	Std deviation	observations
Utilities					
AAA	0.930	0.349	1.0975	0.034	180
AA	1.276	0.431	1.1314	0.038	190
A	1.660	0.667	1.1696	0.054	190
BAA	2.077	0.758	1.2116	0.057	190
Industrials					
AAA	0.481	0.373	1.0560	0.051	190
AA	0.809	0.452	1.0888	0.059	190
A	1.231	0.580	1.1321	0.071	190
BAA	1.835	0.654	1.1972	0.084	190
Railroads					
AA	0.191	0.869	1.0284	0.092	149
A	0.794	0.770	1.0887	0.088	149
BAA	1.240	0.821	1.1337	0.097	149

The credit spread is the difference between the corporate yield and the yield of a Treasury bond with the same maturity. The relative spread is the ratio of the corporate yield to the yield of a Treasury bond with the same maturity. Yields and spreads are in percentage terms. The sample period is from April 1977 to December 1992.

The two-factor model has a number of interesting implications for the coefficients in these regressions. First, the fixed-rate valuation expression in equation (6) can be shown to imply that

$$b < 0 \qquad (10)$$

Thus, the model implies that credit spreads narrow as interest rates increase. The reason for this counterintuitive implication is that an increase in the interest rate increases the drift of the risk-neutral process for V, which in turn makes the risk-neutral probability of a default lower. Consequently, the credit spread is inversely related to the level of interest rates in this model. In addition, the inverse relation is more pronounced for firms with higher default probabilities.

A second implication of the model is that credit spreads are negatively related to returns on the firm's assets or equity:

$$c < 0 \qquad (11)$$

The reason for this is simply that an increase in the value of a firm's assets or equity reduces the probability that the default boundary will be reached. Again, this negative relation between credit spreads and returns should be stronger for firms with higher probabilities of default.

Finally, numerically differentiating credit spreads implied by equation (6) shows that the interest rate sensitivity of credit spreads, holding X fixed, increases with the value of ρ. The intuitive reason for this is similar to that for why the credit spread itself increases with ρ. When ρ is negative, changes in r tend to be reversed by changes in X. Thus, a change in r has less of an effect on the credit spread than when the value of ρ is zero or positive. The correlation with changes in the 30-year Treasury yield is -0.5894 for the returns on the utility stock index, -0.2652 for the returns on the industrial stock index and -0.1609 for the returns on the railroad stock index. Since b measures the interest rate sensitivity of credit spreads, this implies that the value of b estimated for utility spreads should be closer to zero than the value of b estimated for industrial spreads, which in turn should be closer to zero than the value of b estimated for railroad spreads. Thus, we can test this implication of the two-factor model by comparing the values of b across bonds with different values of ρ but with similar values of c.

Table 2 reports the regression results. The empirical results appear to be consistent with the implications of the two-factor model. The estimated coefficients b are negative

---

Table 2. Results of regressing monthly changes in credit spreads on monthly changes in the 30-year Treasury bond yield and the return on the corresponding Standard & Poor's stock index

	a	b	c	t_a	t_b	t_c	R^2	N
Utilities								
AAA	0.00583	−0.04413	−0.54885	0.63	−1.46	−1.45	0.015	179
AA	0.00548	−0.07725	−0.77623	0.49	−2.10	−1.68	0.025	189
A	0.00766	−0.21993	−1.25687	0.63	−5.55	−2.52	0.146	189
BAA	0.00928	−0.18386	−1.62075	0.77	−4.69	−3.28	0.107	189
Industrials								
AAA	0.00822	−0.26066	−0.63411	1.09	−12.57	−3.01	0.459	189
AA	0.01318	−0.43914	−1.23965	1.19	−14.58	−4.04	0.533	189
A	0.01750	−0.50627	−1.88404	1.41	−14.94	−5.47	0.548	189
BAA	0.01852	−0.62645	−2.02645	1.23	−15.23	−4.84	0.556	189
Railroads								
AA	0.02089	−0.78428	−0.66597	1.18	−18.12	−2.15	0.694	148
A	0.01139	−0.77246	−0.17902	0.63	−17.53	−0.57	0.680	148
BAA	0.01750	−0.82324	−0.59208	1.06	−20.44	−2.05	0.742	148

The regression equation is $\Delta S = a + bY + cl + \varepsilon$, where ΔS is the change in the credit spread, ΔY is the change in the 30-year Treasury bond yield and I is the return on the corresponding stock index.

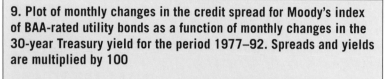

9. Plot of monthly changes in the credit spread for Moody's index of BAA-rated utility bonds as a function of monthly changes in the 30-year Treasury yield for the period 1977–92. Spreads and yields are multiplied by 100

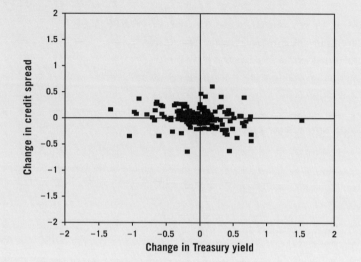

10. Plot of monthly changes in the credit spread for Moody's index of BAA-rated industrial bonds as a function of monthly changes in the 30-year Treasury yield for the period 1977–92. Spreads and yields are multiplied by 100

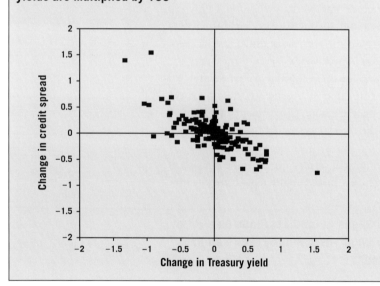

for each of the 11 credit spreads. With the exception of the triple A-rated utility bonds, all of the estimates of b are statistically significant. The t-statistics for the estimates of b for the industrial and railroad bonds are all in excess of 12.

The magnitude of the estimates of b implies that the relation between credit standards and interest rates is economically important as well as statistically significant. For example, the regression results imply that a 100-basis-point increase in the 30-year Treasury yield reduces BAA-rated utility credit spreads by 18.4 basis points, BAA-rated industrial credit spreads by 62.6 basis points and BAA-rated railroad credit spreads by 82.3 basis points. This effect is illustrated in Figures 9, 10 and 11, which plot changes in BAA-rated credit spreads for utility, industrial and railroad bonds against changes in the 30-year Treasury yield. The net effect of this negative relation between credit spreads and interest rates is to make the duration of corporate bonds shorter than would be the case for Treasury bonds. The reason for this is that an increase in the riskless rate is partially offset by a decline in the credit spread, implying that the change in price is less for a risky bond than for a riskless bond. As implied by the model, the coefficient b generally decreases with the credit rating of the bonds. Exceptions include the BAA-rated utility and A-rated railroad credit spreads.

Table 2 also shows that all of the estimates of c are negative. In addition, most of the estimates are statistically significant although not as significant as the estimates of b. With the exception of the railroad credit spreads, the estimates of c decline monotonically with the credit rating of the bonds. The economic magnitude of these estimates is also important. For example, a 10% return (l = 0.10) reduces BAA-rated utility credit spreads by 16.2 basis points, BAA-rated industrial credit spreads by 20.2 basis points and BAA-rated railroad credit spreads by 5.9 basis points. These results are consistent with the evidence of Jones, Mason and Rosenfeld (1984), who find that equity returns are related to prices of below-investment-grade bonds and argue that allowing interest rates to be stochastic may improve the performance of the traditional model.

These results for b and c provide clear evidence against the traditional approach to valuing risky debt in which the interest rate is assumed to be constant and firm value is the only factor determining credit spreads. In fact, the variation in credit spreads due to changes in the level of interest rates is more important for these investment-grade bonds than the variation due to changes in the value of the firm. To see this, note that the standard deviation of monthly changes in the 30-year Treasury yield during the sample period is 36.8 basis points. Similarly, the standard deviations of monthly returns for the utility, industrial and railroad stock indexes are 0.029, 0.036 and 0.053, respectively. Multiplying these values by the parameter estimates b and c implies that a one standard deviation increase in the 30-year yield reduces the BAA-rated utility credit spread by 6.8 basis points, while a one standard deviation positive return for the utility index reduces the credit spread by 4.7 basis points. The corresponding measures for the BAA-rated industrial credit spread are 23.1 basis points and 7.3 basis points, and those for the BAA-rated railroad credit spread are 30.3 basis points and 3.1 basis points.

11. Plot of monthly changes in the credit spread for Moody's index of BAA-rated railroad bonds as a function of monthly changes in the 30-year Treasury yield for the period 1977–89. Spreads and yields are multiplied by 100

The third implication of the two-factor model focuses on the relation between the values of b and the correlation coefficient ρ, holding c fixed. As shown in Table 2, the implications of the model appear to be supported by the regression estimates. For example, the value of c is roughly comparable across AAA-rated utility and industrial and AA-rated railroad bonds. The corresponding ranking of b coefficients for these bonds is precisely as implied by the two-factor model. Similar results hold for the other rating categories. Casual observation of Figures 9, 10 and 11 shows clearly that the interest rate sensitivity of credit spreads is as predicted by the model. These results suggest that the correlation between asset returns and changes in the interest rate has an important effect on the interest rate sensitivity of credit spreads, which in turn is the major source of variation in the credit spreads of these investment-grade bonds. Equivalently, these results imply that the correlation coefficient ρ is a major determinant of a risky bond's duration.

Finally, it is important to acknowledge that the two-factor model does not capture all of the variation in credit spreads. This is particularly true for utility bonds, where the R^2 values for the regressions range from 0.015 to 0.146. For the other bonds, however, the regression R^2s are quite high and range from 0.459 to 0.742. Thus, most of the variation in credit spreads is captured by the two-factor model for these bonds. Note that the R^2 values are generally higher for lower-rated bonds.

To provide additional insights into the properties of credit spreads, we also regress changes in relative credit spreads on percentage changes in the 30-year Treasury yield as well as on the returns on the various stock indexes. Let ΔR be the change in the relative credit spread and let PY be the percentage change in the 30-year Treasury yield. Table 3 reports the results of estimating the regression

$$\Delta R = a + b\,PY + cI + \varepsilon \qquad (12)$$

The implications of the two-factor model for the regression parameters can be shown to be similar to those described earlier.

In general, the results given by this regression parallel those reported in Table 2. If anything, the implications of the two-factor model are more strongly supported by these results. In particular, the estimates of b now decrease monotonically as we move from higher to lower credit ratings. Similarly, the relation between b and the correlation coefficient ρ, holding c fixed, is even more striking. One major difference between the two regressions is that the R^2 values in Table 3 are generally much higher than those in Table 2. For example, the two-factor model is able to explain 65% and 77% of the variation in the relative spreads of BAA-rated industrial and railroad bonds. Similarly, this

CREDIT RISK: MODELS AND MANAGEMENT

130

A SIMPLE
APPROACH TO
VALUING RISKY
FIXED AND FLOATING
RATE DEBT

Table 3. Results of regressing monthly changes in credit spreads on monthly percentage changes in the 30-year Treasury bond yield and the return on the corresponding Standard & Poor's stock index

	a	b	c	t_a	t_b	t_c	R^2	N
Utilities								
AAA	0.00082	−0.19300	−0.07061	0.86	−5.77	−1.79	0.177	179
AA	0.00078	−0.26897	−0.08993	0.72	−7.10	−2.00	0.241	189
A	0.00088	−0.40640	−0.10928	0.73	−9.67	−2.19	0.382	189
BAA	0.00106	−0.41996	−0.14890	0.89	−10.01	−2.99	0.383	189
Industrials								
AAA	0.00115	−0.36209	−0.06507	1.31	−14.21	−2.70	0.522	189
AA	0.00164	−0.53685	−0.11352	1.46	−16.44	−3.64	0.593	189
A	0.00203	−0.66144	−0.16940	1.58	−17.65	−4.72	0.625	189
BAA	0.00220	−0.82130	−0.18029	1.44	−18.56	−4.26	0.650	189
Railroads								
AA	0.00279	−0.78723	−0.04965	1.64	−17.59	−1.68	0.680	148
A	0.00183	−0.83482	−0.00805	1.02	−17.53	−0.26	0.680	148
BAA	0.00253	−0.91002	−0.04776	1.61	−22.03	−1.75	0.770	148

The regression equation is $\Delta R = a + bPY + cI + \varepsilon$, where ΔR is the change in the relative credit spread, PY is the change in the 30-year Treasury bond yield and I is the return on the corresponding stock index.

regression specification now allows the two-factor model to explain more than 38% of the variation in the relative spreads of BAA-rated utility bonds.

Conclusion

A simple new framework has been developed for valuing risky corporate debt that incorporates both default risk and interest rate risk. We applied this model to derive closed-form valuation expressions for fixed-rate and floating-rate debt. An important feature of our approach is that it can be applied directly to value risky debt when there are many coupon payment dates or when the capital structure of the firm is very complex. In addition, this approach allows us to relax the assumption of strict absolute priority which underlies the traditional approach to valuing risky debt.

A number of important insights about the valuation of risky debt emerged from this analysis. We showed that the correlation of a firm's assets with changes in the level of the interest rate can have significant effects on the value of risky fixed-income securities. We also showed that the term structure of credit spreads can have a variety of different shapes. In addition, our model implies that credit spreads are negatively related to the level of interest rates. Finally, our model has many implications for hedging the interest rate and default risk of corporate debt.

The empirical results suggest that the implications of this valuation model are consistent with the properties of credit spreads implicit in Moody's corporate bond yield averages. In particular, credit spreads are negatively related to the level of interest rates. Furthermore, differences in credit spreads across industries and sectors appear to be related to differences in correlations between equity returns and changes in the interest rate. We also found that changes in interest rates account for more of the variation in credit spreads for investment-grade bonds than changes in the value of the assets of the firm. The results provide strong evidence that both default risk and interest rate risk are necessary components of a valuation model for corporate debt.

Finally, we observed that although traditional approaches to modelling risky debt give important conceptual insights, they have not provided practical tools for valuing realistic types of corporate securities. The primary advantage of our model is that it is easily applied to all types of corporate debt securities and so can be used to provide specific pricing and hedging results rather than just general implications. In particular, the model provides a simple theoretical benchmark with which the observed properties of risky corporate debt prices can be compared. Future research should concentrate on testing whether this two-factor model is able to explain the actual level of corporate bond yields using detailed cross-sectional and time-series data for individual bonds and firms.

131

A SIMPLE

APPROACH TO

VALUING RISKY

FIXED AND FLOATING

RATE DEBT

Appendix

Proof of Proposition 1 Let $P(X, r, T) = D(r, T)(1 - wQ(X, r, T))$. Differentiation shows that equation (3) is satisfied if $Q(X, r, T)$ is the solution to

$$\frac{\sigma^2}{2} X^2 Q_{XX} + \rho \sigma \eta X Q_{Xr} + \frac{\eta^2}{2} Q_{rr} + (r - \rho \sigma \eta B(T)) X Q_X$$

$$+ (\alpha - \beta r - \eta^2 B(T)) Q_r - Q_T = 0 \qquad (A1)$$

subject to the initial condition $Q(X, r, 0) = I_{\gamma \leq T}$. Using the results given by Friedman (1975), $Q(X, r, T)$ is the probability that the first passage time of $\ln X$ to zero is less than T, where probabilities are taken with respect to the time-dependent processes

$$d \ln X = \left(r - \frac{\sigma^2}{2} - \rho \sigma \eta B(T - t) \right) dt + \sigma dZ_1 \qquad (A2)$$

$$dr = \left[\alpha - \beta r - \eta^2 B(T - t) \right] dt + \eta dZ_2 \qquad (A3)$$

Integrating the dynamics for r from time zero to time τ implies that

$$r_\tau = r \exp(-\beta \tau) + \left(\frac{\alpha}{\beta} - \frac{\eta^2}{\beta^2} \right) \left[1 - \exp(-\beta \tau) \right]$$

$$+ \frac{\eta^2}{2\beta^2} \exp(-\beta T) \left[\exp(\beta \tau) - \exp(-\beta \tau) \right] + \eta \exp(-\beta \tau) \int_0^\tau \exp(\beta s) dZ_2 \qquad (A4)$$

Integrating the dynamics for $\ln X$, substituting in for the value of r from the above equation and evaluating the resulting double integral by applying Fubini's theorem implies that

$$\ln X_T = \ln X + M(T, T) + \frac{\eta}{\beta} \int_0^T \left[1 - \exp(-\beta(T - t)) \right] dZ_2 + \sigma \int_0^T dZ_1 \qquad (A5)$$

Thus, $\ln X_T$ is normally distributed with mean $\ln X + M(T, T)$ and variance $S(T)$. Similarly, the joint bivariate distribution of $\ln X_t$ and $\ln X_T$ implies that $\ln X_T$, conditional on $\ln X_t = 0$, is normally distributed with mean $M(T, T) - M(t, T)$ and variance $S(T) - S(t)$. Let $q(0, \tau \mid \ln X, 0)$ be the first passage density of $\ln X$ to zero at time τ starting from $\ln X$ at time zero. From equation (2.2a) of Buonocore, Nobile and Ricciardi (1987), the first passage density is defined implicitly by the integral equation

$$N \left(\frac{-\ln X - M(t, T)}{S(t)} \right) = \int_0^t q(0, \tau \mid \ln X, 0) N \left(\frac{M(\tau, T) - M(t, T)}{S(t) - S(\tau)} \right) d\tau \qquad (A6)$$

where $\tau \leq t \leq T$. Dividing the period from time zero to time T into n equal sub-periods and discretising the above integral equation gives the following system of linear equations:

$$N(a_i) = \sum_{j=1}^{i} q_i N(b_{ij}), \quad i = 1, 2, \ldots, n \qquad (A7)$$

where

$$q_i = \frac{q(0, iT/n \mid \ln X, 0) T}{n} \qquad (A8)$$

These equations are easily solved as a recursive system for the q_i terms. The sum of the q_i terms provides an approximation to the value of $Q(X, r, T)$. As n increases, the approximation $Q(X, r, T, n)$ converges to the value $Q(X, r, T)$.

Proof of Proposition 2 Following the same approach as in Proposition 1 implies that the value of the floating-rate coupon can be expressed as

$$F(X, r, \tau, T) = D(r, T)E[r_\tau] - wD(r, T)E[r_\tau I_{\gamma \leq T}] \qquad \text{(A9)}$$

where the expectations are taken with respect to the processes (A2) and (A3). From equation (A4), the expectation $E[r_\tau]$ is $R(r, \tau, T)$. The results obtained by Buonocore, Nobile and Ricciardi (1987) can also be used to show that

$$E\left[r_\tau I_{\gamma \leq T}\right] = \int_0^T E\left[r_\tau \mid \ln X_t = 0\right] q\left(0, t \mid \ln X, 0\right) dt \qquad \text{(A10)}$$

Standard results for the bivariate normal distribution can be used to derive the conditional expectation

$$E\left[r_\tau \mid \ln X_t = 0\right] = R(r, \tau, T) - \frac{C(\tau, t)}{S(t)} M(t, T) \qquad \text{(A11)}$$

where $C(\tau, t)$ is the covariance between r_τ and $\ln X_t$. This covariance can be obtained from equations (A4) and (A5):

$$C(\tau, t) = \left(\frac{\rho \sigma \eta}{\beta} + \frac{\eta^2}{\beta^2}\right) \exp(-\beta \tau)\left[\exp\left(\beta \min(\tau, t)\right) - 1\right]$$

$$- \frac{\eta^2}{2\beta^2} \exp(-\beta \tau) \exp(-\beta t)\left[\exp\left(2\beta \min(\tau, t)\right) - 1\right] \qquad \text{(A12)}$$

Discretising the integral in equation (A10) gives the following approximation for $E[r_\tau \mid \ln X_t = 0]$

$$= \sum_{i=1}^n q_i \left(R(r, \tau, T) - \frac{C(\tau, iT/n)}{S(iT/n)} M(iT/n, T)\right)$$

$$= R(r, \tau, T)Q(X, r, T) - G(X, r, \tau, T, n) \qquad \text{(A13)}$$

As n increases, the approximation $G(X, r, \tau, T, n)$ converges to the value $G(X, r, \tau, T)$. Substituting into equation (A9), and recalling the definition of $P(X, r, T)$, gives $F(X, r, \tau, T)$.

Both authors are from the Anderson Graduate School of Management, University of California at Los Angeles. This is a substantially revised version of an earlier working paper entitled "Valuing Risky Debt: A New Approach". We are grateful for the comments and suggestions of Brian Betker, Brad Cornell, Darrell Duffie, Julian Franks, Mark Grinblatt, Robert Heinkel, David Hirshleifer, Hayne Leland, Andrew Lo, Victor Makarov, Richard Rendleman, Ehud Ronn, Mark Rubinstein, Chester Spatt, Walter Torous, Bruce Tuckman, Justin Wood, Josef Zechner and seminar participants at the Amex Options and Derivatives Colloquium, the University of British Columbia, the University of California at Berkeley, Duke University, the European Institute for Financial Analysis and Portfolio Management, the University of Rochester, Southern Methodist University, Stanford University, the University of Strathclyde, Texas Christian University, UCLA, and the European Finance Association and Western Finance Association meetings. We are particularly grateful for generous financial support by the Milken Institute for Job and Capital Formation. All errors are our responsibility.

133

A SIMPLE
APPROACH TO
VALUING RISKY
FIXED AND FLOATING
RATE DEBT

1 *For a model with dynamic capital structure choice, see Fischer, Heinkel and Zechner (1989a, 1989b).*

2 *In the Leland (1994) model, the firm faces taxes and bankruptcy costs that imply an optimal capital structure. As a result, firms may have incentives to move towards the optimal capital structure in the Leland model.*

3 *Black and Cox (1976) assume that the default threshold is of the form Ke^{-cT} rather than a constant. This time-dependence of the threshold could easily be incorporated into a more general version of our model.*

4 *For a discussion of these alternatives, see Franks and Torous (1989), Gilson, John and Lang (1990) and Wruck (1990).*

5 *See Weiss (1990), LoPucki and Whitford (1990) and Betker (1992).*

6 *As shown by Franks and Torous (1989) and LoPucki and Whitford (1990), this situation can actually occur. In most cases this results from the bondholder receiving pendency interest at a rate higher than the coupon rate of the bond during the period between the default and the execution of the reorganisation plan. In other cases, a settlement made on the basis of the face amount of a long-maturity, low-coupon-rate bond might benefit the bondholder because of the effective shortening of the maturity date.*

7 *Included in these claims would be any administrative and priority claims such as wages, taxes and debtor-in-possession financing.*

8 *Geske (1977) shows that in the Merton (1974) framework, the value of a coupon bond is related to the value of a compound option. Determining the value of this compound option requires evaluating an N-dimensional integral, where N is the number of remaining coupon payments.*

9 *For example, see Chan et al. (1992).*

10 *The effects of temporal aggregation on moments of continuous-time processes are discussed by Longstaff (1989).*

11 *Since changes in the 10-year and 30-year Treasury yields are almost perfectly positively correlated, the empirical results are robust to the way the 10-year and 30-year Treasury yields are weighted in computing credit spreads.*

BIBLIOGRAPHY

Altman, E. I., 1992, "Revisiting the High-Yield Bond Market", *Financial Management* 21, pp. 78–92.

Anderson, R. W., and S. Sundaresan, 1992, "Design and Valuation of Debt Contracts", Working paper, Columbia University.

Betker, B. L., 1991, "An Analysis of the Returns to Stockholders and Bondholders in a Chapter 11 Reorganization", Working paper, Ohio State University.

Betker, B. L., 1992, "Management Changes, Equity's Bargaining Power and Deviations from Absolute Priority in Chapter 11 Bankruptcies", Working paper, Ohio State University.

Black, F., and J. C. Cox, 1976, "Valuing Corporate Securities: Some Effects of Bond Indenture Provisions", *The Journal of Finance* 31, pp. 351–67.

Black, F., and M. Scholes, 1973, "The Pricing of Options and Corporate Liabilities", *Journal of Political Economy* 81, pp. 637–54.

Buonocore, A., A. G. Nobile and L. M. Ricciardi, 1987, "A New Integral Equation for the Evaluation of First-Passage-Time Probability Densities", *Advances in Applied Probability* 19, pp. 784–800.

Campbell, J. Y., 1986, "A Defence of Traditional Hypotheses about the Term Structure of Interest Rates", *Journal of Finance* 41, pp. 183–93.

Chan, K. C., A. Karolyi, F. Longstaff and A. Sanders, 1992, "An Empirical Comparison of Alternative Models of the Short-Term Interest Rate", *Journal of Finance* 47, pp. 1209–27.

Chance, D. M., 1990, "Default Risk and the Duration of Zero-Coupon Bonds", *Journal of Finance* 45, pp. 265–74.

Cornell, B., F. Longstaff and E. Schwartz, 1993, "Financial Distress, Capital Infusions, and Optimal Defaults", Working paper, UCLA.

134

A SIMPLE
APPROACH TO
VALUING RISKY
FIXED AND FLOATING
RATE DEBT

Eberhart, A. C., W. T. Moore and R. L. Roenfeldt, 1990, "Security Pricing and Deviations from the Absolute Priority Rule in Bankruptcy Proceedings", *Journal of Finance* 45, pp. 1457–69.

Fischer, E. O., R. Heinkel and J. Zechner, 1989a, "Dynamic Capital Structure Choice: Theory and Tests", *Journal of Finance* 44, pp. 19–40.

Fischer, E. O., R. Heinkel and J. Zechner, 1989b, "Dynamic Recapitalization Policies and the Role of Call Premia and Issue Discounts", *Journal of Financial and Quantitative Analysis* 24, pp. 427–46.

Franks, J. R., and W. Torous, 1989, "An Empirical Investigation of U.S. Firms in Reorganization", *Journal of Finance* 44, pp. 747–69.

Franks, J. R., and W. Torous, 1994, "A Comparison of Financial Recontracting in Distressed Exchanges and Chapter 11 Reorganizations", *Journal of Financial Economics* 35, pp. 349–70.

Friedman, A., 1975, *Stochastic Differential Equations and Applications: Volume 1* (New York: Academic Press).

Gennotte, G., and T. A. Marsh, 1993, "The Term Structure, Equity Returns, and Yield Premiums on Risky Bonds", Working paper, University of California at Berkeley.

Geske, R., 1977, "The Valuation of Corporate Liabilities as Compound Options", *Journal of Financial and Quantitative Analysis* 12, pp. 541–52.

Gilson, S. C., K. John and L. H. P. Lang, 1990, "Troubled Debt Restructurings: An Empirical Study of Private Reorganization of Firms in Default", *Journal of Financial Economics* 27, pp. 315–54.

Ginzburg, A., K. Maloney and R. Willner, 1993, "Risk Rating Migration and the Valuation of Floating Rate Debt", Working paper, Dartmouth College.

Harrison, J. M., and S. R. Pliska, 1979, "Martingales and Arbitrage in Multiperiod Securities Markets", *Journal of Economic Theory* 20, pp. 381–408.

Hull, J., and A. White, 1992, *Risk* Magazine.

Ingersoll, J. E., 1977a, "A Contingent-Claims Valuation of Convertible Securities", *Journal of Financial Economics* 4, pp. 289–321.

Ingersoll, J. E., 1977b, "An Examination of Corporate Call Policies on Convertible Securities", *Journal of Finance* 32, pp. 463–78.

Jarrow, R., and S. Turnbull, 1992a, "A Unified Approach for Pricing Contingent Claims on Multiple Term Structures", Working paper, Cornell University.

Jarrow, R., and S. Turnbull, 1992b, "Pricing Options on Financial Securities Subject to Credit Risk", Working paper, Cornell University.

Jarrow, R., and S. Turnbull, 1992c, "The Pricing and Hedging of Options on Financial Securities Subject to Credit Risk: The Discrete Time Case", Working paper, Cornell University.

Jarrow, R., and S. Turnbull, 1992d, "Interest Rate Risk Management in the Presence of Default Risk", Working paper, Cornell University.

Jones, E., S. Mason and E. Rosenfeld, 1984, "Contingent Claims Analysis of Corporate Capital Structures: An Empirical Investigation", *Journal of Finance* 39, pp. 611–25.

Kim, I. J., K. Ramaswamy and S. Sundaresan, 1992, "The Valuation of Corporate Fixed Income Securities", Working paper, New York University.

Leland, H. E., 1994, "Corporate Debt Value, Bond Covenants, and Optimal Capital Structure", Working paper, University of California, Berkeley.

Longstaff, F. A., 1989, "Temporal Aggregation and the Continuous-Time Capital Asset Pricing Model", *Journal of Finance* 44, pp. 871–87.

LoPucki, L. M., and W. C. Whitford, 1990, "Bargaining Over Equity's Share in the Bankruptcy Reorganization of Large, Publicly Held Companies", *University of Pennsylvania Law Review* 139, pp. 125–96.

Maloney, K. J., 1992, "A Contingent Claims Model of Corporate Security Valuation Using a Realistic Model of Financial Distress", Working paper, Dartmouth College.

Mella, P., and W. Perraudin, 1993, "Strategic Debt Service", Working paper, University of Cambridge.

Merton, R. C., 1974, "On the Pricing of Corporate Debt: The Risk Structure of Interest Rates", *Journal of Finance* 29, pp. 449–70.

135

A SIMPLE
APPROACH TO
VALUING RISKY
FIXED AND FLOATING
RATE DEBT

Merton, R. C., 1977, "On the Pricing of Contingent Claims and the Modigliani–Miller Theorem", *Journal of Financial Economics* 5, pp. 241–50.

Nielsen, L., J. Saa-Requejo and P. Santa-Clara, 1993, "Default Risk and Interest Rate Risk: The Term Structure of Default Spreads", Working paper, INSEAD.

Ramaswamy, K., and S. Sundaresan, 1986, "The Valuation of Floating-Rate Instruments: Theory and Evidence", *Journal of Financial Economics* 17, pp. 251–72.

Sarig, O., and A. Warga, 1989, "Some Empirical Estimates of the Risk Structure of Interest Rates", *Journal of Finance* 44, pp. 1351–60.

Shimko, D., N. Tejima and D. van Deventer, 1993, "The Pricing of Risky Debt When Interest Rates are Stochastic", *Journal of Fixed Income* 3, pp. 58–65.

Smith, C. W., and J. B. Warner, 1979, "On Financial Contracting: An Analysis of Bond Covenants", *Journal of Financial Economics* 7, pp. 117–61.

Vasicek, O., 1977, "An Equilibrium Characterization of the Term Structure", *Journal of Financial Economics* 5, pp. 177–88.

Weiss, L. A., 1990, "Bankruptcy Resolution: Direct Costs and Violation of Priority of Claims", *Journal of Financial Economics* 27, pp. 285–314.

Wruck, K. H., 1990, "Financial Distress, Reorganization, and Organizational Efficiency", *Journal of Financial Economics* 27, pp. 419–46.

10

Credit Risk Revisited

Michel Crouhy, Dan Galai and Robert Mark

Canadian Imperial Bank of Commerce; Hebrew University, Jerusalem;
Canadian Imperial Bank of Commerce

An investor who holds a corporate bond is exposed to both market risk and credit risk. Market risk is related to movements in government interest rates and spreads for a given credit quality, while credit risk evolves from defaults, as well as credit migration, whether an upgrade or a downgrade. Ideally, credit risk and market risk should be addressed jointly, as in most cases default, or downgrading, is triggered by changes in asset values and financial rates. This integrated approach to credit and market risk is a continuing challenge to academics and practitioners.

Different approaches have been proposed in financial literature, which are all consistent with the arbitrage-free pricing methodology.[1] The option pricing model, after the seminal paper by Merton (1974), builds on the limited liability rule that allows shareholders to default on their obligations while surrendering the firm's assets to the various claimholders, according to prespecified priority rules. The firm's liabilities are thus viewed as contingent claims issued against its assets, with the payouts to the various debtholders specified by seniority and safety covenants. Default occurs at debt maturity when the firm's asset value falls short of debt value at that time, and then the loss distribution conditional on default is endogenously determined.

An alternative to this approach, proposed by Hull and White (1995) and Longstaff and Schwartz (1995) allows bankruptcy to occur at a random default time. Bankruptcy is triggered the first time the value of the firm's assets reaches some prespecified default boundary, and it also assumes the loss in the event of default is exogenous. This approach simplifies the bankruptcy process by not relying on the priority structure of the debt instruments, but it loses its generality by assuming an exogenous recovery rate for each promised dollar in case of default. These models allow for stochastic interest rates.

The most recent approach, developed independently of each other by Duffie and Singleton (1994), Jarrow and Turnbull (1995) and Jarrow, Lando and Turnbull (1997), characterises bankruptcy as an exogenous process, eg, a Markov process in the firm's credit ratings, which does not explicitly depend on the firm's assets and the priority rules for the various debt instruments. However, they still need to assume the recovery factor as given in the event of default. Contrary to the previous approach, the default event is not defined and occurs at a random time.[2] These models allow one to derive the term structure of default probabilities from credit spreads, while assuming an exogenous and somewhat arbitrary recovery rate.[3]

In this chapter, we adopt the traditional option pricing framework to value corporate securities and show that it allows us to retrieve results derived by Jarrow and Turnbull (1995). That is, the credit spread on a corporate bond is the product of the probability of default and the loss rate. However, in our model, the loss rate is endogenously determined and depends on the firm's asset value, volatility, and the default-free interest rate for the same maturity. We then present the economic value of default as a put option. A numerical example is used to illustrate the application of option pricing theory to the

This paper was originally published in Risk *magazine, March 1998. This research was partially sponsored by a research grant from the Zagagi Center, the Hebrew University, Jerusalem.*

assessment of credit risk. We also analyse the probability of default and the conditional expected recovery value. Then we show how credit risk can be assessed according to share value rather than the firm's asset value. In many cases, the results that are based on mathematical approximations are subject to small errors. The systematic risk of credit risk is derived in the final section.

The model presented in this chapter assumes a simple capital structure with one type of (zero-coupon) debt. However, it can easily be extended to the case where the firm has issued both senior and junior debt. Then the loss rate for each type of debt is endogenously derived, together with the default probability.[4] Corporate taxation can also be incorporated in the model to show the impact of taxes on the risk sharing rule between not only the bank and the borrower, but also the government.

Assessing credit risk as a put option

Consider the case of a firm with risky assets V, which is financed by equity S, and by one debt obligation, maturing at time T with face value (including accrued interest) F and market value B. The loan to the firm is subject to credit risk, namely the risk that at time T the value of the firm's assets, V_T, will fall below the obligation to the debt holders, F. Credit risk exists so long as the probability of default, $\text{Prob}(V_T < F)$, is greater than zero, which implies that at time 0, $B_0 < Fe^{-rT}$, ie the yield to maturity on the debt, y_T, is higher than the risk-free rate, r, where $\pi_T = y_T - r$ denotes the default spread which compensates the bond holders for the default risk they bear. If we assume that markets are frictionless, with no taxes, and there is no bankruptcy cost, then the value of the firm's assets is simply the sum of the firm's equity and debt:

$$V_0 = S_0 + B_0 \qquad (1)$$

From the viewpoint of a bank that makes a loan to the firm, the questions are whether it can eliminate/reduce credit risk and at what price. What is the economic cost of reducing credit risk and what are the factors affecting this cost? In this simple framework, credit risk is a function of the financial structure of the firm, ie, its leverage ratio $LR \equiv Fe^{-rT}/V_0$ (where V_0 is the present value of the firm's assets and Fe^{-rT} is the present value of the debt obligation at maturity, assuming no default), the volatility of the firm's assets, σ, and the time to maturity of the debt, T. The model was first suggested by Merton (1974) and Galai and Masulis (1976).

The value of credit risk for the bank loan, when this loan is the firm's only debt instrument and assuming the only other source of financing is equity, is equal to the value of a put option on the assets of the firm, V, at a strike price of F, maturing at time T. If the bank buys such a put option, it eliminates the credit risk associated with the loan (see Table 1).

By purchasing the put on V for the term of the debt, with a strike price equal to the face value of the loan, the bank can eliminate all the credit risk and convert the risky corporate loan into a riskless loan with a face value of F. If the riskless interest rate is r, then in equilibrium it should be that $B_0 + P_0 = Fe^{-rT}$. Thus, the value of the put option is the cost of eliminating the credit risk of providing a loan to the firm. If we make the assumptions needed to apply the Black–Scholes model to equity and debt instruments (see Galai and Masulis (1976) for a detailed discussion), we can write the value of the put as

$$P_0 = -N(-d_1)V_0 + Fe^{-rT}N(-d_2) \quad (2)$$

where P_0 is the current value of the put, $N(\cdot)$ is the cumulative standard unit normal distribution and

Table 1. Bank's payout matrix for making a loan and buying a put option

Time	0	T	
Value of assets	V_0	$V_T \le F$	$V_T > F$
Bank's position:			
(a) make a loan	$-B_0$	V_T	F
(b) buy a put	$-P_0$	$F - V_T$	0
Total	$-B_0 - P_0$	F	F

$$d_1 = \frac{\ln(V_0/F) + \left(r + \frac{1}{2}\sigma^2\right)T}{\sigma\sqrt{T}} = \frac{\ln(V_0/F^{-rT}) + \frac{1}{2}\sigma^2 T}{\sigma\sqrt{T}}$$

$$d_2 = d_1 - \sigma\sqrt{T}$$

and σ is the standard deviation of the rate of return of the firm's assets.

The model illustrates that the credit risk and its costs is a function of the riskiness of the assets of the firm σ, and this risk is also a function of the time interval until debt is paid back, T. The cost is also affected by the risk-free interest rate, r: the higher r is, the less costly it is to reduce credit risk.

The cost is a homogeneous function of the leverage ratio, $LR = Fe^{-rT}/V_0$, ie, it stays constant for a scale expansion of Fe^{-rT}/V_0. We can now derive the yield-to-maturity for the corporate discount debt, y_T, as

$$y_T = -\frac{\ln\left(\frac{B_0}{F}\right)}{T} = -\frac{\ln\left(\frac{Fe^{-rT} - P_0}{F}\right)}{T}$$

so that the default spread, π_T, defined as $\pi_T = y_T - r$, can be derived from equation (2):

$$\pi_T = y_T - r = -\frac{1}{T}\ln\left[N(d_2) + \frac{V_0}{Fe^{-rT}}N(d_1)\right] \qquad (3)$$

The default spread can be computed as a function of the leverage ratio, $LR \equiv Fe^{-rT}/V_0$, the volatility of the underlying assets, σ, and the debt maturity, T. Table 2 shows the default spread for various levels of volatility and different leverage ratios. In Table 2, by using the Black–Scholes model when $V_0 = 100$, $T = 1$, $r = 10\%$ and also $\sigma = 40\%$, with the leverage ratio $LR = 70\%$,[5] we obtain the value of equity, $S_0 = 33.37$ and the value of the risky corporate debt, $B_0 = 66.63$. The yield on the loan is $77/66.63 - 1 = 0.156$, ie there is a 5.6% risk premium on the loan to reflect the credit risk.

The model also shows that the put value is $P_0 = 3.37$. Hence the cost of eliminating the credit risk is $3.37 for $100 of the firm's assets, for the case when the face value of the one-year debt is 77. This cost drops to 25 cents when volatility decreases to 20% and to 0 for 10% volatility. The riskiness of the assets as measured by the volatility, σ, is a critical factor in determining credit risk. To see that the bank eliminates all its credit risk by buying the put, we can compute the yield on the bank's position as

$$\frac{F}{B_0 + P_0} = \frac{77}{66.63 + 3.37} = 1.1$$

which translates to a riskless yield of 10% per annum. The box overleaf shows how the conventional analysis, based on yield spreads, can be transformed to the options approach.

The dynamics of default

From equation (2) one can extract the probability of default for the loan. In a risk-neutral world $N(d_2)$ is the probability that the firm's value at time T will be higher than F, and $1 - N(d_2) = N(-d_2)$ is the probability of default.

Table 2. Default spread for corporate debt

Leverage ratio	Volatility of underlying assets			
	0.05	0.10	0.20	0.40
0.5	0	0	0	1.0%
0.6	0	0	0.1%	2.5%
0.7	0	0	0.4%	5.6%
0.8	0	0.1%	1.5%	8.4%
0.9	0.1%	0.8%	4.1%	12.5%
1.0	2.1%	3.1%	8.3%	17.3%

$V_0 = 100$, $T = 1$ and $r = 10\%$. 10% is the annualised interest rate discretely compounded, which is equivalent to 9.5% continuously compounded.

Integrating yield spread with options approach

Consider the following table of US Treasury and corporate bond yields and the zero coupon curves derived from them

A. Prevailing market yields and zero-coupon curves

Maturity (years)	US Treasury par yields (%)	Company X par yields (%)	Credit spread	US Treasury zero (%)	Company X zero (%)
1	5.60	5.85	0.25	5.52	5.76
2	5.99	6.34	0.35	5.91	6.25
3	6.15	6.60	0.45	6.07	6.51
4	6.27	6.87	0.60	6.19	6.80
5	6.34	7.04	0.70	6.27	7.18
6	6.42	7.22	0.80	6.36	7.37
7	6.48	7.38	0.90	6.42	7.54

Semi-annual 30/360 yields.
Continuously compounded 30/360 zero coupon rates.

The zero-coupon table is used to derive the one-year forward rates' N-year forward.

B. One-year forward rates N-year forward

Maturity (years)	US Treasury forwards (%)	Company X forwards (%)	One-year forward credit spreads N-year forward
1	5.52	5.76	0.24
2	6.30	6.74	0.44
3	6.40	7.05	0.65
4	6.56	7.64	1.08
5	6.56	7.71	1.15
6	6.81	8.21	1.40
7	6.81	8.47	1.65

One year continuously compounded 30/360.

We use the data of the zero-coupon curves to evaluate the implied parameter for a firm with a T-year bond outstanding. If company X has a two-year bond, it should have a yield consistent with 6.25% per annum for a zero-coupon bond. In other words, by converting the two-year corporate coupon bond into its two-year zero-coupon equivalent, its economic discrete-time yield should be 6.25%. The risk-free yield on an equivalent two-year zero-coupon government bond is 5.91%.

If we also assume that the bond has a face value of $F = 100$ at $T = 2$, its present value, B_0, should be: $B_0 = F/(1.0625)^2 = 88.58$. If the standard deviation of the rate of return on the firm's assets, σ, is equal to 20%, we can calculate the equity value S_0 for any given firm's value, V_0. The problem is to find V_0 and hence S_0 so that $88.58 + S_0 = V_0$. This problem is equivalent to finding V_0 so that the put value is equal to $P = F/(1.0591)^2 - F/(1.0625)^2 = 0.57$. By trial and error, given the above assumptions, we find that by introducing $V_0 = 144$ in the Black–Scholes model, the derived equity value is $S_0 = 55.44$ so that $88.58 + 55.44 = 144.02$ and also $P_0 = 0.58$.

The cost of credit risk for the two-year corporate bond can be derived from the value of a put option on V_0 given $F = 100$, which is 0.58 for the above parameters. The present value of the recovery value of the loan is given by:

$$\frac{N(-d_1)}{N(-d_2)} \cdot V_0 = -\frac{0.033}{0.060} 144 = 79.2$$

By following the same procedure for $\sigma = 15\%$ we find that for $V_0 = 124$, the value of bond and equity are 88.58 and 35.42, respectively. The cost of credit risk is $P_0 = 0.57$ and the present value of the recovery value is 81.5. For $\sigma = 25\%$, the yield spread is consistent with a market value of $V_0 = 170$, which means a leverage ratio, LR, of only 0.524 and an equity value of 81.42.

By purchasing the put, P_0, the bank buys an insurance policy whose premium is the discounted expected value of the expected shortfall in the event of default. So equation (2) can be rewritten as

$$P_0 = \left[-\frac{N(-d_1)}{N(-d_2)} V_0 + Fe^{-rT} \right] N(-d_2) \qquad (4)$$

Equation (4) decomposes the premium on the put into three factors. Firstly, the absolute value of the first term inside the bracket is the expected discounted recovery value of the loan, conditional on $V_T \leq F$. It represents the risk-neutral expected payment to the bank if the firm is unable to pay the full obligation F, at time T.

The second term in the bracket is the current value of a riskless bond promising a payment of F at time T. Hence the sum of the two terms inside the brackets yields the expected shortfall in present value terms, conditional on the firm being bankrupt at time T. The final factor which determines P_0 is the probability of default, $N(-d_2)$. By multiplying the probability of default by the current value of the expected shortfall, we derive the premium for insurance against default.

Using the same numerical example as in the previous section (ie, $V_0 = 100$, $T = 1$, $r = 10\%$, $\sigma = 40\%$, $F = 77$ and $LR = 0.7$), we obtain the results in Table 3. These results are based on a risk-neutrality assumption. For the general case, when the assumption of a risk-neutral world is removed, the probability of default is given by $N(-d_2^1)$ where

$$d_2^1 = \frac{\ln(V_0/F) + \left(\bar{r}_v - \frac{1}{2}\sigma^2\right)T}{\sigma\sqrt{T}}$$

where $\bar{r}_v$ is the expected rate of return on asset V, and V is assumed to be lognormally distributed. (See Boness (1964) and Galai (1978) for an explanation of this result.) Referring to our numerical example, the risk-neutral probability of default is 24.4%. If we assume that the discrete time $\bar{r}_v$ is 16%, the probability of default is 20.5%. The expected recovery value is

$$\frac{N(-d_1^1)}{N(-d_2^1)} V_0 = \frac{0.110}{0.205} \times 100 = 53.7$$

From equation (4) we can compute the expected loss at maturity date T, EL_T, equal to the probability of default multiplied by the loss in case of default:

$$EL_T = N(-d_2)F - N(-d_1)V_0 e^{rT}$$

$$= F - N(d_2)F - N(-d_1)V_0 e^{rT} = F\left[1 - N(d_2) - N(-d_1)\frac{1}{LR}\right] \qquad (5)$$

Again, using our previous numerical example we obtain

$$EL_T = 0.244 \times 77 - 0.137 \times 100e^{0.0953} = 3.718$$

This result is consistent with the definition of the default spread and its derivation in equation (3). Indeed, from equation (5) the expected payout from the corporate debt at maturity is

$$F - EL_T = F\left[N(d_2) + N(-d_1)\frac{1}{LR}\right]$$

so the expected cost of default, expressed in yield, is

Table 3. Default statistics

Discounted expected recovery value	$(0.137/0.244)/100 = 56.1$
Value of riskless bond	$77.e^{-0.0953} = 70$
Expected shortfall	$70 - 56.1 = 13.9$
Probability of default	24.4%
Cost of default*	$0.244 \times 13.9 = 3.39$

*The compound cost of default is slightly different from the put value, due to rounding errors.

$$-\frac{1}{T}\ln\left(\frac{F}{F-EL_T}\right) = -\frac{1}{T}\ln\left[\frac{F\left(N(d_2)+N(-d_1)\dfrac{V_0}{Fe^{-rT}}\right)}{F}\right] = \pi_T$$

which is identical to equation (3).

The result in equation (5) is similar to the conclusion in Jarrow and Turnbull's (1995) model, which is used to price credit derivatives, ie, the credit spread is the product of the probability of default and the loss in the event of default. However, in their model they assume that the term structure of credit spread is known and can be derived from market data. The forward spread can then be easily derived. By assuming that the recovery factor is given and exogenous to the model, they can imply the forward probability of default.

In our model, we reach the same conclusion but both the probability of default and the recovery rate are simultaneously derived from equilibrium conditions. From equations (3) and (4) it is clear that the recovery rate cannot be assumed constant: it keeps varying as a function of time to maturity and the value of the firm's assets.

Credit risk as a function of equity value

We have shown that the cost of eliminating credit risk can be derived based on the value of the firm's assets. A practical problem arises over the frequent unavailability of observations on V. In some cases, if both equity and debt are traded, V can be reconstructed by adding the market values of both equity and debt. However, corporate loans are not often traded and the only observations we have are on equity. The question then is whether the risk of default can be hedged by trading shares and derivatives on the firm's stock.

In our simple framework, equity itself is a contingent claim on the firm's assets. Its value can be expressed as

$$S = VN(d_1) - Fe^{-rT}N(d_2) \qquad (6)$$

Equity value is a function of the same parameters as the put calculated in equation (2). A put can be created synthetically by selling short $N(-d_1)$ units of the firm's assets, and buying $FN(-d_2)$ units of government bonds maturing at T, with a face value of F. If one sells short

$$\frac{N(-d_1)}{N(d_1)}$$

units of the stock, S, one effectively creates a short position in the firm's assets of $N(-d_1)$ units, since

$$\frac{-N(-d_1)}{N(d_1)}S = -VN(-d_1) + Fe^{-rT}N(d_2)\frac{N(-d_1)}{N(d_1)}$$

Therefore, if V is not directly traded or observed, one can create a put option dynamically by selling short the appropriate number of shares. The equivalence between the put and the synthetic put is valid only over short time intervals, and must be readjusted frequently with changes in S and in time left to debt maturity.

Using the data from the previous numerical example:

$$\frac{-N(-d_1)}{N(d_1)} = \frac{-0.137}{0.863} = -0.159$$

This means that to insure against default of a one-year loan with maturity value of 77, for a firm with current market value of assets of 100, the bank should sell short 0.159 of the outstanding equity. (Note that the outstanding equity is equivalent to a short term holding of $N(d_1) = 0.863$ of the firm's assets. Shorting 0.159 of equity is equivalent to shorting 0.863 of the firm's assets.)

The question now is whether we can use a put option on equity to hedge the default risk. Remember that equity itself reflects the default risk, and as a contingent claim its instantaneous volatility, σ_s, can be expressed as

$$\sigma_s = \eta_{s,v}\sigma \tag{7}$$

where

$$\eta_{s,v} = N(d_1)\frac{V}{S}$$

is the instantaneous elasticity of equity with respect to the firm's value, and $\eta_{s,v} \geq 1$. Since σ_s is stochastic, changing with V, the conventional Black–Scholes model cannot be applied to the valuation of puts and calls on S. The Black–Scholes model requires σ to be constant, or to follow a deterministic path over the life of the option. However, it was shown by Bensoussan, Crouhy and Galai (1994 and 1997) that a good approximation can be achieved by using equation (7) in the Black–Scholes model. In practice, for long-term options, the estimated σ_s from (7) is not expected to change widely from day to day. Therefore, equation (7) can be used in the context of Black–Scholes estimation of long-term options, even when the underlying instrument does not follow a stationary lognormal distribution.

The systematic and specific risk of default risk

Credit risk is closely related to the market risk of the firm, since the two major factors in determining the cost of default are the value of the firm, V, and its volatility, σ. We can add further insight by relating V to the general market risk through the capital asset pricing model (CAPM). In the CAPM framework, the current value of the firm is given by

$$V_0 = \frac{E(V_T)}{1+\bar{r}_v}$$

where $E(V_T)$ is the expected value of the firm at time T and $\bar{r}_v$ is the cost of the firm's capital. From the CAPM $\bar{r}_v$ can be expressed as

$$\bar{r}_v = r + \beta_v(\bar{r}_M - r)$$

where r is the riskless interest rate, $\bar{r}_M$ is the expected rate of return on the market portfolio of risky assets, and β_v is the firm's systematic risk. The current value of the firm's assets is a function of the co-movements of its value, with the value of all risky assets in the economy:

$$\beta_v = \frac{cov(r_v, r_M)}{\sigma_M^2}$$

where cov is the covariance function, and σ_M^2 is the variance of the rate of return on the market index of all risky assets.

In a continuous time framework, it can be shown that credit risk has a systematic risk, which is related to market risk, as

$$\beta_P \equiv \frac{cov(r_P, r_M)}{\sigma_M^2}$$

$$= \frac{\partial P}{\partial V}\cdot\frac{V_0}{P_0}\beta_v = -N(-d_1)\frac{V_0}{P_0}\beta_v \tag{8}$$

where r_p is the instantaneous rate of return on the cost of credit risk, P_0, as shown in equation (2). The instantaneous beta risk of the cost of default is a function of, first, the business risk of the firm (as measured by its relative co-movement with market risk, β_v); second, the probability term $N(-d_1)$; and third, the ratio of the firm's value to the cost of default, V_0/P_0. The systematic risk of default risk in equation (8) is negative.

By giving a risky loan to the firm, the bank also assumes a positive beta risk of

$$N\left(-d_1\right)\frac{V_0}{P_0}\beta_v$$

due to the risk of default. Insuring against default risk by purchasing P_0 eliminates this beta risk. In terms of our numerical example, adding the assumption that the firm's systematic risk is equal to 1 ($\beta_v = 1$), we get

$$\beta_P = -N\left(-d_1\right)\frac{V_0}{P_0}\beta_v$$

$$= -0.137\cdot\frac{100}{3.37}1 = -4.065$$

The contract to eliminate the default has high negative beta risk. Its elasticity amplifies market movements by almost four-fold, over a short interval.

In January 1998, the Bank for International Settlement's (BIS) regulatory capital framework came into force. For on-balance sheet securities in the trading book such as bonds and stocks, there is a capital charge for general market risk and for specific risk. Specific risk, according to the BIS, relates to the risk that the price of an individual security moves by more or less than what is expected from general market movements, due to specific credit events related to individual issuers. The capital charge for specific risk can be determined either using the "internal models" or an arbitrary standardised approach. In that context, an internal measure of specific risk, SR, for a one-day horizon, follows directly from (8):

$$SR = N\left(-d_1\right)\frac{V_0}{B_0}\beta_v\sigma_M\sqrt{365} \tag{9}$$

and the capital charge, CC_{SR}, for specific risk of the zero-coupon bond, is[6]

$$CC_{SR} = B_0\cdot SR\cdot\left(2.33\right)\sqrt{10} \tag{10}$$

In our example, assuming $\sigma_M = 20\%$, we find SR = 0.00216 and $CC_{SR} = 3.178$.

1 *See, for example, Duffie (1992).*

2 *See also Litterman and Iben (1991) and Madan and Unal (1996). This approach is consistent with the CreditMetrics methodology suggested by JP Morgan to assess credit risk exposure for banks' portfolio of fixed-income instruments.*

3 *This approach is difficult to implement in practice and, in some instances, the model calibration yields negative default probabilities. This inconsistent result is because the recovery factors not only vary over time, but also should be endogeneously determined in the model, since the loss incurred by the debt-holders should depend on the value of the firm's assets.*

4 *The model builds on Black and Cox's 1976 extension of Merton's 1974 model.*

5 *A leverage factor equal to 0.7 is equivalent to a face value of F = 77.*

6 *The capital charge corresponds to a maximum loss at the one-tailed 99% confidence interval over a 10-day horizon. Assuming normality of the price change variations, and serial independence, the instantaneous volatility needs to be scaled up by the factor 2.33√10. There is an additional multiplier of 3 required by BIS to compensate for additional risks not captured by the model, such as liquidity risk.*

BIBLIOGRAPHY

Bensoussan, A., M. Crouhy and D. Galai, 1997, "Black–Scholes Approximation of Complex Option Values: The Cases of European Compound Call Options and Equity Warrants", *Option Embedded Bonds*, I Nelken (editor) Irwin Professional Publishing.

Bensoussan, A., M. Crouhy and D. Galai, 1994, "Stochastic Volatility Related to Leverage Effect I: Equity Volatility Behavior", *Applied Mathematical Finance* vol 1, no. 1, pp. 63–85.

Boness, J., 1964, "Elements of a Theory of Stock-Option Value", *Journal of Political Economy* 12, pp. 163–75.

Duffie, D., 1992, "Dynamic Asset Pricing Theory", Princeton University Press, Princeton.

Duffie, D., and K. J. Singleton, 1994, "Econometric Modeling of Term Structure of Defaultable Bonds", Working paper, Graduate School of Business, Stanford University, California.

Galai, D., and R. W. Masulis, 1976, "The Option Pricing Model and the Risk Factor of Stock", *Journal of Financial Economics* 3, pp. 53–81.

Galai, D., and M. I. Schneller, 1978, "Pricing of Warrants and the Value of the Firm", *Journal of Finance* 33, pp. 1,333–42.

Galai, D., 1978, "On the Boness and Black–Scholes Models for Valuation of Call Options", *Journal of Financial and Quantitative Analysis*, pp. 15–27.

Hull, J., and A. White, 1995, "The Impact of Default Risk on the Prices of Options and Other Derivative Securities", *Journal of Banking and Finance* 19(2), pp. 299–322.

Jarrow, R. A., and S. M. Turnbull, 1995, "Pricing Derivatives on Financial Securities Subject to Credit Risk", *Journal of Finance* 50(1), pp. 53–85.

Jarrow, R. A., D. Lando and S. M. Turnbull, 1997, "A Markov Model for the Term Structure of Credit Spreads", *Review of Financial Studies*, forthcoming.

Litterman, R. and T. Iben, 1991, "Corporate Bond Valuation and the Term Structure of Credit Spreads", *Financial Analysts Journal* (Spring), pp. 52–64.

Longstaff, F., and E. Schwartz, 1995, "A Simple Approach to Valuing Risky Fixed and Floating Rate Debt", *Journal of Finance* 50(3), pp. 789–819.

Madan, D., and H. Unal, 1996, "Pricing the Risks of Default", Working paper, University of Maryland.

Merton, R. C., 1974, "On the Pricing of Corporate Debt: The Risk Structure of Interest Rates", *Journal of Finance* 29, pp. 449–70.

CREDIT RATINGS

Introduction

Credit Ratings

David Shimko

No book on credit risk management would be complete without a section devoted to credit ratings. Practitioners are of course familiar with published ratings from agencies such as Moody's, Standard & Poor's and Fitch IBCA. Perhaps they may be less familiar with the tens and hundreds of private rating systems available in commercial and investment banks today. Many banks mimic the eight or nine major categories of Moody's and S&P but assign clients private ratings that usually correspond to – but sometimes differ from – the public ratings. These private ratings form the basis of most credit decision-making.

With the advances in credit risk measurement technology in the last 20 years, it is surprising that so many financial institutions cling to the old methods. It seems that no matter how sophisticated the credit models become, they will never beat the "Five Cs of Credit": Capacity, Character, Cashflow, and the like. Furthermore, they will never beat the loan officer's innate sense of smell – if a credit smells bad, the bank simply does not lend or provide lines for derivative transactions.

Public credit ratings themselves have had an interesting history in the finance literature. Ask a fresh MBA what happens to a firm's bond prices when its ratings fall, and he or she will say the prices should fall. Ask a more seasoned pro the same question and he will say that bond prices do not react. Are markets so inefficient? An early study by Professor Mark Weinstein (1977) showed that, in fact, markets are efficient enough that by the time ratings change any adverse information about a company is already included in its security prices.

This observation is critical for the assessment of credit risk on the basis of ratings. Ratings are by their nature old news. As more companies are downgraded each year than upgraded, we can also conclude that anyone who assesses the risks of a credit portfolio on the basis of credit ratings alone is probably overestimating its credit quality.

The study by Marshall Blume, Felix Lim and Craig MacKinlay, "The Declining Credit Quality of US Corporate Debt: Myth or Reality?", documents the apparent drop in credit ratings over time and argues convincingly that part of the drop is due to an implicit or explicit rise in rating standards. The paper, published in 1998 and reprinted here as chapter 14, is an important one for those tempted to believe that ratings are constant or that an AA firm today is the same as an AA firm 20 years ago.

The study was sparked by observations that, over time, the number of downgrades in a year exceeded the number of upgrades and by the desire to find out if this was caused by declining credit quality or increased credit standards. The authors found a surprising third explanation: that had it not been for improvements in firm-specific characteristics over the period 1978–95, the number of downgrades would have been even greater.

The results of their study are carefully qualified. They employ a probit analysis technique, which converts a linear function of observable firm characteristics into credit rating proxies. This is not the technique used by Standard & Poor's but a substitute for it, and, as such, the results should be interpreted in that context.

Improving credit ratings

If static credit ratings present problems, can dynamic models solve them? This question was addressed by Lea Carty and Jerome Fons in their (1994) paper, "Measuring Changes in Corporate Credit Quality", which appears here as chapter 13. The authors, both of Moody's Investor Services, recognise the insufficiency of static ratings and suggest a model in which credit ratings change over time. Using Moody's data on rating changes, they tabulate probability transition matrices giving the likelihoods of a bond migrating from its current rating to any other of the possible ratings in the next quarter. Then, applying the historical frequency of ratings changes to estimate the probability of future ratings changes, they are able to simulate the credit rating experience of an average issue over its lifetime.

This is a clever approach which avoids many of the problems associated with static ratings. Of course, as with any extrapolation from historical data, one has to be very careful to enumerate the assumptions when applying past results to future data. For example, will future credit rating changes resemble past rating change behaviour? Will more aggressive refinancings and restructurings lead to credit ratings that are more volatile? Or will a more aggressive use of credit derivatives cause different outcomes to be more or less likely? The study cannot answer these difficult questions, but it does give us a clear starting point.

The authors are not alone in their view of the value of the "ratings migration" approach. The venerable JP Morgan bank thought enough of the model to adapt and incorporate it along with other credit analytics when introducing its CreditMetrics product. RiskMetrics is a widely popular and simple market risk measurement system. Its popularity can be explained by its universal accessibility, low price (free), frequent updates and the implicit recommendation that Morgan "uses calculations similar to these in assessing its market risks".

Such a claim cannot be made for CreditMetrics. JP Morgan uses a number of competing methodologies internally for the assessment of credit risk, and CreditMetrics was not one of them at the time it was introduced. This may be due to the problems associated with the use of models based on credit ratings, or it may be due to the complexity of the credit risk management process itself.

When CreditMetrics was released Stephen Thieke of JP Morgan stated that "the world does not have, and neither does it need, just one benchmark to analyze credit risk" (a discussion of the release of CreditMetrics can be found in Irving, 1997). This is a sound comment, but many users have been confused. Morgan does not view CreditMetrics as comprehensive, nor does it make substantive use of CreditMetrics to arrive at its own measurements of credit risk.

On the whole, JP Morgan should be applauded for publicising and popularising an important and innovative approach to credit risk measurement. Without doubt, RiskMetrics and CreditMetrics have earned their place in the history of risk management and spurred many senior managers and boards of directors into positive action over the assessment of credit risk.

Analytic models

Should we really bother with more complex analytic models of credit? Those who cling to credit ratings and eschew modern modelling techniques often criticise quantitative models as trying to measure something that is inherently unmeasurable. These people rightly fear the interference of quants who often do not understand the credit markets as well as they do. They also believe that something will be lost when the qualitative assessment of credit is relinquished in favour of quantitative methods.

Following this line of thinking, it is prudent to ask whether quantitative models of credit really provide anything more than the qualitative models. Ross Miller does this in chapter 15, which consists of his short, elegant piece "Refining Ratings", first published in 1998. The author uses simple non-parametric techniques of statistical inference to determine whether quantitative modelling adds information to the estimation of default probabilities. Assuming that ratings and default probabilities are meant to measure the same thing, Miller tests the null hypothesis that KMV Corporation's expected default frequency-based ratings provide no more information about the likelihood that a firm will default over a specified period than is contained in Standard & Poor's ratings. That null hypothesis is rejected at the 95% confidence level out to 48 months. The robustness of this test to other default probability estimation techniques and the non-parametric methods used provide strong support for analytic models of the calibre of KMV's.

This and models like it are based on market data, but there are other techniques based primarily on accounting data and firm-specific characteristics. The classic in this area is Edward Altman's (1968) Z-score analysis. This well-publicised model used discriminant analysis to link corporate ratios such as interest coverage and current assets to default probabilities. An updated paper by Altman with co-authors Robert Handleman and Paul Narayanan, "ZETA Analysis – A New Model to Identify Bankruptcy Risks of Corporations", is reprinted here. In this 1977 version, manufacturing and retailing firms are accurately discriminated (default versus non-default) on the basis of return on assets, earnings stability, debt service, cumulative profitability, liquidity, capitalisation and size.

Although multivariate discriminant analysis has some pitfalls, it has become a popular way to "score" corporations and even individuals to assign them an estimated default likelihood. Some banks use a numerical z-score rather than a category rating to evaluate their debtors and trade counterparts. Some guard their discriminant models keenly for fear that unscrupulous counterparties will try to manipulate their ratios to qualify for more credit or better terms.

BIBLIOGRAPHY

Altman, E. I., 1968, "Financial Ratios, Discriminant Analysis and the Prediction of Corporate Bankruptcy", *Journal of Finance* September.

Irving, R., 1997, "From the Makers of ...", *Risk* 10(4), pp. 22–26.

Weinstein, M., 1977 "The Effect of a Rating Change Announcement on Bond Price", *Journal of Financial Economics* 5, pp.329–50.

11

ZETA Analysis: A New Model to Identify Bankruptcy Risk of Corporations

Edward I. Altman, Robert G. Haldeman and P. Narayanan

Stern School of Business, New York University; Zeta Services Corporation, New York; Private consultant

The purposes of this study are to construct, analyse and test a new bankruptcy classification model which considers explicitly recent developments with respect to business failures. The study also incorporates current refinements in the utilisation of discriminant statistical techniques. Several reasons for building a new model, despite the availability of several fairly impressive "old" models, are presented below and the empirical results seem to substantiate the effort. The new model, which we call ZETA (not from the people who brought you Beta), is effective in classifying bankrupt companies up to five years prior to failure on a sample of corporations consisting of manufacturers and retailers.

Reasons for attempting to construct a new model

There are at least five valid reasons why a new bankruptcy classification model can improve and extend upon those statistical models which have been published in the literature in the last decade.[1] These include:

❑ The change in the size, and perhaps the financial profile, of business failures in recent years. The average size of bankrupt firms has increased dramatically with the consequent greater visibility and concern from financial institutions, regulatory agencies and the public at large. Most of the past studies used relatively small firms in their samples with the exception of Altman's (1973) railroad study and the commercial bank studies. Any new model should be as relevant as possible to the population to which it will eventually be applied. This present study utilises a bankrupt firm sample where the average asset size two annual reporting periods prior to failure was approximately $100 million. No firm had less than $20 million in assets.[2]

❑ Following the above, a new model should be as current as possible with respect to the temporal nature of the data. With the exception of three (out of 53) firms, every bankrupt firm in our sample failed in the last seven years. The entire sample of both bankrupt and non-bankrupt firms is listed in Appendix A.

❑ Past failure models concentrated either on the broad classification of manufacturers

This paper was first published in the Journal of Banking and Finance, *1977. It is an elaboration of a model applied to investment analysis and statistical service by Wood, Struthers & Winthrop (WSW). It was written while Professor Altman was a Visiting Scholar at the Centre d'Enseignement Supérieur des Affaires (France) and a Professor* Associé Visitant *at Université de Paris-Dauphiné, and while Mr Narayanan was a graduate assistant at New York University. The authors appreciate support from both WSW and New York University. Burton Siegel, Director of Research of WSW made several valuable suggestions and we also profited from the insightful comments of Dr Jean-Richard Sulzer of the Université de Paris-Dauphiné.*

or on specific industries. We feel that with the appropriate analytical adjustments, retailing companies, a particularly vulnerable group, could be analysed on an equal basis with manufacturers.

❏ An important feature of this study is that the data and footnotes have been scrupulously analysed to include the most recent changes in financial reporting standards and accepted accounting practices. Indeed, in at least one instance, a change which will be implemented in a very short time was applied. The purpose of these operations is to make the model relevant not only to past failures but to the data that will appear in the future. The predictive as well as the classification accuracy of the ZETA model is implicit in our efforts. The major modifications are discussed in the next section.

❏ To test and assess several of the recent advances and still controversial aspects of discriminant analysis. Recent articles in the literature indicate that this statistical technique is being utilised with increasing frequency but not without controversy.[3]

Principal findings

We conclude in this chapter that the new ZETA model for bankruptcy classification appears to be quite accurate for up to five years prior to failure with successful classification of well over 90% of our sample one year prior and 70% accuracy up to five years. We also observe that the inclusion of retailing firms in the same model as manufacturers does not seem to affect our results negatively. This is probably true due to the adjustments to our data based on recent and anticipated financial reporting changes – primarily the capitalisation of leases.

We also find that the ZETA model outperforms alternative bankruptcy classification strategies in terms of expected cost criteria utilising prior probabilities and explicit cost of error estimates. In our investigation we were surprised to observe that, despite the statistical properties of the data which indicate that a quadratic structure is appropriate, the linear structure of the same model outperforms the quadratic in tests of model validity. This was especially evident regarding the long-term accuracy of the model.

Sample and data characteristics and statistical methodology

SAMPLE CHARACTERISTICS

Our two samples of firms consist of 53 bankrupt firms and a matched sample of 58 non-bankrupt entities. The latter are matched to the failed group by industry and year of the data.[4] Table 1 lists the bankrupt firms by type, size and year of bankruptcy petition. Note that our sample is almost equally divided into manufacturers and retailer groups and that 94% (50 of 53) of the firms failed during the period 1969–1975. As mentioned earlier, the average asset size of our failed group is almost $100 million, indicative of the increasing size of failures.[5] The bankrupt firms represent all publicly held industrial failures which had at least $20 million in assets, with no known fraud involved and where sufficient data were available. Five non-bankruptcy petition companies were included, either due to substantial government support (one) or a forced merger (one), or where the banks took over the business (three) (see Appendix A).

VARIABLES ANALYSED

A number of financial ratios and other measures have been found in other studies to be helpful in providing statistical evidence of impending failures. We have assembled data to calculate these variables and in addition have included several "new" measures that were thought to be potentially helpful as well. The 27 variables are listed in Appendix B along with certain relevant statistics which

Table 1. Sample characteristics

	Bankrupt	Non-bankrupt
Number of firms	53	58
Type of firm		
Manufacturer	29	32
Retailer	24	26
Average size (tangible assets)	$96 million	$167 million

Number of firms by years of bankruptcy	
1975	9
1974	9
1973	14
1972	3
1971	5
1970	5
1969	5
1967	1
1962	2
Total	53

will be discussed shortly. Note that in a few cases – eg numbers 7 and 9, tangible assets and interest coverage – the variables are expressed in logarithmic form in order to reduce outlier possibilities and to adhere to statistical assumptions. The variables can be classified as profitability (1-6), coverage and other earnings relative to leverage measures (8-14), liquidity (15-18), capitalisation ratios (19-23), earnings variability (24-26) and a few miscellaneous measures (7, 27).

REPORTING ADJUSTMENTS

As noted earlier, we have adjusted the basic data of our sample to consider explicitly several of the most recent and, in our opinion, the most important accounting modifications. These adjustments include the following:

Capitalisation of leases   Without doubt, the most important and pervasive adjustment made was to capitalise all non-cancellable operating and finance leases. The resulting capitalised lease amount was added to the firms' assets and liabilities and also we have imputed an interest cost to the "new" liability. The procedure involved preparation of schedules of current and expected lease payment obligations from information found in footnotes to the financial statements. The discount rate used to capitalise leases was the average interest rate for new issue, high grade corporate bonds in the year being analysed plus a risk premium of 10% of the interest rate. For example, if a firm had lease payments of $100,000 a year for the next 10 years and the current interest rate was 7.3%, the capitalised lease equals $671,000. Symbolically,

$$CL = \sum_{t=1}^{N} \frac{L_t}{(1+r+0.1r)^t}$$

CL = capitalised lease,
L_t = lease payment in period t,
r   = average interest rate for new issue high grade corporate bonds,
N   = the number of years of leasehold rights and obligations.

An amount equal to the interest rate used in the capitalisation process times the capitalised lease amount is added to interest costs.

Reserves   If the firms' reserves were of a contingency nature, they were included in equity and income was adjusted for the net change in the reserve for the year. If the reserve was related to the valuation of certain assets, it was netted against those assets.

Minority interests and other liabilities on the balance sheet   These items were netted against other assets. This allows for a truer comparison of earnings with the assets generating the earnings.

Captive finance companies and other non-consolidated subsidiaries   These were consolidated with the parent company accounts as well as the information would allow. The pooling of interest method was used.

Goodwill and intangibles   Deducted from assets and equity because of the difficulty in assigning economic value to them.

Capitalised research and development costs, capitalised interest and certain other deferred charges   These costs were expensed rather than capitalised. This is done to improve comparability and to give a better picture of actual funds flows.

STATISTICAL METHODOLOGY

Bankruptcy classification is attempted via the use of a multivariate statistical technique known as discriminant analysis. In this study, the results using both linear and quadratic structures are analysed. Since 1968, there have been several studies devoted to the failure classification and prediction problem. Most of these which utilised discriminant analysis are referenced in notes 1 and 3. It is now fairly well documented that the test for assessing whether a linear or quadratic structure is appropriate – sometimes referred to as the H_1 test, derived from Box (1949)[6] – will provide the proper guidance when analysing a particular sample's classification characteristics. Essentially, if it is assessed that the variance–covariance matrices of the G groups are statistically identical, then the linear format which pools all observations is appropriate. If, however, the dispersion matrices are not identical, then the quadratic structure will provide the more efficient model since each group's characteristics can be assessed independently as well as between groups. Efficiency will result in more significant multivariate measures of group differences and greater classification accuracy of that *particular sample*. What has not been assessed up to this point is the relative efficiency of the linear versus quadratic structures when the sample data are not the same as that used to construct the model, ie, holdout or secondary samples. We will analyse this point in the next section.

Empirical results
THE SEVEN-VARIABLE MODEL

After an iterative process of reducing the number of variables, we selected a seven-variable model, which not only classified our test sample well but also proved the most reliable in various validation procedures. That is, we could not significantly improve upon our results by adding more variables, and no model with fewer variables performed as well.

Return on assets   Measured by the earnings before interest and taxes/total assets, variable number 1 in Appendix B. This variable has proven to be extremely helpful in assessing firm performance in several past multivariate studies, including two by Altman (1968, 1973) and the leading univariate study (see Beaver, 1967).

Stability of earnings   Measured by a normalised measure of the standard error of estimate around a ten-year trend in *return on assets;* number 24 in appendix B. Business risk is often expressed in terms of earnings fluctuations, and this measure proved to be particularly effective. We did assess the information content of several similar variables which attempted to measure the potential susceptibility of a firm's earnings level to declines which could jeopardise its ability to meet its financial commitments. These variables, numbers 25 and 26 (EBIT drop and margin drop) in Appendix B, were quite significant on a univariate level but did not enter into our final multivariate model.[7]

Debt service (see number 9 in Appendix B)   Measured by the familiar interest coverage ratio, ie, earnings before interest and taxes/total interest payments (including that amount imputed from the capitalised lease liability). We have transposed this measure by taking the log 10 in order to improve the normality and homoscedasticity of this measure.

Cumulative profitability

Measured by the firm's retained earnings (balance sheet)/total assets; number 19 in Appendix B. This ratio, which imputes such factors as the age of the firm and dividend policy as well as its profitability record over time, was found to be quite helpful in past studies including one, Altman (1968), whose results will be directly compared to the results of this study. As our results will show, this cumulative profitability measure is unquestionably the most important variable – measured univariately and multivariately (Table 2 below).

Table 2. Influence of each variable in the ZETA model, order of importance

Variable	Variable number	Forward stepwise discriminant analysis	Backward stepwise discriminant analysis	Scaled vector test (relative contribution)	Separation of means test (relative contribution)	Conditional deletion test	Univariate F-statistic
Overall profitability	1	7	7	7 (5%)	5	7	2
Stability of earnings	2	2	2	2 (20%)	2	2	4
Debt service	3	6	6	6 (6%)	7	6	6
Cumulative profitability	4	1	1	1 (25%)	1	1	1
Liquidity	5	5	5	5 (11%)	4	5	3
Capitalisation	6	3	3	3 (18%)	3	3	5
Asset size	7	4	4	4 (15%)	5	4	7

The actual coefficients and covariance terms for the seven variables cannot be reported due to the proprietary nature of the ZETA™ model to the firm of WSW.

Liquidity

Measured by the familiar current ratio; no. 16 in Appendix B. Despite previous findings that the current ratio was not as effective in identifying failures as some other liquidity measures, we find it slightly more informative than others, such as the working capital/total assets ratio.

Capitalisation

Measured by common equity/total capital; number 22 in Appendix B. In both the numerator and the denominator the common equity is measured by a five-year average of the total market value rather than book value. The denominator also includes preferred stock at liquidating value, long-term debt and capitalised leases. We have utilised a 5-year average to smooth out possible severe, temporary market fluctuations and to add a trend component (along with stability of earnings above) to the study.[8]

Size

Measured by the firms' total assets. This variable, as is the case with the others, is adjusted for recent financial reporting changes. No doubt, the capitalisation of leasehold rights has added to the average asset size of both the bankrupt and non-bankrupt groups. We have also transformed the size variable to help normalise the distribution of the variable due to outlier observations. Again a logarithmic transformation was applied.

RELATIVE IMPORTANCE OF DISCRIMINANT VARIABLES

The procedure of reducing a variable set to an acceptable number is closely related to an attempt to determine the relative importance within a given variable set. Several of the prescribed procedures for attaining the "best" set of variables, eg, stepwise analysis, can also be used as a criterion for ranking importance. Unfortunately, there is no one best method for establishing a relative ranking of variable importance. Hence, we have assessed this characteristic by analysing the ranks suggested by six different tests (Table 2). In several studies that we have observed, the rankings across these tests are not very consistent and the researcher is left with a somewhat ambiguous answer. This was definitely not the case in our study.

As noted in Table 2, regardless of which test statistic is observed, the most important variable is the cumulative profitability ratio, *cumulative profitability*.[9] In fact, our scaled vector analysis indicates that this single ratio contributed 25% of the total discrimination. Second in importance is the *stability of earnings* ratio and, except for the univariate test of significance, it too has a consistent ranking across tests. Similarly, our *capitalisation variable* is almost totally consistent across tests. The least important variable appears to be the overall profitability ratio, *return on assets*, but it still is an important contributor to the model's success.

LINEAR VERSUS QUADRATIC ANALYSIS

The H_1 test of the original sample characteristics equals 6.20 and clearly rejects the hypothesis that the group dispersion matrices are equal. Therefore, the linear structure

158

ZETA ANALYSIS:
A NEW MODEL TO
IDENTIFY
BANKRUPTCY RISK
OF CORPORATIONS

classification rule (excluding error costs),

$$X' \Sigma^{-1} (U_1 - U_2) - \tfrac{1}{2}(U_1 + U_2)' \Sigma^{-1} (U_1 - U_2) \geq \ln P$$

is not appropriate and the quadratic structure with a classification rule: assign a firm to one group, eg, non-bankrupt,

$$X' \left(\Sigma_1^{-1} - \Sigma_2^{-1} \right) X - 2 \left(U_1' \Sigma_1^{-1} - U_2' \Sigma_2^{-1} \right) X + U_1' \Sigma_1^{-1} U_1 - U_2' \Sigma_2^{-1} U_2$$

$$\geq \ln \left| \Sigma_2^{-1} \cdot \Sigma_1^{-1} \right| - 2 \ln P$$

where X = variable vector, U_1, U_2 = mean vectors of groups 1 and 2, Σ_1, Σ_2 = dispersion matrices of groups 1 and 2, and P = prior probability of an observation being drawn from one group ÷ prior probability of being drawn from the other group.[10]

As we will show in the next section, the quadratic and linear models yield essentially equal overall accuracy results for the original sample classifications, but the holdout sample tests indicate a clear superiority for the linear framework. This creates a dilemma and we have chosen to concentrate on the linear test due to (1) the possible high sensitivity to individual sample observations of the quadratic parameters (that is, we observe 35 different parameters in the quadratic model compared with only 7 in the linear case, not including the intercept), and (2) the fact that all of the relative tests of importance discussed in the section "Relative importance of discriminant variables" above, are based on the linear model.

CLASSIFICATION ACCURACY – ORIGINAL AND HOLDOUT SAMPLES

Table 3 presents classification accuracy of the original sample based on data from one year prior to bankruptcy. Lachenbruch validation tests[11] and years 2–5 "holdout" sample results are also presented.[12] These results are listed for both the linear and quadratic structures of the seven-variable model.

The linear model's accuracy, based on one year prior data, is 96.2% for the bankrupt group and 89.7% for the non-bankrupt. The upward bias[13] in these results appears to be slight since the Lachenbruch results are only 3% less for the failed group and identical for the non-failed group. As expected, the failed group's classification accuracy is lower as the data become more remote from bankruptcy, but is still quite high.[14] In fact, we observe 70% accuracy as far back as five years prior to failure. This compares very favourably to the results recorded by Altman (1968), where the accuracy dropped precipitously after two years prior. For a comparison of these two studies' results, see Table 5 below.

An interesting result was outlined by comparing the quadratic structure's results with that of the linear (Table 3). As noted earlier, the total samples' classification accuracy is identical for the two structures in period 1, with the linear showing a slight edge in the bankrupt group and the quadratic in the non-bankrupt group. The most obvious and important differences, however, are in the validation and "holdout" tests of the bankrupt group. Here, the linear model is clearly superior, with the quadratic misclassifying over fifty percent of the future bankrupts five years prior. The Lachenbruch

Table 3. Overall classification accuracy (%)

Years prior to bankruptcy	Bankrupt firms		Non-bankrupt firms		Total	
	Linear	Quadratic	Linear	Quadratic	Linear	Quadratic
1 Original sample	96.2	94.3	89.7	91.4	92.8	92.8
1 (Lachenbruch validation test)	(92.5)	(85.0)	(89.7)	(87.9)	(91.0)	(86.5)
2 Holdout	84.9	77.4	93.1	91.9	89.0	84.7
3 Holdout	74.5	62.7	91.4	92.1	83.5	78.9
4 Holdout	68.1	57.4	89.5	87.8	79.8	74.0
5 Holdout	69.8	46.5	82.1	87.5	76.8	69.7

validation test also shows a large difference (over 7% favouring the linear model). Subsequent analysis will report only the linear results.

One further type of validation test was run involving the random selection of approximately one-half of the observations in order to ascertain the model's parameters with the remaining observations as "holdouts". The holdout observations were examined not only the first year prior to bankruptcy but

	Replication no. 1			Replication no. 2	
Year	Bankrupt	Non-bankrupt	Year	Bankrupt	Non-bankrupt
1	92.5	91.4	1	96.2	79.6
2	84.9	91.4	2	86.8	81.0
3	76.5	91.4	3	80.4	79.3
4	61.7	93.0	4	74.5	82.5
5	62.8	84.0	5	69.8	76.8

Table 4. Random sample validation test results: classification accuracy (%)

for all five years. We made two replications of this test, with the results reported in Table 4. Note that the accuracy is still quite impressive for independent observations and for the five years of analysis. There was some difference, however, in the type I and type II errors from each of the replications.

COMPARISON WITH ALTMAN'S 1968 MODEL

The 1968 model of one of the authors has received a good deal of exposure in leading finance texts (Weston and Brigham, 1975; Van Horne, 1974), in non-academic publications (Dun's Review, 1975, and Metz, 1976), as well as immediate (Johnson, 1970) and delayed (Joy and Tollefson, 1975) criticism. To some extent, it has become a standard of comparison for subsequent bankruptcy classification studies. We have compared the ZETA model developed in this paper with the earlier (1968) model in several ways. First, we compare the five-year accuracy for each model using the particular sample of firms of each study. These results are reported in columns 2–3 and 4–5 of Table 5. Note that the newer ZETA model is far more accurate in bankruptcy classification in years 2–5 with the initial year's accuracy about equal. The older model showed slightly more accurate non-bankruptcy classification in the two years when direct comparison is possible.

Second, we have utilised the 1968 model's five variables and parameters,[15] calculated the five variables for the new sample of firms, arrived at each of these firm's Z-scores and classified them as bankrupt if $Z \leq 2.675$ (the 1968 model's cut-off score) and as non-bankrupt if $Z > 2.675$. The observed accuracy of applying the new sample to the old model is illustrated in columns 6–7 of Table 5. In every year (with the exception of year 5, non-bankrupts) the ZETA model dominates the 1968 model applied to the ZETA sample, especially in years 1 and 5.[16] Finally, we selected the five variables utilised in the 1968 model and calculated the parameters based on the 111-firm ZETA sample. Columns 8–9 list the five-year classification accuracy of the new sample based on the old variables, with year 1 as the standard and years 2–5 as "holdouts". Once again the ZETA model dominates in every year, but notice that the new seven-variable model is, in some years, only slightly more accurate than the "old" five-variable model when the data are comparable, ie, adjusted for more meaningful evaluation.

Unfortunately, direct comparison of the parameters of the five-variable 1968 model for that earlier model's sample and the more recent sample did not make sense since the latest sample's data are adjusted along the lines as outlined in the section on "reporting adjustments" above, while the earlier data were not. One can observe the difference in average ratios for the two samples in Table 6. Note that since the total

Table 5. Comparative classification accuracy between the ZETA model and various forms of a prior bankruptcy model (%)

Years prior to bankruptcy (1)	ZETA model		Altman's 1968 model*		1968 model, ZETA sample		1968 variables, ZETA para.	
	Bankrupt (2)	Non-bankrupt (3)	Bankrupt (4)	Non-Bankrupt (5)	Bankrupt (6)	Non-bankrupt (7)	Bankrupt (8)	Non-bankrupt (9)
1	96.2	89.7	93.9	97.0	86.8	82.4	92.5	84.5
2	84.9	93.1	71.9	93.9	83.0	89.3	83.0	86.2
3	74.5	91.4	48.3	N/A	70.6	91.4	72.7	89.7
4	68.1	89.5	28.6	N/A	61.7	86.0	57.5	83.0
5	69.8	82.1	36.0	N/A	55.8	86.2	44.2	82.1

*Source: Altman (1968). N/A = not available.

Table 6. Comparison of group means and significance tests, 1968 model variables

Variable	Average bankrupt group ratio		Average non-bankrupt group ratio		Univariate F-test	
	1968	ZETA	1968	ZETA	1968	ZETA
Working capital/total assets	(0.06)	0.15	0.41	0.31	32.4	40.6
Retained earnings/total assets	(0.62)	(0.001)	0.36	0.29	58.9	114.6
Earnings before interest and taxes/total assets	(0.13)	(0.01)	0.15	0.11	26.6	54.3
Market value equity/total debt	0.40	0.61	2.47	1.84	33.3	11.6
Sales/total assets	1.50X	1.31X	1.90X	1.62X	2.8	3.3

assets and liabilities of all firms are "inflated" by lease capitalisation (for example), the ratios of both bankrupts and non-bankrupts are quite different ("higher" negatives and lower positives) for the new simple *vis-à-vis* the older one. This will cause the group means to be closer when the bankrupt average is negative and the non-bankrupt average positive, as is the case for the second and third variables.

The higher asset totals will also partly explain the lower capital turnover ratios (sales/assets) in the ZETA sample versus the 1968 model's average. Another item of some interest is that, despite the "inflated" total assets (deriving from higher *fixed assets*) in the ZETA sample, the working capital/total asset ratio of the bankrupt group is significantly larger in the more recent sample *vis-à-vis* the earlier one. The expected ranking is observed, however, for the non-bankrupt sample.

A comparison of univariate F-tests for the five variables shows that in four of the five cases (excepting the market value of equity/total debt), the more recent study has a higher test statistic. This is observed despite the greater mean differentials for the 1968 samples – no doubt due to the considerably smaller within-group variance in the recent samples.

Finally, we note that two of the seven variables in the ZETA model are also found in the 1968 model, and a third 1968 measure (market value of equity/total debt) is very similar to *capitalisation* of the ZETA model.

GROUP PRIOR PROBABILITIES, ERROR COSTS AND MODEL EFFICIENCY

In the section on "linear versus quadratic analysis" above, we showed the classification rules for both linear and quadratic analyses. Note that if one sets equal prior probabilities of group membership, the linear model will result in a cut-off or critical score of zero. All firms scoring above zero are classified as having characteristics similar to the non-bankrupt group and those with negative scores similar to bankrupts. The same zero cut-off score will result if one desired to minimise the total cost of misclassification. That is, assuming multinormal populations and a common covariance matrix, the optimal cut-off score, $ZETA_c$, is equal to[17]

$$ZETA_c = \ln \frac{q_1 C_I}{q_2 C_{II}}$$

where q_1, q_2 = prior probability of bankrupt (q_1) or non-bankrupt (q_2), and C_I, C_{II} = costs of type I and type II errors, respectively.

Further, if one wanted to compare the efficiency of the ZETA bankruptcy classification model with alternative strategies, the following is appropriate for the expected cost of ZETA (EC_{ZETA}),

$$EC_{ZETA} = q_1 \left(\frac{M_{12}}{N_1} \right) C_I + q_2 \left(\frac{M_{21}}{N_2} \right) C_{II}$$

where M_{12}, M_{21} = observed type I and type II errors (misses) respectively, and N_1, N_2 = number of observations in the bankrupt (N_1) and non-bankrupt (N_2) groups.

In our tests, we have implicitly assumed equal prior probabilities and equal costs of errors, resulting in a zero cut-off score. We are acutely aware, however, of the potential bias involved in doing so. Instead of attempting earlier to integrate probability priors

161

ZETA ANALYSIS:
A NEW MODEL TO
IDENTIFY
BANKRUPTCY RISK
OF CORPORATIONS

and error costs, we have assumed equal estimates for each parameter, because to a great extent the two parameters neutralise each other, and it was much easier than attempting to state them precisely.[18] The following is our reasoning.

The "correct" estimate of q_1/q_2 is probably in the 0.01–0.05 range. That is, the prior probability that a firm will go bankrupt in the future is probably in this 0.01–0.05 range. Dun and Bradstreet estimate that, in the last decade, between 0.4 and 0.5 per cent of the firm population failed *in any given year*. Although the ZETA model's parameters are based on data from one year prior to bankruptcy, it is not specifically a one-year prediction model. The procedure in this sense is atemporal.[19] It is, in our opinion, incorrect to base one's prior probability estimates on a single year's reported statistics. In addition, there are many definitions of business failure which, economically, approximate bankruptcy. These include non-judicial arrangements, extreme liquidity problems which require the firm's creditors or other external forces to take over the business,[20] bond default, etc. In the final analysis, we simply do not know the precise estimate of bankruptcy priors, but at the same time assert that one must assume the estimate is greater than a single year's reported data. Hence, we believe the prior probability estimate is in the 2–5% range and in subsequent analysis we utilise the 2% figure.

COST OF CLASSIFICATION ERRORS

Another input that is imperative to the specification of an alternative to the zero cut-off is the cost of errors in classification. No prior study of the type attempted here has explicitly included this element of analysis. In order to attempt to precise the cost component into an analysis of model efficiency, it is necessary to specify the decision-maker's role. In this study we utilise the *commercial bank loan* function as the framework of analysis. The type I bankruptcy classification error is analogous to that of an accepted loan that defaults and the type II error to a rejected loan that would have resulted in a successful payoff. Many of the conceptual factors involved in assessing these error costs were first noted in an excellent discussion by Neter and Beaver at the end of Beaver (1967).

An empirical study was performed to assess the costs of these lending errors with the following specification for the equivalent type I (C_I) and type II (C_{II}) error costs:[21]

$$C_I = 1 - \frac{LLR}{GLL} \quad C_{II} = r - i$$

where

LLR = amount of loan losses recovered,
GLL = gross loan losses (charged-off),
r = effective interest rate on the loan,
i = effective opportunity cost for the bank.

The commercial bank takes the risk of losing all or a portion of the loan should the applicant eventually default. The exact amount is a function of the success the bank has in recovering the loan principal.[22] This recovery aspect is rarely considered in conceptual, as well as practical, analysis.

We have measured C_I based on annual report data from 26 of the largest US commercial banks and questionnaire returns from a sample of smaller, regional banks in the Southeast US.[23] Both data sources encompass a five-year period, 1971–1975 inclusive, and we measure the average loan loss recovery statistics on a contemporary and a one-year lag (recoveries lagging charge-offs) basis. The results of this investigation are illustrated in Table 7 and show that the average C_I on a contemporary basis is in the 76.7–83.0% range; when measured on a one-year lag basis, the averages are lower (68.6–72.2%). The year 1975 was an abnormally high loan charge-off year in the US banking system and since these data are included in the contemporary statistics but not

Table 7. Net loan loss experience, 1971–1975 averages, two samples

Net loan loss (C_1) (%)*	Major banks Number	%	Southeast regional banks Number	%
0–20	0	0.0	0	0.0
20–30	1	3.8	0	0.0
30–40	0	0.0	0	0.0
40–50	0	0.0	1	3.0
50–60	0	0.0	2	6.1
60–70	1	3.8	4	12.1
70–80	4	15.4	12	36.4
80–90	13	50.0	11	33.3
90–100	7	27.0	3	9.1
Total	26	100.0	33	100.0
Average (contemporary)	—	83.0	—	76.7
Average (one-year lag)	—	72.2	—	68.6

*Recoveries and loan loss measured on a contemporary basis.

in the one-year lag data, we believe the more representative result for C_I is in the vicinity of 70%. We use this statistic for C_I.

The simple formula for C_{II} specifies that the decision not to lend to an account that would have repaid successfully foregoes the return on that loan, but the loss is mitigated by the alternative use of loanable funds. In its strictest sense, the bank's opportunity cost implies another loan at the same risk which is assumed to pay off. In this case, C_{II} is probably zero or extremely small. Conservatively speaking, however, an account is rejected due to its high risk characteristics and alternative uses probably will carry lower risk attributes. Hence, $r - i$ will be positive but still quite low. Carried to the other extreme, the alternative use would be an investment in a riskless asset, ie, government securities of the same maturity as the loan, and $r - i$ will be somewhat higher – perhaps 2-4%. The relationship between $r - i$ will vary over time and is particularly sensitive to the demand and supply equilibrium relationship for loanable funds.[24] As an approximation, we specify $C_{II} = 2\%$, hence C_I/C_{II} is equal to 35 times.

REVISED CUT-OFF SCORE AND MODEL EFFICIENCY TESTS
With respect now to the calculation of the critical or cut-off score $ZETA_c$, we have,

$$ZETA_c = \ln\frac{q_1 C_I}{q_2 C_{II}} = \frac{0.02 \cdot 0.70}{0.98 \cdot 0.02} = \ln 0.714$$

$$ZETA_c = -0.337$$

Before comparing the efficiency of the various alternative bankruptcy classification strategies, it should be noted that the observed classification accuracy of a model such as ZETA will change with the new cut-off score.[25] For example, with the cut-off score of –0.337, the number of type I errors increases from two (3.8%) to four (7.6%) while the type II errors decrease from six (10.3%) to four (7.0%). These new estimates will form the basis of comparison along with the more realistic priors and measures of error costs.

The following calculations represent our efficiency comparison tests:

$$EC_{ZETA} = q_1(M_{12}/N_1)C_I + q_2(M_{21}/N_2)C_{II}$$
$$= 0.02(0.076)0.70 + 0.98(0.07)0.02 = 0.00243$$

$$EC_{max} = q_1 C_I = 0.02(0.70) = 0.0140$$

$$EC_{prop} = q_1 q_2 C_I + q_2 q_1 C_{II}$$
$$= 0.02(0.98)0.70 + 0.98(0.02)0.02 = 0.01411$$

where EC_{max} is based on the naïve strategy that all firms are classified as non-bankrupt, eg, all loan applications are accepted, and EC_{prop} is a proportional chance strategy based on observed error rates equalling *a priori* probabilities.

Therefore, the best estimate, or most likely result, shows that $EC_{ZETA} < 5.7 \times EC_{max} \approx EC_{prop}$. That is, both naïve strategies are almost six times less efficient than the ZETA model. Rather than leave the comparison analysis with just one set of estimates of prior probabilities and error costs, we have specified the likely limits of each parameter and calculated the resulting ZETA cut-off score, type I and type II errors, and the expected cost of each of the two naïve models plus the ZETA model under each assumption. That is, we can expect that the true value of q_1/q_2 is between 0.01/099 and 0.05/0.95, the

163

ZETA ANALYSIS:

A NEW MODEL TO

IDENTIFY

BANKRUPTCY RISK

OF CORPORATIONS

Assumptions	ZETA results					
	Cut-off score	Type I error	Type II error	EC_{ZETA}	EC_{max}	EC_{prop}
$q_1 = 0.02$; $q_2 = 0.98$ $C_I = 0.70$; $C_{II} = 0.02$	−0.33	0.076	0.070	0.0024	0.0140	0.0141
$q_1 = 0.01$; $q_2 = 0.99$ $C_I = 0.60$; $C_{II} = 0.05$	−2.11	0.226	0.000	0.0014	0.0060	0.0064
$q_1 = 0.01$; $q_2 = 0.99$ $C_I = 0.80$; $C_{II} = 0.01$	−0.21	0.057	0.070	0.0011	0.0080	0.0080
$q_1 = 0.05$; $q_2 = 0.95$ $C_I = 0.60$; $C_{II} = 0.05$	−0.46	0.076	0.070	0.0056	0.0300	0.0309
$q_1 = 0.05$; $q_2 = 0.95$ $C_I = 0.80$; $C_{II} = 0.01$	1.43	0.000	0.225	0.0021	0.0400	0.0385

Table 8. Model efficiency comparisons under various input assumptions

values of C_I could vary between 0.6 and 0.8 and C_{II} between 0.01 and 0.05. We therefore can specify four new comparison tests and their results as listed in Table 8.[26]

We observe that regardless of the assumptions, the ZETA model is considerably more efficient, and this efficiency differential ranges from 4.3 to 19.0 times.[27] Of course, this is not a mathematical proof of the ZETA superiority, but one can feel confident that under reasonable assumptions this will be the case.

ADJUSTMENTS TO THE CUT-OFF SCORE AND PRACTICAL APPLICATIONS
In addition to the utilisation of prior probabilities of group membership and cost estimates of classification errors for comparative model efficiency assessment, these inputs could prove valuable for practical application purposes. For instance, the bank lending-officer or loan-review analyst may wish to be able to logically adjust the critical cut-off score to consider his own estimates of group priors and error costs and/or to reflect current economic conditions in his environment. One could imagine the cut-off score falling (thereby lowering the acceptance criterion) as business conditions improve and the banker's prior probability of bankruptcy estimate falls from say 0.02 to 0.015. Or, a rise in cut-off scores could result from a change (rise) in the estimate of the type I error cost *vis-à-vis* the type II error cost. The latter condition possibly will occur for different decision-makers. For instance, the cost to a portfolio manager of not selling a security destined for failure is likely to be extremely high relative to his cost of not investing in a stock (which does not fail) due to its relatively low ZETA. The portfolio manager may indeed want to raise the cut-off or threshold level to reduce the possibility of intangible (lawsuit costs) as well as tangible (lower prices) costs involved with holding a failed company's stock.

Another example of a practical application of cut-off score adjustment is the case of an accounting auditor. He might wish to use the model to decide whether a "going concern" qualified opinion should be applied. His expected cost for doing so is likely to be quite high (loss of client) relative to the expected cost of a stockholder lawsuit. This might lead to a fairly low cut-off score. On the other hand, the environment may be such that the lawsuit expected cost is prohibitive.

DISTRIBUTION OF ZETA
Figure 1 illustrates the mean ZETA score for the two groups from five years prior to bankruptcy to one year prior. While the average ZETA for bankrupts diminishes as bankruptcy approaches, the standard deviation for each period remains fairly stable, ie, 2.7, 2.5, 2.5, 2.7 and 3.0 for years 1–5. The non-bankrupt group's variance is also quite stable although slightly higher, averaging 3.0. Figure 2

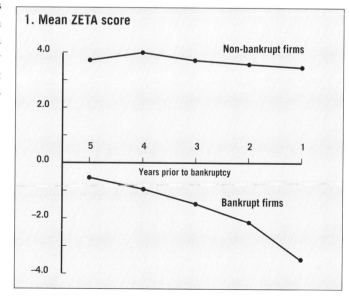

1. Mean ZETA score

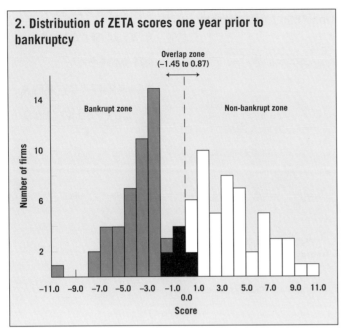

2. Distribution of ZETA scores one year prior to bankruptcy

Overlap zone (–1.45 to 0.87)

Bankrupt zone | Non-bankrupt zone

Number of firms

14

10

6

2

–11.0 –9.0 –7.0 –5.0 –3.0 –1.0 1.0 3.0 5.0 7.0 9.0 11.0
0.0
Score

shows the actual ZETA distribution for the 111 firms (see Appendix A). Note that the overlap area (the interval of ZETA where errors in classification are observed) is relatively small, ie, from –1.45 to +0.87. As expected, the overlap range widens (except in year 5) as the time prior to bankruptcy is more remote.[28]

Conclusions

The ZETA model for assessing bankruptcy risk of corporations developed in this chapter demonstrates significantly improved accuracy over an existing failure classification model and, perhaps more importantly, is based on data most relevant to current conditions. We are concerned with refining existing bankruptcy classification techniques by the use of the most relevant data combined with the most recent developments in the application of discriminant analysis to finance. The model's bankruptcy classification accuracy ranges from over 96% (93% holdout) one period prior to bankruptcy to 70% five annual reporting periods prior. We have assessed the effect of several elements involved with the application of discriminant analysis to financial problems. These include linear versus quadratic analysis for the original and holdout samples, introduction of prior probabilities of group membership and costs of error estimates into the classification rule, and comparison of the model's results with naïve bankruptcy classification strategies.

The potential applications of the ZETA bankruptcy identification model are in the same spirit as previously developed models. These include creditworthiness analysis of firms for financial and non-financial institutions, identification of undesirable investment risk for portfolio managers and individual investors and to aid in more effective internal and external audits of firms with respect to going-concern considerations, among others.

1 *These studies include models for manufacturers by Beaver (1967), Altman (1968), Wilcox (1971, 1976), Deakin (1972, 1977) and Edmister (1972), among others, and models for specific industries such as Altman on railroads (1973), Sinkey on commercial banks (1975), Korobow and Stuhr (1975) and with Martin (1976), also on commercial banks, Altman and Lorris on broker/dealers (1976) and Altman on savings and loan associations (1977a).*

2 *This is in contrast to one of the authors' past efforts on bankrupt manufacturers – Altman (1968) – where the largest firm had assets of less than $25 million.*

3 *For example, see Joy and Tollefson (1975) and the consequent comment by Altman and Eisenbeis (1976) as well as Eisenbeis (1977).*

4 *We have five more non-failed observations than failed because five of the failed firms in our original sample did not have sufficient data for our purposes.*

5 *Dun and Bradstreet (1976) report that the percentage of business failures with short-term liabilities in excess of $1 million has risen from 1.1% in 1970 to 4.5% in 1976. No longer is the large billion dollar enterprise immune to failure. In fact, three S&P 500 firms have failed since 1970 (Penn Central, Arlans Department Stores, and W. T. Grant).*

6 *This test, as well as the actual quadratic algorithm, is incorporated into a computer program known as MULDIS, developed by Eisenbeis and Avery (1972). We have utilised a revised version of their original program in this study.*

7 *Variable no. 25 measures the potential drop in EBIT based on the worst single year's rate of change in EBIT in the past 10 years. Variable no. 26 measures a similar fall in EBIT with respect to the ratio of EBIT/sales over a like period. These earnings "declines" are measured against the current year's interest and debt respectively.*

165

ZETA ANALYSIS:
A NEW MODEL TO
IDENTIFY
BANKRUPTCY RISK
OF CORPORATIONS

8 *Conceptually, the most recent market value should best portray the future earning power of a firm, and we have seen its powerful failure information content before – see Beaver (1968) and Altman (1968). Due to a certain amount of caution for practical and application purposes, we have selected the 5-year average. Note that only the most recent market value is measured in variable no. 21 (Appendix B) and its univariate F-test is approximately identical to the ratio using the 5-year average (variable no. 22).*

9 *These tests include:*
❏ *forwards stepwise; backwards stepwise;*
❏ *scaled vector (multiplication of the discriminant coefficient by the appropriate variance–covariance matrix item);*
❏ *separation of means test – suggested by Mosteller and Wallace (1963) and supported by Joy and Tollefson (1975);*
❏ *the conditional deletion test, which measures the additional contribution of the variable to the multivariate F-test given that the other variables have already been included – supported by Altman and Eisenbeis (1976); and*
❏ *the univariate F-test.*

10 *Essentially, these equations are cut-off scores for classification in a two-group analysis. We will introduce costs of errors into the actual cut-off score when we assume unequal priors and unequal costs.*

11 *Lachenbruch (1967) suggests an almost unbiased validation test of original sample results by means of a type of jackknife, or one isolated observation at a time, approach. The individual observations' classification accuracy is then cumulated over the entire sample.*

12 *Data from the original sample's financial statements 2–5 years prior to failure are applied to the parameters established from one-year prior data and the results observed.*

13 *Mainly due to the classification of the same observations used to construct the model; see Frank, Massy and Morrison (1965) for a discussion of discriminant analysis classification bias.*

14 *Alternative temporal-type bankruptcy modelling strategies would include either completely separate models in each of the five years of analysis or the same variables for each of the five years, only the parameters would change to reflect the differences in data as bankruptcy becomes more remote. The latter approach was first presented by Deakin (1972) using Beaver's (1967) 14 variables. We think this latter approach is of some interest, but for application purposes the analyst is left somewhat confused as to which model to apply to new data. We did in fact, however, experiment with this approach and found that the year 1 model was, overall (five years combined), more accurate than the other years' alternative models. Of course, each individual year's model was the most accurate in reclassifying that particular year's observations. These results, too lengthy to report in full, are available from the authors.*

15 *These variables are: the working capital/total assets; retained earnings/assets; earnings before interest and taxes/total assets; market value of equity/total debt; and sales/total assets.*

16 *This type of test is more akin to an assessment of the "predictive" accuracy of the "old" model as opposed to the "classification" and "validation" accuracy involved with observations from the same periods as that of the model's sample. The bankrupt sample's predictive accuracy (column 6, Table 5) is higher for the ZETA sample than we found in a prior study (Altman and McGough, 1974), ie, 86.8% and 83.0% for years 1 and 2 respectively versus 82.0% and 58.0% in that 1974 study. We would be remiss not to point out that this type of test is not completely valid since the ZETA sample's data has been adjusted before being applied to the 1968 model. Hence, all firms will look worse and the type I error (13.2%) is probably lower than if no adjustments were made, with the opposite effect on the type II error. These adjustments help to explain the fact that the 1968 model applied to the ZETA sample outperforms the same model applied to the 1968 sample in years 2–5.*

17 *See Joy and Tollefson (1975) and Altman and Eisenbeis (1976) for a full discussion of the optimal cut-off score and efficiency tests. Note that if the assumption of multinormality and common dispersion matrices is violated, the cut-off score derived from this formula may not be optimal (see the section on revised cut-off score and model efficiency tests).*

18 *We could have easily adjusted ZETA$_c$ for prior probability estimates, but instead we have deferred this (and also error cost inputs) to a later section.*

19 *For an attempt to add a temporal aspect to failure prediction see Wilcox (1971) and Santomero and Vinso (1977).*

20 *Several large firm problems of this type come to mind, including LTV Corporation, Memorex and, in a different context, Lockheed Aircraft Corp.*

21 *For a more detailed discussion of this investigation see Altman (1977b).*

22 *We are quite aware that there are additional costs involved in the recovery process, including legal, transaction, and loan charge-off officer opportunity costs. These costs are not reported but obviously would*

166

ZETA ANALYSIS:

A NEW MODEL TO

IDENTIFY

BANKRUPTCY RISK

OF CORPORATIONS

increase the type I error cost. In addition, if the type II error (C_{II}) is positive, ie, r > i, then there will be an added cost element in C_I. This added element involves the lost interest on that remaining part of the loan which is not recovered (GLL – LLR) for the duration of the defaulted loan. We will examine C_{II} below, but will not include this added element in our calculation of C_I. Again however, it is clear that we are understating C_I somewhat.

23 *A questionnaire was sent to approximately 100 Southeast banks with 33 possible responses. The range of commercial bank asset sizes in this small-bank sample was between $12 million and $3 billion, with the average equal to $311 million and the median equal to $110 million. The large-bank sample's asset size averaged $13.4 billion with a $10 billion median.*

24 *Various abstractions of the C_{II} calculation are not considered here – such as the loss of the customer's future interest payments on loans. Assuming r – i > 0, we might approximate this loss as the perpetuity of r – i discounted by the bank's cost of capital. Note that if r equals i (C_{II} = 0), the critical cut-off score will equal positive infinity (see the next section) and all loans will be rejected by the model.*

25 *This point is often overlooked in assessing various strategy performances, eg, Joy and Tollefson (1975) overlook this aspect in their critique of the 1968 Altman model.*

26 *In fact, one can specify an alternative equally naïve strategy, ie, all firms will go bankrupt, and arrive at a more efficient result in case number 5 (Table 8) than the EC_{max} strategy. ZETA would, of course, dominate this strategy as well.*

27 *Since the population distributions are not perfectly multinormal, it is possible to search by an iterative process and establish a cut-off score which results in slightly lower overall expected costs. For example, cases 1 and 3 in Table 8 could be very slightly improved in terms of EC_{ZETA}.*

28 *Based on data from two years prior, the overlap interval is from –2.4 to +1.6; three years prior, from –1.9 to +3.1; four years prior, from –3.3 to +5.5; and five years prior, from –3.1 to + 4.6.*

Appendix A

Table A1. Sample failed firms and year of failure

Company	Year of failure	Company	Year of failure
American Beef Packers (M)	1975	Hartfield-Zody's (R)	1974
American Book – Stratford Press (M)	1973	Harvard Industries (M)	1972
Ancorp National Services (R)	1973	Hoe, R. (M)	1969
Arlans Department Stores (R)	1973	Horn & Hardart Baking (R)	1971
Atlas Sewing Centers (R)	1962	Interstate Dept. Stores (R)	1974
Beck Industries (R)	1970	Kenton Corp. (R)	1974
Bishop Industries (M)	1970	Ling-Temco-Vought (M)*	1971
Bohack Stores (R)	1975	Lockheed Aircraft (M)*	1971
Botany Industries (R)	1971	Mangel Stores (R)	1975
Bowmar Instruments (M)[e, r]	1974	Meister Brau (M)	1971
Coit International (R)	1975	Memorex Corp. (M)*	1973
Commodore Corp. (M)	1974	Miller Wohl (R)	1973
Daylin (R)	1975	Mohawk Data Sciences (M)*	1975
Diversa (M)	1969	National Bellas Hess (R)	1974
Dolly Madison Ind. (M)	1970	National Video (R)	1969
Douglas Aircraft (M)*	1967	Omega-Alpha (M)	1973
Dynamics Corp. (M)	1972	Parkview-General (R)	1973
Ecological Science (M)	1970	Penn Fruit (R)	1975
Electrospace (M)[r]	1973	Photon (M)[e]	1972
Esgro Corp. (M)	1973	Potter Instruments (M)	1975
Farrington Mfg. (M)	1969	Roberts Co. (M)	1969
Federals Corp. (R)	1973	Scottex (M)	1973
Fishman, M.H. (R)	1974	Sequoyah Industries (M)	1973
Giant Stores (R)	1973	Simon Stores (R)	1970
Grant, W.T. (R)	1975	Unishops (R)	1973
Gray Mfg (M)	1975	Westgate California (M)	1974
Grayson Robinson Stores (R)	1962		

M, manufacturer; R, retailer.
Asterisk (*) indicates that the firm remained a non-bankrupt only due to extraordinary external support.
Superscript 'e' ([e]) indicates zero cutoff-point error; superscript 'r' ([r]) indicates revised cutoff error, –0.33 score.

167

ZETA ANALYSIS:
A NEW MODEL TO
IDENTIFY
BANKRUPTCY RISK
OF CORPORATIONS

Table A2. Sample non-failed firms

Company	Company	Company
Airco (M)	Franklin Stores (R)	Mays, J.W. (R)
Alexanders (R)	General Dynamics (M)	New Process (R)
American Furniture (M)	Genesco (R)	Outlet Co. (R)
Ampex (M)	Ginos (R)[e]	Pay N'Save (R)
Armada (M)[e]	Grace, W.R. (M)	Penn Traffic (R)
Associated Dry Goods (R)	Grumman Corp. (M)	Phillips Van-Heusen (M)
Automatic Service (R)	Gulf Resources (M)	Reliable Stores (R)
Buffalo Forge (M)	Harris Intertype (M)	Richton Int'l (R)[e, r]
Bunker Ramo (M)	Hewlett Packard (M)	Scovill Mfg (M)
Caldor (R)	High Voltage Eng. (M)	Sterling Precision (M)
Chesebrough Ponds (M)	Hoffman Electronics (M)	Supermarkets General (R)
Cone Mills (M)	House of Fabrics (R)	Varian Associates (M)
Cooper Industries (M)	Ideal Toy (M)	Walgreen (R)
Curtiss-Wright (M)	Itek (M)	Wallace Business Forms (M)
Digital Equipment (M)	Jamesway (R)[e, r]	West Point-Pepperell (M)
Eagle Clothes (R)[e, r]	Kings Dept. Stores (R)	White Consolidated (M)[e, r]
Emporium Capwell (R)	Kroger (R)	Winnebago (M)
Esmark (M)	Kuhns Big K Stores (R)	Zayre (R)
Ford Motor Co. (M)	Lane Bryant (R)	
Foxboro Corp. (M)	Lucky Stores (R)	

M, manufacturer; R, retailer. Superscript 'e' ([e]) indicates zero cutoff-point error; superscript 'r' ([r]) indicates revised cutoff error, −0.33 score.

Appendix B

Table B1. Listing of all variables, group means and F-tests based on one period prior to bankruptcy data

No.	Variable Name	Failed	Non-failed	Univariate F-test
(1)	EBIT/TA	−0.00555	0.11176	54.3
(2)	NATC/TC	−0.02977	0.0742	36.6
(3)	Sales/TA	1.312	1.620	3.3
(4)	Sales/TC	2.107	2.160	0.0
(5)	EBIT/Sales	0.00209	0.07709	30.2
(6)	NATC/Sales	−0.01535	0.04002	33.1
(7)	Long tang. assets	1.985	2.222	5.5
(8)	Interest coverage	−0.5995	5.341	26.1
(9)	Log no. (8) & 15	0.9625	1.162	26.1
(10)	Fixed charge coverage	0.2992	2.1839	15.7
(11)	Earnings/Debt	−0.0792	0.1806	32.8
(12)	Earnings/5 yr. mats	−0.1491	0.6976	8.8
(13)	Cashflow/Fixed charges	0.1513	2.9512	20.9
(14)	Cashflow/TD	−0.0173	0.3136	31.4
(15)	WC/LTD	0.3532	2.4433	6.0
(16)	Current ratio	1.5757	2.6040	38.2
(17)	WC/Total assets	0.1498	0.3086	40.6
(18)	WC/Cash expenses	0.1640	0.2467	5.2
(19)	Ret. earn./Total assets	−0.00066	0.2935	114.6
(20)	Book equity/TC	0.202	0.526	64.5
(21)	MV equity/TC	0.3423	0.6022	32.1
(22)	5 yr. MV equity/TC	0.4063	0.6210	31.0
(23)	MV equity/Total liabilities	0.6113	1.8449	11.6
(24)	Standard error of estimate of EBIT/TA (norm)	1.687	5.784	33.8
(25)	EBIT drop	−3.227	3.179	9.9
(26)	Margin drop	−0.217	0.179	15.6
(27)	Capital lease/Total assets	0.251	0.178	4.2
(28)	Sales/Fixed assets	3.172	4.179	3.5

EBIT, Earnings before interest and taxes.   MV, Market value.
NATC, Net available for total capital.   TC, Total capital.
TA, Total tangible assets.   TD, Total debt.
LTD, Long-term debt.   WC, Working capital.

BIBLIOGRAPHY

Altman, E., 1968, "Financial Ratios, Discriminant Analysis and the Prediction of Corporate Bankruptcy". *Journal of Finance,* September.

Altman, E., 1973, "Predicting Railroad Bankruptcies in America", *Bell Journal of Economics and Management Science,* Spring.

Altman, E., 1977a, "Predicting Performance in the Savings and Loan Association Industry", *Journal of Monetary Economics,* October.

Altman, E., 1977b, "Lending Error Costs for Commercial Banks: Some Conceptual and Empirical Issues", *Journal of Commercial Bank Lending,* October.

Altman, E., and T. McGough, 1974, "Evaluation of a Company as a Going Concern", *Journal of Accountancy,* December.

Altman, E., and T. Lorris, 1976, "A Financial Early Warning System for Over-the-Counter Broker Dealers", *Journal of Finance,* September.

Altman, E., and R. Eisenbeis, 1976, "Financial Applications of Discriminant Analysis: A Clarification", Salomon Brothers Center For the Study of Financial Institutions, working paper no. 79, New York University, Autumn.

Beaver, W., 1967, "Financial ratios as predictors of failure", *Empirical research in accounting: Selected studies,* 1966, *Journal of Accounting Research,* V, supplement.

Beaver, W., 1968, "Market Prices, Financial Ratios and Prediction of Failure", *Journal of Accounting Research,* Autumn.

Box, G .E. P., 1949, "A General Distribution Theory for a Class of Likelihood Criteria", *Biometrika* 36.

Deakin, E., 1972, "A Discriminant Analysis of Predictors of Business Failure", *Journal of Accounting Research,* Spring.

Deakin, E., 1977, "Business Failure Prediction: An Empirical Analysis", in E. Altman and A. Sametz, eds, *Financial Crises: Institutions and Markets in a Fragile Environment* (New York: Wiley-Interscience).

Dun and Bradstreet, 1976, *The Failure Record* (New York).

Dun's Review, October 1975, "How to Tell Who's Going Bankrupt".

Edmister, R., March 1972, "An empirical test of financial ratio analysis for small business failure prediction", *Journal of Financial and Quantitative Analysis.*

Eisenbeis, R., 1977, "Pitfalls in the Application of Discriminant Analysis in Business, Finance, and Economics", *Journal of Finance.*

Eisenbeis, R., and R. Avery, 1972, *Discriminant Analysis and CLassification Procedures: Theory and Applications* (Lexington, MA: D. C. Heath).

Elam, R., 1975, "The Effect of Lease Data on the Predictive Ability of Financial Ratios", *The Accounting Review,* January.

Frank, R., W. Massy and G. Morrison, 1965, "Bias in Multiple Discriminant Analysis", *Journal of Marketing Research,* August.

Johnson, C., 1970, "Ratio Analysis and the Prediction of Firm Failure", *Journal of Finance,* December.

Joy, O., and J. Tollefson, 1975, "On the Financial Applications of Discriminant Analysis", *Journal of Financial and Quantitative Analysis,* December.

Korobow, L., and D. Stuhr, 1975, "Toward Early Warning of Changes in Banks", *Federal Reserve Bank of New York Review,* July.

Korobow, L., D. Stuhr and D. Martin, 1976, "A Probabilistic Approach to Early Warning of Changes in Bank Financial Condition", *Federal Reserve Bank of New York Review,* July.

Lachenbruch, P., 1967, "An Almost Unbiased Method of Obtaining Confidence Intervals for the Probability of Misclassification in Discriminant Analysis", *Biometrics,* December.

Metz, R., 1976, "Market Place: Avoiding the Stock of Shaky Companies", *New York Times,* November 18.

Mosteller, F., and D. F. Wallace, 1963, "Inference in the Authorship Problem", *Journal of American Statistical Association,* June.

Santomero, A., and J. Vinso, 1977, "Estimating the Probability of Failure for Firms in the Banking System", *Journal of Banking and Finance,* September.

Sinkey, J., 1975, "A Multivariate Statistical Analysis of the Characteristics of Problem Banks", *Journal of Finance,* March.

Van Horne, J., 1974, *Financial Management and Policy,* 3rd edition (Englewood Cliffs, NJ: Prentice-Hall).

Weston, J., and E. Brigham, 1975, *Managerial Finance,* 5th edition (New York: Holt, Rinehart and Winston).

Wilcox, J., 1961, "A Simple Theory of Financial Ratios as Predictors of Failure", *Journal of Accounting Research,* Autumn.

Wilcox, J., 1976, "The Gamblers Ruin Approach to Business Risk", *Sloan Management Review,* Autumn.

12

Using Default Rates to Model the Term Structure of Credit Risk

Jerome S. Fons

Moody's Investors Service, New York

As the maturity of a corporate bond increases, its credit spread versus that of a comparable-maturity Treasury bond may widen or narrow, depending on the bond's credit risk. This bond-pricing model illustrates the relationship between credit spread, estimated default likelihood and recovery rate. It explains observed patterns in credit spreads, by rating category, as bond maturity varies. Patterns in marginal default rates reflect a typical firm's life cycle. Lower-rated (smaller, younger, more heavily leveraged) issuers tend to have wider credit spreads that narrow with maturity. Higher-rated (more mature, stable) firms tend to have narrower credit spreads that widen with maturity.

Economists have paid a great deal of attention to the term structure of interest rates but relatively little attention to the term structure of credit risk, defined here as the behaviour of credit spreads as maturity varies. Early studies of the term structure of credit risk noted an upward-sloping risk structure for high-grade bonds. That is, the difference, or spread, between the promised yield to maturity of a default-prone bond and the yield to maturity of a default-free bond of equivalent maturity widens as maturity increases. Conversely, researchers found a downward-sloping risk structure for low-grade bonds.

This unusual pattern was explained by a "crisis-at-maturity" model.[1] This model assumes that highly leveraged firms may encounter financing problems as their near-term debt matures. Their increased default risk is reflected in higher spreads at shorter maturities. Recent theoretical models based on contingent-claims analysis of debt pricing are much more sophisticated.[2]

This chapter introduces a relatively straightforward, risk-neutral model that uses multi-period corporate bond default rates. This simple approach has the advantage of being highly intuitive and easy to implement. It tells us that, for some levels of default risk, credit spreads indeed decrease with maturity. Although the conclusions of this study are based on the results of Moody's corporate bond default studies, the patterns exhibited can be found in other studies of corporate bond defaults.[3]

Patterns in default rates

Moody's default studies summarise the default experience of all corporate, long-term public debt rated by Moody's as of January 1, 1970. More than 473 issuers defaulted between that date and December 31, 1993. By comparing the historical ratings of these defaulting issuers with the ratings for the thousands of public issuers that did not default, we can estimate the default risk associated with each rating category.

Reprinted with permission from Financial Analysts Journal, *September–October 1994. ©1994, Association for Investment Management and Research, Charlottesville, VA. All rights reserved.*

The most important concepts that the Moody's studies present are marginal and cumulative default rates. To find the marginal and cumulative default rate, let $m_t^Y(R)$ be the number of issuers rated R (where R = Aaa, Aa,…) that were originally part of the cohort (or set) of all outstanding issuers with rating R at the start of the year Y (where Y = 1970, 1971,…) and that defaulted in the tth year after Y was formed. Let $n_t^Y(R)$ be the total number of issuers with rating R at the start of the year Y that have *not* defaulted by year t. The marginal default rate, $d_t(R)$, is the average issuer-weighted default rate for R-rated issuers in their tth year. Formally,

$$d_t(R) = \frac{\sum_{Y=1970}^{T} m_t^Y(R)}{\sum_{Y=1970}^{T} n_t^Y(R)} \tag{1}$$

where T equals (1994 – t). The variable T restricts the summations to those cohorts for which t years of history are available – in this example, 1970 through 1993.

For example, $d_5(Baa)$ is the probability that a bond will default in the fifth year after holding the Baa rating. The likelihood that a bond rated R will not default *in* year t is the marginal survival rate, $1 - d_t(R)$. The probability that a bond rated R will not default *by* year t is the cumulative survival rate, $S_t(R)$, defined as follows:

$$S_t(R) = \prod_{i=1}^{t} \left[1 - d_i(R)\right] \tag{2}$$

That is, the cumulative survival rate is the product of the intervening marginal survival rates. The cumulative default rate, $D_t(R)$, is the probability that a bond rated R will default by year t. It is found as follows:

$$D_t(R) = 1 - S_t(R) \tag{3}$$

In other words, the path of marginal default rates through period t completely describes the cumulative survival likelihood, as well as the cumulative default likelihood.

Table 1. Weighted-average marginal default rates, by bond rating and investment horizon, 1970–93

Horizon (years)	Aaa (%)	Aa (%)	A (%)	Baa (%)	Ba (%)	B (%)
1	0.00	0.02	0.01	0.16	1.79	8.31
2	0.00	0.01	0.08	0.35	2.64	7.13
3	0.00	0.05	0.20	0.40	2.66	6.50
4	0.04	0.12	0.18	0.56	2.67	5.52
5	0.09	0.12	0.16	0.52	2.69	4.79
6	0.10	0.11	0.21	0.50	2.19	4.89
7	0.11	0.10	0.24	0.65	1.80	3.59
8	0.12	0.11	0.25	0.68	1.67	3.64
9	0.14	0.13	0.31	0.67	1.67	2.64
10	0.15	0.15	0.35	0.59	1.64	2.57
11	0.17	0.17	0.35	0.64	1.69	1.86
12	0.19	0.20	0.36	0.66	1.74	1.12
13	0.22	0.23	0.35	0.62	1.70	1.22
14	0.25	0.26	0.30	0.73	1.28	1.03
15	0.29	0.00	0.34	0.77	1.24	1.15
16	0.34	0.00	0.35	0.82	1.31	1.30
17	0.21	0.13	0.32	0.85	1.16	1.50
18	0.25	0.16	0.33	0.84	1.06	0.58
19	0.00	0.20	0.40	0.69	1.14	0.00
20	0.00	0.25	0.28	0.71	1.24	0.00

Table 2. Weighted-average cumulative default rates, 1970–93

Horizon (years)	Aaa (%)	Aa (%)	A (%)	Baa (%)	Ba (%)	B (%)
1	0.00	0.02	0.01	0.16	1.79	8.31
2	0.00	0.04	0.09	0.51	4.38	14.85
3	0.00	0.08	0.28	0.91	6.92	20.38
4	0.04	0.20	0.46	1.46	9.41	24.78
5	0.12	0.32	0.62	1.97	11.85	28.38
6	0.22	0.43	0.83	2.46	13.78	31.88
7	0.33	0.52	1.06	3.09	15.33	34.32
8	0.45	0.64	1.31	3.75	16.75	36.71
9	0.58	0.76	1.61	4.39	18.14	38.38
10	0.73	0.91	1.96	4.96	19.48	39.96
11	0.90	1.09	2.30	5.56	20.84	41.08
12	1.09	1.29	2.65	6.19	22.22	41.74
13	1.30	1.51	2.99	6.77	23.54	42.45
14	1.55	1.76	3.29	7.44	24.52	43.04
15	1.84	1.76	3.62	8.16	25.46	43.70
16	2.18	1.76	3.95	8.91	26.43	44.43
17	2.38	1.89	4.26	9.69	27.29	45.27
18	2.63	2.05	4.58	10.45	28.06	45.58
19	2.63	2.24	4.96	11.07	28.88	45.58
20	2.63	2.48	5.23	11.70	29.76	45.58

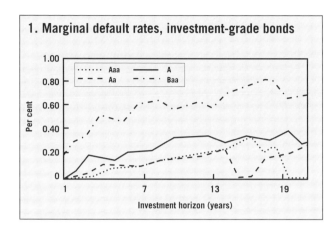

1. Marginal default rates, investment-grade bonds

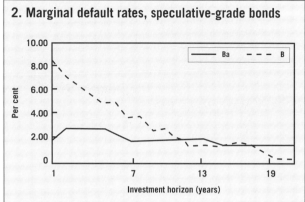

2. Marginal default rates, speculative-grade bonds

Tables 1 and 2 present marginal and cumulative default rates from 1 to 20 years for Moody's broad rating categories. These estimates are derived from Moody's long-term default studies covering the years 1970 through 1993. The cumulative default rates, in particular, show a clear pattern of increasing risk as rating quality declines over any time horizon.

Figures 1 and 2 plot marginal default rates for investment-grade (Aaa, Aa, A and Baa) and speculative-grade (Ba and B) bonds as the investment horizon grows from 1 to 20 years. These rates represent the probabilities, based on past experience, of an issuer defaulting t years after having an R rating. In general, the trend is for investment-grade marginal default rates to rise as the time horizon lengthens and for speculative-grade marginal default rates to decline. Thus, the year-to-year risk of default does not decrease in the cumulative sense, but it does fall for speculative-grade issuers while rising for investment-grade issuers. This shifting pattern of marginal default rates by rating category, which is also supported by changes in corporate credit quality, suggests an underlying mean reversion in company credit outlooks.

Corporate bond issuers are apt to experience life cycles that cause their ratings to settle at average levels in the long run. Small but growing firms, for example, tend to face a great deal of near-term uncertainty in ability to meet their obligations. The same is generally true of mature firms that alter their capital structures significantly by assuming debt. Either type of firm can be rated as speculative and face substantial near-term risks. Having surmounted such obstacles and survived without a default, an issuer may be upgraded or may pay down the borrowings and withdraw from the public debt markets. In other words, the risk of default ten or more years hence is relatively low once a company survives the first few years.

Investment-grade issuers, in contrast, face very low default risk in the near term. They tend to be large, well-established leaders in their industries with a solid track record of meeting obligations. Their credit outlook for the longer term is somewhat less certain; any number of risks can surface over the course of ten or more years. Moreover, top-rated firms have only two credit-quality prospects – stable ratings or declining ratings.

Over the long term, surviving low-rated issuers tend to rise to the middle ratings, middle-rated firms tend to stay middle-rated and top-rated firms tend to slip to the middle ratings. This pattern has implications for the term structure of credit risk.

Risk-neutral bond pricing

The default concepts presented above were used in the context of a standard bond pricing formula to develop a yield-spread model for newly issued bonds. A coupon bond paying an annual coupon, C, and maturing N years from now has a yield to maturity, Y, that solves the expression

$$\text{Price} = \sum_{t=1}^{N} \frac{C}{(1+Y)^t} + \frac{1}{(1+Y)^N} \tag{4}$$

For simplicity, the price, coupon and principal terms are expressed as fractions of unity. Equation (4) states that the price of a coupon bond (default prone or default free) is the present value of a stream of cash flows, C, and a terminal principal payment, 1, where the discount rate is Y.[4]

To use the default date to compute a yield spread over a comparable-maturity, default-free debt instrument, we invoked the following four assumptions:

❑ *Bonds are priced at par.* Typically, a coupon bond is priced at par when first issued. When the price equals 100% of par, the coupon rate, C, equals the promised yield to maturity, Y.

❑ *Investors hold bonds until maturity or default, whichever occurs first.* In the event of default, the bond is sold immediately. This assumption removes the complexity introduced by possible changes in credit rating prior to maturity.

❑ *Investors are risk-neutral.* That is, they are indifferent between taking a gamble with expected payout X and receiving X with certainty. A risk-neutral individual would be indifferent about participating in a lottery with a ticket price of $1.00 and an expected payout of $1.00. Holding the ticket price at $1.00 and raising the expected payout to, say, $1.10, however, would lead the utility-maximising, risk-neutral individual to step up and take a chance.

❑ *Capital markets are arbitrage-free.* In the present context, having arbitrage-free markets means that risk-adjusted expected yields are equal for all securities.

The yield of a default-prone bond is denoted by Y and the yield of a comparable-maturity, default-free issue by i. If a bond has default risk, its yield must be high enough to compensate investors for the risk; the difference $(Y - i)$ is referred to as the credit spread. When the bond is priced at par, the credit spread is $(C - i)$.

A bond's risky coupon and principal payments are then weighted by their probability of being paid when promised. Let S_t be the likelihood that an issuer with a given rating will survive t years from the issuance date without a default. S_t is also the probability that a payment due t years after issuance will be received as promised. Otherwise, the issuer will default on the payment due in year t with probability $S_{t-1}d_t$, which is the probability that the issuer will survive through year $t-1$ times the probability of a default during year t. In the event of a default, the bond holder sells the bond and expects to recover a fraction of the missed coupon plus principal.

This construct gives us a certainty-equivalent version of equation 4:

$$\text{Price} = \sum_{t=1}^{N} \frac{S_t C + S_{t-1} d_t \mu (C+1)}{(1+i)^t} + \frac{S_N}{(1+i)^N} \tag{5}$$

where $S_0 = 1$. The numerator of the summand is a default-risk-adjusted payment stream based on expected default and survival rates. The probability of receiving a coupon payment t years from now is S_t. A default will occur in year t with probability d_t, given that the bond has survived to year t without a default (the probability of this being S_{t-1}). In the event of default, the investor receives a fraction of $(C + 1)$, representing the coupon plus principal owed. S_N is the likelihood of receiving the final principal payment when due.

Equation (5) is identical to equation (4) except that the payment stream in equation (4) is adjusted for default risk. A risk-neutral investor is indifferent between receiving this risk-adjusted payment stream and a certain stream with the same expected value. The appropriate discount rate for this stream is therefore the risk-free interest rate, i.

With the bond price at par (100%) and given an array of marginal default rates (which, in turn, imply a set of survival rates), an estimate of the recovery rate and a default-rate yield of appropriate maturity, equation (5) implicitly determines the risky coupon rate. The difference $(C - i)$ is the credit spread required for the default-prone bond to compensate a buy-and-hold, risk-neutral investor for a set of marginal default rates, d_t, and an expected recovery rate, μ. Such an investor will be indifferent between

173

USING DEFAULT
RATES TO MODEL
THE TERM
STRUCTURE OF
CREDIT RISK

investing in this bond and investing in an equivalent-maturity, default-free bond yielding i. (Of course, most investors are risk-averse and hence would expect to be *more* than compensated for expected default risk, given the uncertainty surrounding point estimates of default likelihood.)

Table 3. Recovery rates by bond seniority

Seniority	Average recovery rate (%)
Senior secured	64.59
Senior unsecured	48.38
Senior subordinated	39.79
Subordinated	30.00
Junior subordinated	16.33

Recovery rates depend on many factors; chief among them is a bond's standing within the firm's capital structure. Moody's long-term default study estimates recovery rates by bond seniority, based on bond prices one month after default. Table 3 shows that average recovery rates decline uniformly with seniority. For our sample of defaulted bonds, the average recovery rate at the senior unsecured level (the rate associated with most debentures, such as bonds and notes) was 48.38% of par, which is the figure used in the simulations presented below.

The term structure of credit risk

Using the model and historical default and recovery rates, the model spreads were compared with recent spreads in the corporate bond market. Figures 3 and 4 plot risk-neutral spreads from 1 to 20 years for each rating category, as determined from equation (5). These figures are from the marginal default rates presented in Table 1 and assume a fixed recovery rate of 48.38%. To arrive at the appropriate default-free yield for each maturity, we fit a (log-linear) regression model to the US Treasury constant-maturity schedule (as of September 30, 1993) and use the modelled value.

Risk-neutral spreads calculated for the investment-grade rating categories exhibit, with minor variations, a steady upward trend as bond maturity increases. To a very small extent, this pattern is attributable to the upward slope of the Treasury yield curve as of September 30, 1993. At the Ba rating level, however, credit spreads rise through the fifth year but then slowly taper off. At the single-B rating, credit spreads fall from Year 1.

Although these patterns roughly match those of the corresponding marginal default rates, it is somewhat surprising to find that spreads against comparable-maturity Treasuries might actually narrow as maturity increases – especially for the lowest rating categories. As the threat of default, even if initially high, recedes, risk-neutral investors require a smaller yield spread to compensate them for expected default loss.

Credit spreads generated using equation (5) are quite sensitive to the recovery rate estimate. Lowering the estimated recovery rate leads to much wider spreads; higher recovery estimates give much smaller spreads. In contrast, the model is much less sensitive to changes in the level of the risk-free yield.

Author Query:
In Figure 4 the y-axis ticks and values don't correspond. Please indicate what should be amended.

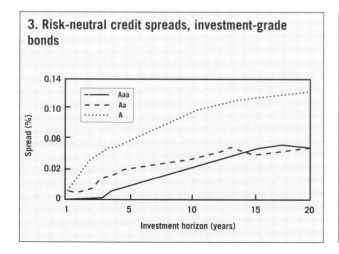

3. Risk-neutral credit spreads, investment-grade bonds

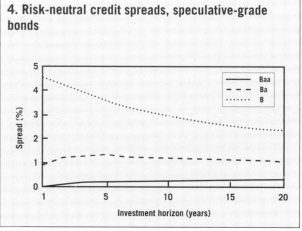

4. Risk-neutral credit spreads, speculative-grade bonds

Market behaviour

Yield spreads calculated using recent market data indicate that our model helps explain observed bond price behaviour. We collected yields as of September 30, 1993, for more than 4,000 rated, straight, US corporate bonds. To minimise the effects of call schedules on yields, all bonds callable within one year were eliminated. After deleting major outliers, as well as those bonds with maturities longer than 20 years, we were left with 2,848 bonds – 108 bonds rated Aaa, 374 rated Aa, 1,235 rated A, 725 rated Baa, 183 rated Ba and 223 rated B.

To compute spreads for each of these rating groups, we fit a spline regression to the US Treasury yield curve as of September 30, 1993. The six panels in Figure 5 show the resulting market credit spreads for each rating category. These scatter plots include a line fitted using standard linear regression methods.

No clear trend emerges in the plot of Aaa spreads against comparable-maturity Treasury bonds as the term varies. Bonds rated Aa and A, however, exhibit a significant, positive relation between spread and maturity. Bonds rated Baa also show a positive relationship, although not as strong as that for bonds rated A.

Consistent with the modelled behaviour, credit spreads for bonds rated Ba decline only slightly as maturity increases. As anticipated, we found a significant negative

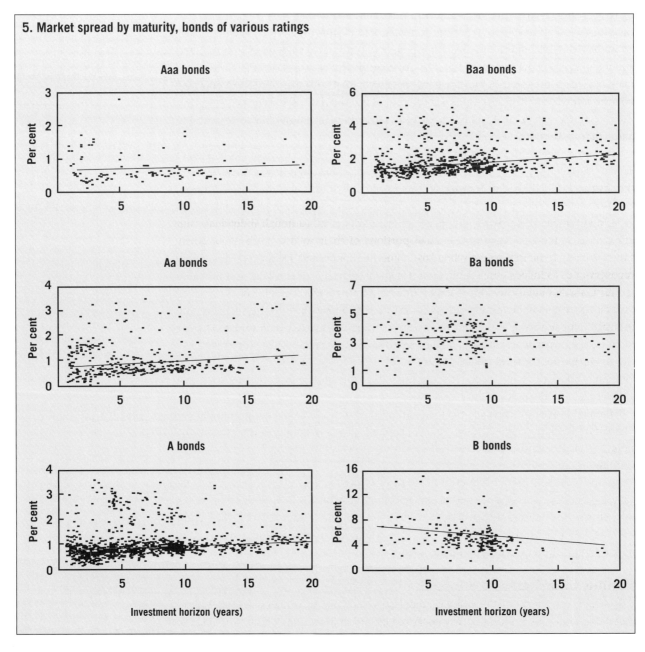

5. Market spread by maturity, bonds of various ratings

Aaa bonds

Baa bonds

Aa bonds

Ba bonds

A bonds

B bonds

Investment horizon (years)

Investment horizon (years)

spread–maturity relationship for B-rated bonds. Furthermore, the lower bounds of the Aa and A spreads exhibit the convexity seen in their corresponding theoretical spread models.

The regression results presented in Table 4 support these observations. In part because of the noise contained in the price data, the overall fit of the regressions is quite low. In two cases – bonds rated Aaa and bonds rated Ba – the slope coefficients of lines fitted through spreads as a function of maturity are not significantly different from zero. All other slope terms are significantly different from zero at the 5% level of confidence. The A-rated bonds have the steepest positive slope, whereas the spreads for

Table 4. Regression results

Bond rating	Slope coefficient	Intercept	Adjusted R² (%)
Aaa	−0.0003	0.742	−0.94
	(−0.04)	(10.04)	
Aa	0.015	0.837	0.94
	(2.13)	(14.70)	
A	0.0174	0.916	1.82
	(4.89)	(31.63)	
Baa	0.0212	1.425	1.06
	(2.96)	(23.02)	
Ba	−0.002	3.372	−0.55
	(0.09)	(18.36)	
B	−0.208	7.254	8.71
	(−4.71)	(19.45)	

Note: Numbers in parentheses are t-statistics.

B-rated bonds are negatively related to maturity. All intercept terms appear to be significant at the 5% level and they rise as credit quality falls.

For each rating category, the fitted line lies above its theoretical counterpart. The difference is particularly apparent for the investment-grade categories. For these bonds, the 20-year theoretical credit spread ranges between 0.06% and 0.31%, and the actual 20-year maturity market spreads (as of September 1993) averaged 0.74% for bonds rated Aaa, 1.14% for bonds rated Aa, 1.27% for bonds rated A and 1.85% for bonds rated Baa.

Theoretical risk-neutral spreads for speculative-grade bonds more closely fit measured spreads. The model spreads for Ba-rated bonds peak at 1.35% in Year 5, whereas market spreads for these bonds averaged 3.37%. Based on historical default rates, risk-neutral spreads for B bonds should range between 4.64% (at one-year maturity) and 2.37% (for 20-year maturity). Market spreads for B bonds averaged 7.05% at one year and 3.09% at 20 years.

The discrepancies between the model estimates and market credit spreads have several explanations. One is that, by virtue of its size and activity level, the liquidity of the market for US Treasury securities far exceeds that of any other bond market. Investors in less liquid issues may require a premium as compensation for liquidity risk.

Second, we assumed that bond investors are risk-neutral. Although individuals may exhibit risk-neutral behaviour with small portions of their wealth (such as lotteries), they are likely to be risk-averse when large sums are concerned. Default-rate (as well as recovery-rate) estimates contain higher-order risk factors.

Third, we assumed that investors could not sell their bonds except in the case of default. Clearly, individuals are free to trade bonds and they may suffer paper losses if the creditworthiness of their bonds declines after the purchase date. Investors in high-rated bonds, in particular, may want compensation for this risk.

Fourth, interest earned on US Treasury securities is exempt from state and local income taxes. As a result, individual investors, in particular, are often willing to accept a lower yield on these securities.

Finally, although we made an effort to minimise complications resulting from the call provisions found in many corporate bonds, residual effects remain. When a firm has the right to call its bonds, investors will demand compensation in the form of a higher promised yield.

As noted earlier, risk-neutral credit spreads are quite sensitive to the recovery rate estimate, but the derived risk-neutral spreads should establish a lower bound on actual market spreads. Although introducing risk aversion will lead to wider theoretical spreads, other risks play a role in the pricing of corporate bonds. These risks could, under certain circumstances, dominate default risk.

Stability of default-rate estimates

The default rates used in the pricing model represent point estimates. History shows that default rates are not particularly stable, especially at low rating levels. By taking the

6. One-year default rates by rating category, 1970–93

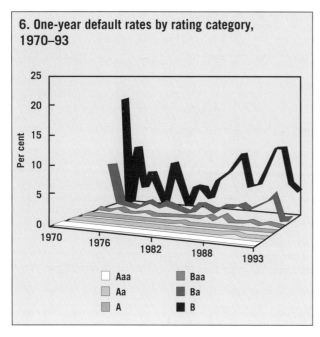

number of issuers with a given rating that default in a year and dividing by the total number of issues with that rating at the beginning of the year, we can form a time series of one-year default rates by rating category.

Figure 6 illustrates the increase in default rate volatility at the lower rating categories after 1970. The figure also suggests at least a mild correlation between default rates and the overall business cycle. The recessions of 1974, 1982 and 1990, as well as the slowdown of 1985, were each accompanied by surges in speculative-grade default rates. (The large spike in 1970 reflects the default of Penn Central Railroad and its affiliates.) Broader trends in corporate leverage are a factor as well, particularly in the second half of the 1980s.

The increased volatility of default rates at lower rating categories, as well as their cyclical nature, introduce uncertainty in pricing. Risk-averse investors may require added compensation for this uncertainty. There is also (although the evidence is not presented here) considerable volatility across recovery rates (measured as the bond's trading price one month after default). This phenomenon also might induce risk-averse investors to seek compensation above actuarially neutral yields.

Left for future research is the question of how the spread-versus-maturity relationship might evolve through time and its role as an indicator of the timing and phases of the credit cycle.[5]

1 See R. E. Johnson, "The Term Structure of Corporate Bond Yields as a Function of Risk of Default," Journal of Finance, vol. 22, no. 2 (1967), pp. 313–45; J. B. Silvers, "An Alternative to the Yield Spread as a Measure of Risk," Journal of Finance, vol. 28, no. 4 (1973), pp. 933–55; and J. C. Van Horne, Financial Market Rates and Flows (Englewood Cliffs, N. J.: Prentice-Hall, 1978), pp. 164–73.

2 See L. T. Nielsen, J. Saa-Requejo and P. Santa-Clara, "Default Risk and Interest Rate Risk: The Term Structure of Default Spreads," INSEAD Working Paper (May 1993); I. J. Kim, K. Ramaswamy and S. Sundaresan, "Does Default Risk in Coupons Affect the Valuation of Corporate Bonds? A Contingent Claims Model," Financial Management, vol. 22, no. 3 (Autumn 1993), pp. 117–31; A. Ginzburg, K. Maloney and R. Willner, "Risk Rating Migration and the Valuation of Floating Rate Debt," Working paper (December 1993); E. P. Jones, S. P. Mason and E. Rosenfeld, "Contingent Claims Analysis of Corporate Capital Structures: An Empirical Investigation," Journal of Finance, vol. 39, no. 3 (1984), pp. 611–25; and R. Litterman and T. Iben, "Corporate Bond Valuation and the Term Structure of Credit Spreads," Goldman Sachs Financial Strategies Group (1988).

3 As a matter of policy, Moody's Investors Service does not make buy or sell recommendations. The model presented here is just one of many possible ways to factor credit risk into the price of a bond.

4 We assume annual coupon payments to simplify the mathematics. The analysis extends easily to semi-annual coupon payments.

5 The author thanks Douglas Lucas, Roger Stein and Pat Corcoran for their comments and Lea Carty for his assistance and comments.

13

Measuring Changes in Corporate Credit Quality

Lea V. Carty and Jerome S. Fons

Moody's Investors Service, New York

M oody's credit opinions assess an issuer's ability to meet its debt obligations in a timely manner. Ratings necessarily look into the future. For many reasons, however, ranging from the unpredictability of the business cycle to event risk, the future of a rated issuer is not deterministic. As a result, ratings may change.

Changes in credit quality are of obvious interest to investors. In the case of default, investors might lose a substantial portion of their investments. The ability of a structured transaction to meet its contractual payments may be dependent on the credit quality of an underlying pool of corporate issues. Loan indentures may offer a rated entity the opportunity to repay a loan before maturity in the event of an upgrade. In each of these cases, there is a value to investors in knowing what to expect in terms of the future evolution of issuer credit.

While the credit paths of rated firms are not predetermined, historically they have exhibited patterns. In this study we have compiled a number of statistics that show various aspects of rating changes for some or all of the last seventy years. These statistics should be helpful in analysing the expected future "credit paths" of rated issuers.

Methodology

The results of this study are drawn from Moody's proprietary database of approximately 4,700 long-term public debt issuers and 2,400 short-term debt issuers. The long-term rating data span the seventy-year period from May 1, 1923, through June 22, 1993, while the short-term data extend from August 20, 1971, through June 22, 1993.

As with Moody's special reports on long-term public debt defaults, the unit of study is the issuer. To keep the focus on changes in corporate credit quality, we have omitted municipal and sovereign issuers. We also omit firms whose rated debt consists solely of issues backed by entities that are not members of the issuer's corporate family, because the ratings of such debt would reflect that backing and not the underlying credit risk of the issuing firm.

Because not all members of a corporate family hold the same rating or have their ratings changed at the same time, we count each legal entity separately. To facilitate this, we track an issuer's actual or "implied" senior long-term rating.

If the issuer has senior unsecured rated debt, we use that rating as the measure of the issuer's credit quality for as long as such obligations are outstanding. When an issuer does not have senior unsecured debt, we infer what this debt would most probably be rated if it did exist. We derive this "implied" senior rating from actual ratings assigned to an issuer's other rated debt.

Fifty-five per cent of our observations use actual senior unsecured ratings. Thirty per cent are derived from actual subordinated debt ratings by assuming a rating of one

This article was first published in The Journal of Fixed Income, *June 1994, pp. 27–41, and appears here with the kind permission of the authors and Institutional Investor Journals.*

letter grade above the subordinated rating (or, following the introduction of numerical modifiers in 1982, one numerical notch above for investment-grade and usually two numerical notches for speculative-grade). The remaining 15% of observations are derived from actual senior secured debt ratings by reducing those ratings one letter grade (or, following the introduction of numerical modifiers, one numerical notch).

We also include data from our long- and short-term default studies. In doing so, we replace downgrades associated with a default (usually to the Ca or C rating) with a "default" category. Since this effectively eliminates the Ca and C categories, we leave these out completely.

Trends in long-term letter rating changes

An important indicator of overall trends in corporate credit quality is the percentage of issuers affected by upgrades or downgrades. To calculate the annual percentage of issuers upgraded or downgraded one or more letter rating categories, we use the number of issuers in our database at the beginning of a given year as the denominator. The numerator is the number of issuers upgraded or downgraded in the course of the year, not counting multiple rating changes for a single issuer. The results are shown in Table 1 and graphically in Figure 1.

This particular indicator illustrates the prolonged deterioration in overall corporate credit quality that started around 1980. For the thirty-year period covering 1950 to

Table 1. Long-term letter rating changes by year 1950–93

	Downgraded issuers		Upgraded issuers		Rating activity (%)	Direction of drift (%)
	Number	Percentage	Number	Percentage		
1950	1	1.09	4	4.35	5.43	3.26
1951	0	0.00	4	4.26	4.26	4.26
1952	6	5.41	2	1.80	7.21	-3.60
1953	0	0.00	3	1.89	1.89	1.89
1954	7	3.89	6	3.33	7.22	-0.56
1955	3	1.45	3	1.45	3.38	-0.48
1956	1	0.47	5	2.35	2.82	1.88
1957	5	2.20	2	0.88	3.08	-1.32
1958	4	1.61	6	2.42	4.44	1.21
1959	6	2.14	6	2.14	4.29	0.00
1960	8	2.69	5	1.68	4.38	-1.01
1961	3	0.97	5	1.61	2.58	0.65
1962	10	2.91	4	1.16	4.07	-1.74
1963	2	0.54	5	1.36	2.45	0.82
1964	3	0.76	17	4.28	6.05	4.53
1965	5	1.22	9	2.20	3.41	0.98
1966	9	2.03	6	1.35	3.38	-0.68
1967	12	2.48	13	2.69	5.37	0.00
1968	6	1.01	3	0.50	1.51	-0.50
1969	16	2.40	7	1.05	3.45	-1.35
1970	36	4.98	16	2.21	10.10	-5.39
1971	18	2.27	10	1.26	4.04	-1.26
1972	17	1.97	15	1.73	3.93	-0.46
1973	18	1.98	20	2.20	4.40	0.44
1974	47	5.08	38	4.10	9.61	-1.19
1975	33	3.39	41	4.21	7.80	0.82
1976	19	1.81	20	1.90	4.00	0.00
1977	34	3.12	30	2.75	6.80	-1.29
1978	27	2.39	23	2.03	5.04	-0.80
1979	38	3.22	32	2.71	6.78	-1.19
1980	67	5.37	30	2.41	8.34	-3.05
1981	61	4.54	43	3.20	9.38	-1.64
1982	87	6.11	55	3.86	11.36	-3.23
1983	113	7.11	66	4.15	13.34	-4.28
1984	110	6.44	85	4.97	13.17	-2.98
1985	173	8.80	76	3.87	15.77	-7.12
1986	219	9.60	95	4.16	18.14	-9.11
1987	178	6.62	84	3.13	13.32	-4.61
1988	215	7.03	99	3.24	13.51	-4.81
1989	231	6.78	86	2.53	12.57	-6.81
1990	297	7.95	63	1.69	12.77	-8.32
1991	291	7.37	84	2.13	12.45	-6.73
1992	256	6.08	87	2.07	9.45	-4.18
1993	258	5.73	140	3.11	9.91	-2.71

1979, the average yearly percentage of upgraded companies (2.26%) slightly exceeded the percentage of downgraded companies (2.18%). By contrast, the period from 1980 through 1993 saw the average yearly percentage of issuers upgraded increase to 3.18%, while the percentage of issuers downgraded more than tripled to 6.82%.[1]

The significant increase in the percentage of issuers downgraded during the latter period is due to a slew of special events and the overall trend toward corporate leveraging. For example, the recession of 1982 proved to be the most severe of the post-World War II era. In 1986, sharply lower oil prices prompted large numbers of industrial and financial company downgrades. Finally, concerns about problem loans in the banking system led to numerous downgrades in 1989, just one year before the onset of another recession.

In addition to a deterioration in credit quality during the 1980s, there appears to have been an increase in the level of rating activity. We summarise annual rating activity in this report by computing the sum of all upward and downward letter rating changes and dividing by the number of issuers outstanding at the beginning of the given year.[2] This measurement captures both the effects of multiple rating changes for a single issuer within a given year and the relative size of rating changes. In effect, it shows the pace at which ratings change, based on units of letter ratings changed per issuer.

In order to measure the increase or decrease in aggregate credit quality, we propose rating drift. Rating drift is calculated by aggregating the number of upward letter rating changes, less the total number of downward letter rating changes, and dividing this difference by the number of issuers outstanding at the beginning of a given year. Hence, rating drift summarises the overall increase or decrease in credit quality of the rated universe as a percentage of one letter grade.

Figure 2 portrays the activity and drift data that are shown in Table 1. Consistent with measurements of overall upgrades and downgrades, rating activity and drift held nearly stationary until the early 1980s. Between 1950 and 1980, yearly activity levels averaged 4.77% and drift averaged –0.07%. During this period the aggregate credit quality of Moody's-rated companies remained unchanged as drift was a meagre –0.07%, even though one out of twenty issuers (4.77%) saw their ratings change each year, on average.

Starting in 1980, however, average yearly activity levels almost tripled to 12.43%, while average yearly drift turned decidedly negative to –4.97%. Activity and drift peaked in 1986, at which point Moody's overall rating activity amounted to roughly one-sixth of a letter grade (18.14%) per rated issuer, and aggregate credit quality of Moody's-rated companies slipped by nearly one-tenth of a letter grade (–9.11%).

Trends in long-term modified rating changes

Moody's added numerical modifiers to its letter rating system in 1982. Table 2 lists upgrades and downgrades (without counting multiple upgrades or downgrades for the same issuer), for each year from 1983 through 1992. It also includes estimates of these numbers through mid-1993.

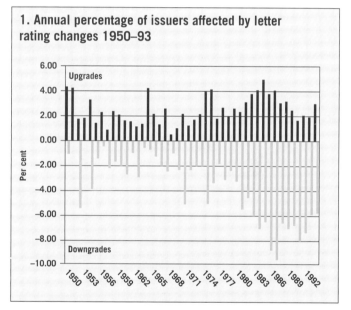

1. Annual percentage of issuers affected by letter rating changes 1950–93

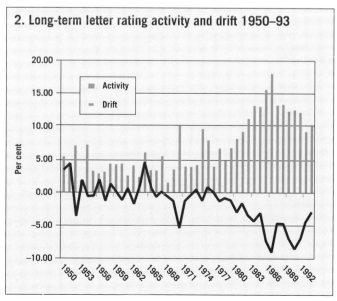

2. Long-term letter rating activity and drift 1950–93

Table 2. Long-term modified rating changes by year 1983–93

	Downgraded issuers		Upgraded issuers		Rating	Direction
	Number	Percentage	Number	Percentage	activity (%)	of drift (%)
1983	122	8.91	148	10.81	32.65	−4.60
1984	191	12.46	173	11.29	42.60	−3.98
1985	169	9.37	237	13.14	47.17	−18.46
1986	171	8.02	345	16.19	50.40	−24.96
1987	159	6.22	274	10.72	35.67	−10.79
1988	176	6.00	324	11.04	36.97	−11.82
1989	168	5.12	337	10.27	32.97	−16.51
1990	138	3.82	489	13.52	33.88	−21.21
1991	153	3.99	485	12.65	29.26	−15.38
1992	178	4.33	451	10.98	25.27	−11.54
1993*	238	5.40	450	10.21	23.86	−6.53

*1993 numbers are annualised from the data available from January 1, 1993, through June 22, 1993.

We calculate activity and drift measurements just as we did for the letter rating changes, except that we use changes in numerical notches rather than letter ratings. Activity and drift figures are also presented in Table 2 and graphically displayed in Figure 3.

Consistent with the results for broad rating categories, rating drift remained negative throughout this period. The averages for yearly rating activity and drift since 1983 are: 35.5% and –13.3%, respectively. These numbers are nearly three times as large as those we report for the letter rating changes for the same period.

To understand this difference, two items must be kept in mind. First, the addition of numerical modifiers to the letter rating system increases the number of possible long-term ratings from nine to nineteen, while leaving the high (Aaa) and low (Caa, Ca, C) ends of the credit scale unchanged. Thus, the middle five letter rating categories are divided into three times as many numerically modified categories. This finer scale for measuring credit risk necessarily induces a greater number of rating changes per issuer.[3]

Second, the 1983–93 average yearly activity of 35.5% indicates that the average issuer experienced rating changes amounting to 35.5% of one numerical notch each year. As there are three numerical notches per letter rating (excluding the Aaa and Caa-and-below categories), this measurement is roughly three times that for letter rating activity (13.1%) over the same period.

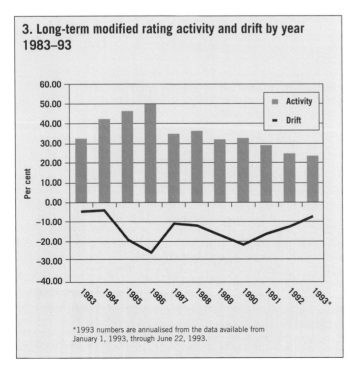

3. Long-term modified rating activity and drift by year 1983–93

*1993 numbers are annualised from the data available from January 1, 1993, through June 22, 1993.

Trends in short-term rating changes

Moody's short-term debt ratings (P-1, P-2, P-3 and NP) represent opinions about the ability of issuers to repay punctually senior debt obligations that have an original maturity not exceeding one year. Prime-1 through Prime-3 are investment-grade ratings, while Not Prime indicates a below-investment-grade opinion. Short-term debt is typically a senior unsecured obligation of a firm. Hence, the implied senior rating adjustment that is sometimes necessary for the long-term calculations is not necessary for short-term rating histories.

Table 3 shows the number and percentage of all upgrades and downgrades for issuers with short-term ratings, as well as the activity and drift measurements defined in previous sections. The numerators of the activity and drift ratios are the number of short-term ratings changed in a given year.

It is noteworthy that the drift of the short-term ratings is highly procyclical. Figure 4 shows the

Table 3. Short-term rating changes by year 1973–93

	Downgraded issuers		Upgraded issuers		Rating	Direction
	Number	Percentage	Number	Percentage	activity (%)	of drift (%)
1973	5	1.13	4	0.90	2.03	–0.23
1974	24	4.92	7	1.43	6.35	–3.48
1975	18	3.81	15	3.18	7.42	–1.06
1976	5	1.06	14	2.98	4.04	1.91
1977	11	2.10	15	2.87	4.97	0.76
1978	10	1.83	8	1.47	3.49	–0.55
1979	13	2.19	8	1.35	3.54	–0.84
1980	29	4.10	9	1.27	5.65	–2.82
1981	26	3.32	10	1.28	4.72	–1.91
1982	66	7.98	10	1.21	10.28	–7.86
1983	30	3.48	17	1.97	5.79	–1.85
1984	40	4.69	32	3.76	8.57	–1.06
1985	60	7.04	16	1.88	11.38	–7.63
1986	93	9.56	19	1.95	14.59	–10.48
1987	52	5.40	19	1.97	9.66	–5.71
1988	62	6.42	32	3.31	11.39	–4.35
1989	85	8.17	24	2.31	14.02	–8.65
1990	124	11.55	12	1.12	17.04	–14.80
1991	74	6.96	26	2.45	10.72	–5.27
1992	59	5.26	47	4.27	10.45	–1.18
1993*	33	5.68	35	6.02	12.91	0.52

*1993 numbers are extrapolated from the data available from January 1, 1993, through June 22, 1993.

downward acceleration in short-term credit quality drift that occurred during the 1973–75 recession, at the slump in the first half of 1980, throughout the 1982 recession, during the slowdown of 1985, and again at the recession of 1990. Accompanying each of these troughs in drift is a spike in activity. The correlation of yearly short-term rating drift with the current year's percentage change in GDP is 42%.

While a firm's long-term health largely determines its ability to pay, liquidity crises can mitigate this ability in the near term. Crises of this type are more prevalent in a slack or contractionary economy. Because liquidity crises have the potential to affect the timely payment of short-term debt, our short-term ratings are especially sensitive to them. The high correlation of short-term rating drift with the growth in GNP reflects this sensitivity.

The pattern of pre-1980 stationarity and post-1980 acceleration of activity, accompanied by an overall deterioration in credit quality, that characterises the long-term rating data also applies to the short-term rating data. Between 1973 and 1979, rating activity averaged 4.55% of one short-term rating level per rated issuer, while rating drift averaged –0.50% of one short-term rating level per rated issuer. After 1979, mean yearly rating activity more than doubled to 10.51%, while rating drift turned, on average, to more than ten times its pre-1980 average: –5.22%. Over the entire period, rating activity averaged 8.52% per year and rating drift averaged –3.65% per year.

Magnitude and dispersion of rating changes

We define the magnitude of a rating change as the number of rating categories that a rating change spans. For example, an upgrade from Ba to Baa spans one letter rating category. A downgrade from Ba to Caa spans two categories. This same concept applies, in the obvious manner, to both our numerically modified ratings and our short-term ratings.

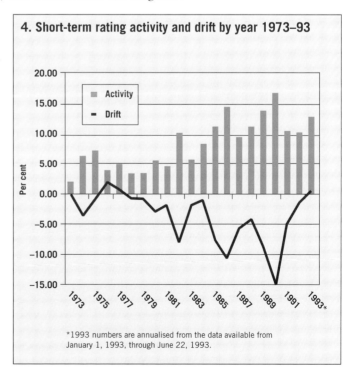

4. Short-term rating activity and drift by year 1973–93

*1993 numbers are annualised from the data available from January 1, 1993, through June 22, 1993.

5. Relative frequency of modified rating change magnitudes

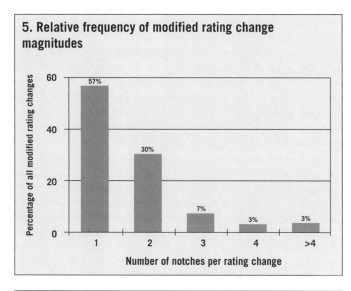

6. Relative frequency of letter rating change magnitudes

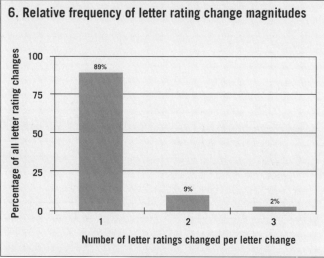

7. Relative frequency of short-term rating change magnitudes

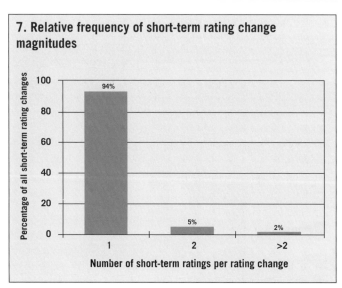

Figures 5, 6 and 7 display the frequency of rating revisions by the magnitude of change for the entire period spanned by our database. As expected, they show that changes of smaller magnitude are relatively more frequent than large rating revisions.

Frequent rating changes of several steps or more would indicate that "surprises" in firms' credit developments are relatively common. In fact the bar charts show just the opposite: Moody's ratings generally anticipate the frequency and severity of unforeseen credit developments by keeping large magnitude rating changes to a minimum. Ninety-four per cent of short-term rating changes are of one rating, 98% of long-term letter rating changes are within two ratings and 94% of changes in the more finely sliced modified ratings are within three notches.

These figures illustrate the frequency of rating changes of varying magnitudes in the database, but they do not show how different rating categories change through time. A concise representation of the state of this evolution at a particular time is a rating transition matrix.

Tables 4–7 depict letter rating transition matrixes for one-year, two-year, five-year and ten-year horizons. The rows indicate the rating at the beginning of the specified period. Each column corresponds to a rating, default or withdrawn status as of the end of the period. Each cell entry, excluding the "default" column, is the weighted-average percentage of issuers that held the row rating at the beginning of the time period and the column status at the end of the time period. For example, 2.5% of all A-rated companies, on average, enjoyed a net improvement of one letter rating (to Aa) by the end of any one-year period.[4]

Care must be taken when interpreting the percentages under the "default" heading. Because of the methodology of this study, not all defaulted firms included in Moody's study of long-term bond defaults are included in this effort.[5] Hence, both the numerators and denominators of Moody's default rates are different for this study. For this reason, these numbers are not directly comparable to those published in our long-term default studies.

Also, by their nature, transition matrixes estimate the probability of an issuer experiencing a net change from the row rating to the column status at the end of a specified time period. They are calculated by comparing beginning-of-period ratings to end-of-period status. By focusing on just two points in time, they ignore the intervening credit history. Clearly, if the history includes a default where interest and/or principal may be lost, it should be flagged.

For this reason, the percentages in the "default" columns are *cumulative* default rates and not necessarily based on the actual status of defaulted issuers at the end of the specified periods.[6] That is, for the transition matrix of a specified time period, the figure reported in the "default" column for a given rating is an estimate of the probability of

Table 4. One-year rating transition matrix (%)

Rating from	Aaa	Aa	A	Baa	Rating to Ba	B	Caa	Default	WR
Aaa	89.6	7.2	0.7	0.0	0.0	0.0	0.0	0.0	2.5
Aa	1.1	88.8	6.9	0.3	0.2	0.0	0.0	0.0	2.8
A	0.1	2.5	89.0	5.2	0.6	0.2	0.0	0.0	2.5
Baa	0.0	0.2	5.2	85.3	5.3	0.8	0.1	0.1	3.0
Ba	0.0	0.1	0.4	4.7	80.1	6.9	0.4	1.5	5.8
B	0.0	0.1	0.1	0.5	5.5	75.7	2.0	8.2	7.8
Caa	0.0	0.4	0.4	0.8	2.3	5.4	62.1	20.3	8.4

Table 5. Two-year rating transition matrix (%)

Rating from	Aaa	Aa	A	Baa	Rating to Ba	B	Caa	Default	WR
Aaa	80.9	12.6	1.6	0.1	0.1	0.0	0.0	0.0	4.6
Aa	2.27	8.6	12.1	1.1	0.6	0.0	0.0	0.1	5.4
A	0.1	4.9	79.6	8.6	1.5	0.5	0.1	0.1	4.6
Baa	0.1	0.5	9.8	73.3	8.6	1.6	0.2	0.4	5.6
Ba	0.1	0.1	0.8	8.4	64.4	10.5	0.7	4.3	10.7
B	0.0	0.2	0.2	1.0	8.2	58.6	2.4	14.7	14.6
Caa	0.0	0.4	0.4	2.2	3.1	8.7	44.5	27.1	13.5

Table 6. Five-year rating transition matrix (%)

Rating from	Aaa	Aa	A	Baa	Rating to Ba	B	Caa	Default	WR
Aaa	62.5	21.8	4.9	0.5	0.7	0.2	0.1	0.2	9.1
Aa	5.5	52.9	22.3	3.9	1.8	0.5	0.0	0.4	12.7
A	0.3	9.9	59.6	15.0	3.9	1.1	0.2	0.6	9.3
Baa	0.2	1.9	18.8	49.7	12.6	3.2	0.3	1.7	11.6
Ba	0.2	0.5	3.6	13.6	37.4	12.6	0.8	10.1	21.2
B	0.1	0.1	0.7	3.1	10.3	31.8	1.7	24.6	27.4
Caa	0.0	0.0	0.6	7.6	5.8	14.0	19.9	35.1	17.0

Table 7. Ten-year rating transition matrix (%)

Rating from	Aaa	Aa	A	Baa	Rating to Ba	B	Caa	Default	WR
Aaa	47.1	31.5	8.8	3.6	1.7	0.2	0.1	1.0	6.0
Aa	8.4	33.6	30.6	9.6	3.3	0.8	0.2	1.3	12.1
A	0.6	14.8	43.0	17.9	5.9	2.5	0.4	1.1	13.9
Baa	0.3	4.7	26.4	29.9	13.2	4.2	0.4	4.0	17.0
Ba	0.4	1.7	10.0	18.6	19.8	10.4	0.6	13.9	24.6
B	0.8	0.0	4.9	6.1	11.6	16.5	0.4	30.2	28.5
Caa	0.0	0.7	4.3	14.5	6.8	8.5	8.5	48.7	8.5

default *within* the specified time period and not a statement as to the probability of an issuer being in default at the end of the specified time period.

Finally, the "WR" column reports the weighted-average percentage of issuers that held the row ratings at the beginning of the period and that had their ratings withdrawn at the end of the period. A senior implied rating might be withdrawn for any number of reasons, from retirement of all rated debt to completion of an exchange offer for all rated debt.

To calculate these probabilities, we tracked the senior implied rating and default status of each issuer in our database as of January 1 of each year beginning with 1970. These matrixes ignore all pre-1970 rating data in order to incorporate Moody's default data, which extend back only to 1970.

Note that the values along the diagonals of the matrixes are the probabilities of an issuer having the same rating at the end of the specified time period as it had at the beginning. As the time period spanned by the transition matrixes expands, the higher-quality ratings have a higher likelihood of remaining unchanged than their lower-quality counterparts. (We discuss this further below.)

For the Aa and A ratings, the frequency of net downgrades exceeds that of net upgrades. For any of the given time horizons, it is more likely for an issuer starting with one of these ratings to have a lower rating at the end of the period than a higher rating. For issuers rated Baa, however, this bias ends. Within a one-year horizon, Baa-rated issuers are about as likely to be rated above Baa as below. Moreover, as the time horizon

Table 8. One-year rating transition matrix (%)

Rating from	Aaa	Aa1	Aa2	Aa3	A1	A2	A3	Baa1	Baa2	Baa3	Ba1	Ba2	Ba3	B1	B2	B3	Caa	D	WR
Aaa	87.0	5.7	2.7	0.2	0.2	0.0	0.0	0.0	0.1	0.0	0.0	0.0	0.0	0.0	0.0	0.0	0.0	0.0	4.1
Aa1	0.9	88.2	3.1	3.5	0.9	0.2	0.1	0.1	0.0	0.0	0.0	0.0	0.0	0.0	0.0	0.0	0.0	0.0	2.8
Aa2	1.0	2.6	73.9	9.3	6.2	1.6	0.9	0.2	0.1	0.0	0.0	0.0	0.1	0.1	0.0	0.0	0.0	0.0	4.2
Aa3	0.1	1.0	2.3	77.3	9.3	4.1	1.1	0.2	0.2	0.2	0.0	0.1	0.1	0.0	0.0	0.0	0.0	0.1	3.9
A1	0.1	0.2	0.9	4.4	76.8	7.6	2.8	1.1	0.3	0.3	0.4	0.5	0.1	0.2	0.0	0.0	0.0	0.0	4.4
A2	0.0	0.1	0.2	0.8	5.0	7.6	7.3	3.7	1.2	0.4	0.3	0.2	0.2	0.0	0.1	0.0	0.0	0.0	3.8
A3	0.0	0.1	0.1	0.3	1.4	8.2	71.0	6.8	4.2	1.7	0.6	0.3	0.4	0.6	0.1	0.0	0.0	0.0	4.4
Baa1	0.0	0.1	0.1	0.1	0.2	2.9	7.0	68.4	9.3	3.7	1.1	0.6	0.6	1.0	0.0	0.0	0.1	0.1	4.9
Baa2	0.0	0.2	0.2	0.2	0.2	1.0	3.6	7.6	67.3	8.4	2.6	0.5	1.0	0.9	0.3	0.3	0.2	0.0	5.7
Baa3	0.0	0.0	0.0	0.0	0.2	0.5	0.4	4.9	9.6	61.5	7.9	3.1	2.4	1.2	0.3	0.1	0.1	0.5	7.2
Ba1	0.0	0.0	0.0	0.0	0.0	0.0	0.8	0.7	3.0	5.7	67.4	4.2	4.3	2.4	0.3	1.1	0.2	1.0	8.7
Ba2	0.0	0.0	0.0	0.0	0.0	0.1	0.0	0.1	0.4	1.9	5.8	66.7	6.5	5.3	0.7	1.4	0.3	0.9	9.9
Ba3	0.0	0.1	0.1	0.0	0.0	0.1	0.1	0.3	0.1	0.8	2.3	3.0	70.0	6.8	1.0	3.3	0.8	3.0	8.4
B1	0.0	0.0	0.1	0.1	0.1	0.0	0.1	0.0	0.1	0.4	0.2	2.3	4.1	68.4	1.1	6.2	0.9	6.3	9.5
B2	0.0	0.0	0.0	0.0	0.4	0.0	0.0	0.4	0.0	0.0	0.4	1.7	3.0	6.0	62.5	6.9	5.6	5.2	7.8
B3	0.0	0.0	0.0	0.0	0.0	0.0	0.0	0.1	0.0	0.1	0.3	0.3	1.5	4.1	1.3	64.7	3.9	15.2	8.5
Caa	0.0	0.0	0.0	0.6	0.6	0.0	0.0	0.0	0.0	0.6	0.0	0.6	1.2	1.2	1.2	1.9	55.9	21.1	14.9

Table 9. Two-year rating transition matrix (%)

Rating from	Aaa	Aa1	Aa2	Aa3	A1	A2	A3	Baa1	Baa2	Baa3	Ba1	Ba2	Ba3	B1	B2	B3	Caa	D	WR
Aaa	79.8	8.1	2.1	0.8	0.3	0.6	0.0	0.0	0.2	0.0	0.1	0.0	0.0	0.0	0.0	0.0	0.0	0.0	8.0
Aa1	2.1	78.4	4.7	3.7	2.6	1.1	0.3	0.2	0.2	0.2	0.2	0.0	0.0	0.0	0.0	0.0	0.0	0.0	6.4
Aa2	1.8	6.1	55.7	12.8	9.6	4.6	1.2	0.8	0.2	0.0	0.0	0.0	0.1	0.1	0.0	0.0	0.1	0.0	6.7
Aa3	0.3	1.0	4.3	62.0	12.9	6.1	2.4	1.1	0.3	0.4	0.3	0.3	0.5	0.1	0.0	0.0	0.0	0.3	7.6
A1	0.2	0.4	2.1	8.9	59.8	10.9	4.7	1.4	1.0	0.6	0.4	0.8	0.7	0.8	0.1	0.1	0.1	0.1	7.0
A2	0.1	0.2	0.2	2.0	8.3	59.2	10.4	5.3	2.5	1.1	0.9	0.6	0.6	0.6	0.3	0.0	0.1	0.1	7.4
A3	0.0	0.2	0.2	0.9	3.6	12.8	49.5	9.8	6.5	3.9	1.4	0.2	1.5	0.6	0.1	0.2	0.0	0.3	8.2
Baa1	0.0	0.1	0.3	0.4	0.8	6.1	9.1	48.4	12.0	6.3	2.5	0.8	2.0	1.5	0.1	0.2	0.1	0.3	8.9
Baa2	0.1	0.5	0.2	0.6	1.1	2.4	7.8	9.1	43.8	10.3	5.0	1.1	1.9	1.8	0.7	0.9	0.0	0.3	12.2
Baa3	0.0	0.0	0.1	0.0	0.1	1.2	2.1	9.2	14.3	37.7	8.0	4.0	2.6	2.9	1.1	0.4	0.4	1.5	14.3
Ba1	0.0	0.0	0.0	0.0	0.0	0.5	1.5	1.2	6.0	7.8	43.9	5.8	5.9	3.4	1.0	2.0	0.6	3.2	17.2
Ba2	0.0	0.0	0.1	0.0	0.0	0.1	0.1	0.5	1.4	3.0	8.8	43.3	7.7	9.2	0.4	2.3	0.7	4.6	17.5
Ba3	0.0	0.1	0.1	0.0	0.0	0.1	0.1	0.7	0.1	0.8	3.9	4.2	50.4	9.1	0.8	5.6	1.2	7.9	14.7
B1	0.0	0.0	0.1	0.2	0.2	0.0	0.1	0.2	0.1	1.0	0.5	2.9	4.2	50.0	1.7	8.2	1.3	13.2	16.3
B2	0.0	0.0	0.0	0.0	0.6	0.0	0.0	0.6	0.0	0.0	0.6	2.2	7.2	5.6	38.9	10.6	6.1	11.7	16.1
B3	0.0	0.0	0.0	0.0	0.0	0.0	0.0	0.2	0.0	0.0	1.0	0.4	2.8	6.0	1.8	46.0	4.6	20.1	17.1
Caa	0.0	0.0	0.0	1.0	1.0	0.0	0.0	0.0	0.0	1.0	0.0	0.0	2.1	2.1	1.0	2.1	35.1	26.8	27.8

Table 10. Five-year transition matrix (%)

Rating from	Aaa	Aa1	Aa2	Aa3	A1	A2	A3	Baa1	Baa2	Baa3	Ba1	Ba2	Ba3	B1	B2	B3	Caa	D	WR
Aaa	51.9	10.8	6.1	4.0	1.9	1.5	0.2	0.6	0.0	0.0	0.0	0.0	0.0	0.0	0.2	0.4	0.0	0.4	22.1
Aa1	4.9	44.8	6.3	8.3	5.7	3.8	2.4	2.5	1.1	0.2	0.2	0.5	0.2	0.0	0.0	0.0	0.0	0.3	19.0
Aa2	3.0	6.3	23.6	14.5	12.6	8.5	4.7	3.3	1.1	1.7	0.5	0.6	0.6	0.0	0.0	0.0	0.2	0.6	18.2
Aa3	1.3	1.7	6.9	30.8	14.1	11.4	5.3	2.8	0.9	0.9	0.5	0.5	0.9	0.0	0.0	0.0	0.1	0.9	20.5
A1	0.8	0.6	2.2	13.3	33.0	13.2	6.2	4.5	2.1	1.9	1.2	0.0	0.9	1.2	0.4	0.2	0.5	1.8	15.9
A2	0.0	0.2	0.1	2.9	10.6	31.9	12.6	7.4	5.5	3.4	1.8	1.1	1.7	1.0	0.4	0.1	0.3	1.0	18.1
A3	0.0	0.2	0.3	2.7	5.2	14.1	22.1	9.1	8.9	6.0	3.2	1.8	4.0	1.8	0.0	0.1	0.0	1.0	19.4
Baa1	0.0	0.2	0.9	1.1	2.2	6.9	12.3	22.7	11.5	5.5	2.5	1.5	3.2	2.6	0.9	0.6	0.2	2.0	23.2
Baa2	0.6	1.0	0.3	0.8	1.3	50.0	8.1	9.1	20.6	9.1	3.8	1.6	2.6	2.6	1.1	0.8	0.8	1.6	29.2
Baa3	0.5	0.0	0.0	0.2	0.5	3.1	4.4	10.1	14.1	12.6	6.8	4.6	2.6	3.5	0.4	0.7	0.0	5.7	30.3
Ba1	0.0	0.0	0.1	0.0	0.3	1.2	2.3	3.6	8.5	7.9	14.0	3.5	6.5	5.3	1.0	2.3	1.2	7.4	34.8
Ba2	0.0	0.0	0.4	0.0	0.0	0.6	1.4	0.4	2.0	2.9	7.3	14.9	5.3	8.3	0.2	4.1	0.6	11.6	40.1
Ba3	0.0	0.2	0.0	0.0	0.0	0.1	0.3	0.4	0.4	1.5	3.0	4.7	19.1	6.4	0.7	6.7	1.0	19.3	36.1
B1	0.0	0.0	0.0	0.1	0.3	0.1	0.5	0.3	0.4	1.1	1.5	3.0	2.8	20.3	1.7	6.4	1.1	27.1	33.3
B2	0.0	0.0	0.0	0.0	0.0	0.0	1.0	0.0	0.0	0.0	1.0	3.0	4.0	12.9	12.9	8.9	4.0	21.8	30.7
B3	0.0	0.0	0.0	0.0	0.0	0.0	0.6	0.3	0.3	1.2	0.0	0.9	3.6	5.7	0.9	15.9	3.9	26.4	40.2
Caa	0.0	0.0	0.0	0.0	0.0	0.0	0.0	0.0	0.0	0.0	0.0	0.0	3.2	6.5	3.2	0.0	19.4	25.8	41.9

expands, Baa-rated issuers are more likely to have a higher rating than lower until, after ten years, there is almost two times as great a chance of having a single-A rating (26.4%) as there is of having a Ba rating (13.3%).

Continuing down the credit spectrum, there is a greater chance of a B-rated issuer enjoying a net up-grade than there is for a Ba-rated issuer. Caa-rated issuers, however, tend to be too weak to make the uphill climb and tend to fall into default.

Tables 8–10 are rating transition matrixes for the modified rating categories and Tables 11–13 show the same for short-term ratings. The patterns in the modified rating transition matrix are roughly similar to those of the letter rating transition matrix.

The salient characteristic of the short-term rating transition matrixes is the lack of staying power for the P-3 and NP ratings. Within just two years, on average, 83% of P-3-rated issuers changed ratings and 40% were to the "withdrawn rating" status.

Distributional aspects of rating lives

The concept of the "average length of time" that an issuer holds a senior rating is difficult to approach. There is no fundamental law stating that an issuer's credit rating has to change over time, but experience shows that the *majority* of firms do experience a change sooner or later. So how does one measure the average length of time that a rating is held?

One way to arrive at a lower bound is to calculate the average time a rating is held, *given that it subsequently changes*. To calculate this, one could take the simple average across issuers of time spans that a particular rating is maintained before the impending change.

This estimate is obviously biased downward since, by definition, it eliminates those issuers that did not undergo rating revisions and whose inclusion would therefore increase the "average." In order to address this bias and examine rating lives more fully, we introduce a statistical model.[7] Details of the estimation of this model appear in the appendix.

By plotting the distributions of historical rating life spans, we found that a Weibull distribution most closely models the life span characteristics of bond ratings.[8] The Weibull distribution is a generalisation of the exponential distribution and is commonly used for modelling "lifetime" data.[9]

Maximum likelihood techniques are available to provide estimates of the distribution's parameters (listed in Table 14) for each long- and short-term rating category. The estimated probability distributions are then used to estimate the mean lifetime of each rating category. For example, Figures 8, 9 and 10 show that higher ratings are relatively more stable as reflected by their longer average "lives".

Such a complete description of the distribution of rating lives permits us to answer many interesting questions. For example, suppose an issuer's senior unsecured debt held a B rating for the previous five years. What is the probability that this rating will change in the current year?

The hazard function ($h(t; a, b)$) is the probability of a rating change at time t, given that no previous change has occurred. It has been developed to answer these questions. Based on our parameter estimates, the answer, given by h(6; 3.90, 0.91), is 0.23, where 6 is the tth year, 3.90 is the scale parameter (a), and 0.91 is the shape parameter (b) for the B rating category.

Table 11. One-year rating transition matrix (%)

Rating from	Rating to					
	P-1	P-2	P-3	NP	Default	WR
P-1	89.9	3.8	0.2	0.3	0.0	5.7
P-2	5.7	80.0	4.0	1.2	0.0	9.1
P-3	0.5	13.0	49.5	12.0	0.2	24.8
NP	0.9	1.9	6.3	63.0	0.0	27.8

Table 12. Two-year rating transition matrix (%)

Rating from	Rating to					
	P-1	P-2	P-3	NP	Default	WR
P-1	80.5	6.4	0.7	0.7	0.0	11.8
P-2	10.0	64.9	4.6	2.0	0.0	18.4
P-3	1.5	21.6	26.7	9.9	0.3	39.9
NP	1.3	4.7	7.8	39.2	0.0	47.0

Table 13. Five-year rating transition matrix (%)

Rating from	Rating to					
	P-1	P-2	P-3	NP	Default	WR
P-1	61.0	10.1	1.4	0.9	0.0	26.6
P-2	17.3	39.7	4.0	1.4	0.0	37.6
P-3	5.0	23.9	5.8	2.7	0.0	62.5
NP	9.8	7.8	3.9	13.7	0.0	64.7

The zero in the (P-3, Default) entry for this matrix is due to the fact that a five-year rating transition matrix uses only data generated before 1988 (in order to have five years of data to examine). This eliminates some short-term defaulters.

Table 14. Estimated scale and shape parameters for the Weibull distribution

Rating	Shape B	Scale A
Aaa	1.10	10.29
Aa	1.16	8.90
A	1.02	9.99
Baa	0.99	7.28
Ba	1.06	5.04
B	0.91	3.90
Caa	0.57	2.27
Aaa	1.38	6.85
Aa1	1.05	7.76
Aa2	1.25	3.66
Aa3	1.12	5.30
A1	1.16	4.02
A2	1.09	3.83
A3	1.09	3.04
Baa1	1.13	2.90
Baa2	1.05	2.66
Baa3	1.15	2.29
Ba1	1.10	2.62
Ba2	1.10	2.47
Ba3	1.20	3.08
B1	1.03	2.64
B2	1.06	2.14
B3	0.82	1.76
Caa	0.70	1.16
P-1	1.16	9.77
P-2	1.00	4.54
P-3	0.90	1.33
NP	0.85	1.86

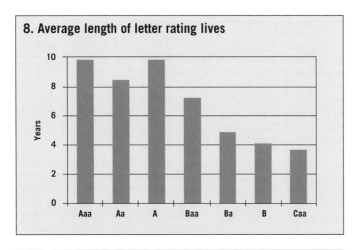

8. Average length of letter rating lives

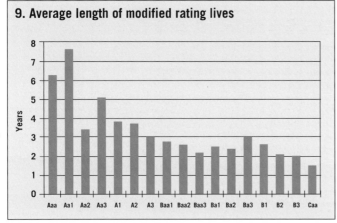

9. Average length of modified rating lives

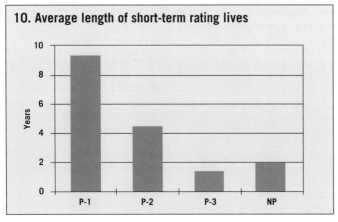

10. Average length of short-term rating lives

In addition, it is interesting to note that this probability gets smaller with time. That is, the probability of a rating change for this issuer is smaller after ten years of holding steady at the B level (0.22) than it is after holding at B for just one year (0.26).

For random variables that are Weibull-distributed, the hazard function has a simple form whose propensity to increase or decrease over time depends on whether the shape parameter is greater than or less than one.[10] Figure 11 shows the hazard functions associated with four long-term rating categories – two investment-grade and two speculative-grade.

In general, the shape parameter falls from just above 1.0 to below 1.0 as credit quality decreases. As this happens, the hazard function changes from increasing with time to decreasing. The intuition behind this pattern is that for the highest-rated companies, there is nowhere to go but down. Hence, over longer periods of time the credit quality of these companies appears slowly to erode, thereby increasing the rate at which a company is downgraded.

For the lowest-rated companies, the probability of a rating change is initially high. But as time progresses, if credit quality has not improved or if the firm has not sunk into default, creditworthiness appears to level off. Hence, over longer time horizons, the probability of a rating change decreases.

Finally, for low-investment-grade issuers, the most populous ratings in our database, there is room to change in either quality direction. The odds of an upgrade or downgrade appear to develop at approximately constant rates as the time horizon expands.

The probability that a rating will not change before a specific date is also of interest. This probability differs from the hazard function in that it is not conditioned upon there having been no rating change. Conditioning requires knowledge (assumed or actual) of the rating experience up to the time in question (in order to assert that there was no rating change prior to time t). It answers the question: "If an issuer receives a senior rating of P-2 today, what is the probability that it will still be at P-2 (without any intervening changes) in one, two, three or more years?"

The survival function, (s(t; a, b)), summarises this probability and is a function of the scale and shape parameters discussed.[11] Figure 12 depicts the survival functions for the four short-term rating categories.

The survival functions are all downward-sloping, as the probability of a rating change increases with the amount of time allowed for the rating to change. Equivalently, the probability that a rating will not change decreases as the amount of time in which it may change increases. As expected, the probability that an issuer rated P-1 will keep its rating for periods up to ten years is higher than for any other short-term rating category. The P-2 survival function lies under that for P-1 but above those for P-3 and NP.

The survival functions for the lowest two rating categories are inverted and much lower than those of the higher-quality ratings. The estimated probability of a P-3- or NP-rated issuer holding steady at the same rating for ten years is very small (s(10, 1.33, 0.90) = 0.002 and s(10, 1.86, 0.85) = 0.016, respectively). These figures show that it is highly unlikely for a low-rated issuer to maintain its rating over a ten-year span.

These ratings appear to be transitory states. In "Defaults and Orderly Exits of Commercial Paper Issuers" (Moody's Special Report, February 1993), Moody's reports that, as of September 30, 1992, P-3- and NP-rated CP constituted just 0.4% and 0.2%, respectively, of the total amount of CP outstanding. Given the relatively short estimated average "lives" of these ratings, the evidence seems to indicate that issuers cannot maintain a low-quality short-term rating for long. Lower-quality short-term issuers must either improve to P-2 or P-1 or exit the market.

Rating momentum

The question of "rating momentum" arises frequently. Rating momentum presupposes that prior rating changes carry predictive power for the direction of future rating changes. For example, the existence of rating momentum would suggest that an issuer upgraded to A is more likely to be subsequently upgraded than downgraded within a one-year period.

The first hypothesis to be tested (for each letter rating category) is that the probability of an upgrade, given that the previous rating change was an upgrade, is less than or equal to the probability of a downgrade, given that the previous rating change was an upgrade. The hypothesis is that there is no upward rating momentum.

The second hypothesis to be tested is that the probability of a downgrade, given that the previous rating change was a downgrade, is less than or equal

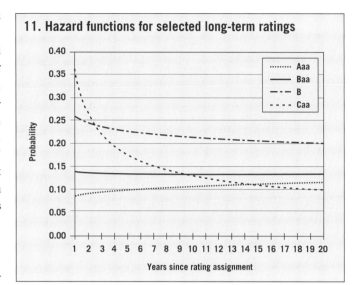

11. Hazard functions for selected long-term ratings

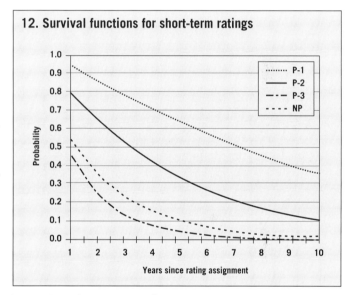

12. Survival functions for short-term ratings

to the probability of an upgrade, given that the previous rating change was a downgrade. Here, the second hypothesis is that there is no downward rating momentum.

To test these hypotheses, we gathered rating histories for all those firms with at least one rating change in our database (this encompasses the rating experience from January 1938 through June 1993). These firms are grouped according to whether their momentum was upward or downward. We then model the probability of an upgrade, downgrade or no change within one year of the prior rating change for each firm as a random variable, X, that assumes the values of $1, -1$ or 0 with probabilities P_u, P_d and P_o, respectively. Since our sample sizes are large, we assume that the sample mean is normally distributed.[12]

"Large" positive values of Z^* are evidence for rejecting the hypotheses. The results of these tests for the rating categories B through Aa and the probabilities of observing a Z^* value at least as great as generated by these tests are given in Table 15.

The test results show that, for the 5% level of confidence, upward momentum is non-existent for all rating categories except B, for which the 7.69% estimated chance of an upgrade following another upgrade within one year is significantly greater than the 0% estimated chance of a downgrade following an upgrade within one year.

The results are very different for downward momentum. For each rating category, the probability of a downgrade following a downgrade within one year significantly exceeds (at the 5% level of confidence) that of an upgrade following a downgrade. The evidence thus supports the hypothesis that a downgraded issuer is more prone to a subsequent downgrade within one year than upgrade.

Table 15. Results of test for rating momentum

Rating	Momentum	Estimated probability (up) (%)	Estimated probability (down) (%)	Upward momentum Z*	Probability of observing Z > Z*	Reject hypothesis at 5%?	Upward momentum Z*	Probability of observing Z > Z*	Reject hypothesis at 5%?
Aa	Up	1.32	3.62	−1.81	0.97	No			
Aa	Down	1.52	5.56				2.16	0.02	Yes
A	Up	1.08	2.37	−1.50	0.93	No			
A	Down	1.19	6.96				4.62	0.00	Yes
Baa	Up	2.87	3.16	−0.22	0.57	No			
Baa	Down	1.85	11.47				6.64	0.00	Yes
Ba	Up	7.66	7.66	0.00	0.50	No			
Ba	Down	4.20	15.38				6.25	0.00	Yes
B	Up	7.69	0.00	2.06	0.02	Yes			
B	Down	5.71	23.82				8.74	0.00	Yes

In light of the drastic deterioration in corporate credit quality associated with the 1980s, it is interesting that evidence for rating momentum is not solely a function of this period's data. An entirely analogous procedure to the above, except that pre-1980 data are examined, reveals that, at the 5% level of confidence, both the Aa and A ratings showed no sign of downward rating momentum, while the Baa, Ba and B categories showed significant downward momentum.

Appendix

The data suffer from Type 1 data censoring. That is, we do not have complete data on all the rating lives in our sample. For example, an issuer may have held the Aaa rating since 1970. In this case, all we know is that there is an Aaa-rated issuer that has held the rating for at least twenty-three years. In a sense, we have some information on this observation but not all (ie, the exact lifetime of the rating). Maximum likelihood estimation takes advantage of the (incomplete) information we have.

Hence, if T_i is the rating lifetime and L_i is the censoring time for the ith observation, our data consist of a series of observations (t_i, δ_i), where $t_i = \min(T_i, L_i)$ and $\delta_i = 1$ if $T_i \le L_i$ and $\delta_i = 0$ if $T_i > L_i$. δ_i is an indicator of whether the ith data point is an observed length of time or an observed censored lifetime. T_i is the actual observed length of time the rating is held, censored or not. The T_i are assumed to be independent and identically distributed.

If $w(t)$ is the probability density function of the T_i, and $W(t)$ is the probability distribution function of each of the T_i observations, then the joint probability distribution function of (t_i, δ_i) is

$$w(t_i)^{\delta_i} \left[1 - W(L_i)\right]^{1-\delta_i}$$

The likelihood function of the data is then

$$L = \prod_{i=1}^{n} w(t_i)^{\delta_i} \left[1 - W(L_i)\right]^{1-\delta_i}$$

Each observed lifetime contributes $w(t_i)$ to the likelihood function while each censored time contributes $(1 - W(t_i))$.

For the Weibull distribution

$$w(t; a, b) = \left(\frac{b}{a}\right)\left(\frac{t}{a}\right)^{b-1} e^{-(t/a)^b}$$

and

$$W(t; a, b) = 1 - e^{-(t/a)^b}$$

Using these functions and optimising the likelihood with respect to the scale, a, and shape, b, parameters, one obtains the equations that implicitly define the maximum likelihood estimators, $\hat{b}$, $\hat{a}$:

$$\left[\frac{\sum_{i=1}^{n} t_i^{\hat{b}} \log t_i}{\sum_{i=1}^{n} t_i^{\hat{b}}}\right] - \frac{1}{\hat{b}} - \frac{1}{r}\sum_{i \in D} \log t_i = 0$$

$$\hat{a} = \left(\frac{1}{r}\sum_{i-1}^{n} t_i^{\hat{b}}\right)^{\frac{1}{\hat{b}}}$$

where

$$r = \sum_{i \in D} \delta_i$$

and D is the set of observations for which $\delta_i = 1$. The first equation can be used to obtain an estimate of b, which can, in turn, be used in the second equation to estimate a.

1 *1982's figures are straight-line interpolations from 1981 and 1983. We use this interpolation because our algorithm for implying senior ratings artificially inflated the numbers of upgrades and downgrades during the 1982 adoption of numerically modified ratings. For example, an issuer with subordinated debt rated Ba prior to 1982 has a senior implied rating of Baa. If, upon adoption of the modified rating system, this issue comes in at the lower end of the Ba scale, say, Ba3, its senior implied rating is now Ba1. This corresponds to the letter rating Ba. Hence our algorithm has artificially created a downgrade from Baa to Ba even though there has been no rating revision. The actual numbers occurred in nearly the same ratio as those presented here. 1993's figures are annualised from the data available as of mid-1993.*

2 *For example, one issuer rating change from Baa to A represents one letter rating change. One issuer rating change from Baa to Aa represents two letter rating changes.*

3 *For example, in the letter rating system, a gradual decline in a hypothetical issuer's credit quality from Aa to A might have been represented by a rating change from Aa to A. Under the modified rating system, the same decline in credit quality might have been signalled through a steady decline from Aa2 to Aa3 to A1, resulting in two modified rating changes in place of one letter rating change.*

4 *The increase in credit quality is net since each rating transition matrix is a snapshot of the evolution of the rating profile at a specific time. Therefore, it does not address the dynamics of how the hypothetical A-rated issuer arrived at the Aa rating one year later. An issuer could have been upgraded to Aaa and then downgraded to Aa between the beginning and end of the one-year period.*

5 *More specifically, as noted earlier, we have excluded from this study firms whose rated debt consists solely of issues backed by entities that are not members of the issuer's corporate family. Hence, defaulters that fall into this category are excluded from the database, as are a number of other issuers.*

6 *We treat the event of default as a terminal state. For example, a Chapter 11 firm may emerge and so not be in default at the end of the specified time period. We treat the emerged firm as a new entity and keep the original firm in default.*

7 *The bias is due to what is called Type I censoring.*

8 *A random variable, t, has the Weibull distribution if it has a probability density function of the form*

$$w(t; a, b) = \left(\frac{b}{a}\right)\left(\frac{t}{a}\right)^{b-1} e^{-(t/a)^b}$$

where a is a scale parameter and b is a shape parameter.

9 *They are equivalent if* b = 1.

10 h(t; a, b) = *probability of a rating change* (W(t; a, b)) *given no previous rating change* (1 − W(t; a, b)), *where* w(t; a, b) *is the density function and* W(t; a, b) *is the distribution function. Hence,* h(t; a, b) = w(t; a, b)/(1 − W(t;, a, b)) = (b/a (t/a)b−1).

11 *The probability of holding a rating for a given number of years is one minus the probability of the rating changing in the given number of years. Hence,* s(t; a, b) = 1 − W(t; a, b), *where* W(t; a, b) *is the distribution function.*

12 $Z^* = \frac{1}{n}\sum_{i=1}^{n} X_i$ *is asymptotically normal with mean* $p_u - p_d$ *and variance* $p_u + p_d - (p_u - p_d)^2$.

14

The Declining Credit Quality of US Corporate Debt: Myth or Reality?

Marshall E. Blume, Felix Lim and A. Craig MacKinlay

Wharton School, University of Pennsylvania; the Vanguard Group;
Wharton School, University of Pennsylvania

In recent years, the number of downgrades in corporate bond ratings has exceeded the number of upgrades, leading some to conclude that the credit quality of US corporate debt has declined. However, an alternative explanation of this apparent decline in credit quality is that the rating agencies are now using more stringent standards is assigning ratings. An ordered probit analysis of a panel of firms from 1978 through 1995 suggests that rating standards have indeed become more stringent, implying that at least part of the downward trend in ratings is the result of changing standards.

Bond ratings play a key role in corporate financing and investment decisions. A corporation that can issue higher rated bonds usually receives better terms than one that can issue only lower rated bonds. By law or policy, some investors can purchase only bonds with an investment-grade rating, a restriction which in some asset pricing models would affect the relative prices of financial assets.

Numerous articles in the popular press have presumed that the credit quality of the debt of US corporations has been declining over the last couple of decades. The comprehensive study by Lucas and Lonski (1992) of Moody's rating changes of corporate debt is consistent with this presumption. To cite their statistics, in 1970 Moody's downgraded 21 issues and upgraded 23 issues, but over the following years the number of bonds downgraded began to exceed by substantial margins the number of bonds upgraded, and by 1990 Moody's downgraded 301 issues and upgraded only 61. Their study includes both investment- and non-investment-grade bonds, but internal data from Donaldson Lufkin & Jenrette confirm that this trend also applies to investment-grade bonds alone. In a somewhat different context, Grundy (1997) documents similar trends in the ratings of preferred shares over the 1965 to 1990 period.

As the credit quality of a firm's corporate debt decreases, that firm will face a greater probability of financial distress, which at the extreme translates into bankruptcy. There is some debate as to the effect of financial distress upon a firm's value and the overall level of economic activity. In the Miller–Modigliani paradigm, the credit quality of a firm's debt should have no impact. However, in a less than perfect world, an increased probability of financial distress may affect a firm's ability and willingness to undertake new investments. Froot, Scharfstein and Stein (1993) present an excellent summary of the avenues through which financial policies can interact with the investment decisions of an individual firm. Gertler (1988) contains a comprehensive survey of the relation between financial structure and aggregate economic activity.

This article was first printed in The Journal of Finance, *Vol. 53 (4), 1998. It is reprinted here with the kind permission of Blackwell Publishers. The authors thank Gary Gorton, Bruce Grundy, Dennis Logue, Krishna Ramaswamy and participants at the Queens University finance seminar, European Financial Management Association meetings, Berkeley Program in Finance, and American Finance Association meetings for helpful comments. The contents of this paper are the sole responsibility of the authors.*

192

THE DECLINING
CREDIT QUALITY OF
US CORPORATE
DEBT: MYTH OR
REALITY?

Those writing about the declining credit quality of US corporate debt have generally accepted this decline in credit quality as fact; yet at least one writer has attributed the observed decline in credit ratings to the use of more stringent rating standards (see Pender, 1992). Under this alternative view, there may have been no real decline in credit quality, and even if there were, the real decline may be less than the data suggest.

The specific question addressed in this paper is the narrow one of whether there is any tendency for a company that maintains the same values for its accounting measures and equity risk measures over time to receive a lower rating today than in prior years. This question is examined using 18 years of ratings for 1978 through 1995. The accounting variables examined in this study are a subset of those accounting variables that Standard and Poor's states that it utilises, and the equity risk measures are those that previous researchers have found to have explanatory power.

The study does find that rating standards have become more stringent in terms of the specific variables used in this study. This finding does not rule out the possibility that the informational content of a specific variable itself has changed over time, however. For instance, it is possible that a firm that had maintained the same leverage ratio over time might still find it more difficult to service its debt in today's environment. Also, it is possible that other information, particularly that available privately to the rating agencies, indicates a decline in credit quality. In either of these cases, more stringent standards in terms of data used in this study would be warranted.

The organisation of the chapter is as follows: the first section contains a discussion of related literature; then the ordered probit model is set forth, and the definitions of the variables used in estimating this model are presented. Finally, the main empirical results are described, and the robustness of these results considered.

Related literature

Moody's and Standard and Poor's (S&P) are the two major rating services for corporate debt. These services employ both publicly available information, such as accounting statements, and non-public information, such as confidential interviews with management, to assign quality ratings to individual corporate bonds. The intent of these quality ratings is to measure the "creditworthiness" of a corporation with "respect to a particular debt security" (Standard and Poor's, 1996, p. 5).

The ratings from S&P in descending order of credit quality are AAA, AA, A, BBB, BB, B, CCC, CC and D. The rating of D is used for a bond that is in default, particularly in its payment of interest or principal. The rating of C is a special rating applied only to income bonds on which no interest is currently being paid. A bond with a rating of BBB or above is known as an investment-grade bond, one with a rating of BB or lower is known variously as a high-yield bond, non-investment-grade bond or junk bond. In an attempt to refine these ratings further, S&P now on occasion assigns a plus or minus to its ratings to indicate that the bond is at the upper or lower end of the rating category. Moody's ratings are similar.

Previous research on quality ratings divides logically into three branches. The first branch addresses the question of whether quality ratings measure what they are supposed to measure. Hickman (1958), one of the first to examine this question, finds generally positive relations between initial quality ratings and default. In another study, Ang and Patel (1975) find that S&P quality ratings have weak power in predicting what they term "financial distress" in the subsequent year. Kao and Wu (1990) find a positive relation between bond yields and quality ratings. These studies and others indicate that quality ratings do have some informational content.

Both the second and third branches examine the type of information contained in quality ratings. The second branch examines whether quality ratings convey information that the market has not already incorporated into prices from other available information. A recent study of this type by Hand, Holthausen and Leftwich (1992) finds that bond and stock prices of an issuing company change in the expected direction when either Moody's or S&P publishes an actual or potential change in rating. From this result, they conclude

193

THE DECLINING
CREDIT QUALITY OF
US CORPORATE
DEBT: MYTH OR
REALITY?

that ratings do contain information beyond what is publicly available. Some previous studies, such as Katz (1974), Grier and Katz (1976) and Ingram, Brooks and Copeland (1983), reach similar conclusions, but other studies, such as Weinstein (1977) and Wakeman (1978), do not detect incremental information effects.

The third branch analyses how the rating agencies use public information in setting quality ratings. The early studies, such as Horrigan (1966), Pogue and Soldofsky (1969) and West (1970), assign ordinal numbers to the quality ratings and regress these numbers on accounting and other variables. Later studies, such as Pinches and Mingo (1973, 1975) and Altman and Katz (1976), use discriminant analysis in place of regression analysis. Kaplan and Urwitz (1979) employ an ordered probit model and find, like the earlier studies, that publicly available data predict with a fair degree of accuracy actual quality ratings. Ederington (1985) compares and contrasts these different statistical approaches.

The empirical results in our study fall into this third and last branch of research, and the methodology generalises and extends that of Kaplan and Urwitz. In contrast to Kaplan and Urwitz, who analyse a single cross-section of firms, the analysis in this study utilises panel data covering the years 1978 through 1995. With panel data, one can examine whether conditional on the included variables, rating standards have become more stringent over time and, if so, the importance of these more stringent rating standards in explaining the recent prevalence of downgrades over upgrades.

The ordered probit model

The empirical analysis in this paper utilises an ordered probit model. This model relates the rating categories to observed explanatory variables through an unobserved continuous linking variable. The rating categories map into a partition of the range of the unobserved variable, which is in turn a linear function of the observed explanatory variables.

Define the following for bond i at year t: R_{it} is the rating category of bond i at time t, Z_{it} is an unobserved linking variable, and X_{it} and W_{it} are vectors of observed explanatory variables measured at time t or before. The number of time periods in the sample is denoted by T. The linking variable Z_{it} is continuous and its range is the set of real numbers. The vector X_{it} will be used in the linear part of the model and the vector W_{it} will be used in modelling the variance of the disturbance terms. The vectors X_{it} and W_{it} may contain variables in common. The variable R_{it} is assigned the value of 4 if bond i at time t has a rating by S&P of AAA, 3 if AA, 2 if A and 1 if BBB.

The ordered probit model consists of two parts. The first part maps the rating categories into a partition of the unobserved linking variable Z_{it} as follows:

$$R_{it} = \begin{cases} 4 & \text{if } Z_{it} \in [\mu_3, \infty) \\ 3 & \text{if } Z_{it} \in [\mu_2, \mu_3) \\ 2 & \text{if } Z_{it} \in [\mu_1, \mu_2) \\ 1 & \text{if } Z_{it} \in [-\infty, \mu_1) \end{cases} \qquad (1)$$

where μ_i are partition points independent of t.

The second part relates the Z_{it}s to the underlying observed variables as

$$Z_{it} = \alpha_t + \beta'X_{it} + \varepsilon_{it} \qquad (2)$$

$$E\left[\varepsilon_{it} \mid X_{it}, W_{it}\right] = 0 \qquad (3)$$

$$E\left[\varepsilon_{it}^2 \mid X_{it}, W_{it}\right] = \left[\exp\left(\gamma_0 + \gamma'W_{it}\right)\right]^2 \qquad (4)$$

where α_t is the intercept for year t and β is the vector of slope coefficients. The random variable ε_{it} is a Gaussian disturbance term with a conditional expectation of zero. To allow for heteroscedasticity, the variance of ε_{it} is modelled as a function of W_{it}, where γ_0 is a constant and γ is a vector of slope coefficients.

194

THE DECLINING
CREDIT QUALITY OF
US CORPORATE
DEBT: MYTH OR
REALITY?

This specification allows the intercept to vary over time while constraining the slope coefficients β to be constant over time. Changes in the intercept over time can be viewed as a measure of changes in standards used in assigning ratings. If α_t is sufficiently less than α_{t-1}, a bond with the same vector of explanatory variables will be associated with a lower rating at year t than at year (t − 1) because the partition points, given by μ_is, are held constant over time. Conversely, if α_t is sufficiently greater than α_{t-1}, the same vector of explanatory variables will be associated with a greater rating at year t than at year (t − 1). An analysis of the robustness of the empirical results to this particular specification, presented in the section on robustness, finds that the main empirical results of the paper are virtually unchanged when the slope coefficients β are allowed to vary over time.

Since the Z_{it}s are unique up to a linear transformation, identification of the model requires two restrictions. The first restriction in this paper is to set the intercept for the first year of the panel to zero. This means that the remaining T − 1 intercepts can be interpreted as changes in rating standards relative to the rating standards of the first year of the panel. The second restriction is to set γ_o in equation (4) to zero. This restriction reduces to the usual restriction in a homoscedastic probit model if the slope coefficients γ in equation (4) are zero, in which case the variance of the error would be equal to 1.0.

The most probable category, and here the most probable rating category, is central to any probit analysis and in this study plays a key role. It is customary to assign the maximum likelihood estimates as values to the parameters in the probit model in determining the most probable rating category, but in fact the most probable rating category can be determined for any arbitrary set of values assigned to these parameters. Specifically, for any observation given by X_{it} and W_{it}, the analyses below set the intercept in the linear part of the probit model to one of the estimates from earlier or later years, and the corresponding most probable category is calculated. In these calculations, all the other parameters of the probit model are equated to their maximum likelihood estimates.[1] Changes in the most probable rating categories as the intercepts vary are a direct measure of changes in rating standards.

Let a be the value assigned to the intercept in the linear part of the probit model, and define θ as the set of parameters of the probit model with the intercept set to a and the other parameters set to their maximum likelihood estimates. Conditional on θ and the explanatory vectors X_{it} and W_{it}, the linking variable Z_{it} will be distributed as a normal variate with an expectation of $a + \beta'X_{it}$ and a standard deviation of $\exp(\gamma'W_{it})$. The probability that a bond falls in rating category j is then given by

$$Pr\left(R_{it}=j|\theta\right)=\begin{cases} Pr\left(a+\beta'X_{it}+\varepsilon_{it}\geq\mu_3|\theta\right) & \text{if } j=4 \\ Pr\left(\mu_j > a+\beta'X_{it}+\varepsilon_{it}\geq\mu_{j-1}|\theta\right) & \text{if } j=3,2 \\ Pr\left(\mu_1 > a+\beta'X_{it}+\varepsilon_{it}|\theta\right) & \text{if } j=1 \end{cases} \quad (5)$$

The value of j that maximises equation (5) is the most probable bond rating category conditional on the parameter vector θ.

The variables

As described in Standard and Poor's (1996), both the business risk and financial risk of a company are analysed in assigning a credit rating. There are no fixed rules, and to use S&P's words, "subjectivity is at the heart of every rating." Nonetheless, it does publish ten financial ratios that are "key" ratios in its analysis of creditworthiness. Five of these ratios measure interest coverage, two measure profitability and three measure leverage. Standard and Poor's uses three-year averages of these ratios and this study follows that practice.

The 1995 annual COMPUSTAT is the source for the accounting ratios used in this paper, and this source includes the industrial, full coverage and research files. The specific accounting ratios used here are: pre-tax interest coverage, operating income to sales, long-term debt to assets and total debt to assets.[2] The first two ratios should be positively related to improvements in credit ratings; the last two ratios should be negatively related to improvements in credit ratings. These accounting ratios are similar to those used in the related studies cited above. The 1995 COMPUSTAT files contain twenty years of data (1976 through 1995), making 1978 the first year for which three-year averages are available; thus, the panel will cover the 18 years from 1978 through 1995.

A number of studies also find a positive relation between credit ratings and firm size, and firm size is therefore included as an explanatory variable in the linear part of the probit model. The rationale is that larger firms tend to be older, with more established product lines and more varied sources of revenues. If so, the explanatory variables used in the linear part of the probit model may be more stable over time for larger firms, and thus for the same set of explanatory variables, a larger firm would tend to receive a higher credit rating.

This study extends this argument by examining explicitly whether the explanatory variables used in the linear part of the probit model are more informative for larger firms. If the explanatory variables for larger firms are more stable over time, the variance of the residuals of the probit model in equation (2) should be similar for larger firms. To examine this conjecture, the variance of the residuals given by equation (4) is modelled as a function of firm size.

Firm size itself is measured in two steps: first, the market value of equity in millions of dollars is deflated by the CPI. Second, the natural logarithm of this deflated market value is taken.[3]

In addition to these accounting ratios, past studies have used beta coefficients and standard errors from the market model. The hypothesis is that a firm will be less able to service its debt for given accounting ratios as its equity risk increases. These equity risk measures take into account both the variability of the underlying cash flows from operations and the degree of leverage. Further separating equity risk into beta and non-beta risk allows for the possibility that these two measures of risk might be related to the debt rating in different ways. For example, for a given degree of leverage, variability to non-market factors might provide more information about the competency of management than variability due to general market movements. Management may have some control over non-market variability, and the type of business itself may largely determine the volatility due to general market movements. If so, how the variability of total returns breaks down into these two sources may convey information. The expected signs on these two relative measures of equity risk are negative.

The CRSP daily stock files are the source of the daily returns used in estimating the betas and standard errors from the market model. For each calendar year in which a company is in the panel and in which it has at least 200 daily returns, a beta and a standard error from the market model are estimated. The market index is taken to be the CRSP value-weighted index. The beta estimates are adjusted for non-synchronous trading effects using the Dimson (1979) procedure with one leading and one lagging value of the market return. There is some variation in the mean levels of the standard errors over time, particularly in 1987. To remove this variation, the standard errors in each year are divided by the cross-sectional mean standard error for that year. Although there is very little variation in the mean betas over time, the betas each year are also standardised in the same way.

The bond ratings themselves come from files of individual bonds that make up the Lehman Brothers Bond Index and were assembled by Professor Arthur Warga – thus, let us call this the "Warga file."[4] Specifically, the Warga file contains among other variables the S&P bond ratings for December of each year for all corporate bonds included in the Lehman Brothers Corporate Bond Index.[5] With a start date of January 1973, this index includes all "publicly issued, fixed rate, nonconvertible investment grade, dollar-denominated, SEC-registered corporate debt." Virtually all of these bonds represent senior debt.

The merger of these files produces a panel of firms over the 18 years from 1978 through 1995, ranging in number from a low of 367 in both 1978 and 1979 to a high of 457 in 1995 (Table 1). The total number of firm-years is 7,324. There is an evident shift in the distribution of quality ratings over these years. The proportion of firms with AAA

Table 1. Companies with rated bonds cross-classified by S&P quality rating and year, 1978–95

The table is based on a panel of companies covering the 18 years from 1978 through 1995. COMPUSTAT, the CRSP daily stock files and the Warga file are the primary sources for the data on this panel of companies. Panel A gives the number of bonds cross-classified by S&P Quality Rating and year as well as the total by year, and Panel B gives the percentage breakdown by year.

			Rating		
Year	AAA	AA	A	BBB	Total
			Panel A: Number		
1978	30	106	173	58	367
1979	37	104	173	53	367
1980	36	105	184	64	389
1981	31	97	180	76	384
1982	25	103	162	90	380
1983	20	107	166	96	389
1984	14	109	178	77	378
1985	11	103	182	98	394
1986	10	106	182	100	398
1987	13	104	181	108	406
1988	14	94	194	109	411
1989	16	94	185	122	417
1990	13	85	172	141	411
1991	16	82	195	126	419
1992	18	86	200	150	454
1993	16	80	186	170	452
1994	14	78	176	183	451
1995	13	78	182	184	457
Total	347	1721	3251	2005	7324
			Panel B: Percentage		
1978	8.2	28.9	47.1	15.8	100
1979	10.1	28.3	47.1	14.4	100
1980	9.3	27.0	47.3	16.5	100
1981	8.1	25.3	46.9	19.8	100
1982	6.6	27.1	42.6	23.7	100
1983	5.1	27.5	42.7	24.7	100
1984	3.7	28.8	47.1	20.4	100
1985	2.8	26.1	46.2	24.9	100
1986	2.5	26.6	45.7	25.1	100
1987	3.2	25.6	44.6	26.6	100
1988	3.4	22.9	47.2	26.5	100
1989	3.8	22.5	44.4	29.3	100
1990	3.2	20.7	41.8	34.3	100
1991	3.8	19.6	46.5	30.1	100
1992	4.0	18.9	44.1	33.0	100
1993	3.5	17.7	41.2	37.6	100
1994	3.1	17.3	39.0	40.6	100
1995	2.8	17.1	39.8	40.3	100

begins at 8.2% in 1978 and declines to 2.8% in 1995, and the proportion of firms with BBB changes over the same time period from 15.8% to 40.3%.

Using 1978 as an example, the following time convention is used in merging these data sources. The bond ratings and market values are those for year-end 1978; the market model estimates are obtained from the daily returns in 1978; and the data for the last year of the three-year averages of the accounting ratios come from the yearly financial statements for 1978. Since many firms have year-end months other than December, COMPUSTAT has developed an algorithm for assigning a calendar year to each yearly financial statement and this paper uses that assignment.

Empirical results

The empirical results in this section are consistent with the hypothesis that over the years 1978 through 1995 S&P has applied more stringent standards in assigning rating categories, at least in terms of the firm characteristics used as explanatory variables in this study. Were it not for improvements in the values of these variables over time, the results suggest that the number of downgrades that occurred over these 18 years would have been even greater.

MODEL ESTIMATES

Estimation of the parameters of the probit model for the panel data covering the years 1978 through 1995 is based on standard maximum likelihood techniques.[6]

The probit model as given by equation (2) assumes that the linking variable Z_{it} is a linear function of the explanatory variables, but this assumption is implausible for the interest coverage variable because the distribution of this variable is extremely skewed with a skewness coefficient of 48.6. The mean is 12.1 and the median is 4.5. This skewness is due to a very few observations: four observations exceed 1,000 and 14 exceed 100. In the sample, the median value for this variable is 10.1 for AAA ratings, 5.6 for AA, 4.5 for A and 3.4 for BBB. A change from 3.0 to 6.0, which brackets the medians for different rating classes, might lead to an upgrade, but the same change from 97.0 to 100.0 would likely have no effect on the rating. Thus, the relation between the linking variable Z_{it} and interest coverage is likely to be monotonically increasing, yet when the interest coverage is extremely large, the effect of small changes in interest coverage should be negligible.

Further, when the interest coverage variable is negative, the magnitude is not meaningful. Since earnings must be negative in this case, the magnitude of the interest rate coverage variable could be large due to either a small interest expense or large negative earnings.

For these reasons, the functional form of the interest coverage variable is modified in two steps: First, before taking the three-year average of the interest rate coverage, any annual component that is negative is set to zero. In the final sample, four observations have zero values for the interest rate coverage ratio. Also, any three-year average of the interest rate coverage greater than 100.0 is set to 100.0 on the assumption that increases in value beyond 100.0 convey no additional information.

197

THE DECLINING

CREDIT QUALITY OF

US CORPORATE

DEBT: MYTH OR

REALITY?

Table 2. Ordered probit model estimates for the panel data, 1978–95

The estimates are for the ordered probit model parameters using a panel data sample of 7,324 observations from 1978 through 1995. The betas are the coefficient estimates for the independent variables in the linear part of the model as defined in the text. The lower boundaries for rating category parameters are the estimates of the partition parameters for the rating categories. The variance parameter is the estimate of the coefficient associated with the market value of equity when the variance of the disturbances is modelled as a function of the deflated market value of equity. The first set of standard errors is calculated under the assumption that the disturbances are uncorrelated. The second, or adjusted set, is calculated using the Newey and West (1987) procedure to account for possible autocorrelation in the disturbances across time for individual firms in the pooled probit model.

	Coefficient	Standard Error	Z-statistic	Adjusted standard error	Adjusted Z-statistic	Coeff. × variable Std dev.
Betas						
Interest coverage κ_1	0.205	0.019	11.05	0.066	3.11	0.206
κ_2	0.020	0.006	3.18	0.011	1.82	0.036
κ_3	0.022	0.005	4.15	0.011	2.07	0.045
κ_4	−0.004	0.002	−2.14	0.003	−1.41	−0.018
Operating margin	1.054	0.111	9.46	0.360	2.93	0.124
LT debt leverage	−1.958	0.158	−12.36	0.543	−3.61	−0.257
Total debt leverage	0.425	0.086	4.94	0.235	1.81	0.063
Market value	0.194	0.014	13.99	0.044	4.41	0.257
Market model beta	−0.198	0.025	−8.05	0.059	−3.36	−0.103
Standard error	−0.530	0.047	−11.36	0.191	−2.78	−0.177
Year dummies						
1978	0.000	—		—		
1979	0.007	0.048	0.14	0.020	0.32	
1980	−0.030	0.047	−0.64	0.027	−1.11	
1981	−0.036	0.048	−0.76	0.035	−1.05	
1982	−0.065	0.048	−1.35	0.041	−1.58	
1983	−0.127	0.048	−2.64	0.052	−2.47	
1984	−0.131	0.049	−2.70	0.050	−2.65	
1985	−0.288	0.051	−5.65	0.081	−3.56	
1986	−0.334	0.052	−6.39	0.091	−3.67	
1987	−0.328	0.052	−6.32	0.091	−3.62	
1988	−0.355	0.052	−6.80	0.095	−3.75	
1989	−0.408	0.054	−7.54	0.106	−3.85	
1990	−0.443	0.056	−7.95	0.119	−3.73	
1991	−0.434	0.054	−7.97	0.112	−3.89	
1992	−0.458	0.055	−8.36	0.123	−3.73	
1993	−0.567	0.061	−9.36	0.151	−3.76	
1994	−0.659	0.065	−10.15	0.175	−3.76	
1995	−0.760	0.070	−10.79	0.205	−3.70	
Lower boundary for rating category						
AAA	2.276	0.176		0.565		
AA	1.472	0.126		0.350		
A	0.573	0.087		0.167		
BBB and below	$-\infty$	—		—		
Variance parameter market value						
	−0.089	0.011	−8.39	0.040	−2.19	

Second, a change in the specification of the model permits the data to determine the shape of the non-linearity. Specifically, let C_{it} be the interest rate coverage for firm i in year t and then include the interest rate coverage variable in equation (2) as

$$\sum_{j=1}^{4} \kappa_j c_{jit} \qquad (6)$$

where c_{jit} is defined as

	c_{1it}	c_{2it}	c_{3it}	c_{4it}
$C_{it} \in [0,5)$	C_{it}	0	0	0
$C_{it} \in [5,10)$	5	$C_{it}-5$	0	0
$C_{it} \in [10,20)$	5	5	$C_{it}-10$	0
$C_{it} \in [20,100]$	5	5	10	$C_{it}-20$

This specification allows different weights for each increment of the interest rate coverage ratio. If the conjecture that further increases in the interest rate coverage from some

1. Plot of the estimates of the intercept from the ordered probit model for the panel data, 1978–95

The estimates of the intercept plotted over time come from the ordered probit model estimated on the panel data of 7324 observations from 1978 through 1995. The variance of the disturbances is modelled as a function of the defaulted market equity. The intercept for 1978 is set to zero as part of the identification of the model. Lower values of the intercept imply more stringent grading standards, given the explanatory variables of the model.

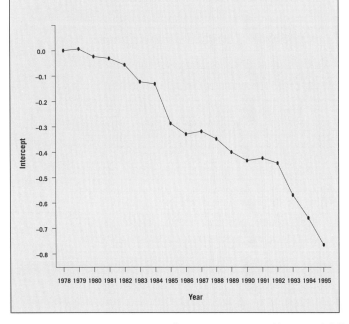

value provide no additional information is true, κ_j associated with higher values should be close to zero.

The probit model further assumes that the generalised residuals are uncorrelated amongst themselves. However, an examination of the generalised residuals from equation (2) suggests that the time series of the residuals of individual companies are autocorrelated, contrary to the assumption of zero correlation. If there is such autocorrelation, the maximum likelihood estimators are still consistent, but the standard errors of these estimators are not. Newey and West (1987) provide a general procedure to obtain consistent standard errors in the presence of such autocorrelation, and this paper utilises their approach to calculate a second "adjusted" set of standard errors.[7]

The estimated coefficients on the firm characteristics all have the correct predicted signs (Table 2) except for the coefficient on total debt leverage. If taken at face value, this exception means that for a given level of long-term debt leverage, a firm with more short-term debt in its capital structure will tend to receive a higher credit rating. However, once the standard error is adjusted for autocorrelation in the residuals, this coefficient does not differ significantly from zero. The coefficients on the interest coverage variables behave as conjectured. The coefficient on the increment of the interest rate coverage from 0 to 5, κ_1, is positive and large and differs significantly from zero. The coefficients on the increments of the interest rate coverage from 5 to 10, κ_2, and from 10 to 20, κ_3, are positive and small but differ significantly from zero. The coefficient on the increment above 20, κ_4, is not significantly different from zero.

In a probit model there are no natural magnitudes for the linking variable, making it difficult to interpret the economic significance of the size of the estimated coefficients. To aid in interpreting these coefficients, Table 2 also presents for each explanatory variable the product of its estimated coefficient and the corresponding standard deviation of the independent variable itself. This product represents the change in the conditional expectation of Z_{it} in response to a change of one standard deviation in the value of this explanatory variable. A comparison of this change to the size of the partitions provides a measure of the economic importance of a variable. As a further aid in interpreting the probit model, Table 3 contains descriptive statistics of the distributions of the explanatory variables by rating category and overall.

The variance of the standard errors of the probit model, which can be interpreted as a measure of confidence of the prediction, decreases with increases in firm size as measured by deflated market equity. This result is consistent with the conjecture that firm characteristics are more informative for larger firms than for smaller firms. As mentioned before, this result – if correct – could have significant implications for regulatory issues and for determining a firm's cost of capital.

The intercepts display a steady downward trend over time (Figure 1 and Table 2). The rank order correlation between the intercepts and time is -0.99, which is significant at the 1% level. This decline in the values of the intercept is consistent with the application of increasingly more stringent standards over time in assigning ratings in terms of the firm characteristics identified in this study.

A comparison of the most probable ratings with the actual ratings can be used to assess the goodness-of-fit of a profit model. For the model in this paper, the most probable rating is within plus or minus one rating category of the actual rating for most companies

199

THE DECLINING
CREDIT QUALITY OF
US CORPORATE
DEBT: MYTH OR
REALITY?

Table 3. Descriptive statistics of the variables used in the probit analyses, 1978–95

This table presents descriptive statistics for the seven variables used in the probit model for each rating class and overall. The statistics are calculated using a panel data sample of 7,324 observations from 1978 through 1995.

Variables	Mean	0.25	Fractiles Median	0.75
A Interest coverage				
AAA	13.21	5.07	10.14	16.54
AA	8.14	4.38	5.60	8.89
A	5.91	3.53	4.45	6.51
BBB	4.34	2.70	3.42	4.68
All	6.35	3.37	4.50	6.77
B Operating margin				
AAA	0.22	0.15	0.19	0.26
AA	0.21	0.12	0.18	0.29
A	0.19	0.12	0.16	0.24
BBB	0.19	0.10	0.14	0.26
All	0.20	0.11	0.16	0.26
C LT debt leverage				
AAA	0.11	0.04	0.08	0.14
AA	0.19	0.09	0.19	0.30
A	0.22	0.14	0.22	0.31
BBB	0.28	0.19	0.28	0.37
All	0.22	0.12	0.22	0.32
D Total debt leverage				
AAA	0.21	0.13	0.17	0.25
AA	0.27	0.17	0.27	0.34
A	0.30	0.21	0.29	0.38
BBB	0.35	0.26	0.35	0.43
All	0.30	0.20	0.30	0.38
E Market value				
AAA	7.92	6.50	8.38	9.26
AA	7.03	6.13	7.11	7.97
A	6.53	5.72	6.60	7.38
BBB	6.21	5.54	6.30	6.97
All	6.63	5.76	6.64	7.46
F Market model beta				
AAA	0.99	0.65	1.00	1.26
AA	0.96	0.58	0.94	1.29
A	1.00	0.60	0.97	1.33
BBB	1.04	0.65	1.00	1.35
All	1.00	0.61	0.97	1.33
G Standard error				
AAA	0.87	0.67	0.83	1.02
AA	0.89	0.72	0.87	1.01
A	0.98	0.79	0.95	1.13
BBB	1.15	0.90	1.10	1.33
All	1.00	0.78	0.96	1.15

(Table 4). The model underpredicts both the high and low rating categories. In general, as the explanatory power of a probit model with multiple categories declines, the underprediction for some categories will become more pronounced with a corresponding overprediction for other categories. In the extreme case of no explanatory power, the most probable category will always be the same – namely, the category with the most observations.

ECONOMIC IMPORTANCE

The decline in the intercepts is consistent with the application of more stringent standards in assigning ratings, but it provides no direct evidence of the economic importance of this statistical result. One way to ascertain the economic significance of this change is to compare the rating that the probit model would predict for a particular year using the firm character-

Table 4. Actual ratings versus predicted ratings using the panel probit model, 1978–95

A measure of the goodness of fit of the probit model that is estimated using a panel data sample of 7,324 observations from 1978 through 1995. The coefficient estimates for the model are presented in Table 2. Presented is the matrix of actual ratings versus predicted ratings. This matrix shows, for instance, that the panel contains 347 companies with bonds carrying a AAA rating. The predicted ratings for these bonds are: AAA for 90, AA for 161, A for 74, and BBB for 22.

Actual Rating	AAA	Predicted Rating AA	A	BBB	Total Actual
AAA	90	161	74	22	347
AA	20	622	1022	57	1721
A	2	362	2399	488	3251
BBB	0	32	894	1079	2005
Total predicted	112	1177	4389	1646	7324

Table 5. Effect of changing rating standards on predicted ratings based on the pooled probit model, 1978–95

One way to measure the effect of changing standards on predicted ratings is, first, to ascertain the predicted rating for a company for the year of its financial and market risk characteristics using the rating standards of that year, termed the base-year prediction, and, second, to compare this predicted rating with the rating that would be predicted using an earlier or later standard. The prediction using an earlier or later standard is based on the financial and market risk characteristics of the base year. To summarise these comparisons, this table presents the net number of firms that would receive a predicted upgraded or downgraded rating as a percentage of the firms in the base year. Such percentages are shown for rating standards of 5 years, 10 years, 15 years and 17 years later or earlier than the base year. The rating standards themselves come from the pooled probit model given in Table 2.

					Percentage upgraded or downgraded (downgraded in parentheses)				
Rating standards						Rating standards			
17 years earlier	15 years earlier	10 years earlier	5 years earlier	Base year		5 years later	10 years later	15 years later	17 years later
				1978		(12.0)	(39.0)	(60.5)	(78.5)
				1979		(17.4)	(51.0)	(72.5)	
				1980		(32.9)	(47.8)	(77.9)	
				1981		(35.7)	(44.8)		
				1982		(26.6)	(40.3)		
			15.2	1983		(24.9)	(45.5)		
			20.4	1984		(30.7)	(55.0)		
			30.2	1985		(18.3)	(48.2)		
			36.2	1986		(7.3)			
			31.5	1987		(15.0)			
		41.6	28.7	1988		(19.5)			
		51.8	35.7	1989		(22.5)			
		46.0	16.8	1990		(31.6)			
		41.8	10.7	1991					
		42.7	12.8	1992					
	64.8	50.2	22.6	1993					
	75.4	59.0	29.5	1994					
84.7	81.6	50.3	35.7	1995					
84.7	73.9	47.9	25.1	Average		(22.6)	(46.5)	(70.3)	(78.5)

istics for that year with the rating that the probit model would predict for an earlier or later year but using the same firm characteristics (Table 5). In short, keep the data the same, but vary the year of the rating standard.

As an illustration, the panel contains 378 companies in 1984. Consider first the predicted rating for a company using its 1984 firm characteristics and the 1984 rating standards, which is determined by the 1984 intercept – in short, the base year prediction. Consider next the predicted rating for that company using its 1984 firm characteristics but using the 1989 rating standards instead of the 1984 rating standards, which means using the 1989 intercept rather than the 1984 intercept. If the more stringent standards were economically important, a substantial portion of companies would have lower predicted ratings using the 1989 standards by comparison with the 1984 standards. In fact, 116 companies, or 30.7%, would have received lower predicted ratings. Also consistent with more stringent rating standards, 77 companies, or 20.4%, would have received higher predicted ratings using the standards of five years earlier, again applied to their 1984 firm characteristics.

On average, 22.6% of the firms would have had lower predicted ratings using the probit model five years forward in time in comparison to the base prediction, 46.5% ten years forward in time, 70.3% 15 years forward in time and 78.5% 17 years forward in time. On average, going back in time, 25.1% of the companies would have had greater predicted ratings using a model five years earlier, 47.9% ten years earlier, 73.9% 15 years earlier and 84.7% 17 years earlier.

Robustness

There are two criticisms that could potentially invalidate the conclusion that rating standards have become more stringent over time. First, the specification that the slope coefficients in the probit model are constant over time is grossly incorrect. It could be that a model with constant coefficients would understate the values of the linking variable before adding in the intercept in early years and overstate the values in the later years.

Table 6. Signs of the ordered probit model estimates for each year of the panel, 1978–95

For each year from 1978 through 1995 using a sample of 7324 observations, a separate ordered probit model is estimated. Table I reports the number of observations each year. The variance of the disturbances in each year is modelled as a function of the deflated market equity. This table presents the signs of the estimated parameters for each year as well as the predicted sign and the number of years for which the estimated sign agrees with the predicted sign. A superscript "a" indicates that the corresponding estimated coefficient is significant at the 5% level, where the standard error is calculated on the assumption that the disturbances are uncorrelated.

| | Linear model | | | | | | | | | | Variance as a function of market value |
| | Interest coverage | | | | Operating margin | LT debt leverage | Total debt leverage | Market value | Beta | Standard error | |
	κ_1	κ_2	κ_3	κ_4							
Predicted sign	+	+/0	+/0	+/0	+	0	0	+	−	−	−
number with sign	18				18	18	7	18	18	18	17
year:											
1978	+	−	+	$-^a$	$+^a$	$-^a$	−	$+^a$	$-^a$	$-^a$	−
1979	+	−	+	−	$+^a$	$-^a$	−	$+^a$	$-^a$	$-^a$	+
1980	$+^a$	−	+	−	$+^a$	$-^a$	−	$+^a$	$-^a$	−	−
1981	$+^a$	−	+	+	$+^a$	$-^a$	$-^a$	$+^a$	−	$-^a$	$-^a$
1982	$+^a$	−	+	+	$+^a$	$-^a$	+	$+^a$	$-^a$	$-^a$	$-^a$
1983	$+^a$	+	+	−	$+^a$	$-^a$	+	$+^a$	−	$-^a$	−
1984	$+^a$	+	+	+	$+^a$	$-^a$	+	$+^a$	−	$-^a$	−
1985	$+^a$	−	+	−	$+^a$	$-^a$	−	$+^a$	−	$-^a$	−
1986	$+^a$	−	+	−	$+^a$	$-^a$	−	$+^a$	−	$-^a$	$-^a$
1987	$+^a$	+	+	−	$+^a$	$-^a$	−	$+^a$	$-^a$	−	$-^a$
1988	$+^a$	+	+	−	$+^a$	$-^a$	+	$+^a$	−	$-^a$	$-^a$
1989	$+^a$	+	−	+	$+^a$	$-^a$	+	$+^a$	$-^a$	$-^a$	−
1990	$+^a$	+	+	+	$+^a$	$-^a$	+	$+^a$	−	−	$-^a$
1991	$+^a$	+	−	+	$+^a$	$-^a$	+	$+^a$	$-^a$	$-^a$	$-^a$
1992	$+^a$	+	+	−	+	$-^a$	$+^a$	$+^a$	$-^a$	$-^a$	$-^a$
1993	$+^a$	$+^a$	+	+	$+^a$	$-^a$	$+^a$	$+^a$	−	$-^a$	$-^a$
1994	$+^a$	$+^a$	+	−	$+^a$	$-^a$	+	$+^a$	$-^a$	$-^a$	$-^a$
1995	+	$-^a$	+	−	+	$-^a$	+	$+^a$	−	$-^a$	$-^a$

Such a time-dependent tendency could manifest itself in the observed decline over time in the intercepts, falsely pointing to more stringent rating standards over time. This criticism can be addressed directly by re-estimating the model year-by-year and also by examining the time-series behaviour of the firm variables themselves.

Second, the analysis omits an important variable whose mean increases or decreases monotonically over time. In this case, the monotonically declining intercept could be just an adjustment for such an omitted variable. This criticism can never be answered definitively without specifying the omitted variable itself. However, it is possible to validate the probit model with a specific prediction of the model: To maintain its rating over time, a firm would have had to improve continuously its firm characteristics.

THE FIRST CRITICISM

As the first step to analysing whether constraining the slope coefficients to be constant over time results in the appearance of greater stringency, the probit model is re-estimated year by year with no constraints on the values of the estimated coefficients between years. The general pattern of the signs of the coefficients that are significant matches the predicted signs most of the time (Table 6). The coefficient on the first increment of the interest rate coverage is positive in all 18 years and significantly different from zero in 15 of these years. With one exception, the coefficients on the third and fourth increments of the interest rate coverage, which are increments in excess of 10, could not be rejected as significantly different from zero. The coefficient on long-term debt leverage is negative and significantly different from zero in each of the 18 years. The coefficient on total debt leverage varies from year to year, and in 15 of the 18 years it is not possible to reject the hypothesis that its value is zero at the 5% level. This randomness suggests that for this panel short-term debt itself has little incremental impact on a firm's rating, which is consistent with the pooled probit analysis. The signs on market value in the linear part of the model are all positive, and the signs on beta and standard error are all negative. Consistent with the overall model, the informativeness of the firm data increases with market values.

That the signs of the significant variables in the yearly probit models are similar to the

Table 7. Effect of changing rating standards on predicted ratings based on the year-by-year probit models, 1978–95

One way to measure the effect of changing standards on predicted ratings is, first, to ascertain the predicted rating for a company for the year of its financial and market risk characteristics using the rating standards of that year, termed the base-year prediction, and, second, to compare this predicted rating with the rating that would be predicted using an earlier or later standard. The prediction using an earlier or later standard is based on the financial and market risk characteristics of the base year. To summarise these comparisons, this table presents the net number of firms that would receive a predicted upgraded or downgraded rating as a percentage of the firms in the base year. Such percentages are shown for rating standards of 5 years, 10 years, 15 years and 17 years later or earlier than the base year. The rating standards themselves come from the year-by-year probit models.

					Percentage upgraded or downgraded (downgraded in parentheses)				
Rating standards						Rating standards			
17 years earlier	15 years earlier	10 years earlier	5 years earlier	Base year		5 years later	10 years later	15 years later	17 years later
				1978		(15.5)	(39.2)	(59.1)	(85.6)
				1979		(14.4)	(53.1)	(72.8)	
				1980		(27.5)	(46.8)	(78.7)	
				1981		(38.5)	(49.0)		
				1982		(32.6)	(50.8)		
			24.9	1983		(29.3)	(54.5)		
			27.0	1984		(37.0)	(68.5)		
			34.3	1985		(24.9)	(70.1)		
			40.7	1986		(13.3)			
			39.9	1987		(20.0)			
		55.0	31.9	1988		(20.9)			
		55.9	41.7	1989		(32.4)			
		53.5	21.7	1990		(45.7)			
		49.6	17.4	1991					
		55.5	20.3	1992					
	74.8	60.2	27.4	1993					
	81.2	71.0	39.0	1994					
86.7	82.5	63.7	47.3	1995					
86.7	79.5	58.0	31.8	Average		(27.1)	(54.0)	(70.2)	(85.6)

signs in the pooled model is supportive of the pooled model, but it does not address the stability of the values of the coefficients themselves. To obtain a more direct measure of the presence of more stringent standards over time, the analysis of the economic importance of the more stringent standards found in the pooled probit is replicated using instead the year-by-year probit models. Specifically, the predicted rating for a firm's financial and market risk characteristics for a base year is calculated using the estimated standards for that year and is compared with the predicted ratings using the standards for later and earlier years as determined by the unconstrained probit models; both of these predictions utilise the firm characteristics of the base year. Again, keep the data the same, but vary the year of the rating standard.

The results of this analysis (Table 7) are very similar to the earlier analysis using the pooled probit model (Table 5). For example, using ten-year-later standards, the year-by-year probit models show that an average of 54.0% of the firms would have received lower predicted ratings. The corresponding percentage for the pooled probit model is similar, 46.5%. Using the ten-year-earlier standards, the year-by-year models show that an average 58.0% of the firms would have received greater predicted ratings. The corresponding percentage for the pooled probit model is again similar, 47.9%.

Except for the steady increase in average market value, there are no obvious time trends in the variables (Table 8). This time trend in average market values could conceivably cause the observed decline in the intercepts in the pooled regression. The argument is the following: Assuming that the correct explanatory variable is not the market value itself, but rather its deviation from the average market value in any year. Since the coefficient on the market value is constrained to be the same over time, the product of the

Table 8. Time-series behaviour of the mean values of the accounting and market value variables used in the probit analyses, 1978–95

This table presents the mean values of the four accounting variables and the market value variable used in the probit model for three periods: 1978–83, 1984–89, and 1990–95. Because of the standardisation of beta and the standard error from the market model, the mean values of these two variables are always one.

	Period		
Variable	1978–83	1984–89	1990–95
Interest coverage	6.80	5.94	6.18
Operating margin	0.19	0.19	0.21
LT debt leverage	0.23	0.21	0.23
Total debt leverage	0.30	0.29	0.32
Market value	6.20	6.67	7.03

203

THE DECLINING
CREDIT QUALITY OF
US CORPORATE
DEBT: MYTH OR
REALITY?

coefficient and market value will be relatively low in the early years of the sample and relatively high in the later years. The relatively larger intercepts at the beginning of the sample and the relatively smaller intercepts at the end of the sample adjust for under- and overstatement.

To assess this argument, the pooled ordered probit model is rerun with the market value variable replaced by its deviation from the yearly average market value. The mathematical effect of this replacement is to shift each year's intercept upward by the product of the average market value for that year and 0.194, the coefficient from the ordered probit model. The new intercepts still decline steadily with time. The rank order correlation is -0.99, which is the same as before and is statistically significant at the 1% level.

THE SECOND CRITICISM

The second criticism is that some critical variable is missing and that the mean value of the variable changes monotonically over time. This criticism can never be answered directly without defining the omitted variable itself. However, the model does contain an internal prediction that can be validated with other data. Specifically, to maintain its rating a firm would have to increase its creditworthiness over time as measured by the variables used in the probit model.

To check this prediction, firms are divided into three groups: those whose current rating is lower than the rating five years earlier, those whose current rating is equal to the rating five years earlier, and those whose current rating is higher than the rating five years earlier. This requirement that a firm have a current rating and a rating five years earlier introduces a potential post-selection bias in the sample, but is unavoidable in validating the model through an analysis of what happens to an individual firm over time. To allow for both possible upgrades and downgrades, the sample for validation includes only bonds rated AA or A five years earlier.

If grading standards are becoming more stringent over time, the difference between the predicted rating using the standards of the current year and the predicted rating using the standards of five years earlier should on average be negative when these predictions are based on firm variables of five years earlier. Even if a firm were subsequently upgraded, the average should still be negative as the firm variables are those of five years earlier, not the improved current variables. As predicted, this average difference is negative regardless of the relation of the current rating to the rating five years earlier (Table 9).

For a firm to maintain or improve its ratings, it would have had to improve its creditworthiness as measured by the firm variables that are used in the probit model. Thus, the difference between the predicted rating on the basis of its current firm variables and the predicted rating on the basis of its firm variables five years earlier where the rating standards are the current standards should vary with the way its actual rating has changed. In fact, this difference is 0.21 when the bond ratings are upgraded. This difference should be 1.0 (or more if some firms are upgraded by two categories) if the model predicts the upgrades perfectly. This difference is 0.11 when the bond ratings are unchanged and -0.24 when the bond ratings are downgraded. These latter two differences would be 0.0 and -1.0 or less if the model predicted perfectly. Although the model is not perfect, it does predict in the correct direction according to the actual change in the rating.

An examination of the changes in the firm variables themselves are consistent with these predictions with the exception of beta. Those firms with upgraded debt show the greatest improvement in their firm characteristics over the five years. Those firms with no change in their debt ratings also show improvement in their firm characteristics, which is consistent with the hypothesis that a firm had to show some improvement just to maintain its rating in the environment of increasingly more stringent standards. Those firms with actual downgrades have worse firm data than five years earlier.

In sum, the predictions of the probit model, both conditional on the actual rating changes and unconditionally, are as expected, which provides validation of the model. Further, the changes in firm characteristics are consistent with actual changes in ratings and the predictions of the model.

204

THE DECLINING
CREDIT QUALITY OF
US CORPORATE
DEBT: MYTH OR
REALITY?

Table 9. Average changes in predicted ratings and firm data from current year to five years earlier cross-classified by actual rating changes for bonds rated AA or A five years earlier

The purpose of this table is to validate the pooled probit model according to the actual change in rating. Panel A shows that regardless of the actual change in rating, the predicted rating using the current standard is lower than the predicted rating using the five-year standard, where both predictions are based on the firm data of five years earlier. Panel B shows that using the current standard, the predicted rating using current firm data is greater than the predicted rating using firm data of five years earlier when there is an actual upgrade, and the reverse when there is an actual downgrade. Panel C shows the change in average values of the firm data from the current values to five years earlier as a function of the actual change in ratings. Those firms with downgrades have worsened firm data. Those with no change or upgrade in ratings have improved firm data.

	Current rating by comparison with rating five years earlier		
	Downgrade	No change	Upgrade
Panel A: Predicted rating using current rating standards less predicted rating using ratings standards of five years earlier based on firm data five years earlier	−0.20	−0.23	−0.20
Panel B: Predicted rating using current firm data less predicted rating using firm data of five years earlier based on current rating standards	−0.24	0.11	0.21
Panel C: Firm data change from five years earlier			
Interest coverage	−2.06	−0.38	3.03
Operating margin	−0.000	0.004	0.008
Long term debt leverage	0.027	−0.012	−0.035
Total debt leverage	0.029	−0.004	−0.035
Market value	0.120	0.369	0.576
Market model beta	−0.022	−0.044	0.006
Standard error	0.057	−0.026	−0.004
Number of firms	716	1867	212

Conclusion

There is a widespread belief among practitioners that the credit quality of US corporate debt has declined over the recent past, and trends in the actual bond ratings are consistent with this belief. However, part of this decline in the level of actual bond ratings could be due to the use of more stringent rating standards in assigning ratings. The empirical results of this paper, which are based on an analysis of a panel of firms over the 18 years from 1973 through 1995, are consistent with this explanation. The data suggest that if it were not for the use of more stringent rating standards, the level of bond ratings might have actually been higher today than in the past.

As a word of caution, all of these results are conditional on the firm characteristics that this study utilises. Another explanation of the empirical results is that this study has omitted a key variable or variables whose yearly average values display a time trend. In this case, the changing intercept in the model could be just compensating for such omitted variables. If this explanation is correct, then the firm characteristics used in this study and similar variants used in prior studies are inadequate to model the rating process. However, analyses in the test suggest that the results are robust to this criticism.

Another explanation of the results is that the meanings of the firm variables used in this study have changed over time. For example, it could be that an interest coverage of 5.0 ten years ago indicated a higher creditworthiness than the same value does today. But even so, the main conclusion of this study is unaltered. In terms of the explanatory variables used in the analysis, the rating standards have become more stringent. In this case, however, the greater stringency would be warranted, and historical comparisons of firm data would be misleading.

Although the main focus of this study is the changing standards used in assigning ratings, the study finds evidence, perhaps for the first time, that accounting ratios and market-based risk measures are more informative for larger companies than smaller companies. If true, the implications are broad. Depending on their design, cross-sectional

205

THE DECLINING
CREDIT QUALITY OF
US CORPORATE
DEBT: MYTH OR
REALITY?

empirical studies of corporations may need to model explicitly the informativeness of the explanatory variables. Regulatory agencies might wish to impose different reporting requirements on corporations as a function of their size.

1 *In subsequent analyses, the slope coefficients in the linear part of the model are also allowed to vary.*

2 *The pre-tax interest coverage is defined as the ratio of* [operating income after depreciation (178) + interest expense (15)] *to* [interest expense (15)], *where the numbers in parentheses are the COMPUSTAT item numbers. The ratio of operating income to sales is defined as that of* [operating income before depreciation (13)] *to* [sales – net (12)]. *The ratio of long-term debt to assets is defined as that of* [long-term debt – total (9)] *to* [assets – total (6)]. *The ratio of total debt to capitalisation is defined as that of* [long-term, debt – total (9) + debt in current liabilities (34) + short-term borrowings – average (104)] *to* [assets – total (6)].

3 *The study also measures firm size by natural logarithm of total assets similarly deflated. When this variable is included in the same probit models with the market value variable, it is insignificant. Thus, the analyses reported in the text do not include this alternative measure of firm size.*

4 *COMPUSTAT contains S&P bond ratings, but only for the last ten years. By using the Warga file, the panel can be extended back eight more years.*

5 *The data for December 1984 are incomplete, so the ratings for November 1984 are substituted.*

6 *See Maddala (1983) and Hausman, Lo and MacKinlay (1992) for details on maximum likelihood estimation of the ordered probit model.*

7 *To calculate the Newey–West standard errors, the partial derivatives of the log likelihood function are interpreted as the moment conditions in Hansen's (1982) generalised method of moments techniques. A lag length of 30 is used, with the data ordered first by firm and then by year. The standard errors are consistent as the number of firms increases. The appendix of Campbell, Lo and MacKinlay (1997) provides further discussion of this approach..*

BIBLIOGRAPHY

Altman, E., and S. Katz, 1976, "Statistical Bond Rating Classification Using Financial and Accounting Data", in *Topical Research in Accounting*, M. Schiff and G. Sorter (eds), (New York: NYU Press).

Ang, J., and K. Patel, 1975, "Bond Rating Methods: Comparison and Validation", *Journal of Finance* 30, pp. 631-40.

Campbell, J. Y., A. W. Lo and A. C. MacKinlay, 1997, *Econometrics of Financial Markets* (Princeton, NJ: Princeton University Press).

Dimson, E., 1979, "Risk Measurement when Shares Are Subject to Infrequent Trading", *Journal of Financial Economics* 7, pp. 197-226.

Ederington, L., 1985, "Classification Models and Bond Ratings", *The Financial Review* 20, pp. 237-62.

Froot, K., D. Scharfstein and J. Stein, 1993, "Risk Management: Coordinating Corporate Investment and Financing Policies", *Journal of Finance* 48, pp. 1629-58.

Gertler, M., 1988, "Financial Structure and Aggregate Economic Activity: An Overview", *Journal of Money, Credit and Banking* 20, pp. 559-96.

Grier, P., and S. Katz, 1976, "The Differential Effects of Bond Rating Changes on Industrial and Public Utility Bonds by Maturity", *Journal of Business* 49, pp. 226-39.

Grundy, B., 1997, "Preferreds and Taxes: The Relative Price of Dividends and Coupons", Working paper, University of Pennsylvania.

Hand, J., R. Holthausen and R. Leftwich, 1992, "The Effect of Bond Rating Agency Announcements on Bond and Stock Prices", *The Journal of Finance* 47, pp. 733-52.

Hansen, L., 1982, "Large Sampling Properties of Generalised Method of Moments Estimators", *Econometrica* 50, pp. 1029-54.

Hausman, J., A. Lo and A. C. MacKinlay, 1992, "An Ordered Probit Analysis of Transaction Stock Prices", *Journal of Financial Economics* 31, pp. 319-79.

Hickman, W., 1958, *Corporate Bond Quality and Investor Experience* (Princeton, NJ: Princeton University Press).

206

THE DECLINING
CREDIT QUALITY OF
US CORPORATE
DEBT: MYTH OR
REALITY?

Horrigan, J., 1966, "The Determination of Long-term Credit Standing with Financial Ratios", *Journal of Accounting Research* 4 (supp.), pp. 44–62.

Ingram, R., L. Brooks and R. Copeland, 1983, "The Information Content of Municipal Bond Rating Changes: A Note", *Journal of Finance* 38, pp. 997–1003.

Kao, C., and C. Wu, 1990, "Two-step Estimation of Linear Models with Ordinal Unobserved Variables: The Case of Corporate Bonds", *Journal of Business & Economic Statistics* 8, pp. 317–25.

Kaplan, R., and G. Urwitz, 1979, "Statistical Models of Bond Ratings: A Methodological Inquiry", *Journal of Business* 52, pp. 231–61.

Katz, S., 1974, "The Price Adjustment Process of Bonds to Rating Reclassifications: A Test of Bond Market Efficiency", *Journal of Finance* 29, pp. 551–9.

Lucas, D., and J. Lonski, 1992, "Changes in Corporate Credit Quality 1970–1990", *Journal of Fixed Income* 1, pp. 7–14.

Maddala, G., 1983, *Limited Dependent and Qualitative Variables in Econometrics*, Econometric Society Monograph No. 3 (Cambridge, UK: Cambridge University Press).

Newey, W., and K. West, 1987, "A Simple, Positive Semi-definite, Heteroskedasticity and Autocorrelation Consistent Covariance Matrix", *Econometrica* 55, pp. 703–8.

Pender, K., 1992, "Demystifying the Ratings Game", *The San Francisco Chronicle*, February 17.

Pinches, G., and K. Mingo, 1973, "A Multivariate Analysis of Industrial Bond Ratings", *Journal of Finance* 28, pp. 1–18.

Pinches, G., and K. Mingo, 1975, "A Note on the Role of Subordination in Determining Industrial Bond Ratings", *The Journal of Finance* 30, pp. 201–6.

Pogue, T., and R. Soldofsky, 1969, "What Is in a Bond Rating?", *Journal of Financial and Quantitative Analysis* 4, 201–28.

Standard & Poor's, 1996, *Standard & Poor's Corporate Ratings Criteria* (New York, NY).

Wakeman, L., 1978, "Bond Rating Agencies and the Capital Markets", Working paper, University of Rochester.

Weinstein, M., 1977, "The Effect of a Rating Change Announcement on Bond Price", *Journal of Financial Economics* 5, pp. 329–50.

West, R., 1970, "An Alternative Approach Predicting Corporate Bond Ratings", *Journal of Accounting Research* 7, pp. 118–27.

15

Refining Ratings

Ross Miller

Miller Risk Advisors

ifficulties in quantifying credit risk mean it is measured with far less precision than market risk. Financial institutions that develop their own internal measures of credit risk usually use a "1" to "9" scale of creditworthiness for their exposures, taking their lead from the rating agencies' alphabetical scales, eg, from triple A to D. Even with the refinement of "notches", designated with a "+" or "-", the vast universe of credit risk is reduced to at most 30 levels. In reality, the broad range of pricing for corporate debt obligations in the market-place indicates that there are far more than 30 categories of credit risk. In the high-yield debt market, the illusion of "stability" provided by a broad categorisation scheme can easily be outweighed by its imprecision.

The better precision of market risk measurements is mainly due to the rich body of quantitative theory that has been developed for it. In particular, there are many cases where the arbitrage-based techniques of option valuation theory can be applied to market risk. Despite the numerous shortcomings of this theory (elaborated upon in this and other journals), its practical application leads to a fairly precise quantification of risk in a wide variety of settings.

Fortunately, these same option-theory roots can be applied to the quantification of credit risk in corporate settings. Indeed, the modern theory's developers – Fischer Black & Myron Scholes (1973) and Robert Merton (1973) – noted in their earliest works on options that the equity in any firm could itself be valued as an option. The value of the equity holder's implicit option is directly related to the likelihood of financial distress, at which point they will choose to limit any further liability from their stake in the firm by "putting" it at a price of zero to the debt holders. Generally, such financial distress will also result in a shortfall to the debt holders and the firm will default on its debt. Hence, the credit risk of the firm, ie, its propensity to default, is directly and quantitatively linked to the value of its equity. (It is usually even more difficult to find the default probability from debt prices because historically debt has been much less liquid than equity.) In those cases where the value of the equity is directly observable, such as when it takes the form of an actively traded security, one should be able, in principle, to "reverse engineer" the probability distribution of default from the market value of the equity, given the volatility and financial structure of the firm's assets. Without delving into the details here, the option-valuation approach to credit risk is far more difficult to make practical than its market risk counterpart.

This chapter develops and applies the statistical machinery needed to determine whether a particular quantitative method of measuring credit risk, using option valuation or other methods, represents a refinement over broader categorisation methods. Here the term "refinement" is used in a technical sense of partitioning the creditworthiness of firms in a way that yields more information than the original partition, in this case the alphabet-based ratings. This is a particularly challenging statistical problem because defaults are infrequent occurrences and the error structure of their estimates cannot be assumed to be normal or to follow any other regular distribution. The solu-

This paper was first published in Risk *magazine, August 1998.*

tion to this problem is to get the most out of the existing data and to apply non-parametric tests (which do not rely on distributional assumptions) to them.

We describe here a methodology for testing whether a quantitative credit rating system is a statistically significant refinement of a broader rating system. We developed it as part of an independent study commissioned by the Capital Markets Assurance Corporation (CapMAC), a financial guarantee company based in New York (which has since merged with another financial guarantee company, MBIA). CapMAC was specifically interested in KMV Corporation's Credit Monitor system – the first options-based credit rating system – and how it compared with Standard & Poor's (S&P's) notch-level ratings for US companies.[1]

S&P ratings are designed to provide intermediate to long-run indications of credit-worthiness.[2] The ratings (in descending order of credit quality) are: AAA, AA+, AA, AA–, A+, A, A–, BBB+, BBB, BBB–, BB+, BB, BB–, B+, B, B– and so on. We did not use ratings below B– (CCC+, CCC, etc) in the study because of the sparseness of these data. We used S&P's senior unsecured debt ratings as reported by S&P's Compustat database service.

In contrast, KMV's ratings take the form of expected default frequencies (EDFs), which range from 0.02% (2 basis points) to 20% and are reported with basis-point precision, making for 1,999 different possible ratings. As the likelihood of default varies over the business cycle, there is no fixed mapping between KMV and S&P ratings. KMV provides EDFs for horizons ranging from one to five years – see Kealhofer, Kwok & Weng (1998) for more information about Credit Monitor and the relationship between EDFs and agency ratings. For this study, the one-year EDF, for which KMV provides the most information, is used. Although the EDF provides a cardinal measure of credit risk, the nonparametric methods used in this study will only examine its ordinal properties relative to S&P ratings.[3]

The test of KMV's predictive power relative to an S&P rating can be expressed as the following null hypothesis: given an S&P rating for a company, the KMV rating (EDF) provides no additional information about the likelihood the firm will default over a specified period of time. Table 1 gives a grid of the EDFs for all companies rated by KMV Credit Monitor at the end of 1989 with an S&P rating of B–. The 87 EDFs are in ascending order (descending creditworthiness). The table also shows which of the 87 defaulted in the following three years. The null hypothesis states that the pattern of defaults should be random within that cohort; however, it is clear from the table that defaults came disproportionately from the companies with the highest EDFs. Of course, this is a single cohort at a single point in time. We will next show how to aggregate all cohorts at all points in time into a single non-parametric statistical test of the null hypothesis.

To do this, we again used companies with both S&P ratings and KMV Credit Monitor EDFs. This time we studied US companies at the end of each month from June 1986 to November 1996 – a total of more than 1,000. Defaults were taken from KMV's default

---

Table 1. The pattern of defaults: 87 companies' "Expected default frequencies" with actual defaults shown for 1990–1992

0.02	0.04	0.13	0.15	0.16	0.16	0.26	0.26	0.28	0.28
0.30	0.30	0.43	0.48	0.51	0.51	0.56	0.63	0.65	0.68†
0.68	0.71	0.74	0.75	0.75	0.76	0.79	0.80	0.86	0.87
0.88	0.88	0.90	0.95	0.99	1.00	1.12	1.12	1.17	1.20
1.20	1.22	1.32	1.33†	1.35†	1.43	1.58	1.72	1.74	1.75
1.87	1.92	1.96	1.99†	2.06	2.07	2.16†	2.23*	2.54	2.64
2.65	2.71†	2.80	3.01	3.03	3.06	3.22	3.31	3.32‡	3.32
3.49	3.63	3.69	3.81	3.91	4.02*	4.12	4.13	4.97	5.75
6.95†	7.09*	7.76†	7.88	8.75	10.42	17.02*			

Note: all companies rated B– by S&P at the end of 1989.
Unmarked: no defaults 1990–1992; *defaulted in 1990; †defaulted in 1991; ‡defaulted in 1992.

database, including those reported by the rating agencies for rated issues as well as those for companies without rated debt.

The trick to aggregating the KMV data over both time and S&P rating categories is to convert each EDF into an ordinal ranking within its month and (notch) rating cohort. A natural ordinal measure is a percentile rank – with 100 being the best (lowest EDF) and 0 the worst (highest EDF). A means for calculating the percentile that both takes account of ties in ranking, which are quite rare for companies with higher EDFs, and is consistent across cohorts of different sizes is given by:

$$\text{Percentile} = 100 \left(\frac{\frac{\text{Worse}}{\text{Total}} + \frac{\text{Total} - \text{Better}}{\text{Total}}}{2} \right)$$

$$= 50 \left(\frac{\text{Worse} + \text{Total} - \text{Better}}{\text{Total}} \right)$$

where Total is the size of the cohort, Worse is the number of the firms in the cohort with worse credit ratings (EDFs) and Better is the number of firms with better ratings.

For example, in a cohort with 20 companies (the smallest allowed in the study), the company with the lowest EDF (assuming it is the only one) has Better = 0 and Worse = 19, so, by substitution above, its Percentile = 97.5. If two companies are tied for third and fourth best EDFs, they would have Better = 2 and Worse = 16, giving Percentile = 85. The reason we set a minimum size for the cohort was to make the distribution of percentiles as continuous as possible, facilitating meaningful comparisons between cohorts. Also note that by converting an EDF to a percentile, we are completely eliminating any bias that might result from EDFs as a whole being more or less optimistic about the overall rate of defaults than S&P ratings.

The null hypothesis that we wish to test is that EDFs provide no more information than is contained in S&P ratings. Given the way the percentiles were constructed, the null hypothesis implies that the percentiles of the population of defaulting firms will have a flat (or uniform) distribution.[4] Furthermore, this distribution should be uniform any number of months prior to default.

The histograms in Figure 1 show that at six months prior to default, this distribution is obviously far from uniform. As the default time nears, the distribution becomes less uniform, which is what one would expect for any system with predictive power, ie, the nearer the event, the greater the predictive power. Nonetheless, just from looking at the graph of the distribution, it is apparent that there is still some predictive power 36 months prior to default.

Applying Kolmogorov–Smirnoff

The Kolmogorov–Smirnoff test is used to quantify the degree to which EDFs provide information not contained in S&P ratings. This test is a basic and well-understood tool of nonparametric statistics (see Siegel & Castellan, 1988, for details). In the one-sample version, we can determine the significance with which a sample of data differs from a given baseline frequency distribution – in this case the uniform distribution.

The Kolmogorov–Smirnoff test works by calculating the maximum distance between the observed distribution of EDFs and the uniform distribution. This maximum distance is known as the D-statistic. By aggregating over all months and ratings we get at least 50 data points, for which both KMV and S&P ratings are known: six, 12, 18, 24, 36 and 48 months prior to default, more than enough to perform a meaningful statistical test.

The results of this test are shown in Table 2. KMV Credit Monitor has very strong predictive value for up to 18 months prior to default. The predictive power

Table 2. Statistical significance of KMV default predictions

Months to default	Number of observations	Kolmogorov–Smirnoff D-statistic	Significance level (%)
6	66	0.5042	>99
12	66	0.4409	>99
18	66	0.3465	>99
24	66	0.2280	99
36	71	0.1775	95
48	54	0.1236	<80

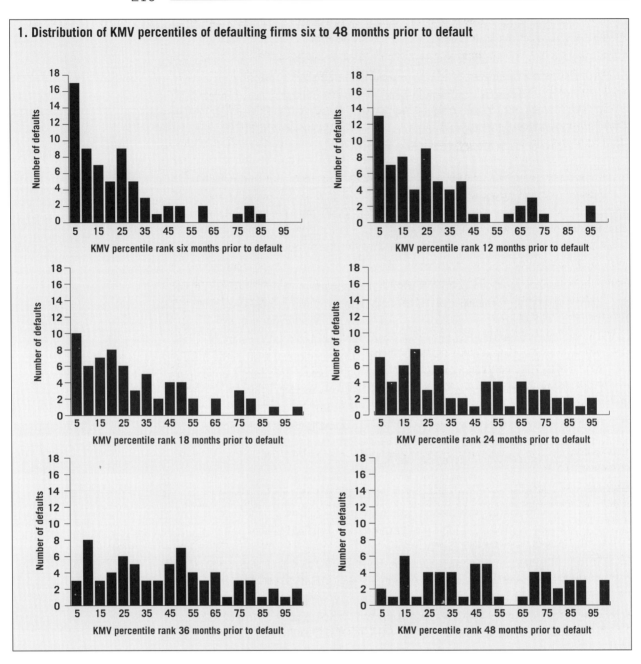

1. Distribution of KMV percentiles of defaulting firms six to 48 months prior to default

remains statistically significant out to 36 months. At 48 months, the significance level finally drops below 95%.[5]

An alternative nonparametric approach to showing the predictive power of EDFs relative to S&P ratings is to apply a binomial test to a division of the sample into two parts, with the fiftieth percentile as a natural cut-off point. The results of this test, which are not given here, as well as those for other natural percentile cut-offs (90th, 75th, etc), confirm the results of the Kolmogorov–Smirnoff test. The advantage of the test is that it does not require the arbitrary choice of a percentile cut-off.

Discussion

This paper has demonstrated a statistical methodology for inferring that a quantitative credit rating system is a refinement of a traditional rating system, ie, it provides additional information. This demonstration was made with the use of a single, innocuous statistical assumption – that the number of firms in a cohort is large enough to make the distribution of percentiles nearly continuous. Generating results beyond those given here almost always comes at the cost of additional assumptions that could affect the validity of the analysis. For example, it is natural to try to turn the analysis around and ask whether, for a given EDF, a letter rating provides additional information. To do this analysis, the technique developed above cannot be applied without making further assumptions. The problem here is that while each letter rating-based cohort has associated with it a near-continuum of EDFs (see Table 1), virtually all cohorts based on a single EDF will contain few, if any, companies because the number of companies is small relative to the number of possible EDFs. The remedy of grouping EDFs together to get around this problem will not only require the use of arbitrary cut-offs but will also throw away information that may then be incorrectly attributed to the letter rating.

Additional assumptions are required to gauge the relative contribution of both the letter-based and quantitative rating systems simultaneously, using regression analysis. In a regression, the two rating systems are used to generate two or more dependent variables. The independent variable is then either the default rate (for grouped data) or a dummy variable representing default (for individual data). Whichever way the analysis is set up, explicit assumptions as to the error distribution of the independent variables must be made to perform the regression. Given that neither rating is generated by a "natural" process that can be expected to have a predictable error term, eg, normally distributed, the results are likely to be quite sensitive to the distributional assumptions that underlie the regression.

On a more positive note, the analysis performed in this paper can be extended to compare two different quantitative credit rating systems with a common letter-based baseline.[6] Such a comparison can be directly implemented using the two-sample version of the Kolmogorov–Smirnoff test, a standard textbook extension of the single-sample version that we used.

1 *All resources and data for this study were provided by CapMAC, who contacted KMV directly for the use of its historical data.*

2 *Additional credit information is available from S&P in the form of CreditWatch indications (positive, negative, stable and developing). However, S&P could not provide this data in a form suitable for a statistical study.*

3 *A rigorous test of the cardinal properties of KMV's Credit Monitor requires more data than was used in this study.*

4 *It is safe to ignore any small error that may be introduced because of the finite sample size and the possibility of ties in rankings*

5 *Technically, the test only shows that the distribution of percentiles is not uniform. However, it is clear from Figure 1 that the difference is such that it confirms that EDFs provide predictive value directly.*

6 *Unfortunately, no other vendors of quantitative credit rating systems contacted by CapMAC would permit the general release of results from such a comparative test.*

BIBLIOGRAPHY

Black, F., and M. Scholes, 1973, "The pricing of options and corporate liabilities", *Journal of Political Economy* 81, pp. 637–59.

Kealhofer, S., S. Kwok and W. Weng, 1998, "Uses and abuses of bond default rates", *CreditMetrics Monitor,* first quarter, pp. 37–55.

Merton, R., 1973, "Theory of rational option pricing", *Bell Journal of Economics and Management Science* 4, pp. 141–83.

Siegel, S., and N. Castellan, 1988, *Nonparametric statistics for the behavioral sciences,* McGraw-Hill, second edition.

CREDIT RISK MITIGATION ALTERNATIVES

Introduction

Credit Risk Mitigation Alternatives

David Shimko

U p to this point the articles in this book have focused on the measurement of credit risk. We now shift our focus to the management of credit risk. This section looks at ways of mitigating risk, focusing on credit derivatives.

Traditionally, there have been several ways to manage credit risk. The first and most obvious method is diversification, whereby those who own portfolios of risky bonds avoid over-concentration in particular credits and ensure that they have investments in a large universe of securities.

A second traditional approach is the insurance or guarantee applied to individual bonds. A third approach – relatively more recent – is an insurance contract on a portfolio of risky bonds. A fourth approach, inspired by option pricing theory, provides hedges for portfolios of bonds by short-selling stocks of the corresponding companies. In the spirit of the third and fourth approaches, a market began to develop for credit derivatives – instruments whose payoffs are contingent on credit-related events.

The simplest such instrument is an insurance policy. For example, if you owned AT&T bonds, you might want to purchase a derivative that would pay you $10 million in the event of a default by AT&T to compensate you for the ensuing loss in value of your bond portfolio. Or, you might want a derivative that paid you the lost value on the bonds only in the event of default, not fixing the $10 million figure. In either case, you could design an instrument to fit the risk profile you were trying to acquire or to shed.

Credit derivatives hit Wall Street with great furore in about 1995. Clients of Wall Street firms were impressed that they could obtain protection against risks they thought they had to bear. For example, a fund manager need not unload his over-bought position in K-Mart bonds if all he has to do is to buy credit derivatives to protect against a loss in a portion of their value. Furthermore, the Wall Street firms themselves could use credit derivatives to modify the credit risks of their own loan portfolios.

The creation of credit derivatives increased the need for bullet-proof analytics. Up until this point, if one held a bond it was not really necessary to distinguish between the probability of default and the loss on default; it was really only the product of the two that mattered. However, if you have to pay out in the event of a default or pay an amount related to the loss on default, the distinction suddenly becomes crucial.

The growth of credit derivatives and their supporting analytics is reminiscent of the growth of the option markets with option analytics. We can expect this trend to continue.

The first paper in this section is by Robert Jarrow and Stuart Turnbull, "Pricing Derivatives on Financial Securities Subject to Credit Risk", first published in 1995. Their study straddles this and the previous section because the results can be used not only to price risky bonds but also to price derivatives on risky bonds. The theoretical content is substantial, and the full potential has yet to be developed.

INTRODUCTION

Jarrow and Turnbull assert that earlier models of risky coupon debt, as pointed out by Robert Geske (1977), generally require a compound option approach to value the debt. This is cumbersome and quantitatively difficult – particularly when there are many coupons, each of which is an option to default on subsequent coupon payments! Furthermore, in valuing any security other than the most senior debt instrument of a firm, one must value all the other instruments senior in priority to the instrument under consideration. Their approach avoids these problems and leads to a far more analytically tractable approach.

Critics have pointed out that Jarrow and Turnbull's approach suffers from an exogenous determination of the payout to the security in the event of default. The authors recognise this limitation but counter that in this new world of US bankruptcy law absolute priority is no longer absolute and managers' claims against the firm may be given arbitrary weight (arbitrary, at least, from the viewpoint of the modeller). One problem that was not resolved in this paper is the importance of their assumption on the assumed independence of the payout on default from the timing of default.

If one is willing to make the assumptions in the last paragraph, the results are theoretically very elegant. In particular, Jarrow and Turnbull show that the price of a risky coupon bond is the sum of the present value of its coupons, with explicit formulas for the discount factors of each of the coupons. This is therefore much more subtle than the usual discounting methods taught to MBA students (ie, discount coupons at a higher rate). But it has the theoretical robustness of the compound option approach with the analytical simplicity of the Finance 101 formulas.

The article is not for the analytically faint-hearted. However, if you have the inclination and analytic arrows in your quiver, further reading of Jarrow and Turnbull is well worth while. A parallel strain of research was developed by Darrell Duffie and Kenneth Singleton and explained in their 1997 working paper "Econometric Modelling of the Term Structures of Defaultable Bonds".

Duffie brings the analytics down a notch in "Credit Swap Valuation", published earlier this year and reproduced here as chapter 17. This paper provides a solid foundation for the quantitative professional looking to build up his or her skills in the valuation of credit-sensitive instruments and derivatives on those instruments. It begins with a "starter case" wherein counterparties to the swap exchange a periodic cash premium in exchange for a (possible) lump-sum default-triggered payment. The cases graduate to others that include accrued swap premia between payments and accrued interest on the underlying notes. Then, the reader learns how to use a reference floating-rate payment instead of a fixed rate.

Far from being a review of previously rehashed materials, Duffie's paper goes on to explain how to calculate implied hazard rates on bonds, a concept parallel to Jarrow and Turnbull's cumulated conditional default rates. It ends with a build-up to a term-structure of hazard rates, a key component in building a credit curve for valuation.

Some readers will welcome the further simplification of the Duffie and Duffie–Singleton papers that is presented in chapter 18: "Constructing a Credit Curve" (1998) by David Li of the RiskMetrics Group. Li introduces his topic with a discussion of credit derivatives, suggesting that these are becoming so important in emerging markets that their notional volumes may well exceed the actual amount of emerging market debt issued!

For the sake of exposition, Li assumes that there is a sequence of bonds of different maturity but equal credit quality on a given name. This is an unrealistic assumption at best, since a bond that matures before another is *de facto* more senior. Nevertheless, the simplification greatly facilitates the analysis that follows: a primer on how to build a credit curve in the spirit of Duffie–Singleton.

As in the Duffie piece earlier, the glue that holds the analysis together is the hazard rate curve, ie, the probability that a firm will default in a given period provided that it has not defaulted by the beginning of that period. Li explains the theoretical reasoning – but, importantly for practitioners, uses a numerical example that readers can replicate for themselves to make sure they understand the fundamental concepts.

Li rightly argues that this calculation is the basis for all credit derivative valuation, but he also recognises that the assumption of known recovery in default may limit one's complete confidence in this technique.

The section ends with Tanya Beder and Frank Iacono's 1997 article "The Good, the Bad – and the Ugly?", which describes a number of pricing issues concerning credit derivatives that are usually not addressed in academic pieces. First, the authors explain the economics of credit derivatives – who uses them and why. Given these motivations, they argue convincingly that credit derivatives cannot behave as pure "derivatives" – instruments whose value is determined solely by the underlying market on which they depend. No, if a regional bank purchases credit derivatives to insulate its portfolio against losses in a local name, the incentives of the bank to manage the default process are altered. Why bother to squeeze more value out of a defaulting borrower if one has insurance to cover the loss? This well-known problem of moral hazard has not been addressed comprehensively in the credit derivatives literature, and this is a good introduction.

Beder and Iacono go on to give analysts another reason to doubt the validity of historical default data – if credit derivatives change the way institutions manage default, assumptions about default rates and recoveries made from historical data are at best questionable. The authors rightly go on to state that because of this and other factors, model risk may be a greater risk in credit derivatives than in any other market.

In summary, this section opens with theoretical treatments of pricing credit-sensitive instruments at an analytical level that will be accessible to many practitioners. Li's article provides a bridge between theory and practice, and Beder and Iacono end with a discussion of work that must be done in the future in order to produce a comprehensive model of credit derivative pricing.

BIBLIOGRAPHY

Duffie, D., and K. Singleton, 1997, "Econometric Modelling of the Term Structures of Defaultable Bonds", Working paper, Stanford University.

Geske, R., 1977, "The Valuation of Corporate Liabilities as Compound Options", *Journal of Financial and Quantitative Analysis*.

16

Pricing Derivatives on Financial Securities Subject to Credit Risk

Robert A. Jarrow and Stuart M. Turnbull

Johnson Graduate School of Management, Cornell University;
School of Business, Queen's University, Ontario

The purpose of this chapter is to provide a new theory for pricing and hedging derivative securities involving credit risk. Two sources of credit risk are identified and analysed. The first is where the asset underlying the derivative security may default, paying off less than promised. This is the case, for example, with embedded options on corporate debt. The second is the credit risk introduced by the writer of the derivative security, who may also default. Examples include over-the-counter writers of options on Eurodollar futures, swaps and swaptions.

For pricing derivative securities involving credit risk, there are currently two approaches. The first views these derivatives as contingent claims not on the financial securities themselves, but as "compound options" on the assets underlying the financial securities. This is the case, for example, with the pricing of embedded options on corporate debt (see Merton, 1974, 1977; Black and Cox, 1976; Ho and Singer, 1982; Chance, 1990; and Kim, Ramaswamy and Sundaresan, 1993) or the pricing of vulnerable options (see Johnson and Stulz, 1987). In practice, however, the valuation methodology is difficult to use. First, the assets underlying the financial security are often not tradable and therefore their values are not observable. This makes application of the theory and estimation of the relevant parameters problematic. Second, as in the case of corporate debt, all of the other liabilities of the firm senior to the corporate debt must first (and simultaneously) be valued. This generates significant computational difficulties. As a result, this approach has not proven very effective in practice for pricing corporate liabilities (see Jones, Mason and Rosenfeld, 1984). Unfortunately, these same complications arise when this technology is applied to pricing swaps (see Cooper and Mello, 1990, 1991). It has shown more promise, however, for valuing commercial mortgages where these problems are present to a lesser extent (see Titman and Torous, 1989).

As a pragmatic alternative, the second approach to the pricing of derivative securities involving credit risk is to ignore the credit risk and price the embedded options as default-free interest rate options (see Ho and Singer, 1984, and Ramaswamy and Sundaresan, 1986). This, however, is inconsistent with the absence of arbitrage and the existence of spreads between the yields on corporate debt and Treasuries.

The purpose of this article is to present a third approach for pricing derivatives securities involving credit risk. This approach uses the foreign currency analogy of Jarrow and Turnbull (1998), which takes as given a stochastic term structure of default-free

This paper was originally published in the Journal of Finance, *Vol 50 (1), 1995, pp. 53–85, and is reprinted here with the kind permission of Blackwell Publishers. It was originally entitled "Pricing Options on Financial Securities Subject to Credit Risk." Helpful comments from an anonymous referee, the Editor of the* Journal of Finance, *the finance workshops at Cornell University, Queen's University, Warwick University and the Derivative Securities Symposium at Queen's University are gratefully acknowledged.*

PRICING
DERIVATIVES ON
FINANCIAL
SECURITIES
SUBJECT TO CREDIT
RISK

interest rates *and* a stochastic maturity-specific credit-risk spread.[1] Given these two term structures, option type features can then be priced in an arbitrage-free manner using the martingale measure technology.[2]

Three alternative approaches have recently and independently been developed for pricing derivative securities involving credit risk. These are: (i) Hull and White (1991), (ii) Litterman and Iben (1991) and (iii) Longstaff and Schwartz (1992) and Nielsen, Saá-Requejo and Santa-Clara (1993). Hull and White only study the pricing of options whose writer may default, called vulnerable options.[3] They do not price options on assets with credit risks, nor do they analyse the hedging of vulnerable options. Litterman and Iben (1991) is a limiting case of the discrete-time model presented below where there is zero payoff in default. Litterman and Iben do not study vulnerable options. The third approach is a modification of the compound options approach previously discussed. In this approach, capital structure is assumed to be irrelevant. Bankruptcy can occur at any time and is modelled by assuming that when the identical but unlevered firm's value hits some exogenous boundary, default occurs in the levered firm and the firm's debt pays off a fixed fractional amount. The valuation of options, which would require the explicit determination of the exogenous boundary, is not addressed.

The first section of this chapter provides the notation and formalises the foreign currency analogy and is followed by a section that provides the economic intuition underlying our methodology via a discrete-time model in a two-period economy. This setup allows us to demonstrate how to price and hedge derivatives written on credit-risky assets and vulnerable derivatives using standard and non-technical arguments. This model readily generalises to an arbitrary number of trading dates. A simple continuous-time model is presented in the third section. The analysis here replicates the results from the discrete-time setting. Necessary and sufficient conditions are provided for the existence and uniqueness of the equivalent martingale measure. By imposing various restrictions on the processes for the different term structures, we obtain a number of closed-form results. This section includes Johnson and Stulz (1987) as a special case. We also price equity options when there is a positive probability of default, generalising Merton's (1976) result. Additional generalisations and extensions are discussed. The final section gives a summary of our findings.

The economy

We consider a frictionless economy with a trading horizon $[0, \tau]$. The set of trading dates can be either discrete or continuous. If discrete, the set of trading dates is $\{0, 1, 2,..., \tau\}$. If continuous, the set of trading dates is the entire time interval $[0, \tau]$. Two classes of zero-coupon bonds trade.

The first class is *default-free*, zero-coupon bonds of all maturities. Let $p_0(t, T)$ be the time t dollar value of the default-free zero-coupon bond paying a certain dollar at time $T \geq t$. We assume that the zero-coupon bond prices are strictly positive, ie, $p_0(t, T) > 0$, and default-free, ie, $p_0(t, t) \equiv 1$.

A money market account can be constructed from this term structure by investing a dollar in the shortest maturity default-free zero-coupon bond and rolling it over at each future date. Let $B(t)$ denote the time t value of this money market account initialised with a dollar at time 0.

The second class is XYZ zero-coupon bonds of all maturities. These XYZ zero-coupon bonds are risky and subject to default.[4] Let $v_1(t, T)$ denote the time t value of the zero-coupon bond *promising* a dollar at date $T \geq t$. We assume that the XYZ zeros have strictly positive prices, ie, $v_1(t, T) > 0$. This restriction is imposed for analytic convenience (to avoid dividing by zeros) and is easily relaxed.

Next, to aid our intuition, to help in modelling and to facilitate estimation, we decompose these XYZ zero-coupon bonds into the product of two hypothetical quantities: a zero-coupon bond denominated in a hypothetical currency, a promised XYZ dollar called an XYZ and a price in dollars of XYZs.

221

PRICING

DERIVATIVES ON

FINANCIAL

SECURITIES

SUBJECT TO CREDIT

RISK

First, we define

$$e_1(t) \equiv v_1(t, t) \tag{1}$$

The quantity $e_1(t)$ represents the time t dollar value of one promised XYZ dollar delivered immediately (at time t) and is analogous to a spot exchange rate. If XYZ is not in default, the exchange rate will be unity as each promised XYZ dollar is actually worth a dollar. However, if XYZ is in default, then each promised XYZ dollar may be worth less than a dollar. The exact specification of this exchange rate process is a crucial step in our model and it is given in subsequent sections. Note that the spot exchange rate can alternatively be interpreted as a payoff ratio in default.

Next, we construct a hypothetical, XYZ paying zero-coupon bond. Define

$$p_1(t,T) \equiv \frac{v_1(t,T)}{e_1(t)} \tag{2}$$

This quantity is the time t value in units of XYZs, of one XYZ delivered at time T. Note that by expression (1), these zero-coupon bonds are default-free in XYZs, ie,

$$p_1(T, T) \equiv 1 \tag{3}$$

Rearranging expression (2) gives a tautological decomposition of the XYZ zero-coupon bond

$$v_1(t, T) = p_1(t, T)e_1(t) \tag{4}$$

This decomposition is useful for modelling purposes as we can use it to separately characterise the term structure of XYZs in terms of $p_1(t, T)$ and the payoff ratio $e_1(t)$. It also aids our intuition by revealing the *foreign currency analogy*, ie, the dollar value of an XYZ bond is the XYZ value of the bond times the spot exchange rate of dollars per XYZ. The foreign currency analogy is useful because foreign currency option pricing techniques are well understood (see Amin and Jarrow, 1991), and these same techniques can now be applied in a modified form to price derivatives involving credit risk.

The two-period discrete trading economy
To illustrate the foreign currency analogy as applied to credit-risky options, we first study a two-period economy. The discrete-time example selected for analysis is analytically simple, yet realistic enough that its multiperiod generalisation should prove useful in actual practice. This example is generalised to the continuous-time setting in a subsequent section.

THE SETUP
There are two time periods with trading dates $t \in \{0, 1, 2\}$. We first describe the term structure for the default-free zero-coupon bonds and then the term structure for the XYZ zero-coupon bonds.

The default-free term structure
The bond price process for default-free debt is assumed to depend only on the spot interest rate. The stochastic evolution of the default-free spot interest rate is shown in Figure 1. The current (t = 0) one period spot rate of interest is defined by

$$r(0) = \frac{1}{p_0(0,1)} \tag{5a}$$

In the "up-state," the one period spot interest rate is

1. The default-free zero-coupon bond price process for the two-period economy

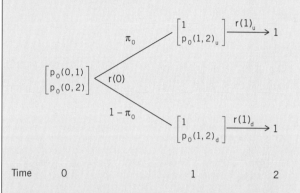

Time   0   1   2

This binomial tree describes the evolution of the spot interest rate process and the zero-coupon bond prices over the time periods 0, 1 and 2, where $p_0(t, T)_\omega$ is the time t price of a zero-coupon bond paying a sure dollar at time T given state $\omega \in \{u, d\}$, $r(t)_\omega$ is the spot interest rate at time t given state $\omega \in \{u, d\}$ and π_0 is the pseudo-probability.

2. The payoff ratio process for XYZ debt in the two-period economy

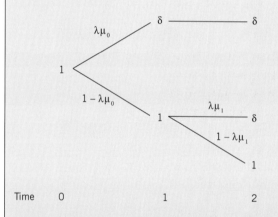

Time   0   1   2

This tree describes the evolution of the payoff ratio for XYZ debt over the time periods 0, 1 and 2, where $\lambda\mu_t$ represents the pseudo-probability at date t, and δ represents the payoff per promised dollar in default.

3. The XYZ zero-coupon bond price process for the two-period economy in XYZs

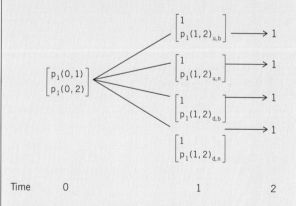

Time   0   1   2

This tree describes the evolution of the XYZ zero-coupon bond prices in XYZs over the time periods 0, 1 and 2, where $p_1(t, T)_\omega$ represents the time t price in units of XYZs of one XYZ paid at time T given state $\omega \in \{ub, un, db, dn\}$.

$$r(1)_u \equiv \frac{1}{p_0(1, 2)_u} \qquad (5b)$$

and in the "down-state"

$$r(1)_d \equiv \frac{1}{p_0(1, 2)_d} \qquad (5c)$$

The pseudo- or risk-neutral probability of state u occurring is denoted by π_0. Without loss of generality we assume that $p_0(1, 2)_u < p_0(1, 2)_d$.

The money market account's values are given by $B(0) \equiv 1$, $B(1) \equiv r(0)$, $B(2)_u \equiv r(0)r(1)_u$ and $B(2)_d \equiv r(0)r(1)_d$. Note that $B(t + 1)$ is known at time t.

The XYZ term structures

We consider zero-coupon bonds belonging to a particular risk class, which we refer to as XYZ. For the one-period zero-coupon bond, two states are possible at maturity. If default has not occurred, the payoff is the face value of the bond. If default has occurred, the payoff is less than the face value of the bond.

Modelling the actual payoff in default is a complex problem. First, the absolute priority rule is often violated.[5] Second, numerous other factors affect the payoff, such as the relative bargaining power of the different stake holders and the percentage of managerial ownership.[6] Consequently, as a first approximation, we take the payoff to the bond holder in the event of default as an exogenously given constant. This payoff per unit of face value is denoted by δ, and it is assumed to be the same for all instruments in a given credit risk class.[7]

In terms of the foreign currency analogy, the spot exchange rate at time 0 is unity, $e(0) = 1$, and at times 1 and 2 the spot exchange rate $e(t)$ takes on the two values shown in Figure 2. This discrete-time binomial process was selected to approximate a continuous-time Poisson bankruptcy process. At time 1, with pseudo-probability $\lambda\mu_0$, default occurs. If in default at time 1, XYZ remains in default at time 2 and the payoff ratio remains fixed at δ per unit of face value. At time 1, with pseudo-probability $(1 - \lambda\mu_0)$, default does not occur. Conditional upon this state, the pseudo-probability that default occurs at $t = 2$ is denoted by $\lambda\mu_1$.

The stochastic evolution of the XYZ zero-coupon bonds in the hypothetical XYZ currency is depicted in Figure 3. This figure is similar to Figure 1 for the default-free bonds except that there are now more states. The states correspond to all possible combinations of spot interest rate movements and bankruptcy. Figure 4 depicts the stochastic evolution of the XYZ zero-coupon bonds in dollars. This process is the multiplicative product of the processes in Figures 2 and 3.

It is assumed that *the spot interest rate process in*

Figure 1 and the bankruptcy process in Figure 2 are independent under the pseudo-probabilities. This is reflected by the fact that the pseudo-probabilities shown in Figure 4 are the product of the separate pseudo-probabilities in Figures 1 and 2. If the market prices of risk are non-random in the economy, then this assumption is equivalent to independence under the true (empirical) process. This assumption is imposed because it simplifies the analysis and facilitates the derivation of numerous results. Its usefulness in practice still needs to be evaluated via empirical investigation.

ARBITRAGE-FREE RESTRICTIONS

In a discrete-time, discrete-state space economy (as analysed above), Harrison and Pliska (1981) show that the non-existence of *arbitrage opportunities* is equivalent to the existence of pseudo-probabilities $\pi_0, \lambda\mu_0, \lambda\mu_1$ such that $p_0(t, 1)/B(t)$, $p_0(t, 2)/B(t)$, $v_1(t, 1)/B(t)$, and $v_1(t, 2)/B(t)$ are martingales; and that market *completeness* is equivalent to uniqueness of these pseudo-probabilities.

4. The XYZ zero-coupon bond price process for the two-period economy in dollars

This tree describes the evolution of the XYZ zero-coupon bond prices in dollars over the time periods 0, 1 and 2. This tree is the multiplicative product of the trees in Figures 2 and 3. π_0 is the pseudo-probability for the spot interest rate process, $\lambda\mu_0$ and $\lambda\mu_1$ are the default process pseudo-probabilities, δ is the payoff ratio in default, and $p_1(t, T)_\omega$ is the time t price in units of XYZs of one XYZ paid at time T given state $\omega \in \{ub, un, db, dn\}$ where $0 \le t < T \le 2$.

Relative prices being martingales implies that trading in these securities is a fair-game, ie, expected values equal current values. Completeness implies that any contingent claim written against these securities can be constructed synthetically via trading in the primary securities. This section characterises the necessary and sufficient conditions of the existence of these unique pseudo-probabilities. Thus, it characterises the necessary and sufficient conditions for arbitrage-free prices and complete markets.

We can obtain these conditions via an investigation of each separate market, the default-free bond market and the risky debt market. The pseudo-probability π_0 is determined in the default-free bond market. From Figure 1 we get

$$p_0(0, 2) = \frac{\pi_0 p_0(1, 2)_u + (1 - \pi_0)p_0(1, 2)_d}{r(0)} \qquad (6)$$

This condition states that the time 0 long-term zero-coupon bond price is its time 1 discounted expected value, using pseudo-probabilities. Using expression (6), π_0 is given by

$$\pi_0 = \frac{p_0(1, 2)_d - r(0)p_0(0, 2)}{p_0(1, 2)_d - p_0(1, 2)_u} \qquad (7)$$

Thus, π_0 exists, is unique, and satisfies $0 < \pi_0 < 1$ if and only if

$$p_0(1, 2)_u < r(0)p_0(0, 2) < p_0(1, 2)_d \qquad (8)$$

These are the standard conditions. They state that the long-term zero-coupon bond should not be dominated by the short-term zero-coupon bond. It earns more return in one state (d) and less in the other (u).

As the time 0 prices for risky debt depend on their time 1 prices, we must first analyse the time 1 risky debt market. This market determines the time 1 pseudo-probability $(\lambda\mu_1)$. From Figure 4 we get

$$v_1(1, 2)_{u,b} = \delta p_1(1, 2)_{u,b} = \frac{\delta}{r(1)_u} \qquad (9a)$$

$$v_1(1, 2)_{u,n} = p_1(1, 2)_{u,n} = \frac{\lambda\mu_1\delta + (1 - \lambda\mu_1)}{r(1)_u} \qquad (9b)$$

224

PRICING

DERIVATIVES ON

FINANCIAL

SECURITIES

SUBJECT TO CREDIT

RISK

$$v_1(1,2)_{d,b} = \delta p_1(1,2)_{d,b} = \frac{\delta}{r(1)_d} \tag{9c}$$

$$v_1(1,2)_{d,n} = p_1(1,2)_{d,n} = \frac{\lambda \mu_1 \delta + (1 - \lambda \mu_1)}{r(1)_d} \tag{9d}$$

Here again, the time 1 long-term XYZ bond price is its time 2 discounted expected value, using the pseudo-probabilities.

Using expression (9), $\lambda \mu_1$ is given by

$$\lambda \mu_1 = \frac{1 - p_1(1,2)_{u,n} \, r(1)_u}{1 - \delta} = \frac{1 - p_1(1,2)_{d,n} \, r(1)_d}{1 - \delta} \tag{10}$$

Thus, $\lambda \mu_1$ exists, is unique, and satisfies $0 < \lambda \mu_1 < 1$ if and only if

$$p_1(1,2)_{u,b} = \frac{1}{r(1)_u} \tag{11a}$$

$$p_1(1,2)_{d,b} = \frac{1}{r(1)_d} \tag{11b}$$

$$\frac{\delta}{r(1)_u} < p_1(1,2)_{u,n} < \frac{1}{r(1)_u} \tag{11c}$$

$$\frac{\delta}{r(1)_d} < p_1(1,2)_{d,n} < \frac{1}{r(1)_d} \tag{11d}$$

$$r(1)_u \, p_1(1,2)_{u,n} = r(1)_d \, p_1(1,2)_{d,n} \tag{11e}$$

Conditions (11a) and (11b) show that in the state of bankruptcy the default-free bonds in units of dollars and the XYZ denominated XYZ bonds are equal. This is because there is no remaining bankruptcy risk, and the only uncertainty left is due to default-free spot interest rates.

Conditions (11c) and (11d) state that given no bankruptcy at time 1, the dollar value of the XYZ zero bond must be less than the dollar value of a claim paying one dollar for sure and greater than a claim paying δ dollars for sure.

Condition (11e) guarantees the independence of the pseudo-probability ($\lambda \mu_1$) from the spot interest rate process. It adds additional structure to the model and, therefore, restricts the possible term structures ($p_0(t, T)$, $v_1(t, T)$) that will be consistent with this specification of the model. This restriction is testable and, if rejected, it could be easily removed.

Finally, the time 0 pseudo-probability ($\lambda \mu_0$) is determined in the time 0 risky debt market. From Figure 4 we get

$$v_1(0,1) = p_1(0,1) = \frac{\lambda \mu_0 \delta + (1 - \lambda \mu_0)}{r(0)} \tag{12a}$$

$$v_1(0,2) = p_1(0,2)$$

$$= \left[\pi_0 (\lambda \mu_0) \delta p_1(1,2)_{u,b} + \pi_0 (1 - \lambda \mu_0) p_1(1,2)_{u,n} + \right.$$

$$\left. (1 - \pi_0) \lambda \mu_0 \delta p_1(1,2)_{d,b} + (1 - \pi_0)(1 - \lambda \mu_0) p_1(1,2)_{d,n} \right] \Big/ r(0) \tag{12b}$$

These conditions guarantee that time 0 prices are their time 1 discounted expected values, using pseudo-probabilities. Substituting conditions (7) and (10) into (12b) and simplifying yields

225

PRICING

DERIVATIVES ON

FINANCIAL

SECURITIES

SUBJECT TO CREDIT

RISK

$$v_1(0, 2) = p_1(0, 2) = p_0(0, 2)[\lambda\mu_0\delta + (1 - \lambda\mu_0)r(1)_d p_1(1, 2)_{d,n}] \quad (13)$$

Using expressions (12) and (13), $\lambda\mu_0$ is given by

$$\lambda\mu_0 = \frac{1 - r(0)p_1(0, 1)}{1 - \delta}$$

$$= \frac{\left[r(1)_d p_1(1, 2)_{d,n} - p_1(0, 2)\right] \big/ p_0(0, 2)}{r(1)_d p_1(1, 2)_{d,n} - \delta} \quad (14)$$

Thus, $\lambda\mu_0$ exists, is unique, and satisfies $0 < \lambda\mu_0 < 1$ if and only if

$$\frac{\delta}{r(0)} < p_1(0, 1) < \frac{1}{r(0)} \quad (15a)$$

$$\delta p_0(0, 2) < p_1(0, 2) < p_0(0, 2)r(1)_d p_1(0, 2)_{d,n} \quad (15b)$$

$$\frac{\left[r(1)_d p_1(1, 2)_{d,n} - p_1(0, 2)\right] \big/ p_0(0, 2)}{r(1)_d p_1(1, 2)_{d,n} - \delta} = \frac{1 - r(0)p_1(0, 1)}{1 - \delta} \quad (15c)$$

Condition (15a) states that the dollar value of the XYZ zero-coupon bond maturing at time 1 must be worth less than receiving a dollar for sure and greater than receiving δ dollars for sure. Condition (15b) states that the XYZ zero-coupon bond maturing at time 2 must be worth more than receiving δ dollars for sure and less than receiving $r(1)_d p_1(1, 2)_{d,n}$ dollars for sure at time 2. Finally, condition (15c) guarantees that under the pseudo-probabilities, the bankruptcy process is independent of the default-free spot interest rate process. This restriction is imposed for analytic convenience and is easily relaxed.

For the remainder of this section, we assume conditions (8), (11), and (15) are satisfied. As argued above, this is equivalent to assuming that there are no-arbitrage opportunities in this economy and that the market is complete.

XYZ ZERO-COUPON BONDS

Under the above structure, XYZ zero-coupon bond prices can be rewritten in an equivalent form. First, note that under the pseudo-probabilities the expected payoff ratios at future dates can be calculated. These are

$$\tilde{E}_1\left(e_1(2)\right) = \begin{cases} \delta & \text{if bankrupt at time 1} \\ \lambda\mu_1\delta + (1 - \lambda\mu_1) & \text{if not bankrupt at time 1} \end{cases} \quad (16a)$$

$$\tilde{E}_0\left(e_1(2)\right) = \lambda\mu_0\delta + (1 - \lambda\mu_0)\left[\lambda\mu_1\delta + (1 - \lambda\mu_1)\right] \quad (16b)$$

and

$$\tilde{E}_0\left(e_1(1)\right) = \lambda\mu_0\delta + (1 - \lambda\mu_0) \quad (16c)$$

where $\tilde{E}_t(\cdot)$ is the time t conditional expected value under the pseudo-probabilities.

Expression (16a) states that at time 1 the expected payoff ratio at time 2 is either δ, if the firm is bankrupt at time 1, or $(\lambda\mu_1)\delta + (1 - \lambda\mu_1)$, if the firm is not bankrupt at time 1. The expected payoff ratio at time 2, as viewed from time 0, is given in expression (16b). It is a weighted average of the payment, δ, from going bankrupt at time 1, plus not being bankrupt at time 1 and the expected payoff at time 2, $[\lambda\mu_1\delta + (1 - \lambda\mu_1)]$. Expression (16c) provides the expected payoff ratio at time 1 as seen at time 0. Note that all of expressions (16a–c) are strictly less than 1.

PRICING
DERIVATIVES ON
FINANCIAL
SECURITIES
SUBJECT TO CREDIT
RISK

Expressions (13), (11) and (9) in conjunction with expression (16) imply

$$v_1(t, T) = p_0(t, T) \tilde{E}_t(e_1(T)) \qquad (17)$$

The XYZ zero-coupon bond price is its discounted expected payoff at time T (using the pseudo-probabilities). The discount factor is the default-free zero-coupon bond price.

This decomposition allows one to implicitly estimate the expected time T payoff $\tilde{E}_t(e_1(T))$ given observations of both bond prices ($v_1(t, T)$ and $p_0(t, T)$). Alternatively, given an estimate of the payoff ratio in default (δ), expression (17) provides us with a recursive estimation procedure for the pseudo-probabilities $\lambda\mu_0$ and $\lambda\mu_1$. This recursive estimation procedure is explained as follows. Given $p_0(0, 1)$ and $v_1(0, 1)$, estimate $\lambda\mu_0$ by expressions (17) and (16c). Second, given these, $p_2(0, 2)$ and $v_1(0, 2)$, estimate $\lambda\mu_1$ by expressions (17) and (16b). This recursive procedure is easily generalisable to multiple periods.

Expression (17) is useful in clarifying the restrictions upon $v_1(t, T)$ (and therefore $p_1(t, T)$) imposed by the no-arbitrage conditions contained in expressions (9) and (12). As the expected payoff ratio is strictly less than 1 ($\tilde{E}_1(e_1(T)) < 1$), we see that the XYZ zero-coupon bond is strictly less valuable than a default-free zero-coupon bond of equal maturity (ie, $v_1(t, T) < p_0(t, T)$). In other words, in the presence of bankruptcy, a strictly positive credit risk spread is a necessary condition for an arbitrage-free price system. This insight generalises and obtains even with the relaxation of the statistical independence assumption in the pseudo-probabilities imposed upon $e_1(t)$ and $p_0(t, T)$. This insight is the reason for rejecting the models of Ho and Singer (1984) and Ramaswamy and Sundaresan (1986) as inconsistent (see the introduction).

The statistical independence condition under the pseudo-probabilities ((11e) and (15c)) is the reason that expression (17) admits such a simple decomposition. This decomposition is an additional restriction imposed upon the economy, and as such it restricts the possible term structures for XYZ zero-coupon debt ($v_1(t, T)$). This is significant as it implies that, in special cases, not all of the XYZ maturity debt must trade to apply the model. For example, consider a multiperiod extension of the above model where the pseudo-default probability $\lambda\mu_t$ is constant over time. In this case, given any two XYZ zero-coupon bonds, one can deduce δ and $\lambda\mu$. With these parameters, the prices for all the remaining XYZ zero-coupon bonds can be computed. Thus, in this case, only two XYZ traded zero-coupon bonds are needed. This observation is significant in applications where there is a sparsity of XYZ zero-coupon bonds trading. In this situation, coupon-bearing XYZ debt may also be useful. This is discussed in the next section.

XYZ COUPON BONDS

Consider an XYZ coupon-bearing bond with promised dollar coupons of k_1 at time 1 and k_2 at time 2, where k_2 includes the principal repayment. Let $D(t)$ represent the time t dollar value of this XYZ coupon-bond. Using the risk-neutral valuation procedure, we know that the XYZ coupon-bond's price equals its discounted expected payoff (using the pseudo-probabilities), ie,

$$D(0) = \tilde{E}_0 \left(\frac{k_1 e_1(1)}{B(1)} + \frac{k_2 e_1(2)}{B(2)} \right) \qquad (18)$$

Simple algebra, along with expression (17), yields

$$D(0) = k_1 v_1(0, 1) + k_2 v_1(0, 2) \qquad (19)$$

The coupon-bearing bond is equivalent to a portfolio consisting of k_1 zero-coupon bonds of maturity 1 and k_2 zero-coupon bonds of maturity 2. This is analogous to an identical result which obtains for default-free coupon bonds. This result is valid even

227

PRICING

DERIVATIVES ON

FINANCIAL

SECURITIES

SUBJECT TO CREDIT

RISK

without the statistical independence assumptions on the pseudo-probabilities contained in expressions (11e) and (15c).

Expression (19) allows one to deduce the term structure of XYZ zero-coupon debt from XYZ coupon-bearing debt prices, in the same manner that it is currently done for default-free debt. In multiperiod generalisations of this model and in conjunction with additional restrictions upon the pseudo-default probabilities (eg, $\lambda \mu_t$ is constant over time), that insight allows one to deduce the prices of the XYZ zero-coupon bonds $(v_1(t, T))$ from the traded prices of only a few issues of XYZ coupon-bearing debt.

OPTIONS ON XYZ DEBT

Options written against the XYZ zero-coupon term structure can now be analysed using the standard procedures. We illustrate this approach with an example. Let $C(t)$ be the time t price of a European call option on the two-period XYZ zero-coupon bond. Let the option's exercise price be K and its exercise date be time 1. Its value at expiration is

$$C(1) = \max[v_1(1, 2) - K, 0] \tag{20}$$

The risk-neutral valuation procedure allows us to compute this option's value at time 0 as the discounted expectation of its time 1 payoff (using the pseudo-probabilities), ie,

$$C(0) = \frac{(1 - \lambda \mu_0)\left[\pi_0 C(1)_{u,n} + (1 - \pi_0)C(1)_{d,n}\right]}{r(0)}$$

$$+ \frac{(\lambda \mu_0)\left[\pi_0 C(1)_{u,b} + (1 - \pi_0)C(1)_{d,b}\right]}{r(0)} \tag{21}$$

The first term on the right hand side in square brackets is the value of the option given default does not occur. The second term in square brackets is the value of the option given that default has occurred.

Because the tree for XYZ zero-coupon debt has four branches, three traded assets and the money market account are needed to hedge the call option. The hedge consists of α shares of the two-period XYZ zero-coupon bond, β shares of the one-period XYZ zero-coupon bond, γ shares of the two-period default-free zero-coupon bond, and ε shares of the money market account such that

$$\alpha v_1(1, 2)_{u,b} + \beta v_1(1, 1)_{u,b} + \gamma p_0(1, 2)_{u,b} + \varepsilon r(0) = C(1)_{u,b} \tag{22a}$$

$$\alpha v_1(1, 2)_{u,n} + \beta v_1(1, 1)_{u,n} + \gamma p_0(1, 2)_{u,n} + \varepsilon r(0) = C(1)_{u,n} \tag{22b}$$

$$\alpha v_1(1, 2)_{d,b} + \beta v_1(1, 1)_{d,b} + \gamma p_0(1, 2)_{d,b} + \varepsilon r(0) = C(1)_{d,b} \tag{22c}$$

$$\alpha v_1(1, 2)_{d,n} + \beta v_1(1, 1)_{d,n} + \gamma p_0(1, 2)_{d,n} + \varepsilon r(0) = C(1)_{d,n} \tag{22d}$$

A unique solution can be shown to exist because the market is complete, ie, conditions (8), (11), and (15) hold. In fact, it can also be shown that the initial cost of constructing this portfolio equals the call's price, ie,

$$C(0) = \alpha v_1(0, 2) + \beta v_1(0, 1) + \gamma p_0(0, 2) + \varepsilon \tag{23}$$

This is a well-known implication of arbitrage-free price systems.

VULNERABLE OPTIONS

Consider options on the XYZ zero-coupon bonds, but written by a third party, who could also default. These options have been labelled *vulnerable options* by Johnson and Stulz (1987). This section studies the valuation and hedging of vulnerable options.

PRICING
DERIVATIVES ON
FINANCIAL
SECURITIES
SUBJECT TO CREDIT
RISK

We assume that this third party has zero-coupon bonds issued against its assets, with prices denoted by $v_2(t, T)$ for $t \leq T$. For simplicity, we suppose these dollar-denominated bonds satisfy the same processes as given in Figure 4, but with the "1" subscript replaced by a "2". Expanding the economy appropriately, we assume that there exist unique pseudo-probabilities such that the relative prices of all bonds, ie, $p_0(t, 1)/B(t)$, $p_0(t, 2)/B(t)$, $v_1(t, 1)/B(t)$, $v_1(t, 2)/B(t)$, $v_2(t, 1)/B(t)$, and $v_2(t, 2)/B(t)$ are martingales. This is the no-arbitrage and complete markets condition. Denote these pseudo-probabilities by the expectations operator $\tilde{E}(\cdot)$. Furthermore, we assume that *the bankruptcy process for the payoff ratio, $e_2(t)$, is independent of the default-free spot interest rate process and independent of the payoff ratio of XYZ, both under the pseudo-probabilities.*

Consider the European call option valued in expression (21), but this time, let it be written by the third party. At maturity, the cashflow to the buyer represents a promise by firm 2 to make the payment $C(1)$, ie,

$$e_2(1)C(1) \tag{24}$$

The value to the buyer at time 0, $C_2(0)$, is therefore the discounted expected value of this payment (under the pseudo-probabilities).

$$C_2(0) = \tilde{E}_0\left(\frac{e_2(1)C(1)}{B(1)}\right)$$
$$= \tilde{E}_0\big(e_2(1)\big)C(0) \tag{25}$$

The statistical independence of the bankruptcy process for the option writer from both the bankruptcy process for XYZ and the spot interest rate process under the pseudo-probabilities implies the second equality. The price of a call option written by a risky firm is equal to the price of a call written by a default-free writer discounted by the expected payoff from the risky writer. Given expression (17), we can rewrite this as

$$C_2(0) = \frac{v_2(0, 1)}{p_0(0, 1)}C(0) \tag{26}$$

As $v_2(0, 1)/p_0(0, 1) < 1$, we see that a vulnerable option is always less valuable than a non-valuable option (ie, $C_2(0) < C(0)$).

A NUMERICAL EXAMPLE
In Table 1 we are given two sets of prices of zero-coupon bonds. The first column is for default-free bonds and the second column is for XYZ zero-coupon bonds. These prices are taken as exogenous. For this credit class, if default occurs the bond holder receives $\delta = 0.32$ dollars per promised dollar. First we need to determine the pseudo-probabilities of default.

For the one period bond using equations (17) and (16c) we have

$$v_1(0, 1) = p_0(0, 1)[\lambda\mu_0\delta + (1 - \lambda\mu_0)] \tag{27}$$

Using the prices in Table 1, this implies that $\lambda\mu_0 = 0.01$. For the two-period bond, using equations (17) and (16b), we have that

$$v_1(0, 2) = p_0(0, 2)\{\lambda\mu_0\delta + (1 - \lambda\mu_0)[\lambda\mu_1\delta + (1 - \lambda\mu_1)]\} \tag{28}$$

implying $\lambda\mu_1 = 0.03$.

Table 1. The initial term structures of default-free debt and XYZ debt

Maturity	Prices of default-free zero-coupon bonds	Prices of XYZ zero-coupon bonds
T	$p_0(0, T)$	$v_1(0, T)$
1	94.8627	94.2176
2	89.5343	87.1168

This table gives the initial prices, in dollars, for default-free and XYZ zeros with maturities 1 and 2. The symbol T represents the maturities of the zeros, $p_0(0, T)$ represents the time 0 price of the default-free zero with maturity date T, and $v_1(0, T)$ represents the time 0 price of the XYZ zero with maturity T.

The process for the default-free spot interest rate is shown in Figure 5, Panel A. This process is consistent with Black, Derman and Toy (1990).

Option on a credit-risky bond

Consider a European put option with maturity one year on an XYZ zero-coupon bond with maturity date time 2. At the maturity of the option, the option holder can sell the XYZ zero-coupon bond for the strike price of 92. Let the face value of the XYZ zero-coupon bond be 100. The option's value at maturity is shown in Figure 5, Panel B. Using equation (21), the time 0 value of this option is

$$C(0) = (1 - 0.01)[0.5(0.07) +$$
$$0.5(0)]0.9486 +$$
$$0.01[0.5(61.97) + 0.5(61.62)]0.9486 =$$
$$0.62 \tag{29}$$

Vulnerable options

Consider a European put option with maturity one year and a strike price of 95 on a default-free zero-coupon bond with maturity date time 2. Let the face value of the zero-coupon bond be 100. If there is no risk of the writer defaulting, the value of the option at maturity is

$$C(1) = \begin{cases} 95 - 93.84 = 1.16 \\ 95 - 94.93 = 0.07 \end{cases} \tag{30}$$

and the value of the option today is

$$C(0) = (0.5(1.16) + 0.5(0.07))0.9486 =$$
$$0.5834 \tag{31}$$

5. A spot-interest rate for the default-free term structure, and B zero-coupon bond prices and option values

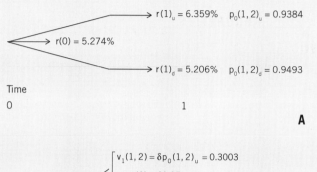

$r(1)_u = 6.359\%$ $p_0(1,2)_u = 0.9384$

$r(0) = 5.274\%$

$r(1)_d = 5.206\%$ $p_0(1,2)_d = 0.9493$

Time 0   1   **A**

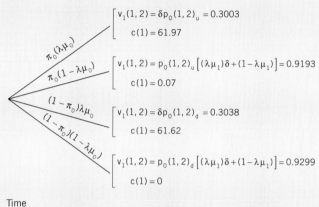

Time 0   1   **B**

Panel A describes the evolution of the spot interest rate and bond price process over the time periods 0 and 1 where $\pi_0 = 0.5$. $r(t)_\omega$ is the spot interest rate at time t given state $\omega \in \{u,d\}$ and $p_0(t,T)_\omega$ is the time t price of a default-free bond paying a dollar at time T given state $\omega \in \{u,d\}$. Panel B describes the evolution of the dollar values of XYZ zero-coupon bonds and the call option's values over the time periods 0 and 1 where $\pi_0 = 0.5$, $\lambda\mu_0 = 0.01$, $\lambda\mu_1 = 0.03$ and $\delta = 0.32$. π_0 is the pseudo-probability for the spot interest rate process, $\lambda\mu_0$ and $\lambda\mu_1$ are the default process pseudo-probabilities, δ is the payoff ratio in default, and $p_0(t,T)_\omega$ is the time 1 value of a default-free dollar paid at time 2 given state $\omega \in \{u,d\}$, $v_1(1,2)$ is the time 1 dollar value of an XYZ paid at time T, and C(1) is the value of a call option at time 1.

Let the institution writing this option belong to the XYZ credit class. Using equation (26), the value of the vulnerable option is

$$C(0) = \left[\frac{94.2176}{94.8627}\right]0.5834$$
$$= 0.5794 \tag{32}$$

Swaps

Consider an existing off-market interest rate swap with two periods remaining where we are receiving fixed payments of 6% from a counterparty belonging to the credit class XYZ, and we are making floating rate payments. For simplicity, we assume that there is no chance of default on the floating rate payments. The time 0 value of the first floating rate payment is

$$\text{Float}(0,1) \equiv 1 - p_0(0,1) \tag{33a}$$

and the second payment is

$$\text{Float}(0,2) \equiv p_0(0,1) - p_0(0,2) \tag{33b}$$

PRICING

DERIVATIVES ON

FINANCIAL

SECURITIES

SUBJECT TO CREDIT

RISK

In a standard swap, the bankruptcy rules are such that if default occurs, all future payments are null and void.[8] We can incorporate this provision into our model by defining a new payoff ratio conditional upon no default at time $t - 1$, ie,

$$\bar{e}(t) = \begin{cases} 1; & \text{probability } 1 - \lambda\mu_{t-1} \\ 0; & \text{probability } \lambda\mu_{t-1} \end{cases} \tag{34a}$$

If default has occurred at $t - 1$, then

$$\bar{e}(t) = 0 \text{ with probability } 1 \tag{34b}$$

implying that the swap is null and void. The value of the swap today at $t = 0$ is

$$v_s(0) \equiv \left[\bar{R}p_0(0, 1) - \text{Float}(0, 1)\right]E_0\left[\bar{e}(1)\right]$$

$$+ \left[\bar{R}p_0(0, 2) - \text{Float}(0, 2)\right]E_0\left[\bar{e}(2)\right] \tag{35}$$

where $\bar{R}$, the fixed payment, equals 6%.[9] We can compute these terms, given that we have determined $\lambda\mu_0$ and $\lambda\mu_1$ from the term structure. From Table 1, the value of the swap, assuming a notational principal of \$100 million is

$$v_s(0) = \left\{\left[0.06(0.9486) - (1 - 0.9486)\right](1 - 0.01) + \right.$$

$$\left.\left[0.06(0.8953) - (0.9486 - 0.8953)\right] + \left[(1 - 0.03)(1 - 0.01)\right]\right\}100\text{m}$$

$$= 55,160(1 - 0.01) + 4,180(1 - 0.03)(1 - 0.01)$$

$$= 58,622 \tag{36}$$

If we ignore the credit risk, the value of the swap is 59,340, a difference of 718. In comparison with the notational principal, this difference is insignificant, though in comparison with the value of the swap (calculated ignoring default), it represents approximately 1% of the total value.

GENERALISATIONS

As discussed earlier, it is a straightforward exercise to generalise this two-period example. Four extensions will prove useful in applications. The first is the multiperiod generalisation that follows by augmenting the number of periods in the previous model. Retaining the statistical independence assumption of the bankruptcy processes from the spot rate process under the pseudo-probabilities implies that the separations exhibited in the expressions for the XYZ zero-coupon bond price (expression (17)), the XYZ coupon bond price (expression (19)), the option value on XYZ debt (expression (21)) and the vulnerable options (expression (26)) still obtain.

The second extension (in the multiperiod setting) is to introduce a correlation (in the pseudo-probabilities) between the bankruptcy process on XYZ debt and the default-free term structure. This is equivalent to changing the probabilities in Figure 4 to a different distribution. In the discrete-time, discrete-state space setting, this generalisation imposes no additional complication, except that the separation exhibited in the previous sections will not obtain. All the previous results generalise in a straightforward fashion.

The third extension is to introduce traded common equity on XYZ into the above economy. This entails the introduction of additional randomness (additional branches on the tree). This extension, albeit messy, is straightforward and is illustrated in the next section.

231

PRICING

DERIVATIVES ON

FINANCIAL

SECURITIES

SUBJECT TO CREDIT

RISK

The fourth extension is to analyse the continuous-time limit of the discrete-time model. The continuous-time limit is useful for estimation and computation. It aids estimation because the pseudo-probabilities for the default-free term structure (π_0) can be re-parameterised in terms of instantaneous volatilities. Volatilities can be easily estimated and interpreted. This same statement is not true for the pseudo-probabilities themselves.

The continuous trading economy

This section extends the previous two-period example to its multiperiod, continuous-time limit. For pedagogical reasons, we retain the statistical independence assumption under the pseudo-probabilities between the bankruptcy process for XYZ debt and the default-free term structure. This allows a direct comparison of the results across the two models. Generalisations to more complicated economies will be subsequently discussed. To be consistent with Heath, Jarrow and Morton (1992), we specify the exogenous stochastic processes followed by the forward rates and the payoff ratio. Although various parameterisations are possible, we choose one convenient for application of the techniques available in Jarrow and Madan (1995).

THE SETUP

We consider continuous trading over the time interval $[0, \tau]$. Let τ_1^* denote the time of bankruptcy of firm XYZ. We assume that τ_1^* is exponentially distributed over $[0, \infty]$ with parameter λ_1. Alternative distributions for the bankruptcy time could have been utilised (see Longstaff and Schwartz (1992) for an endogenously derived process based on a lognormally distributed random variable for the firm's value).

The default-free forward rate is defined by

$$f_0(t, T) \equiv \frac{-\partial \log p_0(t, T)}{\partial T} \tag{37a}$$

The default-free spot interest rate is defined by

$$r_0(t) \equiv f_0(t, t) \tag{37b}$$

and the default-free money market account is defined by

$$B(t) = \exp\left\{ \int_0^t r_0(s)\,ds \right\} \tag{37c}$$

Analogously, we define for XYZ debt

$$f_1(t, T) \equiv \frac{-\partial \log p_1(t, T)}{\partial T} \tag{37d}$$

$$r_1(t) \equiv f_1(t, t) \tag{37e}$$

and

$$B_1(t) \equiv \exp\left\{ \int_0^t r_1(s)\,ds \right\} \tag{37f}$$

We now impose the exogenous stochastic structure directly on the forward rates $f_0(t, T)$, $f_1(t, T)$, and payoff ratio $e_1(t)$.

ASSUMPTION 1 *Default-free forward rates*

$$df_0(t, T) = \alpha_0(t, T)\,dt + \sigma(t, T)\,dW_1(t) \tag{38}$$

232

PRICING

DERIVATIVES ON

FINANCIAL

SECURITIES

SUBJECT TO CREDIT

RISK

where $W_1(t)$ is a Brownian motion, $(\alpha_0(t, T), \sigma(t, T))$ satisfy some smoothness and boundedness conditions,[10] and $\sigma(t, T)$ is deterministic (non-random).

The default-free forward rate's change over a small instant in time is seen to be equal to a drift $(\alpha_0(t, T))$ plus a random shock with volatility $(\sigma(t, T))$. The assumption of a deterministic volatility function is made only to facilitate the derivation of closed-form solutions. This assumption can easily be replaced. The deterministic volatility $\sigma(t, T)$ makes this a Gaussian economy. As such, it is a convenient limit of the process given in Figure 1. If $\sigma(t, T) \equiv \sigma > 0$ is a positive constant, one gets the continuous-time analogue of Ho and Lee (1986). If $\sigma(t, T) = \sigma e^{-\xi(T-t)}$ for σ, ξ constants, one gets the model of hull and White (1990) and Musiela, Turnbull, and Wakeman (1993). Assumption 1 is easily generalised to multiple, independent Brownian motions.

ASSUMPTION 2 *XYZ forward rates*

$$df_1(t,T) = \begin{cases} \left[\alpha_1(t,T) - \theta_1(t,T)\lambda_1\right]dt + \sigma(t,T)dW_1(t) & \text{if } t < \tau_1^* \\ \left[\alpha_1(t,T) - \theta_1(t,T)\lambda_1\right]dt + \sigma(t,T)dW_1(t) + \theta_1(t,T) & \text{if } t = \tau_1^* \\ \alpha_1(t,T)dt + \sigma(t,T)dW_1(t) & \text{if } t > \tau_1^* \end{cases} \quad (39)$$

where $\alpha_1(t, T)$, $\theta_1(t, T)$ satisfy some smoothness and boundedness conditions.[11]

The process for XYZ forward rates mimics the stochastic process for default-free forward rates. Indeed, XYZ forward rates change over a small instant in time by a drift plus a random shock. Prior to bankruptcy $(t < \tau_1^*)$, the drift is adjusted downward to reflect the expected change $\theta_1(\tau_1^*, T)\lambda_1$ that occurs at the bankruptcy time. After bankruptcy $(t > \tau_1^*)$, the forward rate process is identical to expression (38), except for subscripts. Without loss of generality, the coefficient preceding the Brownian motion component equals that in the default-free forward rate process.[12]

ASSUMPTION 3 *The XYZ payoff ratio*

$$e_1(t) = \begin{cases} 1 & \text{if } t < \tau_1^* \\ \delta_1 & \text{if } t \geq \tau_1^* \end{cases} \quad (40)$$

where $0 < \delta_1 < 1$.

The payoff ratio is unity until bankruptcy, at which time it is equal to $\delta_1 < 1$. This is a continuous-time limit of the bankruptcy process in Figure 2. As in the discrete-time setting, the payoff ratio (δ_1) can differ depending on the seniority of the debt. Although the payoff ratio is constant, this restriction is imposed for simplicity. It is a straightforward mathematical exercise to make $e_1(t)$ random and dependent on an additional Brownian motion representing the randomness generating the value of the firm. Given trading in a sufficient number of XYZ zeros, the market for XYZ debt will still be complete, and our methodology still applies. This generalisation would include Merton's (1974) model as a special case. The difficulty with this generalisation is that the valuation formulae become more complex, and estimation/computation becomes more involved. Empirical validation of the simpler model is needed to determine whether this additional complexity is warranted.

One can derive the following stochastic processes for $p_0(t, T)$, $v_1(t, T)$, and $B_1(t)e_1(t)$.[13] These are the continuous-time analogues of Figures 1 and 4. For default-free zeros

$$\frac{dp_0(t,T)}{p_0(t,T)} = \left[r_0(t) + \beta_0(t,T)\right]dt + a(t,T)dW_1(t) \quad (41a)$$

233

PRICING

DERIVATIVES ON

FINANCIAL

SECURITIES

SUBJECT TO CREDIT

RISK

where

$$\beta_0(t,T) \equiv -\int_t^T \alpha_0(t,u)\,du + \frac{1}{2}a(t,T)^2 \tag{41b}$$

and

$$a(t,T) \equiv -\int_t^T \sigma(t,u)\,du \tag{41c}$$

Expression (41) gives the return process followed by the default-free zeros. The random return equals the spot interest rate $r_0(t)$, an adjustment for risk $((\beta_0(t,\ T))$, plus a random shock with volatility $a(t,\ T)$. By construction, the volatility $a(t,\ T)$ approaches 0 as the bond matures.

For the XYZ zeros

$$\frac{dv_1(t,T)}{v_1(t-,T)} =$$

$$\begin{cases} \left[r_1(t) + \beta_1(t,T) - \Theta_1(t,T)\lambda_1 \right] dt + a(t,T)\,dW_1(t) & \text{if } t < \tau_1^* \\ \left[r_1(t) + \beta_1(t,T) - \Theta_1(t,T)\lambda_1 \right] dt + a(t,T)\,dW_1(t) + \left(\delta_1 e^{\Theta_1(t,T)} - 1 \right) & \text{if } t = \tau_1^* \\ \left[r_1(t) + \beta_1(t,T) \right] dt + a(t,T)\,dW_1(t) & \text{if } t > \tau_1^* \end{cases}$$

$$\tag{42a}$$

where

$$\beta_1(t,T) \equiv -\int_t^T \alpha_1(t,u)\,du + \frac{1}{2}a(t,T)^2 \tag{42b}$$

and

$$\Theta_1(t,T) \equiv -\int_t^T \theta_1(t,u)\,du \tag{42c}$$

Expression (42) gives the return process followed by the XYZ zeros. The random return mimics the default-free return process. Indeed, prior to bankruptcy $(t < \tau_1^*)$, the random return consists of a drift, adjusted for the change at the time of bankruptcy, and a random shock with volatility $a(t,\ T)$. At bankruptcy $(t = \tau_1^*)$, the return changes discretely by $(\delta_1 e^{\Theta_1(t,\ T)} - 1)$. Subsequently to bankruptcy $(t > \tau_1^*)$, the return process is that given by expression (41) with only the subscripts changed.

$$\frac{d\left[B_1(t)e_1(t) \right]}{B_1(t-)e_1(t-)} = \begin{cases} r_1(t)\,dt & \text{if } t < \tau_1^* \\ \left[r_1(t)\,dt \right] + (\delta_1 - 1) & \text{if } t = \tau_1^* \\ r_1(t)\,dt & \text{if } t > \tau_1^* \end{cases} \tag{43}$$

Expression (43) gives the return process (in dollars) followed by the XYZ money market account. It returns the XYZ interest rate, except at bankruptcy $(t = \tau_1^*)$, where it drops $(\delta_1 - 1) < 0\%$.

ARBITRAGE-FREE RESTRICTIONS

To ensure that the economy has no-arbitrage opportunities and that the market is complete, using Harrison and Pliska (1981) we need to provide conditions that guarantee the existence of a unique equivalent probability making the relative prices $v_1(t,\ T)/B(t)$, $B_1(t)e_1(t)/B(t)$ and $p_0(t,\ T)/B(t)$ martingales. This is analogous to conditions (8), (11) and (15) derived in the discrete-time setting. To obtain these conditions, we impose[14]

ASSUMPTION 4 *The existence of unique equivalent martingale probabilities*

$$(\delta_1 e^{\Theta_1(t,\ T)} - 1) \neq 0 \text{ for all } t \leq \tau_1^* \text{ and } T \in [0, \tau] \tag{44}$$

234

PRICING

DERIVATIVES ON

FINANCIAL

SECURITIES

SUBJECT TO CREDIT

RISK

This assumption can be understood by referring to the XYZ bond process in expression (42). The bankruptcy process's impact on the XYZ bond's return is the quantity $(\delta_1 e^{\Theta_1(t, T)} - 1)$. For this risk to be relevant (and hedgeable), this coefficient must be non-zero. This condition is satisfied as long as XYZ bond prices change at the time of bankruptcy.

Under this assumption, the following system of equations can be shown to have a unique solution $(\gamma_1(t), \mu_1(t))$.

$$\beta_0(t, T) + \gamma_1(t)a(t, T) = 0 \qquad (45a)$$

$$r_1(t) - r_0(t) + \beta_1(t, T) + \gamma_1(t)a(t, T) - \Theta_1(t, T)\lambda_1 + (\delta_1 e^{\Theta_1(t, T)} - 1)\lambda_1\mu_1(t) = 0$$
$$\text{if } t < \tau_1^* \qquad (45b)$$

$$r_1(t) - r_0(t) + \beta_1(t, T) + \gamma_1(t)a(t, T) = 0 \quad \text{if } t \geq \tau_1^* \qquad (45c)$$

$$r_1(t) = r_0(t) + (1 - \delta_1)\lambda_1\mu_1(t) \quad \text{if } t < \tau_1^* \qquad (45d)$$

$$r_1(t) = r_0(t) \quad \text{if } t \geq \tau_1^* \qquad (45e)$$

The quantities $(\gamma_1(t), \mu_1(t))$ have the interpretation of being market prices of risk. This is most easily seen via expressions (45a) and (45b). Expression (45a) shows that the excess expected return on the T-maturity default-free zero $(\beta_0(t, T))$ is proportional to its volatility $(a(t, T))$. The proportionality factor is the risk premium $\gamma_1(t)$, which is independent of the T-maturity bond selected. This is the standard no-arbitrage condition for the default-free debt market as given in Heath, Jarrow and Morton (1992). It implies their forward rate drift restriction.

Expressions (45b) and (45c) are the analogous restrictions for the XYZ zero-coupon bond market. To interpret these conditions, we combine them with (45a) and (45e).

$$\beta_1(t, T) - \Theta_1(t, T)\lambda_1 = \beta_0(t, T) - \delta_1(e^{\Theta_1(t, T)} - 1)\lambda_1\mu_1(t) \quad \text{if } t < \tau_1^* \qquad (46a)$$

$$\beta_1(t, T) = \beta_0(t, T) \quad \text{if } t \geq \tau_1^* \qquad (46b)$$

Expression (46a) is (45b) rewritten. We see that prior to bankruptcy $(t < \tau_1^*)$, the excess expected return on the XYZ zero $(\beta_1(t, T) - \Theta_1(t, T)\lambda_1)$ is equal to the excess expected return on the default-free zero $\beta_0(t, T)$ plus an adjustment for default risk. The adjustment is proportional to the bankruptcy shock $\delta_1(e^{\Theta_1(t, T)} - 1)$. The proportionality factor is the risk premium $(\lambda_1\mu_1(t))$, which is independent of the T-maturity bond selected. Subsequent to bankruptcy $(t \geq \tau_1^*)$, as there is no more bankruptcy risk, the excess expected return on both XYZ zeros and default-free zeros is identical (see expression (46b)).

Expressions (45e) and (46b) imply that the return processes for the XYZ zeros and the default-free zeros are identical after bankruptcy $(t \geq \tau_1^*)$, which implies that $v_1(t, T) = \delta_1 p_0(t, T)$. That is, after bankruptcy, the Treasury and XYZ term structures are identical, ie, $p_0(t, T) = p_1(t, T)$. This result was seen in the discrete time setting as expressions (11a) and (11b).

An additional implication of Assumption 4 is that the market is complete (see Harrison and Pliska, 1981). Define a *contingent claim* X as a suitably bounded random cashflow at time $T < \tau$.[15] Then, the time t "arbitrage-free" price of this contingent claim is its expected discounted value under the martingale probabilities, ie,

$$\tilde{E}_1\left[\frac{X}{B}(T)\right]B(t) \qquad (47)$$

where $\tilde{E}_t(\cdot)$ is the time t expectation under the martingale probabilities. This expression provides the method for pricing derivative securities involving credit risk.

235

PRICING

DERIVATIVES ON

FINANCIAL

SECURITIES

SUBJECT TO CREDIT

RISK

Next, for simplicity, we add

ASSUMPTION 5 *The Poisson bankruptcy process under the martingale probabilities*

$$\mu_1(t) \equiv \mu_1 > 0 \ a \ positive \ constant \tag{48}$$

The previous structure implies that the bankruptcy process is independent of the spot interest rate process under the true (empirical) probabilities. This additional Assumption 5 implies the statistical independence of the bankruptcy process from the default-free interest rate process *under the martingale probabilities*. It does so because it also makes the time of bankruptcy process an exponential distribution under the martingale probabilities with parameter $\lambda_1\mu_1$, which is independent of the spot interest rate process. It is imposed to simplify the subsequent analysis. This is a subtle condition as it imposes implicit structure on the risk premia in the economy. This assumption can easily be relaxed, with correspondingly more complex valuation formulae. We retain Assumption 5 to facilitate the understanding of the subsequent material. Empirical validation of the model under Assumption 5 is needed to determine whether this additional complexity is warranted.

XYZ BONDS

Under Assumptions 1 to 5, we can simplify $v_1(t, T)$ further

$$v_1(t,T) = \tilde{E}_t\left[\frac{e_1(T)}{B(T)}\right]B(t) = \tilde{E}_1[e_1(T)]p_0(t,T)$$

$$= \begin{cases} \left[e^{-\lambda_1\mu_1(T-t)} + \delta_1\left(1 - e^{-\lambda_1\mu_1(T-t)}\right)\right]p_0(t,T) & \text{if } t < \tau_1^* \\ \delta_1 p_0(t,T) & \text{if } t \geq \tau_1^* \end{cases} \tag{49}$$

This decomposition is the continuous-time analogue of expressions (16) and (17). In this form, we see that to compute the stochastic process for $v_1(t, T)$, we only need the parameters $(\lambda_1\mu_1)$ and σ_1. As in the discrete-time model, these can be obtained via a recursive estimation procedure. In bankruptcy, $v_1(t, T) = \delta_1 p_0(t, T)$.

Merton (1974) also derives an expression for the value of a zero-coupon corporate bond. In Merton's model, default occurs if the value of the firm's assets are less than the amount owed to bondholders at maturity. If default occurs, it is assumed that bond-holders take over the firm without any cost to themselves. In the simplest version of Merton's model, to compute the value of the zero-coupon bond, it is necessary to know both the current value of the firm's total assets and the total asset's volatility. At this point, the two models appear quite similar, each involving two unknowns. The relevant differences in the models appear in the application. Typically a firm has many different forms of liabilities outstanding. To use Merton's model, it is necessary to simultaneously solve for the value of all of these claims, which is a non-trivial exercise (see Jones, Mason and Rosenfeld, 1984) and necessitates strong assumptions about the relevance of capital structure and the treatment of claims in the event of bankruptcy. Secondly, to use Merton's model, one must also be able to measure the current value of the firm's assets. This is a difficult task.

In contrast, our model circumvents these difficulties by taking as given the term structure of interest rates for the relevant credit risk class. This, however, introduces its own set of problems. The bonds used to construct this term structure must have the same probability of default, and if default occurs, the payment rule must be known. In default, we assume that the claim holders receive some fixed amount per promised dollar. This assumption can, in fact, be relaxed to include Merton's (1974) bankruptcy condition as a special case.

236

PRICING

DERIVATIVES ON

FINANCIAL

SECURITIES

SUBJECT TO CREDIT

RISK

In a generalised version of Merton's model, the value of the firm and the term structure of interest rates can be correlated. In our model, we assume independence because it facilitates the derivation of closed form solutions. This assumption can also be relaxed.

An examination of expression (49) reveals that nowhere does the parameter $\Theta_1(t, T)$ appear. This implies that the martingale restrictions under Assumption 5 completely specify $\Theta_1(t, T)$ in terms of the parameters of the bankruptcy process under the martingale probabilities. These restrictions could prove useful for empirical estimation and for testing this particular form of the model. They are provided in the following lemma.

LEMMA 1 *Martingale restrictions under Assumption 5*[16]

$$\left(\delta_1 e^{\Theta_1(t,T)} - 1\right) = \frac{e^{-\lambda_1 \mu_1 (T-t)} (\delta_1 - 1)}{e^{-\lambda_1 \mu_1 (T-t)} + \delta_1 \left(1 - e^{-\lambda_1 \mu_1 (T-t)}\right)} \quad \text{for} \quad t < \tau_1^* \tag{50}$$

See the Appendix for proof of this equation.

Lemma 1 is the additional restriction imposed on the bond's volatilities by the statistical independence assumption under the martingale probabilities, Assumption 5. It is the analogous restriction to that given in the discrete-time setting via expressions (11e) and (15c).

OPTIONS ON XYZ DEBT
This section provides a closed-form solution for a European type call option with exercise price K and maturity m on an XYZ zero-coupon bond with maturity $M \geq m$. Let $C_1(t, K)$ denote the call's time t value with exercise price K. Using risk-neutral valuation, we have that

$$C_1(t, K) = \tilde{E}_t \left[\frac{\max\left[v_1(m, M) - K, 0\right]}{B(m)} \right] B(t) \tag{51}$$

Expression (49) implies that this can be written as

$$C_1(t, K) = \tilde{E}_t \left[\frac{\max\left[p_0(m, M)\tilde{E}_m\left(e(M)\right) - K, 0\right]}{B(m)} \right] B(t) \tag{52}$$

Using the fact that

$$\tilde{E}_m\left[e_1(M)\right] = \begin{cases} \left[e^{-\lambda_1 \mu_1 (M-m)} + \delta_1\left(1 - e^{-\lambda_1 \mu_1 (M-m)}\right)\right] & \text{if} \quad m < \tau_1^* \\ \delta_1 & \text{if} \quad m \geq \tau_1^* \end{cases} \tag{53}$$

and the specifics of Assumptions 1 to 5, we can rewrite this as

$$C_1(t, K) = \delta_1\left(1 - e^{-\lambda_1 \mu_1 (m-t)}\right) C_0(t, K')$$

$$+ \left[e^{-\lambda_1 \mu_1 (M-m)} + \delta_1\left(1 - e^{-\lambda_1 \mu_1 (M-m)}\right)\right] e^{-\lambda_1 \mu_1 (m-t)} C_0(t, K'') \quad \text{if} \quad t < \tau_1^* \tag{54}$$

where

$$C_0(t, L) \equiv \tilde{E}_t \left[\frac{\max\left[p_0(m, M) - L, 0\right]}{B(m)} \right] B(t)$$

$$= p_0(t, M)\Phi\left(h(L)\right) - Lp_0(t, m)\Phi\left(h(L) - q\right) \tag{55a}$$

237

PRICING

DERIVATIVES ON

FINANCIAL

SECURITIES

SUBJECT TO CREDIT

RISK

and

$$h(L) \equiv \frac{\log\left[\frac{p_0(t,M)}{p_0(t,m)L}\right] + \frac{1}{2}q^2}{q} \qquad (55b)$$

$$q^2 \equiv \int_t^m \left[a(u,M) - a(u,m)\right]^2 ds \qquad (55c)$$

$$K' \equiv \frac{K}{\delta_1} \qquad (55d)$$

$$K'' \equiv \frac{K}{e^{-\lambda_1 \mu_1 (M-m)} + \delta_1 \left(1 - e^{-\lambda_1 \mu_1 (M-m)}\right)} \qquad (55e)$$

Expression (54) gives a closed-form solution for the value of a European option on XYZ risky debt, and it is the continuous time analogue of expression (21). It is a linear combination of the value of two distinct European options on otherwise identical *default-free debt*. This result is important because it allows one to compute option values on risky debt using software developed for riskless debt. Indeed, the first term is equal to the risk-neutral probability that default occurs prior to time $m (1 - e^{-\lambda_1 \mu_1 (m-t)})$ times the value of XYZs option in that case $(\delta_1 C_0(t, K'))$. After bankruptcy, recall that XYZ debt is riskless. The second term is equal to the risk-neutral probability that default occurs after time $m (e^{-\lambda_1 \mu_1 (m-t)})$ times the value of the option in that case $((e^{-\lambda_1 \mu_1 (M-m)}) + \delta_1 (1 - e^{-\lambda_1 \mu_1 (M-m)})C_0(t, K''))$. If bankruptcy occurs after the option matures (m), then XYZ debt is again riskless at the option's expiration date, but for a different reason. Note that $C_0(t, K') < C_0(t, K'')$ as $K' > K''$. The option on the default-free debt is valued under Assumption 1, and the formula (55a–e) is obtained from Heath, Jarrow and Morton (1992). When $\sigma(t, T) \equiv \sigma > 0$, we get Ho and Lee's (1986) model, or when $\sigma(t, T) \equiv \sigma e^{-\xi(T-t)}$, we get the model of Hull and White (1990) and Musiela, Turnbull and Wakeman (1993). For $\mu_1 \lambda_1 \equiv 0$, no default risk, expression (54) reduces to $C_1(t, K) = C_0(t, K)$, which is the standard no default interest rate option pricing formula in a Gaussian economy.

Expression (54) is easily computed, and easily extended to multiple factors for the Brownian motion risk.[17]

Equation (54) is for a time prior to bankruptcy. After bankruptcy, the call's value is

$$C_1(t, K) = \delta_1 C_0(t, K') \text{ for } t \geq \tau_1^* \qquad (56)$$

Hence, at bankruptcy, there is a discrete and negative drop in the call's value. This is most easily seen by comparing expressions (54) and (56).

VULNERABLE OPTIONS

The previous sections value options on financial securities subject to default. Implicit in this procedure is that the secondary market buyer/seller of these options are default free. This would happen, for example, when the option transaction is guaranteed by a regulated and organised exchange. In the absence of such a guarantee, the writer of the option contract can also default.[18] Such options are called vulnerable options (see Johnson and Stulz, 1987).[19] This section extends the pricing methodology of the previous sections to price vulnerable options.

To price these vulnerable options, the economy in the previous section needs to be extended. Let the writer of the option be another firm, whose risky zero-coupon bonds $(v_2(t, T))$ are also traded. Using the foreign currency analogy, we can decompose these zero-coupon bonds into

238

PRICING

DERIVATIVES ON

FINANCIAL

SECURITIES

SUBJECT TO CREDIT

RISK

$$v_2(t, T) = e_2(t)p_2(t, T) \quad \text{where } p_2(T, T) = 1 \text{ for all } T \tag{57}$$

It is assumed that the forward rates $f_2(t, T)$ and the payoff ratio $e_2(t)$ satisfy Assumptions 2 and 3 with the index "2" replacing the index "1". Following the same analysis as before, a sufficient condition for the existence of unique equivalent martingale probabilities is Assumption 4 applied to $v_2(t, T)$. Adding Assumption 5, all the preceding results apply in an identical manner.

Next, we consider the option writer, writing a European call option with exercise price K and maturity m on the XYZ zero-coupon bond with maturity $M \geq m$. This is the option valued in the last section. The option's time t price will be denoted $C_2(t, K)$, the "2" subscript indicating the fact that the option writer is involved.

The option writer *promises* to pay $C_1(m, K)$ dollars at time m. However, the option writer may default. Thus, this option contract has a time m value equal to

$$C_2(m, K) = e_2(m)C_1(m, K) \tag{58}$$

Using the risk-neutral valuation procedure, we get that

$$C_2(t, K) = \tilde{E}_t\left[\frac{e_2(m)C_1(m, K)}{B(m)}\right]B(t) \tag{59}$$

Using the statistical independence of the bankruptcy processes from each other and the spot rate process under the martingale probabilities, expression (59) simplifies to:

$$C_2(t, K) = \tilde{E}_t\left[e_2(m)\right]\tilde{E}_t\left[\frac{C_1(m, K)}{B(m)}\right]B(t)$$

$$= \tilde{E}_t\left[e_2(m)\right]C_1(m, K) \tag{60}$$

where

$$\tilde{E}_t\left[e_2(m)\right] = \begin{cases} \delta_2 & \text{if } t \geq \tau_2^* \\ e^{-\lambda_2\mu_2(m-t)} + \delta_2\left(1 - e^{-\lambda_2\mu_2(m-t)}\right) & \text{if } t < \tau_2^* \end{cases} \tag{61}$$

Expression (60) provides (along with expression (54)) a simple closed-form solution for this option's value. Again, as with non-vulnerable options, to compute this value we only need to slightly modify software written for default-free debt options. This is the continuous-time analogue of expression (25).

We can alternatively use expression (49) for $v_2(t, T)$ to write

$$\tilde{E}_t\left[e_2(m)\right] = \frac{v_2(t, m)}{p_0(t, m)} \tag{62}$$

giving an alternative expression

$$C_2(t, K) = \left[\frac{v_2(t, m)}{p_0(t, m)}\right]C_1(t, K) \tag{63}$$

This is a continuous-time analogue of expression (26). In the case of no default for the option writer, expression (63) collapses to $C_1(t, K)$.

EQUITY DERIVATIVES

This section demonstrates how to augment the previous economy to include trading in common equities on XYZ. This extension is significant in that it would allow, for

PRICING

DERIVATIVES ON

FINANCIAL

SECURITIES

SUBJECT TO CREDIT

RISK

example, the pricing and hedging of convertible XYZ debt without using the compound options approach of Merton (1974, 1977). The discrete-time model can be augmented in a similar fashion.

Let the common equity for firm XYZ trade and its time t price be denoted by $S(t)$. We assume its stochastic process satisfies.

$$S(t) = \begin{cases} S(0)e^{\int_0^t \xi(s)ds - \frac{1}{2}[\eta_1^2 + \eta_2^2]t + \eta_1 W_1(t) + \eta_2 W_2(t) + \lambda_1 t} & \text{if } t < \tau_1^* \\ 0 & \text{if } t \geq \tau_1^* \end{cases} \qquad (64)$$

where $\xi(s)$ satisfies some smoothness and boundedness conditions,[20] and η_1 and η_2 are constants.

Prior to bankruptcy, expression (64) is a geometric Brownian motion with instantaneous expected return $\xi(s)ds$.[21] The volatility of this stock is generated by changes in the first Brownian motion, $W_1(t)$, which also affects the term structure of interest rates, and changes in the second Brownian motion, $W_2(t)$, which is unique to the stock. The instantaneous volatility is $(\sqrt{(\eta_1^2 + \eta_2^2)})$. After bankruptcy, the XYZ stock has zero value. This occurs when XYZ debt defaults and pays off $\delta_1 < 1$ dollars per dollar promised.[22]

To use the risk-neutral valuation methodology, it is shown in the Appendix that there exists a unique martingale probability such that $S(t)/B(t)$, $p_0(t, T)/B(t)$, and $v_1(t, T)/B(t)$ are martingales. Under this martingale probability, prior to bankruptcy $(t < \tau_1^*)$, $S(t)$ follows a geometric Brownian motion with modified drift $(r_0(t) + \lambda_1 \mu_1)$. After bankruptcy $(t \geq \tau_1^*)$, $S(t)$ is again zero.

The risk-neutral valuation methodology can now be used to price derivative securities involving XYZ stock. For example, consider a European-type call option on the stock with exercise date T and exercise price K. Denoting its time t value as $C(t)$, its payoff at time T is

$$C(T) = \max [S(T) - K, 0] \qquad (65)$$

Its time 0 value is

$$C(0) = \tilde{E}_0 \left[\max \left(\frac{S(T) - K}{B(T)}, 0 \right) \right] \qquad (66)$$

Using Amin and Jarrow (1992), it is shown in the Appendix that

$$C(0) = \left[S(0)e^{\lambda_1 \mu_1 T} \Phi(g) - Kp_0(0, T)\Phi(g - h) \right] e^{-\lambda_1 \mu_1 T}$$

$$= S(0)\Phi(g) - Kp_0^*(0, T)\Phi(g - h) \qquad (67)$$

where

$$p_0^*(0, T) = p_0(0, T)e^{-\lambda_1 \mu_1 T} = \tilde{E}_0 \left(e^{-\int_0^T [r_0(s) + \lambda_1 \mu_1]ds} \right) \qquad (68a)$$

$$g = \frac{\log \left[\frac{S(0)}{Kp_0^*(0, T)} \right] + \frac{1}{2}h^2}{h} \qquad (68b)$$

and

$$h^2 = \left[\eta_1^2 + \eta_2^2 \right]T - 2\eta_1 \int_0^T a(t, T)dt + \int_0^T a(t, T)^2 dt \qquad (68c)$$

This is the generalisation under stochastic interest rates of Merton's (1976; (17), p. 135)

PRICING
DERIVATIVES ON
FINANCIAL
SECURITIES
SUBJECT TO CREDIT
RISK

formula for the value of a call option on a stock that can go bankrupt.[23] This is the Black–Scholes equation with volatility (h) and the interest rate factor "e^{-rT}" replaced by $p_0^*(0, T) = p_0(0, T)e^{-\lambda_1\mu_1 T}$. This value reflects the credit risk spread on XYZ debt as determined in the market (see expression (45d). In equation (67) the option value depends upon the pseudo-probability of default. In Merton (1976) the risk of default is assumed to be fully diversifiable implying that $\mu_1 \equiv 1$.

This application gives additional markets in which we can estimate the default pseudo-probability $(\lambda_1\mu_1)$. In the equity option market, it is reflected in the value of the option where it can be implicitly estimated.

GENERALISATIONS AND EXTENSIONS

The above continuous-time economy can be generalised in numerous ways. First, vector stochastic processes for $W_1(t)$ and the bankruptcy processes can be included. These would give a multiple factor model for the default-free term structure of interest rates, and it would allow different credit classes for firm XYZ.

Second, as with the discrete-time model, the bankruptcy process can be correlated with the default-free term structure. This could be handled, for example, by making the pseudo-default probability $(\lambda_1\mu_1)$ a function of the spot rate process. These generalisations follow in a straightforward manner using the martingale pricing technology. Computations, however, become more complicated and numerical approximation procedures need to be employed.

The methodology can be extended to the pricing and hedging of over-the-counter foreign currency derivatives. It also provides a general framework for risk management, as it directly addresses market risk and credit risk. Drawing on the result described by equation (19) for credit-risky bonds, the methodology can be applied to credit-linked notes, credit swaps and over-the-counter derivatives.

Conclusion

This chapter presents a technique for valuing options on a term structure of securities subject to credit risk. Both a stochastic process for the evolution of the default-free term structure and the term structure for risky debt are exogenously specified. Arbitrage-free dynamics for these term structures and a risk-neutral valuation procedure are derived. This methodology is applied to corporate debt, but the technique is applicable to other securities as well.

Appendix

PROOF OF LEMMA 1 Define $N_1(t) \equiv 1(t \geq \tau_1^*)$. Under Assumptions 1 to 5,

$$\tilde{E}_t(e_1(T)) = 1(\tau_1^* \leq t)\delta_1 + 1(\tau_1^* > t)\left[e^{-\lambda_1\mu_1(T-t)} + \delta_1\left(1 - e^{-\lambda_1\mu_1(T-t)}\right)\right]$$

$$\tilde{E}_t(e_1(T)) = N_1(t)e^{-\lambda_1\mu_1(T-t)}\left[\delta_1 - 1\right] + \left[e^{-\lambda_1\mu_1(T-t)} + \delta_1\left(1 - e^{-\lambda_1\mu_1(T-t)}\right)\right]$$

Thus,

$$d\tilde{E}_t(e_1(T)) = e^{-\lambda_1\mu_1(T-t)}(\delta_1 - 1)\left[dN_1(t) - 1\left(t \leq \tau_1^*\right)\lambda_1\mu_1 dt\right]$$

or

$$d\tilde{E}_t(e_1(T)) = \tilde{E}_t(e_1(T))\left[\frac{e^{-\lambda_1\mu_1(T-t)}(\delta_1 - 1)}{e^{-\lambda_1\mu_1(T-t)} + \delta_1\left(1 - e^{-\lambda_1\mu_1(T-t)}\right)}\right]d\tilde{N}_1(t)$$

where $d\tilde{N}_1(t) = dN_1(t) - \lambda_1\mu_1 dt$. Next, $v_1(t, T) = p_0(t, T)\tilde{E}_t(e_1(T))$. Using Itô's lemma and Jacod and Shiryaev (1987; 4.49, p. 52), yields

241

**PRICING
DERIVATIVES ON
FINANCIAL
SECURITIES
SUBJECT TO CREDIT
RISK**

$$dv_1(t, T) = dp_0(t, T)\tilde{E}_t(e_1(T)) + p_0(t, T)d\tilde{E}_t(e(T))$$

Substitution and simplification generates

$$dv_1(t,T) = v_1(t-,T)\left[r_0(t)dt + a(t,T)d\tilde{W}_1(t)\right]$$

$$+ v_1(t-,T)\left[\frac{e^{-\lambda_1\mu_1(T-t)}(\delta_1-1)}{e^{-\lambda_1\mu_1(T-t)} + \delta_1\left(1 - e^{-\lambda_1\mu_1(T-t)}\right)}\right]d\tilde{N}_1(t)$$

where $d\tilde{W}_1(t) = dW_1(t) - \gamma_1(t)dt$. Comparison of expression (42) under expression (45b) gives the result. $\qquad\qquad\qquad\qquad$ *QED*

PROOF OF EXISTENCE AND UNIQUENESS OF A MARTINGALE PROBABILITY FOR XYZ EQUITIES   Let (Ω, Q, F) be the probability space. There exists a unique measure $\tilde{Q}$ making $v_1(t, T)/B(t)$, $p_0(t, T)/B(t)$ and $S(t)/B(t)$ martingales. The probability measure $\tilde{Q}$ is given by

$$\frac{d\tilde{Q}}{dQ} = \exp\left\{\int_0^\tau \gamma_1(s)dW_1(s) + \int_0^\tau \gamma_2(s)dW_2(s) - \frac{1}{2}\int_0^\tau \gamma_1^2(s)ds +\right.$$

$$\left.\int_0^\tau \log\mu_1(s)dN_1(s) + \int_0^\tau \left(1 - \mu_1(s)\right)\lambda_1(s)ds\right\}$$

This can be seen as follows. First, define

$$\tilde{W}_2(t) \equiv W_2(t) - \int_0^\tau \gamma_2(s)ds \qquad\qquad (A)$$

where $\gamma_2: \Omega \times [0, \tau] \to \Re$ is predictable with respect to $(G_t: t \in [0, \tau])$ and uniformly bounded. $(G_t: t \in [0, \tau])$ is defined in note 15.

Using equation (A), we can write $S(t)/B(t)$ as

$$d\left(\frac{S(t)}{B(t)}\right) = \left(\frac{S(t-)}{B(t)}\right) \times$$

$$\left(\xi(t) + \gamma_1(s)\eta_1 + \gamma_2(s)\eta_2 + \lambda_1 1\left(t \le \tau_1^*\right) - \lambda_1\mu_1 1\left(t \le \tau_1^*\right) - r_0(t)\right)dt +$$

$$\left(\frac{S(t-)}{B(t)}\right)\left(\eta_1 d\tilde{W}_1(t) + \eta_2 d\tilde{W}_2(t)\right) - \left(\frac{S(t-)}{B(s)}\right)\left(dN_1(t) - \lambda_1\mu_1 1\left(t \le \tau_1^*\right)dt\right) \quad (B)$$

Selecting $(\gamma_1(t), \gamma_2(t), \mu_1(t))$ to satisfy expression (45) and

$$\xi(t) - r_0(t) + \gamma_1(s)\eta_1 + \gamma_2(s)\eta_2 + \lambda_1 1(t \le \tau_1^*) - \lambda_1\mu_1 1(t \le \tau_1^*) = 0 \qquad (C)$$

makes $p_0(t, T)/B(t)$, $v_1(t, T)/B(t)$ and $S(t)/B(t)$ martingales under $\tilde{Q}$. In this solution, $(\gamma_1(t), \mu_1(t))$ are predictable with respect to the augmented filtration $(G_t: t \in [0, \tau])$. For example, under equation (C), we can rewrite expression (64) as

$$S(t) = \begin{cases} S(0)e^{\int_0^t r_0(s)ds - \frac{1}{2}\left[\eta_1^2 + \eta_2^2\right]t + \lambda_1\mu_1 t + \eta_1\tilde{W}_1(t) + \eta_2\tilde{W}_2(t)} & \text{if } t < \tau_1^* \\ 0 & \text{if } t \ge \tau_1^* \end{cases} \qquad (D)$$

which is a martingale (when divided by $B(t)$) under $\tilde{Q}$.

PRICING
DERIVATIVES ON
FINANCIAL
SECURITIES
SUBJECT TO CREDIT
RISK

In stochastic differential form,

$$\frac{dS(t)}{S(t-)} = r_0(t)\,dt + \eta_1 d\tilde{W}_1(t) + \eta_2 d\tilde{W}_2(t) - \left[d\tilde{N}_1(t) - \lambda_1 \mu_1 dt\right] \tag{E}$$

PROOF OF EXPRESSION (67)

$$\overline{S}(t) \equiv S(0)e^{\int_0^t r_0(s)ds - \frac{1}{2}\left[\eta_1^2 + \eta_2^2\right]t + \lambda_1 \mu_1 t + \eta_1 \tilde{W}_1(t) + \eta_2 \tilde{W}_2(t)} \tag{F}$$

for all $t \in [0, \tau]$. The stochastic process $\overline{S}(t)$ follows a geometric Brownian motion with instantaneous drift $(r_0(t) + \lambda_1 \mu_1)$.

Substitution of equation (F) into equation (64), and algebra, yields

$$C(0) = \tilde{E}\left[\max\left(\frac{\overline{S}(T) - K}{B(T)}, 0\right)\right]\tilde{Q}\left(T < \tau_1^*\right)$$

$$= \tilde{E}\left[\max\left(\frac{\overline{S}(T) - K}{B(T)}, 0\right)\right]e^{-\lambda_1 \mu_1 T} \tag{G}$$

1 *This is similar to spirit to the stated purpose of Ramaswamy and Sundaresan (1986; Section 4). Unfortunately, their valuation equation (11) combined with their terminal condition (p. 269) implies that their debt is* default-free. *The imposition of the local expectation hypothesis (9), p. 268 (versus (5) p. 260) uniquely identifies their premium* p(t) *as a stochastic market price for risk. Thus, they are still valuing riskless debt, albeit with an equilibrium model in which the market price of risk is pre-specified by their expression (10).*

2 *The existence of the credit spread is taken as exogenous. Anderson and Sundaresan (1994) allow for strategic interaction between the debtholders and equityholders and value the claims of the firm in a general dynamic setting, so that the credit spread is endogenous. They do not consider counterparty risk.*

3 *Hull and White (1991) obtain a similar result to our expression (26); however, there is a technical problem with the Hull–White article. Their model is in continuous time where the event of default causes a discontinuity in the option's value. The existence and uniqueness of the equivalent probability measure is simply assumed, without comment about the significance of such discontinuities.*

4 *Strictly speaking, the entire term structure of zero-coupon XYZ debt need not trade directly. Enough XYZ coupon-bearing debt must trade, however, so that the prices of all the zeros can be recovered.*

5 *Eberhart, Moore and Rosenfeldt (1990) report that in a sample of 24 firms, the absolute priority rule was violated in 23 cases. Weiss (1990) examines 37 firms and reports violations of the absolute priority rule in 27 cases.*

6 *These issues are discussed in Weiss (1990) and Schwartz (1993).*

7 *Bankruptcy often involves the acceleration of claims in that all debt becomes immediately payable. This acceleration of debt can be partially incorporated into our model by recognising that different risk classes of debt within the same firm can have different recovery rates at different times (δ_t's). δ_t can be greater for those classes of debt that would receive larger payoffs at different times due to acceleration.*

8 *For a more complete description of different possible contingencies, see Cooper and Mello (1991).*

9 *When the swap is first entered into, $\overline{R}$ is determined such that $v_s(0) = 0$. $\overline{R}$ is then called the swap rate.*

10 *These measurability and boundedness conditions can be found in Jarrow and Madan (1995).*

11 *See Jarrow and Madan (1995) for these measurability and integrability conditions.*

12 *See note 14. This is a no-arbitrage restriction.*

13 *For the derivation, see Jarrow and Madan (1995). Note that $t- \equiv \lim_{\substack{\varepsilon \to 0 \\ \varepsilon \geq 0}} (t-\varepsilon)$.*

14 *See Jarrow and Madan (1995). Expressions (45a)–(45c) make the stochastic processes in expressions (41–43) martingales under the transformation $d\tilde{W}_1 = dW_1 - \gamma_1(s)ds$ and with τ_1^* distributed exponentially with parameter $\lambda_1 \mu_1(t)dt$.*

15 *That is, letting $\tilde{Q}$ be the martingale probability with expectation operator $\overline{E}(\cdot)$, $\tilde{E}\left(\left[X/B(T)\right]^2\right) < +\infty$.*

16 *If we had allowed $\sigma(t, T)$ in Assumption 1 to differ from $\sigma(t, T)$ in Assumption 2, then this lemma would have implied their equality as well.*

243

PRICING
DERIVATIVES ON
FINANCIAL
SECURITIES
SUBJECT TO CREDIT
RISK

17 *If there are* b *independent Brownian motions,* $W_i(t)$ *for* $i = 1,..., b$ *with volatilities* $a_i(t, T)$ *for* $i = 1,..., b$, *then* q^2 *in* (55) *becomes* $\sum_{i=1}^{b} \int_t^m [a_i(u, M) - a_i(u, m)]^2 ds$. *Otherwise, the formula remains unchanged.*

18 *The position of an option writer is of unlimited liability and, therefore, default risk to the purchaser is relevant. In contrast, the purchaser of the option contract has limited liability, so the writer does not face a symmetric default risk from the purchaser. In addition, when creating a synthetic long position in an option, the borrowed funds are default-free as their value is always covered by the long position in the underlying security. Recall that the (synthetic call) portfolio's value is non-negative with probability* 1

19 *Johnson and Stulz's (1987) approach is easily understood using our methodology. Our equation (57) corresponds to their equation (1) where,*

$$e_2(T) \equiv \begin{cases} 1 & \text{if } V(T) \geq S(T) - X > 0 \\ \dfrac{V(T)}{S(T) - X} & \text{if } S(T) - X > V(T) \geq 0 \end{cases}$$

The notion $V(T)$, $S(T)$, *and* X *are from Johnson and Stulz (1987). In addition, Johnson and Stulz assume constant interest rates. Unlike our simple model, they allow* $e_2(T)$ *to be random and to depend on the asset underlying the option* ($S(T)$). *This correlation is easily included within our framework. With the* $e_2(T)$ *process as above, Johnson and Stulz (1987) is a special case of our more general methodology.*

20 *Let* $(G_t: t \in [0, \tau])$ *be the augmented filtration generated by* W_1, N_1 *and* W_2 *where* $(W_2(t): t \in [0, \tau])$ *is a Brownian motion independent of* $\{W_1(t): t \in [0, \tau]\}$ *and* $\{N_1(t): t \in [0, \tau]\}$ *where* $N_1(t) \equiv 1(t \geq \tau_1^*)$. *Then, we require that* $\xi: \Omega \times [0, \tau] \to \Re$ *is predictable with respect to* $(G_t: t \in [0, \tau])$ *and uniformly bounded.*

21 *The* $\lambda_1 t$ *term appears in the first line of expression (64) so that* $E_0(dS(t)/S(t)) = \xi(s)ds$, *see the stochastic differential equation (E) in the Appendix.*

22 *Deviations from absolute priority rules typically imply that XYZ stock does not have zero value after bankruptcy. This can be incorporated into the above model (64) by letting* $S(t)$ *have a constant residual value after bankruptcy. The analysis with this extension follows in a straightforward manner. Alternatively, after bankruptcy, one could allow* $S(t)$ *to follow a different (lower valued) stochastic process. This generalisation is left for future research.*

23 *For put options, a similar analysis gives*

$$Put(0) = Kp_0^*(0, T)\Phi(-g + h) - S(0)\Phi(-g) + Kp_0(0, T)[1 - e^{-\lambda_1\mu_1 T}]$$

and the usual put-call parity result holds.

BIBLIOGRAPHY

Amin, K., and R. Jarrow, 1991, "Pricing Foreign Currency Options under Stochastic Interest Rates", *Journal of International Money and Finance* 10, pp. 310-29.

Amin, K., and R. Jarrow, 1992, "Pricing Options on Risky Assets in a Stochastic Interest Rate Economy", *Mathematical Finance* 2, pp. 217-37.

Anderson, R. W., and S. Sundaresan, 1992, "Design and Valuation of Debt Contracts", Working Paper, Columbia University.

Black, F., and J. Cox, 1976, "Valuing Corporate Securities: Some Effects of Bond Indenture Provisions", *Journal of Finance* 31, pp. 351-67.

Black, F., E. Derman and W. Toy, 1990, "A one factor model of interest rates and its application to treasury bond options," *Financial Analyst Journal* 46, pp. 33-9.

Chance, D., 1990, "Default Risk and the Duration of Zero Coupon Bonds", *Journal of Finance* 45, pp. 265-74.

Cooper, I., and A. Mello, 1990, "Pricing and Optimal Use of Forward Contracts with Default Risk", Working Paper, London Business School.

Cooper, I., and A. Mello, 1991, "The Default Risk of Swaps", *Journal of Finance* 45, pp. 265-74.

Duffie, D., 1989, *Futures Markets* (Prentice-Hall: Englewood Cliffs, N.J.).

Eberhart, A. C., W. T. Moore and R. L. Rosenfeldt, 1990, "Security Pricing and Derivations from the Absolute Priority Rule in Bankruptcy Proceeding", *Journal of Finance* 45, pp. 1457-1489.

Harrison, J. M., and S. Pliska, 1981, "Martingales and Stochastic Integrals in the Theory of Continuous Trading", *Stochastic Processes and Their Applications* 11, pp. 215-60.

244

PRICING
DERIVATIVES ON
FINANCIAL
SECURITIES
SUBJECT TO CREDIT
RISK

Heath, D., R. Jarrow and A. Morton, 1992, "Bond Pricing and the Term Structure of Interest Rates: A New Methodology for Contingent Claims Valuation", *Econometrica* 60, pp. 77-105.

Ho, T., and S. Lee, 1986, "Term Structure Movements and Pricing Interest Rate Contingent Claims", *Journal of Finance* 41, pp. 1011-30.

Ho, T., and R. Singer, 1982, "Bond Indenture provisions and the Risk of Corporate Debt", *Journal of Financial Economics* 10, pp. 375-406.

Ho, T., and R. Singer, 1984, "The Value of Corporate Debt with a Sinking Fund Provision", *Journal of Business* 57, pp. 315-36.

Hull, J., and A. White, 1990, "Pricing Interest Rate Derivative Securities", *Review of Financial Studies* 3, pp. 573-92.

Hull, J., and A. White, 1991, "The Impact of Default Risk on Options and Other Derivative Securities", *Journal of Banking and Finance.*

Jacod, J., and A. N. Shiryaev, 1987, *Limit Theorems for Stochastic Processes* (Springer Verlag: New York).

Jarrow, R., and D. Madan, 1995, "Option Pricing Using the Term Structure of Interest Rates to Hedge Systematic Discontinuities in Asset Returns", *Mathematical Finance*, Forthcoming.

Jarrow, R., and S. Turnbull, 1998, "A Unified Approach for Pricing Contingent Claims on Multiple term structures: The foreign currency analogy", *Review of Quantitative Finance and Accounting* 110, pp. 5-19.

Johnson, H., and R. Stulz, 1987, "The Pricing of Options with Default Risk", *Journal of Finance* 42, pp. 267-80.

Jones, E., S. Mason and E. Rosenfeld, 1984, "Contingent Claims Analysis of Corporate Capital Structures: An Empirical Investigation", *Journal of Finance* 39, pp. 611-27.

Kim, J., K. Ramaswamy and S. Sundaresan, 1993, "Does Default Risk in Coupons Affect the Valuation of Corporate Bonds? A Contingent Claims Model", *Financial Management*, pp. 117-31.

Litterman, R., and T. Iben, 1991, "Corporate Bond Valuation and the Term Structure of Credit Spreads", *Financial Analysts Journal* Spring, pp. 52-64.

Longstaff, F., and E. Schwartz, 1992, "Valuing Risky Debt: A New Approach", Working paper, University of California, Los Angeles.

Merton, R. C., 1974, "On the Pricing of Corporate Debt: The Risk Structure of Interest Rates", *Journal of Finance* 29, pp. 449-70.

Merton, R. C., 1976, "Option Pricing when Underlying Stock Returns Are Discontinuous", *Journal of Financial Economics* 3, pp. 125-44.

Merton, R. C, 1977, "On the Pricing of Contingent Claims and the Modigliani–Miller Theorem", *Journal of Financial Economics* 5, pp. 241-9.

Musiela, M., S. M. Turnbull and L. M. Wakeman, 1993, "Interest Rate Risk Management", *Review of Futures Markets* 12, pp. 221-61.

Nielsen, L. T., J. Saá-Requejo and P. Santa-Clara, 1993, "Default Risk and Interest Rate Risk: The Term Structure of Default Spreads", Working paper, INSEAD, France.

Ramaswamy, K. and S. Sundaresan, 1986, "The Valuation of Floating-Rate Instruments", *Journal of Financial Economics* 17, pp. 251-72.

Schwartz, A., 1993, "Bankruptcy Workouts and Debt Contracts", *Journal of Law and Economics* 36, pp. 595-632.

Titman, S. and W. Torous, 1989, "Valuing Commercial Mortgages: An Empirical Investigation of the Contingent Claims Approach to Pricing Risky Debt", *Journal of Finance* 44, pp. 345-73.

Weiss, L. A., 1990, "Bankruptcy Resolution: Direct Costs and Violations of Priority of Claims", *Journal of Financial Economics* 27, pp. 285-314.

17

Credit Swap Valuation

Darrell Duffie

Stanford University Graduate School of Business

T his review of the pricing of credit swaps, a form of derivative security that can be viewed as default insurance on loans or bonds, begins with a description of the credit swap contract, turns to pricing by reference to spreads over the risk-free rate of par floating-rate bonds of the same quality, and then considers model-based pricing. The role of asset swap spreads as a reference for pricing credit swaps is also considered.

Credit swaps pay the buyer of protection a given contingent amount at the time of a given credit event, such as a default. The contingent amount is often the difference between the face value of a bond and its market value and is paid at the time the underlying bond defaults. The buyer of protection pays an annuity premium until the time of the credit event or the maturity date of the credit swap, whichever is first. The credit event must be documented with a notice, supported with evidence of public announcement of the event in, for example, the international press. The amount to be paid at the time of the credit event is determined by one or more third parties and based on physical or cash settlement, as indicated in the confirmation form of the OTC credit swap transaction, a standard contract form with indicated alternatives.

The term "swap" applies to credit swaps because they can be viewed, under certain ideal conditions to be explained in this article, as a swap of a default-free floating-rate note for a defaultable floating-rate note.

Credit swaps are currently perhaps the most popular of credit derivatives.[1] Unlike many other derivative forms, in a credit swap, payment to the buyer of protection is triggered by a contractually defined event that must be documented.

The basics

The basic credit swap contract is as follows. Parties A and B enter into a contract terminating at the time of a given credit event or at a stated maturity, whichever is first. A commonly stipulated credit event is default by a named issuer – say, Entity C, which could be a corporation or a sovereign issuer. Credit events may be defined in terms of downgrades, events that could instigate the default of one or more counterparties, or other credit-related occurrences.[2] Swaps involve some risk of disagreement about whether the event has, in fact, occurred, but in this discussion of valuing the credit swap, such risk of documentation or enforceability will be ignored.

In the event of termination at the designated credit event, Party A pays Party B a stipulated termination amount. For example, in the most common form of credit swap, called a "default swap", if the termination is triggered by the default of Entity C, A pays B an amount that is, in effect, the difference between the face value and the market value of the designated note issued by C.

Reprinted with permission from Financial Analysts Journal, *January/February 1999. ©1999, Association for Investment Mangement and Research, Charlottesville, VA. All rights reserved. Research assistance by Jun Pan is gratefully acknowledged. Discussions with Angelo Aravantis, David Lando, Jean-Paul Laurent, Wolfgang Schmidt, Ken Singleton and Lucie Tepla are much appreciated. This work was supported in part by the Gifford Fong Associates Fund at the Graduate School of Business, Stanford University. A previous version of this document can be found at http://www.stanford.edu/-duffie/working.htm.*

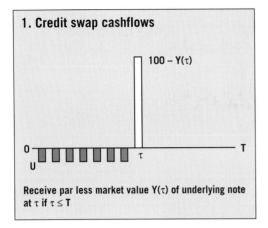

1. Credit swap cashflows

Receive par less market value Y(τ) of underlying note at τ if τ ≤ T

In compensation for what it may receive in the event of termination by a credit event, until the maturity of the credit swap or termination by the designated credit event, Party B pays Party A an annuity at a rate called the "credit swap spread" or, sometimes, the "credit swap premium".

The cashflows of a credit swap are illustrated in Figure 1, where U is the swap's annuity coupon rate, τ is the default event time, Y(τ) is the market value of the designated underlying note at time τ, and T is the maturity date. The payment at credit event time τ, if before maturity T, is the difference, D, between the underlying note's face value – 100 units, for example – and Y(τ), or in this case, D = 100 − Y(τ).

For instance, in some cases, the compensating annuity may be paid as a spread over the usual plain-vanilla (non-credit) swap rate.[3] For example, if the five-year fixed-for-floating interest rate swap rate is 6% versus Libor and B is the fixed-rate payer in the default swap, then B pays a fixed rate higher than the usual 6%. If, for example, B pays 7.5% fixed versus Libor and if the C-issued note underlying the default swap is of the same notional amount as the interest rate swap, then in this case, the default swap spread is 150 basis points. If B is the floating-rate payer on the interest rate swap, then B pays floating plus a spread in return for the usual market fixed rate on swaps or, in effect, receives fixed less a spread. The theoretical default swap spread is not necessarily the same in the case of B paying fixed as in B paying floating.

In general, combining the credit swap with an interest rate swap affects the quoted credit swap spread because an interest rate swap whose fixed rate is the at-market swap rate for maturity T but has a random early termination does not have a market value of zero. For example, if the term structure of forward rates is steeply upward sloping, then an at-market interest rate swap to maturity T or the credit event time, whichever is first, has a lower fixed rate than a plain-vanilla at-market interest rate swap to maturity T. A credit spread of 150 bp over the at-market plain-vanilla swap rate to maturity T, therefore, represents a larger credit spread than does a credit swap without an interest rate swap that pays a premium of 150 bp.

Apparently, when corporate bonds are the underlying securities, default swaps in which the payment at default is reduced by the accrued portion of the credit swap premium are not unusual. This variation is briefly considered later.

In short, the classic credit swap can be thought of as an insurance contract in which the insured party pays an insurance premium in return for coverage against a loss that may occur because of a credit event.

The credit swap involves two pricing problems:

❑ At origination, the standard credit swap involves no exchange of cashflows and, therefore (ignoring dealer margins and transaction costs), has a market value of zero. One must, however, determine the at-market annuity premium rate, U, for which the market value of the credit swap is indeed zero. This at-market rate is the credit swap premium, sometimes called the "market credit swap spread".

❑ After origination, changes in market interest rates and in the credit quality of the issuing entity, as well as the passage of time, typically change the market value of the credit swap. For a given credit swap with stated annuity rate U, one must then determine the current market value, which is not generally zero.

When making markets, the first pricing problem is the more critical. When hedging or marking to market, the second problem is relevant. Methods for solving the two problems are similar. The second problem is generally the more challenging because off-market default swaps have less liquidity and because pricing references, such as bond spreads, are of relatively less use.

This chapter considers simple credit swaps and their extensions.[4] In all the following discussions, the credit swap counterparties A and B are assumed to be default free in order to avoid dealing here with the pricing impact of default by counterparties A and B, which can be treated by the first-to-default results in Duffie (1998b).

Simple credit swap spreads

For this section, the contingent payment amount specified in the credit swap (the amount to be paid if the credit event occurs) is the difference between the face value of a note issued by Entity C and the note's market value $Y(\tau)$ at the credit event time, τ – that is, the contingent-payment amount is $D = 100 - Y(\tau)$.

STARTER CASE

The assumptions for this starter case are as follows:

❑ The swap involves no embedded interest rate swap. That is, the default swap is an exchange of a constant coupon rate, U, paid by Party B until termination at maturity or at the stated credit event (which may or may not be default of the underlying C-issued note.) This constraint eliminates the need to consider the value of an interest rate swap with early termination at a credit event.

❑ There is no payment of the accrued credit swap premium at default.

❑ The underlying note issued by C is a par floating-rate note (FRN) with the maturity of the credit swap. This important restriction will be relaxed later.

❑ For this starter case, the assumption is that an investor can create a short position by selling today the underlying C-issued note for its current market value and can buy back the note on the date of the credit event, or on the credit swap maturity date, at its then-current market value, with no other cashflows.

❑ A default-free FRN exists with floating rate R_t at date t. The coupon payments on the FRN issued by C (the C-FRN) are contractually specified to be $R_t + S$, the floating rate plus a fixed spread, S. In practice, FRN spreads are usually relative to Libor or some other benchmark floating rate that need not be a pure default-free rate. Having the pure default-free floating rate and reference rate (which might be Libor) differ by a constant poses no difficulties for this analysis. (Bear in mind that the short-term US Treasury rate is not a pure default-free interest rate because of repo (repurchase agreement) "specials" (discussed later) and the "moneyness" or tax advantages of Treasuries.[5] A better benchmark for risk-free borrowing is the term general collateral rate, which is close to a default-free rate and has typically been close to Libor, with a slowly varying spread to Libor in US markets.) For example, suppose the C-FRN is at a spread of 100 bps to Libor, which is at a spread to the general collateral rate that, although varying over time, is approximately 5 bp. Then, for purposes of this analysis, an approximation of the spread of the C-FRN to the default-free floating rate would be 105 bp.

❑ In cash markets for the default-free note and C-FRN, there are no transaction costs, such as bid–ask spreads. In particular, at the initiation of the credit swap, an investor can sell the underlying C-FRN at its market value. At termination, the assumption is that an investor can buy the C-FRN at market value.

❑ The termination payment if a credit event occurs is made at the immediately following coupon date on the underlying C-issued note. (If not, the question of accrued interest arises and can be accommodated by standard time value of money calculations, shown later.)

❑ If the credit swap is terminated by the stated credit event, the swap is settled by the physical delivery of the C-FRN in exchange for cash in the amount of its face value. (Many credit swaps are settled in cash and, so far, neither physical nor cash settlement seems to have gained predominance as the standard method.)

❑ Tax effects can be ignored. (If not, the calculations to be made are applied after tax and using the tax rate of investors that are indifferent to purchasing the default swap at its market price.)

With these assumptions, one can "price" the credit swap; that is, one can compute the at-market credit swap spread on the basis of a synthesis of Party B's cashflows on the credit swap, by the following arbitrage argument.

An investor can short the part C-FRN for an initial cash receivable of, say, 100 units of account and invest the 100 units in a par default-free FRN. The investor holds this portfolio through maturity or the stated credit event. In the meantime, the investor pays the floating rate plus spread on the C-FRN and receives the floating rate on the default-free FRN. The net paid is the spread.

If the credit event does not occur before maturity, both notes mature at par value and no net cashflow occurs at termination.

If the credit event does occur before maturity, the investor liquidates the portfolio at the coupon date immediately following the event and collects the difference between the market value of the default-free FRN (which is par on a coupon date) and the market value of the C-FRN – in this example, the difference is $D = 100 - Y(\tau)$. (Liquidation calls for termination of the short position in the C-FRN, which involves buying the C-FRN in the market for delivery against the short sale through, for example, the completion of a repo contract.)

Because this contingent amount, the difference D, is the same as the amount specified in the credit swap contract, the absence of arbitrage implies that the unique arbitrage-free at-market credit swap spread, denoted U, is S, the spread over the risk-free rate on the underlying floating-rate notes issued by C. (That is, combining this strategy with Party A's cashflows as the seller of the credit swap results in a net constant annuity cashflow of $U - S$ until maturity or termination. Therefore, in the absence of other costs, for no arbitrage to exist, U must equal S.)

This arbitrage under its ideal assumptions, is illustrated in Figure 2.

EXTENSION: THE REFERENCE PAR SPREAD FOR DEFAULT SWAPS

Provided the credit swap is, in fact, a default swap, the restrictive assumption that the underlying note has the same maturity as the credit swap can be relaxed. In this case, the relevant par spread for fixing the credit swap spread is that of a (possibly different) C-issued FRN that is of the same maturity as the credit swap and of the same priority as the underlying note. This note is the "reference C-FRN." As long as absolute priority applies at default (so that the underlying note and the reference note have the same recovery value at default), the previous arbitrage pricing argument applies. This argument works, under the stated assumptions, even if the underlying note is a fixed-rate note of the same seniority as the reference C-FRN.

Some cautions are in order here. First, often no reference C-FRN exists. Second, absolute priority need not apply in practice. For example, a senior short-maturity FRN and a senior long-maturity fixed-rate note may represent significantly different bargaining power, especially in a reorganisation scenario precipitated by default.

EXTENSION: ADDING REPO SPECIALS AND TRANSACTION COSTS

Another important and common relaxation of the assumptions in the starter case involves the ability to freely short the reference C-FRN. A typical method of shorting securities is via a reverse repo combined with a cash sale. That is, through a reverse repo, an investor can arrange to receive the reference note as collateral on a loan to a given term. Rather than holding the note as collateral, the investor can immediately sell the note. In effect, the investor has then created a short position in the reference note through the term of the repo. As shown in the top part of Figure 3 (with Dickson as the investor), each repo involves a collateralised interest rate, or repo rate, R. A loan of L dollars at repo rate R for a term of T years results in

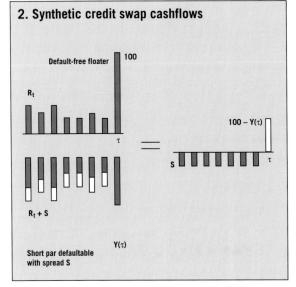

2. Synthetic credit swap cashflows

Default-free floater   100

R_t

τ

$R_t + S$

$Y(\tau)$

Short par defaultable
with spread S

$100 - Y(\tau)$

S τ

a loan repayment of $L(1 + RT)$ at term. As shown in the bottom part of Figure 3, the repo counterparty – in this case, Jones – who is offering the loan and receiving the collateral may, at the initiation of the repo, sell the collateral at its market value, $Y(0)$. Then, at the maturity date of the repo contract, Jones may buy the note back at its market value, $Y(T)$, so as to return it to the original repo counterparty, in this case, Dickson. If the general prevailing interest rate, r, for such loans, called the "general collateral rate", is larger than the specific collateral rate R for the loan collateralised by the C-issued note in question, Jones will have suffered costs in creating the short position in the underlying C-issued note.[6]

In many cases, one cannot arrange a reverse repo at the general collateral rate (GCR). If the reference note is "scarce", an investor may be forced to offer a repo rate that is below the GCR in order to reverse in the C-FRN as collateral. This situation is termed a repo special (see, eg, Duffie, 1996). In addition, particularly with risky FRNs, a substantial bid–ask spread may be present in the market for the reference FRN at initiation of the repo (when one sells) and at termination (when one buys).

Suppose that a term reverse repo collateralised by the C-FRN can be arranged, with maturity equal to the maturity date of the credit swap. Also suppose that default of the collateral triggers early termination of the repo at the originally agreed repo rate (which is the case in many jurisdictions). The term repo special, Z, is the difference between the term GCR and the term specific collateral rate for the C-FRN. Shorting the C-FRN, therefore, requires an extra annuity payment of Z. The arbitrage-based default swap spread would then be approximately $S + Z$. If the term repo does not necessarily terminate at the credit event, this spread is not an exact arbitrage-based spread. Because the probability of a credit event occurring well before maturity is typically small, however, and because term repo specials are often small, the difference may not be large in practice.[7]

Now consider the other side of the swap. For the synthesis of a short position in the credit swap, an investor purchases the C-FRN and places it into a term repo to capture the term repo special.

If transaction costs in the cash market are a factor, the credit swap broker/dealer may incur risk from uncovered credit swap positions, transaction costs, or some of each, and may, in principle, charge an additional premium. With two-sided market making and diversification, how quickly these costs and risks build up over a portfolio of positions is not clear.[8]

The difference between a transaction cost and a repo special is important. A transaction cost simply widens the bid–ask spread on a default swap, increasing the default swap spread quoted by the broker/dealer who sells the default swap and reducing the quoted default swap spread when the broker/dealer is asked by a customer to buy a default swap from the customer. A repo special, however, is not itself a transaction cost; it can be thought of as an extra source of interest income on the underlying C-FRN, a source that effectively changes the spread relative to the default-free rate. Substantial specials, which raise the cost of providing the credit swap, do not necessarily increase the bid–ask spread. For example, in synthesising a short position in a default swap, an investor can place the associated long position in the C-FRN into a repo position and profit from the repo special.

In summary, under the assumptions stated up to this point, a dealer can broker a default swap (that is, take the position of Party A) at a spread of approximately $S + Z$ with a bid–ask spread of K, where

❑ S is the par spread on a reference floating-rate note issued by a named entity, called here Entity C, of the same maturity as the default swap and of the same seniority as the underlying note;

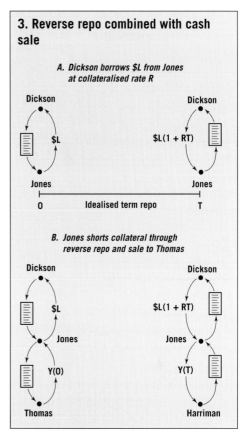

3. Reverse repo combined with cash sale

A. Dickson borrows $L from Jones at collateralised rate R

0   Idealised term repo   T

B. Jones shorts collateral through reverse repo and sale to Thomas

❑ Z is the term repo special on par floating-rate notes issued by C or else an estimate of the annuity rate paid, throughout the term of the default swap, for maintaining a short position in the reference note to the termination of the credit swap; and

❑ K contains any annuitised transaction costs (such as cash market bid–ask spreads) for hedging, any risk premium for unhedged portions of the risk (which would apply in imperfect capital markets), overhead and a profit margin.

In practice, estimating the effective term repo special is usually difficult, because default swaps are normally of much longer term than repo positions. In some cases, liquidity in the credit swap market has apparently been sufficient to allow some traders to quote term repo rates for the underlying collateral by reference to the credit swap spread.

EXTENSION: PAYMENT OF ACCRUED CREDIT SWAP PREMIUM

Some credit swaps, more frequently on underlying corporate rather than sovereign bonds, specify that, at default, the buyer of protection must pay the credit swap premium that has accrued since the last coupon date. For example, with a credit swap spread of 300 bp and default one-third of the way through a current semi-annual coupon period, the buyer of protection would receive face value less recovery value of the underlying asset less one-third of the semi-annual annuity payment, which would be 0.5% of the underlying face value.

For reasonably small default probabilities and intercoupon periods, the expected difference in time between the credit event and the previous coupon date is approximately half the length of an intercoupon period. Thus, for pricing purposes in all but extreme cases, one can think of the credit swap as equivalent to payment at default of face value less recovery value less one-half of the regular default swap premium payment.

For example, suppose there is some risk-neutral probability $h > 0$ per year for the credit event.[9] Then one estimates a reduction in the at-market credit swap spread for the accrued premium that is below the spread that is appropriate without the accrued-premium feature – approximately $hS/2n$, where n is the number of coupons per year of the underlying bond. For a pure default swap, spread S is smaller than h because of partial recovery, so this correction is smaller than $h^2/2n$, which is negligible for small h. For example, at semi-annual credit swap coupon intervals and for a risk-neutral mean arrival rate of the credit event of 2% per year, the correction for the accrued-premium effect is less than 1 bp.

EXTENSION: ACCRUED INTEREST ON THE UNDERLYING NOTES

For calculating the synthetic arbitrage described previously, the question of accrued interest payment on the default-free floating rate note arises. The typical credit swap specifies payment of the difference between face value *without* accrued interest and market value of the underlying note. However, the arbitrage portfolio described here (long a default-free floater, short a defaultable floater) is worth face value *plus accrued interest on the default-free note* less recovery on the underlying defautable note. If the credit event involves default of the underlying note, the previous arbitrage argument is not quite right.

Consider, for example, a one-year default swap with semi-annual coupons. Suppose the Libor rate is 8%. Then, the expected value of the accrued interest on the default-free note at default is approximately 2% of face value for small default probabilities. Suppose the risk-neutral probability of occurrence of the credit event is 4% per year. Then, the market value of the credit swap to the buyer of protection is reduced roughly 8 bp of face value and, therefore, the at-market credit swap spread is reduced roughly 8 bp.

Generally, for credit swaps of any maturity with relatively small and constant risk-neutral default probabilities and relatively flat term structures of default-free rates, the reduction in the at-market credit swap spread for the accrued-interest effect, below the par floating rate-spread plus effective repo special, is approximately $hr/2n$, where h is the annual risk-neutral probability of occurrence of the credit, r is the average of the default-free forward rates through credit swap maturity, and n is the number of coupons per year of the underlying bond. Of course, one could work out the effect more precisely with a term-structure model, as described later.

EXTENSION: APPROXIMATING THE REFERENCE FLOATING-RATE SPREAD

If no par floating-rate note of the same credit quality is available whose maturity is that of the default swap, then one can attempt to "back out" the reference par spread, S, from other spreads. For example, suppose C issues an FRN of the swap maturity and of the same seniority as the underlying note and it is trading at a price, p, that is not necessarily par and paying a spread of $\hat{S}$ over the default-free floating rate.

Let AP denote the associated annuity price – that is, the present value of an annuity paid at a rate of 1 unit until the credit swap termination (default of the underlying note or maturity).

For reasonably small credit risks and interest rates, AP is close to the default-free annuity price because most of the market value of the credit risk of an FRN is associated in this case with potential loss of principal. A more precise computation of AP is considered later.

The difference between a par and a non-par FRN with the same maturity is the coupon spread (assuming the same recovery at default); therefore,

$$p - 1 = AP(\hat{S} - S)$$

where S is the implied reference par spread. Solving for the implied reference par spread produces

$$S = \hat{S} + \frac{1 - p}{AP}$$

With this formula, one can estimate the reference par spread, S.

If the relevant price information is for a fixed-rate note issued by C of the reference maturity and seniority, one can again resort to the assumption that its recovery of face value at default is the same as that of a par floater of the same seniority (which is again reasonable on legal grounds in a liquidation scenario). And one can again attempt to "back out" the reference par floating-rate spread.

Spreads over default-free rates on par fixed-rate notes and par floating-rate notes are approximately equal.[10] Thus, if the only reference spread is a par fixed-rate spread, F, using F in place of S in estimating the default swap spread is reasonably safe.

An example in Figure 4 shows the close relationship between the term structures of default swap spreads and par fixed-coupon yield spreads for the same credit quality.[11] Some of the difference between the spreads shown in Figure 4 is, in fact, the accrued-interest effect discussed in the previous subsection.

If the reference pricing information is for a non-par fixed-rate note, then one can proceed as before. Let p denote the price of the available fixed-rate note, with spread $\hat{F}$ over the default-free rate. Then,

$$p - 1 = AP(\hat{F} - F)$$

where AP is again the annuity price to maturity or default. So, with an estimate of AP, one can obtain an estimate of the par fixed spread, F, which is a close approximation of the par floating-rate spread, S, the quantity needed to compute the default swap spread.[12]

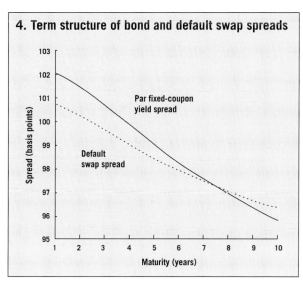

4. Term structure of bond and default swap spreads

Estimating hazard rates and defaultable annuity prices

The hazard rate for the credit event is the arrival rate of the credit event (in the sense of Poisson processes). For example, a constant hazard rate of 400 bps represents a mean arrival rate of 4 times per 100 years. The mean time arrival, conditional on no event arrival data by T, remains 25 years after T for any T. Begin by assuming a constant risk-neutral hazard rate, h, for the event. In this simple model (to be generalised shortly), at any time, given that the credit event has not yet occurred, the amount of time until it does occur is risk-neutrally exponentially distributed with parameter h. For small h, the probability of defaulting during a time period of small length, Δ, conditional on survival to the beginning of the period, is then approximately $h\Delta$. This section contains some intermediate calculations that can be used to estimate implied hazard rates and the annuity price.

THE CASE OF CONSTANT DEFAULT HAZARD RATE

Suppose default by Entity C occurs at a risk-neutral constant hazard rate of h. In that case, default occurs at a time that, under "risk-neutral probabilities", is the first jump time of a Poisson process with intensity h. Let

❑ $a_i(h)$ be the value at time zero of receiving 1 unit of account at the ith coupon date in the event that default is after that date and
❑ $b_i(h)$ be the value at time zero of receiving 1 unit of account at the ith coupon date in the event that default is between the $(i-1)$th and the ith coupon date.

Then,

$$a_i(h) = \exp\{-[h + y(i)]T(i)\}$$

where $T(i)$ is time to maturity of the ith coupon date and $y(i)$ is the continuously compounding default-free zero-coupon yield to the ith coupon date. Similarly, under these assumptions,

$$b_i(h) = \exp[-y(i)T(i)]\{\exp[-hT(i-1)] - \exp[-hT(i)]\}$$

The price of an annuity of 1 unit of account paid at each coupon date until default by C or maturity $T(n)$ is

$$A(h, T) = a_1(h) + \cdots + a_n(h)$$

The market value of a payment of 1 unit of account at the first coupon date after default by C, provided the default date is before maturity date $T(n)$, is

$$B(h, T) = b_1(h) + \cdots + b_n(h)$$

Now, consider a classic default swap:
❑ Party B pays Party A a constant annuity U until maturity T or the default time τ of the underlying note issued by C.
❑ If $\tau \leq T$, then at τ, Party A pays Party B 1 unit of account minus the value at τ of the underlying note issued by C.

Suppose now that the loss of face value at default carries no risk premium and has an expected value of f.[13] Then, given the parameters (T, U) of the default swap contract and given the default-risk-free term structure, one can compute the market value of the classic default swap as a function of any assumed default parameters h and f:

$$V(h, f, T, U) = B(h, T)f - A(h, T)U$$

The at-market default swap spread, $U(h, T, f)$, is obtained by solving $V(h, f, T, U) = 0$ for

U, leaving

$$U(h,T,f) = \frac{B(h,T)}{A(h,T)}$$

For more accuracy, one can easily account for the difference in time between the credit event and the subsequent coupon date. At small hazard rates, this difference is slightly more than half the intercoupon period of the credit swap and can be treated analytically in a direct manner. Alternatively, one can make a simple approximating adjustment by noting that the effect is equivalent to the accrued-interest effect in adjusting the par floating-rate spread to the credit swap spread. As mentioned previously, this adjustment causes an increase in the implied default swap spread that is on the order of $hr/2n$, where r is the average of the intercoupon default-free forward rates through maturity. (One can obtain a better approximation for a steeply sloped forward-rate curve.)

Estimates of the expected loss, f, at default and the risk-neutral hazard rate, h, can be obtained from the prices of bonds or notes issued by Entity C, from risk-free rates, and from data on recovery values for bonds or notes of the same seniority.[14] For example, suppose a C-issued FRN, which is possibly different from the note underlying the default swap, sells at a price p, has maturity $\hat{T}$, and has spread $\hat{S}$. And suppose the expected default loss of this note, relative to face value, is $\hat{f}$. Under the assumptions stated here, a portfolio containing a risk-free floater and a short position in this C-issued FRN (with no repo specials) has a market value of

$$1 - p = A(h, \hat{T})\hat{S} + B(h, \hat{T})\hat{f}$$

This equation can be solved for the implied risk-neutral hazard rate, h.

Provided the reference prices of notes used for this purpose are near par, a certain robustness is associated with uncertainty about recovery. For example, an upward bias in f results in a downward bias in h and these errors (for small h) approximately cancel each other out when the mark-to-market value of the default swap, V(h, f, T, U), is being estimated. To obtain this robustness, it is best to use a reference note of approximately the same maturity as that of the default swap.

If the C-issued note that is chosen for price reference is a fixed-rate note with price p, coupon rate c, expected loss $\hat{f}$ at default relative to face value, and maturity $\hat{T}$, then h can be estimated from the pricing formula

$$p = A(h, T)c + B(h, \hat{T})(1 - \hat{f})$$

To check the sensitivity of the model to choice of risk-neutral default arrival rate and expected recovery, one can use the intuition that the coupon yield spread of a fixed-rate bond is roughly the product of the mean default intensity and the fractional loss of value at default. This intuition can be given a formal justification in certain settings, as explained in Duffie and Singleton (1997). For example, Figure 5 contains plots of the risk-neutral mean (set equal to initial default) intensity $\bar{h}$ implied by the term-structure model and that mean intensity implied by the approximation $S = f\bar{h}$, for various par 10-year coupon spreads S at each assumed level of expected recovery of face value at default, $w = (1 - f)$.

Figure 5 shows that, up to a high level of fractional recovery, the effects of varying h and f are more or less offsetting in the fashion previously suggested. (That is, if one overestimates f by a factor of 2, even a crude term-structure model will underestimate h by a factor of roughly 2 and the implied par-coupon spread will be relatively unaffected, which means that the default swap spread is also relatively unaffected.) This approximation is more accurate for shorter maturities. The fact that the approximation works poorly at high spreads is mainly because par spreads are measured on the basis

5. Hazard rate implied by spread and expected recovery

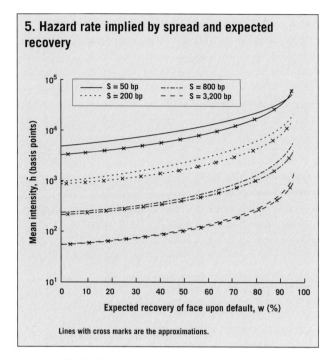

Lines with cross marks are the approximations.

6. Two-year default swap spread by expected response of default intensity to change in short-term default-free rate

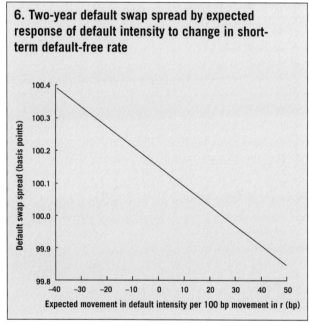

of bond-equivalent yield (compounded semi-annually), whereas the mean intensity is measured on a continuously compounded basis.

If multiple reference notes with maturities similar to that of the underlying default swap are available, an investor might average their implied hazard rates, after discarding outliers, and then average the rates. An alternative is to use non-linear least-squares fitting or some similar pragmatic estimation procedure. The reference notes may, however, have important institutional differences that will affect relative recovery. For example, in negotiated workouts, one investor group may be favoured over another for bargaining reasons.

Default swaps seem to serve, at least currently, as a benchmark for credit pricing. For example, if the at-market default swap quote, U^*, is available and an investor wishes to estimate the implied risk-neutral hazard rate, the process is to solve $U(h, T, f) = U^*$ for h. As suggested previously, the model result depends more or less linearly on the modelling assumption for the expected fractional loss at default. Sensitivity analysis is warranted if the objective is to apply the hazard-rate estimate to price an issue that has substantially different cashflow features from those of the reference default swap.

THE TERM STRUCTURE OF HAZARD RATES

If the reference credit's pricing information is for maturities different from the maturity of the credit swap, an investor is advised to estimate the term structure of hazard rates. For example, one could assume that the hazard rate between coupon dates $T(i-1)$ and $T(i)$ is $h(i)$. In this case, given the vector $h = [h(1), ..., h(n)]$, and assuming equal intercoupon time intervals, we have the more general calculations:

$$a_i(h) = \exp\{-[H(i) + y(i)]T(i)\}$$

where

$$H(i) = \frac{h_1 + \cdots + h_i}{i}$$

and

$$b_i(h) = \exp[-y(i)T(i)]\{\exp[-H(i-1)T(i-1)] - \exp[-H(i)T(i)]\}$$

Following these changes, the previous results apply.

Because of the well-established dependence of credit spreads on maturity, the wise analyst will consider the term structure when valuing credit swaps or inferring default probabilities from credit swap spreads.

When information regarding the shape of the term structure of hazard rates for the reference entity C is critical but not available, a pragmatic approach is to assume that the shape is that of comparable issues. For example, one might use the shape implied by Bloomberg par yield spreads for issues of the same credit rating and sector and then scale the implied hazard rates to match the pricing available for the reference entity. This ad hoc approach is subject to the modeller's judgement.

A more sophisticated approach to estimating hazard rates is to build a term-structure model for a stochastically varying risk-neutral intensity process, as in Duffie (1998a), Duffie and Singleton (1997), Jarrow and Turnbull (1995), or Lando (1998). Default swap pricing is reasonably robust, however, to the model of intensities, calibrated to given spread correlations and volatilities. For example, Figure 6 shows that default swap spreads do not depend significantly on how much the default arrival intensity is assumed to change with each 100 bp change in the short-term rates. The effect of default-risk volatility on default swap spreads becomes pronounced only at relatively high levels of volatility of h, as indicated in Figure 7. For this figure, volatility was measured as percentage standard deviation, at initial conditions, for an intensity model in the style of Cox–Ingersoll–Ross. The effect of volatility arises essentially from Jensen's inequality.[15]

Even the general structure of the defaultable term-structure model may not be critical for determining default swap spreads. For example, Figure 8 shows par coupon yield spreads for two term-structure models. One, the RMV model, is based on Duffie and Singleton (1997) and assumes recovery of 50% of *market value* at default. The other, the RFV model, assumes recovery of 50% of *face value* at default. Despite the difference in recovery assumptions, with no attempt to calibrate the two models to given prices, the implied term structures are similar. With calibration to a reference bond of maturity similar to that of the underlying bond, the match of credit swap spreads implied by the two models would be even closer. (This discussion does not, however, address the relative pricing of callable or convertible bonds with these two classes of models.)

Some cautions or extensions are as follows:

❑ The risk-neutral hazard-rate need not be the same as the hazard rate under an objective probability measure. The "objective" (actual) hazard rate is never used here.

❑ Even if hazard rates are stochastic, the previous calculations apply as long as they are independent (risk-neutrally) of interest rates. In such a case, one simply interprets $h(i)$ to be the rate of arrival of default during the ith interval, conditional only on survival to the beginning of that interval. This "forward default rate" is by definition deterministic.[16]

❑ If the notes used for pricing reference are on special in the repo market, an estimate of the "hidden" specialness, Y, should be included in the preceding calculations as an add-on to the floating-rate spreads, $\hat{S}$, or the fixed-rate coupon, c, when estimating the implied risk-neutral hazard rate, h.

❑ If necessary, one can use actuarial data on default incidence for comparable companies and adjust the estimated actual default arrival rate by a multiplicative corrective risk-premium factor, estimated cross-sectionally perhaps, to incorporate a risk premium.[17]

❑ If one assumes "instant" payment at default, rather than payment at the subsequent coupon date, the factor $b_i(h)$ is replaced by

$$b_i^*(h) = \exp\left\{-\left[y(i-1)+H(i-1)\right]T(i-1)k_i\left[h(i)\right]\right\}$$

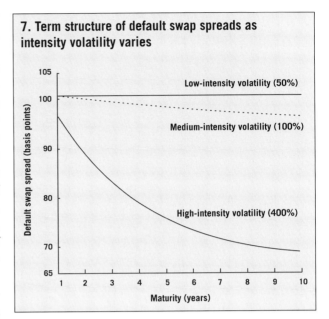

7. Term structure of default swap spreads as intensity volatility varies

Low-intensity volatility (50%)

Medium-intensity volatility (100%)

High-intensity volatility (400%)

Default swap spread (basis points) / Maturity (years)

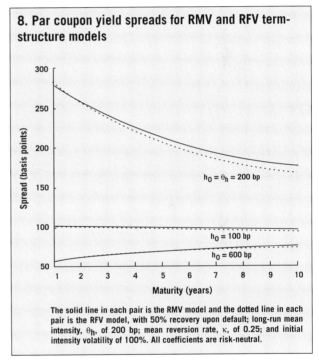

8. Par coupon yield spreads for RMV and RFV term-structure models

$h_0 = \theta_h = 200$ bp

$h_0 = 100$ bp

$h_0 = 600$ bp

Spread (basis points) / Maturity (years)

The solid line in each pair is the RMV model and the dotted line in each pair is the RFV model, with 50% recovery upon default; long-run mean intensity, θ_h, of 200 bp; mean reversion rate, κ, of 0.25; and initial intensity volatility of 100%. All coefficients are risk-neutral.

where

$$k_i\big[h(i)\big] = \frac{h(i)}{h(i)+\varphi(i)}\left\langle 1 - \exp\left\{-\big[h(i)+\varphi(i)\big]\big[T(i)-T(i-1)\big]\right\}\right\rangle$$

is the price at time $T(i-1)$, conditional on survival to that date, of a claim that pays one unit of account at the default time provided the default time is before $T(i)$ and where φ_i is the instantaneous default-free forward interest rate, assumed constant between $T(i-1)$ and $T(i)$. This equation can be checked by noting that the conditional density of the time to default, given survival to $T(i-1)$, is over the interval $[T(i-1), T(i)]$. For reasonably small intercoupon periods, default probabilities and interest rates, the impact of assuming instant recovery rather than recovery at the subsequent coupon date is relatively small.

The role of asset swaps

An asset swap is a derivative security that can be viewed in its simplest version as a portfolio consisting of a fixed-rate note and an interest rate swap that pays the fixed rate and receives the floating rate to the stated maturity of the underlying fixed-rate note. The fixed rate on the interest rate swap is conventionally chosen so that the asset swap is valued at par when traded. An important aspect is that the net coupons of the interest-rate swap are exchanged through maturity even if the underlying note defaults and its coupon payments are thereby discontinued.

Recently the markets for many fixed-rate notes have sometimes been less liquid than the markets for associated asset swaps, whose spreads are thus often used as benchmarks for pricing default swaps. In fact, because of the mismatch in termination with default between the interest rate swap embedded in the asset swap and the underlying fixed-rate note, the asset swap spread does not on its own provide precise information for default swap pricing. For example, as illustrated in Figure 9, a synthetic credit swap *cannot* be created from a portfolio consisting of a default-free floater and a short asset swap.

The asset swap spread and the term structure of default-free rates together, however, can be used to obtain an implied par floating-rate spread from which the default swap spread can be estimated. For example, suppose an asset swap is at quoted spread $\hat{S}$ to the default-free floating rate. (In the following, repo specials and transaction costs are ignored, but they can easily be added.) Suppose the stated underlying fixed rate on the note is c and the at-market default-free interest-rate swap rate is c^*. Then, the interest rate swap underlying the asset swap is an exchange of the floating rate for $c-\hat{S}$. An analyst can compute the desired par fixed-rate spread, F, over the default-free coupon rate of the same credit quality from the relationship implied by the price of a portfolio consisting of the asset swap and a short position in a portfolio consisting of a par fixed-rate note of the same credit quality as the underlying C-issued fixed-rate note combined with an at-market interest rate swap. This portfolio is worth

$$1-1=0$$

$$= AP(c-F) + AP^*(c^*-c+\hat{S})$$

where AP is the defaultable annuity price described previously and AP^* is the default-free annuity price to the same maturity. All the variables c, c^*, $\hat{S}$, and AP^* are available from market quotes. Given the defaultable annuity price AP, which can be estimated as discussed previously, an analyst can thus solve this equation for the implied par fixed-rate spread:

$$F = c - \frac{AP^*}{AP}(c-\hat{S}-c^*)$$

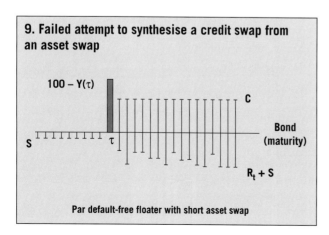

9. Failed attempt to synthesise a credit swap from an asset swap

$100 - Y(\tau)$

c

Bond (maturity)

S

τ

$R_t + S$

Par default-free floater with short asset swap

The implied par rate F is approximately the same as the par floating-rate spread, S, which is then the basis for setting the default swap spread. For small default probabilities, under the other assumptions given here, the default swap spread S and the par asset swap spread are approximately the same.

To assume that the asset swap spread is a reasonable proxy for the default swap spread is dangerous, however, for premium or discount bonds. Figure 10 shows the divergence between the term structures of asset swap spreads for premium bonds (coupon rate 400 bp above the par rate), par bonds and discount bonds (coupon rate 400 bp under the par rate).

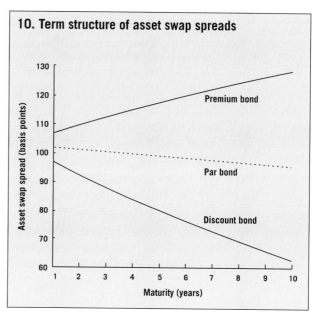

10. Term structure of asset swap spreads

Concluding remarks

This article has explained how the superficially simple arbitrage pricing (and synthesis) of a credit swap through a portfolio of default-free and defaultable floating-rate notes may, in fact, be difficult. Key concerns are, first, the ability to short the underlying note without incurring the cost of repo specials, and second, the valuation and recovery of reference notes used for pricing purposes in relation to the actual note underlying the swap. Model-based pricing may be useful because it adds discipline to the measurement and use of default probabilities and recoveries. For additional modelling of default swaps, see Davis and Mavroidis (1997).

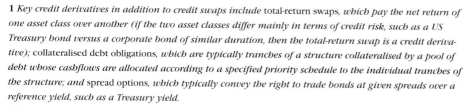

1 *Key credit derivatives in addition to credit swaps include* total-return swaps, *which pay the net return of one asset class over another (if the two asset classes differ mainly in terms of credit risk, such as a US Treasury bond versus a corporate bond of similar duration, then the total-return swap is a credit derivative);* collateralised debt obligations, *which are typically tranches of a structure collateralised by a pool of debt whose cashflows are allocated according to a specified priority schedule to the individual tranches of the structure; and* spread options, *which typically convey the right to trade bonds at given spreads over a reference yield, such as a Treasury yield.*

2 *At a presentation at the March 1998 International Swap Dealers Association conference in Rome, Daniel Cunningham of Cravath, Swaine, and Moore reviewed the documentation of credit swaps, including the specification of such credit event types as "bankruptcy, credit event upon merger, cross-acceleration, cross-default, downgrade, failure to pay, repudiation, or restructuring".*

3 *My discussions with a global bank indicate that of more than 200 default swaps, approximately 10% of the total were combined with an interest rate swap.*

4 *I do not consider here "exotic" forms of credit swaps, such as "first-to-default" swaps, for which credit event time τ is the first of the default times of a given list of underlying notes or bonds, with a payment at the credit event time that depends on the identity of the first of the underlying bonds to default. For example, the payment could be the loss relative to face value of the first bond to default.*

5 *The moneyness of Treasuries refers to their usefulness as a medium of exchange in, for example, securities transactions that are conducted by federal funds wire or for margin services. This usefulness conveys extra value to Treasury securities.*

6 *As to the costs, a haircut would normally apply. For example, at a haircut of 20%, a note trading at a market value of $100 would serve as collateral on a loan of $80. At a general collateral rate of 5%, a specific collateral rate of 1%, and a term of 0.5 year, Jones incurs an extra shorting cost of which the present value is* $80 × (5% − 1%) × [0.5/1 + 5% × 0.5)] = $1.56.

7 *If the term repo rate applies to the credit swap maturity, then S + Y is a lower bound on the theoretical credit swap premium.*

8 *This article does not consider these effects directly, but traders have noted that, in practice, the credit swap spread for illiquid entities can vary substantially from the reference par FRN spread.*

9 *This rate may be interpreted as a Poisson arrival rate, in the sense of hazard rates explained later in the chapter.*

10 *The floating-rate spread is known theoretically to be slightly higher than the fixed-rate spread in the case of the typical upward-sloping term structure, but the difference is typically on the order of 1 bp or less on a five-year note per 100 bp of yield spread to the default-free rate. See Duffie and Liu (1997) for details.*

11 *Figures 4-10 are based on an illustrative correlated multi-factor Cox-Ingersoll-Ross model of default-free short rates and default arrival intensities. The short-rate model is a three-factor Cox-Ingersoll-Ross model calibrated to recent behaviour in the term structure of Libor swap rates. The model of risk-neutral default-arrival intensity is set for an initial arrival intensity of 200 bp, with 100% initial volatility at 25% per year to 200 bp until default. Recovery at default is assumed to be 50% of face value. For details, see Duffie (1998b). The results depend on the degree of correlation, mean reversion and volatility among short-term rates and default-arrival intensities.*

12 *Sometimes the statement is made that if the underlying asset is a fixed-rate bond, the reference par floating-rate spread may be taken to be the asset swap spread. The usefulness of this assumption is considered in the last section of this article.*

13 *Recovery risk is sometimes viewed as reasonably diversifiable and relatively unrelated to the business cycle. No rigorous test of these hypotheses is available.*

14 *Sources of recovery data include annual reports by Moody's Investors Service and Standard & Poor's Corporation, Altman (1993) for bonds, and Carey (1998) and sources cited in it for loans. The averages reported are typically by seniority.*

15 *The risk-neutral survival probability to term* T *for a risk-neutral intensity process* h *under standard regularity assumptions is given by*

$$E^* \left\{ \exp\left[-\int_0^T h(t)\,dt \right] \right\}$$

where E* *denotes risk-neutral expectation. See Lando for a survey. Because* exp(·) *is convex, more volatility of risk-neutral intensity causes, other things being equal, a higher risk-neutral survival probability and thus narrower credit spreads.*

16 *This idea is based on the "forward default probability" introduced by Litterman and Iben (1991).*

17 *Multiplicative factors are preferred to additive factors in light of general economic considerations and the form of Girsanov's Theorem for point processes, as in Protter (1990). Fons (1994) provides information on the pricing of notes at actuarially implied default rates, but Fons does not provide an estimate of default arrival intensity.*

BIBLIOGRAPHY

Altman, E., 1993, "Defaulted Bonds: Demand, Supply and Performance 1987-1992", *Financial Analysts Journal* 49(3), pp. 55-60.

Carey, M., 1998, "Credit Risk in Private Debt Portfolios", *Journal of Finance* 53(4), pp. 1363-88.

Davis, M., and T. Mavroidis, 1997, "Valuation and Potential Exposure of Default Swaps", Technical Note RPD-18 (Tokyo: Mitsubishi International).

Duffie, D., 1998a, "Defaultable Term Structure Models with Fractional Recovery of Par", Working paper, Graduate School of Business, Stanford University.

Duffie, D., 1998b, "First-to-Default Valuation", Working paper, Graduate School of Business, Stanford University.

Duffie, D., 1996, "Special Repo Rates", *Journal of Finance* 51(2) June, pp. 493-526.

Duffie, D., and J. Liu, 1997, "Floating-Fixed Credit Specials", Working paper, Graduate School of Business, Stanford University.

Duffie, D., and K. Singleton, 1997, "Modeling Term Structures of Defaultable Bonds", Working paper, Graduate School of Business, Stanford University (forthcoming in *Review of Financial Studies*).

Fons, J., 1994, "Using Default Rates to model the Term Structure of Credit Risk", *Financial Analysts Journal* 50(5), pp. 25-32; reprinted as Chapter 12 of the present volume.

Jarrow, R., and S. Turnbull, 1995, "Pricing Derivatives on Financial Securities Subject to Default Risk," *Journal of Finance* 50(1), pp. 53-86.

Lando, D., 1998, "On Cox Processes and Credit Risky Securities", Working paper, Department of Operations Research, University of Copenhagen (forthcoming in *Review of Derivatives Research*).

Litterman, R., and T. Iben, 1991, "Corporate Bond Valuation and the Term Structure of Credit Spreads", *Journal of Portfolio Management* 17(3), pp. 52-64.

Protter, P., 1990, *Stochastic Integration and Differential Equations* (New York: Springer-Verlag).

18

Constructing a Credit Curve

David Li

The RiskMetrics Group

Τhe structuring and trading of credit derivatives has grown tremendously in recent years. As banks, security firms and corporations continue to hedge and realign their credit risks, and mutual funds strive to enhance their yield and control their credit risk exposure, this growth is expected to continue. The emergence of new credit derivative instruments on Wall Street is now commonplace. In addition to the standard products, such as credit default swaps, total return swaps, credit spread options, collateralised bond obligations and collateralised loan obligations, many new structures incorporating exotic option features have started to appear (for example, the credit default swaption). Many credit derivative products are associated with emerging market sovereign debt: in fact, the volume of emerging market credit derivatives has raised concerns that the total value of underlying assets in emerging market credit derivatives is much larger than that of the actual underlying assets.

How to value these instruments in practice is an interesting, but challenging task. Because most credit derivative transactions are over-the-counter trades, how each transaction is priced is not transparent to outsiders. Different firms may use dramatically different techniques and information in valuing similar instruments. As the credit derivative market develops, the bid and ask spread for typical products shrinks, and standard valuation techniques appear.

Central to the valuation of credit derivatives is the question of how to build a credit curve. A credit curve gives the instantaneous default probability of a party at any time in the future. It is as important to credit derivative pricing as the yield curve is to fixed-income derivative pricing. While many articles have been written about how to build a yield curve based on the current market price information of traded securities – such as futures, bonds and swaps – little has been written on credit curve construction.

This article presents a credit curve construction method based on the yield spread curve of a corporation. We assume that there exists a series of bonds with maturity 1, 2,..., n years, which are issued by the same company and have the same seniority. All the information used here is market-observable. From the market price of these bonds, we can calculate their yields to maturity. Using the yield-to-maturity of corresponding treasury bonds, we obtain a yield spread curve. The credit curve construction is based on this yield spread curve and an exogenous assumption about the recovery rate based on the seniority and the rating of the bonds and the industrial sector to which the corporation belongs.

The approach suggested here is contrary to the use of historical default experience information provided by rating agencies such as Moody's Investors Service or Standard & Poor's. We use market information rather than historical information for the following reasons:

❑ The calculation of profit and loss for a trading desk can only be based on current market information. This current market information reflects the market-agreed

The views expressed here are those of the author only, and not necessarily those of CIBC/Oppenheimer or any other organisations of CIBC World Markets Company. The author thanks Philippe Hatstadt and Tareq Hoque of CIBC/Oppenheimer for helpful discussions and Harry Turtle of the Washington State University for helpful comments. This paper was written while the author was an Executive Director in the Financial Products Group at CIBC/Oppenheimer.

perception about the evolution of the market in the future, on which the actual profit and loss depend. The default rate derived from current market information may be considerably different to historical default rates.

❑ Rating agencies use classification variables in the hope that homogeneous risks will be obtained after classification. This technique has been used elsewhere; for example, in pricing automobile insurance. Unfortunately, classification techniques often omit some firm-specific information.

❑ Rating agencies react much more slowly than the market in their anticipation of future credit quality. A typical example would be the rating agencies' belated reaction to the recent Asian crisis.

❑ Ratings are primarily used to calculate default frequency, rather than default severity. However, much of a credit derivative's value often depends on default severity as well as frequency.

❑ The information available from a rating agency is usually the one-year default probability for each rating group and the rating migration matrix. Neither the transition matrices nor the default probabilities are necessarily stable over long periods of time. In addition, many credit derivative products have maturities beyond one year, which requires the use of the long-term marginal default probability.

Of course, using only market information creates problems as well. Except for a few very large companies, the majority do not have a series of outstanding debts with the same seniority and multiple maturities. In the absence of this information, we could still use the asset swap spreads of similar firms as a proxy, or the aggregate spread information of a rating group for the specific company.

When default occurs we assume that the bondholder receives a fixed percentage of the bond price (ie, a recovery rate) immediately prior to default. This is consistent with the approach of Duffie and Singleton (1997). But it differs from the legal treatment of bond default in the US. Under US law, in the case of default on a coupon bond, the bondholder has claim only to the current accrued interest plus the face amount; for a zero coupon bond, the bondholder has claim to a linearly interpolated value of issue price and maturity value based on when default occurs.

The Duffie–Singleton approach provides a particularly good approximation to the legal treatments if the legal treatment is reflected in the market price of the bonds. This default treatment would also simplify modelling in more complicated situations with stochastic hazard rates or interest rates.

In this chapter, we consider both the discrete and continuous cases. In the discrete case, the credit curve consists of a series of default probabilities over each period, conditional on survival to the beginning of the period. These probabilities are sometimes referred to as conditional marginal martingale default probabilities (after Jarrow and Turnbull, 1997). In the continuous case, the credit curve can be expressed in terms of a hazard rate function, which characterises the instantaneous probability of default at any time in the future if it is still "alive". The analysis also demonstrates that under a risk-neutral probability measure, the rate of return of risky bonds is not the risk-free interest rate, but rather equals the risk-free rate plus the mean loss due to default (given by the product of the probability of default and the loss given default). It is also shown that the discrete model converges with the continuous one.

The remainder of the chapter is organised as follows: in the first section, we describe the characterisation of a default event. Next we define a random variable to denote the survival time of a firm or "time-until-default". The characterisation of time-until-default using a probability density function, an accumulative distribution function, a survival function or a hazard rate function are then presented. Some basic survival notations from actuarial science are used to simplify the analysis. Subsequent sections describe the discrete and continuous models using our framework. The main result in Duffie and Singleton (1997) is reformulated here using our framework. We then give a numerical example and a conclusion.

Time-until-default and the survival function

In the study of default, interest centres on a group of individual companies for each of which there is defined a point event, often called default (or survival), occurring after a length of time. We introduce a random variable called the time-until-default for a security A, for this length of time, and denote it T_A. This random variable is the basic building block for the valuation of cashflows subject to default. To determine time-until-default precisely requires:

❏ an unambiguously defined time origin;
❏ a time scale for measuring the passage of time; and
❏ an entirely clear definition of default.

We choose the current time as the time origin to allow use of current market information to build credit curves. The time scale is defined in terms of years for continuous models, or number of periods for discrete models. The meaning of default has been defined by a number of rating agencies, such as Moody's.

Now consider a security A with time-until-default, T_A, defined as a continuous random variable measuring the length of time until default occurs. For notational simplicity we will, for the moment, omit the use of the subscript A. Then let F(t) denote the distribution function of T,

$$F(t) = Pr(T \le t) \quad t \ge 0 \tag{1}$$

and set

$$S(t) = 1 - F(t) = Pr(T > t) \quad t \ge 0 \tag{2}$$

Assume $F(0) = 0$, which implies $S(0) = 1$. The function $S(t)$ is called the survival function, and it provides the probability that a security will attain age t. The distribution of T_A can be defined by specifying either the distribution function $F(t)$ or equivalently the survival function $S(t)$. We can also define the probability density function as

$$f(t) = F'(t) = -S'(t) = \lim_{\Delta \to 0^+} \frac{Pr[t < T \le t + \Delta]}{\Delta}$$

To make probability statements about a security having survived x years, we use the notation $T - x | T > x$ to denote its future survival time. In a simple manner we define

$$_t q_x = Pr\left[T - x \le t \mid T > x\right] \quad t \ge 0$$

and

$$_t p_x = 1 - {_t q_x} = Pr\left[T - x > t \mid T > x\right] \quad t \ge 0 \tag{3}$$

The symbol $_t q_x$ can be interpreted as the conditional probability that the security A will default within the next t years conditional on the survival in x years. In the special case of $x = 0$, we have

$$_t p_0 = S(t) \quad x \ge 0$$

If $t = 1$, we use the actuarial convention of omitting the prefix 1 in $_t q_x$ and $_t p_x$. Thus

$$p_x = Pr\left[T - x > 1 \mid T > x\right]$$

$$q_x = Pr\left[T - x \le 1 \mid T > x\right]$$

The symbol q_x is usually called the marginal default probability, which represents the probability of default in the period of $[x, x + 1]$ conditional on the survival to the beginning of the period. A credit curve in a discrete world can be expressed as the sequence of $q_0, q_1, \ldots, q_n$.

Hazard rate function

The distribution function $F(t)$ and the survival function $S(t)$ provide two mathematically equivalent ways of specifying the distribution of the random variable of time-until-default. There are, of course, other ways of characterising the problem. A familiar approach used by statisticians is the hazard rate function, which gives the instantaneous default probability for a security that has attained age x.

$$\Pr\left[x < T \le x + \Delta x \,\middle|\, T > x\right] = \frac{F(x + \Delta x) - F(x)}{1 - F(x)}$$

$$= \frac{f(x)\Delta x}{1 - F(x)}$$

The hazard rate function

$$h(x) = \frac{f(x)}{1 - F(x)}$$

has a conditional probability density interpolation as the conditional probability density function of default at exact age x, given survival to that time. The relationship between the hazard rate function, the distribution function and the survival function is

$$h(x) = \frac{f(x)}{1 - F(x)}$$

$$= -\frac{S'(x)}{S(x)} \tag{4}$$

The survival function can then be expressed in terms of the hazard rate function using

$$S(t) = e^{-\int_0^t h(s)\,ds}$$

We can also express $_tq_x$ and $_tp_x$ in terms of the hazard rate function as follows:

$$_tp_x = e^{-\int_0^t h(s+x)\,ds}$$

$$= e^{-\int_x^{x+t} h(s)\,ds} \tag{5}$$

In addition,

$$F(t) = 1 - S(t)$$

$$= 1 - e^{-\int_0^t h(s)\,ds}$$

and

$$f(t) = S(t) \cdot h(t)$$

$$= h(t) \cdot e^{-\int_0^t h(s)\,ds}$$

which is simply the density function for T. We need to put a constraint of positiveness on $h(x)$ so that the probability $_tp_x$ is less than 1. The hazard rate function can have different forms. A typical assumption is that the hazard rate is a constant, h. In this case, the density function is

$$f(t) = he^{-ht} \quad t > 0, \, h > 0$$

which shows that the density function follows an exponential distribution with parameter h. Under this assumption, the survival probability over the time interval $[0, t]$ is

$$_tp_x = e^{-\int_0^t h(x+s)\,ds}$$

$$= e^{-ht}$$

$$= (p_x)^t$$

where p_x is the probability of survival over one a year period. This assumption has been implicitly assumed in studies such as Jonkhart (1979) and Yawitz (1977). The aforementioned research can be found in survival analysis books, such as Bowers *et al* (1997).

The discrete version

Let us begin with the valuation of a corporate bond subject to default. Suppose that a bond promises to pay a stream of cashflows $C_1, C_2, ..., C_n$ at times $t_1, t_2, ..., t_n$ in the future. We assume that the current time is t_0. The discount factor calculated from the Treasury yield curve is $P(t_0, t)$, and is defined as the value of a zero coupon bond at time t_0 which pays \$1 at time t. Denote $V(t_i)$ as the bond's market value at time t_i immediately after the cashflow C_i is paid. Since the present value of the risky bond depends on when default occurs and the recoverable value depends on the price just prior to default, its value is path dependent.

We first establish a recursive relationship between the bond price at time t_i and the bond price one period later at time t_{i+1}. The current bond price can then be solved by a recursive formula.

Consider the period $[t_i, t_{i+1}]$. If the bond survives, its terminal value is $C_{i+1} + V(t_{i+1})$; if it defaults (and assuming the Duffie and Singleton's treatment of default) the recoverable value is $R(t_{i+1})[C_{i+1} + V(t_{i+1})]$. In the discrete model we assume that recoverable value is made at the end of the default period $[t_i, t_{i+1}]$, ie, at time t_{i+1}. The conditional survival probability over the period is p_i. So we have the following recursive formula:

$$V(t_i) = \frac{P(t_0, t_{i+1})}{P(t_0, t_i)}\left\{P_i\Big[C_{i+1} + V(t_{i+1})\Big] + (1 - p_i)R(t_{i+1})\Big[C_{i+1} + V(t_{i+1})\Big]\right\}$$

$$= \frac{P(t_0, t_{i+1})}{P(t_0, t_i)}\Big[p_i + (1 - p_i)R(t_{i+1})\Big]\Big[C_{i+1} + V(t_{i+1})\Big] \qquad (6)$$

where $i = 0, 1, 2, ..., n - 1$, and the boundary condition is

$$V(t_n) = 0$$

By consecutive substitution in (6) we obtain

$$V(t_0) = \sum_{i=1}^{n} P(t_0, t_i)\left\{\prod_{j=0}^{i-1}\Big[p_j + (1 - p_j)R(t_{i+1})\Big]\right\}C_i \qquad (7)$$

Let

$$DC(t_i) = \left\{\prod_{j=0}^{i-1}\Big[p_j + (1 - p_j)R(t_{i+1})\Big]\right\} \qquad (8)$$

be the credit discount factor, and

$$Q(t_0, T_i) = P(t_0, t_i)DC(t_i)$$

be the credit risk adjusted discount factor, then we have initial bond value

$$V(0) = \sum_{i=1}^{n} Q(t_0, t_i) \cdot C_i \qquad (9)$$

Equation (9) shows that the defaultable bond may still be valued as if the promised cashflows are default free if the discount factor is adjusted for default. In general, the credit risk-adjusted discount factor or the total discount factor is the product of the risk-free discount factor and the pure credit discount factor if the underlying factors affecting default and those affecting the interest rate are independent. To extract the marginal default probability, we can just use expression (7) and the following relationship

$$p_i = e^{-\int_{t_i}^{t_{i+1}} h(s)\,ds}$$

If we assume a piecewise constant hazard rate, that is

$$h(s) = h_i \qquad s \in (t_{i-1}, t_i]$$

then we have

$$p_i = e^{-h_{i+1}(t_{i+1} - t_i)}$$

The continuous model

The continuous version of the Duffie and Singleton model can be obtained from equation (7). Recall from equation (5), we have

$$p_j = e^{-\int_{t_j}^{t_{j+1}} h(s)\,ds}$$

Then,

$$p_j + (1 - p_j)R(t_{j+1}) = e^{-\int_{t_j}^{t_{j+1}} h(s)\,ds} + \left(1 - e^{-\int_{t_j}^{t_{j+1}} h(s)\,ds}\right) R(t_{j+1})$$

$$\approx e^{-\left[1 - R(t_{j+1})\right]\int_{t_j}^{t_{j+1}} h(s)\,ds}$$

if $\Delta_t = t_{j+1} - t_j$ is small. Then the credit discount factor can be written as

$$\prod_{j=0}^{i-1} p_j + (1 - p_j)R(t_{i+1}) \approx \prod_{j=0}^{i-1} e^{-\left[1 - R(t_{j+1})\right]\int_{t_j}^{t_{j+1}} h(s)\,ds}$$

$$\approx e^{\sum_{j=0}^{i-1} \int_{t_j}^{t_{j+1}} \left[1 - R(t_{j+1})\right] h(s)\,ds}$$

If we divide the time interval $(0, t_i]$ into many smaller time intervals with a length of $\Delta t = t_i / n$, then we would have

$$\lim_{n \to \infty} \left[p_j + (1 - p_j)R \right] = \lim_{n \to \infty} e^{-\sum_{j=0}^{i-1} \int_{t_j}^{t_{j+1}} \left[1 - R(t_{j+1})\right] h(s)\,ds}$$

$$= e^{-\int_0^{t_i} \left[1 - R(s)\right] h(s)\,ds}$$

If we also assume

$$P(t_0, t_i) = e^{-\int_0^{t_i} r(s)\,ds}$$

where $r(s)$ is the short rate, then we can rewrite equation (7) as

$$V(t_0) = \sum_{i=1}^{n} C_i \cdot e^{-\int_0^{t_i} \left\{ r(s) + [1-R(s)]h(s) \right\} ds} \qquad (10)$$

This is the fundamental result of Duffie and Singleton for a zero coupon bond, shown here for a coupon-bearing bond and using only elementary mathematics.

A numerical example

We give a numerical example in this section to illustrate how to build a credit curve. The market information used can be either a series of bond prices or asset swap spreads. We assume a corporation has a series of outstanding bonds with maturities of 1, 2, 3, 4, 5, 7 and 10 years. For simplicity, assume the asset swap spreads of these bonds are known and that each bond is priced at par with semi-annual coupon payments, then the coupon rate can be solved. We assume the following information for the bonds:

Coupon	Spread (bp)	Maturity	Price
10.95%	500	1 year	100.00
11.21%	500	2 years	100.00
11.37%	500	3 years	100.00
11.47%	500	4 years	100.00
11.55%	500	5 years	100.00
11.69%	500	7 years	100.00
11.85%	500	10 years	100.00

And if the spread drops to 200 basis points, we have:

Coupon	Spread (bp)	Maturity	Price
7.89%	200	1 year	100.00
8.13%	200	2 years	100.00
8.30%	200	3 years	100.00
8.40%	200	4 years	100.00
8.48%	200	5 years	100.00
8.62%	200	7 years	100.00
8.78%	200	10 years	100.00

The discount curve used is the US dollar Libor curve on June 3, 1998. Discount factors corresponding to coupon payment dates are given in Table 1.

We also assume that the hazard rate function is a constant from one maturity date to another. Suppose the current time is $t_0 = 0$, and the maturity dates of bonds are t_1, t_2,..., and t_n. We assume that

$$h(t) = h_i, t_{i-1} \leq t < t_i$$

For the first bond we have the following valuation formula by using equation (10).

$$100 = \frac{10.95}{2} \cdot e^{-\int_0^{0.5} \left\{ r(s) + [1-R(s)]h(s) \right\} ds} + \left(100 + \frac{10.95}{2} \right) \cdot e^{-\int_0^{1.0} \left\{ r(s) + [1-R(s)]h(s) \right\} ds}$$

or

$$100 = \frac{10.95}{2} \cdot P(0, 0.5) e^{-[(1-R)h_1] \cdot 0.5} + \left(100 + \frac{10.95}{2} \right) \cdot P(0, 1.0) e^{-(1-R)h_1 \cdot 1.0}$$

If we assume an exogenous and constant recovery rate R, we can solve for h_1 in the

Table 1. Discount factors on June 3, 1998

Date	Discount factor
08-Jun-98	0.9993
08-Dec-98	0.9715
08-Jun-99	0.9433
08-Dec-99	0.9147
08-Jun-00	0.8861
08-Dec-00	0.8577
08-Jun-01	0.8303
08-Dec-01	0.8034
08-Jun-02	0.7774
08-Dec-02	0.7518
08-Jun-03	0.7271
08-Dec-03	0.7023
08-Jun-04	0.6784
08-Dec-04	0.6554
08-Jun-05	0.6332
08-Dec-05	0.6109
08-Jun-06	0.5896
08-Dec-06	0.5689
08-Jun-07	0.5491
08-Dec-07	0.5298
08-Jun-08	0.5112

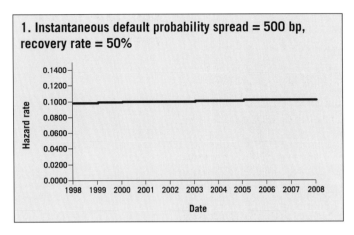

1. Instantaneous default probability spread = 500 bp, recovery rate = 50%

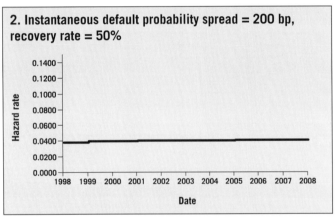

2. Instantaneous default probability spread = 200 bp, recovery rate = 50%

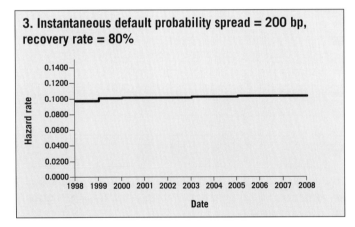

3. Instantaneous default probability spread = 200 bp, recovery rate = 80%

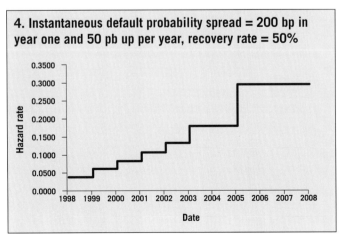

4. Instantaneous default probability spread = 200 bp in year one and 50 pb up per year, recovery rate = 50%

above equation. Having solved for h_1 we can solve for h_2, so that the second bond maturing at time t_2 is also priced at par. Continuing in this manner we can determine a hazard rate function up to the maturity of the last bond.

Figure 1 gives the hazard rate function when the spread curve is flat at 500 bp and the recovery rate is 50%. For a flat spread curve we see that the instantaneous default probability is also flat at 10%. In general, we have $s = (1 - R)h$ where s denotes the spread. For a fixed recovery rate, the instantaneous default probability decreases as the spread decreases.

Figure 2 shows that the instantaneous default probability decreases from 10% to 4% when the spread changes from 500 bp to 200 bp. Also to keep the spread constant, a high recovery rate would result in high default probability.

Figure 3 gives the default probability when the spread is 200 bp and the recovery rate is 80%.

The spread curve of a corporation is usually an increasing function of maturity. This reflects the fact that the market values bonds as if corporations have a higher probability of default each year into the future. Litterman and Iben (1991), and Dybvig and Marshall (1996) argue that the market overestimates the risk of long term bonds.

Figure 4 gives the hazard rate function when the spread is an increasing function of maturities. We see clearly that the conditional default probability increases as the maturity increases in this case.

Conclusion

This chapter presents a credit curve construction method based on the Duffie and Singleton approach to default settlement. Only observable market information is employed, in a manner similar to yield curve construction. The basic properties of a hazard rate function and its relationship with default probability are presented. We also present an alternative proof of the basic theorem in Duffie and Singleton in both the discrete and continuous case.

Only elementary mathematics are used to prove the discrete case result. The continuous model is shown to be a limiting case of the discrete case. The suggested approach may be used to value many credit derivatives accurately, including credit default swaps and credit linked notes.

BIBLIOGRAPHY

Bowers, N., H. Gerber, J. Hickman, D. Jones and C. Nesbitt, 1997, *Actuarial Mathematics,* 2nd edition (Schaumburg, Ill.: Society of Actuaries).

Duffie, D., and K. Singleton, 1997, "Modeling Term Structure of Defaultable Bonds", Working paper, Graduate School of Business, Stanford University.

Dybvig, P., and W. J. Marshall, 1996, "Pricing Long Bonds: Pitfalls and Opportunities", *Financial Analyst Journal* January-February, pp. 32-9.

Jarrow, R. A., and S. M. Turnbull, 1995, "Pricing Derivatives on Financial Securities Subject to Credit Risk", *Journal of Finance* 50(1), pp. 53-85.

Jarrow, R. A., and S. M. Turnbull, 1997, "When Swaps Are Dropped", *Risk* May, pp. 70-5.

Jonkart, M., 1979, "On the Term Structure of Interest Rates and the Risk of Default", *Journal of Banking and Finance* 3(3), pp. 253-62.

Litterman, R., and T. Iben, 1991, "Corporate Bond Valuation and the Term Structure of Credit Spreads", *Financial Analyst Journal,* pp. 52-64.

Yawitz, J. B., 1977, "An Analytic Model of Interest Rate Differentials and Different Default Recoveries", *Journal of Financial and Quantitative Analysis* September, pp. 481-90.

19

The Good, the Bad – and the Ugly?

Tanya Styblo Beder and Frank Iacono

Caxton Corporation; Chase Securities

D ealers saw explosive growth in the credit derivatives market during the first half of 1997. Many major dealers and banks established specialised desks and brokers also leapt in, hoping to capitalise on the expected higher spreads typically seen in the early stages of market development.

Credit derivatives are certain to drive a paradigm shift in the relationships between several markets. The likely result will be the ability to separate and manage certain risks better with more consistent pricing across markets. Concomitantly, model risk may find its most fertile ground yet. This chapter discusses what is good, bad and potentially ugly about credit derivatives.

Let us begin by defining a credit derivative: it is a derivative product that makes payments based on the credit performance of some credit-sensitive instrument or instruments. Credit performance is typically measured by yield or price spreads relative to benchmarks, credit ratings or default status.

Three of the most common types of credit derivatives are asset swaps, total return swaps and default swaps. An asset swap in this context is a swap under which one party makes payments equal to the actual cashflows (principal and interest) on a credit-sensitive instrument. Typically, the other party makes payments based on Libor, or, in some cases, on another credit-sensitive instrument.

A total return swap is a swap under which two parties periodically pay each other the total return on two reference assets or baskets of assets. When at least one of the reference assets is a credit-sensitive instrument, the swap is a credit derivative.

A default swap is a swap under which one party (the beneficiary) pays the other party (the guarantor) a fixed amount, or an amount based on a generic interest rate. This is in exchange for the guarantor's promise to make a fixed or variable payment in the event of default in one or more reference assets.

"Credit risk derivatives" were first publicly introduced in 1992, at the International Swaps and Derivatives Association annual meeting in Paris. After a slow start,[1] the size of the credit derivatives market is now estimated at between $40 and $50 billion with expectations for it to grow to $100 billion in 1997 (*Risk* June, 1996, page 47). But even before modern credit derivatives, there were financial arrangements which were economically similar. Examples of such products include letters of credit (LCs),[2] bond insurance[3] and call and put options embedded in corporate debt securities.[4] Figure 1 shows a timeline of key credit-based financial instruments since 1700.

Burgeoning interest in the credit derivatives market brings news – some good, some bad, some potentially ugly. Increased activity will encourage a broader array of counterparties to participate in credit risk products, stimulate more competitive pricing, promote arbitrage across capital markets and prod participants to standardise documentation. The less attractive side effects may include diminished returns, less assistance in loan workouts, unforeseen liabilities and potentially ugly model risk issues.

This paper originally appeared in Risk *Magazine, July 1997, Credit Risk Supplement, pp. 30–4.*

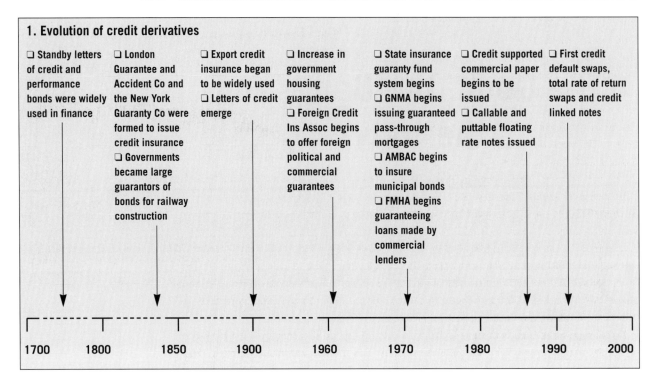

1. Evolution of credit derivatives

❏ Standby letters of credit and performance bonds were widely used in finance

❏ London Guarantee and Accident Co and the New York Guaranty Co were formed to issue credit insurance
❏ Governments became large guarantors of bonds for railway construction

❏ Export credit insurance began to be widely used
❏ Letters of credit emerge

❏ Increase in government housing guarantees
❏ Foreign Credit Ins Assoc begins to offer foreign political and commercial guarantees

❏ State insurance guaranty fund system begins
❏ GNMA begins issuing guaranteed pass-through mortgages
❏ AMBAC begins to insure municipal bonds
❏ FMHA begins guaranteeing loans made by commercial lenders

❏ Credit supported commercial paper begins to be issued
❏ Callable and puttable floating rate notes issued

❏ First credit default swaps, total rate of return swaps and credit linked notes

1700   1800   1850   1900   1960   1970   1980   1990   2000

The good

Credit derivatives will encourage more participants in many markets: in particular, in high-yield debt, bank loans and credit enhancement products. Until recently, more or less all the credit risk of commercial lending was borne by the banking sector. For example, of the $250 billion-plus in leveraged syndicated loans, institutional investors such as insurance companies and pension funds hold only $10 billion. Credit derivatives will allow more players – including broker-dealers, insurance companies, pension funds and other institutional investors – to alter their returns by absorbing or reducing the credit risk of these loans. More competitive pricing of this risk is the likely result, with savings being enjoyed by the borrowers.

Credit derivatives will also allow banks to turn their inventory without alienating customers. Many banks, especially smaller and regional/local banks, often find themselves faced with a difficult trade-off. On the one hand, regulation and economic prudence require their loan portfolios to be well diversified (ie, have limited exposure to a single issuer or industry). On the other hand, once the time and effort has been expended to build a banking relationship, it is advantageous for both bank and customer to do more business with each other. Credit derivatives offer a means by which these banks can dispose of or diversify this credit exposure, while at the same time maintaining the banking relationship.

These banks' inventories are just one of the new asset classes that credit derivatives will make available to investors. Some market participants argue that bank loans have had historically high risk-adjusted returns, and that this risk-return profile allows banks to compensate potential counterparties to credit derivatives well for taking on credit risk.[5] In the past few years, several large US commercial banks have begun issuing structured notes based on pools of loans originated by themselves. The notes offer investors highly customised risk-return profiles, ranging from limited participation in the first losses on a portfolio to highly-leveraged structures in which modest losses in the underlying pool can result in substantial losses in principal.

Another effect will be the creation of more efficient pricing across several market sectors. The pricing of letters of credit, standbys, guarantees, insurance and capital market spreads should become more aligned. Despite the economic similarities of these products, their pricing has historically been quite divergent. For example, long-term, single-A corporate bond spreads have ranged between 50 and 340 basis points since 1977, as shown in Figure 2. During this same time period, banks have charged 10 to 200 bp annually to guarantee performance on comparable risks.

Huge new arbitrage opportunities now exist, many as dramatic as those created by the early currency swap market. For example, one arbitrage that has been driving many trades is created by the difference between dealer and end-user funding costs. Assume ABC Investments is interested in taking on credit exposure to XYZ Corp, a BBB issuer. XYZ's debt currently yields Treasury plus 85 bp. Assume further that ABC does not want interest rate exposure, nor does it want to make a large upfront investment of its own funds. Given these parameters, one possible solution is to borrow fixed rate funds (or synthetic fixed rate funds) in order to pur-

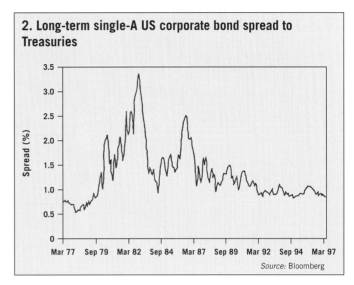

2. Long-term single-A US corporate bond spread to Treasuries

Source: Bloomberg

chase XYZ's bond. If ABC can borrow fixed at Treasury plus 55 bp, it can capture 30 bp (85 – 55) for taking the credit exposure of XYZ through this mechanism.

Now assume the bank can fund at Treasury plus 25 bp. In this scenario, the bank can offer ABC a total return swap on Treasuries versus XYZ bonds, or simply a default swap on XYZ. The swap can be priced so that ABC captures much more than 30 bp for taking the credit risk of XYZ. Specifically, ABC will earn 60 bp per annum, less adjustments for the bank's profit and loss, reserves and additional hedging costs.

Credit risk theory will take a great leap forward, with portfolio-level approaches being adopted over the next few years (hopefully by the regulators as well as the regulated). In the area of credit derivatives, it is important to understand how an institution views the potential exposure of basket transactions. An example is a $25 million credit derivative in which the seller guarantees any one of four credits that defaults, but must only pay for one (ie, if more than one of the credits default, the seller is only liable for one).

If the seller has a maximum allowable exposure (or line) of $25 million to each of the four names, should the institution view the basket transaction as a use of the $25 million exposure limit for each name, or otherwise? To the degree that $25 million in exposure is not counted for each name, the institution may find itself in a position in which a $25 million loan is made to a defaulting name which compounds the credit derivative exposure of $25 million, resulting in a $50 million loss on one of the individual names.

Loan documentation is likely to become much more standardised in order to facilitate liquid and active trading for loans that become the subject of credit derivatives trading, just as in the case of interest rate swap documentation. Traders will demand the ability to make distinctions based on name, without having to worry about the specifics of particular loan agreements. This development, however, should not preclude the possibility of more customised loan documentation when special circumstances so require (eg, specific collateral).

The bad

Returns may not be high enough for the intrinsic risks. The global decrease in the rates of return on loans may translate into lenders/investors taking inadequate return for the risk of default, whether on junk bonds, collateralised bond obligations (CBOs), credit derivatives or loans.

For example, returns in Japan languish in the 3–5% range, returns in Italy have dropped by more than 5% relative to other European returns (eg, Germany) and returns in the US are at 6–7% (a 10-year low). As Europe prepares for monetary union, the primary distinguishing feature between countries will be credit. Trading in these instruments, despite the lack of data regarding whether returns are at adequate levels, may be expensive for those who have not established sufficient exposure limits for loan trading and credit derivatives.

A recent academic study (Gilson and Warner, as reported by Institutional Investor, March 1997) of 1,376 junk bonds outstanding today reports that covenants and collateralisation are significantly weaker, yet maturities are much longer, for junk bonds versus bank loans. The question is whether the higher return of about 2% is sufficient compensation for these risks.

The greater ability to trade distressed debt may reduce the impetus for creditors to assist aggressively in the work-out process, thereby reducing recovery amounts and increasing the time to recovery. This in turn may reduce the long time series of classic default data to questionable value. Many regulators and market participants look to the classic default data to determine whether new instruments such as credit derivatives are priced properly. Those who do not perform stress testing to analyse sensitivity to small changes in the default data, probability of default, timing of recovery and the recovery amount may be in for some nasty surprises.

An alternative perspective on this paradigm shift is that resources will be devoted more efficiently once the free trading of credit risk allows banks to sell credit exposure easily and allows different players to participate in the work-out process. An example might be vulture funds who are more efficient than bank work-out areas. Whether efficiency will demand more or less effort and zeal remains to be seen, but there can be little doubt that this dramatic change in regime will call, at the very least, for new interpretation of the old data.

The lack of standard terms and codes of practice for trading bank loans, and credit derivatives thereon, are creating huge potential liabilities for the future. The thin margins in the business and the increased speed of transactions may discourage an expensive legal review of all of the documents in a particular loan sale or CBO transaction. This may create situations in which a seller's obligations actually increase with a loan sale.

As an example, consider an environment of increasing defaults during the next downturn in the economic cycle. At that time, a nightmarish situation could arise in which a participant to a syndicated loan sells a participation, but does not properly extinguish its obligation to contribute additional capital if a guarantee is called in under the default. In such a situation, the seller may be called on not only to provide additional funds to support the original borrower under a syndicate capital call, but also to provide support to the buyer of the original loan. Those who do not determine whether existing documentation and procedures provide adequate protection for the buyer and seller; and whether legal assignment includes the entire exposure of the seller may have expensive experiences.

...and the potentially ugly

There are basically four approaches used by market participants to price credit derivatives today – default models based on ratings or credit spreads, by reference to guarantee products, and replication analysis. They each have their own strengths and weaknesses, as described below, which sometimes result in substantially different pricing across models.

RATINGS-BASED DEFAULT MODELS

These models approximate the probability of the default or downgrade of a given underlying instrument based on its credit rating and on published transition matrices.[6] To supplement the default or downgrade data, one also needs to make an assumption regarding the impact such an event has on the price of the underlying (ie, the recovery rate).[7] One widely used source of default loss data is the Altman Dataset. Some of these models used fixed recovery rates, others stochastic (roughly speaking, random) ones. An example of the first approach is Jarrow, Lando and Turnbull (1994), which models the default process based on credit ratings. Specifically, the model assumes that the credit rating of a risky bond follows a Markov chain, and employs a matrix of probabilities for the transition between credit ratings (including default). Das and Tufano (1996) build on this approach with a model that allows for a stochastic recovery rate in the event of default. An advantage of this type of model is that it is relatively light in terms of data requirements. Pricing is based on aggregate statistics. Moreover, this approach is a good solution to the problem of inadequate (or missing) issuer-specific data. But this strength is also the source of a key weakness – issuer-level information is lost. So to the extent that a particular issuer is more or less likely to default than other issuers in its rating category, the model may be unreliable.

CREDIT-SPREAD-BASED DEFAULT MODELS

These models use the term structure of an issuer's credit spread over default-free instruments of similar maturity to estimate the probability of default or the recovery rate in default. Once this term structure is built, the user can make an assumption about the probability of default over time, to back out the expected recovery rate or vice versa.

For example, under a simple version of this model, if a US corporate issuer's credit spread over the Treasury rate is 1%, the expected default losses are 1% annually or $1 million per $100 million at risk. Hence, for the $100 million risk, if the expected recovery rate is assumed to be 50%, the resulting default probability is 2% annually (2% of $100 million times the default rate of 50%). One strength of this approach is that once issuer-specific information is available, it is easy to use. Moreover, if one is willing to interpolate on the basis of only a few data points or to make an assumption with respect to recovery rates (possibly based on the Altman Dataset), one can back out a time varying default probability based on credit spreads. Arbitrages and anomalies in the term structure of an issuer's credit spread become readily apparent.

A weakness of this approach is that a complete term structure is not available for most issuers, so the modeller is again left to interpolate on the basis of only a few data points or to make assumptions based on aggregate data. Another weakness is that the model implicitly assumes the entire spread over Treasuries to be due to credit risk. Other factors, such as tax, liquidity and investor appetite can also have a profound effect on this spread. Determining which portion of the spread is attributable to each factor is not an easy task.

PRICING BASED ON GUARANTEE PRODUCT MARKETS

This approach simply looks to other forms of credit enhancement as a reference for the amount by which a guarantor should be compensated, or how much the beneficiary of credit protection should be willing to pay for the commitment of a specific guarantor. The basic idea is that if Bank A is willing to pay Bank B 50 bp annually to guarantee the debt of XYZ Corp, a default swap which in essence provides similar protection should be priced similarly.

The strength of this approach is that it is easy to use. The weaknesses are that it is only available for a limited number of names and product structures (specifically, products which offer full default protection only). And even if the credit derivative is a full default swap, there are often material contractual differences which might make pricing by reference to a guarantee contract unreliable.

REPLICATION/COST OF FUNDS

This approach prices a credit derivative in terms of hedging costs. The dealer determines the positions necessary to hedge the derivative contract, and how much it costs the dealer to enter into each position. The net hedging cost (plus reserves and the dealer's profit and loss) is the price of the credit derivative. For example, assume a dealer pays fixed in order to receive default losses, if any, on a five-year note issued by XYZ Corp. Assume the bond yield to maturity of the note is 7%, and the dealer can fund this position at 6.5%. As a first approximation, the dealer would be willing to pay 0.5% for default protection (less a reduction to allow for reserves and profit and loss).

The strength of this approach is that, if a hedge can be constructed, it is the most straightforward pricing methodology available, and its result is the most useful to a dealer. Dealers often employ a hedging/replication approach as one methodology for pricing derivatives. The problem with this approach is that, for many structures, a complete hedge is not available, or would be prohibitively costly. In these cases, a dealer is forced either to rely on a more theoretical approach or to accept the risk that the theoretical pieces will not behave as the whole, or forego the transaction.

To illustrate the potential variances across these models, we have performed a theoretical (mid-market) pricing of a simple credit derivative product under two of the four approaches using market data from June 11, 1997. The product we analyse is a default swap on the 7.25% November 1, 2002, note issued by IBM. Under our hypothetical contract, A makes fixed payments to B based on a fixed rate $10 million notional amount. These payments are made semi-annually and cover the period November 1, 1997, through November 1, 2002: the first payment therefore falls on May 1, 1998. In exchange, B agrees to make a payment to A, should there be a default event on the IBM note between November 1, 1997, and November 1, 2002. The payment amount is to be calculated one month after the event of default, and is computed as the difference between: (i) the price at which the note would be trading if its yield to maturity were equal to that of the US Treasury bond or note maturing closest to November 1, 2002; and (ii) the actual market price of the IBM note. The IBM note is rated A1 by Moody's and A by Standard & Poor's.

Using the term structure of credit spread approach, the fixed amount paid by A to B is approximately 32 bp annually. This is based on the spread to Treasury of the November 1, 2002, note of 33 bp and the spread of another IBM note, maturing on November 1, 1997, of 42 bp. Using the replication/cost of funds approach, A is only willing to pay 3 bp annually if it funds at Libor flat. This is based on the forward-start yield-to-maturity of the November 1, 2002, note of 6.85% (compared with 6.78% spot), and the five-year forward-start swap rate of 6.82% (compared with 6.735% spot). If A can fund at Libor-10 bp, then it is willing to pay 13 bp per annum. This illustrates the sensitivity of credit derivative pricing across the modelling approach used, as well as within the same modelling approach.

1 *As of 1995, market estimates were no higher than $10 million in notional amount, showing growth that had been far less spectacular than the early growth of the interest rate swaps market.*

2 *Under an LC, an issuer pays a bank an annual fee in exchange for the bank's promise to make debt payments on behalf of the issuer, should the issuer fail to do so. LCs are utilised to provide credit support for financial products which trade in markets which demand a high degree of credit quality, such as the commercial paper market. LCs are known to go back at least as far as the turn of the century. (See Cleveland and Huertas, 1985)*

3 *Under a bond insurance contract, an issuer pays an insurer, such as FGIC, CapMac or AMBAC, to guarantee performance on a bond. Bond insurance is used largely in the Municipal Bond Market, where some 35% of the new issues in 1993 were insured (see Fabozzi and Fabozzi). Bond insurance dates back to 1971 (see Das, 1993)*

4 *For example, callable and puttable floating rate notes (FRNs), are one type which became popular in the 1980s. Under a callable FRN, the issuer has the right to redeem the note prior to maturity at a pre-specified price (eg par). Under a puttable FRN, the investor has the right to force early redemption. Since FRN coupons periodically reset to market interest rates, fluctuations in market value due to changes in interest rates are minimised. For this reason, the credit risk of the issuer will be the primary driver of an FRN's market value.*

5 *It should be noted, however, that since bank loans carry large administrative costs, as well as regulatory capital requirements, comparisons to other markets should be used with caution. The extent to which banks will be able to compensate their credit derivative counterparties will depend largely on whether regulatory capital requirements change to reduce the amount of capital that must be held against an asset which has been hedged through a credit derivative.*

6 *For an example of these transition matrices, see Standard & Poor's* Ratings Performance 1996: Stability and Transition.

7 *This is true whether or not the payout on the trigger event is fixed or variable. Even if the payout is fixed, an expectation of the conditional decline in value is necessary for the dealer to determine the appropriate hedge ratio.*

BIBLIOGRAPHY

Cleveland, H., and T. Huertas, 1985, *Citibank 1812-1970*, p. 43.

Das, S., 1993, "Credit Risk Derivatives", *Journal of Derivatives,* pp. 7-23.

Das, S., and P. Tufano, 1996, "Pricing Credit Sensitive Debt when Interest Rates, Credit Ratings and Credit Spreads are Stochastic", *Journal of Financial Engineering* 5(2), pp. 161-98.

Fabozzi, F., and T. Dessa Fabozzi, 1995, *The Handbook of Fixed Income Securities* (Fourth edition) p. 176.

Jarrow, R., D. Lando and S. Turnbull, 1994, "A Markov Model for the Term Structure of Credit Risk Spreads", Working paper, Cornell University.

PRACTITIONER'S GUIDE TO MANAGING CREDIT RISK

Introduction

Practitioner's Guide to Managing Credit Risk

David Shimko

The title of this volume suggests that credit risk measurement and credit risk management are inseparable. This is surely true. On the one hand, a credit department with good analytics but without the capacity for thoughtful action brings no value to anyone save the analyst, who may improve his career prospects elsewhere. On the other hand, those who execute on the basis of inferior credit models, or in many cases no model at all, will find that their intuition can easily fail them in markets as complex as these.

To be successful in its mission, therefore, this book must not only present state-of-the-art credit analytics but it should also provide a road map for the implementation of credit risk management policy informed by these analytics. That is the purpose of this final section – to make a start on that map.

The first two articles, "A Credit Risk Toolbox" and "Reconcilable Differences", were written by credit risk management practitioners and are reprinted from *Risk* magazine, where they appeared in 1998. The last two contributions, "Practical Use of Credit Risk Models in Loan Portfolio and Counterparty Exposure Management" by Robert Jarrow and Donald van Deventer, and "Portfolio Management and Stress-Testing using CreditMetrics" by Christopher Finger and Aidan McNulty, were commissioned especially for this volume. We asked each of the participating companies to define a key credit risk management issue and to address it using the analytics that are covered in the previous sections.

Each makes its unique contribution to the overall text. "A Credit Risk Toolbox", by Angelo Arvanitis and Jon Gregory at Paribas, is an excellent example of smart implementation of modern credit risk analysis. The traditional approach to credit risk management – that default rates and recoveries determine prices – becomes extremely difficult when more than a few names are analysed and gives little guidance on how to model the correlations between defaults. The Paribas team offers an elegant solution to both problems. First, rather than assuming approximating loss distributions, the authors explain that the actual individual binary (default/no default) distributions can be used. Furthermore, the moment-generating function (MGF) approach is used to simplify the complex expressions that arise.

Of course, inverting the MGF to get the aggregate default probability distribution is difficult, but the authors make the shrewd observation that we do not need the whole distribution for most applications but only the tail defining the worst-case losses. The methods they reference and apply are the "steepest descent" or "saddle-point" procedures.

To work out implied pairwise correlations between default probabilities, the authors use a multivariate normal approach and force the correlations from a calibration of the normal distributions to the actual distributions. One could argue that this is theoretically the weaker part of the paper, but it stands as an example of how practitioners need to be able to get around theoretical hurdles to arrive at answers they can act on. In the latter sense, I find this approach to credit risk assessment compelling.

The results are intriguing. The authors rightly claim that models based on "constant exposures will almost always underestimate the true economic capital." Their model generates stochastic exposures that allow for a more realistic expression of the default process and the correlations between defaults.

The second chapter in this section, "Reconcilable Differences", by H. Ugur Koyluoglu and Andrew Hickman of Oliver Wyman and Credit Suisse Financial Products, respectively, advances a general model framework that attempts to integrate four major credit assessment models under a single umbrella. The four models are: CreditMetrics (The RiskMetrics Group – previously JP Morgan), PortfolioManager (KMV), CreditPortfolio-View (McKinsey) and CreditRisk+ (CSFP). Impressively, the authors develop a somewhat technical but not inaccessible framework that includes all these models as special cases – with one proviso. The generalisation comes at the expense that each model is reduced to its single-period-equivalent form with fixed recovery rates and fixed exposures.

If you are willing to accept this assumption for the time being, you will find that the study has much to offer. Adopting a multifactor framework, the authors use systemic variables to produce correlated default rates. This provides distributions of default rates that are conditional on the state of the factors at any given point in time. The distribution is a very general one – the Poisson distribution (CreditRisk+) and the binomial distribution (CreditMetrics and CreditPortfolioView) are special cases.

Combination (ie, convolution) of the conditional probability distributions leads to unconditional distributions for loss probabilities. At this point the models can really only differ in the way they are parameterised. This is not to say that the different models themselves cannot generate widely different default probability estimates. However, it does suggest that if all the models fit within this framework, comparing them should be easier given the common, more general framework.

As the typical practitioner does not have the time or inclination to reinvent the credit risk assessment wheel, he (or she) will probably value the ability to compare existing credit models with each other. The Wyman–CSFP contribution hints at theoretical integrability, but the practitioner's first decision on the job may be whether to buy or build a credit risk assessment system. If he chooses to buy a system, he will have to know why it is better than the others, and also where it is weaker. Where can he begin?

This topic is addressed by Robert Jarrow and Donald van Deventer of the Kamakura Corporation in their article "Practical Use of Credit Risk Models in Loan Portfolio and Counterparty Exposure Management" (the first author is also Professor of Finance at Cornell University). To decide which model is best, they argue that within the class of Merton-esque models, which are built on the foundations of contingent claims theory, there is no test as appropriate or effective as one that tests hedging performance.

How does this work? If you were testing the Black–Scholes model on option prices, you could always find an implied volatility that makes the model price fit the market price. Therefore, even if a model can match market prices, that does not necessarily make it a good model. What *would* make it a good model? Suppose that Model A generates a proposed hedging portfolio A and that Model B generates a corresponding hedging strategy B. Which hedged portfolio yields the best performance in terms of the lowest volatility of residual price variations? The model that produced it should be judged the best.

It is precisely this intuition that Jarrow and van Deventer apply to determining which credit pricing model works the best. But, rather than coming to a pat conclusion, the study is better described as a road map for the practitioner who is keen to compare the models he has and to use the data that are available to determine which model performs the best. This analysis should help him choose which model he should use to make his credit risk management decisions.

The authors make two points very strongly. First is the failure of what they call "static reduced-form models" – ie, Merton-esque models – to stand up to tests of hedging performance. They simply do not describe reality well. Second, many practitioners and vendors compare their model results to historical default frequencies, but the authors show that there is so much variability in those estimates that this is at best a very weak test for the appropriateness of a model. They prove the point convincingly using a First Interstate data set and the Merton model as an example.

Readers will be left with the conclusion that benchmarking and assessing the performance of models are an important part of the credit risk management process. This paper provides an example of how the process should work.

"Portfolio Management and Stress-Testing using CreditMetrics", by Christopher Finger and Aidan McNulty of the RiskMetrics Group, addresses another very practical issue. Specifically, how can one compare models or benchmark performance without having a clear example of the correct implementation of any given model? Although, for obvious reasons, their contribution focuses on the CreditMetrics methodology, readers will find the openness of the data sources and the general nature of the questions raised about the data appropriate for any model.

The authors begin by describing the data requirements for the CreditMetrics system. This involves understanding the states of nature (eg, credit ratings), credit exposure as a function of the state, and interaction or correlation among the exposures. Most importantly for credit risk managers, they also discuss where the greatest sensitivities are. For example, one would not want to spend 90% of one's time refining an estimate that contributed only 10% of the error in estimating default probabilities.

Using a somewhat typical global credit portfolio, the authors show how to implement credit analysis in CreditManager, and they examine a case in which Asian credits weaken and correlations between defaults increase (a not unlikely scenario at the time of this writing). Their approach supports a "what-if" culture of credit risk management – those with user-friendly, fast models who can ask, and expect answers to, questions such as "What happens when the mutual default correlations increase by 5%" or "How will a shift in the relative value of international stock markets affect my rating transition probabilities?"

The final result is a floor-plan for a proactive risk management approach. Once unattractive scenarios are identified, model users should be able to overlay multiple risk mitigation strategies on their portfolios to see which strategies achieve the desired distribution of results at the lowest possible cost. Although the authors do not provide detail here, this is clearly the direction they are suggesting the reader should go.

Conclusion

Where do we go from here? The sensible credit risk manager is now in a better position to ask the following questions:

❏ What are our credit portfolio objectives?
❏ How do these objectives translate into measurable and actionable quantities?
❏ What are the underlying value-drivers in the credit portfolio?
❏ What is the analytical link between these drivers and portfolio value?
❏ What kind of system do I need to make this link continuously accessible?
❏ How do I compare different risk mitigation or risk-taking strategies?
❏ How can I maximise portfolio performance vis-à-vis the objectives?
❏ How will my own performance be measured over time?

The answers to these questions will make the difference between a successful credit risk manager and an unsuccessful one.

20

A Credit Risk Toolbox

Angelo Arvanitis and Jon Gregory

Paribas

This chapter presents new insights and techniques for the computation of credit loss distributions for capital allocation and active portfolio management. It focuses on portfolios whose exposures are marked-to-market and therefore vary randomly over time. The analysis is thus applicable to both loan and capital market derivative portfolios. We develop analytical expressions under restricted assumptions and a general simulation procedure. We demonstrate how default correlations, stochastic recovery rates, stochastic exposures and credit migration affect the capital computation. We present two Monte Carlo acceleration techniques that significantly reduce the simulation time. Finally, we discuss how portfolio optimisation can be developed within this framework.

The management of credit risk is becoming a standard responsibility of risk departments. There are several commercially available products for credit risk management (see Bibliography). In this paper, we present techniques for faster and more accurate calculation of credit loss distributions.

There are two general approaches for calculating credit loss distributions. The first is to make simplifying assumptions about the portfolio and derive analytical expressions. The accuracy of such an approach will vary with the characteristics of the portfolio and quite large errors can be introduced. Nevertheless, the method we describe here (which has not previously been applied in credit risk management) gives good results. The second approach is to use Monte Carlo simulation, which is flexible but slow. We describe two techniques that significantly speed up the simulation.

Another objective of this paper is to deal with the problems of modelling default correlations. No assumption needs to be made about the capital structure of the firm, nor are equity returns required to estimate the correlations. An important question that arises in this context is the simulation of correlated binary variables, corresponding to default events, given only marginal probabilities and pairwise correlations.

We introduce a new approach for modelling stochastic recovery rates that intuitively links the recovery amount to the severity of the default. This induces correlation between the recovery rates and also leads to a reduction in simulation time.

Unexpected loss

A common measure in risk management is the unexpected loss. This is the worst loss incurred at a specified level of confidence and for a specified observation period; it is therefore used to measure economic capital. The period used in credit risk is generally in terms of years (rather than days as for market risk) since the underlying positions cannot be readily traded. The level of confidence is defined by the (100 – x) percentile of the loss distribution where x is determined according to the institution's credit rating.

This is an updated version of a paper originally published in Risk *(December 1998), pp. 50–55. The authors are grateful to Jean-Michel Lasry for helpful comments and discussions. A longer version of the paper is available from the authors upon request.*
E_mail: angelo_arvanitis@paribas.com; john_gregory@paribas.com

For a normal distribution, the confidence level can be determined as a multiple of its standard deviation. But losses due to credit risk are highly skewed as adverse credit events are rare but give large losses. This means that a normal approximation is not valid, as illustrated in Figure 1. This shows the error $(UL_{stdev} - UL_p)/UL_{stdev}$ that would arise if one used the appropriate multiple of the portfolio's standard deviation (UL_{stdev}) rather than the true percentile (UL_p). For example, for a portfolio of 1,000 facilities each with default probability 2%, the unexpected loss is underestimated by 300%. To manage a portfolio of credit exposures one must estimate the whole loss distribution, without relying on the normality assumption.

For a portfolio consisting of n assets or netted positions, the portfolio loss due to defaults up to a given time T is given by

$$L(T) = \sum_{i=1}^{n} (1 - \delta_i) X_i(T) d_i(T) \tag{1}$$

where $X_i(T)$ is a stochastic exposure given by the greater of the present value of the asset and zero, $\max(PV_i, 0)$, $d_i(T)$ is a binary default function that is 1 indicating default and 0 otherwise and δ_i is the recovery rate. The above expression cannot be calculated explicitly except when the number of assets is small.

Saddle-point approximation

When considering sums of independent random variables, it is convenient to consider the moment generating functions (mgf). The mgf of a random variable V is

$$M_V(s) = E\left[e^{sV}\right] = \int_{-\infty}^{\infty} e^{st} p_V(t) dt \tag{2}$$

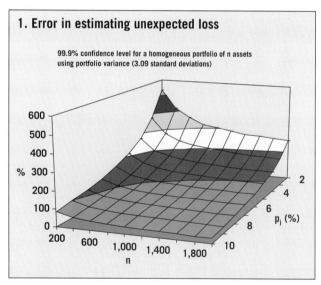

1. Error in estimating unexpected loss

99.9% confidence level for a homogeneous portfolio of n assets using portfolio variance (3.09 standard deviations)

This can be thought of as the Fourier transform of the pdf. When independent random variables are added, their distributions are convolved but their mgfs are multiplied. As multiplication is such a simple operation, a summation of independent random variables is best tackled by examining their mgfs. For the example we are considering – a weighted sum of binary variables with weights (w_i) and default probabilities (p_i) – the mgf is just

$$M_L(s) = \prod_{i=1}^{n} \left(1 - p_i + p_i e^{w_i s}\right) \tag{3}$$

One then has the problem of "undoing" the transform, ie, obtaining the pdf of L from the mgf M_L. This can be achieved by an inversion integral similar to equation (2). By suitably approximating the shape of the integrand one obtains an analytical approximation to the pdf of L. This

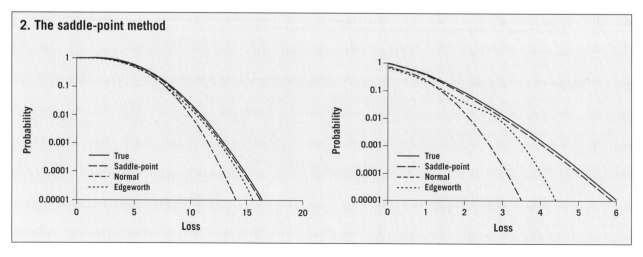

2. The saddle-point method

True
Saddle-point
Normal
Edgeworth

technique is known as the method of steepest descents or saddle-point method (Davison and Hinkley, 1988). The method also allows one to obtain analytical approximations to the tail probability without having to integrate the density function. The saddle-point method does not make any prior assumption about the shape of the loss distribution. The shape of the approximated pdf may have fat or thin tails, be symmetric or asymmetric, be uni-modal or multimodal, and be bounded or unbounded. In the case of a loss distribution we know that it is bounded by 0 and the sum of all the exposures.

Figure 2 compares the saddle-point approximation with the true distribution in the $B(50, 0.10)$ and $B(50, 0.01)$ cases, ie, $n = 50$, p_i all equal. It is apparent that the saddle-point method gives better results than the normal approximation, especially in the tails, and also outperforms the Edgeworth series (using two correction terms to the central limit theorem; see, for example, Johnston, Kotz and Balakrishnan, 1995). To quantify its performance, consider estimating the unexpected loss at the 99.9th percentile for the $B(50, 0.01)$ example. This corresponds to a tail probability of 0.001. The saddle-point method underestimates the economic capital by 3%, the Edgeworth correction by 17% and the normal approximation by 37%.

We have been able to use the saddle-point approximation to derive expressions for loss distributions that include variable exposures and default probabilities and we have also been able to incorporate correlation into the analysis. The calculations are at virtually no computational cost, and we believe the saddle-point approximation to be an excellent method for calculating tail probabilities of credit loss distributions.

Simulation methods

The analytical expressions presented in the last section are very powerful in calculating loss distributions, and may be used for arbitrary (but deterministic) recovery rates, unequal exposures and unequal default probabilities. However, to include all the effects present in a real portfolio – such as stochastic exposures, stochastic recovery rates, correlations and credit migrations – we must use simulation. The method presented is not based on Merton's "firm value model" model (1974), though it has an interpretation in terms of the asset returns of the firm.

Default events are positively correlated, which increases the unexpected loss. The correlations are mostly influenced by macroeconomic factors reflected in the general state of the economy. The estimation of default probabilities and correlations can be done dynamically based on the credit spreads of bonds issued by the firm or the returns of the underlying equity. Alternatively, static estimates can be made using historical data. We estimate default correlations from historical data supplemented with information according to the industrial and geo-graphical characteristics of each counterparty. We empha-sise that our correlation model is not based on equity returns and allows any procedure for estimating the default correlations to be used.

A correlation structure for binary variables is not com-pletely specified by its pairwise correlations. We must therefore define the higher-order correlations. To do this, we assume that the entire correlation structure can be determined from a multivariate normal distribution, for which the higher-order correlations are defined by the pairwise ones. It must be emphasised that this is by no means the only way to build the higher-order structure, although the approach has the intuitive interpretation that

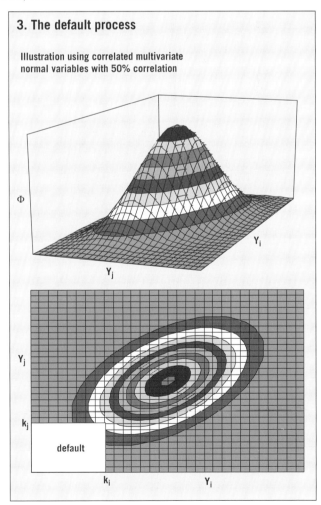

3. The default process

Illustration using correlated multivariate normal variables with 50% correlation

4. Maximum value for default correlation

As a function of the default probabilities of the two assets

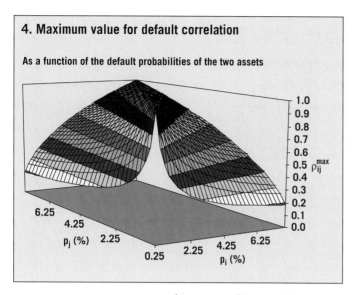

the multivariate normal distribution represents the standardised (zero mean and unit variance) asset returns of the counterparties.

The correlation framework is defined by mapping the binomial default probabilities (p_i) on to thresholds $k_i = \Phi^{-1}(p_i)$ of a normal distribution. The probability that the two assets default is given by integrating the bivariate normal pdf, which is plotted in Figure 3 showing a correlation of 50%. The area bounded by the two normal variables, $k_i = \Phi^{-1}(p_i)$ and $k_j = \Phi^{-1}(p_j)$, defines the probability of joint default of assets i and j. As the correlation increases, the density function is "squashed" along the diagonal, increasing the joint default probability.

We need to relate the correlations between the normal variables λ_{ij} to the correlations between binary variables ρ_{ij}. This can be achieved by equating the expectation of pairs of joint Binary events to the joint probability of a correlated bivariate normal distribution:

$$E\left[d_i d_j\right] = \Phi\left(\lambda_{ij}, k_i, k_j\right) \tag{4}$$

Using the standard definition of the correlation coefficient:

$$\rho_{ij} = \frac{\Phi\left(\lambda_{ij}, k_i, k_j\right) - p_i p_j}{p_i(1-p_i)p_j(1-p_j)} \tag{5}$$

establishes a relationship between ρ_{ij} and λ_{ij} that can be solved numerically.

It is important to understand the full implication of the above formula. Without loss of generality, $p_i \le p_j$; so $\Phi(\lambda_{ij}, k_i, k_j) \le p_i \le p_j$ (as the probability of a pair of events occurring is necessarily less than or equal to either of their individual probabilities), which gives:

$$\rho_{ij} \le \sqrt{\frac{p_i(1-p_j)}{p_j(1-p_i)}} \tag{6}$$

So the default correlation can reach unity if and only if the individual probabilities are equal. The maximum value that the pairwise default correlation may take with respect to the individual probabilities is shown in Figure 4.

Using this representation for the binary default events, it is possible to derive analytical formulae for the loss distribution. We do not discuss this approach further but instead proceed with Monte Carlo simulation for full flexibility. The same analysis can be performed by sampling from the alpha-stable instead of the normal distribution.

For a Monte Carlo simulation, we need a way of simulating correlated binary (default) events that involves drawing from the correlated multivariate normal distribution:

$$Y \sim N\left[\begin{pmatrix} 0 \\ 0 \end{pmatrix}, \begin{pmatrix} 1 & & \lambda_{ij} \\ & \ddots & \\ \lambda_{ij} & & 1 \end{pmatrix}\right] \tag{7}$$

The underlying correlation matrix represents the correlation between the multivariate normal variables and not the default events themselves.

We know that the covariance matrix can always be factorised as $C = AA^T$ for some matrix A (by Cholesky factorisation or diagonalisation on C). If u is a multivariate process with components independently drawn from the standard normal distribution, the vector Au has the required covariance matrix C.

Having determined the correlation between the normal random variables, the binary default variable d_i is given by the indicator function $I(Y_i < k_i)$, where Y_i is the ith element of the vector Au. The additional structure we have imposed ensures that the binary default variables match the default probabilities and correlations in the input data.

The simulation method we present includes stochastic exposures. It is important to compare this with the case in which the exposures are treated as constant, known as the loan equivalent approach. This approach makes three crucial assumptions. The first is that there is zero covariance between the exposures of the assets, which is unlikely. The second assumption is that the recovery rate is constant. We later present an analysis of a real portfolio in which this assumption leads to an underestimate of 25% of the unexpected loss. The last assumption is that the unexpected loss can be defined by the portfolio variance. The argument presented previously shows that this is not appropriate.

Our treatment of stochastic recovery rates follows from the default and migration model. In the event of default, the recovery rate is defined by a series of further thresholds below the default threshold. Intuition suggests that a more extreme default leads to a lower recovery rate. This approach means that further random numbers need not be drawn and introduces correlation between the recovery rates. The form of the correlation is determined by the default correlation structure. The position of the recovery rate thresholds can be determined by matching the historical mean and variance, which depend on the seniority of the debt (eg, see CreditMetrics).

If default occurs at some time in the future, it is necessary to know the exposure distribution at the risk horizon. If the exposure is negative, default does not lead to a loss. A loss of up to the maximum exposure can be incurred when it is positive. The exposure distributions are estimated by simulating underlyings over many paths. Assets are then revalued, on a deal-by-deal basis, at a number of discrete time points on these paths. The exposure data is aggregated on a counterparty basis to account for the covariances between exposures, netting agreements and collateral.

We now apply the methodology above to a hypothetical example to illustrate the effect of the various factors on the loss distribution for a portfolio of swaps. Our initial analysis will consider only default events since they account for the majority of losses. We can estimate the distribution for the variable defined in equation (1) by averaging over many simulations.

Figure 5 shows the loss distributions for the swap portfolio obtained from four scenarios of varying complexity: a basic case (constant exposures and recovery rates and no default correlation) and then including default correlation, stochastic recovery rates and stochastic exposures. Table 1 summarises the findings. It shows the increase in the 99.9th percentile for the effects studied and also shows the estimate for the loan equivalent methodology.

The most dramatic effect in the estimation of capital comes from the introduction of stochastic exposures. This has important implications for loan equivalent methodologies. Using constant exposures will almost always underestimate the true economic capital. The loan equivalent measure accounts for only 69% of the true economic capital in this instance.

We have so far restricted our analysis only to losses from default events, but for a complete model we also need to consider credit downgrades and the volatility of the credit spreads even without credit migration. The migration process is defined as a simple extension to the default model where further thresholds are added for each migration probability

5. Tail of loss distributions

For swap portfolio under different assumptions

Front row: Basic case
2nd row: Stochastic recovery rates
3rd row: Default correlation
Back row: Stochastic exposures

Table 1. Economic capital estimates for swap portfolio under different assumptions

	Economic capital	Relative increase (%)
Basic case	36	–
Stochastic recovery rates	45	25
Correlated defaults	66	83
Stochastic exposures	124	244
All effects	177	392
Loan equivalent	122	229

6. Forward credit spread curves

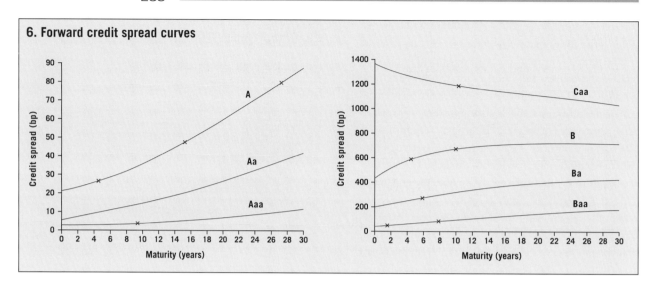

(see CreditMetrics for a complete description of this procedure). Credit migration has two effects. First, credit downgrades lead to a loss in the market value of assets and facilities. Second, a downgraded counterparty is more likely to default.

To calculate the loss due to credit migration, we have to be able to compute credit spread curves at future points in time for all credit classes. Jarrow, Lando and Turnbull (1997), and Arvanitis, Gregory and Laurent (1999) present a pricing model that is consistent with this framework. The latter model also accounts for the volatility of credit spreads within a rating class. This would be important for capital market portfolios, where losses are marked-to-market even if there is no downgrade. In Figure 6, we show the estimation of forward credit spread curves using the model presented in Arvanitis, Gregory and Laurent (1999), calibrated with US telecommunication bond prices on December 30, 1997.

The credit migration events have a significant effect on the mean of the loss distribution (16% increase for the swap portfolio considered in this example) but the tail is not affected as much (4% increase in unexpected loss). This is due to the fact that the tails of the distribution are defined by the most extreme losses from default events. The loss distribution for credit migration events only is much closer to normal but still has a fatter tail, an important observation for building models to assess the specific risk of bond portfolios.

Credit migration also causes a drift in default probabilities that must be taken into account when considering losses for multiple periods. For investment-grade portfolios, this will increase the probabilities of default over time since there is more chance of worsening credit quality.

Many simulations are required to get a good estimate of the loss distribution because the events that determine the tail of the distribution are rare. We describe two ways to speed up the convergence of the Monte Carlo simulation. The first is importance sampling, where the aim is to concentrate the simulations in the regions of most interest. Figure 7 shows the effect on convergence. The second uses the analytical formulas discussed earlier to control the variation of a Monte Carlo estimator (see Figure 8). This approach represents a combination of the analytical and simulation methods, which is particularly powerful when the analytical approximation is close to the true distribution. Note that it is also possible to combine the importance sampling and control variate methods.

Default data

To estimate expected loss and capital for risk management, we need to use "real" default probabilities. A straightforward way of estimating these numbers is from historical data, since they reflect actual default experience. It is important to point out that as the default process is non-stationary (more defaults during recession than expansion of the economy), particular attention should be paid to the choice of the estimation interval.

From the prices of traded instruments we can only derive risk-neutral default probabilities, which reflect a combination of the real default probabilities and the risk premia.

7. Importance sampling

Example using importance sampling to speed up the convergence of the Monte Carlo simulation

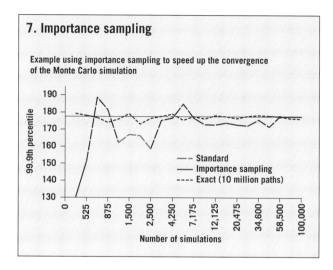

8. Control variate

Example using the saddle-point approximation as a control variate in the Monte Carlo simulation

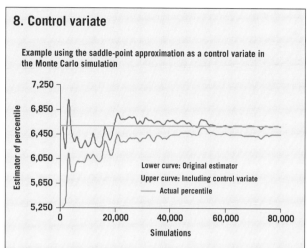

They are therefore inappropriate for risk management. Risk-neutral default probabilities are substantially more volatile than the real ones, resulting in high volatility for the computed capital – which is not acceptable for most applications. On the other hand, for arbitrage-free pricing and hedging we should use risk-neutral default probabilities. They could be derived from the prices of standard default swaps, since these are the natural instruments for hedging counterparty risk in loan and derivative portfolios. If default swaps are not traded for a specific name, bonds would be the best alternative.

Similarly, default correlations can be estimated from either historical defaults or historical credit spreads, or ideally, they can be implied from the prices of securities that are sensitive to correlation, such as spread options or first-to-default swaps. Unfortunately, the latter instruments tend to be very illiquid.

9. Credit portfolio optimisation

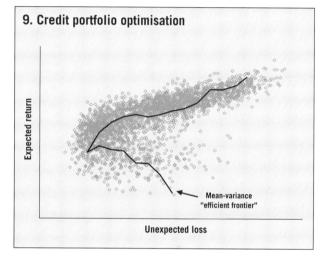

Credit portfolio optimisation

As the loss distributions are skewed, the usual mean-variance optimisation can lead to inefficient portfolios, as shown in Figure 9. Credit portfolio optimisation aims to increase the ratio of expected return to capital (unexpected loss) by either increasing the former or reducing the latter. The lack of exact analytical results forces us to use simulation to compute the efficient frontier.

BIBLIOGRAPHY

Arvanitis, A., J. K. Gregory and J.-P. Laurent, 1999, "Building Models for Credit Spreads", *Journal of Derivatives* Spring, pp. 27–43.

Credit Suisse Financial Products, 1997, *CreditRisk+*.

Davison, A., and D. Hinkley, 1988, "Saddlepoint Approximations in Resampling Methods", *Biometrika* 75(3), pp. 417–31.

Jarrow, R.A., D. Lando and S. Turnbull, 1997, "A Markov Model for the Term Structure of Credit Risk Spreads", *Review of Financial Studies* 10(2), pp. 481–523.

Johnston, N., S. Kotz and N. Balakrishnan, 1995, *Continuous Univariate Distributions* volumes I and II, John Wiley.

JP Morgan, April 1997, CreditMetrics.

KMV Corporation, Portfolio Manager, Description, Usage and Specification, Version 4.0.

Merton, R., 1974, "On the Pricing of Corporate Debt: The Risk Structure of Interest Rates", *Journal of Finance* 29, pp. 449–70.

Wilson, T., 1997, "Portfolio Credit Risk", *Risk* September, pp. 111–17; October, pp. 56–61.

21

Reconcilable Differences

H. Ugur Koyluoglu and Andrew Hickman

Oliver, Wyman & Company; Credit Suisse First Boston

I n the past few years, major advances in credit risk analytics have led to the proliferation of a new breed of sophisticated credit portfolio risk models. Several models have been developed, including proprietary applications developed for internal use by leading-edge financial institutions, and third-party applications intended for sale or distribution as software. Several have received a great deal of public attention, including JP Morgan's CreditMetrics/CreditManager, Credit Suisse Financial Products' CreditRisk+, McKinsey & Company's CreditPortfolioView and KMV's PortfolioManager. These new models allow the user to measure and quantify credit risk comprehensively at both the portfolio and contributory level. As such, they have the potential to cause profound changes to the lending business, accelerating the shift to active credit portfolio management[1] and, eventually, leading to an "internal models" reform of regulatory credit risk capital guidelines.[2]

But before these models can deliver on their promise, they must earn the acceptance of credit portfolio managers and regulators. To these practitioners, this seemingly disparate collection of new approaches may be confusing, or may appear as a warning sign of an early developmental stage in the technology. While these misgivings are understandable, this paper will demonstrate that these new models in fact represent a remarkable consensus in the underlying framework, differing primarily in calculation procedures and parameters rather than financial intuition.

This paper explores both the similarities and the differences among the new credit risk portfolio models, focusing on three representative models:
❑ "Merton-based", eg, CreditMetrics and PortfolioManager;[3]
❑ "econometric", eg, CreditPortfolioView; and
❑ "actuarial", eg, CreditRisk+.

Note that this paper examines only the default component of portfolio credit risk. Some models incorporate credit spread (or ratings migration) risk, while others advocate a separate model. In this aspect of credit risk there is less consensus in modelling techniques, and the differences need to be explored and resolved in future research. The reader should strictly interpret "credit risk" to mean "default risk" throughout.

Additionally, for comparability, the models have been restricted to a single-period horizon, a fixed recovery rate and fixed exposures.

Underlying framework

At first, the models appear to be quite dissimilar – CreditMetrics is based on a microeconomic causal model of default; CreditPortfolioView is a macroeconomic causal model; and CreditRisk+ is a top-down model, making no assumptions about causality.

This paper was originally published in Risk *magazine, October 1998. The authors wish to thank Andrew Cross, Frank Diebold, Tom Garside, Marc Intrater, Andrew Kuritzkes, Hashem Pesaran, Til Schuermann, James Wiener and Tom Wilde for providing helpful comments and discussions. All errors are the responsibility of the authors alone. The opinions expressed herein are those of the authors and do not necessarily reflect those of Credit Suisse Financial Products, CSFP Capital Inc., or Oliver, Wyman & Company. This paper is an abridged version of "A Generalised Framework for Credit Portfolio Models", a working paper that may be obtained from the authors on request.*

Despite these apparent differences, the models fit within a single generalised underlying framework, consisting of three components:

❑ *Joint default behaviour.* Default rates vary over time – intuitively, as a result of varying economic conditions. Each borrower's default rate is conditioned on the "state of the world" for the relevant economic conditions. The degree of "correlation" in the portfolio is reflected by borrowers' conditional default rates varying together in different states.

❑ *Conditional distribution of portfolio default rate.* For each state, the conditional distribution of a homogeneous sub-portfolio's default rate can be calculated as if borrowers are independent because the joint default behaviour is accounted for in generating conditional default rates.

❑ *Convolution/aggregation.* The unconditional distribution of portfolio defaults is obtained by combining homogeneous sub-portfolios' conditional default rate distributions in each state and then simply averaging across states.

This generalised framework allows a structured comparison of the models, as follows.

CONDITIONAL DEFAULT RATES AND PROBABILITY DISTRIBUTION OF DEFAULT RATE.
All three models explicitly or implicitly relate default rates to variables describing the relevant economic conditions ("systemic factors"). This relationship can be expressed as a "conditional default rate" transformation function (see Figure 1). The systemic factors are random and are usually assumed to be normally distributed. Since the conditional default rate is a function of these random systemic factors, the default rate will also be random.

The Merton-based model relies on Merton's model of a firm's capital structure:[4] a firm defaults when its asset value falls below its liabilities. Default probability then depends on the amount by which assets exceed liabilities and the volatility of those assets. If standardised changes in asset value, ΔA_i, are normally distributed, the default probability can be expressed as the probability of a standard normal variable falling below some critical value, c. Joint default events among borrowers in the portfolio are related to the extent that the borrowers' changes in asset value are correlated.

Since the Merton model neither assigns the transformation function, nor assumes a probability distribution for default rates explicitly, these relationships must be derived. The change in asset value can be decomposed into a set of normally distributed orthogonal systemic factors, x_k, and a normally distributed idiosyncratic component ε_i:

$$\Delta A_i = b_{i,1} x_1 + b_{i,2} x_2 + \cdots + \sqrt{1 - \sum_k b_{i,k}^2} \, \varepsilon_i$$

where $b_{i,k}$ are the factor-loadings, and $x_k, \varepsilon_i \sim \text{iid } N[0,1]$.

Given the values of the systemic factors, the change in asset value will be normally distributed with a mean given by the factor loadings and factor values, and a standard deviation given by the weight of the idiosyncratic factor. The default rate, conditioned on the systemic factors' values, can then be expressed as[5]

$$p_i \big|_x = \Phi \left[\frac{c - \sum_k b_{i,k} x_k}{\sqrt{1 - \sum_k b_{i,k}^2}} \right]$$

For the single borrower or homogeneous portfolio case, the systemic factors can be summarised by a single variable, m, reducing the transformation function to

$$p \big|_m = \Phi \left[\frac{c - \sqrt{\rho} \, m}{\sqrt{1 - \rho}} \right]$$

where $m \sim N[0,1]$ and

$$\rho = \sum_k b_k^2$$

is the asset correlation.

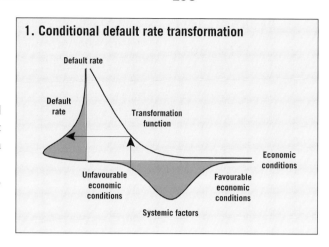

1. Conditional default rate transformation

Since the cumulative normal function is bounded $[0,1]$ and concave in the relevant region, the resulting default rate distribution is bounded $[0,1]$ and skewed right, as in Figure 1.

The probability density function for the default rate, $f(p)$, can be derived explicitly, as follows:

$$f(p) = \varphi(m(p))\left|\frac{dm}{dp}\right| = \frac{\sqrt{1-\rho}\, \varphi\left(\dfrac{c - \sqrt{1-\rho}\,\Phi^{-1}(p)}{\sqrt{\rho}}\right)}{\sqrt{\rho}\,\varphi\left(\Phi^{-1}(p)\right)}$$

where $\varphi(z)$ is the standardised normal density function.

The econometric model[6] drives the default rate, $p_{i,t}$, according to an "index", $y_{i,t}$, of macroeconomic factors. The index is expressed as a weighted sum of macroeconomic variables, $x_{k,t}$, each of which is normally distributed and has lagged dependency.

$$x_{k,t} = a_{k,0} + a_{k,1} x_{k,t-1} + a_{k,2} x_{k,t-2} + \cdots + \varepsilon_{k,t}$$

and

$$y_{i,t} = b_{i,0} + b_{i,1} x_{1,t} + b_{i,2} x_{2,t} + \cdots + \upsilon_{i,t}$$

where $\varepsilon_{k,t}$ and $\upsilon_{i,t}$ are normally distributed random innovations.

The index is transformed to a default probability by the Logit function:

$$p_{i,t} = \frac{1}{1 + e^{y_{i,t}}}$$

The index and macroeconomic variables can be combined in a single equation:

$$y_{i,t} = \left[b_{i,0} + \sum_k b_{i,k}\left(a_{k,0} + \sum_j a_{k,j} x_{k,t-j}\right)\right] + \sum_k b_{i,k}\varepsilon_{k,t} + \upsilon_{i,t}$$

consisting of a constant term and random terms representing systemic and index-specific innovations. For the single borrower or homogeneous portfolio case, these random terms can be summarised by a single normally distributed variable, m, so that the conditional default rate can then be expressed as:

$$p\Big|_m = \frac{1}{1 + e^{U+Vm}}$$

where $m \sim N[0, 1]$, and U and V represent the summarised constant term and coefficient to the random term, respectively.

Since the Logit function is bounded $[0, 1]$ and concave, the resulting distribution is bounded $[0, 1]$ and skewed, as in Figure 1.

The implied probability density function for the default rate, $f(p)$, is

$$f(p) = \varphi(m(p))\left|\frac{dm}{dp}\right| = \frac{1}{Vp(1-p)}\,\varphi\left[\frac{1}{V}\ln\left(\frac{1-p}{p}\right) - \frac{U}{V}\right]$$

The actuarial model[7] assumes explicitly that the default rate distribution follows the gamma distribution. Joint default behaviour is incorporated by treating the default rate as a random variable common to multiple borrowers. Borrowers are allocated to "sectors", each of which has a gamma-distributed default rate with specified mean and volatility. A borrower's conditional default rate is a scaled weighted average of sector default rates:

$$p\big|_x = \bar{p} \sum_k \omega_k \frac{x_k}{\mu_k}$$

where $\bar{p}$ is the borrower's unconditional default rate, ω_k represents the weight in sector k,

$$\sum_k \omega_k = 1$$

and

$$x_k \sim \Gamma\left[\alpha_k, \beta_k\right] \text{ with } \alpha_k = \frac{\mu_k^2}{\sigma_k^2} \text{ and } \beta_k = \frac{\sigma_k^2}{\mu_k}$$

The gamma distribution is skewed right, as in Figure 1, but has unbounded positive support.

It is possible to derive the actuarial model's implied transformation function such that when applied to a normally distributed systemic factor, m, it results in a gamma-distributed default rate. The transformation function consists of all points (χ, ξ) that satisfy

$$\int_0^\xi \Gamma(p; \alpha, \beta)\,dp = \int_\chi^\infty \varphi(m)\,dm$$

Hence, the transformation function is given by

$$p\big|_m = \Psi^{-1}\left(1 - \Phi(m); \alpha, \beta\right)$$

where

$$\alpha = \frac{\bar{p}^2}{\sigma^2}, \quad \beta = \frac{\sigma^2}{\bar{p}}$$

$m \sim N[0, 1]$ and $\Psi(z; \alpha, \beta)$ is the cumulative density function of the gamma distribution.

CONDITIONAL DISTRIBUTION OF PORTFOLIO DEFAULT RATE
Given fixed or conditional default rates, a homogeneous sub-portfolio's distribution of defaults follows the binomial distribution $B(k; n, p)$, which provides the probability that k defaults will occur in a portfolio of n borrowers if each has default probability p. CreditMetrics implicitly uses the binomial distribution by calculating the change in asset value for each borrower and testing for default – exactly equivalent to the binomial case of two states with a given probability. CreditPortfolioView explicitly uses the binomial distribution by iteratively convoluting the individual obligor distributions, each of which is binomial.

CreditRisk+ uses the Poisson distribution $P(k; pN)$, which provides the probability that k defaults will occur in a portfolio of n borrowers given a rate of intensity per unit time p. The binomial and Poisson distributions are quite similar; indeed, the Poisson distribution is the limiting distribution for the binomial distribution.[8]

AGGREGATION
The unconditional probability distribution of portfolio defaults is obtained by combining the conditional distributions of homogeneous sub-portfolio defaults across all "states of the world". Mathematically, this is expressed as a convolution integral.

The Merton-based and econometric models are conditioned on normally distributed systemic factors, and the independent loans' defaults are binomially distributed. Hence, the convolution integral for a homogeneous sub-portfolio with a single systemic factor is expressed as

$$\int_{-\infty}^{\infty} B\left(k; n, p\big|_m\right) \varphi(m)\, dm$$

The actuarial model's homogeneous sub-portfolio convolution integral, with gamma-distributed default rate and Poisson-distributed conditional defaults, is

$$\int_{0}^{\infty} P\left(k; np\right) \Gamma\left(p; \alpha, \beta\right) dp$$

These integrals are easily evaluated; in particular, the convolution of the Poisson distribution and gamma distribution yields a closed-form distribution, the negative binomial distribution. It is the differences between sub-portfolios – differing exposure size or default probabilities, or multiple systemic factors, complex correlation structure, etc – that create difficulty in aggregation. In practice, then, the convolutions are evaluated by Monte Carlo simulation in CreditMetrics and CreditPortfolioView, while CreditRisk+ uses a numeric algorithm based on "banding" exposures. In all three cases, the procedures are exact in the limit.

Figure 2 depicts the models as they are redefined in relation to the generalised framework.

Harmonisation of parameters

The preceding discussion shows that all three models critically depend on the unconditional default probability and joint default behaviour. While unconditional default probability is relatively straightforward, joint default behaviour appears in a different form in each model. The Merton-based model uses pairwise asset correlations; the actuarial model uses sector weightings and default rate volatilities; and the econometric model uses coefficients to common macroeconomic factors. Although these parameters are very different in nature, they contain equivalent information to characterise joint default behaviour.

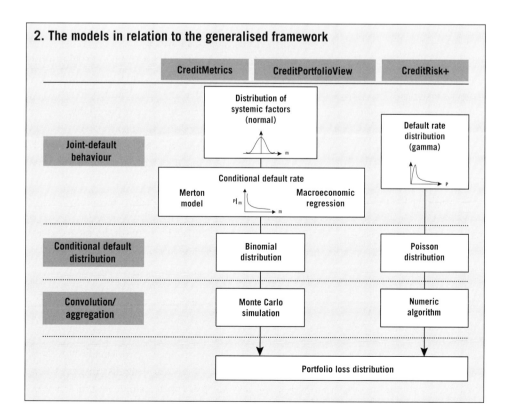

2. The models in relation to the generalised framework

COEFFICIENTS AND CORRELATIONS

The Merton-based model represents joint default behaviour with a set of asset factor-loadings or, equivalently, a pairwise asset correlation matrix:

$$\Delta A_i = b_{i,1} x_1 + b_{i,2} x_2 + \cdots + \sqrt{1 - \sum_k b_{i,k}^2} \varepsilon_i$$

The systemic factors are defined to be orthonormal, so that

$$\text{correlation}\left[\Delta A_i, \Delta A_j\right] = \frac{E\left[\Delta A_i \Delta A_j\right] - E\left[\Delta A_i\right] E\left[\Delta A_j\right]}{\sqrt{\left(E\left[\Delta A_i^2\right] - E\left[\Delta A_i\right]^2\right)\left(E\left[\Delta A_j^2\right] - E\left[\Delta A_j\right]^2\right)}}$$

$$= b_{i,1} b_{j,1} + b_{i,2} b_{j,2} + \cdots$$

The econometric model's "index" regression coefficients closely resemble the asset factor-loadings of the Merton-based model. An "index correlation" is easily defined in a similar fashion to an asset correlation, and will be treated as equivalent, though they may provide slightly different results to the extent of differences in their respective conditional default rate functions.

UNCONDITIONAL DEFAULT RATE AND DEFAULT RATE VOLATILITY

The unconditional default rate and default rate volatility are specified directly in the actuarial model. For the Merton-based and econometric models, they are calculated by

$$\bar{p} = \int_{-\infty}^{\infty} p\big|_m \, \varphi(m) \, dm$$

and

$$\sigma^2 = \int_{-\infty}^{\infty} \left(p\big|_m - \bar{p}\right)^2 \varphi(m) \, dm$$

The parameters for the Merton-based (c and ρ) and econometric models (U and V) can then be solved to yield a specified unconditional default rate and default rate volatility. This defines the relationship between default rate volatility and asset correlation (see Figure 3).

DEFAULT CORRELATION

Some models take a Markowitz variance–covariance view of credit risk portfolio modelling. Each borrower has a variance of default given by the variance for a Bernoulli variable:

$$\text{var}\left(\text{default}_i\right) = \bar{p}_i \left(1 - \bar{p}_i\right)$$

For a large homogeneous portfolio, the portfolio variance approaches

$$\sigma^2 = \bar{p}\left(1 - \bar{p}\right)\rho_{\text{default}}$$

This provides the relationships between default correlation and default rate volatility and, therefore, asset correlation.

Mappings such as these allow parameter estimates to be "triangulated" by multiple methods, to the extent that model differences are not significant. For example, default rate volatilities can be used to estimate implied asset correlations in the absence of asset value data.

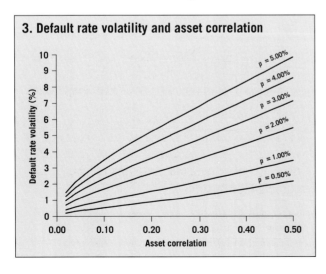

3. Default rate volatility and asset correlation

Differences in default rate distribution

The discussion above ("Underlying framework") demonstrates that substantial model differences could arise only from the differing treatment of joint default behaviour – the conditional default distributions are effectively the same and the aggregation techniques are all exact in the limit. The section "Harmonisation of parameters" provides the means to compare the joint default behaviour on an apples-to-apples basis.

This comparison will be illustrated for a homogeneous portfolio with an unconditional default rate, $\bar{p}$, of 116 basis points and a standard deviation of default rate, σ, equal to 90bp.[9] Since each model produces a two-parameter default rate distribution, the mean and standard deviation are sufficient statistics to define the relevant parameters for any of the models, as above. To yield $\bar{p} = 116$bp and $\sigma = 90$bp, the parameters for each model are as follows:

❑ Merton-based: $c = -2.27$, $\rho = 0.073$
❑ econometric: $U = 4.684$, $V = 0.699$
❑ actuarial: $\alpha = 1.661$, $\beta = 0.0070$.

In this example, the models' conditional default rate functions are virtually indistinguishable when the systemic factor is greater than negative two standard deviations. For extremely unfavourable economic conditions, the econometric model predicts a somewhat higher default rate, and the actuarial model predicts a somewhat lower default rate. The default rate distributions (see Figure 4) are also very similar, with only minor discrepancies in the tails.

The degree of agreement in the tails of these distributions can be assessed with the following statistic:

$$\Xi_z(f, g) = 1 - \frac{\int_z^\infty |f(x) - g(x)| dx}{\int_z^\infty f(x) dx + \int_z^\infty g(x) dx}$$

where $f(x)$ and $g(x)$ are probability density functions and z defines the lower bounds of the "tail", which will be defined arbitrarily as the area more than two standard deviations above the mean, ie, $z = \bar{p} + 2\sigma$. This statistic measures the amount of the probability distributions' mass that overlaps in the tail, normalised to the total probability mass of the two distributions in the tail. The statistic will be bounded [0, 1], where zero indicates distributions with no overlapping probability mass, and one indicates exact agreement. Table 1 provides the tail-agreement statistics for the example distributions.

Without a credible alternative distribution, this tail-agreement statistic provides a relative rather than an absolute measure. However, it can be used to test the robustness of the similarity to the parameters (see Table 2).

The results in Table 2 demonstrate that the similarity of the models holds for a reasonably wide range of parameters. The models begin to diverge at a very high ratio of default rate volatility to default probability, particularly for very low or very high default probabilities. Accordingly, in very high quality (AA or better) or very low quality (B or worse) portfolios, model selection can make a difference, though there are scant data on which to base such a selection. In a portfolio with only moderate weight in very high or very low quality sub-portfolios, these differences should not be significant in aggregation.

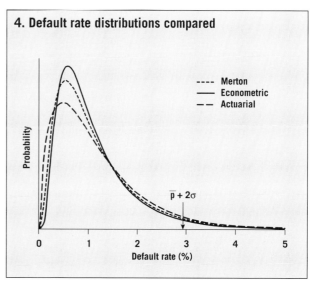

4. Default rate distributions compared

Table 1. Tail-agreement statistics for the example distributions

Merton versus econometric	94.90%
Merton versus actuarial	93.38%
Econometric versus actuarial	88.65%

Table 2. Tail-agreement statistics versus parameter values

$\bar{p}$	$\sigma/\bar{p}$ 0.50	1.00	2.00	3.00
0.05%	98.10% 93.53% 91.71%	95.94% 88.50% 84.70%	91.16% 81.17% 73.13%	89.12% 78.99% 69.04%
0.10%	97.92% 93.75% 91.73%	95.57% 88.94% 84.78%	91.15% 82.16% 73.95%	88.40% 80.40% 69.73%
0.25%	97.61% 94.11% 91.79%	94.93% 89.73% 84.97%	90.35% 83.87% 74.83%	87.86% 82.92% 71.60%
0.50%	97.33% 94.42% 91.88%	94.41% 90.56% 85.30%	89.91% 85.71% 76.15%	88.09% 85.61% 74.28%
1.00%	97.06% 94.93% 92.04%	93.97% 91.69% 85.93%	89.89% 88.29% 78.57%	88.97% 89.38% 78.72%
2.50%	96.62% 95.82% 92.62%	93.62% 93.94% 87.79%	90.77% 93.65% 84.77%	91.33% 94.68% 87.53%
5.00%	96.33% 97.02% 93.55%	93.85% 96.70% 90.87%	92.79% 95.24% 91.38%	94.59% 81.79% 79.96%
10.00%	96.21% 98.55% 95.45%	94.92% 95.57% 95.22%	95.79% 72.95% 72.41%	na na na

na = not applicable because it is an unreasonable combination of parameters – model results become unstable. Each cell contains tail-agreement statistics for Merton v. econometric, Merton v. actuarial and econometric v. actuarial.

IMPACT OF PARAMETER INCONSISTENCY

This finding of similarity should be taken with caution, as it hinges on harmonising parameter values. In practice, the parameters vary with the estimation technique. The different estimation techniques appropriate to different joint default parameters may result in inconsistent default rate volatility. Even mean default probabilities may vary considerably depending on the estimation technique, sample, etc. Unsurprisingly, when the parameters do not imply a consistent mean and standard deviation of default rate distribution, the result is that the models are significantly different. This case is illustrated by an example of three parameter sets that are not consistent, though plausibly obtainable for the same portfolio (see Table 3). Within any one of these three parameter sets, a comparison of the models yields results similar to Figure 4 and Table 1 – tail-agreement statistics average 91% and range from 82% to 95%. Large differences arise when the models are compared across the inconsistent parameter sets (see Figure 5) – tail-agreement statistics average only 76% and range from 65% to 85%, even when comparing the same model applied to each of the inconsistent parameter sets. The differences in parameters – well within the typical range of estimation error – have much greater impact than model differences in this example.

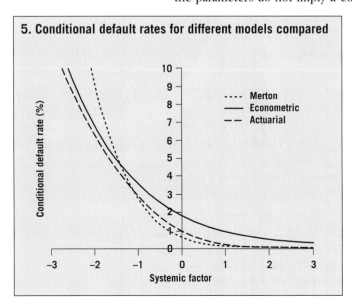

5. Conditional default rates for different models compared

Merton
Econometric
Actuarial

Conditional default rate (%)

Systemic factor

Table 3. Hypothetical inconsistent parameter values

	$\bar{p}$	s	c	r	a	b	U	V	Model for comparison*
1	**2.26%**	**1.70%**	−2.00	8.5%	1.767	0.0128	**4.00**	**0.70**	Econometric
2	**1.52%**	**1.71%**	−2.16	14.4%	**0.790**	**0.0192**	4.60	0.95	Actuarial
3	**1.54%**	**2.63%**	−2.16	**26.2%**	0.343	0.0449	4.95	1.30	Merton

*In the inconsistent parameter case, the parameter sets' "models for comparison" were selected arbitrarily. Bold figures indicate parameters appropriate to selected model.

Conclusions

On the surface, the credit risk portfolio models studied here seem to be quite different. Deeper examination reveals that the models belong to a single general framework, which identifies three critical points of comparison – the default rate distribution, the conditional default distribution, and the convolution/aggregation technique. Differences were found to be immaterial in the last two of these, so that any significant differences between the models must arise from differences in modelling joint default behaviour which manifest in the default rate distribution. Further, when the joint default parameter values are harmonised to a consistent expression of default rate and default rate volatility, the default rate distributions are sufficiently similar as to cause little meaningful difference across a broad range of reasonable parameter values. Any significant model differences can then be attributed to parameter value estimates that have inconsistent implications for the observable default rate behaviour.

Parameter inconsistency is not a trivial issue. A "naïve" comparison of the models, with parameters estimated from different data using different techniques, is quite likely to produce significantly different results for the same portfolio. The conclusions of empirical comparisons of the models will vary according to the degree of difference in parameters.[10] In such comparisons, it is important to understand the proportions of "parameter variance" and "model variance" if different results are produced for the same portfolio. The findings in this paper suggest that "parameter variance" is likely to dominate. Future studies should focus on the magnitude of parameter differences and the sensitivity of results to these differences.

Parameter inconsistency can arise from two sources: estimation error, which could arise from small sample size or other sampling issues; or model mis-specification. While default rate volatility may be immediately observable, even long periods of observation provide small sample size and risk non-stationarity. At the other extreme, asset correlations can be measured with reasonable sample size in much shorter periods, albeit with the risk of mis-specification in the return distributions and default causality assumptions in the translation to default rate volatility. Rather than conclude that parameter inconsistency potentially constitutes irreconcilable differences between the results of these models, this paper concludes that because the models are so closely related, the estimates are complementary and should provide improved accuracy in parameter estimation within the generalised framework as a whole.

A useful metaphor can be drawn from the success of the value-at-risk framework in modelling market risk. VAR has become the industry standard and the basis for regulatory capital requirements. But in practice, VAR encompasses a variety of significantly different modelling and parameter estimation techniques – eg, historical simulation versus variance–covariance, delta–gamma versus exact Monte Carlo simulation, etc. The underlying coherence of the VAR concept – that risk is measured by combining the relationship between the value of trading positions to market variables with the distribution of those underlying market variables – ensures a consistency sufficient for widespread acceptance and regulatory change. Similarly, the underlying coherence of these new sophisticated credit risk portfolio models should allow them to overcome differences in calculation procedures and parameter estimation. Rather than dissimilar competing alternatives, these models represent an emerging industry standard for credit risk management and regulation.

1 *For example, see Kuritzkes (1998).*

2 *See International Swaps and Derivatives Association (1998).*

3 *The discussion that follows will focus on CreditMetrics as the example, but will also apply reasonably well to PortfolioManager.*

4 *See Merton (1974), Kealhoffer (1995) and Gupton, Finger and Bhatia (1997).*

5 *Vasicek (1987) develops this representation of the Merton model for a single factor.*

6 *See Wilson (1997).*

7 *See Credit Suisse Financial Products (1997).*

8 *See Freund (1992).*

9 *These parameters were selected to match Moody's Investors Service's "All Corporates" default experience for 1970-1995, as reported in Carty and Lieberman (1996).*

10 *For example, Isda (1998) and Roberts and Wiener (1998) compare the results of several models on test portfolios. The former finds that model results are fairly consistent, while the latter finds that the models may produce quite different results for the same portfolio using parameters independently selected for each model.*

BIBLIOGRAPHY

Carty, L., and D. Lieberman, 1996, *Corporate Bond Defaults and Default Rates 1938-1995,* Moody's Investors Service Global Credit Research, January.

Credit Suisse Financial Products, 1997, *CreditRisk+ - A Credit Risk Management Framework.*

Freund, J., 1992, *Mathematical Statistics,* fifth edition (New Jersey: Prentice Hall).

Gupton, G., C. Finger and M. Bhatia, 1997, *CreditMetrics Technical Document,* Morgan Guaranty Trust.

International Swaps and Derivatives Association, 1998, *Credit Risk and Regulatory Capital,* March.

Kealhoffer, S., 1995, "Managing Default Risk in Derivative Portfolios", in *Derivative Credit Risk: Advances in Measurement and Management* (London: Risk Books).

Kuritzkes, A., 1998, "Transforming Portfolio Management", *Banking Strategies,* July-August, pp. 57-62.

Merton R., 1974, "On the pricing of corporate debt: the risk structure of interest rates", *Journal of Finance* 29, pp. 449-70. (Reprinted as chapter 4 of this volume.)

Roberts, J., and J. Wiener, 1998, "Handle With Care", Oliver, Wyman & Company, Working paper.

Vasicek, O., 1987, "Probability of Loss on Loan Portfolio", KMV Corporation, February 12.

Wilson, T., 1997, "Portfolio Credit Risk, Part I", *Risk,* September 1997, pp. 111-17. (Reprinted as chapter 2 of this volume.)

Wilson, T., 1997, "Portfolio Credit Risk, Part II", *Risk,* October 1997, pp. 56-61. (Reprinted as chapter 3 of this volume.)

22

Practical Use of Credit Risk Models in Loan Portfolio and Counterparty Exposure Management

Robert A. Jarrow and Donald R. van Deventer

Cornell University; Kamakura Corporation

The state of the art in credit risk modelling is advancing rapidly, with a wide variety of improvements, generalisations and extensions made to the original Merton model since its publication in 1974.[1] The Merton model is called a "structural" model of credit risk. "Structural" because the assumptions underlying the model are imposed on the firm's balance sheet – the firm's structure. An alternative approach to credit risk modelling, called the "reduced-form approach", was introduced by Jarrow and Turnbull (1995) just over two decades later. "Reduced form" because the assumptions underlying the model are imposed on the prices of the firm's traded liabilities that can be deduced from the structural models – the reduced form. A recent survey summarises the characteristics of 13 different credit models that have been introduced since 1993.[2]

Given the plethora of credit risk models now available, how should a banker who seeks to use them in credit risk management assess their relative performance and, then, implement them in practice? The answer to this difficult question is the subject of this chapter.

The form of the chapter is as follows. The first section briefly reviews the various credit risk models available. In the second section we discuss how these models should be evaluated, arguing that they need to be verified on the basis of their ability to hedge market prices and not through comparison of implied default probabilities with historic default probabilities. The third section illustrates this assertion with a short empirical study involving the Merton model, and a fourth section concludes the paper.

The credit risk models

Selection of the appropriate credit risk model is an important aspect of credit risk management. An inappropriate model contains model error, and model error introduces risk into the credit risk management process. This model risk is as "real" in terms of profit/loss volatility as is market, credit, liquidity or operational risk.

For example, a recent $80 million loss at the New York branch of a major international bank stemmed from a derivatives dealer's activities who believed that his pricing model was better than "the market". Generating biased quotes outside the rest of the market, the model caused his trades to dominate new transactions. This imbalanced position continued until outside auditors called a halt to his trading activity.

Historically, the first class of credit risk models to be formulated was based on the structural approach. Such models include the original Merton model (1974) and the extension of this model to random interest rates by Shimko, Tejima and van Deventer

302

PRACTICAL USE OF
CREDIT RISK MODELS
IN LOAN PORTFOLIO
AND COUNTERPARTY
EXPOSURE
MANAGEMENT

(1993). This class of models imposes assumptions on the evolution of the value of the firm's underlying assets. The liability structure of the firm, in conjunction with the firm's asset value fluctuations, determines the occurrence of bankruptcy and the payoffs (recovery rates) in the event of default. See Jones, Mason and Rosenfeld (1984), *Risk* Magazine (September, 1998) and Jarrow and van Deventer (1998) for a summary of the empirical results relating to this class of models.

Extensions of the structural approach, assuming exogenous recovery rates, include the work by Nielsen, Saá-Requejo and Santa Clara (1993) and Longstaff and Schwartz (1995). The Longstaff and Schwartz paper contains some empirical results.

The original Merton model, like the Black–Scholes model, assumed constant interest rates. Constant interest rates are inconsistent with market realities, and this assumption is one of the reasons why implementations of the original Merton model have not performed well in empirical tests.

Random interest rates, from both an intuitive and a theoretical perspective, should be an essential feature of any credit risk model. Indeed, the US taxpayers' trillion dollar experience with the interest rate-induced failures of many banks in the savings and loan industry provides anecdotal evidence for the validity of this claim. More anecdotal evidence also comes from the current troubles experienced by firms in Asia, where high interest rates (used to defend national currencies) have triggered record bankruptcies. Random interest rates, in fact, have been a standard assumption underlying all recent models of the credit risk process.[3]

It was the desire to include random interest rates and the discovery of the Heath-Jarrow–Morton (1992) term structure modelling technology that led to the reduced-form approach to modelling credit risk (Jarrow and Turnbull, 1995, and Jarrow, Lando and Turnbull, 1997). Empirical verification of these models is just becoming available, for which see Duffee (1999) and references therein.

Reduced-form models impose their assumptions directly on the prices of the firm's traded liabilities – primarily its debt – and on the default-free term structure of interest rates. Intuitively, the assumptions on the firm's debt prices relate to the credit spread, which is decomposable into the probability of bankruptcy (per unit time) multiplied by the loss (per promised dollar) in the event of bankruptcy. Exogenous assumptions are imposed on these quantities (the bankruptcy and recovery rate process) directly. This procedure gives the reduced-form models added flexibility in fitting market realities.

This is especially true of the implicit assumptions embedded in the structural approach regarding corporate capital structure policy. The structural approach assumes that the corporate capital structure policy is static, with the liability structure fixed and unchanging. For example, the Merton model (and its extension by Shimko, Tejima and van Deventer, 1993) assumes that management puts a debt structure in place and leaves it unchanged even if the value of corporate assets (and therefore equity) has doubled. This is too simplistic to realistically capture management behaviour and the dynamics of bankruptcy. It is our belief that management attempts to maintain a more constant debt/equity ratio across time. For example, a real estate entrepreneur would confirm that, when a building purchased for $100 million and financed with an $80 million loan doubles in value, he would refinance for $160 million. The Merton model cannot capture this behaviour, whereas the reduced-form model can.

The common implementation of the Merton model uses accounting data and equity prices to estimate the relevant parameters. The common implementation of the reduced-form models uses Treasury and corporate debt prices. Reduced-form models have been criticised for this reason because corporate debt markets are known to be less liquid than equity markets (with a scarcity of available quotes and wider bid/ask spreads), the implication being that corporate debt prices are useless and that they contain little if any useful information. This is a narrow point of view, not reflecting market efficiency. All corporate securities contain some information concerning the potential default of the issuer. Although perhaps noisier than equity prices, debt prices do provide valuable information.

303

PRACTICAL USE OF
CREDIT RISK MODELS
IN LOAN PORTFOLIO
AND COUNTERPARTY
EXPOSURE
MANAGEMENT

To accommodate the wider bid-offered spreads in thinly traded debt, reduced-form models need to model liquidity risk explicitly. Then, however, they can reliably use debt prices to extract relevant information. In fact, such models, if properly constructed, can be used to extract implied parameters from all or any subset of the available market prices: equity prices, debt prices, subordinated debt prices or credit derivative prices.

Evaluation of credit risk models

All credit risk models are based on the option pricing technology underlying the famous Black–Scholes formula. This technology is sometimes called the "risk-neutral" valuation technology. But, regardless of its name, the basic framework underlying these models is the same. Derivatives are priced by synthetic replication in complete markets that are arbitrage-free. Pricing by "synthetic replication" means that a derivative is priced by determining the cost of synthetically constructing the derivative using other traded securities. For example, a call option on a stock is priced in a Black–Scholes model by determining the cost of constructing the option using a dynamic portfolio of the underlying stock and riskless borrowing.

This means that a model is valid if and only if its implied "hedge" works.[4] The implied "hedge" is the synthetic replication portfolio used in reverse. This insight implies that the only valid way to test the outputs[5] of a credit risk model is to test its hedging performance. Hence, a model that fails a hedging test is misspecified. A misspecified model, if used to infer default probabilities, will only generate misspecified estimates.

It could be argued that the implicit default probabilities obtained from a credit risk model could be empirically verified by comparing them to historical default frequencies. In theory this is correct, but in practice it does not work. In Japan, for instance, Nippon Credit Bank and Long-Term Credit Bank of Japan were both nationalised and neither defaulted. A hedging test of the pricing of both firms' equity and bonds would have provided an informative test of model performance. No test based on default experience could have been performed. As with this example, empirical comparisons of estimated and historical default probabilities do not work for one of two reasons.

One, it can be argued that standard statistical procedures do not apply. Indeed, default is a firm-specific event that has not yet occurred. Since it has not, there are no historical data of relevance. For example, how many IBMs are there, or have there been?

Two, it can be argued that even if standard statistical procedures apply, default is a rare event and not enough observations are available to obtain reliable estimates. Indeed, if one believes that existing firms are samples from a population of similar firms, some of which have defaulted in the past, then statistical methods do apply. But here defaults are so rare that the standard errors of the default likelihoods are too large and the power of standard statistical procedures is too small. The bottom line is that any reasonable estimate of default probability is consistent with the data. Therefore, comparisons of estimates with historical default probabilities are not very informative.

To illustrate this last point, we perform an empirical investigation of the Merton model to demonstrate the wide range of default probabilities that are consistent with a reasonable specification of the model's parameters, thereby casting doubt on the reliability of the estimates obtained.

An empirical investigation of the Merton model

This section presents an empirical investigation of the Merton model using a unique data set to determine the implied default probabilities. The unique data set employed is the First Interstate Bancorp data set previously used by Jarrow and van Deventer (1998). The set contains weekly quotes on potential new issues of various maturity bonds of First Interstate Bancorp from January 3, 1986, to August 20, 1993. For this illustration the two-year debt issue is employed. For these data, we show that the range of the implied default probabilities obtained for reasonable specifications of the input parameters is too wide and too time-varying to be verifiable using historical default data. This evidence casts doubt on the reliability of using historical default data to test a credit risk model.

PRACTICAL USE OF
CREDIT RISK MODELS
IN LOAN PORTFOLIO
AND COUNTERPARTY
EXPOSURE
MANAGEMENT

DEFAULT PROBABILITIES FROM MERTON'S MODEL

Merton's model of risky debt views debt as a put option on the firm's value. In this simple model debt is a discount bond (no coupons) with a fixed maturity. Firm value is represented by a single quantity that is interpreted as the value of the underlying assets of the firm. The firm defaults at the maturity of the debt if the asset value is less than the promised payment. Using the Black–Scholes technology, an analytic formula for the debt's value can easily be obtained. In this solution it is well known that the expected return on the value of the firm's assets does not appear. In fact, it is this aspect of the Black–Scholes formula that has made it so useable in practice.

From Merton's risky debt model, one can infer the implied *pseudo* default probabilities. These probabilities are not those revealed by actual default experience but those needed to do a valuation. They are sometimes called *martingale* or *risk-adjusted* probabilities because they are the empirical probabilities, after an adjustment for risk, used for valuation purposes. If we are to compare implied default probabilities from Merton's model with historical default experience, we need to remove this adjustment.

Removal of the adjustment is akin to inserting expected returns back into the valuation procedure. To do this, we need a continuous-time equilibrium model of asset returns consistent with the Merton risky debt structure. Merton's (1973) intertemporal capital asset pricing model provides such a structure. We now show how to make this adjustment.

Let the value of the ith firm's assets at time t be denoted by $V_i(t)$, with its expected return per unit time denoted by a_i and its volatility per unit time denoted by σ_i. Under the Merton (1974) structure, we have that

$$V_i(t) = V_i(0)\, e^{\mu_i t + \sigma_i Z_i(t)}$$

where $\mu_i = a_i - \sigma_i^2/2$ and $Z_i(t)$ is a normally distributed random variable with mean 0 and variance t.

The evolution of $V_i(t)$ above is under the empirical probabilities.[6] In Merton's (1973) equilibrium asset pricing model, when interest rates and the investment opportunity set[7] are constant, the expected return on the ith asset is equal to

$$a_i = r + \frac{\sigma_i \rho_{iM}}{\sigma_M}\left(a_M - r\right)$$

where r is the risk-free rate,[8] the subscript M refers to the "market" portfolio or, equivalently, the portfolio consisting of all assets of all companies in the economy, and ρ_{iM} denotes the correlation between the return on the asset value of firm i and the market portfolio.

Using this equilibrium relationship, the drift term on the ith company's assets can be written as

$$\mu_i = -\frac{1}{2}\sigma_i^2 + \left(1 - b_i\right)r + b_i a_M$$

where $b_i = \sigma_i \rho_{iM}/\sigma_M$ is the ith firm's beta.

For expositional purposes, we parameterise the expected return on the market, a_M, as equal to a constant, k, times the risk-free interest rate, r:

$$a_M = kr$$

This is without loss of generality. Using this relation, we have that

$$\mu_i = -\frac{1}{2}\sigma_i^2 + \left(1 - b_i + b_i k\right)r$$

In Merton's risky debt model, the firm defaults at the maturity of the debt if the firm's asset value is below the face value of the debt. We now compute the probability that this event occurs.

305

PRACTICAL USE OF
CREDIT RISK MODELS
IN LOAN PORTFOLIO
AND COUNTERPARTY
EXPOSURE
MANAGEMENT

Let t be the maturity of the discount bond and let B be its face value. Bankruptcy occurs when $V_i(t) < B$; formally,

$$\text{Probability}\left(\text{Default}\right) = \text{Probability}\left(V_i(t) < B\right) = N\left(\frac{\ln\left(B/V_i(0)\right) - \mu_i t}{\sigma_i \sqrt{t}}\right)$$

where $N(\cdot)$ represents the cumulative normal distribution function.

We see from this expression that default probabilities are determined given the values of the parameters $(B, V_i(0), \sigma_i, r, \sigma_M, \rho_{iM}, k)$. The estimation of these parameters is discussed in the next section.

EMPIRICAL ESTIMATION OF THE DEFAULT PROBABILITIES
As mentioned previously, this estimation is based on First Interstate Bancorp bond data. The time period covered is from January 3, 1986, to August 20, 1993. Over this period the bank solicited weekly quotes from various investment banks regarding new issue rates on debt issues of various maturities. The two-year issue is employed in the analysis that follows; see Jarrow and van Deventer (1998) for additional details.

To estimate the default probabilities, we need to estimate the seven parameters $(B, V_i(0), \sigma_i, r, \sigma_M, \rho_{iM}, k)$.

The face value of the firm's debt, B, can be estimated using balance sheet data. To do this, we choose B to be equal to the total value of all of the bank's liabilities, compounded for two years at the average liability cost for First Interstate.

The firm value at time 0, $V_i(0)$, and the firm's volatility parameter, σ_i, are both unobservable. This is one of the primary difficulties with using Merton's model and with the structural approach in general. For this reason, both the market value of First Interstate's assets and the firm's asset volatility were implied from the observable values of First Interstate common stock and First Interstate's credit spread for a two-year straight bond issue. We choose those values that minimise the sum of squared errors of the market price from the theoretical price (see Jarrow and van Deventer, 1998, for details).

The spot rate, r, is observable and the volatility of the market portfolio, σ_M, can easily be estimated from market data. As a proxy for the market portfolio we used the S&P500 index. The volatility of the index over the sample period was 15.56%.

This leaves two parameters: the expected return on the market and the correlation between the firm's assets and the market portfolio. As both quantities are unobservable and arguably difficult to estimate, we allow them to be "free" parameters. That is, we leave them unspecified and estimate default probabilities for a range of their values. The range of values we use for the correlation, ρ_{iM}, is from –1 to 1, and the range of ratios, k, of the market return to the risk-free rate is from 1 to 5.

Finally, in order to compare the derived two-year default probabilities with the observable credit spread, which is quoted on an annual basis, we convert the actual two-year default probability to a discrete annual basis using the following conversion formula:

$$\text{Probability}\left[\text{Annual}\right] = 1 - \sqrt{1 - \text{Probability}\left[\text{Two year}\right]}$$

Table 1 gives these annualised default probabilities for November 17, 1989.[9] One can see the surprisingly wide range of default probabilities that are possible as we vary the free parameters. Across the entire table the annualised default probability varies from 0.06% to 92.68%. For a correlation of 1 (the typical asset),[10] the range of default probabilities for a market return to risk-free rate ratio, k, of between 2 and 3 is 9.09% to 2.57%. These ranges are quite large and they cast doubt on our abilities to validate the model credibly using historical default frequencies.

More insight into the imprecision of the Merton default probability estimates can be obtained by looking at the variability of these estimates across time. For illustrative purposes, we set the correlation between First Interstate assets and the market portfolio to be 1. We look at the two extreme market return to risk-free rate ratios $k = 5$ and $k = 1$.

306

PRACTICAL USE OF
CREDIT RISK MODELS
IN LOAN PORTFOLIO
AND COUNTERPARTY
EXPOSURE
MANAGEMENT

Table 1. Merton model default probabilities (%)

Correlation of asset returns with market returns	Ratio of expected return on market to risk-free rate				
	5.00	4.00	3.00	2.00	1.00
1.00	0.06	0.49	2.57	9.09	22.83
0.75	0.49	1.76	5.06	11.79	22.83
0.50	2.57	5.06	9.09	14.99	22.83
0.25	9.09	11.79	14.99	18.67	22.83
0.00	22.83	22.83	22.83	22.83	22.83
−0.25	43.08	37.64	32.38	27.42	22.83
−0.50	64.78	54.16	43.08	32.38	22.83
−0.75	82.14	69.70	54.16	37.64	22.83
−1.00	92.68	82.14	64.78	43.08	22.83

Date: November 17, 1898; actual credit spread, 1.220%.

Time-series graphs of the annualised default probabilities are displayed in Figures 1 and 2.[11] The line connecting the data is drawn chronologically from point to point. The highest end of the line represents the newest data points. The primary observation from these graphs is the high degree of instability that the estimates exhibit across time. This is especially true for the larger market return to risk-free rate ratio, $k = 5$. The more stable estimates for $k = 1$, however, appear to be implausibly high.

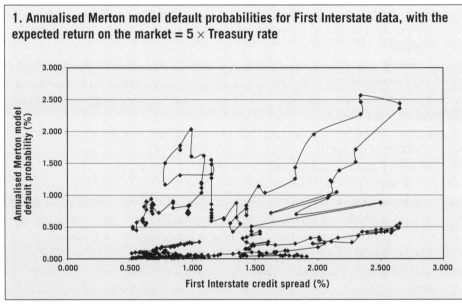

1. Annualised Merton model default probabilities for First Interstate data, with the expected return on the market = 5 × Treasury rate

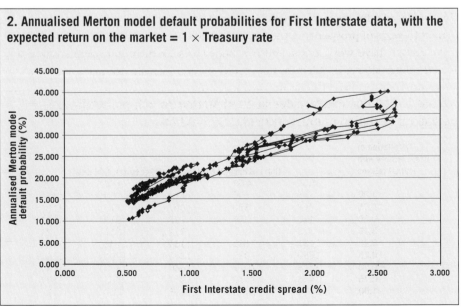

2. Annualised Merton model default probabilities for First Interstate data, with the expected return on the market = 1 × Treasury rate

PRACTICAL USE OF
CREDIT RISK MODELS
IN LOAN PORTFOLIO
AND COUNTERPARTY
EXPOSURE
MANAGEMENT

Table 2. Standard deviation of Merton default probabilities, 1986–93 (%)

Correlation of asset returns with market returns	Ratio of expected return on market to risk-free rate				
	5.00	4.00	3.00	2.00	1.00
1.00	0.48	1.13	2.34	4.10	6.41
0.75	1.13	1.98	3.16	4.61	6.41
0.50	2.34	3.16	4.10	5.17	6.41
0.25	4.10	4.61	5.17	5.76	6.41
0.00	6.41	6.41	6.41	6.41	6.41
−0.25	9.52	8.68	7.87	7.11	6.41
−0.50	12.56	11.16	9.52	7.87	6.41
−0.75	13.84	13.10	11.16	8.68	6.41
−1.00	12.88	13.84	12.56	9.52	6.41

To obtain a better sense of the magnitude of the variability in these default probability estimates, we computed the standard deviations of the estimates across time. The results are given in Table 2, from which they can be seen to be quite large. To put them in perspective, the standard deviation of First Interstate Bancorp's two-year credit spread over the sample period was only 0.566%.

In Table 3 we consider the ratio of the annualised default probability standard deviations to the standard deviation of First Interstate's two-year credit spread. The results emphasise further the instability of the estimated default probabilities. Except for the case where the correlation coefficient is 1 and the market return to risk-free rate ratio, k, is 5, the variation in default probabilities far exceeds the volatility of the underlying credit spread.

In summary, given the wide variation in default probabilities for small changes in the input parameters, this illustration supports the statement that comparing estimated default probabilities with historical default frequencies does not provide a very powerful test of a credit risk model.

Concluding comments

The successful implementation and practical use of a credit model involves critical choices. In these choices, bank management and bank regulators have a fiduciary responsibility to shareholders and depositors to completely "vet" or audit all the models that are used. A black box approach to modelling fails this test. All credit models used should be subjected to critical analysis and review, either publicly or privately.

All models should be tested "out of sample" by the user (or an auditor employed by the user). The richest tests involve historical periods with substantially different market conditions (say the high-interest period 1979–85 in the United States) or tests based on other countries with quite different market conditions. Japan and the rest of Asia over the last decade, for example, provide a much better testing ground than just using the almost 15 years of prosperity in the United States.

All models have weaknesses, and it is better to seek them out aggressively than to identify them after a problem has occurred. An ideal credit risk management system

Table 3. Ratio of standard deviation of Merton default probabilities to standard deviation of credit spread, 1986–93 (%)

Correlation of asset returns with market returns	Ratio of expected return on market to risk-free rate				
	5.00	4.00	3.00	2.00	1.00
1.00	84	200	413	723	1131
0.75	200	350	557	815	1131
0.50	413	557	723	912	1131
0.25	723	815	912	1017	1131
0.00	1131	1131	1131	1131	1131
−0.25	1680	1533	1390	1256	1131
−0.50	2218	1971	1680	1390	1131
−0.75	2443	2312	1971	1533	1131
−1.00	2274	2443	2218	1680	1131

PRACTICAL USE OF
CREDIT RISK MODELS
IN LOAN PORTFOLIO
AND COUNTERPARTY
EXPOSURE
MANAGEMENT

should perhaps utilise many credit models to help to "diversify" this model risk. Such a system would allow the user full control of the model audit and performance testing process. This kind of system would end the debate about relative model performance because it is "agnostic". Through its use the user would obtain definitive proof of "best model performance".

Despite their inherent difficulties, models are the key ingredient of a successful credit risk management system. This is because they can be used to estimate true credit-adjusted valuations that correctly reflect the risk-adjusted value of a borrower's promise to repay. Such credit-adjusted valuations can and should be used for:

❏ all major derivative exposures;
❏ callable bonds;
❏ standby letters of credit;
❏ other contingent credit lines;
❏ all value-at risk calculations;
❏ all risk-adjusted capital calculations;
❏ middle office exposure management;
❏ mark-to-market real-time trade authorisations;
❏ net income simulation with default adjustment.

Finally, a good credit risk model should be rich enough to allow extension to retail credit scoring as well as small-business credit scoring.

Credit model risk management has much in common with loan portfolio management. Diversification of model risk is essential, and so is the transparency and comprehensiveness of the analytics used. The pursuit of perfection in credit risk modelling will continue for decades, and practical bankers should plan for and implement smooth transitions from one model to the next as the state of the art improves.

1 *See Chen* et al. (*1998*).

2 Ibid., *p. 100.*

3 Ibid.

4 *It is sometimes believed that if a derivatives model matches market prices correctly, the model is "proven". This is not a sufficient test. Any reasonable model (with enough time-varying parameters) can be calibrated to match the relevant market prices. Given that this is true for many models, matching market prices cannot be used to differentiate them.*

5 *It can be argued that another way to test a model is to test its inputs – ie, its assumptions. For example, if the model assumes constant interest rates, one can test to see if this assumption is empirically valid.*

6 *Under the pseudo-probabilities* $a_i = r$.

7 *The investment opportunity set is the means and covariances of all the assets' returns. This implies that the mean and covariances with the market return are also deterministic.*

8 *In this structure this is the spot rate of interest on default-free debt.*

9 *This date was chosen because it is the mid-point of the First Interstate data set.*

10 *The typical asset has a beta of 1. If the volatility of the market and the firm's asset are equal, the correlation is one as well.*

11 *As in Jarrow and van Deventer (1998), we omit two outlying data points August 14 and 21, 1992.*

PRACTICAL USE OF
CREDIT RISK MODELS
IN LOAN PORTFOLIO
AND COUNTERPARTY
EXPOSURE
MANAGEMENT

BIBLIOGRAPHY

Chen, D. H., H. H. Huang, R. Kan, A. Varikooty and H. N. Wang, 1998, "Modelling and Managing Credit Risk", in *Asset & Liability Management: A Synthesis of New Methodologies* (London: Risk Publications), pp. 97–115.

Duffee, G., 1999, "Estimating the Price of Default Risk", *Review of Financial Studies* 12(1), pp. 197–226.

Heath, D., R. Jarrow and A. Morton, 1992, "Bond Pricing and the Term Structure of Interest Rates: A New Methodology for Contingent Claim Valuation", *Econometrica* 60(1), pp. 77–105.

Jarrow, R., and S. Turnbull, 1995, "Pricing Derivatives on Financial Securities Subject to Credit Risk", *Journal of Finance* 50(1), pp. 53–85; reprinted as Chapter 16 of the present volume.

Jarrow, R., and D. van Deventer, 1998, "Integrating Interest Rate Risk and Credit Risk in ALM", in *Asset & Liability Management: A Synthesis of New Methodologies* (London: Risk Publications), pp. 87–96.

Jarrow, R., D. Lando and S. Turnbull, 1997, "A Markov Model for the Term Structure of Credit Risk Spreads", *Review of Financial Studies* 10(2), pp. 481–523.

Jones, E. P., S. P. Mason and E. Rosenfeld, 1984, "Contingent Claims Analysis of Corporate Capital Structure: An Empirical Investigation", *Journal of Finance* 39, pp. 611–26; reprinted as Chapter 8 of the present volume.

Longstaff, F. A., and E. S. Schwartz, 1995, "A Simple Approach to Valuing Risky Fixed and Floating Rate Debt", *Journal of Finance* 50, pp. 789–820; reprinted as Chapter 9 of the present volume.

Merton, R. C., 1973, "An Intertemporal Capital Asset Pricing Model", *Econometrica* 41 (September), pp. 867–87.

Merton, R. C., 1974, "On the Pricing of Corporate Debt: The Risk Structure of Interest Rates", *Journal of Finance* 29, pp. 449–70; reprinted as Chapter 4 of the present volume.

Nielsen, L., J. Saá-Requejo and P. Santa-Clara, 1993, "Default Risk and Interest Rate Risk: The Term Structure of Default Spreads", Working paper, INSEAD.

Shimko, D., N. Tejima and van Deventer, 1993, "The Pricing of Risky Debt when Interest Rates are Stochastic", *Journal of Fixed Income* September, pp. 58–66; reprinted as Chapter 7 of the present volume.

23

Portfolio Management and Stress-Testing using CreditMetrics

Christopher C. Finger and Aidan McNulty

The RiskMetrics Group, LLC

This chapter focuses on the practical application of the CreditMetrics model. Recognising that the accuracy of any credit portfolio risk measure is largely dependent on the quality of the supporting data, we will give particular emphasis to the role of stress-testing and scenario analysis in effective portfolio risk management. Credit spreads can be affected by liquidity; default rates and rating changes behave differently at different points in the credit cycle, and recovery rates on distressed debt can vary with industry sector. Historical summaries of these factors and derived data based on them may not adequately reflect the true range of possible realisations in the near future. For this reason, any decision based on a credit portfolio model – whether to allocate assets in the medium term or to identify opportunities to reduce exposure – should reflect the impact of parameter uncertainty.

We begin by outlining the CreditMetrics model and describing the required data. We then illustrate, using a realistic bond portfolio, the sensitivity of the portfolio to uncertainty in these data. We develop a standard CreditManager[1] analysis of the portfolio and utilise the application's stress-testing capabilities to compare the analysis across a variety of economic conditions. We conclude by describing how this type of analysis can support a proactive risk management approach that better reflects the risk/return appetite of the risk manager under a broad range of future market assumptions.

Overview of the CreditMetrics model

CreditMetrics is a portfolio credit model. It takes information on the individual obligors in the portfolio as inputs, and produces as output the distribution of portfolio values at some fixed horizon in the future. From this distribution it is possible to produce statistics that quantify the portfolio's absolute risk level, such as the standard deviation of value changes or the worst-case loss at a given level of confidence. This gives a picture of the total risk of the portfolio, but we may also analyse our risks at as fine a level as by exposure. In this way, we may quantify the risk contribution of each exposure in the portfolio, identifying concentration risks or diversification opportunities, or evaluate the effect of a potential new exposure. In all these cases it is important to bear in mind that the value changes being modelled are only those due to significant credit quality changes (rating changes and defaults) and do not include changes due to moves in the prevailing risk-free interest rates or incremental changes in the spread for a particular obligor or rating.

The model is best described in three parts:

❑ The definition of the possible "states" for each obligor's credit quality, and a description of how likely obligors are to be in any of these states at the horizon date.

❑ The revaluation of exposures in all possible credit states.

❑ The interaction and correlation between the credit migrations of different obligors.

312

PORTFOLIO

MANAGEMENT AND

STRESS-TESTING

USING

CREDITMETRICS

STEP 1 – THE STATES OF THE WORLD

Typically, the definition of an obligor's possible credit states amounts to selecting a rating system – whether an agency system or an internal one, or whether a coarse system with seven states or a fine one with plus or minus states added. The crucial element here is that we know the probabilities that the obligor migrates to any of the states between now and the horizon date. That we have to provide this information to the model is what distinguishes CreditMetrics from a credit-scoring model. Thus, the model does not aim to put credit analysts out of their jobs but to put their work to use. The most straightforward way to present the probabilities is through a transition matrix, an example of which appears as Table 1.

A transition matrix characterises a rating system by providing the probabilities of migration (within a specified horizon) for all of the system's states. Among the most widely available transition matrices are those produced by the major rating agencies, which reflect the average annual transition rates over a long history (typically 20 years or more) for a particular class of issuers (eg, corporate bonds or commercial paper).

Although this information is useful and the agency default rates have become benchmarks for describing the individual categories, the use of average transition matrices for credit portfolio modelling is often criticised for not capturing the credit cycle. In other words, since the matrices represent only averages over many years, they cannot take into account the relative benigness or severity of the current year's credit transitions. A number of methods are now available to address this. One is to select shorter periods of the agency history and create matrices based, for example, only on the transitions in 1988 to 1991.[2] A second is to model explicitly the relationship between transitions and defaults and macroeconomic variables, such as spread levels or industrial production. This method has been popularised by McKinsey and Company; see Wilson (1997a and 1997b) for more details.

A second criticism of the agency matrices has been that they are subject to the same drawbacks as the agencies' rating systems themselves. One of these is coverage; the matrices seem to be valid only for obligors rated by the agencies, thereby excluding obligors in emerging markets and US obligors that are too small to qualify for an agency rating. In these cases the most desirable solution is a rating system (either an institution's internal system or a local rating agency) for which a long, consistent history of transitions is available. Though transition histories for most internal or local rating systems are not usually adequate, it is still possible to implement CreditMetrics by mapping the alternative rating system to an agency system and taking advantage of the agency transition matrices. A second drawback is the tendency for agency ratings to be "sticky", meaning that the agencies might not downgrade a particular issuer until well after the issuer's credit has truly deteriorated. For this reason, the high probabilities on the diagonal of the matrix in Table 1 (those probabilities corresponding to no change in rating) might give an overly optimistic view of future transitions, particularly for investment-grade issuers. Kealhofer, Kwok and Weng (1998) document this phenomenon, and tackle it by mapping the KMV expected default frequencies into bins; they then use historical transitions between the bins to produce a transition matrix with notably lower probabilities on the diagonal.

In the end, the agencies' long-term transition matrices tend to be used simply because

Table 1. Example transition matrix – Moody's rating system (%)

	Aaa	Aa	A	Baa	Ba	B	Caa	D
Aaa	93.38	5.94	0.64	0.00	0.02	0.00	0.00	0.02
Aa	1.61	90.53	7.46	0.26	0.09	0.01	0.00	0.04
A	0.07	2.28	92.35	4.63	0.45	0.12	0.01	0.09
Baa	0.05	0.26	5.51	88.48	4.76	0.71	0.08	0.15
Ba	0.02	0.05	0.42	5.16	86.91	5.91	0.24	1.29
B	0.00	0.04	0.13	0.54	6.35	84.22	1.91	6.81
Caa	0.00	0.00	0.00	0.62	2.05	4.08	69.19	24.06
D	0.00	0.00	0.00	0.00	0.00	0.00	0.00	100.00

313

PORTFOLIO

MANAGEMENT AND

STRESS-TESTING

USING

CREDITMETRICS

they are reliable and readily available. In all of the cases mentioned above, the intent is not to abandon the CreditMetrics framework but to improve on these matrices and obtain better inputs to the CreditMetrics model – that is, transition matrices which give better forecasts of future credit events. And, regardless of which transition matrix is ultimately chosen as the "best", because of the difficulties inherent in default rate estimation it is prudent to examine the portfolio under a variety of transition assumptions.

STEP 2 – REVALUATION

The first step concerns the description of migrations of individual credits, and to complete the picture we need a notion of the impact of these moves on value. This brings up the issue of revaluation. In short, we assume that the value of a particular instrument today is known, and we wish to estimate its value, at our risk horizon, conditional on any of the possible credit migrations that the instrument's issuer might undergo.

Consider a Baa-rated, three-year, fixed 6% coupon bond, currently valued at par. With a one-year horizon, the revaluation step consists of estimating the bond's value in one year under each possible transition. For the transition to default, we value the bond through an estimate of the likely recovery value. Many institutions use their own recovery assumptions here, although public information is available. (See chapter 7 of Gupton, Finger and Bhatia, 1997, for references.) For the non-default states, we obtain an estimate of the bond's horizon value by utilising the term structure of bond spreads and risk-free interest rates. Thus, for a transition to Ba, we create the term structure of Ba bond yields and value a two-year (the remaining maturity), 6% fixed coupon bond. Repeating this procedure for every rating state, we arrive at the values in Table 2. With the information in this table, we have all of the stand-alone information for this bond; consequently, we can calculate the expectation and standard deviation of the bond's value at the horizon.

As before, it is important to be cognisant of the data used in the calculation and the limitations that these imply. The spread data available represent averages by industry sector and by rating. This implies that, for any bond, it is necessary to assume that its value today is comparable to the average value of other bonds in its sector and rating; furthermore, the value impact in the model of a rating move, eg, from Baa to Ba, is equal to the average difference in value between comparable bonds in the Baa and Ba categories. The spread information is customisable, but, in general, customisation requires assumptions such as that, if a bond trades at a premium today to its rating category, it will continue to trade at a premium to its new category if it is downgraded. Clearly, as spread information becomes available for finer categories this valuation step will improve without the basic model framework changing.

To incorporate other types of exposures involves only defining the values in each possible future rating state of the underlying credit. Essentially, this amounts to constructing something like Table 2. For some exposure types, all that is necessary to build this table is recovery assumptions and spreads, while for others further information is required. Table 3 summarises the information necessary for a variety of instrument types.

The set of exposure types in Table 3 can be extended to instruments whose value depends on the credit quality of more than one name. An example would be a default

Table 2. Values at horizon for a three-year, 6% Baa bond

Rating at horizon	Probability (%)	Accrued coupon	Bond value	Bond plus coupon
Aaa	0.05	6.0	100.4	106.4
Aa	0.26	6.0	100.3	106.3
A	5.51	6.0	100.1	106.1
Baa	88.48	6.0	100.0	106.0
Ba	4.76	6.0	98.5	104.5
B	0.71	6.0	96.2	102.2
Caa	0.08	6.0	93.3	99.3
D	0.15	6.0	40.1	46.1
Mean			99.8	105.8
Standard deviation			2.36	2.36

314

PORTFOLIO

MANAGEMENT AND

STRESS-TESTING

USING

CREDITMETRICS

Table 3. Information for revaluation – single obligor exposures

Exposure type	Information required
Bonds	Credit spreads
Loans	Credit spreads
Amortising loans	Credit spreads, amortisation schedule
Receivables	Credit spreads
Letters of credit	Credit spreads
Loan commitments	Credit spreads, commitment fees, expected drawdown in new rating or default
Market-driven instruments (swaps, forwards, derivatives, etc)	Credit spreads, exposure estimates based on volatility of underlying market rate

swap, where the investor pays one counterparty in return for default protection on a reference name. Here, the analogue of Table 2 would be a grid representing all possible combinations of credit states for the pair (counterparty and reference name), and it would reflect the payoff in the event of a default by the reference name as well as the counterparty exposure to the seller of the protection.[3]

STEP 3 – BUILDING CORRELATIONS

As mentioned above, the information in Table 2 is sufficient to describe the behaviour of an individual exposure. However, to describe a portfolio of exposures, we need to construct correlations between them. To do this we posit an unseen "driver" of credit migrations, which we think of as the changes in asset value. Our approach is conceptually similar to, and certainly inspired by, structural models such as Merton's (1974), in which actual firm asset levels and volatilities are estimated and linked to default probabilities. In our case, we do not seek to observe asset levels nor to use asset information to predict defaults; as mentioned before, the stand-alone information for each name (in particular the name's probability of default) is provided as a model input through the specification of the transition matrix. Assets are used only to build the interaction between obligors but not to predict their individual behaviour.[4]

To begin our construction of correlations, we assume that changes in asset value are normally distributed. We then partition the distribution of asset value changes for each name according to the name's transition probabilities. For the Baa-rated obligor above (with default probability 0.15%), the default partition is chosen as the point beyond which lies 0.15% probability; the CCC partition is then chosen to match the obligor's probability of migrating to CCC, and so on. The result is illustrated in Figure 1.

A common misconception with this step is that by using a normal distribution for asset value changes we are somehow not accounting for the well-documented non-normality in the returns of credit-driven assets. This is not the case, as it is only the driver of credit changes for which we assume a normal distribution and not the changes in asset values themselves. In fact, if we overlay the values (from Table 2) corresponding to the rating changes on to the partition in Figure 1, this becomes more clear. In Figure 2 we see that a two-standard deviation increase in asset value produces an appreciation of 0.1, whereas an equally likely two-standard deviation decrease produces a depreciation of 1.5; similarly, a three-standard deviation increase in asset value yields an appreciation of 0.3, but an equivalent decrease yields a depreciation of 59.9. This is the type of skew that is expected in credit distributions.

In the portfolio framework, once the partitions are defined for every obligor it only remains to describe the correlation between changes in asset value. Rather than attempting to observe these changes directly, we may take correlations in equity returns as a proxy for the asset value correlations. This is primarily a practical decision, which then allows us to estimate correlations using reliable and directly observable data. As in the preceding two steps, however, it is crucial to examine the sensitivity of the model to uncertainties in the data. Although the correlation estimates are designed to be stable and applicable over long horizons, such as one year, market events may change correlation structures rapidly; to evaluate the effect of these changes it is advisable to analyse the portfolio under both normal and "stressed" correlation conditions.[5]

315

PORTFOLIO

MANAGEMENT AND

STRESS-TESTING

USING

CREDITMETRICS

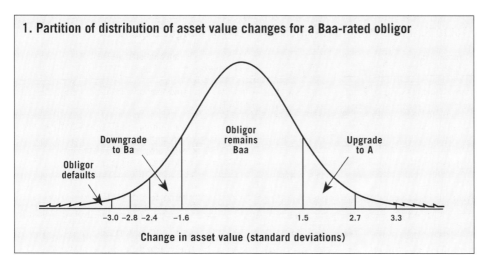

1. Partition of distribution of asset value changes for a Baa-rated obligor

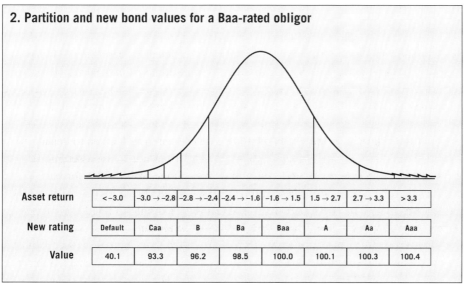

2. Partition and new bond values for a Baa-rated obligor

Asset return	< −3.0	−3.0 → −2.8	−2.8 → −2.4	−2.4 → −1.6	−1.6 → 1.5	1.5 → 2.7	2.7 → 3.3	> 3.3
New rating	Default	Caa	B	Ba	Baa	A	Aa	Aaa
Value	40.1	93.3	96.2	98.5	100.0	100.1	100.3	100.4

With the correlations defined, the model is completely specified. In principle, it is possible to calculate explicitly the probabilities of all joint rating transitions (eg, obligor 1 defaults, obligor 2 downgrades, obligor 3 maintains its rating, etc). In practice, it is faster to obtain the portfolio distribution by using a Monte Carlo approach. Thus, for a single scenario, we draw from a multivariate normal distribution to produce asset value changes, read from the partitions to identify these with new rating states and exposure values and aggregate the individual exposures to arrive at a portfolio value for the scenario. Examples of this procedure for strongly and weakly correlated two-obligor portfolios are illustrated in Figures 3 and 4. Repeating this process over a large number of scenarios, we accumulate a large number of equally likely portfolio values and are able to estimate the value-at-risk (VAR), and other descriptive statistics, of the portfolio.

Bond portfolio example

Now that we have outlined the CreditMetrics methodology, we will illustrate a practical application by analysing a "real" portfolio of 133 bonds. We begin with a determination of the total risk of the portfolio, move on to an identification of risk concentrations, and finally analyse the risk contributions of the individual exposures in the portfolio. Using this analysis as a benchmark, we assess the likely behaviour of the portfolio under a stressed market scenario. This analysis highlights the portfolio's sensitivity to assumptions about future market conditions and, in particular, to the input data as discussed earlier. The objective of the analysis is to demonstrate how this approach helps to determine the risks in a portfolio and, in doing so, supports the risk manager in making appropriate asset allocation decisions.

3. Two Baa-rated bonds with strong correlation (mean, 199.6; standard deviation, 4.13)

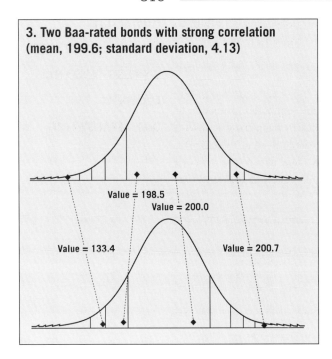

Value = 198.5
Value = 200.0
Value = 133.4
Value = 200.7

4. Two Baa-rated bonds with weak correlation (mean, 199.6; standard deviation, 3.35)

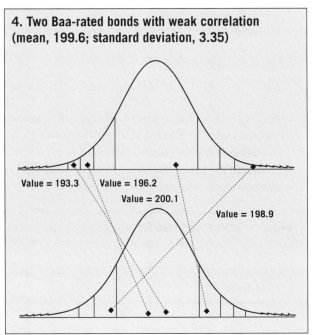

Value = 193.3
Value = 196.2
Value = 200.1
Value = 198.9

Although this example relates to a bond portfolio, the principles and steps involved in the analysis are identical for other credit portfolios. In other words, *the process* followed in this example would be exactly the same for portfolios containing loans, commitments, swaps, letters of credit, receivables or other instruments.

We consider a portfolio of corporate bonds with an approximate marked-to-market value of $1 billion. This is a relatively simple portfolio of 133 bonds of varying maturities issued by 119 different obligors (issuers). The issuers have Standard & Poor's credit ratings ranging from AA to B and do business in 11 countries and nine industries.

So, where are the risks in this portfolio? How well diversified is it? How can we improve the asset allocations across the portfolio while staying fully invested? The first step is to look at exposure concentrations.

EXPOSURE CONCENTRATIONS
The portfolio's exposure concentration across countries and industries is given in Table 4. This information indicates that:

❑ Exposures are spread across seven countries, but there is a concentration (in value terms) in the US, the UK, Germany and Japan.

❑ Exposures are spread across all industries with a concentration (in value terms) in the financial and consumer cyclical sectors. However the overall portfolio appears to be reasonably diversified, with a bias toward G7 country exposure.

Table 4. Exposures by country and sector

Sector	Exposure ($ million)												As % of
	Australia	Brazil	Canada	France	Germany	Japan	S. Korea	Malaysia	Sweden	UK	US	Aggregate	portfolio
Basic material	13.1		6.0	1.8	0.9	10.9		0.6	3.0	4.6	24.0	65.0	5.7
Consumer cyclical			1.3	4.1	47.7	10.7		8.2		6.5	146.0	228.0	20.0
Consumer non-cyclical			1.2	1.5	6.8	2.5		1.3	1.1	10.0	56.0	80.0	7.0
Energy			10.1			3.0		0.2		14.1	28.1	56.0	4.9
Financial		7.4	2.8		30.0	0.1	13.4	2.7		41.0	198.0	295.0	25.9
Industrial	1.6		2.1	7.5	4.8	21.0		2.7	2.0	7.8	105.0	157.0	13.8
Technology				1.8	0.9	24.0		1.2		37.1	104.0	172.0	15.1
Utilities					0.4	0.0	4.8	3.6		14.0	63.0	85.0	7.5
Independents					0.0			2.3				2.3	0.2
Aggregate	14.8	7.4	24.2	16.8	91.0	72.1	18.3	22.8	6.0	134.0	724.0	1114.0	
As proportion of portfolio (%)	1.3	0.7	2.1	1.5	8.0	6.3	1.6	2.0	0.5	11.8	63.4		

While this is a useful starting point for understanding the portfolio, it is important to realise that exposure concentrations do *not* always reflect risk concentrations.

RISK CONCENTRATIONS

We now turn to the measurement of credit risk. The mean value of the portfolio in one year's time is $1.15 billion, taking into account interest income, expected losses due to downgrades and default, and other term effects. The uncertainty in value associated with unexpected losses is reflected in the different risk measures summarised in Table 5. The interpretation of the VAR figures in Table 5 is as follows: on average, in only one year out of 100 should the losses due to credit events exceed $31.6 million, and in only one year out of 1,000 should they exceed $64.5 million.

Table 5. Risk measures for the example portfolio

Mean value	$1.15 billion
VAR 99%	$31.6 million
VAR 99.9%	$64.5 million
Standard deviation	$8.4 million

Knowing the total VAR of the portfolio is useful, but it is of limited value without a breakdown by country, industry, maturity, rating, etc. The question that should be asked is where these risks come from. Thus, our next step is to examine the VAR profile across countries and industries. Table 6 shows the breakdown of credit risk measured in terms of VAR at a 99.9% confidence interval. We see that the VAR profile is quite different from the exposure profile.

In terms of countries, the VAR profile in Table 6 shows that, other than in the US, there are no significant country risk concentrations. Moreover, the UK and the US have a considerably smaller VAR than the size of the exposures would suggest. This is because the issuers in these countries have relatively high ratings (AA or A), and in the US the risks are diversified across several different industries. The result is similar for industries, with concentrations in financial and consumers. What is notable, however, is that the VAR associated with South Korea and Malaysia is disproportionate relative to the present value of the investment in those countries.

The analysis at this point would suggest that the portfolio is reasonably diversified. However, the portfolio VAR is unduly sensitive to our investments in two countries (Malaysia and South Korea); further, our investment in the financial sector is quite large. Thus, we would like a better idea of the contribution of these countries and sectors to the portfolio risk.

MARGINAL RISK

Although we now have a complete picture of the credit risk profile of the portfolio in VAR terms, to understand how different sectors or individual investments contribute to the total portfolio risk we need to consider *marginal VAR*.

Table 6. VAR by country and sector

	VAR ($ million)											
Sector	Australia	Brazil	Canada	France	Germany	Japan	S. Korea	Malaysia	Sweden	UK	US	Aggregate
Basic material	6.1		1.7	0.9	0.1	2.3		0.2	0.7	1.1	3.7	3.7
Consumer cyclical			0.6	1.2	6.4	1.0		1.0		1.2	17.0	17.0
Consumer non-cyclical			0.4	0.2	1.4	0.6		0.4	0.3	1.0	11.0	11.0
Energy			0.9			1.4		0.1		2.0	5.7	6.0
Financial		2.3	0.2		1.4	0.1	5.5	0.7		6.0	24.7	25.0
Industrial	0.5		0.8	3.5	0.5	6.0		0.5	0.5	2.2	12.0	12.0
Technology				0.2	0.2	1.1		0.1		1.9	10.0	10.0
Utilities					0.1	0.0	1.4	1.0		0.4	13.0	13.0
Independents								0.6				0.6
Aggregate	6.1	2.3	2.0	4.7	7.0	6.8	6.9	4.1	1.5	8.0	55.0	

Table 7. Marginal VAR of the portfolio by country ($ million)

Australia	0.1
Brazil	0.5
Canada	0.5
France	0.5
Germany	0.7
Japan	0.1
South Korea	0.5
Malaysia	0.2
Sweden	0.3
United Kingdom	1.0
United States	20.0
Aggregate	31.2

Marginal VAR measures the impact of an individual exposure (or a collection of exposures) on the portfolio as a whole. Marginal VAR is defined as the contribution of the exposure to the total risk of the portfolio. In other words, it is the amount by which the total portfolio VAR would be reduced if the position were removed. The benefit of marginal VAR lies in its ability to identify key sources of risk, quantify the impact of hedging and determine the effect of removing a position from the portfolio.

The next step in the process is to look at the portfolio's risk concentrations in marginal terms. Table 7 gives a breakdown of marginal VAR by country. From this we can see our diversification benefit from different country exposures. For example, the Australian exposure brings a significant diversification benefit in that the stand-alone VAR is $6.0 million (from Table 5), whereas the marginal VAR is $0.1 million. Looking further at our South Korean exposure, we can see that it too contributes a diversification benefit to the portfolio but to a much lesser extent than Australia, although the exposure levels are at the same level of magnitude. Though the absolute marginal VAR number associated with the South Korean exposure is not significant in the context of the overall portfolio VAR, the relationship between those two numbers could change dramatically under different market conditions. To a portfolio manager, the behaviour of specific assets under forecast market conditions is important information when making asset allocation decisions.

STRESS-TESTING

The next task is to investigate the portfolio under hypothetical market conditions. This may take the form of a stress test in which extreme market assumptions are applied; alternatively, we may apply economic forecasts that underlie our investment strategy. For the purposes of this analysis, we will apply a series of market parameters that we predict would accompany a general downturn in the health of the global financial services sector, brought about by a sudden deterioration in the condition of Far Eastern economies. Specifically, we will assume the following:

❏ A credit crunch in Asia manifests itself in a 200 basis point widening of spreads on Asian corporate debt.
❏ The credit crunch in turn has a significant effect on the credit quality of Asian companies, characterised by an increase in the rate of credit downgrades and corporate defaults.
❏ Recovery rates on defaulted debt shrink by 50%.
❏ There is an increase in the average asset correlation between companies operating in the global financial services sector from 27% to 40%.

Under these new market parameters, we run the same VAR and marginal VAR analysis as before to isolate any extreme sensitivities in the portfolio to the forecast market conditions. As we would expect, the overall VAR levels in the portfolio increase. The new levels are:

VAR 99%	$35.8 million
VAR 99.9%	$70.5 million
Standard deviation	$9.4 million

Additionally, we see that the relative contributions to the portfolio VAR of our different country exposures has changed. The new marginal VAR figures are presented in Table 8.

| Table 8. Marginal VAR of the portfolio by country under stress scenario | | | | | | | | | | | |

Sector	Australia	Brazil	Canada	France	Germany	Japan	S. Korea	Malaysia	Sweden	UK	US	Aggregate
					Marginal VAR ($ million)							
Basic material	0.9		0.7								1.4	1.7
Consumer cyclical				0.9	0.6	0.8		0.1		0.2	12.8	20.4
Consumer non-cyclical			0.1								1.7	2.6
Energy			1.0								0.2	1.3
Financial		0.5	0.2		0.5		2.9	0.1		2.5	24.3	32.5
Industrial			0.1		0.1				0.1	1.1	7.1	7.9
Technology					0.1	0.1					1.6	2.0
Utilities							1.8	0.1			0.1	2.5
Independents												
Aggregate	0.9	0.5	1.7	0.1	1.0	0.9	4.7	0.2	1.0	3.8	50.5	

What is notable now is that most of the diversification benefit we were gaining from the South Korean investments has disappeared, in that the marginal VAR contribution has increased from $0.5 million to $4.6 million. On further examination we see that the portfolio has become significantly more sensitive to its concentration in the financial sector, where the marginal VAR has increased from $27.9 million to $32.5 million. On the other hand, the portfolio gains substantial diversification benefits from its exposure to the non-financial sectors, particularly in France and the UK.

Having identified the exposures to South Korea and financial services generally as the major sources of risk concentration, the next step is to experiment with different risk-reducing strategies.

For example, consider a switch out of South Korea financial paper into a bond issued by a French energy company which has the same maturity, credit rating and yield. In this way the portfolio would achieve exactly the same expected return, since the new bond has the same stand-alone parameters (rating, maturity, coupon, etc) as the old one. However, the effect of this switch would be that much of the portfolio's exposure to South Korea would be shifted into a country and an industry that are largely uncorrelated with the rest of the portfolio. This would lead to better diversification of credit risk and a reduction in the total VAR for the portfolio of $2 million.

In practice, whether a portfolio manager would implement this switch depends on a number of factors. However, if he or she is comfortable with the market forecast that is represented in the stress-test parameters, a reallocation of assets is a realistic course of action. For example, it may be that the outlook for the particular South Korean issuer is positive and the manager expects a ratings upgrade or a tightening of spreads, leading to a significant capital gain. In this case he/she may be perfectly happy with the risk concentration.

Lower credit risk for the same level of return is just one possible result of this type of analysis. Alternatively, a manager might prefer to explore opportunities that give higher returns for the same level of risk. This would involve looking for a switch out of a highly-rated bond into one with a lower rating in a different country and/or industry. In this way, it may be possible to benefit from the higher return associated with the lower-rated bond, while its additional credit risk is diversified away.

Conclusion

Focused credit risk analysis extends the scope and breadth of the information available to portfolio managers. By exploring credit risk in a structured way and, in particular, modelling the risk of the portfolio under a variety of market conditions, credit managers can develop a thorough understanding of the risk profile of even the most complex portfolio, pinpointing risk concentrations and identifying sources of diversification. This information provides a unique insight into the nature of potential problems and the viability of new opportunities. It can be an important input into tactical and strategic portfolio decisions.

320

PORTFOLIO
MANAGEMENT AND
STRESS-TESTING
USING
CREDITMETRICS

1 *CreditManager is the software implementation of the CreditMetrics model.*

2 *Standard & Poor's markets a software tool, CreditPro+, to facilitate this approach.*

3 *For more details, see Finger (1998).*

4 *In this sense, asset value distributions are used in a similar way to copula functions in the insurance literature. Wang (1998) provides an excellent survey of these techniques.*

5 *Stressing correlations is possible but is more involved than simply imposing new correlation levels. See Finger (1997) for further discussion.*

BIBLIOGRAPHY

Finger, C. C., 1997 "A Methodology to Stress Correlations", *RiskMetrics Monitor* Fourth quarter.

Finger, C. C., 1998 "Credit Derivatives in CreditMetrics", *CreditMetrics Monitor* Third quarter.

Gupton, G. M., C. C. Finger, and M. Bhatia, 1997, *CreditMetrics® - Technical Document* (New York: Morgan Guaranty Trust Co.).

Kealhofer, S., S. Kwok and W. Weng, 1998, "Uses and Abuses of Bond Default Rates", *CreditMetrics Monitor* First quarter.

Merton, R. C., 1974, "On the Pricing of Corporate Debt: The Risk Structure of Interest Rates", *Journal of Finance* 29, pp. 449-70; reprinted as Chapter 4 of the present volume.

Wang, S. S., 1998 "Aggregation of Correlated Risk Portfolios: Models and Algorithms", CAS Committee on Theory of Risk.

Wilson, T., 1997a, "Portfolio Credit Risk I", *Risk* September, pp. 111-17; reprinted as Chapter 2 of the present volume.

Wilson, T., 1997b, "Portfolio Credit Risk II", *Risk* October, pp. 56-61; reprinted as Chapter 3 of the present volume.

GLOSSARY

This glossary provides short definitions of terms and abbreviations that are used, often without further explanation, in the risk management industry. The glossary has been designed for general reference, so not all of the terms defined below are used elsewhere in this book. Longer definitions are available in an industry-standard glossary, called The Chase/Risk Magazine Guide to Risk Management, *which is also available from Risk Publications.*

Accreting swap Swap whose notional amount increases during the life of the swap (opposite of amortising swap)

Accrued benefit obligation Present value of pension benefits that have been earned by an employee to date, whether "vested" in the employee or not. It can be an important measure when managing the asset/liability ratio of pension funds

Add-on factor Simplified estimate of the potential future increase in the replacement cost (qv), or market value, of a derivative transaction

All-or-nothing Digital option (qv). This option's put (call) pays out a predetermined amount (the "all") if the index is below (above) the strike price at the option's expiration. The amount by which the index is below (above) the strike is irrelevant; the pay-out will be "all" or nothing

American option Option exercisable at any time up to expiration (*see also* European option)

Amortising option Option whose notional amount decreases during the life of the option, such as an amortising cap, collar or swaption

Amortising swap Swap whose notional amount decreases during the life of the swap (opposite of accreting swap)

Annuity swap Swap where, on the fixed payment side, the principal amount is amortised over the life of the swap

Arch (autoregressive conditional heteroscedasticity) A discrete-time model for a random variable. It assumes that variance is stochastic and is a function of the variance of previous time steps and the level of the underlying

Asian option (*see* average price (rate) option)

Asset-backed security A financial instrument which is collateralised by bundled assets such as mortgages, real estate or receivables

Asset-risk benchmark Benchmark (qv) against which the riskiness of a corporate's assets may be measured. In sophisticated corporate risk management strategies, the dollar risk of the liability portfolio may be managed against an asset-risk benchmark

Asset-sensitivity estimates Estimates of the effect of risk factors on the value of assets

Asset swap Swap involving cashflows on assets

Average cap Also known as an average rate cap, a cap on an average interest rate over a given period rather than on the rate prevailing at the end of the period (*see also* average price (rate) option)

Average price (rate) option Option on a currency's average exchange rate or commodity's average spot price in which four variables have to be agreed between buyer and seller: the premium, the strike price, the source of the exchange rate or commodity price data and the sampling interval (each day, for example). At the end of the life of the option, the average spot exchange rate is calculated and compared with the strike price. A cash payment is then made to the buyer of the option equal to the face amount of the option times the difference between the two rates (assuming the option is in the money; otherwise it expires worthless)

Average worst-case exposure The expression of an exposure in terms of the average of the worst-case exposures over a given period

Back-testing The validation of a model by feeding it historical data and comparing the model's results with the historical reality

Backwardation Description of a market in which commodity forward prices are lower than the spot price

Barrier option Option where the ability of the holder to exercise is activated or, alternatively, extinguished if the value of the underlying reaches a specified level. Also known as a limit option or trigger option

Basis point value (BPV) The price movement due to a one basis point change in yield

Basis swap Interest rate swap between two counterparties with floating-rate debt issued on two different bases, eg, three-month Libor, six-month Libor, US commercial paper, US Prime

Basket option Option based on an underlying basket of bonds, currencies, equities or commodities

Benchmark Criterion against which to measure the performance of any of a variety of variables, including interest rate, foreign exchange, liability and pension fund portfolios. Also used to judge the performance of risk managers or fund managers

Bid/ask (offer) spread Difference between the buying price and the selling price of an asset at a particular moment in time

Bilateral netting The ability to offset amounts owed to a counterparty under one contract against amounts owed to the same counterparty under another contract, for example, where both transactions are governed by one master agreement. Also known as "cherry picking"

Blended interest rate swap Result of adding a forward swap (qv) to an existing swap and blending the rates over the total life of the transaction

Break forward Forward contract which the customer can break at a predetermined rate, allowing him or her to take advantage of any favourable exchange rate movements

Business intelligence tools Term used to describe latest generation of access tools expected to support both data extraction and subsequent analysis

Call option Contract which gives the purchaser the right to buy an underlying at a certain price on or before a certain date (*see also* put option)

Cancellable swap Swap in which the payer of the fixed rate has the option, usually exercisable on a specified date, of cancelling the deal (*see also* swaption)

Cap Ceiling on the price level of an underlying (eg, commodity or interest rate), constructed from a strip of European options (qv). For example, if on prescribed reference dates a standard interest rate such as Libor or US Treasury bills is above a rate agreed between the seller of the cap and the buyer, the seller pays the buyer the extra interest costs until the next reference date (the opposite of a floor (qv))

Capped option Option where the holder's ability to profit from a change in value of the underlying is subject to a specified limit

Caption Option on a cap (qv)

Central line theorem The assertion that as sample size, n, increases, the distribution of the mean of a random sample taken from practically any population, approaches a normal distribution

Cherry picking (*see* bilateral netting)

Close-out netting The ability to net a portfolio of contracts with a given counterparty in the event of default (*see also* bilateral netting)

CMTM Current mark-to-market

value (*see also* current exposure and replacement cost)

Collar Combination of the purchase of a cap (qv) and the sale of a floor (qv), or, vice versa, to create the desired band within which the buyer of the collar wants the price of the underlying (eg, interest rate costs) to be held

Commodity swap Swap in which one of the cashflows is based on a fixed value for the underlying commodity and the other is based on a floating index value. The commodity is often oil or natural gas, although copper, gold, other metals and agricultural commodities are also commonly used. The end-users are consumers, who pay a fixed rate, and producers

Compound option Option on an option, the first giving the buyer the right, but not the obligation, to buy the second on a specific date at a predetermined price. There are two kinds. One, on currencies, is useful for companies tendering for an overseas contract in a foreign currency. The interest rate version comprises captions (qv) and floortions (qv)

Contango Description of a market in which the forward price of a commodity is higher than the spot price

Contingent option Option where the premium is higher than usual but is only payable if the value of the underlying reaches a specified level. Also known as a contingent premium option

Contingent premium option (*see* contingent option)

Controlled foreign company (CFC) In US tax parlance, a CFC is a foreign corporation where 50% of the total combined voting power of all classes of stock entitled to vote, or of the total value of the stock of the corporation, is held by US shareholders

Correlation matrices Statistical constructs used in the value-at-risk (qv) methodology to measure the degree of relatedness of various market factors

Corridor Collar (qv) on a swap using two swaptions (qv)

Cost volatility Volatility relating to operational errors, fines and losses a business unit may incur. Reflected in excess costs and penalty charges posted to the profits and losses (*see also* revenue volatility)

Counterparty risk weighting (*see* risk weighting)

Country risk The risks, when conducting business in a particular country, of negative economic or political conditions arising in that country. More specifically, the credit risk of a financial transaction or instrument arising out of those conditions

Credit derivatives Financial contract that involves a potential exchange of payments in which at least one of the cashflows is linked to the performance of a specified underlying credit-sensitive asset or liability

Credit equivalent amount As part of the calculation of the risk-weighted amount (qv) of capital the Bank for International Settlements (BIS) advises each bank to set aside against derivative credit risk, banks must compute a "credit-equivalent amount" for each derivative transaction. The amount is calculated by summing the current replacement cost (qv), or market value, of the instrument and an add-on factor (qv)

Credit (or default) risk The risk that a loss will be incurred if a counterparty to a derivatives transaction does not fulfil its financial obligations in a timely manner

Credit risk (or default risk) exposure The value of the contract exposed to default. If all transactions are marked to market each day, such positive market value is the amount of previously recorded profit that might have to be reversed and recorded as a loss in the event of counterparty default

Credit swaps Agreement between two counterparties to exchange disparate cashflows, at least one of which must be tied to the performance of a credit-sensitive asset or to a portfolio or index of such assets. The other cashflow is usually tied to a floating-rate index (such as Libor), or a fixed rate, or linked to another credit-sensitive asset

Credit Value at Risk (CVAR) (*see* value-at-risk (VAR))

Cross Two non-dollar currencies in relation to each other, eg, Deutschmark/yen

Cross-currency swap Also known as (cross-) currency coupon swap, an interest rate swap with the fixed rate payable in one currency and the floating rate in another

Cumulative default rate (*see* probability of default)

Currency option The option to buy or sell a specified amount of a given currency at a specified rate at or during a specified time in the future

Currency swap Swap where payment (typically a default or credit downgrade) occurs. It can be linked to the price of a particular security, set at a predetermined recovery rate, or it can take the form of an actual delivery of the underlying security at a predetermined price

Current exposure (*see* replacement cost)

DEaR Daily earnings at risk

Default correlation Degree of covariance between the probabilities of default of a given set of counterparties. For example, in a set of counterparties with positive default correlation, a default by one counterparty suggests an increased probability of a default by another counterparty

Default probability (*see* probability of default)

Default risk (*see* credit risk)

Default risk exposure (*see* credit risk exposure)

Deferred pay-out option American option (qv) where settlement is at expiry

Deferred start options Options purchased before their "lives" actually commence. A corporation might, for example, decide to pay for a deferred start option to lock into what it perceives as currently advantageous pricing for an option it knows that it will need in the future

Deferred strike option Option where the strike price is established at a future date based on the spot foreign exchange price prevailing at that future date

Defined benefit plan Contractual obligation established between a corporation and its employees to provide them with an agreed level of financial support at their retirement

Delegation costs Incentive costs incurred by banks in delegating monitoring activities

Delta The delta of an option describes its premium's sensitivity to changes in the price of the underlying

Diffusion effect The potential for increase over time of the credit exposure generated by a derivative as time progresses, there is more likelihood of larger changes in the underlying market variables. Depending on the instrument type and structure, this effect may be moderated by the amortisation effect

Digital option Unlike simple European and American options, a digital option has fixed pay-outs and, rather like binary digital circuits, which are either on or off, either pays out this amount or nothing at all. Digital options can be added together to create assets that exactly mirror investors' anticipated index price movements (*see also* one touch all-or-nothing)

Direct risk Risk of loan default on the lending of money (*see also* Credit risk)

Discount swap Swap where the fixed rate payments are below the internal rate of return on the swap, the difference being made up at maturity by a balloon payment

Dividend discount model Theoretical estimate of market value that computes the economic or the net present value of future cashflows due to an equity investor

Down-and-in option Barrier option (qv) where the holder's ability to exercise is activated if the value of the underlying drops below a specified level (*see also* up-and-in option)

Down-and-out option Barrier option (qv) where the holder's ability to exercise expires if the value of the underlying drops below a specified level (*see also* up-and-out option)

Drill-down capabilities When a potential future credit exposure profile reveals that an institution's exposure could become unacceptably high, the methodology/system used to calculate future exposure provides a clear breakdown of the types of potential market event that are responsible for the result

Dual currency option Option allowing the holder to buy either of two currencies

Dual currency swap Currency swap where both the interest rates are fixed rates

Dual strike option Interest rate option, usually a cap or a floor, with one floor or ceiling rate for part of the option's life and another for the rest

EAFE Europe, Australia and the Far East Equity Index

Efficient frontier method Technique used by fund managers to allocate assets

Embedded option Interest rate-sensitive option in a debt instrument that affects its redemption. Such instruments include mortgage-backed securities and callable bonds

Employee stock option programme Plan tying a portion of a company's employees' compensation to the company's long-term performance

Equity-linked swap Swap where one of the cashflows is based on an equity instrument or index, when it is known as an equity index swap

Equity warrant Warrant (qv), usually attached to a bond, entitling the holder to purchase share(s)

ERISA Employee Retirement Income Security Act

European option Option that can only be exercised at expiry (*see also* American option)

Exchange rate agreement Contract for differences or synthetic agreement for forward exchange (qv) that does not reflect changes in the spot market

Exercise The act of a call (put) option holder buying (selling) the underlying product (*see also* American option; European option)

Expected default rate Estimate of the most likely rate of default of a given counterparty, expressed in terms of a given level of probability

Expected (credit) exposure Estimate of the most likely future replacement cost, or positive market value, of any given derivative transaction, expressed in terms of a given level of probability. More exactly, it is the mean of all possible probability-weighted replacement costs, where the replacement cost in any outcome is equal to the mark-to-market present value if positive, and zero if negative

Expected (credit) loss Estimate of the amount a derivatives counterparty is likely to lose as a result of default from a derivatives contract, with a given level of probability. The expected loss of any given derivatives position can be derived by combining the distributions of credit exposures (qv), rate of recovery (qv) and probabilities of default (qv)

Expected rate of recovery *see* rate of recovery

Exposure profile The path of worst-case or expected exposures over time. Different instruments reveal quite differently shaped exposure profiles, due to the interaction of the diffusion (qv) and amortisation effects

Extinguishable option Option in which the holder's right to exercise disappears if the value of the underlying passes a specified level (*see also* barrier option)

Floor Series of European call options protecting the buyer from a fall in interest rates below a specified rate (the opposite of a cap (qv))

Floortion Option on a floor (qv)

Forward Agreement to exchange a predetermined amount of currency, commodity or other financial instrument at a specified future date and at a predetermined rate

Forward band Zero-cost collar (qv), that is, one in which the premium payable as a result of buying the cap (qv) is offset exactly by that obtained from selling the floor (qv)

Forward break (*see* break forward)

Forward exchange agreement (FXA) Contract for differences or synthetic agreement for forward exchange that also reflects changes in the spot market

Forward/forward Short-term exchange of currency deposits (*see also* forward/forward deposit)

Forward/forward deposit Agreement by one party to make a deposit with another at a specified future date and at a predetermined rate

Forward rate agreement (FRA) Short-term interest rate hedge. Specifically, a contract between buyer and seller for an agreed interest rate on a notional deposit of a specified maturity on a predetermined future date. No principal is exchanged. At maturity, the seller pays the buyer the difference if rates have risen above the agreed level, and vice versa

Forward swap Swap arranged at current rate but entered into at some time in the future

Fraption Option on a forward rate agreement (qv). Also known as an interest rate guarantee

FTSE 100 (Footsie 100) Index comprising 100 major UK shares listed on The International Stock Exchange in London. Futures and options on the index are traded at the London International Financial Futures and Options Exchange (Liffe)

Function In information technology (IT), within an institution, part of the organisation that has specific responsibilities, such as credit control, human resources, finance, etc (*see also* process)

Future Obligation to buy or sell a standard amount of currency, commodity, financial instrument or service at a predetermined price and at a specified date. Futures are normally traded on exchanges and involve margin payments (daily payments to or from the holder of the position that vary according to the profit or loss of the position)

Future benefit obligation (FBO) Present benefit obligation (PBO) (qv) of benefits earned by employees plus an estimate of the present value of future PBO that current employees will accrue, assuming that they keep working for the company until retirement

Future exposure (*see* potential exposure)

Gamma Gamma describes the rate of change in the delta (qv) of an option for a small change in the underlying

Gap analysis Gap analysis involves the numerical comparison between maturing assets and maturing liabilities in order to ascertain a financial institution's exposure to changes in interest rates. A positive "gap" indicates that a financial institution will incur a loss if interest rates rise, while a negative gap indicates exposure to a fall in interest rates

Gapping Feature of commodity markets whereby there are large and very rapid price movements to new levels, followed by relatively stable prices

Garch Generalised Arch (qv)

GIC Guaranteed investment contract

Gold warrant Naked or attached warrant exercisable into gold at a predetermined price

Hedge To hedge is to reduce risk by engaging in transactions that offset the exposure of one instrument or position with another which reduce exposure to market fluctuations

Herstatt risk (*see* settlement risk)

High coupon swap Off-market coupon swap (qv) where the coupon is higher than the market rate. The floating-rate payer pays a front-end fee as compensation. Opposite of low coupon swap (qv)

Historical simulation methodology Method of calculating value-at-risk (VAR) (qv), using historical data to assess the likely impact of market moves on a portfolio

Indexed notes Contract whereby the issuer usually assumes the risk of unfavourable price movements in the instrument, commodity or index to which the contract is linked, in exchange for which the issuer can reduce the cost of borrowing (compared with traditional instruments without the risk exposure)

Interest rate cap (*see* cap)

Interest rate floor (*see* floor)

Interest rate guarantee Option on a forward rate agreement (qv). Also known as a fraption

Interest rate option Option to pay or receive a specified rate of interest on or from a predetermined future date

Interest rate swap (IRS) Swap where the cashflows exchanged are based on two different ways of calculating interest, most commonly where one is a fixed rate and the other a floating rate

IRS Internal Revenue Service

ISE International Stock Exchange of London

Issuer risk Risk to an institution when it holds debt securities issued by another institution (*see also* credit risk)

Knock-in option Option where the holder's ability to exercise is activated if the value of the underlying reaches a specified level (*see also* barrier option)

Knock-out option Option where the holder's ability to exercise is extinguished if the value of the underlying reaches a specified level (*see also* barrier option)

Lender option Floor (qv) on a single-period forward rate agreement (qv)

Leptokurtosis Phenomenon when the probability distribution has a larger mass on the "tail" (qv) and a sharper hump than is consistent with a normal assumption

Level payment swap Evens out those fixed rate payments that would otherwise vary, for example, because of the amortisation of the principal

Limit option (*see* barrier option)

Loan-equivalent amount Description of derivative exposure used to compare the credit risk of derivatives with that of traditional bonds or bank loans

Lognormal distribution The assumption that the log of today's interest rate, for example, minus the log of yesterday's rate is normally distributed

London interbank offered rate (Libor) Rate of interest at which funds are offered in the London interbank market, for maturities ranging from overnight to five years. Three- and six-month Libor are widely used as reference rates for payments on floating-rate loans

Long-dated forward Forward foreign exchange contract with a maturity of greater than one year. Some long-dated forwards have maturities as great as 10 years

Lookback option Option that allows the purchaser, at the end of a given period of time, to choose as the rate for exercise any rate that has existed during the life of the option

Low coupon swap Tax-driven swap in which the fixed-rate payments are significantly lower than current market interest rates. The floating-rate payer is compensated by a front-end fee. Opposite of high coupon swap (qv)

Mapping The process whereby a treasury's derivative positions are related to a set of risk "buckets"

Marginal default rate (*see* probability of default)

Market comparables technique Technique for estimating the fair value of an instrument for which no price is quoted by comparing it with the quoted prices of similar instruments

Market maker Market participant who is committed, explicitly or otherwise, to quoting bid and offer prices in a particular market

Market risk Risks related to changes in prices of tradable macroeconomic variables, such as exchange rate risks or interest rate risks

Min–max option One of the strategies for reducing the cost of options by forgoing some of the potential for gain. The buyer of a currency option, for example, simultaneously sells an option on the same amount of currency but at a different strike price

MLIV Maximum likely potential increase in value

Monetised equity collar Transaction comprising three stages. First, a protective put option is purchased, guaranteeing the client a minimum value on the underlying equity position. Second, a call option is sold to reduce the cost of the put in exchange for sacrificing some of the potential appreciation of the stock. Third, there is an advance of cash equal to a percentage of the value of the put strike price. The transaction enables the client to retain some equity exposure to major moves in the underlying stock

Monte Carlo simulation Technique used to determine the likely value of a derivative or other contract by simulating the evolution of the underlying variables many times over. The discounted average outcome of the simulation gives an approximation of the derivative's value. Monte Carlo simulation can be used to estimate the value-at-risk (VAR) (qv) of a portfolio. Here, it generates a simulation of many correlated market movements for the markets to which the portfolio is exposed, and the positions in the portfolio are revalued repeatedly in accordance with the simulated scenarios. This results in a probability distribution of portfolio gains and losses from which the VAR can be determined

Mortgage-backed security (MBS) Security guaranteed by pool of mortgages. MBS markets include the US, UK, Japan and Denmark

Multi-index option Option giving the holder the right to buy the asset that performs best out of a number of assets, usually two. The investor would typically buy a call allowing him to buy the equity index that has performed best over the life of the option

Net present value (NPV) Technique used to assess the worth of future payments by looking at the present value of those future cashflows discounted at today's cost of capital

Novation Replacement of a contract or, more usually, a series of contracts with one, new contract

Off-market coupon swap Tax-driven swap strategy in which the fixed-rate payments differ significantly from current market rates. There are high and low coupon swaps (qv)

One touch all-or-nothing Digital option (qv). This option's put (call) pays out a predetermined amount (the "all") if the index goes below (above) the strike price at any time during the option's life. How far below (above) the strike price the index moves is irrelevant; the pay-out will be the "all" or nothing

Operational risk Risk of loss occurring from inadequate systems and control, human error or management failure

Opportunity cost Value of an action that could have been taken if the current action had not been chosen

Option Right, but not the obligation, to buy or sell a given commodity, stock, interest rate instrument or currency in the future at a mutually agreed price, known as the strike price (qv). The right is given in exchange for a premium

Option-dated forward contract, or **option forward** Forward foreign exchange contract with an option on the date of exchange

Option on Libor An interest rate option (cap or floor) that uses Libor (qv) as the benchmark

Ornstein–Uhlenbeck equation A standard equation that describes mean-reversion. It can be used to characterise and measure commodity price behaviour

OTC (*see* over-the-counter)

Over-the-counter (OTC) Customised derivative contracts usually privately arranged with an intermediary such as a major bank, as opposed to a standardised derivative contract available on an exchange

Over-the-top warrant Warrant with the same characteristics as an up-and-out option (qv)

Participating forward Also known as a profit-sharing forward, an adaptation of the range forward (qv) in which only a floor (qv) is fixed. Instead of paying a premium, the owner undertakes to pass a percentage of any gain to the seller. The percentage (known as the seller's participation rate) varies in direct proportion to the level of the floor. For a low participation rate, the buyer must accept a low floor. The buyer is allowed to choose the level of either the participation rate or the floor. Based on his choice, the seller fixes the other variable

Participating option Option where the holder forgoes a predetermined percentage of any profits in return for paying a reduced premium

Participating swap Swap where a counterparty incurs lower costs in return for giving up a percentage of any gain on the swap

Passive foreign investment company (PFIC) In US tax parlance, a foreign corporation that has either 75% or more of its gross income as passive income or at least 50% of its assets held for the production of passive income

Path-dependent option Generic term for options where the pay-off, or sometimes the exercise style, depends not just on the current price of the underlying asset or commodity but also on the path it follows

Peak exposure If the worst-case or the expected credit risk exposures of an instrument are calculated over time, the resulting graph reveals a credit risk exposure profile. The highest exposure marked out by the profile path is the "peak exposure" generated by the instrument

Periodic resetting swap Swap where the floating-rate payment is an average of floating rates that have prevailed since the last payment rather than the interest rate prevailing at the end of the period. For example, the average of six one-month Libor rates rather than one six-month Libor rate

Portfolio variance The square of the standard deviation (qv) of the portfolio's return away from the mean

Positive cashflow collar Collar (qv) other than a zero-cost collar

Potential exposure Estimate of

the future replacement cost, or positive market value, of a derivatives transaction. Potential exposure should be calculated using probability analysis based on broad confidence intervals (eg, two standard deviations) over the remaining term of the transaction

Present benefit obligation (PBO) Measure of the present value of pension benefits earned by employees to date, adjusted for the estimated salary level at which the actual pay-outs of the benefits will be calculated. It can be an important measure when managing the asset/liability ratio of pension funds (*see also* future benefit obligation)

Pre-settlement risk As distinct from credit risk arising from intra-day settlement risk (qv), this term describes the risk of the loss that may be suffered during the life of the contract if a counterparty to a trade were to default and if, at the time of default, the instrument were to have a positive economic value

Probability of default The likelihood a counterparty will not honour an obligation on a timely basis when it becomes due

Probit procedures Methods for analysing qualitative dependent methods where the dependent variable is binary, taking the values zero or one

Process In information technology (IT), within an institution, the detailed set of activities that each function (qv) performs or is required to perform

Projected benefit obligation (PBO), or accrued liability The steady-state (going concern) actuarial liability of a pension fund

Quanto options (quantos) Options in which the strike price for the underlying is denominated in a second currency. A common example is a foreign currency Bund option

Quasi-American options These allow the option holder to exercise at agreed times other than maturity

Range forward Forward contract in which, instead of an individual spot rate for exchange, a range is agreed, allowing for exchange at any rate prevailing within that range at maturity. If the spot rate at maturity is outside that range, the exchange takes place at the end of the range nearest that rate. The buyer

of the contract fixes only one end of the range, the seller retaining the right to fix the other

RAPM Risk-adjusted performance measurement

RAROC Risk-adjusted return on capital

Rate of recovery Estimate of the percentage of the amount exposed to default, ie, the credit risk exposure (qv) that is likely to be recovered by an institution if a counterparty defaults

Reduced cost option Generic term for options for which there is a reduced premium, either because the buyer undertakes to forgo a percentage of any gain, or because he or she offsets the cost by writing other options (eg, min-max, range forward). (*See also* zero-cost option)

Relative performance option Option whose value varies in line with the relative value of two assets

Replacement cost The present value of the expected future net cashflows of a derivative instrument. Aside from various conventions dealing with the bid/ask spread, synonymous with the "market value" or "current exposure" of an instrument

Return on value-at-risk (Rovar) An analysis conducted to determine the relative rates of return on different risks, allowing corporations to compare different risk capital allocations and capital structure decisions effectively

Revenue volatility Volatility reflecting the extent to which each business unit is exposed to financial loss as a result of a mismatch between the variability of income and costs in each financial year (*see also* cost volatility)

Reversal The act of switching from a fixed to a floating basis in a swap, or vice versa

Risk weighting When calculating the amount of capital the Bank for International Settlements (BIS) advises should be set aside to cover the credit risk generated by derivative transactions, banks first calculate a "credit equivalent amount" (qv) and then multiply this figure by the appropriate counterparty "risk weighting" (eg, 20% for OECD incorporated banks). The product of this calculation is the final "risk-weighted amount"

Roller-coaster swap Swap in which a counterparty alternately pays a fixed then a floating rate

S&P 100 (*see* Standard & Poor's 100)

S&P 500 (*see* Standard & Poor's 500)

Sensitivity analysis Analysis of the possible loss of future earnings, fair values or cashflows arising from selected hypothetical changes in market rates and prices

Settlement risk The risk that occurs when there is a non-simultaneous exchange of value. (Also known as "delivery risk" and "Herstatt risk" (qv))

Sharpe ratio Measure of the attractiveness of the return on an asset by comparing how much risk premium the investor can expect it to receive in return for the incremental risk (volatility) the investment carries. It is the ratio of the risk premium over the volatility of the asset

Skewness Bias introduced when calculating probability by having more observations on the left or right "tail" (qv)

SLA Savings and Loan Association

SOLB LPF Salomon Brothers Large Pension Fund Bond Index

SPDA Single premium deferred annuity

Spot price Price paid for commodities when they are offered for immediate payment and physical delivery

Spread lock Fixes a given spread over, for example, US Treasuries for a borrowing at some time in the future

Spread lock swap Swap with an option to fix the floating-rate payment at a given spread over a benchmark fixed rate, such as US Treasuries, at some time or for some period in the future

Standard & Poor's 100 (S&P 100) Index of 100 US stocks whose average performance gives an indication of broad stock market trends. It is made up of transport, financial and utility stocks

Standard & Poor's 500 (S&P 500) Index of 500 US stocks whose average performance gives an indication of broad stock market trends. It is made up of 400 industrial stocks plus those in the S&P 100 (qv)

Standard deviation Single number representing the

deviation or dispersion from the mean (*see also* portfolio variance)

Step-down swap Swap in which the fixed-rate payment decreases over the life of the swap

Step-up swap Swap in which the fixed-rate payment increases over the life of the swap

Stock index future Future on a stock index allowing a hedge against, or bet on, a broad equity market movement

Stock index option Option on a stock index future

Stock option Option on an individual stock

Straddle The sale of a put and a call with the same strike price on the same underlying and with the same expiry. The strike is normally set at the money. For purchasing two premiums, the purchaser benefits if the underlying moves enough either way. Straddles therefore enable the purchaser to hedge against an expected increase in volatility in the underlying

Stress testing Analysis that gives the value of a portfolio under a range of worst-case scenarios

Strike price The price level of the underlying asset at which an option may be exercised

Structured note Structured notes are OTC products that bundle several disparate elements to create a single product, generally by embedding options in a debt instrument such as a medium-term note

Swap The exchange of one sort of cashflow for another (*see also* asset swap; cancellable swap; commodity swap; currency swap; interest rate swap; swaption)

Swaption Option to enter into a swap at a future date and predetermined fixed rate. The terms "payer's option" and "receiver's option" indicate whether the owner has the right, but not the obligation, to pay or to receive fixed rate payments (*see also* cancellable swap)

Synthetic agreement for forward exchange (SAFE) Contract for differences on the spread between two currencies between two future dates

Synthetic option Replicating the payment of an option using cash or, more often, futures

Tail probability An event with low probability

Tax-exempt swap Swap in which the fixed rate cashflows are in line with those of tax-exempt bonds, especially US municipal bonds

Termination Cancellation of a swap agreement, with settlement based on the current value of the swap

Theory of economic capital Theory that economic or risk capital is the equity capital required to support unexpected losses

Theta A measurement of the effect on an option's price in relation to a one-day decrease in the expiration

Tobit procedures Methods for analysing qualitative dependent methods where the dependent variable is censored and assigned a zero value if the event does not occur

Total return swap Swap agreement in which the total return of bank loans or credit-sensitive securities is exchanged for some other cashflow, usually tied to Libor, or other loans or credit-sensitive securities. It allows participants to effectively go long or short on the credit risk of the underlying asset

TPS Transfer pricing system

Traded option Option that is listed on and cleared by an exchange, with standard terms and delivery months

Transaction risk Extent to which the value of transactions that have already been agreed is affected by market risk (qv)

Translation risk The foreign currency assets and liabilities of a firm have to be translated into the domestic currency at the end of the firm's financial year. Translation risk is the risk that this translation will dramatically affect the value of the company's assets and liabilities due to exchange rate fluctuations

Trigger option (*see* barrier option)

Tunnel option Set of collars, typically zero-cost, covering a series of maturities from the current date. They might, for example, be for dates six, 12, 18 and 24 months ahead. The special feature of a tunnel is that the strike price on both sets of options, not just on the options bought, is constant

Underwriting risk Risk of loss occurring from underwriting an issue for sale or unexpected levels of claims (insurance)

Unexpected default rate The distribution of future default rates is often characterised in terms of an expected default rate (eg, 0.05%) and a worst-case default rate (eg, 1.05%). The difference between the worst-case default rate and the expected default rate is often termed the "unexpected default rate" (ie, 1% = 1.05% − 0.05%)

Unexpected loss The distribution of credit losses associated with a derivative instrument is often characterised in terms of an expected loss (qv) or a worst-case loss (qv). The unexpected loss associated with an instrument is the difference between these two measures

Up-and-away option (*see* up-and-out option)

Up-and-in option Type of barrier option (qv) which is activated if the value of the underlying goes above a predetermined level (*see also* down-and-in option)

Up-and-out option Type of barrier option (qv) that is extinguished if the value of the underlying goes above a predetermined level (*see also* down-and-out option)

Value-at-risk (VAR) Formally, the probabilistic bound of market losses over a given period of time (known as the holding period) expressed in terms of a specified degree of certainty (known as the confidence interval). More simply, the VAR is the worst-case loss expected over the holding period within the probability set out by the confidence interval. Larger losses are possible but with a low probability. For instance, a portfolio whose VAR is $20 million over a one-day holding period, with a 95% confidence interval, would have only a 5% chance of suffering an overnight loss greater than $20 million

VAR (*see* value-at-risk)

Variance–covariance methodology Methodology for calculating the value-at-risk (qv) of a portfolio as a function of the volatility of each asset or liability position in the portfolio and the correlation between the positions

Vega A measure of the change in an option's price caused by changes in volatility (qv)

Vested benefit obligation (VBO) Measures the present value of pension benefits that have been earned by, and are due to, the employee regardless of whether he or she continues working for the firm. It can be an important measure when managing the asset/liability ratio of pension funds

Volatility Measure of the variability (but not the direction) of prices or rates

Warehouse Applies principally to swaps. To run a book without matching transaction for transaction. The object is to allow the management of a book as a whole rather than as a set of individual deals. In theory, all market-makers should warehouse

Warrant Certificate, often issued as part of a package together with a bond, giving the purchaser the right, but not the obligation, to buy a specified amount of a given asset, such as the issuer's equity (equity warrants), bonds (debt warrants), currency, oil, gold or other commodity, at a specified price during the course of a given period of time

Warrant-driven swap Swap with a warrant attached allowing the issuer of the fixed-rate bond to go on paying a floating rate in the event that he or she exercises another warrant that allows him or her to prolong the life of the bond

Worst-case default rate The highest rates of default that are likely to occur at a given moment or period in the future, with a given level of confidence

Worst-case (credit risk) exposure Estimate of the highest positive market value a derivative contract or portfolio is likely to attain at a given moment or period in the future, with a given level of confidence

Worst-case (credit risk) loss Estimate of the largest amount a derivatives counterparty is likely to lose, with a given level of probability, as a result of default from a derivatives contract or portfolio

Worst-case rate of recovery (*see* rate of recovery)

Yield curve Graphical representation of the term structure of interest rates, usually depicted as spot yields on bonds with different maturities but with the same risk factors plotted against maturity

Yield-curve option Option that allows purchasers to take a view on a yield curve without having to take a view about a market's direction

Yield-curve swap Swap in which the index rates for the two interest streams are at different points on the yield curve. Both payments are refixed with the same frequency, whatever the index rate

Zero-cost collar Purchase of a put option at a desired strike price and the simultaneous sale of a call at a strike set so that the premium collected on the call matches the premium paid for the put. This results in a zero-cost transaction

Zero-cost option (*see* zero premium option)

Zero-coupon bond Bond on which no coupon is paid. It is either issued at a discount or redeemed at a premium to face value

Zero-coupon swap Swap converting the payment pattern of a zero-coupon bond (qv) either to that of a normal, coupon-paying fixed-rate bond or to that of a floating rate

Zero premium option Generic term for options for which there is no premium, either because the buyer undertakes to forgo a percentage of any gain or because he or she offsets the cost by writing other options (*see also* reduced cost option)

INDEX